THE OXFORD HISTORY OF
CHRISTIANITY

John McManners is a Fellow of All Souls College, and Regius Professor Emeritus of Ecclesiastical History at the University of Oxford. He has written extensively on French and European history. His fifth book, *Death and the Enlightenment* (OUP, 1981), was awarded the Wolfson Literary Prize for History, and was one of *The Times* ten best non-fiction books of the year.

THE CONTRIBUTORS

Henry Chadwick, Regius Professor Emeritus of Divinity, and Master of Peterhouse, Cambridge

Robert Markus, Professor Emeritus of Medieval History, University of Nottingham

Henry Mayr-Harting, Fellow and Tutor in History, St Peter's College, Oxford

Kallistos Ware, Bishop of Diokleia, Spalding Lecturer in Eastern Orthodox Studies, and Fellow of Pembroke College, Oxford

Jeremy Johns, Lecturer in Islamic Archaeology, University of Oxford

Colin Morris, Professor of Medieval History, University of Southampton

Patrick Collinson, Regius Professor of Modern History, University of Cambridge

John McManners

Owen Chadwick, Regius Professor Emeritus of Modern History, University of Cambridge

Martin Marty, Fairfax M. Cone Distinguished Service Professor, University of Chicago

Fredrick B. Pike, Professor Emeritus of History, University of Notre Dame, Indiana

Peter Hinchliff, Fellow of Balliol College, Oxford

Kenneth Ballhatchet, Emeritus Professor of the History of South Asia, University of London, and **Helen Ballhatchet**, Associate Professor, Keio University, Japan

Sergei Hackel, Formerly Reader in Russian Studies, University of Sussex, and Vicar-General of the Russian Orthodox Church in the British Isles

Maurice Wiles, Regius Professor of Divinity, University of Oxford

Bryan Wilson, Reader in Sociology, University of Oxford, and Fellow of All Souls College, Oxford

Basil Mitchell, Nolloth Professor Emeritus of Philosophy of the Christian Religion, and Fellow of Oriel College, Oxford

John V. Taylor, Formerly General Secretary of the Church Missionary Society, and Bishop of Winchester

THE OXFORD
HISTORY
OF
CHRISTIANITY

Edited by
JOHN McMANNERS

Oxford   New York
OXFORD UNIVERSITY PRESS
1993

Oxford University Press, Walton Street, Oxford OX2 6DP

Oxford New York Toronto
Delhi Bombay Calcutta Madras Karachi
Kuala Lumpur Singapore Hong Kong Tokyo
Nairobi Dar es Salaam Cape Town
Melbourne Auckland Madrid

and associated companies in
Berlin Ibadan

Oxford is a trade mark of Oxford University Press

British Library Cataloguing in Publication Data
Data available

Library of Congress Cataloging in Publication Data
Data available
ISBN 0–19–285291–4

1 3 5 7 9 10 8 6 4 2

Typeset by Best-set Typesetter Ltd., Hong Kong

Printed in Great Britain by
Clays Ltd.
Bungay, Suffolk

Contents

List of Maps

Introduction

JOHN McMANNERS

'JESUS, Jesus of Nazareth: I can't remember him'. Pontius Pilate, in retirement, talks over the old days in Jerusalem; the name of a crucified miracle-worker, Jesus of Nazareth, comes up; it eludes him. The story was published by Anatole France in an anticlerical newspaper on Christmas Day 1891, to alarm pious ladies and enrage the *curés*. Yet this tale for agnostics has a double edge. A spark had been ignited which was to burn on through the centuries long after Rome had fallen, but the intellectuals and rulers of the empire had been blind to the significance of the newly kindled flame. Despairing as he did of human intelligence and foresight, France was ironically conceding a point to the providentialist religious apologetics of his day. Christianity had won against all the odds: it was an astonishing success story.

The theme of God's domination of history and of his providential oversight of the church has continually recurred in Christian thought, and has often been used as an apologetical argument. From time to time the general concept was made specific, as in speculations about an allocation of miracles to ensure the success of the initial preaching, or about a millenarian climax when the faithful will be vindicated. The God of the Old Testament, who uses Assyria and Egypt and all worldly lordships as his instruments, was accepted as the Christian deity. For Augustine, Rome had grown great not, as Cicero held, because its rule was established on justice, but to form the cadre of recruitment for the 'City of God'. The concept of divine control ran through the chronicle writers of the Middle Ages, and was finally elevated by Bossuet, in his *Universal History* (1681), onto a plane of baroque splendour. 'Remember, Monseigneur', he tells the heir to the French throne, for whom the book was written, 'the whole long chain of individual causes which create and destroy empires depends on the secret orders of the Divine Providence. From the highest heaven, God holds the reins of every kingdom; all hearts are in his hand'. While it was a warning to kings, the central theme was wider: 'Empires crumble: religion alone endures'. As the idea of continuous and indefinite progress became acclimatized in European thought, it was annexed by Christians as well as by secular humanists, though with questions about God's 'reserve power' as against human freedom and the laws of nature. Progress and providence become interdependent. The Victorian hymn-writer saw God working out his purpose 'as year succeeds to year' until the consummation 'when the earth shall be filled with the glory of God as the waters cover the sea'.

Yet the Christian view of the operation of God in history was not—except when crudely used as propaganda—a simple gloating over assured success in the shadow of omnipotence, nor was it assumed—in spite of many a rhetorical flourish to the contrary—that men can know how and when supernatural oversight is exercised. The church consciously inherited from the Jews the role of God's chosen people, but how often in the Old Testament the elect had been subjected to educative punishments and arbitrary rejections. As voices from whirlwind and darkness warned Job and the prophets, the ways of God are mysterious, unfathomable to mortals. The two great philosophical thinkers who dominated the formation of the Christian Middle Ages did not identify divine guidance to the church with success in the world or progress. To Augustine, every age is equidistant from eternity, and the City of God belongs to a redemptive process above ordinary history; to Boethius, God has provisionally delegated power to Fortuna (originally a goddess of the Romans) ensuring chance and chaos will be ever with us, teaching the futility of earthly possessions. Medieval chroniclers inherited and revelled in the Old Testament notion of God sending portents and punishments, yet if they spoke of these naïvely, they were conscious of the inscrutability of the divine will. Rodolfus Glaber, a Burgundian historian of the eleventh century, was confident the church would travel in safety over the sea of the world, as Peter had walked on the water supported by his Lord; but when the bell rang for matins in the cold and darkness, how could he be sure his fasts and vigils would avail him while, all around, carnal men prospered?

With the splitting of the churches at the Reformation it became less possible than ever to be dogmatic about the workings of the divine purpose. Bossuet's view of the *modus operandi* of Providence promptings deep in men's minds, sowing courage or fear, wisdom or folly—was identical with that of his English contemporary Gilbert Burnet, though Burnet had the nice additional touch of God raising up 'unlikely and unpromising instruments to do great services in the world . . . not always employing the best men', lest they acquire praise which is due only to their creator. These 'instruments' could hardly have met with Bossuet's approval: Burnet was writing an enthusiastically Protestant *History of the Reformation*.

For long, Christian speculation on history assumed that creation was recent and the judgement would not long be delayed; against this narrow time-scale, it seemed reasonable to expect God to hasten on his interventions; hence, for example, the great and long-continuing influence of the prophecy of Abbot Joachim of Fiore at the end of the twelfth century, proclaiming the approach of the Age of the Holy Spirit, when the church, led by 'Spiritual men', would rule. Providential speculation was bound to change when the comfortable calculation of

Archbishop Ussher (1650), settling the creation of the world at 8 a.m. on Saturday 22 October 4004 BC, was abandoned for geological epochs and the long climb to intelligent life forms, with the future extended to millions of years, against a background of myriads of galaxies where other beings may be enacting other histories. In the nearest we have to a theological *Summa* for our times, John Macquarrie speaks of 'Providence' as the inherent drive, in a continuous divine creation, 'towards richer and fuller kinds of being', but a drive which we must not presume to trace in the events of our own brief history. Paradoxically, as our horizons have extended towards infinity, the precariousness of our tenure of the planet has become more evident. The linkage of indefinite progress with Providence no longer has a secure hold on the imagination. Will the centuries of Christianity ahead be a story of monks amid the ruins of an atomic war, preserving the books to fulfil a Toynbeesque role of 'chrysalis' for the emergence of a new civilization? Or of Teilhard de Chardin's *homo progressivus*, half-Christian, half-Marxist, 'for whom the future of the earth counts more than its present'—an ominous formula.

There had always been an ambiguity in the events of history for those who sought to tease out a providentialist interpretation; 'whom the Lord loveth he chasteneth' had to be set against 'yet saw I never the righteous forsaken'. But there is an even greater discouragement from triumphalist boasting and the facile apologetics of success: Christianity is a religion distinctive in being centred on an instrument of torture; by its credo, God created man free, and himself bears the tragic consequences of human freedom. The disciple is not above his master: Providence for the individual is guidance through tragedy—the message of Bonhoeffer's letters from prison:

All we may rightly expect from God, and ask him for is to be found in Jesus Christ . . . If we are to learn what God promises . . . we must persevere in quiet meditation on the life, sayings, deeds, sufferings, and death of Jesus . . . it is certain that our joy is hidden in suffering, and our life in death; it is certain that in all this we are in a fellowship that sustains us . . . You must never doubt that I am travelling in gratitude and cheerfulness along the road where I am being led.

What then of the church? Perhaps the future of institutional Christianity, both in the relations of Christian bodies with each other, and in their relations with other religions and with the world, may be a sacrificial one, abandoning so much the past has cherished, in striving to represent the Christ-like spirit. This idea is beginning in Christianity today, even in matters of doctrine, over which so much blood and ink has been spilt, and where assumptions of providential guidance have been so ruthlessly made. In the new atmosphere, there are those who regret the great alliance between imperial power and the church which was forged under Constantine, the beginning of the Christian civilization of the Middle Ages. Is success of this kind an example of the working of Providence, or should a theology of incarnation, of God becoming man, imply a Providence of total vulnerability? Was the Constantinian alliance a betrayal of the pure essence of Christianity, with religion contributing to society and culture at the risk of its own soul, at the expense of its eternal mission?

The modern way of writing history (which may be called 'scientific' if we remember how science works by hypotheses, inspired guess, and selective concentration, as well as by amassing and classifying facts, and does not exclude sympathy) is a product, essentially, of the thought of Western Europe, of Christendom. Though the apologetical argument from success had been used, in strict logic the Christian view of Providence cannot explain specific happenings or chains of events. And there were, in the implications of Christian belief, encouragements to writing history in an austere, uncommitted fashion, and with wide cultural concern. Firstly, there was the conviction that everything men do or think matters intensely and eternally, as coming under the judgement of God; secondly, there was the concept of a creator entirely distinct from his creation, ruling the universe by general laws, whose ways are inscrutable, and who gives men the gift of freedom. Hence the obligation to treat seriously and with reverence all men and the social orders they build, to study everything, to explain without partisanship, insisting on the logical coherence of all things, without professing to know what the great design might be. Like other aspects of our culture—science, art, music, philosophy (philanthropy even)—historiography now exists as a discipline independent of the Christian preoccupations with which it was once cocooned and by which it was nourished. No longer concerned with puzzling over the workings of Providence, it has emerged from the labyrinth to independent existence in the harsh light of a secular day.

The writers of the various chapters of this book belong to the confraternity of professional historians of the 'scientific' kind; whatever as individuals they believe about human destiny, whatever spiritual contacts they expect or do not expect in their own lives, they write, within their lights, impartially, with detachment from their convictions. This does not mean with indifference, for an historian would hardly choose to spend his life researching on a subject about which he did not care, or attempting to relive the thoughts and emotions of people with whom he could not sympathize. Indeed, sympathy of some kind is necessary for the historian to break through to understanding: 'nemo nisi per amicitiam cognoscitur'. And impartiality does not come naturally, as it were by voiding the mind; it comes by training and conscious effort, using passionate feelings yet having discovered how to bridle them, knowing when to hold them in check, when to give free rein. In handling such an emotive subject as Christianity, the difficulties are enormous. The contributors to this volume agreed to write as individuals, unconstrained by overall directives or by the views of our colleagues. Our book has no conclusions, for we did not write to a common formula, and a history of Christianity raises problems which outrun by far the scope of the professional techniques available to us. Each of us could have written an epilogue, but it would not have been as an historian.

The scope of a history of Christianity must be wide. The devout might argue for a limitation to 'real Christianity', the story of those who found God and lived by their faith, and the movements of reformation and renewal which they inspired—the bright inner core of a vast confusion of compromises with the world. We should not concern ourselves too much, they would say, with the paraphernalia which overlie the spirit of the original Gospel, Kierkegaard's 'complete inventory of churches, bells, organs, footwarmers, alms-boxes, hearses etc.' Nothing could be further from the mentality of the historian. Kierkegaard's supercilious catalogue is of things which have mattered to ordinary people, pointers to the environment where they found fraternal and spiritual experiences. One might wonder too if 'real Christianity', uncontaminated by the world, could have survived. 'Can Jesus be preached in the whole world without ecclesiasticism?' asked Friedrich Naumann, an exponent of charismatic religion in the early years of this century, 'can molten gold be carried from place to place in anything but crucibles of iron and steel?' The historian is prepared to examine any evidence, indeed, the crucibles probably concern him most, because vessels of iron and steel, their construction and manipulation, are more susceptible to his explanations than the stream of molten gold. A religion is a social institution and, as such, a routine subject for analysis. It is more than that, of course; the historian must go as far as he can into that 'more', but the point is reached when his instruments are too clumsy to handle the evidence. The contrast between the institution and the ideal has been continually pointed out by preachers from within and anticlericals from without. A religion 'which must be divine because it survives such scandalous representatives' has been a standard theme of European conversation and writing—perhaps no topic has produced such a volume of satirical observations. Dean Swift, with masochistic irony, wondered whether 'the abolition of Christianity . . . might possibly bring the Church in danger'. Both Christianity and the church are the subjects of the historian's investigations.

Why was Christianity successful? Among the explanations which are found in this book, some belong to the 'gold', the inherent qualities of the religion, and some to the 'crucible', the compromises incorporating it into the social order. Renan's suggestion that Mithraism might have become the official cult of the Roman Empire breaks down when the 'gold' of the two religions is compared. 'A man used Mithraism', writes A. D. Nock, 'he did not belong to it body and soul'. Gibbon's picture of the Saracens—had they not gone down in defeat before Charles Martel at Poitiers in 732—sweeping on to Poland and Scotland, their fleet in the Thames and the Qur'ān being expounded in the pulpits of Oxford, is equally fallacious, for it ignores the 'crucible' aspect, the long build-up and integration of religion and the social order which formed the Christian Middle Ages. Christianity flourished where it had become, not just an ally of power (though that counted), but also the heart and inspiration of a social complex. This never happened with the Nestorian Church, which in the tenth century had fifteen metropolitan provinces from the Caspian Sea to the Persian Gulf, whose missionaries reached China, Samarkand, and India, and whose scholars translated works of the Greek philosophers into Arabic. It did not integrate with Persian civilization, lost the Mongols to Islam, and finally, amid barbarous invasions from the East, was reduced to a few scattered communities. By contrast, the Coptic Church in Egypt survived under the Arabs because of its affinities with the people, just as the Armenian Church, identified with the nation, kept alive even when divided among Persians, Arabs, Turks, and Russians. Only in Europe did Christianity assume the role of the moulder of a great civilization, and as Europe expanded, Christianity went with the conquerors to make mass conversions, and with the settlers to occupy vast open spaces. Even so, the point may be conceded to Toynbee, Butterfield, and others: the decline of the social and cultural complex of Christian Europe is the painful beginning of a new opportunity, enabling the true mission of converting the world to begin again, at the point where gregarious conformity ends and individual decision becomes obligatory.

As he welcomes this 'spiritual mutation', Toynbee rejoices in the separation of religion from cosmogony, astronomy, geology, biology, and, indeed, Hellenic philosophy as well, since it distorted the church's doctrinal definitions. What of art? Does this also come into his category of 'obnoxious lumber', obstructing the soul on its pilgrimage to higher things? As the tide of religion swept forward in Europe, with its exuberant and eclectic use of all the resources of artistic skill, there has been a continuing undertow, a tradition of reticence and austerity. The Iconoclastic movements in the Eastern church, from the end of the seventh century to the middle of the ninth, was the result of outside pressures: images were hindrances in controversy with the Monophysites (who concentrated on the divine and not the human nature of Christ), Manichaeans (who regarded all matter as evil), and Muslims (who rejected representations of the human form). As the Gothic cathedrals were rising in the twelfth century, aspiring to heaven with spire and pinnacle, rich in pictorial glass and statuary, doubts of a different kind were inspired in Bernard of Clairvaux, doubts about relevance: 'What use are carvings of centaurs and tigers with stripes and spots', he asked, 'will they melt a sinner's heart?' There were similar reservations about the elaboration of music, about instruments and polyphony as against the Gregorian chant. These austere pastoral considerations were evident in the Reformation, as well as a sinister and literally knock-down argument derived from the biblical texts concerning graven images. To Luther's disgust, Professor Karlstadt published *On the Abolishing of Images* (1533), which led to an early bout of iconoclasm in Wittenberg. In the following year, Zwingli (himself a sensitive musician and lover of art) proposed the ending of idolatry in Zurich, so that paintings were ripped from churches and whitewash took over. He wrote to a friend rejoicing in the completion of the work: 'we have churches which are positively luminous; the walls are beautifully white'. Calvin's concern was more sophisticated; he was dominated by an overwhelming sense of the majesty of God. 'Only those things are to be carved or painted', he said, 'which the eyes are capable of seeing. Let not the majesty of God, which is far above the perception of the eyes, be debased through unseemly representation.' Regarding art and music as 'gifts of God', he was no exponent of universal destruction; he merely wished to exclude 'unseemly representations' from the church buildings. The trail of havoc left by Scottish Calvinists and French Huguenots in the sixteenth century and by English Puritans in the seventeenth was only indirectly a reflection of his teaching; rather, it was a result of passions aroused by civil war, of literal-minded imitation of the kings of the Old Testament who destroyed 'the groves and high-places of idolatry', and the back-up given by worldly entrepreneurs who saw profits to be made out of ecclesiastical property. Though the Counter-Reformation ceilings with the cloud-borne hosts of heaven were a dramatic repudiation of Calvinist restrictions, the Roman church, like its rivals, tried to use the Bible as a control of aesthetic inspiration. The Council of Trent wanted New Testament incidents depicted with no other details than the gospels supplied, and writers like the Jesuit Menestrier, reflecting in awe on the imaginative creations of Bernini and Le Brun, still had reservations about allegorical figures with no scriptural warrant.

In our own century, the swing to austerity has been, in part, the result of the rediscovery of the virtue of humility. The papal tombs in St Peter's have evolved to total simplicity, the barest possible memorials to the servants of the servants of God. Enthusiasts for a church of the people have cast disapproval on the symbolism of the cathedral aloofly dominating the city skyline. More significant still is the change in the ideal of liturgical worship, which has now become egalitarian, with full community participation. The words are everyday prose, the music elementary and congregational; baroque splendours and 'the dim religious light' of Victorian churches are out of favour. Anton Henze in Germany, regarding all church architecture as a sublimation of the style of the ruling class, turned to the stark simplicities of modern technology, and in England, Eric Gill campaigned for 'mass for the masses', with worship around a central altar, getting rid of 'the whole caboodle of pharasaic ceremonies and mystògogism'. In 1960, Peter Hammond published an indictment of English church-building since the war, comparing it unfavourably with the French and German churches of the Catholic liturgical revival. Looking at his photographs of bare arenas devoid of mystery, one wonders—and turns in relief to the high altar of Coventry cathedral, adorned with Graham Sutherland's majestic tapestry.

Austerity also arises as a refuge from self-doubt about the means of artistic expression. In the Middle Ages, when all art was in a religious context, its practitioners worked with confident single-mindedness. Even in the eighteenth century, a Boucher or a Mengs moved from secular portraiture, or rococo, classical, or erotic fantasy to an *Adoration of the Shepherds* or a *Noli me tangere* with unselfconscious mastery. In the nineteenth century came a hiatus; there was a search for a distinctive style which was 'religious' and would be recognized as such—Ingres and Flandrin are examples of the quest. In our own day, with an almost entirely secular visual culture which adds television, cinema, photographs, and cartoons to the established art forms, swamping the imagination, the artist lacks the basic conventions within which he can be sure that his portrayal of religious themes will meet with the emotional response which leads to spiritual awareness or, at least to religiosity. Instead of the collaboration of many craftsmen in a masterpiece (like a cathedral) which is understandable by everybody, the most characteristic manifestation of spirituality in art today is the 'testimony', the individual artist witnessing to his view of the universe in his total *œuvre*. Chagall was such a one, claiming to be 'something of a Christian' of the kind of St Francis of Assisi, with 'an unconditional love for other beings'. In his art, Christian icons, Jewish severities, and pagan mythologies blend; there is the crucifixion and the holocaust, the Madonna and Aphrodite, against a background of solemn clowns, fabulous beasts, flowers, and musical instruments, bathed in a blue, etherial brightness. But we lack a common artistic form applicable to public worship and private meditation. Among the spectators of modern art there must be many like the writer of this preface, yearning for their religious experience to be relevant for the present and the future, yet finding their imagination tied to a past whose magic cannot be updated.

Christianity is a religion of the word—the 'Word made Flesh', the word preached, the word written to record the story of God's intervention in history. Every story needs a picture. Pope Gregory the Great defined the role of the artist thus: 'painting can do for the illiterate what writing does for those who can read'. Augustine had gone further in praise of music: written words are in themselves inadequate—'language is too poor to speak of God . . . yet you do not like to be silent. What is left for you but to sing in jubilation'. The visual artist as well as the musician is entitled to the benefit of the Augustinian argument. Words constitute a record exerting a long-term pressure: a work of art has an instantaneous impact. It bridges the gap between cultures with a single gesture, with an immediacy denied to translations of the record. Whatever the culture from which it derives, a great work of art is a potential source of spiritual insight, falling short of words in the power of syllogistic argument and even in the ability to suggest the content of the imagination's inward eye, but far superior in the evocative power to haunt and illuminate. Wassily Kandinsky, the pioneer of abstract painting, who published a study of *The Spiritual in Art* in 1912, spoke of art as resembling religion in taking what is known and transforming it, showing it 'in new perspectives and in a blinding light'. Some of the masterpieces of painting and sculpture in the Christian tradition have been produced by artists whose status as believers is doubtful. In Kandinsky's view of the breakthrough to spiritual perception, this is no paradox. 'It is safer to turn to geniuses without faith than to believers without talent', said the French Dominican Marie-Alain Couturier—an aphorism which he tested by persuading Matisse, Braque, Chagall, and other great names of the day to do work for the church of Assy in the French Alps. Couturier was not subordinating religious considerations to élitism; to him, 'all great art is spiritual since the genius of the artist lies in the depths, the secret inner being from whence faith also springs'. Jacques Maritain has drawn out a further implication of the supposition of the unity of all spiritual experience. To the Christian who wishes his art to reflect his religious convictions he says: keep this desire out of the forefront of the mind, and simply 'strive to make a work of beauty in which your entire heart lies'.

An artist has his living to make and patrons to please; he works within traditions and fashions or reacts against them; his performances may be distorted by technical limitations on the one hand, or by the temptation to displays of virtuosity on the other. There is never a straightforward uncomplicated 'spiritual' inspiration. Even so, the testimony of art to the Christian vision is dramatic. A religion of transcendency, creation, and judgement, of incarnation, and of the indwelling spirit, provides an inexhaustible supply of themes—the life, parables, miracles, death, and resurrection of Jesus, his prophetic precursors and his saints, the triune God and the heavenly hosts—as well as the stocks of allegories, virtues, and, even, gods and goddesses of classical antiquity, cheerfully annexed in the Middle Ages on the analogy of 'spoiling the Egyptians'. The catalogue does not end there. A century ago, Bishop Westcott, starting from the indifference of the New Testament to artistic representations, built up an argument to annex the whole of nature as a Christian theme, a continual potential revelation of the divine. And he encouraged the artist to lavishness. 'To what purpose hath this waste . . . been made?' they asked when 'the ointment of spikenard, very costly' had been poured—it was 'a witness of love', Westcott replied.

There is a view of the faith which is essentially triumphalist: the cross was a victory over the devil, while the Son, the eternal judge, reigns at God's right hand. Romanesque art in the West about the year 1000 made much of the Last Judgement—a warning to the baptized warlords whose primitive passions the waters of regeneration had failed to cool. At the same time in Byzantium, in mosaic and fresco, the stylized transcendent Christ, the Ancient of Days of Daniel's vision, looked down on his people, their creator and judge. In both East and West, art was presenting a Saviour congruous with the alliance with power and the mission of overawing the barbarians surging against the frontier lines. With immeasurably greater resources of technical skill, baroque triumphalism was the characteristic art form of the Counter-Reformation—the heavenly hosts in glittering tiers welcoming the victorious Christ or the transfigured Virgin, and the whole life of Jesus and his saints shot through by intimations of divine splendour.

The mind of the Christians of the first half of the third century was very different. In the paintings in the catacombs the figurations of power are absent—they were to come later from Roman models after the conversion of Constantine. There are pictures of Daniel, Jonah, Noah, Lazarus: 'enumerating the precedents for divine intervention for one of the faithful', says André Grabar. Christ is represented as the Good Shepherd and by the acrostic symbol of the fish. There is no cross or crucifixion scene. The reticence of these early believers is moving. They shrink from the recollection of the servile and degrading death inflicted on their Lord, and they conceive salvation in the gentle terms of the friendship of Christ, not in the panoply of imperial triumphs. The twelfth and early thirteenth centuries saw the rediscovery of the friendship theme, exemplified in Abelard's theory of the atonement ('our redemption is the great love awakened in us by the Passion of Jesus') and in the life of St Francis. Artists turned to the Annunciation, the Infancy, and the Madonna and Child, and patrons, now wealthy laymen or great churchmen rather than monks, welcomed this reversion to tenderness, to the magic spring time of the sacred story. When the Renaissance saw the perfection of the naturalistic portrayal of the human frame and the inner luminosity of living flesh, the theme was adorned with masterpieces of astonishing perfection. In his *Annunciation*, Botticelli, touched by the preaching of Savonarola, moved from the charm of his pagan goddesses into a new, etherial dimension.

Triumphalism, friendship; and there is a third driving emotion in Christian art—sorrow. The cult of the friendship of Jesus could never forget his sufferings. Even the crucifixion scenes of the Renaissance, avoiding the agony of the sacred figure and portraying him as 'the Adonis of Galilee', have tragedy implicit everywhere, in the darkening sky, the despair on the faces of the beholders, the compassion on the faces of the angels. The *Resurrection* of Piero della Francesca (1462–4) seems to be a triumphalist allegory with Christ emerging from his tomb with banner unfurled—until we look into the eyes, fixed and staring with the memory of pain. In Germanic Europe in the fifteenth century, under the influence of the mystics, the cult of Christ and his mother became focused on the passion. The times were evil, there was a deepening sense of sin and fear of death in the piety of the day. Hence, the harrowing crucifixion scenes. The grimmest and best known of all is Grünewald's (1515); there is no hope here—we see, in Huysmans' words, 'the God of the morgue'. Yet there is a degree of tragedy more subtlely sombre evident in Pieter Bruegel's *Christ Carrying the Cross* and in modern treatments of the theme. The suffering is suffering in loneliness: no one cares.

Those who share the sorrows of Christ, and seek his friendship, will share in his triumph—and how may the artist depict the believers' ultimate fulfilment and reward? If heaven is limited (as in the extreme view of the more austere schoolmen, Jansenists, and Puritans) to the soul alone with its God, artistic representation is virtually impossible. Yet, if the doctrine of the church as a divine institution is taken seriously, however theo-centrically eternity is viewed, it must comprise a community of the redeemed. Or, at least, they must serve attendance at a heavenly court, for which there was a standard imagery used by countless baroque painters—cloud-borne hierarchies reaching up to the Virgin and the Godhead in a luminous infinity. If one imaginative decor, why not others, more comfortable ones, where the weary pilgrim may feel at home: the white turrets of the city of the Book of Revelation and the Middle Ages, the paradisial garden watered by the fountain of life of Renaissance imagery? In a city or a garden, the setting cries out for socia-bility, and hence the way was open for the popular modern concept of heaven, which arose in the eighteenth century, owing something to hymn-writers, but more to Rousseau's *Nouvelle Héloïse* and the visions of Swedenborg. Here, the redeemed have work to do, their spiritual development continues, and they renew and perfect their earthly loves. Modern theologians in their élitism have reservations, but this seems to be a case where the insight of ordinary Christians, in its naïve way, is nearer to the heart of the gospel of love than theirs. True, in this comfortable heaven, the artist does not easily find themes rising above banality. The upgrading of terrestrial experience into eternity lends itself to facile, sentimental representations of the Forest Lawn variety, and tempts the imagination to cling to a familiar environment rather than reaching out to the strange shores and sunlit uplands of a new world of the spirit. Besides, there is the problem for the artist which Chateaubriand posed: 'no one is interested in beings who are perfectly happy'. Even so, the sublimation of erotic passion into heaven (by Charles Kingsley in his fulfilment, and Emily Dickinson in her loneli-ness) provides the artist with a bridge to carry over an inspiration of this world into the next; witness William Blake's fond reunions on Judgement Day, and Dante Gabriel Rossetti's *Blessed Damozel* at the golden barrier, waiting to lead her earth-bound lover into the 'deep wells of light'.

Theologically (and perhaps artistically), the best description of the end and aim of the Christian is one which makes heaven incidental: 'to be with Christ', in St Paul's words. Arguably, the greatest works of spirituality in art are those which convey the inwardness of that simple but mysterious phrase. The mystics had described the journey to union—deserts of dryness and the night of the soul on the way to the meeting with the divine love in all the intensity and immediacy of erotic passion, infinitely sublimated. Bernini's *Ecstasy of St Teresa* is the most astonishing of the attempts which have been made to seize the moment of ecstasy. The entranced saint on the edge of another universe, and the ambiguously smiling angel wielding the cruel dart reveal the disquieting intensity of a love which has no limits. But the way of St John of the Cross and of St Teresa is not for the generality of believers; it is, rather, meditation on the life, teaching, and death of Jesus and the hope that, in his resurrection, he will remember them. Rembrandt, a contemporary of Bernini, was the supreme artist of such every-day discipleship. Restrained by Calvinist austerity from lofty allegorical flights and disciplined by unhappiness, he portrayed the life of Jesus in a fashion which compels the spectator to sympathetic self-identification, up to the final despair of his *Descent from the Cross*, etched in pallor and hopelessness on the face of the Virgin Mary. There was a triumphalist strain in Christian art in the presentation of the resurrection, but there was also a muted one, nearer to the heart of discipleship—the moment of recognition, found in so many versions of *Noli me Tangere*, Mary Magdalen and the risen Christ at dawn in the garden. The moment of recognition is at the heart of Rembrandt's piety, though he prefers the meeting with the two disciples at Emmaus. 'Abide with us for it is towards evening' they say, and in the twilight, with the breaking of the bread, they suddenly know, even as also they are known.

The writer of this preface hopes for that moment of recog-nition. But his hope does not arise from, and does not deter-mine his judgements as an historian. The record of events

is ambiguous about the claim to a supernatural, inward significance. With more information than other people and with an
array of techniques for interpreting it, the historian is in the
same lifeboat as everyone else when it is a question of ultimate
meaning. He can but wonder—with hope or, like Flaubert,
without it. In August 1850, after a tour of the Near East
divided between archaeological monuments and brothels, Flaubert arrived at Jerusalem and the Holy Sepulchre. 'There came
over me', he wrote, 'that strange feeling which two men like
you and me experience when we are alone by our firesides,
striving with all the might of our being to look into that age-
old abyss represented by the word "love", and imagine what it
might be, if it could possibly be so'.

FROM THE ORIGINS
TO 1800

1

The Early Christian Community

HENRY CHADWICK

Jesus and the Apostles

THE earliest Christian communities were marked out by their allegiance to Jesus of Nazareth. They believed that in his teaching and life, God had 'visited his people' and sent a prophet and more than a prophet, an example and teacher of the way of truth and righteousness surpassing John the Baptist; the 'Messiah' or anointed leader of ancient expectation. He performed cures of both body and mind but from compassion, not to impress doubters. People who demanded miracles to prove his divine mission were refused: his power came from the presence of the Father and was discerned by those 'with ears to hear'. Also disappointed were some who hoped for an inauguration of a holy war against the Roman occupation of Judaea: he taught non-resistance, love to enemies. Yet he certainly taught the relativity of earthly authority, and even that by his bringing in of God's kingdom the Mosaic law and Temple cult ceased to be final. By the high-priestly families of Jerusalem he was felt to be a threat both to their authority and to their political collaboration with the Roman power. The claim that with his coming God was inaugurating his rule on earth laid him open to a charge of blasphemy, which was without difficulty transformed into a plea to the prefect Pontius Pilate that Jesus was instigating sedition. Betrayed by one of the inner circle of disciples, Judas, he was arrested and, at passover-time probably in the year 30 of our era, executed by crucifixion—a method of killing in which the preceding torture is prolonged as long as possible, death being certain. Four centuries earlier Socrates at Athens observed that a really righteous person would be so unacceptable to human society that he would be subjected to every humiliation and crucified.

For the community of disciples the crucifixion was not the end. The rising again of Jesus is described in the earliest Christian texts in two related but distinguishable streams of language. The first speaks of the empty tomb or rising again after burial, of appearing to apostles, women disciples, and other witnesses. The second stream speaks of the Lord now delivered from the limitations and particularity of human life to be present to his people at all times and places. As an act of God, Easter is not accessible to the methods of historical investigation. The historian knows that something important occurred to transform the disciples from a huddle of frightened men into bold missionaries risking their lives for their faith. But resurrection is not resuscitation (even in those texts where the this-worldly nature of the event is most stressed), but a mysterious 'going to God'.

The apostolic community experienced his presence in their worship, in the proclamation of divine forgiveness and renewal, visibly embodied in the 'sacraments' (a much later Latin term for a religious symbol with instrumental effect). This presence in and with the community was to them the sign of the kingdom of God on earth.

Faith that Jesus was God's anointed prophet and king (Messiah) was basic to self-definition for the first church. The Christians did not initially think of themselves as separate from the Jewish people, though Jesus had had severe things to say about Pharisees. (But then, so has the Talmud.) God's call was to the Jew first. The call to Gentiles was a disputed matter for a time. To the earliest Christian communities Jesus was not the founder or originator of the community of God's people, but the climax of an already long story of a divine education of humanity through the special illumination given to the prophets of Israel. To interpret his significance they turned to the Hebrew sacred books, the Mosaic law as well as the prophetic writings. The Christians fully shared with Judaism the ethical passion characteristic of monotheism. Monotheism is first a critique of nature religion, but then of tribalism—that is, of the notion that the function of religion is to ensure the coherence, survival, and prosperity of the tribe. The Hebrew scriptures contained prescriptions that enforced a separateness and particularity of the Jewish people, in tension with the universalism of monotheistic belief: if there is but one God, he is Lord of all peoples, even if some of them feel after him more coherently than others. Like some Greek-speaking liberal Jews, the early Christians read the prophets as foretelling a universal mission of the Jews to illuminate all peoples. Yet the law imposed prescriptions apparently designed to mark off the Jews from other nations. The Christians believed that by the death of Jesus, the suffering servant of Isaiah, God had formed a new covenant not only with the Jews but with all peoples of the earth. The Hebrew scriptures imposed a law not to be binding on Gentiles, yet (for all its moral imperfections) not to be set in sharp antithesis to the new and more excellent way of love embodied in Jesus' life and teaching.

These last propositions were hotly contested in the apostolic community. Many adherents of the young church were Pharisees, a meticulously devout party among the Jews anxious to preserve their national religion from liberal assimilation to the surrounding Gentile world. To many of them it seemed abhorrent to suggest that the Mosaic law was other than final.

The controversy ran contemporaneous with a delicate question of authority. Was the representative of the ascended Lord to be found in the members of his family, in particular in 'James the Lord's brother'? James emerged as generally acknowledged head of the community at Jerusalem. Side by side with him were the 'apostles', those commissioned by Jesus to proclaim repentance in view of God's imminent kingdom. The risen Lord had appeared not only to women, Peter, and the rest of the Twelve but also to James (1 Cor. 15: 5–7). James embodied strict conservatism in regard to observance of both the moral and the ceremonial law. Among the apostles Peter held a generally recognized position of leadership: the gospel tradition preserves explicit commissions given to him by Jesus (Matt. 16: 16–18; Luke 22: 31–2; John 21: 16–17), and his prominent role is conceded in the Pauline letters. According to the Acts of the Apostles Peter took the lead in opening membership of the church to Gentiles. He appears to have occupied a middle position, holding that while Gentile Christians need not be circumcised or keep traditional Jewish festivals, they should respect Jewish food laws.

St Paul

A more radical position, at least in principle, was held by the most prominent figure (though not the originator) of the Gentile mission—Saul or Paul of Tarsus, a Hellenized Jew with Roman citizenship. A Pharisee by training and once a vehement conservative, he had at one stage harassed the infant church but was dramatically converted by confrontation with a vision of the risen Lord. From then onwards, he knew himself commissioned to carry the way of Jesus beyond the particularity of Judaism to the Gentile world. His rejection of the view that non-Jewish believers should keep the Mosaic law implied a break between church and synagogue; his theology had vast social consequences. At the same time he profoundly believed that in the church Jew and Gentile were to be united in one fellowship. Peter's apostolate to the Jews was paralleled by Paul's in the Gentile world, which was to have its own focus in the capital of the empire at Rome.

'Freedom from law', however, was heady language for Gentile converts without the strong moral training provided by an orthodox Jewish family. At a very early stage the apostle

Paul was confronted by opposed parties, the one contending that the freedom of the Spirit so emancipated them from social convention that they could act as they pleased, especially in sexual indulgence, the other with more plausibility holding that the life of the Spirit required renunciation of marriage. The pagan world was familiar with the widespread beliefs that sexual contact between man and woman hindered the soul's rise to higher things, and even that one who has been favoured with the love of a god ought to forgo mortal love. The apostle insisted that marriage is no sin, and celibacy, a gift not granted to all, is better for the missionary service of God's kingdom.

The Gentile world was full of gods, local regional deities for the most part, who needed to be placated with sacrifices to ensure good crops, fertile spouses, successful commercial ventures, or even military victory for the emperor's army. Philosophers could argue against them, playwrights could mock them, but their following remained strong among the many who felt that one cannot be too careful not to offend the cosmic powers. To the rituals myths were attached. If the myths were incompatible, that hardly mattered, since no one with education really supposed them to be plain prose. Few thought the stories about Zeus were historical.

St Paul understood the distinctive heart of Christianity to lie in the historic facts of the gospel; the Jesus of history was one with the Christ of his faith, who was also the eternal wisdom of God in creation. St John likewise believed that God was uniquely present in Jesus. But even as early as St John's Gospel (undated but often hypothetically dated late in the first century— it cannot be later) the 'incarnation' implies a manifestation within time and history of the eternal Word of God. In the epistle to the Hebrews (by an unknown Christian of learning and sophistication) there is equal emphasis both upon the spontaneity and fullness of Jesus' humanity and upon the faith that in him the eternal Son of the Father has come to unite believers to himself; he is the pioneer of our salvation, our

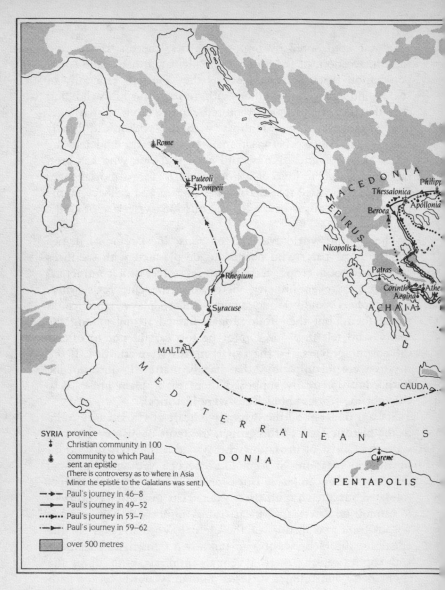

Rome

Puteoli
Pompeii

MACEDONIA

EPIRUS

Philippi
Thessalonica
Beroea
Apollonia

Nicopolis

Patras

Rhegium

Corinth   Athe
Aegina

ACHAIA

Syracuse

MALTA

M E D I T E R R A N E A N   S

CAUDA

SYRIA province

Christian community in 100

community to which Paul
sent an epistle
(There is controversy as to where in Asia
Minor the epistle to the Galatians was sent.)

DONIA

Cyrene

PENTAPOLIS

Paul's journey in 46–8
Paul's journey in 49–52
Paul's journey in 53–7
Paul's journey in 59–62

over 500 metres

THE JOURNEYS OF ST PAUL AND
CHRISTIAN COMMUNITIES IN 100

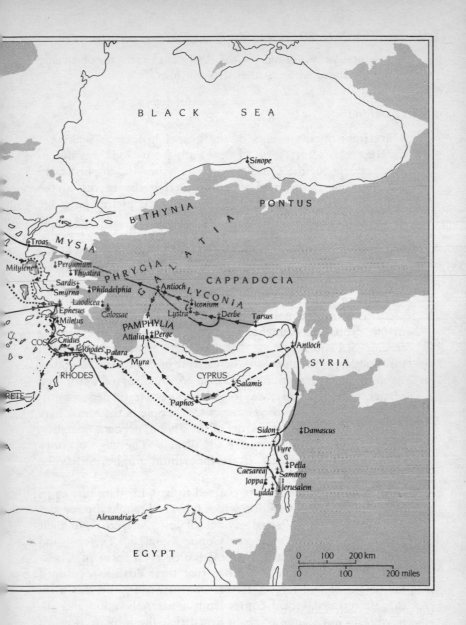

BLACK SEA

Sinope

BITHYNIA

PONTUS

MYSIA

Troas

Pergamum

Mitylene

Thyatira

Sardis

Smyrna

Philadelphia

Laodicea

Colossae

Ephesus

Miletus

PHRYGIA

GALATIA

CAPPADOCIA

Antioch

Iconium

LYCAONIA

Lystra

Derbe

Tarsus

COS

Cnidus

PAMPHYLIA

Attalia

Perge

Antioch

SYRIA

Rhodes

Patara

RHODES

Myra

CYPRUS

Salamis

CRETE

Paphos

Sidon

Damascus

Tyre

Pella

Caesarea

Samaria

Joppa

Jerusalem

Lydda

Alexandria

EGYPT

0   100   200 km

0   100   200 miles

representative bringing to the Father and to the heavenly company those who put their trust in him.

Gnosticism

This stress on the events of the gospel history as making a difference, as a revelation of new light from God, was not an easy concept for the Gentile world to assimilate. Sophisticated pagans were accustomed to reinterpreting the myths of the gods allegorically, either as an imaginative picture-language describing the natural order of the world or as a projection of human psychological states. To treat the Christian story in this way was to produce the phenomenon of Gnosticism in which a claim to disclose secret revelation is combined with a mixing of myths and rites drawn from a variety of religious traditions. Gnosticism was (and still is) a theosophy with many ingredients. Occultism and oriental mysticism became fused with astrology, magic, cabbalistic elements from Jewish tradition, a pessimistic reading of Plato's doctrine that man's true home does not lie in this bodily realm, above all the catalyst of the Christian understanding of redemption in Christ. A dualism of spirit and matter, mind and body, was joined with a powerful determinism or predestinarianism: the Gnostics (or 'people in the know') are the elect, their souls fragments of the divine, needing liberation from matter and the power of the planets. The huge majority of humanity are earthy clods for whom no hope may be entertained.

Most of the Gnostic sects claimed to be Christian; that is, to represent the secret tradition which Jesus had taught the apostles in private. They collected sayings of Jesus shaped to fit their own interpretation (as in the Coptic *Gospel of Thomas*), and offered their adherents an alternative or rival form of Christianity. Gnostic teachers claimed that their dualism explained the origin of evil far better than the orthodox church's view that the created world comes from a perfectly good and all-powerful God. Some of them urged that the imperfections of the creation cohere with those of the Hebrew scriptures, of which they held a low opinion. The Creator was incompetent or malevolent.

Only one second-century sect—the Mandeans of Iraq—remains alive today. But the version of Gnostic mythology and practice propagated by the third-century heretic, Mani (from Mesopotamia), enjoyed a millennium of diffusion from Cadiz to China: one text from a Christian writer of late fourth-century Spain, Priscillian of Avila, first becomes intelligible in the light of a Manichee catechism of AD 800 extant in Chinese. In one form or another Gnosticism has permanently remained an underground concomitant of the church. The church soon constructed fences against it.

In antiquity the Gnostic separation of spirit from matter had consequences for two prominent features of mainstream Christianity. The Gnostics could not believe that in Christ the eternal God could have polluted himself by taking flesh and enduring crucifixion; in the first epistle of John this denial is directly combated. Secondly (and relatedly) the Gnostics tended to deny significance to the sacraments of baptism in water and eucharist. Some of the sects offered their adherents 'baptism of fire', an inward psychological elevation perhaps. Mani attacked the church for using wine (an invention of the devil, he thought), and for believing in any special significance for the sanctified bread. The early prevalence of such opinions probably illuminates the intensity with which St John's Gospel (chapters 3, 6, and 15) stresses the necessity of being reborn 'of water and the Spirit' and of participating in the bread of heaven and the true vine. St Paul was emphatic that by receiving the broken bread and poured out wine, the believer is participating in the self-offering of the Son to the Father in his broken body and shed blood. Only the baptized were admitted to the thanksgiving (*eucharistia*). To share in it was so distinctive a mark of membership that, in time of persecution in the second and third centuries, pieces of the consecrated bread were taken round to baptized believers languishing in prison or on a sickbed.

A characteristic of many Gnostic sects was to treat the sacraments either as magic or as mere symbols for a subjective psychological state within the individual believer. Bishops, priests, and deacons were held in scorn by them; but they allowed positions of leadership and liturgical presidency to women, as orthodox communities did not. The closer the Gnostics stood to orthodoxy, the more likely they were to wish to infiltrate the catholic community; this was especially the case among the Manichees, but they could be detected by their refusal to drink of the eucharistic cup (since they regarded wine as an invention of the devil) and to make the sign of the cross (since to them the suffering of Jesus was no actual event but a symbol for the universal condition of the human race).

Other features of Gnosticism especially objectionable to orthodox teachers were the radical dualism of spirit and matter, the determinism which assured a small elect minority of salvation with everyone else being predestined to annihilation, perhaps worse, and the tendency to merge myths and cults, incorporating a few Christian elements with adaptations of Mithraism, astrology, magical spells, and anything else lying to hand. Moral virtue was of little interest to Gnostics, whose confidence in their own salvation made all that seem a matter of indifference. Although the Gnostics claimed to offer a higher knowledge than the simple faith of the church, their teachings were highly mythological and encountered an opposition, no less vehement than that of the church, from the late pagan Platonists, such as Plotinus (mid-third century) and his successors. Plotinus wrote his most impassioned tract to attack Gnosticism as pretentious mumbo-jumbo. He particularly disliked their deep pessimism about the visible material world.

Marcion

The Gnostic critique and rejection of the Creator God of the Old Testament was taken to extremes by Marcion in the first half of the second century. He and his followers listed moral contradictions between the Old and New Testaments, and abominated allegory as a sophisticated device for evading difficulty. But the apostolic writings themselves had been corrupted, he thought, by unknown persons determined to keep Christianity Jewish, preserving the new wine of Jesus in old bottles. Marcion felt that even the apostles themselves had seriously misunderstood the intentions of their Master by failing to see how utterly new his message was. He therefore set out to produce a corrected text first of the letters of Paul his hero, then of the gospel of Paul's companion Luke (the other gospels being scrapped), which he thought the work of Paul himself in its original form.

New Testament Canon

Marcion's principle of exclusion gave sharp impetus to the early church's need to define which books did or did not rank as authoritative documents to which appeal could be made. Unlike Marcion, many Gnostic sects welcomed numerous gospels other than the four which were finally included in the canon, and enjoyed producing 'secret' or apocryphal gospels, acts, epistles, and apocalypses (the choice of these and not other literary genres being a silent testimony to the existence and currency of the canonical texts). Many of these 'apocryphal' texts portrayed Jesus as a strenuous advocate of sexual renunciation. Some developed the reticent traditions of Jesus' infancy to provide stories about Mary's parents, and her (miraculous) birth and perpetual virginity.

To the Gnostics it was a commendation to label a text 'secret' or 'apocryphal'. The orthodox gave the latter term a pejorative sense; the apocryphal texts were correctly seen as an attempt to replace the books accepted by the mainstream communities and included in their church lectionary as authentic representatives of the apostolic tradition of faith.

In later Christian debate the history of the formation of the biblical canon has at times become a sensitive issue: were the books admitted to the church's canon because they were self-authenticating, and a passive act of the community was to *acknowledge* their inherent authority? Or did the church actively *create* the canon in response to Marcion and other sectarian leaders whose 'inspired' writings were either more or less than the church accepted? Both questions have to receive affirmative answers, and they are not mutually exclusive. The books were acknowledged because of their content as witnesses to the apostolic gospel; their formal acceptance as canonical scripture was a matter of discussion and decision by gradual consensus among the communities of the late second century and afterwards. But the term 'canon' was being used for the standard of authentic teaching given by the baptismal confession of faith well before it came to be used for the list of accepted books. The criterion for admission was not so much that traditions vindicated an apostolic authorship as that the content of the books was in line with the apostolic proclamation received by the second-century churches.

Montanism

Gnosticism and Marcion's onslaught on everything Jewish in the Christian tradition were not the only factors in precipitating the formation of the canon. The early churches had charismatic prophets who, in some cases, spoke with 'tongues', that is, unintelligible sounds of ecstatic excitement. At Corinth St Paul found the phenomenon deeply divisive and productive of censoriousness; he taught the Corinthian church that the authenticity of a gift of the Spirit should be tested by whether or not it contributed to love and edification of the community as a whole. The gifts of the Spirit being many and diverse, it is a mistake to make the recognition of one gift the supreme criterion, as some of the Corinthian charismatics wanted to do.

In the mid-second century in Phrygia a vehement anti-Gnostic reaction helped to inflame a powerful movement of charismatic prophecy, led by Montanus and two women, Prisca and

Maximilla. Their inspired utterances, which were cast in the first person as direct statements by the Paraclete, were collected. A touch of regional pride appeared in the expectation that the New Jerusalem, of which the Apocalypse of John had spoken, would descend to earth on a hill in their own Phrygia. The Montanist prophets required everyone to acknowledge their utterances as the true work of the Holy Spirit. Despite the conversion of some entire communities in Asia Minor to the sect, and despite the advocacy in the West given by their most eminent convert Tertullian, the great church did not concede recognition. Instead, there came to be a powerful emphasis on the ending of the age of miracle and revelation now that the last of the twelve apostles was dead. To Irenaeus, the normal ministry of word and sacrament is in principle the point where the Spirit of God is encountered, not at emotional ecstasies which reject rationality and tradition. Anti-Montanist reaction reinforced the belief that the apostolic canon is closed; but it did nothing to diminish millenarian hopes which long retained orthodox defenders. But there were also second-century interpreters of the Apocalypse who did not think intended to be literal and earthly the seer's vision of Christ returning to a rebuilt Jerusalem.

A Book Religion?

The outcome of this development was to give Christianity something of the character of a 'book religion', a concept hardly known to the pagan world but significant in Judaism. This shift in emphasis created a theological problem. The books of the Bible are marked by a rich diversity of genre, content, and manner. By the first half of the third century some expositors (Cyprian, Origen) begin to speak of the books as a single book, because given by the one author, God. That in turn led to the assumption that diversity was embarrassing, that different standpoints within the biblical books should be harmonized, lest the authority of the sacred writings be diminished. The first beginnings of this process can be discerned as early as Irenaeus, c.180. The obscurity of parts of scripture was also a source of embarrassment if one took the books collectively to be the essential medium of divine revelation; but that could be mitigated by allegory, or by the principle that obscure texts are interpreted by what is clear.

Before the time of Irenaeus, the sacred books of the Christians were in the main the Hebrew Bible, 'law, prophets, and writings' or 'Old Testament'. The tradition of the words of the Lord was largely oral, and even after the canonical gospels were freely circulating, second-century citations of Jesus' teaching often suggest oral rather than written transmission. About AD 130 Papias of Hierapolis in Asia Minor recorded traditions about the authorship of the gospels of Matthew and Mark, but also knew a story about Jesus found in the non-canonical 'Gospel according to the Hebrews' and was quite convinced that the mind of Jesus was captured less from written books than from the oral teaching of those seniors who had known apostles personally.

To form a New Testament canon was to give special importance to the written tradition, imparting a fixity which protected it against adulteration. Nevertheless, the formation of the canon of writings did not mean that the living tradition of the teaching Church was downgraded. The 'writtenness' of the apostolic tradition was of the accidents rather than the substance of the apostolic proclamation concerning Christ.

At the same time, to set a New Testament canon beside the Old carried implications for the concept of 'inspiration'. That the apostle Paul thought of his letters to his churches as constituting inspired revelation to instruct all subsequent generations is unlikely. But to treat the apostolic writings as 'prophecy' given by Spirit-inspired men altered the perspective.

In pre-Christian antiquity two theories of inspiration were widely current. According to the first view, inspiration is an enhancement of natural, rational discernment, not a suspension or abolition. This view allowed room for disagreement between prophets and for the recognition of limitations in the human factor. According to the second view, inspiration was mantic possession: the divine afflatus took over the voice of prophet or prophetess, and employed the human agent as a musician plays a lyre which has no mind of its own. Both these theories are found among Christians seeking to interpret biblical authority. The mantic view implied that the words are divinely given; so any text can be interpreted in the light of other texts where the same word occurs.

This theory of a 'verbal inspiration' especially held good for the Greek translation of the Old Testament, commonly called that of the Seventy (Septuagint), begun at Alexandria in the third century BC. The legend recounted how seventy translators had worked in independent cells and had all come up with the identical version of the sacred text. Among the church Fathers some thought the legend ridiculous, others (like Augustine) firmly adhered to it. Nevertheless, both Origen and Augustine could also presuppose the first view of inspiration. At times this took the sophisticated form of explaining contradictions between biblical texts at the literal, historical level as being deliberately placed there by the divine author to teach the point that a deeper meaning lies beyond the literal sense. But Origen and Augustine could also explain differences between (for example) the evangelists by observing that different eyewitnesses normally give different accounts of the same event. Augustine added that the same story is seldom repeated in precisely the same words by a single person.

In the second century a variant of this theme appeared in the assumption made by writers in the orthodox tradition that on the essentials all Christians rightly believing are agreed: the cacophony of dissension is a characteristic either of heretics or of pagan philosophers. The modern historian sees greater variety than the thesis's defenders wished to concede. Nevertheless it is instructive that the Christians of the 'great church' (as a pagan writer, Celsus, called it *c*.177–80) thought in this way about unity in diversity. There was a pressure towards standardization.

Bishops

The formation of the New Testament canon from late in the second century was only one feature of this process. A much earlier development than the biblical canon was the evolution of the threefold ministry of bishop, presbyter, and deacon. The apostles of Jesus were not merely witnesses to the Lord's resurrection (clearly an unrepeatable function in the historical sense), but also a source of decision-making or pastoral jurisdiction in the early communities. The tradition recorded that Jesus had entrusted his church with the power of the keys, that is, a commission to decide disputes and to give rulings about erring individuals. As the early church came to see that history was not coming to an immediate end, they also saw some permanent ministerial structure was needed.

The mother church at Jerusalem in the apostolic age had a single head in the person of James, the Lord's brother. In the Gentile churches spiritual leadership might be in the hands of 'presbyters' (Acts 20: 17) under the overall authority of an apostle such as St Paul. But it soon seemed natural for one man to be held first among equals; or the first prominent convert in a city, like Stephanas at Corinth (1 Cor. 16: 15–16), might form a community round his household. At Philippi there were bishops and deacons, officers also mentioned in the Pastoral Epistles to Timothy and Titus. Evidently the general itinerant care exercised by Paul and his helpers is supplemented by permanent resident officeholders. Several other first-century texts speak of the two 'orders' of bishop and deacon; the title bishop is also applied to people called presbyters. In the Pastoral Epistles the noun presbyters often appears in the plural, bishop in the singular, suggesting that one man was beginning to have a special position in both worship and charitable administration.

For many centuries it was common form for a bishop to address a presbyter as 'fellow-presbyter'. The main function of early presbyters was not to preach or celebrate but to give counsel to bishops.

The emergence of the 'monarchical' bishop seems to have been more rapid in some regions and cities than others. The bishop and his clergy formed a visible manifestation of the continuity of the community in consequence of the fact that their due succession was treated with care. A bishop went to represent his people at the ordination of bishops in neighbouring churches. He also conducted correspondence with other churches. He was the normal minister of baptism, the president of the eucharistic assembly, 'blamelessly offering the gifts' as the first epistle of Clement put it (before the end of the first century). The gifts offered no doubt included the alms of the faithful as well as bread and wine. The Christians soon acquired a reputation even among the pagans for being generous with their money; they thought it better to give than to enquire too closely into the merits of the recipients, and were therefore occasionally easy game for confidence tricksters. A vivid portrait of a successful charlatan exploiting the second-century Christians is given by Lucian in his *Peregrinus*.

Of the manner of making clergy, very early texts speak of prayer and laying on of hands, by which was conferred a charismatic gift appropriate to the office (2 Tim. 1: 6). In antiquity no insignia such as cup or Bible were handed to the person ordained, and the clergy did not initially wear special vestments; they were simply instructed to see that what they wore was 'wholly clean'. By the third century it became common for at least some clergy in at least some places to wear either white or black—black being the more penitential. One group in fourth-century Asia Minor was distinctive in that all, both clergy and laity, wore an extremely uncomfortable black sackcloth. But the garments modern Christians think of as Western ecclesiastical vestments developed from the 'Sunday best' of late Roman aristocrats, which the clergy (always the guardians of the old tradition) continued to wear after their barbarian congregations had put on trousers or Lederhosen.

A particularly striking feature of the early Christian communities is that they were urban, and only slowly penetrated rural societies. (We hear of farmers alarmed to learn from 1 Cor. 9: 9 that 'oxen are of no concern to God'.) The *plebs* elected their bishop but because their community was part of the universal or catholic church, they needed the consent and the consecrating hands of neighbouring bishops.

Episcopal elections were not always peaceful, especially if tension arose between influential families or groups. Popular suffrage meant that rival factions would shout for their own candidate. At Rome in the mid-third century the presbyter Fabian found himself elected bishop because a dove settled on his head. The Lord had promised his presence to two or three agreeing in his name: consecrations by only two bishops occasionally occurred, but three were usually thought the minimum, all the bishops of the province being desirable. To restrain partisan appointments, the great Council of Nicaea called by Constantine in 325 invested the bishop of the metropolis of the civil province with a veto. Simultaneously the council affirmed that just as the bishops of the great cities of Rome and Syrian Antioch exercised jurisdiction beyond the confines of their own diocese and province, so also the bishop of Alexandria should hold jurisdiction throughout Egypt and Libya. This canon marks the first and crucial step to the creation of 'patriarchates', a dignity soon to be shared by Constantinople (founded 330) and Jerusalem, giving the Greek East four patriarchates to the West's one.

Rome

Combating second-century Gnosticism, Irenaeus appealed to the 'public' doctrine taught in the churches of apostolic foundation by the successive bishops, and especially cited the succession-list of Rome, 'the very large, ancient, and universally known

church founded by the two glorious apostles Peter and Paul'—
for (Irenaeus adds) all believers everywhere in every church are
necessarily in agreement with Rome as an apostolic foundation
with a cosmopolitan membership and extensive dealings with
other churches. The Christian community in Rome was Greek-
speaking until the mid-third century, and had frequent contacts
with churches of the Greek East. Towards the latter part of the
first century, Rome's presiding cleric named Clement wrote
on behalf of his church to remonstrate with the Corinthian
Christians who had ejected clergy without either financial or
charismatic endowment in favour of a fresh lot; Clement
apologized not for intervening but for not having acted sooner.
Moreover, during the second century the Roman community's
leadership was evident in its generous alms to poorer churches.
About 165 they erected monuments to their martyred apostles,
to Peter in a necropolis on the Vatican Hill, to Paul on the road
to Ostia, at the traditional sites of their burial. Roman bishops
were already conscious of being custodians of the authentic
tradition or true interpretation of the apostolic writings. In the
conflict with Gnosticism Rome played a decisive role, and
likewise in the deep division in Asia Minor created by the
claims of the Montanist prophets to be the organs of the Holy
Spirit's direct utterances.

The earliest known example of the Roman bishop exercising
jurisdiction is painful. In Asia Minor Easter was celebrated on
the date of the Jewish Passover festival, that being the date of
the crucifixion in St John's Gospel (a work closely associated
with the tradition of Ephesus). But the gospels of Matthew,
Mark, and Luke make the Last Supper the Passover meal, and
place the crucifixion a day later, which affected the calculation
of the date for the Easter festival elsewhere. In Rome Easter
was celebrated on the Sunday following the full moon after the
spring equinox, and was a memorial of the resurrection. In the
150s Polycarp of Smyrna visited Rome; no agreement was
reached. In the 190s it seemed intolerable to the then bishop
of Rome, Victor, that the churches in Asia Minor celebrated

Easter on a different date, and to the distress of many he threatened excommunication on those who did not adopt the Roman date. Since the churches of Asia Minor in all probability had the more ancient observance, they refused submission, and the difference continued.

In the mid-third century Bishop Stephen of Rome asserted that all should observe the tradition of Peter and Paul: viz. those baptized outside the church by schismatic clergy should be readmitted as penitents by imposition of hands, but not treated as if the majesty of Christ's name had never been pronounced. The sacrament was Christ's, not the minister's. Bishop Cyprian of Carthage vehemently dissented, and had the support of the Greek East. Cyprian thought it absurd to suppose that where there is no true eucharist (in schism), there can be valid baptism. The debate was to mark a lasting difference between East and West. It was also the first occasion on which the bishop of Rome is known to have invoked the text of Matthew 16: 18 to justify his primatial jurisdiction. The Roman church was exercising leadership long before anyone appealed to this text. Most ancient exegetes take the 'rock' on which Jesus will build his church to be St Peter's faith.

The Latin *papa*, or Greek *pappas*, 'Daddy', was used by early Christians of a bishop to whom they stood in a filial relation. North African Christians called the bishop of Carthage *papa*, but his colleague at Rome was 'bishop of Rome'. From the sixth century the title *papa* became especially Roman in the West. Until the fourth century his authority lay in being 'successor of Peter and Paul'. The influence of Matthew 16: 16 led to the dropping of Paul. Not until Innocent III (d. 1216) is the title 'successor of Peter' replaced by 'vicar of Christ'.

Montanism, the Easter controversy, and the debate about baptism were all complex issues which required consultation between bishops. In Acts 15 scripture recorded the apostles meeting in synod to reach a common policy about the Gentile mission. The 'synod' or, in Latin, 'council' (the modern distinction making a synod something less than a council was unknown in antiquity) became an indispensable way of keeping a common mind, and helped to keep maverick individuals from centrifugal tendencies. During the third century synodical government became so developed that synods used to meet not merely at times of crisis but on a regular basis every year, normally between Easter and Pentecost. Synods were not like the parliaments of liberal democracies. On fundamental questions of doctrine or canon law their decisions were expected to be unanimous. Cyprian of Carthage repeatedly upheld the principle that 'a bishop is responsible to God alone'. But he did not mean that a bishop was utterly free to act and think as he thought fit. He had obligations to the universal episcopate which had to act in harmony for the unity of the church. In Cyprian's conception of the church, it also followed that the bishop is the vehicle of sacramental order, and to be authentically Christian is always to be in communion with the catholic bishop. To go into schism is to break that love between believers which is constitutive in the church. 'He cannot have God for his Father who has not the Church for his mother.' To be outside the one visible communion is to be outside the Ark drowning in the flood. 'Outside the Church there is no salvation.'

The Social Role of the Clergy

'We Christians', said Tertullian, 'have everything in common except our wives.' The church of the apostolic age sought to identify itself with the 'poor' whom Jesus had declared blessed (Luke 6: 20); or had he meant the 'poor in spirit' (Matt. 5: 3), the humble-hearted, who could hold their property without pride as means to support the destitute? The churches in the great cities like Rome acquired resources to maintain the clergy, initially paid on a dividend basis from the monthly total of offerings, and the very poor or oppressed. The absence of endowments before the time of the Emperor Constantine inevitably meant that well-to-do Christians had much influence on their local communities, which could be decisive when a new bishop was being chosen. But care for the poor remained a prime task of bishops. The Roman empire was no welfare state, and before Christian times in the West (unlike the East) care for the poor was rare. Poverty is a relative term. The Latin *pauper* means a person of modest means rather than someone without food, roof, or clothing; Ovid defined him as 'a man who knows how many sheep he owns'. The Christians sought to protect the destitute, or those who had fallen in status and resources like widows, and orphans. They provided hospices for the sick or for raising the innumerable foundlings. In the mid-third century the Roman church was feeding 155 church officials of various grades, and more than 1,500 widows and distressed persons. At Antioch in Syria late in the fourth century, the number of destitute persons being fed by the church had reached 3,000. It became common for a register or *matricula* of names to be kept.

Church funds also came to be used in special cases to buy the emancipation of Christian slaves, but the church did not have a general programme for the abolition of slavery. Christian preachers could declare how wrong it was for an individual to be dominated by another so as to be his legal property, and to be bought for much less than the rich would give for a racehorse. But slaves in good households were far better fed, clothed, and housed than the free wage-labourers who formed the majority of the labour force. And the freedom of the emancipated slave was relative rather than absolute.

The principle long continued to be agreed that Christian aid to the destitute should not discriminate in favour of church members, but had no criterion other than need. When the plague struck Carthage in 252, Bishop Cyprian sent his people out to nurse the sick and bury the dead. More than a century later the emperor Julian 'the Apostate' was complaining that the Christians look after 'not only their own beggars but ours as well'.

The clergy did not only minister word and sacraments;

they also performed social roles for their flock. Pagans were accustomed to using temples as safe-deposits for their treasures. So the Christians came to use their clergy as bankers. Although the Old Testament disapprobation of usury continued within the church (above all when people of slender means took out loans on the security of their house or smallholding and ended by being evicted—a situation liable to cause urban riots), even the clergy were willing to make loans for Christian merchants. The Council of Nicaea (325) forbade them to charge more than 12 per cent a year. The ordinary commercial rate, at least for maritime loans, would have been far higher.

Certain occupations were held to be unfitting for baptized believers; magic, idolatry, eroticism, games in the amphitheatre ranked as unsuitable occupations. There was controversy in the second-century churches whether a Christian could be a magistrate or bear public authority, activities which might require apparently compromising with idolatry or condemning criminals to execution. Capital punishment was unacceptable to the ancient church.

Sex and Marriage

The church found it hard to enforce chastity within marriage when a pagan man took it for granted that he had the right to sleep with his slavegirls. But we must not suppose that the rigid Christian sex ethic was shaped by reaction against pagan debauchery. The characteristic Christian theme was most at variance with pagan assumptions in that bishops asked husbands to be as faithful to their wives as they expected their wives to be to them. That was news. In the second century the medical writer Galen was impressed by Christian continence and especially the fact that many were celibate. Justin in 150 presented his fellow-believers as heroes of restraint, rejecting remarriage after divorce, even discouraging second marriages for the widowed. Tertullian wished well-to-do Christians to take widows into their houses as 'spiritual spouses'. The

Christians were strongly opposed to child exposure, actively rescuing foundlings, and deplored abortions which they did not think defensible except with arguments that equally justified infanticide.

A striking difference between pagan and Christian attitudes to sex and marriage appears in a curious duality. On the one hand, many pagan religious and philosophical moralists frowned on sexual activity as carnal and obstructive to the higher aspirations of the soul; yet the reproductive impulse ensures the survival of human society and its exercise must be good when directed to procreation rather than pleasure. On the other hand, the Christians (who could also echo the philosophers' sentiments) read the story of the Fall of Adam and Eve as implying a flaw in human sexuality, not necessarily as a *cause* of sin but as a prime *expression* of selfish egotism.

Attached to many early Christian communities were groups of ascetics, both men and women, some of whom demonstrated the supernatural character of their chastity by the sexes cohabiting, yet without sexual contact. Despite episcopal censures, the practice continued for a surprisingly long time; measures were taken to stop Irish clergy so cohabiting as late as the sixth century. John Chrysostom was declaiming against the practice at Antioch in Syria in the 380s.

Writing to the Corinthians who thought sex in marriage incompatible with the spiritual life, the apostle had insisted that marriage and procreation are no sin, while conceding to his opponents that, though good, marriage is not as good as celibacy. St Peter was certainly married and on apostolic journeys took his wife with him. Philip the evangelist begat four daughters. But in the mid-second century the apocryphal 'Acts of John' presented St John as a lifelong virgin. Jerome was confident that even married apostles lived in mutual continence, after the example of their unmarried Lord and his ever virgin mother. For bishops, then for presbyters, finally for deacons, Western churches came to expect and ultimately to require celibacy (though the canonical compulsion was not seriously enforced until medieval times and even thereafter in parts of Europe, like Southern Germany or Wales, it was common for village priests to have a consort and a family, with the support of their flock and the connivance of their bishop who derived income from the annual fee or tax to allow the arrangement).

The Church and the 'World'

The Christian community inherited from its Jewish matrix a strong sense of being 'called out' (the root meaning of *ecclesia*) from the surrounding society which they felt to be possessed by different values. The 'world' was, in terms of nature and by creation, a great good, a gift of the omnipotent and good Creator. Yet the 'world' is also a term in Christian usage for something alienated from God and hostile to him, corrupted and, apart from the sustaining hand of grace, hellbent for chaos and destruction. In this aspect the world's values find expression in the driving lust for power, wealth, and sexual indulgence. The inexplicable weight of cumulative malevolence in the human race made it natural to personify the power of evil as Satan, 'the adversary', in Greek *diabolos* or 'slanderer', a cosmic 'god of this world' (2 Cor. 4: 4). From the devil's power, from planetary fate, Christ is redeemer, and his values as expressed in, for example the 'Beatitudes' (Matt. 5) are a reversal of those current in society. The Jewish–Christian tradition identified the gods of polytheism with subordinates of the devil, malevolent spirits entrapping their worshippers, impelling them to worship the created order (hence the images in temples where polytheists believed their gods to be resident) rather than the Creator. Both St Paul and his elder contemporary, the Jew Philo of Alexandria, saw in sexual perversion and disorder a symptom of idolatry.

Endeavours to enforce assimilation to Graeco-Roman culture upon the Jews had provoked fierce resistance. 'Hellenism' meant not only speaking Greek as the main language of communication in the eastern half of the Mediterranean, but also games, gymnasia, theatres, and the diffusion of polytheistic cult. The Maccabees fought rather than acquiesce in the placing of a statue of Zeus in the Temple. Caligula proposed to put his own statue there, and the resulting furore is echoed in the New Testament (e.g. 2 Thess. 2: 4). The imperial cult was to Jews and Christians sacrilege. Insensitive Roman government provoked the Jewish revolts of AD 66, 116, and 132–5, the last ending in their expulsion from Jerusalem and its transformation by Hadrian into a wholly Gentile city, Aelia (Hadrian's family name) Capitolina (because a shrine of Jupiter of the Capitol was built). The Temple Mount was left in ruins. The Roman empire was not experienced by the Jews as a regime of toleration, and pagan society was in some degree anti-Semitic. Educated Greeks and Romans thought strange the Jewish religion without images and with no sacrifices except at Jerusalem, with bizarre food laws excluding pork, with circumcision, and a distinctive calendar.

The acceptance of the Gentile Christians without a requirement that they keep the Mosaic law seemed to the rabbis an excessive liberalism, and relations between church and synagogue after their separation had become final (probably about AD 85) were not comfortable. The infant churches experienced from the synagogues persecution which, when full grown, they were to be in a position to return.

Martyrs

But persecution mainly came upon the church from the Roman government. The precedent was set by Nero at Rome in AD 64. St Paul had been sent to Rome a prisoner, and suffered eventual execution. The precedents guided provincial governors. The crime was paradoxical, namely, the mere profession of Christianity, the name itself, rather than any crimes that might be attributed to the name by association. A Christian defendant could gain release by offering incense on a pagan altar. The external act sufficed. So the prime offence was a refusal to acknowledge respect to the gods, including the emperor, by whose favour the empire was preserved. An oath by the emperor's genius (tutelary spirit) seemed simple enough. To refuse it was to suffer imprisonment, torture, being flung to wild beasts in the amphitheatre, or, in the case of a Roman citizen, being beheaded. The Christians called such heroes of integrity 'witnesses', martyrs. (Why this word was specially chosen has been the subject of scholarly controversy; the probable answer is that the Christian who died for Christ was believed to be uniquely united with his crucified Master, thereby linking the concept of witness with sacrificial dying; but in martyrdom the cause is primary, the dying secondary.)

The Christian neglect of the gods, indeed the propensity of the more militant to hiss in disapproval as they walked by a temple, offended polytheists, who feared that heaven would not be propitious: floods, plagues, famines, earthquakes were sent by angry spirit-powers who had not been placated with the customary offerings. Barbarian invasion or civil war could also bring vast unpopularity on the Christians, cast as scape-goats. In the second and early third centuries persecution was often haphazard, caused by mob violence or by delation to the local governor who might be quite reluctant to react to the information handed in by complainants. Threats to the survival of the empire and resentment at the Christian attitude to the celebrations of Rome's millennium in 248 precipitated per-secution on the initiative of the Emperor Decius in 250; he began his brief reign with a fierce and lethal attack, especially on bishops. The government was well aware that the very survival of the church had been in no small degree due to the coherence and discipline imparted by the episcopate. Moreover, by 250 the church was freely penetrating the upper levels of Roman society; at Carthage Cyprian was well-to-do, with his own villa and private resources which he devoted to his church. His fellow bishops addressed him as 'lord' (a compliment he did not reciprocate). The severest of persecutions under

Diocletian, from 303 for a decade, was caused by fear of Christian penetration into the army, including even officers of the high command, and into the higher echelons of the Civil Service.

Some enthusiastic Christians courted martyrdom by smashing religious images or, under cross-examination, appearing contumacious, dissident, and disrespectful to the governor. What was a Roman proconsul to do with a Christian who explained that he paid his taxes not in the least because the emperor's laws and edicts required that, but because it was the command of the Lord? Or with another who, when asked for his 'home' (*patris*), answered that it was the heavenly Jerusalem? The radical other-worldliness of such people seemed incomprehensible to the authorities. The church discovered in persecution, provided that it was inefficient (as most of it was), that even if some pagan observers thought the martyrs merely theatrical suicides (so the Emperor Marcus Aurelius), many others were led to ask questions. The church became the subject of incredulous and not necessarily friendly discussion, but it was a kind of publicity from which the church came to gain recruits. 'The blood of the martyrs is seed' (Tertullian). On the other hand, the unpopularity of the Christians was also caused by unpleasant stories that at their nocturnal meetings they indulged in cannibalism and incest (charges easily explicable from misunderstandings of language about the eucharist). Some of honest and good heart would not even speak to a Christian as late as the mid-third century, by which date the Christian story and way of life had become well known, because they suspected them of enormities. In Asia Minor about 110 the younger Pliny, the governor of Bithynia, asked Trajan whether the profession of Christianity was in itself culpable or 'the vices associated with the name', especially since after investigation by torture he had discovered that there were no frightful vices: the accused said their custom was to meet before dawn on a particular day to sing a hymn to Christ as a god and to take an oath (*sacramentum*) to abstain from wrongdoing. Two 'women servants' (*ministrae*) were found to confess to nothing vicious and to hold only 'squalid superstition'. Group sex in the dark simply did not occur. Pliny was astonished. But the obstinacy seemed intolerable.

The effects of persecution on the Christians themselves were various. In North Africa a Christian militancy developed, and the supreme ambition was to be granted a martyr's crown. In Numidia (southern Algeria) zealous believers greeted one another with the wish 'May you gain your crown'. The anniversaries, called 'birthdays', of the martyrs were carefully remembered, and so came to create the earliest church calendars (so that the historian can know on what day of what month a martyr died, but not necessarily in what year, that being of no liturgical significance). By about AD 200 there were Christians in Rome celebrating the memory of St Peter and St Paul on 29 June. (During the third century they were celebrating Easter and Pentecost, which were inherited and then modified from Judaism and so dependent on a lunar year. By 300 the West added the birth of Jesus integrated into a solar calendar by being placed at the winter solstice. A rival distraction was needed to the pagan festival at this time when presents were exchanged and much liquor consumed. Christian preachers attempted, without much success, to persuade their congregations to fast while inebriated pagans feasted and to give alms to the very poor who could give no present in return.)

There were internal arguments about the honouring of martyrs and about the proper way of ensuring that the honours did not become confused with old heathen practices, such as offering food and wine at the tombs of ancestors. In Carthage an inveterate schism (Donatism) originated when a devout and wealthy lady who treasured the relic of a martyr was rebuked for lavishing kisses on it at the commemoration of the faithful departed at the eucharist; 'she went off in a huff', we are told, and when the archdeacon who rebuked her became the next bishop of Carthage she had her majordomo appointed as a rival, with the support of the main body of Numidian bishops.

The issue was not merely personal, however. The question was whether, when a pagan government forbade Christian meetings for worship and required the surrender of Bibles and vessels and vestments, any kind of compromise was morally possible. Rigorists rejected compromise: they would surrender nothing and understood it to be of the essence of their Christian allegiance that every Lord's day they would unfailingly celebrate the eucharist. Compromisers, such as the archdeacon, disapproved of confrontations, and wanted to lie low until the storm was past. The police were not uncooperative, and were willing to accept heretical or medical volumes in lieu of Bibles.

During the persecutions those who had most to lose in terms of this world's goods were the rich Christians, whose property was liable to confiscation unless they 'apostatized'. Naturally this had immediate consequences for the destitute fed by the church chest that rich believers funded. But the number of those who compromised their faith was largest among the propertied and those well up in the social hierarchy. When persecution died down, many wished for restoration, and there were sharp disagreements about the terms, conditions, and proper authority under which restoration could and should be granted. At Rome in the 250s a split occurred between the rigorists led by Novatian who believed that for apostates there could be no restoration in this life, and those who saw no restriction in the Lord's committal of the power of the keys to bind and loose. At Rome there had been some disagreement and even contention for more than a century on the possibility of restoration for believers who committed adultery, murder, or apostasy (participation in idolatrous rites). A subtle tract, the *Shepherd* of Hermas, early in the second century sought to undermine the rigorist position as inhuman, yet without surrendering the church's obligation to maintain moral standards among its members. Sanctity could easily merge into separation and censoriousness.

In the debate about restoration scripture could be quoted both for rigour and for mercy. Since it was desirable that penitents should not be treated with rigour by one bishop and with mercy by a neighbouring bishop, a common policy was needed. Canon law originated in the agreements of third-century church councils concerning the terms of restoration of the lapsed. Mercy should be shown to the contrite, but the community needed to be reassured that the contrition was genuine. Cheap grace was to be avoided. Moreover, there were degrees of culpability. How should one estimate the faults of those who offered incense without any torture, those who gave way only after cruel torture by rack and fire, and those who had not actually offered incense at all but had bribed a friendly official to sell them a certificate to say they had done so? In 303 a Christian named Copres from the Nile valley, engaged in a lawsuit over property, went to Alexandria to present his case and was disconcerted to discover that he would be required to participate in some act of idolatry, such as a sacrifice or an oath by the emperor's genius, as a condition of litigation. He was able to give a pagan friend power of attorney to act on his behalf, and so found an elegant way of keeping his conscience clear and his standing with the church unaffected. His letter home to his wife discloses the inconvenience, but not more, which the persecution caused him. For others it became an issue of life or death. The martyr's conflict was seen not as a fight against duly constituted authority in government, but against Satan. It was a struggle in which the heroic confessor of the faith was understood to be uniquely assisted by the Spirit of God, and more than one account tells of the 'victims' being granted visions to strengthen them. In fact the extant Acts of the Martyrs (where based on contemporary records and not legends) do not portray the martyrs as human heroes, but as very frail mortals who are being given supernatural strength.

In the visionary revelation granted to him in exile on Patmos St John saw the martyrs beneath the altar crying 'How long O Lord?' (Revelation 6: 9–10). By the fourth century, relics of martyrs would be placed beneath the altar in the Christian basilica. Surely they were interceding for the faithful on earth.

Their acceptance by God was symbolized by the fact that while the ancient churches prayed for God's continuing grace for the faithful departed, they did not pray for martyrs. The martyrs prayed for them.

Defenders of the Faith: Justin Martyr

The Christians found themselves under attack not only from the Roman government but also from Greek philosophers and representatives of high literary culture, orators, historians (but not natural scientists). From the middle years of the second century the converts included some philosophically trained minds, at least the equal of most pagan contemporaries. Justin came from Nablus in Palestine to Ephesus where, according to his own account (which may not be plain prose), he studied with teachers of several different schools—Stoic, Aristotelian, Pythagorean, Platonist—expecting from the last named not only clarity for his mind but light for his soul. One day, however, walking by the seashore he met an elderly Christian who told him about the Hebrew prophets, undermined his naïve confidence in the moral guidance of philosophers, and converted him to Christianity. Justin moved on to Rome where he offered lectures in his own school on the Christian philosophy. This brought him into conflict with a pagan critic, and the exchange of argument can be deduced from the defence (*Apologia*) for Christianity which Justin composed and which he later supplemented with a further appendix. We have also from his pen a long *Dialogue with Trypho the Jew*. In a style modelled on the Platonic dialogues, Justin here interpreted Old Testament prophecies which he saw fulfilled in Jesus and in the present life of the church, already spreading throughout the known world.

Justin was convinced that in the highminded Stoic ethics of human brotherhood, and especially in the other-worldly Platonic metaphysics, there was much for a Christian to welcome. With varying results the divine Sower had sown the seed of truth, admittedly not always in wholly fertile ground. Plato was surely mistaken to think the soul inherently immortal by nature rather than in dependence on God's will, and to suppose it capable of reincarnation. Yet Justin's list of what Plato said aright is long and serene. He regretted that Plato had not broken with the gods of the old cults and myths even though he had evidently known them to be false. For Plato perceived God to be immutable, incorporeal, nameless, transcendent beyond all time and space. In debate with Trypho, Justin exploited this principle: because the almighty Father is transcendent, the God who appeared to Moses at the burning bush cannot have been the Father but his Word and Reason (*Logos*) who is therefore 'other than the Father in number though not in will'.

In the universal reason of the divine Word all rational beings share, and both Abraham and Socrates are 'Christians before Christ'. Christ's ethical teaching proclaimed the way to true happiness, for he was not only man but God, acknowledged in the manger by the magi, vindicated by his wonderful acts, by the fulfilment of prophecy in the gospel story, and by the astounding diffusion of the gospel in the world. So the truths only partially apprehended in the aspirations of the greatest classical philosophers of Greece find their fulfilment, and correction, in the framework of the Christian faith. Should anyone ask how Plato's discernment of divine creation and even of the divine Triad could be so close to the now known truth, the answer is that he had read the books of Moses on his visit to Egypt. To one pagan philosopher of Justin's age Plato was only 'Moses in Attic idiom'.

Justin had such confidence in the rationality of the gospel that the phenomenon of unbelief had to be explained on the hypothesis of evil spirits spreading misinformation and prejudice in the interests of polytheism and superstition. Indeed, in the mystery religions such as that of Mithra, the worshippers shared in a kind of sacramental meal by which evil spirits had parodied the Christian eucharist. Justin held in abhorrence the Gnostic mixing of myths and cults to make an unpalatable bouillabaisse of religions. He wrote not only to defend the faith against persecuting governors, sceptical philosophers, and combative rabbis, but also to uphold the authentic tradition against Simon Magus' followers (Acts 8: 9) or the adherents of Marcion and the Gnosticizing Platonist Valentine. Their rejection of the Old Testament set aside the argument from fulfilled prophecy which had played a notable part in his conversion. Justin saw Adam as prefiguring Christ, Eve as a 'type' of Mary, and called the correspondences of Old and New Testament figures the principle of 'recapitulation'; that was to say that redemption is not from the created order but of it and within it.

Justin's themes here became important to Irenaeus, bishop of Lyons in the Rhône valley *c.*180, where his Greek congregation had close links to the churches of Asia Minor. Irenaeus asserted the unity of the two Testaments in his *Refutation of the Knowledge falsely so called*, a work principally directed against those heretics standing close to orthodox Christianity and therefore offering a dangerous threat to orthodox congregations. Picking up from St Paul the idea that the Old Testament law was a kind of 'tutor', Irenaeus saw the relation of the Testaments as a progressive education of humanity. This way of thinking allowed him to concede some shortcomings of moral insight in the Old Testament. An unfolding of the divine purpose he also discerned in the revelation that in relation to the world God is active by his word and wisdom, like 'two hands' shaping the world and guiding the church.

Neither of the two principal works of Irenaeus to survive complete is extant in his original Greek. The anti-Gnostic treatise as a whole is preserved in a Latin translation made in North Africa *c.*395. His *Demonstration of the Apostolic Preaching* is preserved only in Armenian. His understanding of the faith is strongly biblical. His ideal theologian was a person submissive to authority through the tradition authenticated by the apostolic Bible, not someone with bright new ideas, certainly not someone claiming to offer fresh revelations.

The Father and the Son

Justin's language about the distinction of the Father as God transcendent from the Son as God immanent, which Irenaeus had made his own, precipitated sharp debate (the so-called monarchian controversy) at Rome *c.*190–225. In combating Gnostic dualism orthodox writers had insisted on the divine monarchy: there is only one ultimate principle. But Justin's language about the otherness of the divine Word suggested a dyarchy. What had St John meant when he said that the Word was '*with* God'?

The distinction of the Son from the Father was a theme vehemently taken up by the Roman presbyter Hippolytus. Hippolytus fell out with Callistus, the archdeacon in charge of the cemeteries in the catacombs, and found Callistus' election to be bishop more than he could endure, so he became bishop in rivalry. Callistus had publicly accused him of being a ditheist, and used language offering cover to those (soon associated with a presbyter named Sabellius) who held that Father, Son, and Spirit are names for one God under different aspects. Callistus also offended Hippolytus' moral rigorism by asserting that the power of the keys entrusted by the Lord to his church did not exclude authority to restore to communion penitent adulterers. Hippolytus composed a strange book entitled the *Refutation* arguing the dependence of a row of Gnostic sects upon a row of pagan philosophers, and finally turning his weapons on Callistus, who seemed to him the abomination of desolation sitting where he ought not. The cantankerous tone of Hippolytus cannot be denied. Nevertheless, he was certainly a learned man. He wrote a substantial commentary on the book of Daniel, to discourage fervent apocalyptic expectations of an imminent end to the world which had lately led one bishop to lead his flock out into the desert to meet the returning Lord, requiring a rescue operation by government authority. He compiled a chronicle of world history, fitting together the calculations of Greek chroniclers with the indications of date found in the Bible. He composed an Easter table. Admirers of his scholarship dedicated a statue in his honour, inscribed on the base with a catalogue of his writings. One, entitled *Apostolic Tradition*, has been plausibly conjectured to be a church order (directions for liturgy and the proper ordering of the community) certainly of the early third century and probably from Rome. Whether or not the work is by Hippolytus, the document is a major source for early liturgy and is the first text to witness to liturgical patterns which have remained in use.

Tertullian

The most important and eloquent theologian in the West at the end of the second century was Tertullian, a lay Christian of Carthage. A brilliant polemical writer, he overwhelmed his opponents (heretics, Jews, pagans, and, after he became a Montanist, orthodox bishops) with a combination of rapier and bludgeon. The earliest writer of Christian Latin (and a fascinating witness to the emergence of a specifically Christian Latin vocabulary), he coined the terminology which was to dominate Western theology—for example, *trinitas*, 'three persons in one substance', or of Christ 'two substances or natures in one person'. A particularly influential and characteristic tract is his *Against Praxeas*, a Christian who came from Asia Minor to Rome to express opposition both to the pluralistic theology of Justin and Hippolytus and to any recognition that Montanist prophecy might be an authentic work of the Paraclete. In Tertullian's trenchant phrase, 'he accomplished two bits of the devil's business: he put to flight the Paraclete and crucified the Father.' For Tertullian stood with Justin in defending the distinctness of Son and Father. Among other works Tertullian composed a riveting tract *On the Soul*, its nature and origin, and the problem of 'its inherited flaw'. In some of his tracts he is outspokenly hostile to philosophy as mother of heresy, strident in his insistence that for a true believer everything is decided by the authority of the apostolic rule of faith and scripture so that further enquiries are superfluous. In other tracts he is strikingly positive to the 'naturally Christian soul' and its rational powers.

Aristotle once recommended to the would-be polemical orator that paradox could be effective. Tertullian enjoyed paradox. To him the divine character of Christianity was vindicated not by its reasonableness but by the very fact that it was the kind of thing no ordinary mind could have invented. The crucifying of the Son of God sounds ridiculous and scandalous: 'I believe because it is outrageous.'

To the east of Carthage in Libya sharp disputes between the monarchian followers of Sabellius and upholders of the Logos theology occurred half a century after Tertullian's time. The Libyan quarrel was referred to Bishop Dionysius of Alexandria, a very well-educated man, who sided with those theologians who stressed the distinctness of Father and Son; they should not be said to be of one being but to be as distinct as the husbandman and the vine. The Sabellian group complained to the bishop of Rome who reproached his Alexandrian colleague for careless language, and proclaimed that in God unity is prior to all plurality, which is found not in God as he is in and to himself, but in God in his providential relationship with the world. In making his defence Dionysius of Alexandria found useful matter in the pages of Tertullian's *Against Praxeas*.

Tatian

Justin's pupil Tatian from Mesopotamia developed with a sarcastic pen the philosophers' dependence on Moses, which he argued with elaborate synchronisms from ancient chroniclers proving the priority of Moses. Tatian was also influential for making a harmony of the four gospels which in the Syriac-speaking churches of the East long remained the standard lectionary text. He wrote a book expounding 1 Corinthians 7 to imply that the apostle was not really defending marriage, since his arguments fatally conceded that it was not the most perfect state for the believer, and no true believer could aspire to less than the perfection to which God called. A number of Gnostic themes also entered his theology so that his reputation suffered. Nevertheless, his chronographic calculations were gratefully exploited by Clement of Alexandria, *c.* 190–200.

Clement

Clement of Alexandria's principal achievement was his trilogy: (1) an Exhortation to conversion (*Protreptikos*), in the style of ancient homilies commending the study of philosophy to men of affairs inclined to think it a waste of time; (2) the *Paidagogos* or Tutor, providing a guide to ethics and etiquette, which is a major source for social history of the age; (3) *Stromateis*, or Miscellanies, a deliberately rambling work, constantly changing the subject, but from which the discerning reader can reconstruct a remarkable, carefully thought out system.

Clement's prose puts him in a higher class than any of his extant pagan contemporaries, and he was able obliquely to refute pagan critics (such as Celsus, writing 177–80) who thought Christians an anti-cultural lot, by decorating his pages with a rich variety of quotations and allusions taken from classical poetry and philosophy. At first it looks like namedropping until one finds the same sort of thing in Athenaeus or Aelian. Clement's purpose was to make cultured persons under instruction for baptism, called 'catechumens' (by contrast with 'the faithful' who are the baptized), feel that they would be at home in the church. He wanted to show that one could be an educated and intelligent believer without abandoning the apostolic rule of faith and life. The by-product of his work is to vindicate the proper place of the Christian intellectual within the community. After all, bishops could not announce the correct date for Easter if they had no mathematicians to call upon. Thanks to their extensive plagiarism from the Old Testament, Clement argued, Plato and the Greek philosophers had found out many true things and expressed them in beautiful language.

Clement combined his highly positive evaluation of culture with a severe puritanism towards any concessions to polytheistic myth and cult. He was wholly against eroticism in art and literature, and thought that, in the event of any conflict, aesthetic value must yield to morality. He wrote an exposition of Jesus' saying to the rich young ruler that to be perfect he must sell all. He explained that the Lord required a strict use of wealth for the service of God, but did not condemn mere possession. In this distinction between possession and use, Clement picked up language from St Paul in 1 Corinthians 7, recommending that married couples treat sexuality as a means to a higher end, not as an end in itself. Clement wrote the third book of his *Miscellanies* to attack the Gnostic denial of the goodness of the created order, which lay at the root of their contradictory attitudes to sex, either as a repulsive carnality or as a source of phallic ecstasy. So too wealth should be used as a means to good ends, but never be sought or enjoyed for its own sake. A rich Christian would wisely put himself and his purse under the guidance of a prudent and austere spiritual director, pointing him along the path to perfection.

Almost all philosophically minded people of Clement's age, except for only a tiny handful of Epicureans, took it for granted that the order of the world reflects a designing providential hand. Platonists and Stoics in different ways expended much effort, therefore, in accounting for the evils of experience. Pagan Platonists, however, could not stomach the Christian notion of incarnation which they understood to imply change in God. Clement circumvented the difficulty by interpreting the incarnation in one particular corner of the world as a specially significant moment in a universal care for all humanity at all times and in all places. A general, diffused providence which has no particular manifestations whatever is an inherently problematic concept. For Clement, God does not change his will by the incarnation; he wills a change in humanity. The incarnation is therefore an extreme instance of divine immanence within the creation.

Origen

Clement was a convert from paganism. His Alexandrian successor Origen (184–254) was the son of Christian parents. The martyrdom of his father in 203 left him with a cold antipathy to the pagan establishment, whether in government or in high culture. This lasting antipathy coexisted in his mind with a rare mastery of philosophical debate and classical literature. There are intricate philosophical and logical disputes of the Hellenistic schools which we now understand only because Origen gave a clear account of the points at issue. A steely ascetic renunciation marked his character, and Eusebius of Caesarea reports a tradition that in the zeal of youth he had subjected himself to castration to free him to instruct female pupils without scandal. The story may be true since instances of such zeal are well attested for Christian antiquity. When, however, Origen himself came to write a commentary on Matthew 19: 12 he strenuously opposed a literal exegesis. His ascetic determination led him to sell his non-Christian books. But a prodigious memory enabled him to retain to the end of his life a total recall, whether of a text of scripture or a line of the *Iliad* or a passage in Plato's *Dialogues*. Learning by heart was standard procedure in ancient and medieval education. After his father's death he was taken into the house of a rich Christian lady of liberal sympathies—for Origen too liberal since she had a Gnostic chaplain. Soon he set up his own lecture school. An anti-Christian riot (215) made him take refuge in Palestine; but the bishop of Alexandria, Demetrius, recalled him to be head of the catechetical school (217). There he delegated elementary instruction to an assistant, while he took advanced students, following the example of Jesus (Mark 4: 34).

Out of his advanced lectures emerged a powerful refutation of the entire Gnostic world-view and principles of biblical interpretation, a work entitled *On First Principles*. However, the book, which as a whole survives only in a revised and partially expurgated Latin translation by Rufinus made in 398, damaged his reputation for pure orthodoxy. This was mainly because of his belief that, if God is pure goodness, so that divine punishments are always therapeutic, not merely retributive, and if freedom is alienable in all created rational beings, then ultimately even the most wicked will be purified by divine love and fit for salvation. Then Christ will deliver up the kingdom to the Father, and God will be all in all. This 'all' includes even Satan himself, for he felt that to concede that any rational creature is irredeemable would be to surrender to Gnostic dualism. 'One could pity but not censure a being totally deprived of all capacity for recognizing goodness and doing what is right.' The fuss these ideas created, and a storm when the bishop of Caesarea in Palestine ordained Origen presbyter without reference to the bishop of Alexandria, moved Origen to migrate to Caesarea (231). His universalism seemed to offer unending real misery punctuated by periods of illusory bliss.

To interpret the Bible Origen exploited the Platonists' tri-partite division of the cosmos into matter, soul, and mind. Origen first launched the theme, developed in the eighteenth century by Joseph Butler and Isaac Newton, that revelation is to be understood on the analogy of nature. There is no difficulty in the former which is not met in the latter. Scripture accordingly has three levels of meaning corresponding to the three levels of reality: (*a*) a literal historical sense, (*b*) a moral meaning, and (*c*) a spiritual interpretation. The existence of (*b*) and (*c*) he thought proved by the presence of some biblical texts where the literal sense seemed absurd or contradictory; such texts must have been placed there as signposts to a spiritual allegorical exegesis. An axiom is that nothing unworthy of God can be intended. Just as the believer in Christ seeks to rise through the historical Son of man to the Son of God, so also in scripture the literal sense is the first rung on the ladder to the eternal spiritual meaning.

The exegesis of scripture by homily or commentary became Origen's main life work, the commentaries being on so vast a scale that none survives complete. The transmission of the majority of the homilies depends on Latin translations by Rufinus and Jerome. Origen also compiled a huge edition of the various Greek versions of the Old Testament. The purpose was to give solid ground for disputations, especially with rabbis who would not recognize the canonical authority of books which, though in the Septuagint (the Bible of the Gentile mission), were absent from the Hebrew canon. The overplus of the Greek over the Hebrew was not regarded by Origen as less than fully canonical; the suggestion that the overplus should be read for example of life and instruction of manners, but not to establish disputed doctrine, was left to Jerome. For Origen that was no more than a matter of tactics in controversy, not one of principle.

Origen's doctrine of God bequeathed a legacy of problems (and some solutions) to his successors. He insisted that Father and Son must be distinct realities or hypostases, not mere adjectives of one personal divine substance. A vehement reaction against this view came in Syria in the decade after his death.

Paul of Samosata

Paul, a native of Samosata on the Euphrates, became bishop of Antioch-on-the-Orontes, third city of the empire, at a time when Syria ceased to be under Roman control but was briefly part of the kingdom of Palmyra under Queen Zenobia (266–71). Paul distressed other bishops by offensive remarks about 'dead exegetes', and especially about Origen's notion that the pre-existent divine Word, a kind of second-level God, became incarnate by the Virgin Mary. He preferred to explain divine presence in Christ on the analogy of inspiration: Jesus was a man, essentially like all others except in being perfectly good. In him the Word and Wisdom of God dwelt in a unique degree.

Disturbed bishops gathered in synod at Antioch to express

their disapproval. They also disliked changes Paul had made in the liturgy, and his encouragement of enthusiastic audience-participation in sermons. They heard accusations that his manner of life in public and private affairs was secular. He had women not only in his church choir (it is the first known instance) but also in too close association with the life and pastoral work of the clergy. It was also alleged that he amassed wealth by exploiting his high credit with the Palmyra court, accepting douccurs from citizens wanting favours.

Paul's opponents found it easier to agree in synod on his unworthiness for office than to eject him from the episcopal residence. The Palmyra authorities gave them no assistance. But the fall of Palmyra to the Emperor Aurelian (271) re-established Roman power in Syria. If St Paul could appeal to Caesar, so could the bishops opposed to Paul of Samosata. Aurelian ruled that the latter's continued occupation of the bishop's residence was a matter to be decided by the bishop of Rome and his Italian synod.

Diocletian and the Rise of Constantine

In the middle decades of the third century, political crises, a drastic trade recession, inflation, civil war, and barbarian invasions almost produced the collapse of the Roman empire. In 257 the Emperor Valerian ordered the harassment of the church. He was soon to be taken prisoner in battle against the Persians. In 284 the Emperor Diocletian, a soldier from Illyricum (Dalmatia), took power with army support. He massively reorganized the empire on a military basis, splitting provinces to prevent ambitious governors from becoming too powerful, attempting to control inflation by fixing prices by edict (and thereby driving goods off the market). He enhanced his own powers, reducing those of aristocratic senators, and poured out a huge volume of edicts to establish law and order. He divided the government between East and West, taking the East himself. For the first nineteen years of his reign persecution of the church was not his policy, and the church prospered in numbers. But the infiltration of Christianity in high places, mainly through governors' wives, and in the high command of the army caused alarm. Apollo's oracle at Didyma near Miletus recommended an attack on the church.

Persecution severely affected the East and North Africa. Disagreements in the church about the point at which one could not compromise left a legacy of schisms in the Nile valley and in North Africa, where the rancour of the Donatist schism persisted until the Muslim invasions swept them away four centuries later. But in Gaul and Britain no one was martyred under the rule of Constantius Chlorus. He died at York in July 306, and the army at once acclaimed his son Constantine. Constantine's mother may have had Christian sympathies. Before a battle where the odds were much against him, Constantine successfully invoked the aid of the God of the Christians. He won. He had put a Greek monogram of the first letters of the name of Christ (CHR) on his standards, and it had been a talisman of victory.

In 313 Constantine, having eliminated other rulers in the West, was able to persuade his eastern colleague, the pagan Licinius, to join in a general policy of toleration for all cults including Christianity. It became legally possible for the church to own property. In 323–4 civil war ended with the elimination of Licinius, and Constantine was at last sole ruler. He was persuaded that disunity in the church was displeasing to heaven and bad for the empire's success and prosperity. The embittered schism of the Donatists in North Africa from 311 onwards brought him sharp disappointment.

In 324 on arriving in the East he felt sure that soon he would go to the Holy Land to see the sacred sites and to be baptized in Jordan. But that romantic plan was abruptly aborted. He found the Greek churches of Egypt, Palestine, Syria, and Asia Minor seething with controversy about the opinions of an Alexandrian priest named Arius. Arius had been excommunicated by his bishop, Alexander, for denying that Christ is on the divine side of the gulf between the Creator and his creation.

Arius

Arius was not a fool. If one affirms that there is and can be only one ultimate and self-sufficient principle, the transcendent Father, and also that the divine Triad is three distinct realities (as Origen had taught), it is not easy then to affirm that the Son and the Father are in being identical or 'of one substance'—not at least without fairly complicated explanations. Origen had himself felt the difficulty. He mitigated the problem by saying that the Son's generation by the Father is no event in time but is eternal. In other words, the Father–Son relationship is intrinsic to the divine life. Arius differed from Origen in seeing the coming forth of the divine Word as a service to the inferior created order. He reasoned that the Lord who was physically born of Mary, grew in wisdom, suffered dereliction and death, must be less than the unbegotten, impassible, deathless Father. God is beyond Jesus. Arius made the coming forth of the Son depend not on the Father's inherent being but on his sovereign will. It was, so to speak, not something that had to happen. The theological implication is that the Son must be somewhere midway between the Creator and the contingent creation now in need of redemption. Arius therefore clashed with a principle strongly stated by Irenaeus: 'Through God alone can God be known.' Only one who transcends the world can redeem it.

Arius received support from scholarly and politically powerful bishops, in particular from the learned church historian Eusebius of Caesarea in Palestine, a man for whom Constantine came to have great respect. An admirer of Origen, Eusebius probably thought he was facing a repetition of the situation of eighty years previously when a learned theologian harassed by a bishop of Alexandria needed support from his church. So a domestic Alexandrian dispute became a wide conflagration.

A synod of bishops, assembled from several Greek provinces, was already planned for the spring of 325 at Ankara. There an attempt was to be made to reach agreement on the date of

Easter and to end the discord between Egypt and Rome on the one hand and Syria and Asia Minor on the other. This synod was transferred by Constantine to the lakeside town of Nicaea, not far from his own palace and more accessible for the two priests sent to represent bishop Silvester of Rome.

The Council of Nicaea was the largest assembly of bishops hitherto, and though the great majority of the members were from the Greek East, the presence of Roman legates and the prominent role played by the sees of Alexandria and Antioch made it possible for the council to be given the title 'ecumenical'. The title 'ecumenical synod' was already in use for a world-wide association of repertory actors.

The council put Arianism at the head of its agenda. Arius and his friends had suggested that his critics must presuppose the (to him) unacceptable proposition that the Son's relation to the Father is one of 'identity of being', language unprotected against the heresy of Sabellius. Taking the term as a challenge, the council wrote 'identical in being' into their confession of faith, to which they appended anathemas on propositions attributed (in some cases rightly) to Arius.

In the notion of sameness there are ambiguities and ambivalences only dimly noticed by few people at the time. Because of the happy ambiguity Constantine found that all but two bishops were willing and able to sign the creed and canons, including Eusebius of Caesarea who promptly published an open letter indicating in what sense he interpreted the creed and anathemas. The following half-century saw intense debate revolving round various interpretations of the creed and the possibility of either supplementing or replacing it by something either wider or narrower.

Signs of Constantine's new deal for the church were that the council petitioned and obtained from the emperor a degree of tax exemption for the sake of the church's welfare for the poor, and that exile was imposed on the two bishops who withheld their signature to the creed and canons. The Alexandrian and Roman dating for Easter was imposed. All the decisions of the council were notified to Silvester of Rome.

At the time of the Council of Nicaea Constantine was not yet baptized, but his support to the Christian cause was not in serious doubt. To the assembled bishops he described himself as 'bishop of external things'—presumably external to the church. But he certainly wanted the church to be both united and free of heresy. In the civil war of 324 he had represented his military campaign as a crusade against a corrupt paganism. From 326 onwards pagan temples began to suffer the gradual loss of old endowments. The emperor had begun to think polytheistic cult a veneration of evil spirits and therefore perhaps a danger to his realm. In 330 he inaugurated his new eastern capital, the 'city of Constantine' at Byzantium on the Bosphorus, planned as a 'New Rome'. The dedication ceremonies were conducted by Christian clergy.

Before about 400 AD it was common for baptism to be deferred until near the end of life because of the formidable nature of the penances and discipline required after the confession of post-baptismal sin. Constantine finally set aside all hesitation. On his deathbed at Pentecost 337 he was baptized by a bishop whose sympathies happened to be Arian; much later legend made Pope Silvester bestow the lifegiving baptismal water. His solemn burial was at Constantinople alongside the cenotaphs of the twelve apostles which he had placed in the church of the apostles on the city's highest hill. He was to be the thirteenth, the equal of the Twelve.

That his conversion was momentous for the church cannot be doubted. He had conferred great material benefits, providing Bibles and building great basilicas such as St John Lateran and St Peter's at Rome, the church of the Resurrection (later called the Holy Sepulchre) at Jerusalem, and that of the Nativity at Bethlehem. Gratitude to him has always been greater in the Orthodox churches of the East than in the West, where his domination of the church has often not been regarded as an altogether unmitigated good, at least in its consequences. But the Arian controversy was a nightmare to the Greek East and Constantine's role in supporting orthodoxy was not quickly forgotten.

Retrospect

A retrospect on the progress of the church in the two and a half centuries between St Peter and Constantine must include substantial astonishment. That a movement beginning as a breakaway group within Judaism should end by capturing the imperial palace could hardly have been foreseen by the Emperors Tiberius or Nero. Tacitus regarded Christianity as one more contemptible superstition, to the pessimist additional evidence of the sad capacity of human beings to believe strange things. That these people would one day be enthroned in the citadel of power could not have seemed conceivable to him. Moreover, the Christians were predominantly, if not entirely, world-renouncing. They were dissenters from and critics of the worldly values of power, pleasure, and opulence, and therefore in the long term the creators of the modern secularizing notion that such pursuits are irrelevant to religion and vice versa. Yet from Justin onwards, they were seeing the destinies of the empire mysteriously bound up with God's purposes being worked out through his church. Melito, bishop of Sardis (*c.*160–70), reckoned Augustus' ending of civil wars and establishment of peace in the generation immediately before Christ's birth as a providential dispensation to foster the spread of the gospel. Eusebius of Caesarea discerned in the rise of Constantine the time promised by the prophet when the earth would be full of the knowledge of God as the waters cover the sea. Augustine would see biblical prophecies of the ending of idolatry fulfilled in his lifetime by the edicts of Theodosius I.

Most Christians had a strong reserve towards that polytheism that pervaded society, which is not to say that there were not quiet compromisers, like the Christians of southern Spain early in the fourth century who held official cultic positions in the worship of Jupiter, or the bishop of Troy who could painlessly apostatize under Julian because he had never ceased to pray to the sun-god. Origen was convinced that the gospel had brought 'a new song' to the world, breaking up ancestral customs. The egalitarianism by which aristocrats and their slaves shared in one and the same eucharist was extraordinary. The Christian writers of the Roman imperial period write with a freshness and excitement which is absent from most of the non-Christian authors. The Christian rejection of polytheism was encapsulated in their argot for heathen cult and myth: 'paganismus'. A 'paganus' in Latin was either a country peasant or, in the language of the army, a civilian. The Christians called 'pagans' those who had not in baptism enlisted in Christ's militia for the battle against satanic idolatry and superstition. Thoughtful pagans regarded the ethical demand of the Christian proclamation as too tough to be practicable, and feared that the proclamation of peace and love to enemies would make the empire pusillanimous in self-defence. The Christian ideal was more the saint than the sage: men and women who made the world to come seem present now rather than those who knew how to live and survive in a stormy and dangerous society. Origen once remarked that the high moral ideal of the old polytheistic world was one of individual or family self-respect and honour, whereas the Christian ideal was one of service to the community in humility.

The pagan contemporaries of Constantine were not wrong in saying that he had carried through a huge religious and social revolution. To change the religion of the Roman empire was to change the world.

2

From Rome to the Barbarian Kingdoms

(330–700)

ROBERT MARKUS

IF one were writing the history of Western Europe in the period from about 330 to about 700 AD, there would, inevitably, be two major themes. The first would tell of the late Roman empire and its fate after the reorganization by the Emperors Diocletian and Constantine, until most of its Western provinces were superseded by barbarian kingdoms. The second theme would be the story of these new nations, the Germanic kingdoms whose foundations were laid during the years from about 400 to 600 AD.

Within the orbit of the late Roman world, Christianity was primarily receptive; it inherited a set of institutions ready-made, conformed to a social and political structure which had developed over a long period, and learned to live with a culture which it had little part in creating. Among the Western barbarian nations, however, Christianity could play a more creative role. Though it still needed to learn to live with the ways of the new peoples, it had its own mature traditions, and cultural and institutional development, encapsulating much of Roman civilization and fitting it to play a decisive role in shaping the new Germanic societies. If the characteristic stance of Christianity in the Roman world was that of learning, its characteristic stance in the Germanic West was that of teaching. And a large part of what it was teaching to the Germans it had learned from the Romans.

The Age of Hypocrisy: Christianization and its Problems

Eusebius, the 'father of church history' and biographer of the first Christian emperor, commented in his *Life of Constantine* on the 'hypocrisy of people who crept into the church' with an eye to the emperor's favour. Many people doubtless came to embrace the emperor's religion for worthier motives; but Eusebius put his finger on the radical novelty of the condition in which Christians now found themselves. There had been rich Christians before the time of Constantine, there had been educated or upper-class people to be found in Christian communities, and in growing numbers during the century before Constantine. But rarely can their Christianity have contributed to their standing in society, their wealth or power. But, from now on, their religion could itself become a source of prestige, and did so, to the dismay of bishops who, like Eusebius himself, were sometimes inclined to look for less worldly motives for conversion to Christianity. A hundred years after Eusebius Augustine, bishop of Hippo, looked with anxiety at the hordes of 'feigned Christians' driven into his congregations by social pressures and legal compulsion. To adopt the emperor's religion could promote one's chances in the world. During the hundred years or so after Constantine Christianity could be a passport to office, power, and wealth. But by the 430s it had become the religion of most educated Roman town-dwellers. With only very few exceptions, the ruling élites were Christian. In 437 one of the last pagan aristocrats allowed himself to be converted on his deathbed by his conspicuously pious niece, perhaps from fear of less gentle pressure from the emperor. General conformity brought the age of hypocrisy to an end. Hypocrisy, the tribute paid to the establishment by nonconformity, could no longer flourish in a society overwhelmingly if not always profoundly

Christianized, at least in and around the towns, and in the central provinces of the empire.

We cannot be sure either about the speed of this mass Christianization or the means which brought it about. There can be little doubt that at the time Constantine took control of the Western empire, Christianity can have been the religion of only a minority, though perhaps not so tiny a minority as has sometimes been thought. Fifty years later, the brief reign of his nephew, Julian (d. 363), allows us a glimpse of the inhabitants and local dignitaries of Eastern towns divided in religion. Some places welcomed Julian's pagan revival; others, including some large and important cities, were much less enthusiastic about his attempt to reimpose it after a generation of rule by Christian emperors. Julian's main impact was confined to the Eastern provinces. Here, however, Christians could be found—at least in some areas—in greater concentration than in the West; socially and culturally they were on a level not very different from their non-Christian peers. Within a few years of this last attempt by an emperor to rally the Roman empire to paganism, a Greek bishop could speak of Julian's pagan revival as a misguided attempt to introduce 'novelties' in place of the traditional religion; but at much the same time in the West, Christians were still regarded as outside the mainstream of respectable upper-class culture, as the foolish minority who rejected the wise and hallowed traditions of their forefathers which had made Rome great. Christianity was slower to make its way in the West and its adherents slower to assimilate the culture of their pagan contemporaries.

By the 430s this assimilation had come about. But it had not been a smooth process. During the preceding fifty or sixty years Christians were often seen as outsiders, especially in Western aristocratic circles. Here a determined attempt was made in the last decades of the fourth century to uphold the ancient Roman religion along with the classical culture with which it was associated. The opposition of these pagan aristocrats flared into open conflict with the Christian court in the

390s. But their sons and grandsons were all won over to Christianity. By the 430s, the cultural and religious divisions between Christian bishops and pagan senators had ceased to divide. The Roman aristocracy rallied to Christianity and made common cause with their bishop in turning Rome itself into a city reborn under the protection of its patrons, Peter and Paul, into a Christian version of its former self. If the urban élites were largely won over to Christianity by about 430, the masses had drifted into it even sooner. In the last two decades of the fourth century a fair number of cities, scattered all over the empire, experienced riots in which fanatical Christian mobs destroyed temples and 'purged the idols'. There were not many pagans left in Roman towns by the middle of the fifth century.

How this came about must remain obscure. The pressure of legal penalties, not only against pagans but eventually also against heretics, schismatics, and Jews, no doubt had a part to play; but to judge by the extent to which Christian mobs could get their way without restraint years before the emperors' coercive legislation, enacted in the years after 390, it was no more than a minor part. Other social pressures, chief among them that of patronage in an age in which patronage had unprecedented importance in Roman society, must have had at least as great an importance. Of the influence of Christian spouses on their pagan families we have a good many examples. And we must not discount those who became converts to the new religion, whether on account of the superiority of its miracles—especially its apparently superior powers of healing—or of its doctrine or the example of those who taught it. The mutual support and warmth that membership of a Christian group could provide will also have played its part.

If we cannot really be sure about the way this Christianization of the urban population was brought about, we can, however, discern some of the anxieties that accompanied it. For the most part these arose from the almost heedless manner in which Christians were prepared to identify themselves with the dominant values of secular Roman society. So far as the artistic, literary, and intellectual culture of the Roman world is concerned, that was rapidly, and on the whole smoothly, absorbed by late Roman Christianity. The Christian church had never set up its own system of education to rival or to parallel the available secular educational provision. If Christians wished to be educated, as some always had, and as more and more inevitably did after Constantine, they shared the education received by their non-Christian fellows. By the middle of the fourth century, Christianity had gone a long way towards assimilating the dominant culture of pagan Romans. An easy symbiosis had come into being between the cultivated pagan and the educated Christian. It could seem as if nothing except attendance at the church's services divided a pagan intellectual such as the professor Marius Victorinus from the educated clergy of a city such as Milan. Right across the social scale, religion made little perceptible difference to the outward shape of life. Many Christians continued to take part in traditional Roman festivities; they sometimes shocked their bishops by dancing in church, getting drunk at celebrations in the cemeteries, consulting magicians, or resorting to charms to cure their troubles, just as did other people.

Anxiety on this score became acute during the last decades of the fourth century, and the first of the fifth. In the 380s and 390s pagan aristocrats such as Q. A. Symmachus, Vettius Agorius Praetextatus, or Nicomachus Flavianus, alienated from the Christian court and from the men newly risen through its patronage into the upper ranks of society, saw themselves as the guardians of ancient Roman values, including Roman religion, literature, and even artistic styles. Some of the most learned Christians of the time, including Augustine of Hippo and the biblical scholar Jerome, were ill at ease with the culture they were conscious of sharing with these pagans. Such anxieties, however, were soon dispelled. They were forgotten, along with the conflict which had, briefly, and perhaps not very deeply, divided the generation of Ambrose and Symmachus in the 380s and 390s. Within a generation or two aristocratic

Christians were pursuing the same interests as their pagan ancestors. In the later fifth century Christian aristocrats, now frequently bishops, had made their own the literary and rhetorical culture of the pagan aristocracy. For men such as Sidonius Apollinaris (*c.*431–*c.*480), the Gallo-Roman aristocrat who became bishop of Clermont, saw his inherited traditional culture as an integral part of his Roman Christianity, distancing him from the barbarian heretic.

The *malaise* about a shared intellectual and literary culture was short-lived, the product of passing confrontation. Latin literature continued to be copied by Christian aristocrats; classical learning survived in the teaching available, now in episcopal households rather than public schools; Roman art continued to adorn the walls of churches and the sides of sarcophagi. Upper-class Christians were indistinguishable from their pagan fellows in their life-style. This is what worried many of them, especially the more serious-minded. The heated debates in Western Europe around the year 400 on the meaning of perfection had their roots in the uncertainty about what it meant to be a genuine Christian in a society of fashionable Christianity. In a world in which outward conformity with the religion of the establishment was hard to distinguish from real commitment, the call to authentic Christianity often took the form of conversion to some form of the ascetic life. Virginity, voluntary poverty, and self-denial had long been admired. The leaders of the community and the religious élites differentiated themselves from society at large by adopting these virtues; monastic communities had come into being dedicated to their observance. From the later fourth century, this ideal offered puzzled Christians a means to define their identity without ambiguity. The ascetic life, previously most popular in the Eastern provinces, now came to appeal widely to Western aristocrats, men and women, virgins and widows. The explosion of asceticism worried many churchmen. Some, like Jerome's enemy Jovinian, saw in the ascetic movement a chasm opening within the church between an élite of the perfect and the ordinary faithful.

Others, notably the British monk Pelagius and his followers, wanted all Christians to be dedicated to an austere struggle with mediocrity, an arduous quest for perfection.

The theological debates occasioned by this crisis of identity occupied the generation of Jerome and Augustine. From these debates crystallized, eventually, the doctrine of grace and merit, finally in a form which fell short both of the teaching of Pelagius and of the extreme views (ruthless predestination, divine election irrespective of human merits) propounded by Augustine in his old age. Western monasticism, too, turned away—as had already some Greek monastic founders such as St Basil—from the extremes of asceticism. With the *Rule* of St Benedict (*c.*550), supremely, the monastic community was launched on the road of catering for ordinary people rather than a spiritual élite. Its influence was slow to make itself felt, and it did not make a clean sweep of Western monasticism until the ninth century. But already by the time of Pope Gregory I (d. 604) the monastic movement, widely diversified as it was, was being integrated into the life of the church at large and open to the demands made on it by the church's interests and needs.

Like the monastic calling, marriage and sexuality were revalued in the course of the debates around 400. It is difficult to assess the impact of Christianity on a sector of experience which was undergoing profound change in the course of late antiquity. The inequality of the partners was already becoming attenuated during the early centuries of our era, and there are widespread symptoms to suggest the emergence of a notion of the married couple as a partnership of equals. The relationship of marriage was becoming impregnated by the ideals of mutual affection and respect, and considered as the exclusive area for the partners' sexual activities. If we can trust the figures which suggest that Christians tended to marry at a notably higher age than their pagan contemporaries, Christianity would appear to have re-inforced these shifts towards marriage as a more personal and free partnership of equals. But equally, it provided a home for some of the darkest forms of distrust of and revulsion from sex and marriage. In this respect, too, the ground had been prepared by what Michel Foucault has described as a 'pathologization of sex' in late antiquity: anxiety about sex and the sexual regime began to dominate the thought of medical writers and the advice they offered to clients intent on achieving balanced lives. Sex took the place of diet as the main preoccupation of the late Roman valetudinarian. Among Christians anxiety about sex was intensified, especially in the course of the crisis of identity around AD 400.

The superiority of virginity and sexual abstinence over marriage was generally taken for granted. But a dark undercurrent of hostility to sexuality and marriage became interwoven with the more benign attitudes towards the body and sexuality current as late as the second century. Attitudes diverged, and mainstream Christianity became infected with a pronounced streak of distrust towards bodily existence and sexuality. This permanent 'encratite' tendency was given powerful impetus in the debates about Christian perfection at the end of the fourth and the beginning of the fifth centuries. Pelagius thought Jerome's bitter hostility to marriage akin to Manichaean dualism, and his disciple Julian of Eclanum—with less justice—accused Augustine of the same betrayal. But, though Jerome's intemperate denigration of the married state met with little sympathy, Augustine did not manage to dispel the sombre cloud that continued to hover over sexual relations. His name could, indeed, be invoked through the medieval centuries to reinforce the exaltation of virginity at the expense of marriage and to curtail the role of sexuality even within Christian marriage.

In the public realm Christians identified themselves almost without reservation with the political and social order of the Roman empire. The seeds of the ideology behind this had been sown long before the time of Constantine. But it was Eusebius who rounded off these hints into an image which came to dominate fourth-century minds. In his eyes Christianity and the Roman empire were made for each other. God's providential intentions were realized by Constantine: Augustus had united the world under Roman rule, Christ under God's, and Constantine welded together the two unities in a Christian society which was, in principle, universal. Church and empire were fused in a single entity; the empire was an image of the heavenly kingdom, its boundaries the limits of Christendom, the emperor the representative of divine authority in the world. This commonplace became something like an orthodoxy in the Christian empire of the fourth century. The official imposition of Christian orthodoxy at the end of the century reinforced the tendency to merge church and empire; the Christian emperors became God's agents in bringing their subjects under the yoke of Christ. Heresy became a kind of revolt akin to treason, and Christian missions within imperial territory a means of securing public order. Of missions sent by Roman bishops beyond the imperial frontiers we hear nothing until the sixth century. The empire was the natural home of Christianity; beyond it lay barbarity, all that was un-Roman and uncivilized. Political, cultural, and religious exclusiveness combined to create a new sense of *Romania* which was synonymous with civilization and Christianity.

This image of Christian destiny was widely accepted until Augustine of Hippo came to reject it, late in his career. Before him it had sometimes been questioned by dissident groups. The Donatists in North Africa upheld the ancient image of the church as a gathered élite, a foreign body in the midst of secular society and an apostate church. Defenders of the orthodoxy agreed at the Council of Nicaea (325) sometimes denounced emperors such as Constantius II as heretics, and repudiated the authority of secular rulers over the church. Others, like Ambrose, bishop of the imperial city of Milan (d. 397), were determined to subject the exercise of imperial power to the spiritual authority of bishops. But until Augustine's *City of God* (413–27) most Christians unquestioningly accepted the Roman political and social order as the earthly form of the Christian society.

The fourth and fifth centuries saw the wholesale Romanization of Christianity and Christianization of Roman society. But they were also the golden age of doctrinal clarification. If, during this period, the social boundaries of Christianity in the late Roman world were vanishing, its doctrinal definition, by contrast, gained in sharpness. Uncertainties over the church's Trinitarian teaching came to a head under Constantine, who thought himself divinely commissioned to secure the church's unity. The council held under him at Nicaea in 325 enacted an agreement with the emperor's support. But its formula of the Son's 'consubstantiality' with the Father was slow to gain general acceptance, despite Constantine's efforts to impose it. It was only after protracted debate, in which Athanasius of Alexandria, Hilary of Poitiers, and others fought a stubborn campaign of resistance to the Eastern court that Nicene orthodoxy finally triumphed, both in the government's legislation and in the creed adopted by the Council of Constantinople in 381. It was not long, however, before doubts on another central doctrinal issue began to cause deep divisions among Christians. From around 430, debates on the relation between human and divine in the person of Christ were finally resolved—though further disagreement by no means eliminated—by the Council of Chalcedon (451). While councils were defining the central doctrines of the faith, the Fathers of the fourth and fifth centuries were bringing the conceptual equipment of antique thought and the rhetorical techniques of classical literature to its exposition and interpretation.

Doctrinal self-definition was accompanied by institutional development. The church's organization had crystallized, almost from its beginnings, around the urban centres in which the Christian communities were established. The Council of Nicaea set its seal on the structure that had thus come into being: a network of urban bishoprics, grouped into provinces headed by a metropolitan bishop, usually in the capital city of the civil province. The ecclesiastical organization thus came to reduplicate the structure of the civil administrative geography, though not quite exactly, and least in the less Romanized areas where the Roman network of cities with their administrative territories was less regular. The emergence of 'parishes' within the area under a bishop's jurisdiction was, however, a much slower, later, and more uneven process, depending on the gradual penetration of Christianity into rural areas.

Adaptation to Roman society and culture; doctrinal self-definition, and organizational solidification: the century and a half after Constantine's conversion was all this; but more than anything else, it was the time in which Christians learnt to live in the new conditions of their existence. The 'Constantinian revolution' was far more than the sudden breaking out of peace over the church and demanded a drastic reconstruction of the framework of experience. A sense of insecurity and emotional tension had been the permanent feature of Christian existence during most of the previous three centuries. Even though individual Christians might never have suffered any harassment, their corporate existence and their way of thinking were determined by this condition. Their miraculous transformation from a persecuted minority into a privileged élite, soon to become a dominant majority, was not an experience for which they were intellectually or spiritually well prepared.

Kairoi: The Christianization of Time

Christians had always lived—like most late antique people—in a universe which included an unseen world as large and as varied as the visible. They were pilgrims in this world, aliens in the society of their pagan fellows, but they knew they were part of a vast community: 'this church which is now travelling on its journey, is joined to that heavenly church where we have the angels as our fellow-citizens', said Augustine, faithfully echoing the conviction of all early Christians. The worshipping community here on earth was an outlying colony, its prayer a distant echo of the perfect and unceasing praise offered to God in heaven by his angels and his saints. It was especially in its worship that the apparent distance between the earthly and the heavenly community was bridged. Angels hovered around the eucharistic altar and carried the congregation's self-offering to the throne of God, bringing back his blessing. Angels also attended their eating and their drinking. The Christian community lived in perpetual proximity, even intimacy, with the larger community of which it felt itself to be a part. The threshold of death was a way of access rather than a barrier between the two parts of the community. The dead linked heaven and earth. At their graves their families would unite with their beloved over a memorial meal and a drink, easing their grief in recreating the family intimacy, only transiently ruptured. Every anniversary was a celebration of the larger family. Dead bishops and local martyrs received public commemoration by the whole community: this is where the real, large family came solemnly alive. At the centre of this familiarity of human and divine was the assurance of being linked with a community which stood in God's direct, face-to-face, presence. The saints were God's friends, but they also remained men's kin. Together with them, the whole community was in God's presence. The divine was always *there*, waiting like lightning to break through the cloud, to be earthed by the conductors of worship, of the altar, the church building, the saint, alive or dead.

It is hard not to view this axiom of early Christian imagination from a post-Reformation perspective. But we shall mistake its real substance if we begin with the cult of saints and relics seen, as they were seen in the Reformation, in terms of channels through which a distant, concealed world of the holy is made present and accessible. The holy, rather, formed the permanent context of life, always and everywhere present, animating a community larger than the little group gathered around the altar, ready at any moment to manifest blessing or power, at special moments or special places. The organization of special moments and places took place in the rituals of communal worship. The liturgical seasons and the cycle of commemorative festivals defined both a weekly and an annual rhythm of Christian living.

Christian festivals had coexisted for a very long time with ancient non-Christian celebrations. While the Christian communities occupied a place on the edges of society and kept aloof from most of other people's festivities, their own sacred time was well enough defined. But with their full entry into Roman secular society in the course of the fourth century, two systems of sacred time came to coexist. The old Roman calendar of festivals contained a cycle of urban celebrations reaching back to the city's legendary foundation. Around the middle of the fourth century Christians seem to have observed these traditional festivals along with their own; some ancient celebrations kept their appeal for centuries. Christians never entirely clarified to their own satisfaction the questions about how much of this appeal they could afford to yield to. On one hand, they had a vivid sense of a deep gulf between sacred and profane. Some festivities were irremediably tainted with profanity, while others might just be excused as games people play, devoid of religious significance. Such a distinction was perhaps the greatest novelty imported into the world of classical antiquity by Christianity: no Greek or Roman would have tried to disentangle sacred from profane in his ceremonials, or even have understood the distinction. On the other hand, while Christians felt the pressure to make such a distinction and to separate the sacred sharply from the profane, they had no clear criteria to show where the line was to be drawn. What carried pagan religious significance, and thus had to be shunned, and what was mere urban romping, and might therefore be—just— tolerated?

The choice was put brutally before Christians who saw no harm in taking part, around 490, in the ancient festivities of the Lupercalia. 'Make up your minds', the pope urged; 'either celebrate it in the full-blooded manner of your pagan ancestors', or acknowledge that 'it is superstitious and vain, and manifestly incompatible with the profession of Christianity'. The pope was forcing a choice on his congregation of 'neither Christians nor pagans'. Neutrality was, to his mind, impossible; there could be no area, such as his opponents wished to protect, of customs rooted in a pagan past, but now deprived of religious significance. This frontier between that which belonged to what Peter Brown has described as the 'neutral technology of civilized living' and what still carried 'a heavy charge of diffused religiosity' was shifting and never quite fixed. For Christians its precise location was a question of supreme importance; but they had no criteria for answering it. The crucial boundary between what is 'Christian' and what is 'pagan' was set by the limits of official clerical tolerance. The tolerable was always becoming suspect, and the suspect often tolerated. The history of clerical suspicion of 'secular' celebrations is still only patchily written; it would reveal not only a remarkable—though by no means even—development over time, but a no less remarkable variation from place to place. Many no doubt sincere Christians continued to celebrate the first day of January in defiance of their clergy's disapproval, or liked to greet the rising sun from the steps into the church, and, most of all, to attend the great festive games and shows. As bishops like Augustine and Pope Leo I (like their Eastern colleagues such as John Chrysostom) often complained, the people who filled the churches on the festivals of Jerusalem also filled the theatres on the festivals of Babylon. Their efforts were directed towards drawing more and more of the Christian life into the sacred time of the liturgy. 'We fast for them on their feast days', Augustine had said of the few remaining pagans, 'so that they themselves might become the spectacle'. Thus Leo I thought it better that his congregation should keep their fasting for the proper liturgical seasons publicly set aside for it, rather than carry it out as a private ascetic exercise. In ways such as these, late Roman bishops worked slowly, by piecemeal additions and elaborations of regularly recurrent observances, to define a new sacred time in which the Christian life was to be wholly caught up, until the sacred time of the old pagan past was slowly forgotten, or emptied of its charge of religiosity.

The central events of the Lord's life had always been the pivots of the Christian year and the week; the day of the Resurrection and Sunday, the Lord's day, were at the centre of a cycle of festivals. A second series clustered around celebrations of the Lord's Incarnation. Both continued to develop; but it was the commemoration of the martyrs that came to swamp the Christian calendar during the fourth century, filling the interstices left in it. The heroes of the faith who died at the hands of the persecutor had long enjoyed special honour among Christians, as, before them, among Jews. The cult of the martyr became detached from the general cult of the community's dead members. He was one of the 'very special dead', his tomb a gathering place where the anniversary of his 'deposition' would be celebrated by the whole community gathered in his memory. From the fourth century, popes, bishops, and emperors competed in fostering the memorials of the martyrs, rediscovering or restoring their burials, adorning them with inscriptions recording their deeds, erecting great basilicas in the cemeteries to accommodate the crowds of worshippers. The celebration of the martyr's anniversary had grown out of the commemoration of the departed dead; but it soon outgrew the limits of its origins and became far more than the expression of that larger family solidarity which embraced heaven and earth. It helped fourth-century Christians to come to terms with the paradox that the privileged, wealthy, and powerful post-Constantinian church actually was also the church of the martyrs.

The most urgent need for the triumphant post-Constantinian church was to annex its own past. It had to find a way of being able to think of itself as the true heir of the persecuted church, not its betrayer. This is the task to which the church historians of the fourth and fifth centuries, above all dedicated themselves: their work, more than anything else, helped to shape a sense of the church's identity with the church of the martyrs, rooted in its own past, continuous and undisturbed by any emperor's conversion. But these ecclesiastical histories appealed to restricted, educated circles. For the vast majority, the historical gap between the age of the martyrs and the age of the established church was more effectively bridged by the cult of the martyrs. African Christianity inherited a particularly exuberant cult, which councils tried repeatedly to restrain. The Donatists considered themselves to be the church of the martyrs, and kept alive the old posture of the persecuted church in the new, much altered, times after Constantine. The recurrent celebration of the martyrs' feast days catered for the need to make the church's past present, linked the sacred time of the Christian year into the sacred history of God's holy people, and so helped to reconcile a triumphant faith which had emerged dominant in society, with the tenacious sense that blessedness lay in being persecuted for his name, and it kept alive a sense that Christ's kingdom was not of this world. Other forms of holiness—that of the virgin and the ascetic—were assimilated to martyrdom. Isidore of Seville (d. 636) summed it all up thus: 'many who bear the attacks of the adversary and resist the desires of the flesh are martyrs, even in the time of peace, in virtue of this self-immolation to God in their heart: they would have been martyrs in the time of the persecutions'.

Topoi: The Christianization of Space

Thus the church made its past its own: the martyrs were made present in time; but they also had to become present in space. Traditionally, their burials lay in the suburban cemeteries. There the city would, in Jerome's phrase, 'upheaving itself', turn its back on the ancient temples and civic monuments within the city, to pay its respects in throngs to the martyrs beyond the walls. By the end of the fourth century the martyrs were coming into the city. Despite the Roman law prohibiting interference with the grave, and the taboo safeguarding the city-enclosure from pollution by corpses, relics of the saints were being moved into urban churches, 'translated', rehoused in splendid buildings, enshrined under altars. Inhibitions about moving bodily remains survived, sometimes for centuries, especially in Rome itself. But substitutes for parts of the saint's body would be found no less efficacious in guaranteeing his or her presence. With astonishing speed, cults such as that of the first martyr, Stephen, spread over the whole Mediterranean world, and, eventually, beyond. Early in the fourth century the Carthaginian clergy disapproved of a local lady addicted to the habit of venerating a martyr's bone; but a hundred years later we hear of only isolated protests. The cult of the saints in particular places associated with their memory was transferred to movable relics. The cult was detached from the place of its own original environment, and thus opened European routes to sacred travel, sacred commerce, and, eventually, sacred theft.

The martyrs' role in turning late antique towns into Christian cities can hardly be exaggerated. Pope Damasus rehabilitated and adorned the burials of the martyrs in Rome's suburban cemeteries: the army of martyrs surrounded the pagan city like a besieging force. In 386 Ambrose moved relics he had just discovered in a Milan suburb to one of the new churches he had built to ring the growing city with prestigious sanctuaries; it was a well thought out act. It met a popular demand, and it gave 'the church of Milan, hitherto barren of martyrs, the ability to rejoice in its own sufferings'. The relics under the altar took the place intended for the bishop's burial, so that 'He who suffered for all might be upon the altar, and those redeemed by his passion beneath it'. In the discovery of its martyrs, the church of Milan had recovered its ancient distinction and gained new protectors. In city after city the focal points of the martyrs' cults shifted from the suburban cemeteries to the splendid new churches, both in the suburbs and in the town centres; the celebration of their memory was integrated into the normal eucharistic worship of the urban community. The old African prohibition of multiplying sites of popular devotion to legions of homemade martyrs was turned inside out: every altar now had to have a martyr's relic beneath it.

The first and chief result of the enhanced importance of the martyr's cult was thus the reshaping of the sacred topography of late antique towns. The Roman town enclosure, marked off from its environment by the foundation rite, had itself been sacred; and it contained temples, the sacred edifices of public worship. A learned pagan philosopher might occasionally question the necessity for temples or sacrifices: Seneca anticipated many a Christian with his insistence that 'God is close to you, with you, within you', so that temples and sacrifices were otiose. Here, as so often, the protesting voices of the philosophic counter-culture became the norm accepted by Christians: for them no place could be inherently sacred. 'The God who made the world and everything in it, being the Lord of heaven and earth, does not live in shrines made by man' (Acts 17: 24), St Paul had told the Athenians, with one eye on the great shrine of their city's divine protectress on the next hill. Unlike the pagan temple, the Christians' churches housed no divinity; for they themselves were 'the temple of the living God' (2 Cor. 6: 16). Their churches were simple gathering places to shelter the community at worship. For centuries they were 'consecrated' by the first celebration in them of the eucharist: what made them holy was the use made of them.

Until the fourth century, Christians inhabited an undifferentiated spatial universe. Their God was wholly present everywhere at once, allowing no site, no building, or space any specially privileged holiness. Christians had a sacred history: in the fourth century they acquired a sacred geography which was its spatial reflection. A place could become holy through some historical event, a memory of a work of God done at the site at a particular time. The martyr's grave had been one type of such sites. Now, the presence of the martyrs in city churches began to create new sites of holiness: churches were no longer simply the gathering places of the faithful for worship, but shrines of the saints, holy places. The church building was a microcosm of the heavenly kingdom. To enter a church was to enter a world separated from the work-a-day environment by its interior layout, its decor, all designed to enhance the sense of the saint's solemn presence in his shrine. To walk the length of a great basilica from porch to apse was to make the journey of salvation and find oneself in 'a place of perfection, the heavenly Jerusalem, its walls and buildings made in heaven, transferred to this spot'. The solemnity was heightened at the actual times of worship by the colourful splendour of clerical pomp. As the inscription over the sanctuary arch told the worshipper in St Martin's church at Tours, 'How awesome is this place! This is none other than the house of God, and this is the gate of heaven.' (Gen. 28: 17.)

As such gateways to heaven multiplied, they came to outline a new map of sacred urban topography. Christians now had what they had never had before: a network of holy places in their towns. The transformation of an ancient city into a new Christian city is best documented at Rome. Constantine had sponsored the building of a cathedral adjoining a palace he had assigned to the bishop, and of some great memorial churches on the edges of the city. His successors continued the programme. In the fifth century the popes embarked, in alliance with the local aristocracy, on a programme of urban renewal. They created a new Christian area centred on some of the great city basilicas, away from the traditional civic centres. The ancient monumental centre, heavy with pagan memories, was gradually transformed by the erection of churches and the conversion of public buildings into churches. Eventually a network of humble welfare-stations under ecclesiastical auspices completed the Christian topography of Rome. Similar developments can sometimes be traced in less detail in less magnificent places, and must have taken place, on a more modest scale, almost everywhere.

The location of the earliest episcopal churches—in the inhabited suburbs, within the walls, near the edge of the walled town, or near the centre?—is often doubtful and in many cases has been much debated. The pattern was certainly not uniform. Ancient and well-established episcopal churches tended to stabilize subsequent urban development. Suburban sanctuaries often became the foci for further urban growth. Sometimes, as in some Rhineland towns, new settlements came to cluster around them, dislocating the town, turning old centre into suburb and old suburb into new centre. Whether their sites shifted or not, everywhere towns became transformed by the great churches and the smaller shrines built both near their centres and in their suburbs in the fourth and fifth centuries.

Thus late Roman towns became a web of holy places through the shrines of the martyrs, later of other saints, 'honorary martyrs', determining spatial relationships within the town. But there was another reason why some places were holy—not intrinsically—but through their association with a past even more venerable than that of the martyrs: the sites of the lives of the apostles and the Lord. Just as the shrines of martyrs and saints came to define a sacred topography of holy places within and around a town, so the sites of the New (and, for that matter, the Old) Testament stories came to define a larger sacred geography. Jerusalem occupied the centre of this sacred universe, as it had done among the Jews. Jewish men had been expected—unrealistically in the conditions of the Diaspora—to make regular pilgrimages to the Holy City. Now, in Christian times, pilgrimage from the ends of the earth, organized and elaborated into regular re-enactments of the episodes of sacred history, carefully fostered by great architectural enterprises, sponsored by bishops and emperors, linked the most distant towns with the sacred sites. The short pilgrimage from town to the martyr's tomb in the suburban cemetery and the longer routes to the shrines of apostles or of the Holy Land interlocked to create a nexus of sacred topography; pilgrims' tales, literary accounts, guides, and itineraries helped to familiarize Western Christians with a new religious ordering of space.

As saints became ubiquitous, they also changed their functions. In the early Christian community the living faithful prayed to God for their dead; now the dead saint is asked to pray for the living: a whole new liturgy comes into being. As the martyr is, literally, detached from the place of his martyrdom and made present wherever his relics have become the centre of a cult, so relics begin to be seen in a new way. A man as highly educated as Augustine changed his mind about them in the course of his life. As a middle-aged bishop he was reluctant to believe that miracles still happened in his world as they had in the time of the Lord and his apostles. His thought had been moving towards an idea of nature, not unlike that found in some Stoic philosophers, as a complex of processes subject to their own natural law. This conception, however, dissolved in his mind as, towards the end of his life, he came to accept the prevalent belief in the everyday occurrence of miracles. 'The world itself is God's greatest miracle', he wrote, defending God's freedom to work miracles at the cost of dissolving the idea of a nature which is subject to its own laws in the freedom of the divine will. Now he was ready to see daily miracles wrought by the relics of St Stephen, recently discovered and brought to Africa, and to make use of them in his pastoral work among his congregations. In minds less critical and less sophisticated than Augustine's, relics soon became themselves the seats of holy power, God's preferred channels for miraculous action. A new nexus of local social relationships came to centre around their shrines; their cult provided ways of securing social cohesion in the locality, and one of the means on which bishops depended to consolidate their authority.

The Order of Society

The chief mutations of Christianity in late antiquity stem from two sources: first, its takeover of the Roman world, second its takeover of the Germanic world. We have been considering some of the ways in which the late Roman world inhabited by Christians was transformed in fact and in their imagination. This transformation provided the skeleton for the Christianity which was to take over the Germanic world, to mould it and modify it in turn. But this second mutation of Christianity was the work more of a change in the nature of the Roman world itself, its social and its political structure as well as its intellectual assumptions and its culture, than of anything we might call 'the impact of the barbarians' on it.

It is a collapse into simplicity. To pass from the world of Augustine and his pagan contemporaries into the world of Gregory the Great (pope 590–604) is to move by imperceptible stages from a world in which the basic question was 'What is a Christian?' to one in which it has become 'How should a Christian live, behave, be a *good* Christian?' In the early fifth century, Roman society was still a complex fabric of strands of very varied origin. Institutions, customs, political and cultural traditions stemming from a long pagan past, were still very much alive in it. It was within such a milieu that Christians were faced with the task of defining their identity. The kind of society which came into being in Europe was a more homogeneous Christian society, less differentiated than Augustine's. The multiformity of late antique culture had collapsed into the homogeneity of a Christian culture. By the time of Pope Gregory I the world of cultivated Roman paganism had receded into a past now only dimly seen through the distorting medium of legend and folklore. Augustine's world had still contained blocks refractory to the light of the gospel. The 'opaque' areas of experience, of institutions, and daily living, if they had not disappeared by Gregory's time, had become absorbed into a Christian universe as translucent parts. In principle, there was nothing that could not be absorbed into this radically Christianized world.

The categories of classification available to a bishop like Gregory the Great, or his contemporary in Gaul, Gregory of Tours, divided mankind into orthodox Catholics, heretics, pagans, and Jews. A Catholic accepted the doctrines taught by his bishop and his authority over the pattern of his moral and his cultic behaviour. The existence of imperfectly Christianized 'rustic' masses posed no serious problem except the pastoral one of how to improve the quality of their religious life. Customs and beliefs deriving from a pagan past may have been frowned upon, but they did not necessarily exclude their adherents from the community of Christians. Baptism turned a pagan into a Christian. Much work might remain for the clergy both in imposing a code of Christian morals, and in determining where the line was to run between what could and what could not form a respectable part of the Christian life. What constituted a 'pagan' was a matter of definition by clerical authority; in practice it meant what evaded the bishop's control. Gregory the Great's decision that English converts to Christianity might continue to use their traditional places of worship provided they were sprinkled with holy water was a revolutionary extension of clerical tolerance, with momentous implications for later missionary activity. But once they had received baptism, the existence of such superficially Christianized people ceased to present any challenge to the self-confidence of a Christian society. Heretics posed a more serious problem, but, happily, after the elimination of the aggressively Arian Vandal kingdom in North Africa, and the conversion of the Arian Goths and Burgundians to Catholicism, it ceased to be a pressing practical one. Pagans could not, of course, belong to the community of Christians. Through the eyes of bishops we can catch an occasional glimpse of little groups of them; but with the conversion of the Franks from *c.*500 and of the English from *c.*600 onwards, they could only be found in large numbers on the fringes of Western Christendom and in the outer darkness beyond. (Their conversion, in part through the work of English missionaries, in the period after *c.*700, is dealt with in the next chapter.)

There was, however, one troubling group inherited from the Roman past, which remained a permanent feature of the social landscape of Western Europe: the Jews who existed in most Roman towns, in large numbers or small. In many towns they had for generations lived peaceably with, and often trusted by, their Christian neighbours. But in a community whose contours were defined by religion more than by Roman law, they were an anomalous, marginal group, who could not, by definition, form part of the 'Christian people'. Thus when a Gallic bishop in 576 'converted' the local Jewish community to Christianity, those who refused baptism were expelled from the city. Gregory the Great, interestingly, seems to represent the survival of an older tradition in upholding the civil rights of Jews within the community defined by Roman law rather than by religion; but such a survival could not long resist the powerful pressures towards conformity where Roman legal inhibitions were less strong. In practice, toleration and coexistence came under growing threat, especially in later times, with new emphasis being laid on ecclesiastical uniformity.

An ever-larger proportion of the 'Christian people' of Western Europe after 500 were no longer the subjects of the Roman emperor. By about AD 600 his authority was acknowledged only in parts of the Italian peninsula, and even there, in the following century, it became remote and ineffectual. In areas settled by Germanic peoples and governed by their kings new forms of government and new political institutions often coexisted with older political traditions of Roman origin. The horizons within which most people's lives were confined became narrower; the far-flung contacts which had linked distant provinces became attenuated, local clerical and military élites came to form cohesive, small-scale groupings with local or regional interests and loyalties, sometimes intense local pride. It was a world in which clerical power and the military power of the local representatives of secular rulers eclipsed the civilian administrator. In many towns—including, supremely, Rome itself—municipal authority drained towards the bishop. At the end of the sixth century a Frankish king complained that all the riches were flowing into the hands of bishops at the expense of the royal fisc, and that royal authority was being eclipsed by that of the bishops of cities. It was the bishop who had the standing and the resources to carry out work originally incumbent on the local gentry: constructing new channels for a river, securing water supplies, maintaining fortifications, as

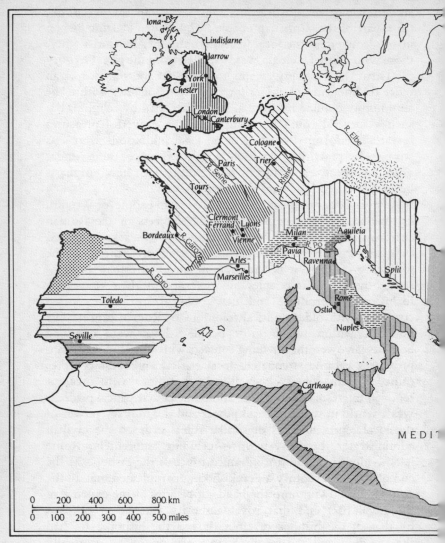

Iona
Lindisfarne
Jarrow
York
Chester
London
Canterbury
Cologne
Paris
Trier
R. Seine
R. Rhine
R. Elbe
Tours
Clermont
Ferrand
Lyons
Milan
Aquileia
Bordeaux
Vienne
Pavia
R. PO
Ravenna
Split
R. Garonne
Arles
R. Ebro
Marseilles
Rome
Toledo
Ostia
Naples
Seville
Carthage

MEDIT

0   200   400   600   800 km
0   100   200   300   400   500 miles

THE ROMAN WORLD TO *c.*600

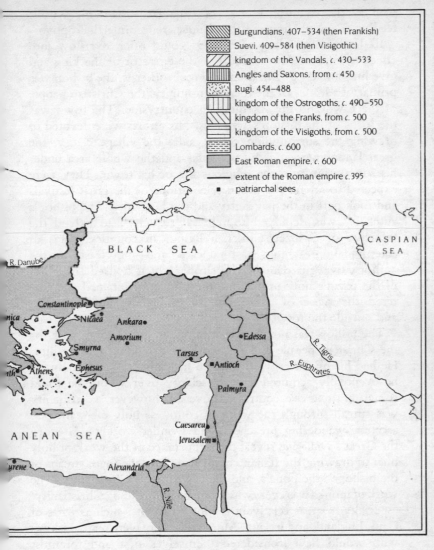

Burgundians, 407–534 (then Frankish)
Suevi, 409–584 (then Visigothic)
kingdom of the Vandals, c. 430–533
Angles and Saxons, from c. 450
Rugi, 454–488
kingdom of the Ostrogoths, c. 490–550
kingdom of the Franks, from c. 500
kingdom of the Visigoths, from c. 500
Lombards, c. 600
East Roman empire, c. 600
— extent of the Roman empire c. 395
▪ patriarchal sees

CASPIAN SEA

BLACK SEA

R. Danube

Constantinople

nica

Nicaea

Ankara

Amorium

Smyrna

Edessa

R. Tigris

Tarsus

Athens

Ephesus

Antioch

R. Euphrates

th

Palmyra

Caesarea

ANEAN SEA

Jerusalem

yrene

Alexandria

R. Nile

well as the traditional tasks of organized charitable works: feeding the poor, housing the refugee, redeeming the captive.

If the local standing of bishops could often overflow into effective influence at the court of the emperor or the king and give him influence with them and their officials, the bishop was primarily a leader of the local community: the Christian people of the town and the surrounding countryside. The town was the focus of the bishop's activities. His efforts were devoted to drawing the surrounding countryside, the village clergy, the great landowners and the peasants, and the whole area under his supervision into the religious life of his town. They were expected to attend the urban celebrations of the great festivals and took part in the pageantry and the festivities. The bishop's authority was deployed to repress 'rusticity', to extend the franchise of civilized Christian living. In countless ways of ceremonial, preaching, pastoral care, and—not least—as the authoritative guardian of the shrine which housed the relics of the town's holy protectors, the bishop maintained and fostered the sense of a community embracing all classes, in and outside the town.

The bishop was not, however, alone in his pastoral work for the Christian people and the work of extending Christianity. He had his own clergy attached to his cathedral, and gradually he eventually acquired a parish clergy over whom he could sometimes exercise control. Above all, however, Christianity was spread through the work of countless holy men, monks, ascetics, wandering preachers, and wonder-workers. Gregory the Great's *Dialogues* reveal the importance of the work of holy men in drawing the Italian countryside into the main stream of the bishops', the pope's, and the townsmen's Christianity. The work of monks was everywhere crucial in spreading Christianity, especially in areas relatively lacking in towns, such as parts of Gaul, England, and Ireland. Moreover, there were many bishops who would have considered themselves first and foremost monks: St Cuthbert of Lindisfarne (d. 687) had a respectable ancestry reaching back to St Martin of Tours (d. *c*.397).

A Byzantine historian remarked of the Franks in the sixth century that 'although they have become Christians, they still keep a greater part of their ancient religion'. The judgement could be applied more widely than its immediate target. To read Gregory of Tours' *History of the Franks* or Bede's of the English people, or a poem like *Beowulf*, is to experience a world in which the new and the traditional, in culture and in religion, in law and institutions, are inextricable. The early history of Germanic Christianity is dominated by the paradox that mass conversion required some considerable continuity. The new religion had to be seen to meet existing needs, and not to overtax the courage its converts would need to break with the religion of their ancestors. But, once converted, they needed to define their new identity: they had to create discontinuities which would draw a line between their Christian present and their pagan past. The realignment of these societies was necessarily slow, their central value-systems resistant to change. Gregory of Tours and Bede both knew that the conversion of their peoples to Christianity had done something to the religion to which they were converted. This is what made them anxious about the attitudes of powerful men in their societies—rulers, great magnates—towards the churches of which they considered themselves the lords. They perceived that the acquisition of wealth and privilege exposed churches and monasteries to new dangers. They were also aware of an even deeper change in the texture of Christianity: it had become the religion of a warrior nobility whose values and culture it had necessarily to absorb in the process of Christianizing them.

A century separates the 'conversion' of the English, beginning in the years around 600, from that of the Franks, and even more years divide Bede's *Ecclesiastical History of the English People* (c.720) from Gregory's *History of the Franks* (c.590). Yet there is much that these two great historians have in common, and not only their sense of foreboding, their anxiety about the future, and a vision of past greatness; they share, above all, a need to give the Christianity of their compatriots,

Franks or English, roots in the Roman past. Like Eusebius and the other ecclesiastical historians, their great achievement was to articulate a sense of a 'Christianity' identical with the 'Christianity' embodied in societies profoundly different in character from their own. In the permeation of both English and Frankish society by Christian values the work of Irish monks was crucially important. Bede was conscious of the debt the English owed to saints such as Columba and Aidan, and loved to contrast their holiness with the 'slothfulness' of Christians of his own day. Gregory wrote before Columbanus and his monastic foundations made their impact on Frankish society; but everywhere monks and nuns—not only of Irish origin—helped to give some moral and devotional definition to the Christianity of royal courts, aristocratic households, and small local communities.

The English church owed much to Gaul, and shared many of its features. The Roman past lay more heavily over the Iberian peninsula. Its Gothic settlers were already far advanced along the road of assimilating the culture and the religion of their Roman subjects at the time of their conversion to Catholicism in the 580s. St Isidore of Seville (d. 636) saw Spain as a Christian land, in which the separate identities of Goth and Roman were no longer of any but historical interest. North Africa had been reconquered from the Vandals in the 530s, but was never to become securely integrated into the Byzantine empire. In the sixth century its ancient Christian traditions were strong enough to sustain resistance to Justinian's attempts to dictate doctrine to the church. It had been singularly successful in achieving a synthesis of local and cosmopolitan, rural and urban, into a religious culture of remarkable vitality and tenacity, even in the seventh century. Of its 'underground' survival after the Arab conquest of the African provinces we have only patchy evidence. In Italy, soon after the collapse of the Gothic regime under Byzantine attack, the Lombards, a nation largely pagan at the time of its arrival in Italy in the 560s, settled in the northern and much of the central part of the peninsula. Slowly they came to conform to the Catholicism of their Italian subjects. But it would be anachronistic to think of Western Europe around *c.*700 as homogeneous Western, Christian, Latin culture, shared among nations with any definite sense of forming a community aspiring to be 'Western Christendom'.

True, the foundations had been laid for a cultural revival, a breakdown of the isolation in which individual centres of learning, art, and devotion had existed. During this period following the collapse of Roman rule in the West, sometimes still called the 'dark ages', Western Christians rethought the culture they had inherited from the ancient world. This rethinking went on in episcopal households and monasteries as well as in some urban schools which survived in some areas well into the sixth century. Above all, the English in the age of Bede created a vigorous culture whose ripples were to be felt across Western Europe for decades. The vitality of a pre-Christian Celtic past was fused with the newly discovered artistic and intellectual traditions of the late antique Mediterranean world. The history written, the gospel books copied and illuminated, in Northumbrian monasteries in the decades around 700 left a permanent mark on Christian art and on history-writing. This 'Northumbrian renaissance', most creative in the cultural development of Western Europe, was not an isolated one. Throughout the Germanic West, in the decades 680–700, 'appear the first elements of a renaissance, a forerunner of the great Carolingian renewal'. The political leadership within this cultural area assumed by the Franks, the alliance of their kings with the popes, and the achievement of Western Christianity under this leadership are dealt with in the next chapter. Here we may note one fact with an importance in a long perspective which overshadows all others: the conquests by Islam.

For fifty years since the posthumous publication of Henri Pirenne's *Mahomet et Charlemagne* (1937) scholars have been debating what they have labelled its 'thesis': that the ancient rhythms of an undivided Mediterranean civilization had enough tenacity to survive Germanic invasions and settlements, and were disrupted and transformed only as a consequence of the spread of Muslim power, cutting the Mediterranean in half. From the debate on this 'thesis' we may here stand aside. However we assess the impact of Islam on the economy, the society, and the culture of Europe, its significance for the history of Christianity is immeasurable. If, looking at the Mediterranean world from our Western and Northern viewpoint, we do no more than take note of the removal of North Africa from the scene of Latin Christianity, we shall scarcely have begun to come to grips with the size of the problem. Yet even to note this is to identify a radical shift in the shape, not only geographical but spiritual, of Christendom. The submergence of North Africa beneath the tide of Islam in the seventh century meant far more than the loss of one of the most intellectually vital parts of the Latin church. For the North African church had long clung to its own traditions of autonomy with a tenacity which made it a power with which the emperors and popes had to reckon. For the Western church the removal of the African church meant the removal of a permanent focus of fruitful tension. The Roman see emerged as the sole religious authority and centre of a barbarian West. The Western church could forget the tensions that had enriched her life while Rome was one among several great sees. Increasingly cut off from the Eastern churches, and with Carthage eclipsed, Rome could become the unchallenged teacher and mistress of new nations; and they were only too prepared to learn. Pirenne was undoubtedly right in making Mahomet the creator of medieval Western Christendom.

3

The West: The Age of Conversion
(700–1050)

HENRY MAYR-HARTING

THE period which here concerns us is not notable for great theologians, great popes, or great heretics. The Christian achievement turns less on individual geniuses than in any other period of remotely comparable length in the history of this ever fermenting religion. The Emperor Charlemagne (768–814) is said to have lamented to the leader of his court school, the York man Alcuin, that he had not twelve learned men like Jerome or Augustine. This remark did not go down well with Alcuin, who thought he was being criticized, but we can see what it meant to the late ninth-century writer who reported it. The great constructive developments of this period were missionary (and one can never draw a hard distinction between internal and external missionizing), liturgical, monastic, and political.

The Missionary Church

Missionary drive was virtually a necessity of political security in the early medieval West. The Rhine was the eastern boundary of the Carolingian Franks up to the time of Charlemagne. But it was also an artery of their communications in a burgeoning world of churches, palaces, and trade. Never could they securely hold the Rhine until the Frisians at the lower end of it and the Saxons across it were tamed and Christianized. The empire of Charlemagne was divided in the ninth century, and its eastern division came to be dominated in the tenth century by the now Christianized Saxons. From their rule of the eastern Frankish kingdom developed Germany. Now the same process occurred all over again. For the eastern border of the Saxons was the River Elbe, and that too was an artery of Saxon communication. But never could the Elbe be securely held until the Slavs across it, the Danes near the lower end of it, and the Bohemians on its upper reaches, were all tamed and Christianized. The Danes, and the Swedes, were already perceived to pose a missionary problem in the ninth century; their Christianization was one response to what would become known to historians as the Viking threat. Similarly, the Hungarians became the principal external threat to the Christianized Germanic peoples of Europe in the late ninth and tenth centuries, particularly in conjunction with the Slavs; and after the former's defeat and settlement on the Middle Danube, it was a natural instinct of the Saxon rulers to draw them into the orbit of western Christian kingdoms. Further east, Bulgaria eventually became firmly attached to the Byzantine church, but in the 860s Louis the German, king of the East Franks, even tried to become involved in the Bulgarian conversion. The reason was a familiarly political one: the desire to apply a lever to the other side of the threatening Moravians. His action only had the effect of helping to throw the Moravians too into the arms of Byzantine Christianity. A century later, at about the time that Otto I was crowned Holy Roman Emperor (962), he sent a mission (albeit unsuccessful) to Princess Olga of Kiev. Here missionizing passes almost from the defensive to the offensive. The Russians 800 miles to the east of the Elbe scarcely threatened Otto I, but the Byzantines could be expected to react unfavourably to his imperial coronation, and Kiev was already in the orbit of Byzantine trade and political influence. Saxon Christianity in Kiev would have been tantamount to an attack, at least culturally, on the Byzantine flank.

But one can be too political about mission, or the work of preaching, as contemporary churchmen would have called it. Two formative influences on the early Middle Ages were Pope Gregory the Great's preaching of Christianity to the Lombards and (through Augustine of Canterbury) to the Anglo-Saxons; and the *peregrinatio*, or self-imposed exile for God's sake, of Irish monks like St Aidan at Lindisfarne, St Columbanus in Burgundy, and St Gall in Suabia, who had a vast effect in spreading Christianity. The Anglo-Saxons felt the full force of both influences, which made English Christianity from the start strongly missionary in character. The greatest missionary of our whole period was the Devonian St Boniface. More than any other single individual, he created the ecclesiastical frame-work of what would become Germany. When Boniface was consecrated bishop by Pope Gregory II in 722, it was not to a particular see, but to a very wide commission of preaching to heathens, such as, for instance, the Aquitanian St Amand had had in northern Gaul during the previous century. Only in the last eight or nine years before his death (754) was he archbishop of Mainz. Much as he mistrusted almost every Irishman with whom he came in contact on the Continent (Bishop Clement for his disrespect of patristic authority, the priest Sampson for his cavalier attitude to the baptismal rite, Virgil of Salzburg for sowing dissension between himself and the duke of Bavaria as well as for believing that the world was round), Boniface's establishing of monasteries as the learned back-up to missionary work and his devotion to the papacy and to Rome both owed something to the Irish background in England. More par-ticularly, his sense that his calling as a monk, far from being incompatible with preaching to pagans, positively required it, owes much to the Gregorian influence. Pope Gregory (590–604) had sent Roman monks to the English. His writings, particularly his *Homilies on Ezechiel*, composed while he was pope, show that he thought the contemplative life of monks would be best validated if it bore fruit in action. Of the two wives of Jacob, whom spiritual writers regarded as the biblical types of the contemplative and active lives, Rachel was beautiful, but Liah was the fertile one. Gregory himself thought he had married Rachel when he became a monk; but being pope was like waking up in the night to find oneself in the arms of Liah. It was a shock, but while there were those who still lacked the Christian faith, it was a necessary shock.

The character of St Boniface comes through strongly in his letters. Notwithstanding his devotion to the papacy, he was an embryonic English Protestant. He had a strong sense of responsibility to his vocation of preaching and loved to compare himself to St Paul. He was very aware of his duty to his conscience. Important as were his contacts with the Frankish rulers for his preaching in Hesse and Thuringia, he could scarcely bring himself to share the company of the fast-living Frankish bishops whom he met at court—Milo of Trier 'and others like him', as he said dismissively—until his mentor, Bishop Daniel of Winchester, had to cite to him texts from Augustine and the Bible against separating oneself from sinners and in favour of dissimulation. But there are moments when we experience the charm and courtesy which drew English men and women to him as helpers in his continental mission. A monk of Glastonbury called Wigbert, on his way to Hesse, was touched by the distance which Boniface travelled to meet him. Boniface's devotion to the papacy is shown in his name. Both Willibrord, English apostle to the Frisians, and Wynfrith, were consecrated bishop by the pope in Rome and were given the names of Roman martyrs whose feasts fell around the time of their consecration: Willibrord Clement and Wynfrith Boniface. But the one remained known as Willibrord (despite an unimpeachable Roman allegiance), while the other called himself thereafter Boniface. Before twelfth-century English bishops helped to propagate a canon law based on papal direction by appealing constantly to Rome for guidance, Boniface had done the same in the eighth century. He consulted a succession of popes on marriage law, on priestly mores, on ordinations, on liturgy, on whether nuns might wash each other's feet, and on the eating of bacon fat, the last a subject about which the Fathers had remained curiously silent. Indeed, as Rome and the Eastern churches were drifting apart, not least through the Iconoclastic Controversy, Boniface and his mission were preparing a new Rome-centred area of authority in the North.

Yet Boniface's mission was not simply Rome-centred. His own ecclesiastical authority as an archbishop and metropolitan, though a reflection of papal authority at one level, was too important to him in itself to allow of such a thing. He complained at length about a Gallic bishop called Aldebert, who held services at springs and groves instead of in properly consecrated churches, spurned the established saints' cults by distributing his own finger-nails as saintly relics, and invoked the names of archangels which were not to be found in the Bible. These were all implicit attacks upon higher ecclesiastical authority. When Boniface wrote to other bishops, he had a way of invariably reminding them that Christian authority meant service. The service of the pastor was exemplified in Christ's washing of his disciples' feet, and so, whatever little present he might have received from another bishop, back went a towel from a seemingly inexhaustible linen cupboard. Thus was episcopal authority symbolically reinforced. Malcolm Parkes has powerfully suggested that an eighth-century Fulda manuscript, containing the Epistle of St James, has been glossed in the very handwriting of St Boniface. The hand is a strong one, and the sentiments, emphasizing the apostolic succession of bishops, are magisterially expressed. Some historians have seen St Pirmin's monastic foundations (the most famous at Reichenau), by which Pirmin made an important contribution to the Christianization of the south-west German world in the first half of the eighth century, as an attack upon Boniface's episcopal authority among the Germans, or at least as the creation of a counter-sphere of influence. There is, however, no evidence that Boniface viewed Pirmin in this way, and in the next generation the followers of Boniface and Pirmin worked in harmony to create the foundations of the Carolingian church.

But in general Boniface was one of the greatest exponents of a high view of metropolitan and episcopal power which would confront the reformers who asserted papal authority in the eleventh century.

In 723–4, soon after his episcopal consecration, Boniface received a letter from Bishop Daniel of Winchester advising him how to argue with pagans. He should stress, said Daniel, that the creation of the universe and the existence of its ruler must be anterior to the Germanic gods. The pagans think it important to propitiate gods with sacrifices, yet they have no idea which is the most powerful of them, so that they might be offending the one who most needs propitiating by paying him insufficient attention. They do not know what sort of sacrifice most propitiates them, so that they might be wasting their sacrifices. And Boniface should ask them what sort of gods have allowed the Christians to have all the lands rich in wine and oil and other goods, and have left the heathens only with the frozen North. The arguments were not to be put in an insulting or irritating way, but calmly and with great moderation. This letter sets a tone for much missionary work in the early Middle Ages. Its arguments may raise a smile now, but it came from an experienced pastor to an intelligent and dedicated missionary, and was clearly directed to some of the major preoccupations of Germanic and other pagans. Sir Raymond Firth's study of the conversion to Christianity in this century of the Tikopians, with their gods, their ancestor cults, and their propitiatory sacrifices, has shown how interested these Pacific islanders were to discuss a kind of theology of god-power. Could the pagan or Christian cults be demonstrated to be the more correct, judged by practical effects in crops, fish, and health? Another great missionary, St Anskar, had to engage in similar arguments when he preached (under the sponsorship of Louis the Pious) to the Swedes at the prosperous port of Birka in the ninth century. We know from archaeology that Birka was at the northern end of a flourishing trade route which was beginning in the 830s and 840s to bring in huge quantities of silver from the Muslim-controlled trade routes between Byzantium and China. The arrival of Christianity in Birka sparked off one of the sternest tussles between Christianity and paganism anywhere in this period. Some merchants there maintained that the old gods had served them well and would not be pleased by the withdrawal of sacrifices in favour of a foreign and untried god. But there were others who had traded with the Carolingian West (coins of Louis the Pious and other Frankish objects have been found at Birka), who had come to know Christianity from their trading connections, and who formed the bedrock of Anskar's support. It should not be supposed from such criteria for choosing Christianity or retaining paganism that pagans were so simple-minded as to think prosperity and material adversity automatic grounds for conversion or retention of paganism as the case might be. We all have to interpret our fluctuating fortunes in the light of deeper states of mind and in relation to profound and sometimes shifting beliefs. But missionaries constantly encountered the idea of an interaction between supernatural power and material prosperity, and the complexity of this idea only served to increase the sensitivity which they needed to make an impact on the discussion.

Historical writers have often stressed the greed and economic exploitation, as well as the politics, which motivated much missionary work in the early Middle Ages. This can easily be overdone; it fails to take account of the inextricably intertwined motives with which Christian societies addressed themselves to their pagan neighbours. The brutality with which Charlemagne's armies brought the Saxons to enforced Christianity and extracted tithes from them through new ecclesiastical foundations stands clearly revealed. But it is exposed above all in a letter of Alcuin (796) criticizing the whole policy. Careful thought, said Alcuin, should be given to the right method of teaching and baptizing. It was useless to baptize people who had no understanding of the faith, or who had not been persuaded by teaching to espouse Christianity. The ideal book, he thought, for teaching would-be converts systematically what they needed to know was

Augustine of Hippo's *De Rudibus Catechizandis*. This would give them the outline: the immortality of the soul, heaven and hell, the Trinity, the saving mission of Jesus Christ, his passion, resurrection, and ascension, his judgement of the world, the gospel. Alcuin's ideas must to some extent have become Carolingian practice. Recently, Susan Keefe has listed no fewer than sixty-one treatises on baptism which have come down to us in manuscripts from the Carolingian age.

Time and again when we think that we have nailed the political, military, and economic aspects of huge missionary undertakings, another point of view makes itself apparent, sometimes quite unexpectedly, in the sources. The foundation of the archbishopric of Magdeburg provides an example. Otto I founded the monastery of St Maurice at Magdeburg in 937, and from 955 at the latest he intended this church to become an archbishopric, heading the missionary organization amongst the Slavs to the east of the River Elbe. He endowed it with vast lands and rights, including tithes of silver and other rights of tribute from the Slavs. Never was economic gain, as well as the consideration of military security which we mentioned earlier, more clearly in evidence.

Yet when the archbishopric finally became a reality in 968, one sees that the emperor also had religious and pastoral considerations in mind. The first archbishop he appointed, Adalbert (not to be confused with the martyr of that name who preached to the Liutizi Slavs and was greatly venerated by Otto III), was rather a grandee, and not above gratuitously forceful interventions in the feuds of the Saxon aristocracy. But he also had another side. He showed a scrupulous concern for the monastic observance of those monks who had formerly composed the community of what became his cathedral church. Moreover there is a tenth-century manuscript of various patristic writings from the monastery of St Maximin of Trier (Berlin, MS Lat. fol. 759), which contains a short catechism on the Trinity, the Our Father, and the Apostles' Creed. Here is a sample of it: 'What is the second petition? Thy Kingdom come. What is to be understood by it? We pray that Christ will reign in us and not the devil.' St Maximin of Trier was on the other side of Otto I's kingdom from Magdeburg and the Slavs, but this was the monastery from which Adalbert came. It adds to the interest of the concern for preaching shown in this manuscript that Adalbert was the bishop whom Otto had in 960–1 sent to Princess Olga of Kiev. Thus Adalbert's monastic background, so far in geographical distance from the Slav missions (but not on that account far from people who needed to be taught the basics of Christianity), shows pastoral awareness. Quite as striking, for Otto I's approach, is some evidence relating to the appointment of a suffragan bishop. In the document by which Otto I established the archbishopric, the following words occur: 'and because the venerable man Boso has sweated much amongst the Slav people to convert them to God, he is to have the choice of election [as bishop] to whichever church as between Merseburg and Zeitz [both new suffragan sees] he prefers.' The obscure Boso, an alumnus of the monastic school at Regensburg, looks like the perfect exemplar of everything for which Alcuin had argued.

We have said that no real distinction can be made between internal and external missionizing. The Christianization of early medieval society in depth required constant teaching of Christianity, and that required organization. The history of parish organization, for that is what is in question here, cannot be written in a paragraph. A pattern of parishes, as we know it, took centuries to come into existence anywhere in Europe. One starts with communities of monks or canons or clerics serving a wide area from their church, until aristocrats founded small churches, served by one priest, on their estates, probably from a mixture of religious, social, and economic motives. This latter development gathered momentum at different times in different places. There appear to be many small churches, often of wood, served by a single priest, in ninth-century Europe; in England, on the other hand, the first signs of such a phenomenon occur in the tenth century. Yet this much can be said: that in the research of these days, the evidence of some form of parochial structure is more likely to take one by surprise for its earliness than its lateness. A list of Cornish saints recently studied in an early tenth-century manuscript, where in several cases the saints are listed according to geographical contiguousness of parochial dedications, suggests that the parochial structure of Cornwall, as we know it today, was already in existence at that time. On the other side of Europe, a century earlier, researches have shown the monastery of Fulda in the time of its abbot Hrabanus Maurus (822–42) to be administering a large network of parish churches. Whether these were parish churches in the full jurisdictional sense of the high Middle Ages, with burial rights and established revenues, is a moot point. But in terms of pastoral provision much development had already occurred long before 1050. This evidence matches that of the many handbooks of canonical, theological, and liturgical material compiled by (or for) bishops, which shows their determination to teach their flocks.

Christianity and the Political Order

During the eighth and ninth centuries the Christian church effected nothing short of a revolution in the forms of Western politics. Put briefly, there developed an idea of the pervasive religious and moral responsibility of the ruler. Christianity enormously expanded the perspectives in which rulers could think of themselves, and these perspectives in turn became an engine of expanded royal government. If one looks at seventh-century England, as described by the Venerable Bede, it is hard (for all his efforts) to see much difference between the pagan Penda of Mercia and the Christian Oswald of Northumbria as rulers. Both were marauding, tribal war-leaders whose main aim was to bring military glory to themselves and their followers. Or, put more sympathetically, both belonged to a Heroic Age whose culture achieved a high standard of the goldsmith's art and fine poetry to commemorate its warriors. This culture persisted in many aspects into the Christian period. But already by the late eighth century, Germanic kings, though still war-leaders, had come to think of themselves as much more. The single greatest genius in this transformation was Charlemagne, king of the Franks and crowned Holy Roman emperor at Rome in 800. One of his court scholars, Einhard, wrote a biography of the emperor which was very influential as a model of royal biographies in the Middle Ages. It was a masterly synthesis of the ancient Roman ideal of a ruler (as presented in Suetonius' *Lives of the Caesars*) and a new Christian ideal of the ruler as a generous builder of churches and a devout man of prayer (though Einhard was careful to avoid hagiographical over-piety). But when we move from Einhard to the Christian ideal of rule in general, it is at once necessary to point out an important fact about Christianity: that its book, the Bible, consists of two Testaments, which are very different from each other in ethic. However much the Christian religion taught of Christ, the Old Testament played a vital part in the reconciling of Germanic society and Christianity.

Charlemagne thought of himself, and was viewed by his court scholars as, a 'new David'. That was not in itself a new idea, but its content and significance were greatly enlarged by him. David was a war-leader of the Israelites (who looked rather like the Franks to Charlemagne), but he was also the builder of the Jerusalem Temple. Charlemagne's self-image was not confined to David. In the preamble to his *Admonitio Generalis* of 789, which above all embodied his conception of a regenerated society based on sound religious worship and a soundly educated clergy with sound mores, he compared himself to Josiah, the Jewish king who had attacked idolatry and reformed the religious worship of Israel. The rite of anointing kings became important under the Carolingians. The Old Testament kings had been initiated with unction; and in any case the Carolingians, unlike their Merovingian predecessors amongst the Franks, could not depend for their sacrality upon a long royal genealogy stretching back into the past. But if

Charlemagne had a priestly character as a ruler, it lay more in the duty of a priest to teach and preach, than in any function of administering sacraments. Later rulers extended Charlemagne's Old Testament concepts. Both Charles the Bald, his grandson, and Alfred in England, compared themselves to Solomon, ruling in accordance with divine wisdom, and Alfred as a lawgiver saw himself in a succession of lawgivers beginning with Moses.

To focus on Charlemagne is not to say that any one individual could have Christianized the political order single-handed. The foundations of Old Testament kingship were laid by scholars who wrote on the Old Testament, not least the Venerable Bede in the early decades of the eighth century. To us Bede is above all famous for his *Ecclesiastical History of the English People* (731), but his contemporaries attached more importance, judging by manuscript circulation, to his scriptural commentaries. In these commentaries—on Solomon's rebuilding of the Temple, on Esras and Nehemiah, especially on Samuel—he constantly addressed himself to passages about kings. It is true that he was not very interested in kingship as such, and treated every passage possible as an allegory of the church. But to his scholarly readers in Carolingian Europe that probably only served to emphasize the lesson that the interests of good kings and a flourishing church were closely intertwined. In one way or another Bede helped to concentrate educated minds in the succeeding generations on the Old Testament. In particular, he was a strong influence on Alcuin, who probably drafted Charlemagne's *Admonitio Generalis*. A court school, such as Alcuin led, may be defined as an institution for harnessing learning to political purposes, all kinds of learning including biblical learning. As Alcuin looked back from the high days of his own collaboration with Charlemagne, which also involved his many pupils who became bishops and abbots, he obviously saw a model of this relationship at the York of his younger days, when Eadbert ruled Northumbria while his brother Egbert was archbishop of York and built up the cathedral library. York was not a monastic school as was that of Wearmouth and

Jarrow in Bede's day. It has a claim to be considered the first court school of the Middle Ages.

If Charlemagne strove to achieve the regeneration and salvation of the society over which he ruled, this could only be done in association with the clergy. The *Admonitio Generalis* was a programme for giving the clergy social power. It seems to have worked. The clergy educated under the dispensation of Charlemagne stood at the elbows of his successors like Old Testament prophets advising them how to rule—from the Old Testament. Smaragdus, abbot of St Michael's, Verdun, in his *Via Regia*, illustrated many kingly virtues from the Old Testament. David showed prudence in doing the things committed to him by Saul; Job exemplified simplicity (in the good sense) for it was said of him that he was a simple man; Solomon, in Proverbs, highlighted patience, where he said that a prince is made mellow by patience. Under Charles the Bald, the most powerful of his bishops, Hincmar, archbishop of Reims, even used the analogy of bishops to suggest, though in a purely theoretical way, that kings who failed to fulfil their coronation oaths might be deposed. He dwelt on the *pondus sacerdotum*: the burden of priests, and more particularly of bishops (and especially of archbishops), was that they would be responsible for the souls of kings at the Last Judgement. The gathering momentum of clericalism under the Carolingians can be seen from the fact that while Alcuin still addressed his learning in many ways to the laity, his pupil Hrabanus Maurus, abbot of Fulda, wrote the *De Institutione Clericorum*, a compendium of theology and law exclusively for the clergy.

The power of the clergy, and their role in the salvation of society, was central to virtually every issue of theological discussion at this time. In the 840s, for instance, Charles the Bald elicited two treatises on the real presence of Christ in the eucharist, one (a reissue of an earlier work) from Paschasius Radbertus, abbot of Corbie, which stressed transubstantiation and the corporeal presence; the other from Ratramnus, a monk of Corbie, with a very different emphasis. The presence of

Christ, to Ratramnus's mind, was a spiritual presence; the sacrament was primarily a memorial of Christ's passion. These two treatises gave classic expression to the opposing arguments about the eucharist, and they have been of great interest to theologians ever since. Charles the Bald was presumably not seeking to stir up trouble in Corbie. Perhaps he saw a comprehensive theology, with the great disputes all ironed out, as a necessary basis for salvation through Christian society. If that is so he might almost be considered the initiator of scholasticism with its dialectic method. Many intellectual strands of the Carolingian Renaissance, subsequently dropped, were taken up again in the eleventh and twelfth centuries. For our present purposes, however, one should notice that both writers agreed on the necessity of priestly consecration before Christ could be present in any sense in the sacrament of the altar. Again, when the Irishman Scotus Eriugena, one of the two finest minds of the ninth century (the other was Gottschalk, close student of Augustine's works and initiator of the controversy on pre-destination), translated from Greek into Latin the *Heavenly Hierarchy* of Pseudo-Denis (*c.*860), he might at first sight have been engaged in something purely academic. Eriugena himself was never part of the Carolingian ecclesiastical establishment and worked directly under the private patronage of Charles the Bald. He had an unrivalled knowledge of Greek and Greek theology, and the *Heavenly Hierarchy* contained much on the orders of angels. It had been written by a Syrian monk around AD 500 with the idea that contemplative monks were most like the highest orders of angels, closest to the Godhead in heaven. But it was a book about hierarchy, and that is why it became of interest to Carolingian bishops, as there is evidence that within a decade it did.

Amidst all this, there never was a time when any Carolingian ruler saw the clergy as such in the guise of a challenge to secular power. The idea of secular power in itself meant little before the propagandists of the eleventh-century papal reform mounted their assault on it. The idea of church and state as separate entities comes later still, with the development of secular bureaucracies. Indeed, to suppose that any Carolingian ruler would readily see the clergy as a challenge, as Henry II of England could see Thomas Becket in the 1160s, would be radically to misconstrue his mentality. The world might end at any moment; the illustrations of ninth-century Apocalypses are charged with innovation and nervous energy. As time went on, the threat of ferocious barbarians seemed to become more and more intense: the Vikings, the Muslims in the Mediterranean, the Hungarians, not to speak of the internal disorders arising from the division of Charlemagne's empire. But even under Charlemagne, one sees from his letter to Queen Fastrada (791, when he was fighting the Avars) how constant were the prayers, how ascetic the fasts, how generous the alms, needed to stave off defeat and disaster. God could never be taken for granted; even by the just. When one studied the Old Testament closely— and it became almost dangerous not to do so—it was apparent that prayers might not be answered, and that the just might fall in battle. The learned abbot, Lupus of Ferrières, consoling the layman Einhard on the death of his wife, pointed out that God had allowed Absalom to be killed despite the prayers of David; and Agobard, archbishop of Lyon, writing against superstition, asked Louis the Pious what use it was to suppose that God would always show up the just in judicial ordeals, when he had allowed Josiah to perish in battle against the Egyptians. It took an advance in political maturity for Germanic peoples to cope with failure as positively God-given. That is an advance which the Carolingians achieved. Yet what was certain was that God would strike punitively at the first sign of sin, and the worst sin in a ruler was pride. Charlemagne thought that the Byzantine emperors had been denied the Roman empire, which had been conferred on him instead (800), because they had shown the pride of Nebuchadnezzar of Babylon, not least in allowing images of themselves to be idolatrously venerated. He allowed no such thing in his court. On the contrary, he allowed his clergy to criticize him with astonishing freedom, as Alcuin criticized his forcible conversion of the Saxons. From top to bottom this was a society, which as David Ganz has so well observed in connection with the predestination controversy, 'was all too aware of its sins, all too uncertain of their forgiveness'. With sin and corruption, doom and catastrophe, threatening on every side, the only danger from the clergy came if they failed to know or do their job. Then they would be like professional sailors, who, when the ship was caught in a storm, could not handle sails or rudders. The business of a ruler was to force them to know their job and do it.

The gravest doubt which has assailed historians about Charlemagne's moral and educational programme is whether it had much effect. Some would argue that society as a whole was incapable of rising to it morally and that little could be done to enforce it. It is always salutary to question whether edicts are obeyed, and it is true that many of Charlemagne's do not emphasize sanctions but assume a sense of shared moral responsibility throughout society. The above is, however, too pessimistic a view. Charlemagne himself sometimes referred to royal favour as a sanction, and a ruler with as great conquests of territory as his had many rewards to bestow or withhold. More than that, Charlemagne believed in God's sanctions and there is every reason to think that he was not at all alone in this attitude. The Capitulary of Thionville in 805, for instance, forbids usury, the kind of usury which involved buying cheap corn in quantity and selling it at excessive profit in times of scarcity. Old Testament kings had regarded it as their duty to protect the poor, and King David, to whom were attributed all the psalms in Charlemagne's time, was considered very opposed to usury (for example, Psalm 15: 'Lord who shall abide in thy tabernacle? . . . He that putteth not out his money to usury, nor taketh reward against the innocent'; this psalm is illustrated by one of the most inventive miniatures of the Stuttgart Psalter, *c.*830). Now what the Capitulary of Thionville actually says is: 'When famine or plague occurs, men should not wait for our edict but should straightway pray to God for his mercy; as to scarcity of food *in this present year*, let each man help his own people as best he can, and not sell his corn at too high a price.' There was, then, famine in 805 itself; surely this was a punishment of God. To us, profiteering exacerbates famine; to ninth-century people it caused it, in the sense that God punished all immoralities of a society. We saw earlier the strong propitiatory element in the religion of the Germanic pagans with whom St Boniface dealt in the 720s. It had by no means disappeared from the Christianity of their descendants eighty years later.

Between Carolingian times and those of the Saxon (or German) empire of the tenth and early eleventh centuries, the role of Christianity in the public order shifted. Or rather, the moral and educational aspects continued through the work of bishops, cathedrals, monasteries, and parish churches, while upon the image of the ruler in the West a new ceremonial character was superimposed. In a famous book (*The King's Two Bodies*), E. H. Kantorowicz illustrated his theme of the development of Christ-centred kingship with the depiction of the Emperor Otto III on a page of a gospel book made for the imperial church of Aachen probably in the 990s. Even scholars who think that Kantorowicz read too much meaning into this picture would agree that it represents the emperor as if he were Christ seated in majesty. Otto III sought to recreate the image and the empire of Charlemagne. But Charlemagne would have been horrified by the Babylonic pride and the Byzantine iconodulism of this page. Only Charles the Bald, certainly influenced by Eastern concepts of rule, would have begun to appreciate it. As in art so in ceremony the ruler came often to be represented as Christ. When Henry II of Germany was crowned emperor at Rome in 1014, his procession making its way to St Peter's was joined on the Via Cornelia by twelve senators, six of them clean-shaven and six with beards. The symbolism here was Christ and the apostles. One contemporary manuscript shows Henry II crowned by the hand of Christ, while angels invest him with sword and lance.

Christ-centred kingship is totally different in character from

Old Testament kingship. The Israelite kings were actual rulers in the world, some of them good and some bad, exemplifying kingly virtues and actions, rewards and punishments. They could be used as real models of rule. Christ was not a worldly ruler, and some of the virtues which he preached, like meekness, would have been extremely dangerous for rulers to imitate. Christ-centred kingship, therefore, is a liturgical projection of an image, not a quarry of exemplars.

It might be imagined that Christianity would first provide for rulers those ritualistic and magical elements congruent with the expectations of converted pagans, and thereafter, with growing political and religious maturity, the moral dimension. In fact we have just suggested the reverse order of development. This implies, in the earliest age of conversion, the great importance of continuity between Germanic social mores and European Christianity. Adaptations were required of Christianity; biblical colours had to be matched to Germanic ones. *Beowulf* is an Anglo-Saxon epic poem of (probably) the eighth century, shot through with Christian learning and allusions, but all about warrior heroes, their feuds, their treasure, their veneration of pagan ancestors. Of this poem and its cultural milieu, Patrick Wormald has written: 'Christianity had been successfully assimilated by a warrior nobility, a nobility which had no intention of abandoning its culture or seriously changing its way of life, but which was willing to throw its traditions, customs, tastes and loyalties into the articulation of the new faith.' Another Germanic epic, the Old High German *Heliand*, presented Christ the saviour as a great Germanic war-leader with the apostles as his followers in battle. Its text survives in a Fulda manuscript of *c*.820–30, and Fulda was a monastery founded by St Boniface as a convenient centre from which to preach to several Germanic peoples including the Saxons. When the shift of emphasis from moral to liturgical kingship came, it must be seen in the changing political context of ninth- and tenth-century Europe, and the emergence of new dynasties all over the once-unified empire of Charlemagne; one of their principal qualifications to rule was their capacity to defeat external enemies. Hence an increasingly important function of Christianity was the validation or canonization, through symbol and ritual, of power actually achieved.

Bishops, Monks, and Saints

Monasticism was vital to the impact of the Christian church on society in our period. Missionaries were trained in monasteries, their schools and libraries were vital to the educational effort (the learning of Charlemagne's court school had been quickly dispersed to monasteries), their rules of life became yardsticks of Christian living which influenced lay people, and their pioneering character as landlords and organizers of economic wealth should not be overlooked. But when we have said all this, we have said barely half. To a tenth-century man or woman (and Karl Leyser has shown the great importance of nunneries in the aristocratic social order of tenth-century Saxony), as to a modern monk or nun, the *raison d'être* of monasteries was their communal worship, their liturgy. Indeed, this liturgy affected the public order itself. Can we imagine, for instance, that rulers could effectively have articulated their image through Christ, had there been no religious feeling in society as a whole to which appeal could be made, when they projected the Christ-image of rule? The acquisition of the sacred relic of the blood of Christ by the important monastery of Reichenau (on Lake Constance) in the 920s, its veneration there, and Otto I's associating himself with that veneration, is an example of this religious feeling. So are the wonderfully creative cycles of the life of Christ, with lavish application of gold, which illustrate tenth- or early eleventh-century gospel books and other liturgical books, made at monasteries such as Reichenau and St Pantaleon, Cologne. The Aachen Gospels with its Christ-image of Otto III, has itself also a highly dramatic series of Christ illustrations. Monastic worship shaped the religious feeling of early medieval society more than did any other single factor.

Early medieval monasticism was largely based on the Rule of

St Benedict, at least from the time of St Boniface onwards, but with the liturgical side of the Rule greatly elaborated. This liturgical elaboration is sometimes considered to be a special feature of the monastic movements of the tenth century radiating from Gorze–Trier, Cluny in Burgundy, Gerard of Brogne, and from Ethelwold of Winchester and others in England. But the tenth-century reformers based themselves, in Odo of Cluny's case very consciously, on the monastic dispensations of Benedict of Aniane (note the name), Louis the Pious's great monastic adviser (d. 822). More generally, they looked back to Carolingian times in their liturgical practice. Ethelwold of Winchester built organs both at Abingdon and Winchester; their accompaniment probably made a dramatic difference to the sound of the chants. The age of organ-building goes back at least to Louis the Pious, for whom a Venetian priest called George built an organ at Aachen in 826, and it is reflected in the lively illustrations of organs in the Utrecht Psalter, a Reims manuscript of about 830. The abbey church of St Ricquier, built in the 790s, had galleries in its apses, and choir screens round the area of some of its altars, with the idea (as we know from the ritual order of its Abbot Angilbert) of dividing the monks' and boys' choirs; the building must have echoed to the sound of these choirs as they answered each other antiphonally from different parts of it. The triforium galleries of the nunnery at Gernrode (960s), perhaps the best preserved Ottonian church, were surely built with the same idea. While anyone who tests the acoustics of the westwork at St Pantaleon, Cologne, also tenth-century, will be convinced that here, too, sound was a no less important consideration than the visual effect of its cool rhythms.

The sources of Carolingian and Ottonian Europe ring with music, alas! exclusively religious. The *Life of Udalric of Augsburg* refers lyrically to the specially composed chants which were performed at the Palm Sunday services on the hill called 'Perleihc' by the canons and boys of Augsburg cathedral. Odo of Cluny, a famous composer in his day, took care that there should be a congruence of meaning and sound in his antiphons. Another famous composer was an early tenth-century bishop of Liège called Stephen, some of whose chants are first found in compilations of the monastery of St Gall. This shows one way in which the various parts of Charlemagne's empire could retain their cultural unity even when they broke up politically. Charlemagne himself was a singer though not a soloist like David; he sang only when the rest of the congregation was singing, and in a low voice. But he was interested in the chants. Perhaps the most important stimulus to the musico-liturgical development of this whole period was the introduction of Roman chant under Pepin III, father of Charlemagne, at Metz cathedral where a saintly ancestor (Arnulph) had been bishop in the previous century. Here it is necessary to make in parentheses a point of some consequence. Metz cathedral was not a monastic establishment. Indeed, the cathedral monastery, like Canterbury or Durham, was something peculiar to England in the Middle Ages. But its bishop at the time of Pepin III, Bishop Chrodegang, a younger contemporary of St Boniface, had initiated a very influential rule of life for its canons which was quasi-monastic. Within the limits of the canons' active pastoral life, Chrodegang stressed the communal liturgy. This is where the Roman chant fitted in. Our point is that not all liturgical development in this period was strictly monastic, yet monastic ideals strongly influenced cathedral life. The aims of the monastic Boniface and the canonical Chrodegang complemented each other. But whether we speak of monasteries or cathedral churches, music is a touchstone of the liturgical development (also seen in service-books, ritual orders, hymns, and liturgical sermons) which binds the Carolingian and Ottonian periods together.

When historians contemplate the widespread monastic reforms of the tenth century, they often see these reforms as an ideal instrument by which kings and bishops could counteract the power of the lay aristocracies in the regions. This is because the need to reform was felt to arise from the normal attitude of aristocrats in the Germanic world that churches which they had helped to establish were a part of their material property. Such an attitude, though unfavourable to the concept of a universal church, could be of great benefit to cathedrals, monasteries, and parish churches, because it provided them with protectors, and because often a high standard of religious observance could be stimulated by family pride. But it also had potential drawbacks, because the use of a church's income, or part of it, to provide for members of a family could assume a disproportionate weight compared with religious observance. Thus reform could involve a clash with the vested interests of local aristocracies. It could mean the recovery for the communal purposes of the monastery of land which had previously been regarded by an aristocratic family as a private-property share in its endowments. To take on these powerful vested interests, so the argument runs, the reformers needed the support of rulers and bishops (if bishops themselves were not a part of the local familial nexus), and rulers at the same time gained an opportunity to reduce the power of local aristocracies. The most general form of this view is that the tenth-century rulers of Germany and England worked the church, and particularly the reformed monasteries within it, into a system of government. Wide local powers, it is said, were transferred from semi-autonomous secular magnates to wealthy and disciplined ecclesiastical corporations which had a natural interest in sustaining royal power.

But it is easy to exaggerate the conflicting interests of kings and aristocrats in monastic reform. First of all the tenth-century reformers should not be viewed as if they were eleventh-century papal reformers. The latter made a root-and-branch attack on lay control of churches. The former were still happy to recognize lay authority and lay material rights provided that the essentials of communal liturgy and communal living which went with it were safeguarded. Indeed, laymen were often the best protectors of a truly monastic way of life. Secondly, the reformed monasteries of the tenth century were of necessity largely aristocratic in composition, and had they been perceived to have no function in aristocratic society, they could not have been as successful as they were. Therefore, the monastic reforms should be regarded at least as much in the light of co-operation as of combat between king and aristocracy. Moreover, when we speak of the perceived function of reformed monasteries, we do not mean primarily their economic functions as efficient optimizers of agrarian wealth, or even their cultivation of knowledge and production of books. There is rather a lot of evidence that what laymen especially valued was the propitiatory function with God of beautiful worship, with splendid chants, vestments woven by the most skilful women, and lavish expenditure of gold on the book covers seen in church and on the altar crosses. This was a heroic age of gift-giving to reward the soldiers of Christ. In the reign of Canute, an aristocratic woman called Godiva attending a vigil of prayer to St Etheldreda in Ely, was so kindled in her love towards the Ely monks, because of the 'beauty of the place and of their devotion', that she granted three estates to the monastery. The appeal of liturgical monastic religion can also be seen from the fact that when Ethelwold in the 960s expelled the married clergy from the church of Winchester in favour of celibate monks, three of the former clergy, Eadsige, Wulfige, and Wilstan, returned as celibates to the new communal life.

It is undoubtedly true that in this period when new political lordships and principalities were replacing the Carolingian empire, and Europe was recovering from external attacks, the church was far more an upholder than a hammer of kings and other rulers. But rule also depended on a degree of common purpose between kings and at least a proportion of the secular magnates. Tenth-century kings tried to achieve a balance between secular and ecclesiastical power in the localities rather than to crush the former; this was demonstrably the aim of Otto I and Otto II when disposing of the tributes exacted from the Slav peoples. Moreover, before we speak of the transfer of powers, we should remember that these men were not nineteenth-century constitutional lawyers, any more than they were eleventh-century papal reformers. The juristic aspects of power were not uppermost in their minds. Karl Leyser has shown that this was a 'patrimonially', not a 'bureaucratically', governed society; rule was by the personal presence of an itinerant ruler, the exercise of his patronage, the close bonds which he could establish with his followers, and the ceremonial projection of his sacrality. No more than kings, did bishops and abbots rule primarily through bureaucracies or closely defined legal powers. If their power was anything, it was the power of holy men.

Holiness, in early medieval society, was not seen to lie above all in the cultivation of a personal and interior life of prayer, morality, and spiritual meekness. Mystical writings were much less favoured than hagiographies about famous prelates or nuns who had done great deeds. There were recluses in this age, like St Romuald who resigned the archbishopric of Ravenna almost as soon as it had been thrust upon him by Otto III in order to lead a life of private prayer and asceticism. But more characteristic was the visible manipulation of supernatural power by men and women who wielded authority. A proliferation of hermits tends to occur when Christian society perceives a gap between ecclesiastical and spiritual power. The eleventh-century reform movement caused such a gap to open up. In the previous centuries, however, spiritual power was securely earthed in the *Adelsheiliger*, the aristocratic holy men and women who held ecclesiastical office. The vast majority of bishops in this age were aristocrats. Those who were not, but rose by exceptional ability, were invariably the subject of unfavourable comment, and when successful (as in the case of Archbishop Willigis of Mainz, 975–1011), it was because their rule drew on the capital of the *Adelsheiliger* tradition.

One of the most famous and effective bishops of the Ottonian empire was Archbishop Bruno of Cologne (953–65). He was Otto I's brother, and his biographer was not slow to apply to him the biblical phrase, 'a royal priesthood'. To this writer, one of Bruno's most admirable qualities was a capacity to inspire terror. His gift of tears in prayer would have counted for nothing without this. Of course, as archbishop, he could raise quite an army from his estates, and this aspect of a bishop's or abbot's power should not be overlooked. Churchmen justified it in Augustinian terms. The citizens of the heavenly city, during their pilgrimage through this earth towards their fatherland of the world to come, had a duty to secure earthly peace in order to facilitate this pilgrimage. They could not opt out. That is why Bruno was prepared to be duke of Lorraine and archbishop at the same time. But he inspired awe not only because of his military resources, but also because of his lavishly spent wealth, his splendid building projects, the perception of his learning, the magnetism of his personality which brought him a following of other ecclesiastics. The same applies to many other churchmen of the age, in England most obviously to Bishop Ethelwold of Winchester. In the tenth and early eleventh centuries, bishops developed a sacral image similar to that of kings and very closely associated with theirs. Archbishop Egbert of Trier had himself represented on the first page of a book of liturgical gospel readings and in a psalter as if he were a Christlike emperor seated in majesty. The chronicler Bishop Thietmar of Merseburg has this to say in support of his view that bishops should be appointed by none other than kings and emperors:

Our kings and emperors, who take the place of the almighty ruler in this world, are set above all other pastors; and it is entirely incongruous that those whom Christ, mindful of his flock, has constituted princes of this earth [i.e. bishops], should be under the dominion of any but those who excel all mortals by the blessing of God and the glory of their crown.

Let us look at a holy man in action, and the means by which he could exercise local power in a society where constitutionalism by no means ruled. Gauzlin, abbot of Fleury (1004–30), was not a bishop. Indeed, his authority in the Loire region derived partly from the ineffectiveness of both royal power (though he was on good terms with King Robert of France) and episcopal power (he was on bad terms with the bishop of Orléans). But his example will serve for many an abbot and bishop. A local knight called Walter had usurped land belonging to the dependent monastery of Fleury at Sault. Gauzlin rode there, and when Walter threatened to kill any monk whom he found on the land, Gauzlin replied that he had a plentiful supply of confessors at Fleury. 'If you martyr a single one of my monks', said the abbot, 'I shall send two; if you martyr two, you will have four on your hands; however many you kill, I shall double the number.' Soon afterwards, on Good Friday, Walter was seized by a fever; his house was invaded by impure demons; he just had time to struggle to Sault and make his confession; and at dawn on Easter Sunday 'he withdrew from his body'. That is how society was controlled in the early Middle Ages.

It was a well-known fact that not every bishop and abbot could be a holy man, though it is astonishing how many were. Holy men were needed everywhere, but there was naturally a shortfall in the supply. But what function had the saints in heaven if not to make good the deficiency? Particularly was this so, since the Christians of the early medieval West followed their Germanic forebears in locating the holy in physical objects such as stones, trees, groves, and hills. In a society which drew no sharp line between the natural and the supernatural, a very real presence of the saints in heaven was felt to be where their bodily remains rested. Indeed, steal the relics and one could steal the saintly power which went with them. When we look at the lists of saints' resting-places in Anglo-Saxon England, when we see how saints' remains were moved from the outer fringes to the heart of the West Saxon and Mercian kingdoms where they could do more good (for example, St Oswald from Tynemouth to Gloucester, St Judoc from Cornwall to Winchester), when we watch Otto I move the body of St Maurice (the soldier saint) in state from Burgundy to Magdeburg to fight on his eastern frontier, we witness the deployment of heavenly troops on earth as if there were not the slightest difference between the two spheres.

'Dead' saints could perform exactly the same function as living ones. The statue-reliquary of St Faith at the monastery of Conques was carried out to manors which the tenth- and eleventh-century monks claimed belonged to them. This statue can still be seen in the treasury at Conques in the Massif Central. Encased in gold and encrusted with gems, the saint sits in a hieratic posture with staring eyes, looking every inch an oriental potentate. It is an accomplished work of art, and it was made to terrify, and to give noblemen with guilty consciences (especially depredators of the monastery's lands) bad dreams. Such statues were common in this part of France during the later part of our period, though most have not survived. It took much longer for a consolidated kingship to emerge in France than it did in Germany after the break-up of the Carolingian empire. The region of Conques suffered especially at this time from the breakdown of public authority and the rise of an aristocracy exercising local power from newly built castles. But, as Jean Dunbabin has pointed out, the castellans became vulnerable to the concerted criticism of the communities which they dominated. In the orchestration of this criticism, and in the curbing of local aristocrats who were quite unrestrained by royal power, no single factor was more important than the veneration of saints' shrines at a local monastery. This was how the identity of a local community was articulated against its oppressors; this was where local men and women, also, were helped in their illnesses and misfortunes generally; this was a major instrument of social order at the grass roots in an age of political fragmentation. Not surprisingly one finds a greater number of narratives of the miracles of dead saints in France than in Germany, because they were more needed there. France could also boast living saints, however, especially in the line of holy men who ruled Cluny as abbots in the tenth and eleventh centuries. The effect of Odo of Cluny on robbers is comparable to that of Gauzlin of Fleury or of the statue of St Faith at Conques on unscrupulous knights. Odo's biography was written by a monk who had little interest in the miraculous and much in practical virtues. Perhaps the greatness which Cluny achieved amongst Western monasteries shows, amongst other things, that in the final analysis living saints were even more effective than dead ones.

This account of Western Christianity in the early Middle Ages may have been rather weighted towards the political, and perhaps, given the political complexion of the discussion, it may be surprising to many readers that more has not been said about the papacy. The popes pressed their primatial and jurisdictional claims with impressive continuity in this period; using every appeal to them made by Carolingian churchmen seeking to bolster their own positions; making a bid to establish the authority of the papacy over the Bulgarian church; declaring its sole power to establish a new archbishopric as at Magdeburg in 968; and developing the special relationship with the new Polish church at the turn of the first millennium which would ultimately bear fruit in a Polish pope at the turn of the second. But the political story of the Christian church in this age is a story particularly about bishops. Bishop Rathier of Verona wrote in the 930s that the church was one in all its bishops; that not Jerusalem, not Rome, not Alexandria, had received a special prerogative of rule to the exclusion of others (he tucks Rome pointedly into the middle). In the 1080s, when Archbishop Siegfried of Mainz wanted to retire to become a monk, his cathedral clergy wrote to him in horror, stressing a traditional view: 'Nothing in the world surpasses the life of a bishop; every monk or recluse and every hermit, as being of lesser importance, must give way to him.' As one looks along the line of great bishops stretching back to Boniface and Wilfrid and the great Gallic and Spanish bishops of a still earlier age, one understands what impressed these writers. The principal claim to greatness of even the popes themselves, before the mid-eleventh century, lay in their conduct as bishops of Rome, building churches, organizing poor relief, and resisting the attempts of every tinpot contender for the empire to dominate the city and its people.

All that would change with the papal reform to which Pope Gregory VII (1073–85) has given his name. The reformers' ideal was a world ordered by intellectual logic (which would give rise to fully blown scholasticism), by law and jurisdiction, by a centre at Rome. Against them stood a world ordered by ritual, sacrality, and magic. This world was a world of bishops, whose mentality (to use the terminology of Henry Chadwick) was elliptical. The church was not a circle ruled from a centre, but an a-centralized ellipse, the points on which were the bishoprics of the world. This old order was not unchallenged by ideas of the universal church, with an implication of a centralized order, already for instance by Ambrosius Autpertus, eighth-century abbot of Volturno, in his commentary on the Apocalypse. But its character was the natural result of the close intertwining of Christianity with the rule of kings and emperors.

EASTERN CHRISTENDOM

4

Eastern Christendom

KALLISTOS WARE

> And therefore I have sailed the sea and come
> To the holy city of Byzantium . . .

MANY others before Yeats have expressed the same sense of wonder. 'How splendid a city,' exclaimed an eleventh-century visitor to Constantinople, Fulcher of Chartres, 'how stately, how fair, how many monasteries within it, how many palaces raised by sheer labour in its highways and streets, how many works of art, marvellous to behold. It would be wearisome to tell of the abundance of all good things; of gold and silver, garments of varied appearance, and such sacred relics.' Even today, with modern Istanbul no more than a pale shadow of the Byzantine past, a shiver of astonishment still passes down the traveller's spine as she or he enters St Sophia, the church of the Holy Wisdom, and stands under the vast dome. There is light everywhere. In the words of Procopius, writing soon after the rebuilding of the church in the 530s by the Emperor Justinian: 'The interior, you might say, is not illumined by the sun from the outside, but the radiance is generated from within.' So effortlessly does the dome overarch the central space that 'it seems not to rest on solid masonry, but to be suspended from heaven by a golden chain'.

The 'Great Church', as it was called, standing at the heart of the city of Constantinople, may serve as a fitting visual symbol of Eastern Christendom. For more than eleven hundred years— from its dedication as 'New Rome' by the Emperor Constantine the Great on 11 May 330, until its capture by the Ottoman Turks on 29 May 1453—Constantinople was the capital of the Eastern Roman empire, the hub of Orthodox Christianity, except during a relatively brief interlude of crusader occupation from 1204 to 1261. Nor did 1453 mark the end of its history as a Christian centre. Although St Sophia became a mosque (it is now a museum), the patriarch of Constantinople continued to reside in the city, exercising jurisdiction over the Orthodox subjects of the sultan in civil affairs as well as religious. The patriarch is still there today, despite threats of expulsion during the past thirty years. His flock in Constantinople now numbers little more than two or three thousand, but he retains his honorary primacy as 'first among equals' within the world-wide Orthodox communion.

But the story of Eastern Christendom from 330 onwards is by no means the tale of a single city alone. The patriarch of Constantinople is only the senior among the four eastern patriarchs; below him in order of precedence, but independent of him in jurisdiction, come his colleagues at Alexandria, Antioch, and Jerusalem. This pattern of four major sees began to emerge in the fourth century, and was formally ratified at the Council of Chalcedon (451). Yet these four were never the only important centres. Further to the east in this early period Edessa served as a focal point for Syriac-speaking Christianity. Initially all Christians in the East, whether Greek, Syrian, Coptic, or Armenian, were joined in communion, but schisms in the fifth and sixth centuries led to a fragmentation that continues to the present day. Thus alongside the Greek-speaking Byzantine church there came to exist other Eastern churches, separated from it: the Church of the East, often misleadingly called the 'Nestorian' church, and the five non-Chalcedonian churches that are commonly called 'Monophysite'. From the ninth century onwards Byzantine missionary expansion among the Slavs led to the establishment of Orthodox national churches to the north: the church of Bulgaria, the church of Serbia and, most important of all, the church of Russia, with its centre first at Kiev and then at Moscow. All of these have their place together with Constantinople in the varied and intricate tapestry of the Christian East.

The 'Organic Body': Emperor and Patriarch within the Byzantine Polity

How would it have felt to be a Christian at Constantinople in the Byzantine era? Two chief figures dominated the scene. 'The constitution (*politeia*) consists, like the human person, of parts and members', states the *Epanagogē*, a legal textbook drafted at Constantinople around 880, possibly by the patriarch, St Photius; 'and of these the greatest and most necessary are the emperor and the patriarch. Thus the peace and felicity of subjects, in body and soul, depends on the agreement and concord of the kingship and the priesthood in all things.' Of these two dominant figures, by far the more powerful was the emperor. Yet, although the two were never equal partners, both were regarded as essential to the proper functioning of the body politic.

Our modern distinction between church and state would have been meaningless to the Byzantines. They did not envisage church and state as two contrasted entities, subsisting in co-operation or conflict, but they thought of society as a single, integrated whole. The emperor had religious as well as civil responsibilities. He was concerned with the entirety of his subjects' lives, and therefore among other things with the way in which they worshipped God. 'What higher duty have I in virtue of my imperial office', stated Constantine, 'than to dissipate errors and to suppress rash indiscretions, and so to cause all humans to offer to almighty God true religion, honest concord and due worship?' As Patriarch Antony of Constantinople wrote to the Grand Prince Vasilii of Russia around 1395:

The holy emperor has a great place in the church. He is not as other rulers and the governors of other regions are; and this is because the emperors, from the beginning, established and confirmed true religion in all the inhabited earth. . . . It is not possible for Christians to have a church and not to have an empire. Church and empire have a great unity and community; nor can they be separated from each other.

When claims such as this are made on the emperor's behalf, it should not be forgotten that several rulers of the Byzantine empire were women, not just imperial consorts but empresses reigning in their own right. All that is said here about the Christian emperor applies also to them.

The basic principles of Byzantine imperial ideology were formulated in the 330s by the court prelate Eusebius of Caesarea, during the reign of the first Christian emperor, Constantine I; and they prevailed virtually unchanged until the last emperor, Constantine XI, fell fighting the Turks on the walls of the city in 1453. The Eusebian theory can be summed up in the phrase 'As in heaven, so on earth'. The emperor is to be seen as the living icon of Christ, God's vicegerent on earth. The terrestrial rule of the emperor reproduces God's rule in heaven. In Eusebius' words, 'Crowned in the image of the heavenly kingship, gazing upwards, he steers and guides humans on earth according to the pattern of his prototype.' Just as God regulates the cosmic order, so the emperor regulates the social order. God by his divine activity brings all creation into ordered harmony under his absolute rule; and in a similar way the emperor brings all humankind into ordered harmony under his own absolute rule, within the framework of a universal Christian state.

Eusebius' 'image' doctrine, which became normative for the Christian East, differs profoundly from the political theory of the two cities worked out by St Augustine in the West after the fall of Rome to the barbarians in 410. Where Eusebius thinks in terms of continuity—of the prototype reflected in the image— Augustine thinks in terms of discontinuity: the city of God is radically distinct from any human city or society in this fallen world. For Eusebius the conceptual framework is Platonic idealism, for Augustine it is eschatology.

As God's image and vicegerent, the emperor presided day by

day over the 'liturgy' of the palace, with its elaborate court ceremonial and its bureaucratic hierarchy. So through the imperial administration Byzantium was maintained in unity as an 'organic body', to use the phrase of Charles Williams in *Taliessin through Logres*:

> The logothetes run down the porphyry stair
> bearing the missives through the area of empire.
>
> .   .   .   .   .   .
>
> The organic body sang together.

But the 'organic body' had also its religious aspect, and in this too the emperor played his part, although only a layman. His role within the church was given visible expression in the worship at St Sophia, when during the divine liturgy on great feasts he carried the holy gifts into the sanctuary at the offertory and placed them on the altar.

Western writers have sometimes described the Byzantine pattern as 'Caesaropapism', meaning that Caesar, the civil ruler, was also pope, supreme governor of the church; but the label is misleading. Justinian, in his sixth Novel—a classic statement of Byzantine political theory—speaks of a 'happy concord' between priesthood (*sacerdotium*) and kingship (*imperium*), but he does not say that the one is subordinated to the other. In the agreement between John V Palaeologus and the holy synod (*c.* 1380–2), the emperor is termed 'general defender of the church', but not 'head of the church'; the head was Christ. Certainly the emperor's powers in the ecclesiastical sphere were extensive. He selected the patriarch from a list of three names submitted by the holy synod; indeed, sometimes he simply nominated the patriarch without consulting the synod at all. If a patriarch defied him, almost always the emperor could secure his deposition. It was the emperor who summoned a church council; he presided in person, or else appointed lay commissioners to preside in his place, and he could usually determine the agenda discussed by the bishops.

After the conclusion of the council, it rested with him to confirm its decisions and to proclaim them as imperial law.

Yet there were limits to the emperor's domination. On a number of decisive occasions, when the ruling emperor sought to impose a particular religious policy, a large proportion of the clergy and laity successfully resisted his will. This happened, for instance, during the Monothelete controversy in the seventh century, during the iconoclast dispute in the eighth and ninth centuries, and during reunion negotiations with the papacy in the thirteenth and fifteenth centuries. The Byzantine church was never crudely erastian.

The emperor's counterpart at Constantinople, the patriarch, was known from 595 onwards as 'ecumenical patriarch'. Literally this means patriarch of the *oikoumenē* or the whole inhabited earth, 'universal' patriarch, but in reality it signified merely patriarch of the Christian empire. Until the schism with Rome, the patriarch of Constantinople always looked on the pope as his senior, although without ascribing to him direct jurisdiction in the East. He also recognized the autonomy of the other three eastern patriarchs, although in practice, especially after the Arab conquests of the mid-seventh century, their influence was greatly inferior to his own.

Most patriarchs of Constantinople worked in close co-operation with the holy synod, the *synodos endēmousa* or 'home synod', consisting of hierarchs with sees in the immediate environs of the city, and of any other bishops temporarily resident in the capital. This was usually in more or less continuous session. When major doctrinal or disciplinary problems arose, larger episcopal synods were convened, usually at Constantinople itself or not far distant. On exceptional occasions, a 'general' or 'ecumenical' council was held, representing in principle the entire Christian world. Byzantine Christendom recognized seven such councils, the first occurring in 325 and the last in 787. For Eastern Orthodoxy the ecumenical council constitutes, along with the eucharist, the supreme visible expression of God's continuing presence in the church on earth. Whereas the Western church during the Middle Ages grew increasingly monarchical, Orthodox Christians in Byzantine as in modern times have always seen their church as conciliar. As the Italo-Greek Barlaam the Calabrian, sent by the Byzantine emperor to negotiate reunion with the West, told Pope Benedict XII at Avignon in 1339: 'There is only one effective way of bringing about union: through the convocation of a general council to be held in the east. For to the Greeks anything determined by a general council has the authority of law.' At each true council, on the Orthodox understanding, the miracle of Pentecost is renewed; the Holy Spirit descends, the many become one in mind and heart, and the truth is revealed.

Bishops in the Christian East, from the sixth or seventh century onwards, were required to be celibate. In modern Orthodox practice the episcopate is limited specifically to monks, not just to celibates, but probably this was not the invariable rule until around the fourteenth century. Parish priests in the Christian East, on the other hand, in the vast majority of cases have always been married men living with their wives and families. The fact that priests are usually married in the Greek East but celibate (especially from the eleventh century onwards) in the Latin West has made a profound difference to the status and role of the clergy in the two halves of Christendom. Parish priests in the Orthodox world have remained, in their education and in their daily way of life, far less sharply distinguished from the laity than is the case with their Roman Catholic counterparts. Some of the clergy in Byzantine urban parishes, and in particular at St Sophia in Constantinople, were not unlearned, but most of the village priests were probably little better educated than their flock. The majority of them worked for their living in some secular occupation, commonly as farmers, or else in other forms of manual labour, as cobblers, metal-workers, or the like; the better educated might be schoolmasters. The church canons specify a wide range of occupations not permitted to the clergy; they are not to engage in commerce, to become bankers, inn-keepers, or brothel-owners, or to enter the Civil Service. But we know relatively little about the parish clergy in Byzantium, since the surviving sources refer mainly to bishops or monks.

In the West the only education effectively to survive the barbarian invasions was by the clergy and for the clergy, but in Byzantium many of the laity, especially in the upper ranks of the Civil Service, were well read, not only in classical literature and philosophy, but sometimes also in theology. Patriarchs were chosen on occasion from among the learned Civil Servants; Tarasius in 784, Nicephorus in 806, and Photius in 858, were all of them laymen at the time of their election to the patriarchate. As late as 1353 the lay courtier Nicolas Cabasilas, while still in his early thirties, was selected as one of the three candidates for the patriarchate, although in the end he was not chosen. This continuing tradition of secular learning meant that the laity never became a purely passive element in the Byzantine church community. This is an important clue to any true estimate of church–state relations in the East.

The 'Angelic Life': The Witness of Monasticism

'Monks are the sinews and foundations of the Church', said the ninth-century monastic reformer, St Theodore the Studite. Within the 'organic body' of Byzantium, the life of prayer pursued by monks and nuns was seen as an essential support of the social and spiritual fabric. For the fourth-century author of the anonymous *History of the Monks in Egypt*, monasteries form a rampart of defence around the total Christian community: 'There is no town or village in Egypt or the Thebaid that is not surrounded by hermitages as if by walls, and the people depend on their prayers as if on God himself. . . . Through them the world is kept in being.' Monasteries were to be found everywhere in the Christian East. Many were in cities, and at least 300 monastic houses are known to us in Constantinople alone. Others were in the cultivated countryside, and yet others in the remote wilderness, such as St Katherine's at Mount Sinai, the rock monasteries of Cappadocia, the Holy Mountain of Athos, or the monasteries of the Meteora perched on sheer volcanic crags in Thessaly.

Monastic communities varied greatly in size. Some were highly organized landowning and commercial enterprises, with hundreds of brethren sharing the community life. Others had very modest resources, containing perhaps no more than three or four residents. Some were founded by members of the imperial house or the nobility, others by small groups of peasants anxious to ensure that prayers would be said for themselves and their families in their lifetime and after death. The Christian East has no centralized orders, parallel to those that arose in the West during the tenth and eleventh centuries; each Orthodox monastery is a self-governing unit, under the direction of its own abbot. Such is also the pattern envisaged by St Benedict in his *Rule*.

Hermits have always been more common in Eastern Christendom than they were in the medieval and post-medieval West. Isolated holy men were to be found everywhere, sometimes close to a monastery or on the outskirts of a village, sometimes in the forest or the deep desert. Their dwelling might be a hut or cave, even a tree or the top of a pillar. For the Christian East the monk *par excellence* is the solitary rather than the cenobite. As St Isaac the Syrian said, 'The glory of Christ's Church is the life of the solitaries.'

Christian monasticism first emerged as a distinct movement in the early fourth century, but it was not so much an innovation as a fresh expression of the ascetic spirit present in Christianity from the start. It is no coincidence that the organized development of monasticism came precisely in the period after Constantine's conversion, at the moment when the persecutions had come to an end and Christianity was growing ever more privileged. Martyrs inwardly in heart and conscience, the monks kept alive the spirit of self-sacrifice at a time when martyrdom of blood had ceased. They acted as a counterbalance to an established Christianity, reminding the church at large that

God's kingdom is not to be identified with any earthly realm. In this way they fulfilled an eschatological role, serving, in the words of St Gregory Palamas, as the prophets of the second coming of Christ.

The monastic vocation was as much for women as for men; indeed, it is often women who may justly claim the priority as monastic pioneers. St Antony of Egypt and his fellow-countryman St Pachomius are commonly regarded as the 'founders of Christian monasticism' (in reality the origins of monasticism are to be located as much in Syria as in Egypt). But when, as a young man in the 270s, Antony wished to become an ascetic after the death of his parents, he was able to entrust his younger sister to the care of what his biographer St Athanasius calls a *parthenōn*, a convent of virgins. Antony's innovation was to move from the inhabited area into the remote desert; but, long before he or Pachomius had ever thought of adopting asceticism, there already existed in Egypt structured communities of what today would be termed nuns. The pioneering role played by a monastic woman is particularly evident in the case of St Basil of Caesarea, organizer of the ascetic life in Asia Minor and author of the *Rules* that still remain the primary monastic source for the Orthodox Church. His elder sister St Macrina embraced monasticism before he did, and but for her influence he might never have become a monk at all. Too often, in ancient as in modern times, monastic history has been written exclusively from a masculine point of view.

What did the Byzantines expect from the monasteries? Not, on the whole, learning and education. Some monasteries ran a small school, but this was on an elementary level and intended for future monks. The copying of manuscripts was seen as manual labour rather than scholarly research. When the Byzantine looked for scholarship, he turned rather to the senior ranks of the Civil Service. Most Orthodox monks were (and are today) not priests but laymen, working with their hands on agriculture or some form of craftsmanship. Again, this was the way in which St Benedict envisaged the monastic life; it was only later that so many Western monasteries became colleges of priests.

There are some cases of monks undertaking missionary work and evangelism. One such instance is the tenth-century St Nikon, nicknamed *ho metanoeite*—'the "Repent ye"', because of the characteristic opening of his sermons—who reconverted the people of Crete after the Arab occupation and worked among the pagan Slavs in the southern Peloponnese. Another example in the eighteenth century is the 'New Martyr' St Kosmas the Aetolian, who set out from Mount Athos on a series of missionary journeys, preaching to the Greek and Albanian Christians who were in danger of lapsing to Islam. But, on the whole, evangelism was not undertaken by the monasteries in a systematic way.

Much more important was the social and charitable work of the monasteries. From the beginning hospitality was always seen as part of the monk's vocation. Repeatedly the sources insist that a monk, even when a hermit, should care for the sick and provide alms for the poor. He does not beg, but gives to others. Monastic bishops, such as St John Chrysostom, displayed a burning zeal for social righteousness. Chrysostom spoke characteristically of the two altars:

You honour the altar in church, because the Body of Christ rests upon it; but those who are themselves the very Body of Christ you treat with contempt, and you remain indifferent when you see them perishing. This living altar you can see everywhere, lying in the streets and market places, and at any hour you can offer sacrifice upon it.

In the words of the great Byzantinist N. H. Baynes, 'One of the outstanding features of early Byzantine asceticism is . . . its championship of the poor and oppressed. . . . The Byzantine in his hour of need turned instinctively for aid and comfort to the ascete in the full assurance of his sympathy and succour.' Monastic charity often took a highly organized form. St Basil saw *philanthropia*, active love for humankind, as an integral part of the monastic vocation, and founded at Caesarea a vast complex of charitable institutions, hospitals, orphanages, and hostels for the poor. Michael Attaleiates, in the foundation charter of the house that he established at Constantinople in 1077, laid down that the community—a small group of eight monks—should maintain a 'centre for nourishing the poor'. Each day six destitute men were to be given a meal, 'meat, fish, cheese, cooked vegetables, dried or green, or whatever else God shall send. . . . Do not allow a day to pass without some act of mercy; but let the brethren open both the gate of the monastery and their own hearts to everyone who is poor, giving away everything, even to the last scrap.'

But charitable work has never been regarded in the Christian East as the primary function of monasticism. The chief task of the monk or nun was to pray. The monastery was above all a place where the ordered cycle of the Divine Office was offered day by day without interruption. Attaleiates, although assigning social work to his monks, insisted that their main duty was 'carefully to watch over the doxology and liturgy of the Church'. The monk serves the world by standing in God's presence. He helps society not so much by what he *does* as by what he *is*—by his singleminded pursuit of perfection. As St Isaac the Syrian put it, in a deliberate paradox, it is better to 'build one's own soul' than to 'convert whole multitudes of the heathen from error to the worship of God'.

This, then, was what the Byzantine expected from the monasteries: not, on the whole, learning, evangelism, or organized charity, but holiness. He expected to find there men and women who would pray for his sins, and who could offer him at moments of crisis a healing word of counsel. A figure characteristic of Orthodox monasticism at all periods is the *gerōn* or charismatic 'elder' (in Slavonic, *starets*)—not necessarily old in years, but mature in spiritual experience and capable of guiding others. The prototype of the monastic *gerōn* is the hermit St Antony of Egypt, who in later life, as St Athanasius put it, became 'a physician to all Egypt'. Eastern Christendom has its spiritual mothers as well as its spiritual fathers. One example is

Melania, abbess at the Mount of Olives in Jerusalem, who guided the young Evagrius to the monastic life; he later became one of the most influential of Greek spiritual writers. An elder need not necessarily be a monastic, but is sometimes a lay man or woman living in the world.

Such is the true contribution that, in Byzantine eyes, the monasteries made to society: prayer, holiness, spiritual guidance.

'This Faith Has Made Firm the Whole World . . .': The Articulation of Doctrine

The first half-millennium of the Byzantine era, from the early fourth to the early ninth century—the epoch of the seven ecumenical councils—was a period of incessant doctrinal exploration. To modern readers the debates often seem abstruse and arid, but at the time they aroused intense popular interest. The theological hymns of Arius were sung by Alexandrian dockworkers. Gregory of Nyssa, at Constantinople in the early 380s, complained that he could not obtain a straight answer to a practical question: 'If you ask someone to give you change, he philosophizes about the Begotten and the Unbegotten. . . . If you say to the attendant "Is my bath ready?", he tells you that the Son was made out of nothing.' The rival factions at the horse races in the sixth-century Hippodrome, the Blues and the Greens, each championed a particular standpoint in Christology. An enthusiasm for ecclesiastical controversy has continued to be a feature of the Greek people in modern times. In 1901 the publication of a translation of the New Testament in contemporary Greek led to the downfall of the government and to student demonstrations in which eight people were killed. On a recent occasion in central Athens, so I recall, I was delayed by a massive traffic jam. This was caused, as my taxi-driver explained, by 'a riot of unemployed theologians'.

Doctrinal discussions during the epoch of the seven councils can be divided into three main stages. First, during the fourth century the focus of attention was the theology of the Trinity.

What is the relation of Christ to God the Father? In what sense can God be Father, Son, and Holy Spirit, and yet still be one? How can there be in God true unity combined with true diversity? The Council of Nicaea (325), the first ecumenical council, repudiated the view of Arius that God the Son is fundamentally inferior to God the Father. According to Nicaea, Christ belongs to the realm of the eternal and the uncreated, being 'true God from true God', 'consubstantial' or 'one in essence' (*homoousios*) with the Father; what the Father is, the Son is also. During the next sixty years Arianism continued to enjoy widespread support, while the Nicene faith was defended first by St Athanasius of Alexandria, and then by the three Cappadocian Fathers, St Basil of Caesarea, St Gregory of Nazianzus (known in the Christian East as 'Gregory the Theologian'), and St Gregory of Nyssa. The Nicene position was eventually reaffirmed at the second ecumenical council, held at Constantinople in 381. This council spoke also of the Holy Spirit as equal to the other two persons, 'worshipped and glorified together with the Father and the Son'.

During the second stage, from 431 to 681, the centre of interest shifted from the Trinity to the person of Christ. If Christ is true God, in what sense is he also authentically human? And if he is at the same time God and man at once, how can he be one? Emphasizing Christ's personal unity, the third ecumenical council, held at Ephesus in 431 under St Cyril of Alexandria, affirmed that the Virgin Mary is *Theotokos*, 'God-bearer' or 'Mother of God'. What Mary bore, so the council stated, was not merely a human being closely united with God—not merely a superior kind of prophet or saint—but a single and undivided person who is God and man at once. Nestorius, the bishop of Constantinople, who expressed reservations about the title *Theotokos*, was condemned for making too sharp a contrast between Christ's Godhead and his humanity. Nestorius was a follower of Theodore of Mopsuestia, the chief exponent of the Antiochene tradition of Christology, which insisted with great vividness upon the full integrity of Christ's human nature. At Alexandria more emphasis was placed upon the unity of his person.

The Council of Ephesus led, indirectly rather than directly, to a lasting schism. The Christians in East Syria and Mesopotamia, living mainly in the Persian empire outside the boundaries of Byzantium, felt unable to accept the definition of Mary as *Theotokos*. They were heavily influenced by the theological school of Edessa, one of the main centres of Antiochene Christology. In course of time they came to constitute a separate communion, predominantly Syriac in language and culture, divided from the Greek-speaking Byzantine church with its centre at Constantinople. They referred to themselves as 'The Church of the East', and are sometimes called by Western writers 'Assyrians', 'Chaldeans', or 'Nestorians'; but this last term is misleading, for they ascribe no special importance to Nestorius and show far greater admiration for Theodore of Mopsuestia. In the West it was once imagined the Church of the East divided Christ into two different persons. This is certainly unjust; but it has always been concerned to uphold his entire manhood, avoiding any confusion within him between the human and the divine aspects, such as might suggest that his humanity was swallowed up by his Godhead. Once of vast extent, with missionary work extending in the thirteenth century across Asia as far as China, the Church of the East has since then been virtually annihilated by persecution. One of its greatest writers, the seventh-century Isaac the Syrian, also known as Isaac of Nineveh, has been widely read by Greeks and Russians, unaware that he belonged to a church not in communion with their own. This is a striking example of the way in which inner, spiritual unity can continue to exist despite an outward separation.

Unable to obtain a fair hearing at Ephesus, the Christology of Antioch was to some extent reinstated at the fourth ecumenical council, Chalcedon (451). This affirmed that Christ, 'perfect in Godhead and perfect in humanity', is 'made known to us in two natures. . . . The difference of the natures is in no way destroyed because of the union, but rather the property of each nature is preserved, and both concur in one person and one *hypostasis*.' This was an attempt to strike a balance between the Alexandrian and the Antiochene approaches, allowing for both the diversity and the unity within the incarnate Christ. But followers of Cyril of Alexandria, in Egypt, Syria, and elsewhere, felt that it savoured too much of 'Nestorianism', implying a continuing division between the divine and the human in the Saviour. They were willing to say that Christ is '*from* two natures' but not that he is '*in* two natures'.

In the West, the study of early Christian doctrine tends to stop abruptly at 451, whereas in fact debates about the person of Christ continued undiminished for another two centuries. For all its importance, Chalcedon is not an end-point, but no more than an episode in a far lengthier process. Strenuous efforts were made by the imperial government at Constantinople to reconcile the non-Chalcedonians of Egypt and Syria. The fifth ecumenical council, at Constantinople in 553, adopted a 'Neochalcedonian' standpoint, reinterpreting the 451 council in Cyrilline terms. Christ is 'in two natures', but it is also necessary to affirm, as Cyril does, that he is 'one incarnate nature (*physis*)'. Just as Ephesus in 431 had said 'God was born', so Constantinople in 553 said 'God died', using what is known as 'Theopaschite' language, that is, language that attributes suffering to God: 'the Lord of glory and one of the Holy Trinity' was 'crucified in the flesh'.

These Neochalcedonian concessions were rejected as inadequate by most of the non-Chalcedonians. Around 633 a new attempt at a compromise was made by the Emperor Heraclius, supported by Patriarch Sergius of Constantinople: while there are in Christ two natures, he has only a single 'energy' or mode of operation and a single will. This standpoint, known as the Monothelete position, enjoyed some initial success, but failed in the end to satisfy anyone. The non-Chalcedonians wanted nothing less than an explicit condemnation of Chalcedon, while Chalcedonian theologians such as St Maximus the Confessor argued that human nature without a human will is an unreal abstraction. If Christ was genuinely human, then he must have possessed authentic human freedom, being 'tempted in everything just as we are, only without sinning' (Heb. 4: 15). Maximus died in exile, but his theology enjoyed a posthumous triumph at the sixth ecumenical council (Constantinople 681), which ascribed to Christ 'two natural energies' and 'two natural wills', that is to say, a human will as well as a divine will. In this way Chalcedonian two-nature Christology was clearly reaffirmed.

By this time, however, there was little practical motive for the imperial government at Constantinople to seek a compromise with the non-Chalcedonians, for as a result of Muslim expansion during 634–9 they were now almost all of them outside the bounds of the Byzantine empire. In retrospect, the difference between those who said 'in two natures' and those who said 'from two natures' often seems minute. Both parties agreed that Christ is truly human as well as truly divine. It was tragic that in the two centuries following the 451 council a lasting agreement between the two sides proved impossible. The council of Chalcedon led, as Ephesus had done, to an enduring separation.

The non-Chalcedonian Christians of Egypt came eventually to form what is today known as the Coptic Orthodox Church, while those in Syria now constitute the Syrian Orthodox Church, often termed 'Jacobite' (after the sixth-century bishop Jacob Baradaeus or Bar'adai). Closely dependent on the Coptic Church is the Ethiopian Orthodox Church, which only attained full independence in 1959. Linked with the Syrian 'Jacobite' church is the Syrian Orthodox Church of the Malabar, in South India, whose members are known as the St Thomas Christians, after their supposed founder St Thomas the apostle. The fifth member of the non-Chalcedonian family is the Church of Armenia. These five churches are often termed 'Monophysite', because they follow Cyril in describing Christ as 'one nature', although this does not mean that they deny his full humanity. It is less misleading to call them 'Oriental Orthodox', in contrast to the

Chalcedonians who may be styled 'Eastern Orthodox'. Discussions between the two groups of Orthodox, in progress since 1966, have made it clear that the difference between them is largely linguistic, depending on the sense attached to the term *physis*. There is good reason to hope that the schism between Chalcedonians and non-Chalcedonians—one of the most ancient in Christian history—will be fully healed in our own day. For Eastern Christendom this is much the most important and promising of the present-day 'ecumenical dialogues'.

The third main stage during the era of the seven ecumenical councils was the controversy about icons. By an icon is meant an image or visual representation of Christ, the Virgin Mary, the angels, or the saints. It might take the form of a painted panel of wood, but could be equally a mosaic or fresco on the church wall, an embroidery, a portrait in metal, or even a statue, although three-dimensional figures are extremely rare in East Christian art. The first attack on the use of icons lasted from 726 until 780, when it was brought to an end by the Empress Irene. In 787 the seventh ecumenical council—meeting, as the first had done, at Nicaea—decreed that it was theologically correct to depict Christ and the saints in icons, and to show these icons liturgical honour. A further, though less extreme, period of iconoclasm followed in 815–42. The definitive restoration of the holy icons under the Empress Theodora in 843 was remembered by later generations as the 'Triumph of Orthodoxy', and was commemorated annually on the first Sunday in Lent. It is interesting that the imperial protagonists of icon-veneration should both have been women.

The iconodules or venerators of icons saw them not merely as a form of decoration, or an optional extra, but as fundamental to the true profession of Christian faith. As the 787 council insisted in its dogmatic decree on the icons:

> This is the faith of the apostles,
> This is the faith of the fathers,

This is the faith of the Orthodox,
This faith has made firm the whole world.

Most of the discussion involved not icons in general, but specifically the icon of Christ the Saviour. For both sides the dispute was not primarily about the nature of religious art, but about the basic doctrine of Christ's person. In this way the conflict over icons may be seen as a continuation of earlier Christological debates during the fifth to seventh centuries. The iconodules argued that, since Christ did not simply appear on the earth but took a real human body, it is possible and, indeed, essential to portray his face in line and colour. To refuse to depict Christ is somehow to doubt the fullness of his human nature; and icons are therefore a guarantee, in the words of the 787 council, that 'the incarnation of the Word is genuine and not illusory'.

The iconodules made several further points. First, repudiating the iconoclast charge of idolatry, they made a careful distinction between worship in the strict sense (*latreia*), which can be shown only to God the Holy Trinity, and the 'relative honour' (*schetikē timē*) that is given to icons. Secondly, the iconodules appealed to the didactic value of icons, calling them 'opened books to remind us of God'. 'What the written word is to those who know letters,' said St John of Damascus, one of the chief defenders of the icons, 'the icon is to the unlettered; what speech is to the ear, the icon is to the eye.' Thirdly, John and others used what may be termed an 'ecological' argument. Icons, in their view, reveal the spirit-bearing potentialities of material things; God may be worshipped and his glory made manifest not only through words, but through wood and paint and cubes of stone.

The iconoclasts, as John of Damascus saw it, were too intellectualist in their religious stance. 'Do not insult matter,' he protested, 'for it is not without honour. Nothing is to be despised that God has made. That is a Manichaean error.' Icons make explicit the innate holiness of the material world, and call down God's blessing on all human artistic creativity. The iconographer serves as the priest of creation, transfiguring it and rendering it articulate in praise of God. He acts as a 'subcreator', in J. R. R. Tolkien's phrase, as a 'maker' after the image of God the Maker. In the words of St Theodore the Studite, 'The fact that the human person is made in the image and likeness of God means that the making of an icon is in some way a divine work.'

Icons play a central part in the worship of all Orthodox churches of the Byzantine tradition. While also in use among the non-Chalcedonians, they serve far less as a focus of devotion. They are treated in Byzantine Orthodoxy with full liturgical honours: incense is offered and candles are lit before them, the faithful make prostrations in front of them and kiss them, they are carried in procession. They are to be found in the home as well as in church. An Orthodox act of liturgical prayer is unthinkable without the presence of icons. Clearly there are dangers here of superstitious exaggeration, but the cult of icons, resting as it does on a sound doctrine of the creation and the incarnation, possesses a firm theological basis.

The icon is believed to confer grace and to possess sacramental value. In the words of the 787 council, 'When we honour and venerate an icon, we receive sanctification.' It fulfils a mediatorial role. It is not just a visual aid but a means of communion. Standing before Christ's icon, the worshipper is brought face to face with Christ himself. By virtue of the icon, we pass within the dimensions of sacred space and sacred time, entering into a living, effectual contact with the person or mystery depicted. The icon is a way in, a point of meeting, a place of encounter.

With the convening of the seventh and last ecumenical council in 787 and the 'Triumph of Orthodoxy' in 843, many Byzantine Christians came to feel that the articulation of doctrine was now a completed task. The Fathers of the second Nicene Council displayed a typically Byzantine reverence for tradition when they affirmed: 'We take away nothing and we add nothing. . . . We preserve without change or innovation all the ecclesiastical traditions that have been handed down to us, whether written or unwritten.' Such traditionalism could easily lead to a barren 'theology of repetition', and yet it would be a grave mistake to imagine that nothing happened in the Orthodox world after 787. Creative developments in religious thought and art continued uninterrupted at Constantinople up to the final collapse of the empire. When Yeats spoke of Byzantium as a 'bobbin bound in mummy-cloth', he saw only part of the truth. 'Conservatism is always mixed with change', writes Ernest Barker, 'and change is always impinging on conservatism, during the twelve hundred years of Byzantine history; and that is the essence and the fascination of those years.'

The Breaking of Unity

Negatively, the period after 843 was marked by a growing antagonism between the Orthodox East and the papacy. It used to be thought that the schism between Greek and Latin Christendom occurred in two main stages. First came the conflict between Pope Nicolas I of Rome and Patriarch Photius of Constantinople in 863–7. Communion was temporarily broken between the two; and, although in his second period of office (877–86) Photius remained in communion with Rome, no solution was found for the underlying causes of the conflict. Then came a further clash in 1054. Cardinal Humbert travelled to Constantinople as papal legate on what was intended to be a mission of reconciliation, but became exasperated by the uncooperative stance of the patriarch, Michael Cerularius, and issued an anathema against him. Michael retaliated by anathematizing Humbert. These mutual anathemas, eventually revoked by both sides on 7 December 1965, not long before the end of the Second Vatican Council, were formerly believed to mark the final breach between Orthodoxy and Rome, the definitive consummation of the schism.

Today, however, it is generally recognized that the so-called 'Photian schism' of 863–7 and the anathemas of 1054, while certainly significant, are no more than incidents in a much more complex story. The schism between East and West did not occur as a single event at a specific moment in history, accomplished everywhere at once, but it was, in the words of Gervase Mathew, 'a gradual, fluctuating, disjointed process'. The beginnings of that process extend back far before the ninth century, while its final completion did not occur until long after 1054.

More divisive than the anathemas of 1054 were the crusades, which led unhappily to a disastrous increase in Greek–Latin tension. The sack of Constantinople by the Fourth Crusade in 1204 is something that Greek Christendom has never forgotten or forgiven. From that point onwards most Greeks saw the Latins as enemies of their church and nation. Although reunion was proclaimed at two councils attended by the Greeks, Lyon (1274) and Florence (1438–9), in each case this remained no more than an agreement on paper, for the decisions were rejected by an overwhelming majority of clergy and laity throughout the Orthodox world.

Yet as late as the seventeenth century there were frequent occasions on which Orthodox and Roman Catholics in the Eastern Mediterranean shared in communion together. In particular the Jesuits during 1600–1700 were often invited by Orthodox bishops to preach, to open schools, and to hear confessions. If we are to assign a specific date to the 'final breach', then probably the year should not be earlier than 1724, when a schism occurred between pro-papal and anti-papal groups in the church of Antioch, and rival patriarchs were elected. This led to a malign hardening, so that doors open hitherto between Orthodox and Roman Catholics were now slammed shut.

In the controversy between Orthodoxy and Rome, from the time of Photius in the ninth century onwards, there were two fundamental issues. East and West differed, first, concerning the procession of the Holy Spirit. Both the Greeks and the Latins were agreed that the Spirit is fully personal and fully divine. But the Greeks recited the Nicene–Constantinopolitan creed in its original form, stating that the Spirit 'proceeds from the Father', and they regarded the Father, the first person of the Trinity, as the sole source of being, the unique cause of hypostatic origin within the deity. The Latins, on the other hand, had inserted 'Filioque' into the creed, affirming that the Spirit 'proceeds from the Father and the Son'. The addition seems to have originated in Spain during the sixth century, but was not adopted at Rome itself until the early eleventh century. In Byzantine eyes this disagreement over the procession of the Spirit was the main theological issue between the churches, and it still remains a difficulty for contemporary Orthodox, who feel that the Western approach leads to a devaluation of the Holy Spirit, to an underestimation of his distinctive personhood and autonomy. Orthodox suspect that much Western Trinitarian thinking—in Augustine, Aquinas, and also Barth—has overstressed the unity of the divine essence at the expense of the diversity of the persons, and they regard the addition of the *Filioque* as a symptom of this.

The second main point of conflict has been the papal claims. Orthodox look on the pope as the elder brother in the universal Christian episcopate, as the first in honour and in pastoral *diakonia*. But they do not ascribe to him a supremacy of direct power and jurisdiction in the Christian East, and they cannot accept that he has a special charisma, not given to other bishops, whereby in certain circumstances he is infallible. Eastern Christendom sees the church as conciliar in structure, not monarchical. Far greater than the pope or any other single hierarch is the ecumenical council. Truth is preserved within the church on earth, not through the testimony of one see alone, but through the consensus of the whole people of God. As the Eastern patriarchs stated in their letter to Pope Pius IX in 1848, 'The defender of religion is the very body of the Church, that is to say, the people (*laos*) itself.' Relatively little, however, was said about the papal claims by Byzantine controversialists, and many of them regarded the question as a matter not of dogma in the strict sense, but simply of canon law. The dogmatic issue *par excellence* remained always the procession of the Holy Spirit. The Council of Florence spent about nine months debating the *Filioque*, and only nine days on the papal claims.

Conflict arose also over lesser issues, such as the rules of fasting, the Western use of 'azymes' or unleavened bread at the eucharist, the manner of conferring confirmation, the celibacy of the clergy, and divorce (forbidden in the West, but permitted in certain situations by Orthodox canon law). Orthodox also disliked the medieval Western teaching on purgatory and indulgences. Latin theology has always made more use of juridical categories than the Greeks have done, and in its developed scholastic form it is much more systematic, more heavily dependent on logical argument, than is the predominantly mystical approach of the Christian East.

The differences were real, but in the heat of controversy they were unduly exaggerated. Usually there was little attempt to distinguish between primary issues and those that were secondary. Fortunately a few Latins, such as Anselm of Havelberg or Humbert of the Romans (not to be confused with Cardinal Humbert of the 1054 anathemas), were more far-seeing; and so also were a few Byzantines. Theophylact of Bulgaria, writing from the Orthodox side in the late eleventh century, considered that each church should be left free to follow its own customs over such matters as fasting, azymes, or clerical celibacy. He passed over the question of the papacy, and regarded the *Filioque* as the sole point of real importance; and even here he saw the disagreement as basically linguistic. The fundamental problem, he observed, was moral and personal: 'Love has grown cold.' Surely he was right. Divergences in doctrine and custom would never have proved so intractable if the two halves of Christendom, largely for non-theological reasons, had not become strangers to each other. The best hope for East–West reconciliation during our own time lies precisely in the fact that today we are strangers no longer.

The Light of Tabor

On the positive side, in Byzantine theology after the period of the seven ecumenical councils there was a flowering of mystical theology. Two figures are outstanding. The first of them, St Symeon the New Theologian, was a theologian-poet of the late tenth century. His leitmotiv is the nearness yet otherness of the eternal:

> I know that the Immovable comes down;
> I know that the Invisible appears to me;
> I know that he who is far outside the whole creation
> Takes me into himself and hides me in his arms.
>
> .   .   .   .
>
> I know that I shall not die, for I am within the Life,
> I have the whole of Life springing up as a fountain within me.
> He is in my heart, he is in heaven.

One of the most Spirit-centred of all Christian writers, Symeon asserted that it was possible for every baptized Christian, even in this present life, to attain direct, conscious experience of the Holy Spirit:

> Do not say, It is impossible to receive the Holy Spirit;
> Do not say, It is possible to be saved without him.
> Do not say that you can possess him without knowing it . . .

By the grace of the Spirit, the Christian comes face to face with Christ in a vision of divine light. Symeon himself received such visions on a number of occasions. He described the light as 'non-material' and 'spiritual'; for him it was not a physical, created light, but uncreated and eternal—the light is God himself. He felt himself 'oned' with this supranatural light in a union that transformed his human personhood without annihilating it:

O power of the divine fire, O strange energy! . . .
You who dwell, Christ my God, in light wholly unapproachable,
How in your essence totally divine do you mingle yourself with grass?

.   .   .   .

You, the light, are joined to the grass in a union without confusion,
And the grass becomes light; it is transfigured yet unchanged.

What Symeon's writings on the Holy Spirit and the divine light convey above all else is a sense of freshness, of enthusiasm and discovery. With his insistence upon the primacy of personal experience, he shows how unjust it is to dismiss later Byzantine theology as mere formalism, devoid of originality. The same dynamism and the same appeal to personal experience are evident during the fourteenth century in our second dominant figure, St Gregory Palamas, the leading theologian in the hesychast controversy. A hesychast is one who pursues *hesychia*, inner stillness or silence of the heart, in particular through the use of the Jesus Prayer. This is a short invocation, constantly repeated, usually in the form 'Lord Jesus Christ, Son of God, have mercy on me.' Through inner attentiveness and the repetition of this prayer, sometimes accompanied by a physical technique involving the control of the breathing, the hesychasts of Mount Athos believed that they attained a vision of divine light and so union with God.

A Platonist philosopher at Constantinople, Barlaam the Calabrian, originally from South Italy, launched a comprehensive attack on the hesychast standpoint. Underlining the divine transcendence and unknowability, he held that it was possible to attain a direct vision of God, face to face, only in the future life. He considered the light seen by the monks in prayer to be merely created, and he dismissed their physical technique as gross superstition. Palamas, himself a monk of Athos, came to the defence of his fellow hesychasts. He insisted, as Symeon had also done, upon the possibility of a direct, unmediated experience of God, not just in the age to come, but here and now. Where Barlaam's eschatology was futurist, that of Palamas was realized or, more exactly, inaugurated.

Palamas believed, with as much conviction as Barlaam, in the transcendence and mystery of God. But then Palamas took a further step. Employing a distinction found in earlier Greek

Fathers such as Basil of Caesarea, although not used systematically by Symeon, he differentiated between the essence and the energies of God. While God in his essence remains utterly unknowable to humans, alike in this life and in heaven, his energies—which are God himself in action—come down to us, and the saints participate in them by grace through a union of love. According to Palamas the light beheld by the monks in prayer is not a physical light of the senses, although it may be seen through the bodily eyes. It is the uncreated energies of God, the same light that shone from Christ on Mount Tabor at the Transfiguration, and which will shine from him likewise at his second coming in glory on the last day. His understanding of the divine light is thus basically the same as Symeon's, although Symeon did not state with the same clarity that it is a vision of God's energies, not his essence. Palamas did not attach crucial significance to the physical technique of the hesychasts, but he considered it theologically defensible. Developing a holistic anthropology, he argued that the body is called to share with the soul in the work of prayer, just as it can share also in the vision of the divine light.

The Palamite teaching on the energies of God and the divine light was confirmed at three councils in Constantinople (1341, 1347, 1351). In all this Palamas was concerned to safeguard, as Symeon had also striven to do, both the otherness and the nearness of the Deity. In dialectical fashion he wrote of God: 'He is both being and non-being; he is everywhere and nowhere; he has many names and he cannot be named; he is ever-moving and he is immovable; and, in a word, he is everything and nothing.' God is mystery, surpassing all reality and all knowledge, and yet God is at the core of our being, closer to us than our own heart. He is unknowable, yet we meet him face to face. The Palamite distinction between essence and energies has been misunderstood by many Western theologians, who see in it a threat to God's unity and simplicity. Fundamentally, however, Palamas is making the uncontroversial point accepted by mystics in East and West alike, that God is transcendent and yet immanent, utterly beyond our understanding and yet directly united to us in his love.

Symeon and Palamas are both exponents of the negative or 'apophatic' approach that seeks to safeguard the mystery of God, his hiddenness and incomprehensibility. Patristic theology often appears over-subtle to the modern reader, abstract, excessively speculative. But at its best it always allowed, as Symeon and Palamas did, for the dimension of God as mystery. The divine may be experienced in love, but not defined in words. 'Let things ineffable be honoured with silence', said St Basil; as St Isaac the Syrian put it, 'Silence is the mystery of the age to come.' Voluminous writers though they were, St Symeon and St Gregory Palamas would both have agreed.

The Slav Missions

Restricted on its eastern flank through the separation of the non-Chalcedonians and the expansion of Islam, and then on its western flank through the estrangement with Rome, Byzantine Christendom expanded in a startling and dramatic fashion to the north. It was in the middle of the ninth century that the church of Constantinople first embarked, in a systematic manner, upon missionary work among the Slav peoples outside the boundaries of the empire. In 863 Patriarch Photius sent out the brothers St Cyril and St Methodius—honoured in Orthodoxy as 'equal to the apostles'—to preach Christianity in Moravia (roughly equivalent to modern Czechoslovakia). They took with them the Slavonic versions that they had begun to make of the Bible and the service books. These translations constitute the most important single feature in their missionary work. Whereas the Byzantine church used only the Greek language within the territory of the empire, the native vernacular was employed by Greek missionaries outside the imperial frontiers. Unlike the medieval Western church, with its exclusive use of Latin in worship, the Byzantine church employed in its missions the language of the people to whom it preached.

This greatly encouraged the emergence, among the Slavs, of 'autocephalous' or independent churches with a strongly national identity.

The mission of Cyril and Methodius in Moravia failed to take permanent root. German missionaries were also at work in the same area, and the country passed eventually within the orbit of Latin Christendom. But other lands, where the two brothers had not themselves preached, benefited from their work. The Slavonic translations which they and their disciples had made were adopted in Bulgaria, Serbia, and Russia. The ruler of Bulgaria, Boris, was baptized by the Greeks around 865, and in 926–7 an independent Bulgarian patriarchate was created. Serbia was converted by Byzantine missionaries during 867–74. The Serbian church gained partial independence when St Sava, the greatest of the Serbian national saints, was consecrated archbishop at Nicaea in 1219, and in 1346 a Serbian patriarchate was set up. Photius also sent a mission to Russia in the 860s, but the firm establishment of the Russian church came only in 988, with the baptism of St Vladimir, the ruler of Kiev. The Russian church gained its independence from Constantinople in 1448, becoming a patriarchate in 1589. Byzantine and Bulgarian missionaries worked likewise in the Romanian principalities of Wallachia and Moldavia; here, however, the people were not Slavs but claimed descent from Latin-speaking settlers in the Roman province of Dacia.

The early period of Russian church history—the Kievan era, extending from 988 to the early thirteenth century—has a particularly attractive character. Among its most striking features is a 'kenotic' quality, a spirit of loving compassion and humility. The ancient sources contrast the savagery of Vladimir prior to his conversion with his gentleness as a Christian, shown for example in his refusal to employ capital punishment. After his death in 1015, two of his sons, Boris and Gleb, declined to protect themselves against the attacks of their elder brother; choosing the path of non-resistance, they allowed themselves to be killed rather than shed the blood of others in self-defence.

They were not exactly martyrs, for they had died in a political quarrel, but they were seen as sharing in the innocent suffering of Christ, and were given the special title of 'passion-bearers'. Russian history, like Byzantine, has often been marked by cruelty and violence; figures such as Boris and Gleb serve as an important counterbalance. Monasteries played a major role in Kievan Christianity; the chief monastic centre was the Pecherskii Lavra, the Monastery of the Caves at Kiev, founded by St Antony around 1051, and reorganized by his successor St Theodosii.

Kiev was over-run by the Mongol Tatars in 1237, and in the fourteenth century the centre of both political and religious life in Russia shifted to Moscow. The Monastery of the Holy Trinity, founded about 1340 by St Sergii of Radonezh some 45 miles outside Moscow, played the same role in Muscovite Orthodoxy as the Pecherskii Lavra had played in Kievan Russia. Monks setting out from St Sergii's monastery did much to spread the Christian faith in the more remote regions of northern Russia. Sergii himself held in balance the mystical and the social aspects of monasticism, but a split occurred among his followers in the early sixteenth century. One party, the Possessors, led by St Joseph of Volokalamsk, emphasized the importance of liturgical worship in monastic life, and the responsibility of the monks to provide hospitality and to care for the sick and poor. To make all this possible, so Joseph believed, the monasteries were justified in owning large estates. The other party, the Non-Possessors, with St Nil Sorskii as their chief spokesman, gave priority to inner prayer and to the strict observance of ascetic poverty. Joseph's standpoint prevailed at the time, but the tradition of the Non-Possessors survived, often underground, serving as a hidden source of vitality for Russian Christendom.

'Byzantium after Byzantium': The Turkish Era

Under growing Turkish pressure from the late eleventh century onwards, fatally weakened by the Latin sack of Constantinople in 1204, the Byzantine empire dwindled in size throughout the fourteenth century and finally collapsed in 1453. In retrospect what seems surprising is not that it eventually succumbed but that it survived for so long. Sultan Mehmed II, the conqueror of Constantinople, was quick to install a new patriarch, Gennadius, and to grant him protection. 'Be patriarch, with good fortune,' said Mehmed to him, 'and be assured of our friendship, keeping all the privileges that the patriarchs before you enjoyed.' But, though tolerated by their Muslim masters, the Christians of the Ottoman empire were placed in a situation of permanent inferiority. They paid heavy taxes, and as a mark of discrimination were forced to wear a distinctive dress. Their children could be seized to serve in the sultan's court or in the janizary guard. No new churches could be built, and existing churches were liable to confiscation. Visible signs of the Christian faith were reduced to a minimum; no religious processions in the open air were permitted, and no ringing of bells. Christians were strictly forbidden to attempt to convert a Muslim, on penalty of death, but were themselves continually encouraged to apostatize.

These outward restrictions had an unhappy effect on the inner life of Greek Orthodoxy. Corruption was widespread in the higher church administration. The ecumenical patriarch was forced to pay the Turkish authorities for the *berat* confirming him in office, and the fee continually increased. Rival factions formed within the holy synod, each promoting its own candidate, and there were frequent changes of patriarch, with the Turks usually intervening in their appointment and deposition. In the sixteenth century there were 19 patriarchal reigns; in the seventeenth century, no less than 61 patriarchal reigns, with 31 individual patriarchs (often the same person held office on several different occasions); in the eighteenth century, 31 patriarchal reigns, with 23 individual patriarchs. These figures provide some indication of the deep instability in church life.

Yet more seriously, the church found it all but impossible to maintain institutions of higher learning. Despite the efforts of the Patriarchal Academy at Constantinople, the 'Great School of the Nation', the educational level of the clergy fell disastrously low. Greeks desirous of university studies went to the West, especially to Italy, and above all to Padua. Educated abroad under Roman Catholic or Protestant auspices, they were in danger of losing a sense of their true Orthodox identity. Orthodox theology in the seventeenth and eighteenth centuries became heavily Latinized in its style, and the effects of this are apparent even today.

There was a danger that Orthodoxy under the Turks might be extinguished through steady demoralization and sheer ignorance. Defections on a massive scale occurred in Asia Minor, Bosnia, and Albania. Sometimes the local population compromised by becoming 'Crypto-Christians', conforming outwardly to Islam but continuing to practise their Christian faith in secret. Yet, considering the worldly attractions of apostasy, the remarkable fact is not that so many fell away, but that so many continued faithful. Particularly in Greece itself, the bulk of the population resisted the temptation to convert to Muhammadanism. Many chose to die for their faith, and those who suffered in this way during the Turkish period have been given the special title 'New Martyrs'. If there is much to pity in the sufferings of Greek Orthodoxy under the Ottoman rule, there is also much to admire. It showed an impressive power of survival. The Turcocratia was an era not only of decadence but of humble persistence.

The church, however, was placed on the defensive, and this resulted in an understandable stagnation. Orthodoxy remained basically faithful to its Byzantine inheritance, but failed to develop that heritage creatively. The conservative spirit, already apparent in some quarters in the later Byzantine period, now became much more marked. Patriarch Jeremias II of Constantinople gave voice in 1590 to an unyielding traditionalism that was typical:

It is not the practice of our Church to innovate in any way whatsoever, whereas the Western Church innovates unceasingly. . . . We do not dare to remove from the ancient books a single 'jot or tittle', as the saying goes. So we were taught and such is our purpose—to obey and to be subject to those who were before us.

The chief intellectual challenge confronting Greek Orthodoxy in the Turkish period came from the Reformation and the Counter-Reformation. The first major contact between Orthodox and Protestants was in 1573, when Patriarch Jeremias II received a delegation of Lutheran scholars from Tübingen. In his subsequent correspondence with them, touching on such topics as free will and grace, scripture and tradition, the sacraments, prayers for the dead, and the invocation of the saints, he showed no inclination to adopt the Protestant view, but adhered strictly to traditional Orthodoxy. But another patriarch of Constantinople a generation later, the brilliant but ill-starred Cyril Loukaris, in 1629 issued a Confession of Faith that was strongly Calvinist in its teaching. He died nine years later, strangled at the orders of the Turkish authorities. His Confession provoked an anti-Protestant reaction, and was condemned at the Councils of Jassy (1642) and Jerusalem (1672), which produced in their turn statements of faith strongly influenced by Roman Catholic theology. In particular they spoke of the 'transubstantiation' of the elements at the eucharistic consecration; this term, taken from Latin scholasticism, is usually avoided by present-day Orthodox, although they remain firmly convinced of Christ's real presence in the eucharist. A surprisingly constructive exchange occurred between the Eastern patriarchs and the Anglican Non-Jurors during 1716–25, and a large measure of theological agreement was reached; but the correspondence was broken off when the Orthodox became aware that the Non-Jurors did not represent the Anglican Church as a whole. This is much the most fascinating ecumenical encounter in which the Orthodox were engaged during the Turkish period.

With the eclipse of Greek Christendom under the Turks, leadership in the Orthodox world passed to the great church of Russia. By the second half of the fifteenth century the grand dukes of Moscow had effectively shaken off Tatar suzerainty. They began to see themselves as heirs to the Byzantine empire, and to look on Moscow as the Third Rome, superseding the Second Rome on the shores of the Bosphorus. These claims were strengthened when the head of the Russian church became a patriarch in 1589; but the patriarchate of Moscow ranked no higher than fifth in the Orthodox world, taking its place after the four ancient patriarchates of the East.

Russian Orthodoxy was weakened by schism in the middle of the seventeenth century, when the dynamic and authoritarian Patriarch Nikon of Moscow, as part of a wider reforming programme, introduced liturgical changes that were rejected by a substantial number of Russian Christians. These 'Old Believers', as they are termed—it would be more exact to call them 'Old Ritualists'—became permanently separated from the main body of the Russian church. Rigid in their outlook and excessively nationalist, they yet embodied much that is genuinely admirable in the piety of 'Holy Russia'. Their sincerity and strength is readily apparent in the celebrated autobiography by one of their leaders, Archpriest Avvakum.

A further blow befell the Russian church at the start of the eighteenth century. In 1721 Tsar Peter the Great issued the Spiritual Regulation, abolishing the Moscow patriarchate and placing the church under a 'spiritual college' or synod, containing married clergy as well as bishops. Deprived of its leadership, the Russian church was rendered subject to the secular authorities to an extent that had never been the case in Byzantium. Hierarchs and parish priests were treated as Civil Servants. Peter and several of his successors showed a marked hostility towards monasticism, and numerous religious houses were suppressed. Yet beneath the surface the true life of Orthodox Russia continued, finding notable expression during the later eighteenth century in the person of St Tikhon of Zadonsk, a 'kenotic' bishop with a strong social conscience in the tradition of St John Chrysostom.

In 1782 a large folio volume in Greek appeared at Venice,

bearing the title *Philokalia* ('Love of [Spiritual] Beauty'), edited by St Macarius of Corinth, in collaboration with a monk of Athos, St Nicodemus. This was perhaps the most significant single book to be published in the four centuries of the Turcocratia. It is a collection of spiritual texts in the hesychast tradition, dealing with the ascetic life, the Jesus Prayer, inner stillness, and mystical union. Here we see disclosed the true sources of strength that enabled Greek Orthodoxy to survive under the Turks. Translated almost immediately into Slavonic by a Ukrainian monk who had settled in Moldavia, St Paisii Velichkovskii, it proved deeply influential in nineteenth-century Russia. It is symbolically appropriate that a book such as the *Philokalia* should have appeared at the very moment when Eastern Christendom stood on the threshold of the modern era. For the most precious gift that Orthodoxy has been able to make to the Christian West in our own time has certainly been its tradition of mystical theology, its understanding of silence and the prayer of the heart.

Heaven on Earth

To understand Christians in the past, and equally the present-day members of a religious community that is not our own, perhaps the wisest means of approach is to look above all at their experience of prayer. What is their sense of the sacred? How do they perceive the numinous, the 'beyond in our midst'? In what way do they stand before God?

For the Byzantine worshipper, as for the contemporary Eastern Christian, the experience of prayer may best be summed up in the phrase 'heaven on earth'. Such exactly was the impact of the newly restored St Sophia on Procopius. 'The visitor's mind is lifted up to God and soars aloft,' he wrote, 'thinking that he cannot be far away, but must especially love to dwell in this place that he himself has chosen.' Similar language is used in the legendary account of the conversion of Russia in the twelfth-century *Primary Chronicle* attributed to Nestor: 'We knew not whether we were in heaven or on earth', reported the envoys of Prince Vladimir after attending the service in St Sophia. In the words of St Germanus of Constantinople, 'The Church is an earthly heaven, in which the heavenly God dwells and moves.'

Such in brief is the basic sense of the sacred within Orthodoxy. This experience of 'heaven on earth' is realized above all in the central act of worship, the offering of the eucharist or the divine liturgy, as it is called in the Christian East, a more elaborate and expressive rite than the Latin mass. The celebration of the liturgy joins in unity the earthly and the heavenly realms. When the holy gifts are carried into the sanctuary at the great entrance, it is Christ himself who enters, accompanied by the angels. The members of the visible congregation, whether many or few, are taken up into an action far greater than themselves, becoming concelebrants at the celestial altar with Christ the one high priest, with the Mother of God, the bodiless powers of heaven, and the saints. Eastern Christendom attaches the utmost importance to the presence and intercession of the saints, and above all of the *Theotokos*, protectress of Constantinople, mother and guardian of the Orthodox people. The immediate involvement of the invisible church in the earthly celebration is enhanced by the icons which surround the worshipper on every side, enabling him to feel that the church walls, so far from closing him in, open out upon eternity.

'The church', affirms St John Chrysostom, 'is the place of the angels, of the archangels, the kingdom of God, heaven itself.' Here, in this vision of 'heaven on earth', lies the deepest inspiration of Eastern Christendom and its living heart.

5

Christianity and Islam

JEREMY JOHNS

Introduction

THE relationship between Christianity and Islam during the Middle Ages is usually seen, in the West, in terms of military conflict, and, in the East, in terms of the Arab contribution to Western culture. It is symptomatic of the past (and of the continuing) relationship between the two faiths, that each focuses upon an issue which the other regards as peripheral. Moreover, both avoid the question which, today, seems central to the relationship between the two faiths, because, for the first time since the Middle Ages, Christian (and Jewish) society plays host to large communities of Muslims: how and why was it that Islam managed to incorporate successfully Christian communities into Muslim society, whilst Christian Europe failed totally in its attempts to accommodate Muslims within Christendom?

Christianity and the Arabs before Islam

Pompey's conquest of the East (66–63 BC) created the political geography which was to dominate Near Eastern history until Islam: two superpowers, Rome and Persia, faced each other across the Euphrates. The Syrian desert thrust like a wedge between them, pushing upwards and outwards, exerting a constant pressure upon their frontiers. In this desert, and stretching southwards into the Arabian peninsula, was the home of the Arabs.

Until the third century AD, Arab kingdoms dominated the desert between Rome and Persia; independent caravan cities, both capitals of vast commercial empires, and centres of powerful military organizations: Edessa, Petra, Hatra and Palmyra. At first, the superpowers tolerated such rivals but, during the second and third centuries, the Arab caravan cities were suppressed: their destruction had two important repercussions.

First, the settled Arabs of the Roman East were rapidly assimilated into the cultural empire of Rome. Christianity, which had already spread widely amongst the Aramaic-speaking Arabs of the empire, was almost universally accepted during the third to fifth centuries, and developed into the distinctive form of the Syriac church.

Second, both Rome and Persia still needed additional protection along their borders against both each other and the bedouin of the desert, and so semi-nomadic Arabs were encouraged to settle on the frontier. East Rome or Byzantium set about the Christianization of these Arab confederates so that, to the bonds of military service purchased by annual subsidy, was added that of a shared faith. Constantine's militarization of Christianity presented the Arab warriors with Christ Victorious, a God whom they could follow into battle alongside their Byzantine allies, whether against the Zoroastrian Persians, the pagan Arabs, or—eventually—the Muslims.

In the marginal lands of the Arab confederates, monasteries and cult centres were the main agents of conversion: frequently, a seasonal Arab campsite grew up near a monastery, or vice versa, and religious sites were often integrated into the pattern of semi-nomadic life. In the sixth century, the Ghassānids, Byzantium's Arab confederates, built one of their most important seasonal camps outside the walls of Rusāfa (Sergiopolis), the chief shrine of St Sergius. The annual feast of this saint (15 November) coincided with the migration of the tribes south from their summer grazing lands on the Euphrates. In the Arab encampment, the Ghassānid leader built a splendid and elaborate audience-hall in the Byzantine style. At sites like

Rusāfa, one can observe the way in which Christianity had become associated with an Arab military aristocracy, governed by a centralized authority, which was inspired by and modelled on Byzantine rule.

Indeed, the alliance with Byzantium greatly accelerated the development of an Arab sense of national identity and the elevation of Arabic from a purely spoken to a literary language. The imperial administration encouraged the development of a centralized monarchy amongst the Arab confederates and awarded the title of 'phylarch' and the honorifics of the imperial court to the confederate commander and his followers: consequently, the confederate leader began to style himself 'king of all the Arabs'. It is with this title that Imru' al-Qays (d. 328), the client-king of Byzantium, appears in his epitaph, the Namāra inscription, the earliest known occurrence of a linguistic form which can be identified as Arabic. Christianity had a similar cohesive effect and, by the end of the fourth century, there had already developed a mature Arab Christian culture with an Arab episcopate, Arab ecclesiastical and monastic foundations, Arab saints, and, perhaps, an Arabic liturgy and Arabic religious poetry.

The development of a distinctly Arab Christian culture was facilitated in the fifth century by the spread amongst the Christian Arabs of Nestorianism and Monophysitism, which had in common their opposition to the official Byzantine church. Nestorianism was strongest in eastern Syria, within the Persian sphere, where it was established as an official Persian church, hostile to Byzantium, but active almost exclusively amongst the Arabs of Mesopotamia and Babylonia. In contrast, Monophysitism constituted almost a dissident movement within Byzantium. Most of the fifth and sixth centuries saw often violent revolts against imperial and patriarchal authority, and the systematic persecution of the Monophysites of northern Syria. Whole communities of monks were expelled into the desert, where they spread their beliefs amongst the Arabs, consolidating the hostility of the latter towards the established church. The survival of Monophysite Christianity under Islam is remarkable: the Jacobites of Najrān in Yemen were the only Christians in the Peninsula to be tolerated after Islam, while the Mesopotamian tribe of Taghlib retained their Christianity until as late as the eleventh century.

The towns of north-western Arabia, however, remained isolated from the spread of Christianity amongst the Syrian Arabs. One story has the young Muhammad accompany his uncle's caravan from Mecca to Bostra in Syria, where he is identified by an anchorite as the prophet whose mission was foretold by scripture. The story reveals only how ignorant its teller was of Syrian Christianity, for even the name of the monk—Bahīra—is a confusion of the Syriac title *bhīrā*, 'reverend'. None the less, the Qur'ān contains several passages which clearly derive from Christian sources. Some of these reflect accurately the traditions from which they were taken; others, like the account of the Last Supper, appear to be based upon fundamental miscomprehension; still others contradict Christian teaching and challenge central Christian dogmas, such as the divine nature of Christ and the resurrection.

Exactly when these and other Christian influences were incorporated into the Qur'ān cannot now be determined with certainty: Islamic tradition is almost the only source upon which we can draw and there have not yet been identified any satisfactory internal criteria upon which the reliability and the chronology of its many elements may be securely established. Islamic tradition does preserve the names of a few Christians living in pagan Mecca during the life of Muhammad and even asserts that the interior of the Ka'ba at Mecca was decorated with paintings of Jesus and Mary, but this is insufficient cause to conclude the existence of an active Christian community at Mecca, still less one which had so strong an influence upon Islam. It was only after the Arab conquest of Palestine and Syria that the young Muslim community had any significant contact with Christianity, and the principal influence of Christianity upon the new faith was to cause early Islam to define itself in reaction against the practices and beliefs of its new Christian subjects.

The Military Threat

Islam twice posed a universal military challenge to Christianity. First, during the rapid conquests of the mid-seventh to mid-eighth centuries when, for a time, all Christendom seemed in danger of invasion and defeat. And second, in the fifteenth to seventeenth centuries when the Ottomans made their bid for world supremacy. At other times, military conflict between Christian and Muslim powers was confined to limited geographical regions and generally had limited strategic objectives. Western historiographical tradition has largely obscured the significance of the two universal military threats to Christianity by concentrating upon certain regional conflicts and grouping them together as 'the crusades'. In fact, the Western assault upon the eastern Mediterranean (eleventh to thirteenth centuries), even when combined with the Christian conquests of Sicily and the Iberian peninsula, was a minor event which occurred on the periphery of the Muslim world and constituted little more than a nuisance to Islam. The crusades did not amount to a military threat to Islam, nor did the Muslim counter-attack threaten Christianity.

According to Islamic tradition, Muhammad was born at Mecca in the Hijāz (north-western Arabia) in c.570. There, in c.610, he began his prophethood but, in 622, because of opposition within Mecca, he was forced to emigrate with his followers to Medina. Over the next decade, until his death in 632, Muhammad laid the foundations of the polity which, under his successors or caliphs, was to conquer much of the Mediterranean and the Near East. During this decade, there emerged at Medina a ruling élite in which were allied both Muhammad's supporters and the aristocracy which had controlled Mecca since the early sixth century. Muhammad himself belonged to the Meccan ruling class which, at first, constituted his fiercest opponent.

The principal aim of the Medinan élite during the reign of the first caliph, Abū Bakr (632–4), and in the early years of 'Umar (634–44) seems to have been the integration of all the Arabs of the peninsula and of Syria, Egypt, and Iraq into a unified state under Medinan control. The process of integration was not peaceful. Muhammad had secured the allegiance of the Hijāz and much of central and south-western Arabia by force of arms as much as by diplomacy, and on his death a widespread revolt against the Medinan hegemony broke out, which was energetically suppressed by Abū Bakr. This victory of the Medinan élite and its loyal tribal allies extended their authority throughout the peninsula, but the Arabs of Syria remained largely independent. Muhammad himself is said to have dispatched two expeditions to the northern borders of the peninsula, but it was only under Abū Bakr that the tribes of southern Syria were incorporated into the new community. Under 'Umar, in 634–6, these early gains were consolidated by the occupation of the key towns of southern Syria, which prompted a strong Byzantine counter-offensive. The decisive defeat of Byzantium in Syria at the Yarmūk (c.636) paved the way for the conquest of northern Syria during 637–48. The same period saw the conquest of Iraq and Egypt.

The integration of the Arabs of the peninsula and of Syria, Egypt, and Iraq into the new community had created the large class of conquered Arab tribesmen, which was the instrument through which the Medinan polity achieved the early conquests. This is not to suggest that the conquests were the product of tribal migrations, for the Arab armies were small, well-equipped, well-disciplined, and centrally controlled. Their structure and their successes testify to the ability of the Medinan élite to govern their tribal subjects by means of a variety of practical measures, which included the lure of material gain from booty, military stipends, and grants of land; a strict and cohesive military organization, which was largely based upon existing tribal structures; a carefully organized policy of controlled migration into the conquered lands; and a fiscal regime which was designed to encourage the settlement of the conquests, just as it penalized nomadism.

In the absence of any evidence independent of Islamic tradition that the first caliphs embarked upon the conquest of Byzantine Syria and Sassanid Iraq for ideological reasons, it is most probable that direct conflict with Byzantium and Persia did not initially aim at the conquest of the two superpowers but merely at the integration into the Medinan polity of the Arabs dwelling upon and within their borders. The Byzantine and Sassanid counter-attacks of the mid-630s prompted a renewed Arab offensive which, because of the internal weaknesses of the two empires, resulted in the decisive defeat of Byzantium in Syria and in the complete destruction of Sassanid Persia. It may be, therefore, that it was only the success of the first Arab conquests which led the Arab leaders to embark upon the second wave of expansion. In 656–92, internal conflict diverted the energies of the Arabs from expansion and conquest, but, under the Umayyad caliphs 'Abd al-Malik (685–705) and al-Walīd I (705–14), a new impetus propelled the Muslim armies (as they may now be called) in a concerted assault upon Byzantium. In the West, the Muslim advance along the North African littoral culminated in 711 with the invasion of Spain. By 716 the conquest of the Iberian peninsula was all but complete and Arab armies began to probe northwards into France. This dramatic expansion in the West coincided with the last concerted Arab assault against Constantinople (717–18), and these were the two arms of a co-ordinated pincer movement which was designed to attack Byzantium simultaneously from East and West. In the event, neither offensive was successful: the Arabs lifted the siege of Constantinople and, in 733, Charles Martel put an end to the Arab advance north of the Pyrenees. By 750, the first great period of Islamic expansion was over.

There is an important contrast to be made between the conquests of the first four caliphs (632–56) and those of the

Umayyads (692–750). Syria, Egypt, and Iraq belonged to very much the same ethnic and cultural environment as the Arabian peninsula and their conquest was largely motivated by a desire to unite and to integrate the Arabs of this Semitic world. Subsequent conquests, however, were achieved in new and wholly alien cultural worlds: the Turkic East and the Latin West. Whereas the motive force of the earliest conquests had been Arab integration, the Umayyad armies were directed against external non-Arab enemies. Moreover, the second half of the seventh century had been characterized not merely by civil war but also by ideological ferment which had brought Islam to maturity and thoroughly established it amongst the Arab armies. The Umayyad conquests of the pagan East and the Christian West thus assumed the character of ideological conflict. The military threat to Christendom was a real one and, for a few years early in the eighth century, it must have seemed as if both Byzantium and the Christian West would fall to Islam. In the event, the failure of Umayyads to integrate the non-Arab Muslims of the new conquests into the political hierarchy led to revolt in North Africa and in Iran, dissipating the momentum of the conquests in internal strife.

None the less, during the ninth century, Islam did make important advances in the Christian Mediterranean. The conquest of Crete (823) paved the way for the invasion of Sicily (827) and, once the conquest of that island was finally completed in 902, a Muslim army invaded Italy and made a second, and equally unsuccessful, attempt to attack Constantinople from the West. Sicily remained in Arab hands until 1060–92 and, throughout the ninth and tenth centuries, served as a base for raids against Italy's Tyrrhenian and Adriatic coasts: in 846, Rome itself was pillaged. Shorter lived Arab bases were established on the Italian mainland at Bari (843–71), and then at Agropoli and on the Garigliano until as late as 915. Further north, the Muslims established a colony at Fraxinetum (888–972) from where they caused much disruption in Provence and the Ligurian Alps. The Muslim advance in the central Mediterranean was only possible in the absence of any strong and co-ordinated resistance and, during the eleventh century, the vigorous growth of the Tyrrhenian maritime cities and the foundation of the Norman state in southern Italy and Sicily, dislodged the Muslim bridgehead. At the same time, following the collapse of the caliphate of Cordoba (1031), the Christian kingdoms of northern Spain took the offensive and, by the end of the century, had conquered much of the Castilian uplands.

In the Near East, Byzantium had already taken the initiative and, during the 960s, had pushed its frontier beyond the Cilician plain. In 969, both Antioch and Aleppo were captured and, while only the former was held, it served as the forward base for John Tzimisces's (969–76) expedition of 972 which reached far into Palestine. For a century, Armenia and much of Syria once again lay within the empire.

In the mid-eleventh century, however, the Saljūk invasions changed the balance of power in the Near East by permanently detaching Asia Minor from Byzantium. In 1060 the Saljūks had taken Baghdad and gained control of the 'Abbāsid caliphate. Under the Saljūk sultans, Sunnī Islam underwent a revival which was manifested, in part, in a new offensive against Byzantium and, during the 1060s, Turkish raids thrust deep into Armenia, Georgia, and Anatolia. The decisive defeat of the Byzantines at Manzikert in 1071 deprived the empire of its Asian territories and opened the way for the Turkish migrations into the Anatolian plateau. In the wake of Manzikert, Byzantium appealed to Latin Christendom for assistance against the Turks. Twenty-five years later, Western Europe's response was the First Crusade.

The crusades were born, were sustained, and eventually declined because of currents deep within European society: Christendom's assault against the Muslims had less to do with the relationship between Christianity and Islam than with the internal stresses and strains of Christian Europe. And yet, the European historical tradition has tended to portray the relationship between Christianity and Islam during the Middle Ages in terms of military conflict, and has concentrated upon the crusades as the most significant manifestation of that conflict.

The military threat posed by Islam (and by the Vikings) to Western Europe during the ninth and tenth centuries prompted the church to adapt and to extend Augustine's doctrine of just war. While it remained the responsibility of secular leaders to defend Christendom, the church encouraged them and their followers to do so by promising eternal life to those who fell in battle against the heathen. Later, when the external threat to Christendom had declined, leaving unoccupied an increasingly brutal and lawless warrior-class, the reforming papacy sought to harness its violent energies. The so-called 'Peace of God' movement was, in fact, just one of several means by which the church came to organize the warrior-class in order to secure its own political ends. But the transformation of the brutalized warriors of the tenth century into the Christian knights—the *militia Christi*—of the eleventh, was to have a crucial impact upon Christianity's relationship with Islam: the responsibility for the conduct of just war was removed from the secular powers of Christendom and assumed, instead, by the church through the agency of its Christian knights. But, right at the beginning of the crusading movement, the papacy lost control of its agents, and the conduct of war against Islam thus passed from the relatively cautious and well-informed papal, imperial, and royal statesmen of Mediterranean Europe, into the hands of violent, ignorant, and impressionable warriors from the North.

During the second half of the eleventh century, the papacy extended the Peace of God movement beyond the bounds of Christendom, to Spain, Sicily, and North Africa, and lent its support to military expeditions against the Muslims. Now, in addition to the promise of a martyr's crown to those who fell in battle, the papacy offered all participants the remission of any penance imposed by the church. At the Council of Clermont, in November 1095, the papacy itself took the initiative and Pope Urban II urged his audience to undertake another 'just war' against the Muslims, in defence of the Christian churches of the East. Urban's exact words can no longer be recovered, but it is quite clear that either the pope himself, or the preachers who carried his message from Clermont, implanted two potent ideas in the hearts and minds of the knights of Europe.

The first was that the object of the planned expedition was to be Jerusalem. The potency of this image, in which the earthly city was subsumed under the heavenly Jerusalem, was great and, if later propagandists of the crusade are to be believed, Jerusalem was the physical and spiritual objective upon which the unsophisticated apocalyptic and eschatological beliefs of the mass of participants was focused. But no less powerful was the combination of the ancient Christian tradition of pilgrimage to the Holy City with the more recent concept of just war against the Muslims. The early crusaders described their expedition as a 'pilgrimage' (*peregrinatio*), but unlike mere pilgrims the crusaders carried weapons and, in return for their preparedness to fight, they received special privileges from the church.

The second and the more powerful idea which spread from Clermont was that the pope had offered crusaders not just the remission of penance, but nothing less than the full remission of the temporal penalties due to sin, or—perhaps—even the full remission of the sins themselves. Whatever Urban really said at Clermont, and whatever he actually meant by his words, there can be no doubt that the majority of crusaders at Clermont and throughout the twelfth and thirteenth centuries believed that in doing so they had made a contract with God and had assured themselves of a place in Paradise.

This 'good deal', to which repeated reference is made not just in crusading songs but also in the works of such distinguished preachers and theologians as Bernard of Clairvaux, was just part of the package of benefits which knightly participants hoped to acquire in joining the crusade. At Clermont, Urban had promised that those who went on crusade would be able to keep as their own the lands which they conquered, and the prospect of material gain, with the economic and social independence which it would bring, was a powerful incentive in land-hungry Europe. The lure of booty, of an adventure shared with comrades in arms, and of the mysterious Orient, with its fabulous wealth and exotic luxuries, all played their part amongst the heady mixture of religious and worldly motives which drew the knights of Christian Europe into battle with Islam.

The eastern crusades never posed a military threat to Islam. The thin line of Latin States which clung to the Syrian coast in the twelfth and thirteenth centuries constituted only a minor, local nuisance within the Muslim world as a whole, and they were swiftly crippled by the Muslim counter-crusade which culminated in the victories of Saladin (1169–93). The only lasting military gain for Christendom was that it retained naval control of the Mediterranean and its islands: a control that the Ottomans were to challenge but never to win. The principal long-term strategic consequence of the crusades, however, derived from conflict within Christendom, between the Latins and the Greeks, which led to the Fourth Crusade (1204) and to the destruction of the Byzantine defences of Europe's eastern border, opening the way for the Muslim conquest of the Balkans, Greece, and Eastern Europe.

Western Christendom, however, *did* perceive the crusades to be a military assault upon the Islamic world as a whole. Successes in the western and central Mediterranean in the eleventh to thirteenth centuries, combined with the dramatic triumph of the First Crusade and the capture of Jerusalem in 1097, to convince Europe that Islam was on the retreat and could be conquered. Not even the loss of the Holy City (1187) completely awoke Europe from the dream and, until the late thirteenth century, there were repeated efforts to drive back the Muslim counter-offensive. Gradually, Latin attention shifted from Syria to Egypt, which Saladin had developed as the heart of the Muslim Mediterranean and which constituted a potential threat to Latin naval superiority. Fantastical schemes were considered for a Latin advance down the Nile which would unite Western Christendom with the isolated churches of Nubia and Abyssinia, but the disastrous failure of St Louis's Crusade (1249–50) brought an end to the assault on Egypt. At about this time, Christian hopes were raised briefly by the prospect of an anti-Muslim alliance with the Mongols, amongst whom Nestorian Christianity had some superficial influence, but this vain and short-lived hope receded after 1260, when the Mamlūks of Egypt halted the Mongol advance in Palestine, and proceeded to consolidate their eastern frontier by driving the last Franks from Syria (1291).

But, if the crusades never constituted a serious threat to Islam's military control of the Near and Middle East, the very existence of the crusader States caused grave offence to Islam. The profanation of the Holy City, the reduction of the Muslim population of Syria (not to mention Spain and Sicily) to the status of inferior subjects, the interference with the *hajj* and other religious obligations, all amounted to an unforgivable affront to the collective dignity of Islam. So too did the ultimate defeat and expulsion of the crusaders from the East constitute a lasting and bitter humiliation to Christian pride. Both these old wounds were to be reopened in the nineteenth and twentieth centuries by the incorporation of most of the Islamic world into the empires of Christian Europe.

The Doctrinal Challenge

Christianity has largely misunderstood the nature of Islamic militancy. The fiction that Islam was preached by the sword and Christianity by the lamb and the dove appeared early in Christian writing, and still exercises a powerful influence upon the popular perception of Islam. Christian polemicists were quick to contrast the idealized life of Christ with that of Muhammad and his followers, 'who ceased not to go forth in battle and rapine, to smite with the sword, to seize the little ones, and ravish wives and maidens'. In fact, as we have seen, the first Arab conquests of Syria, Egypt, and Iraq were not motivated by religious fanaticism, but by a political ambition for Arab integration. As a result of these conquests, the Arabs found themselves to be rulers of a Judaeo-Christian subject population and Islam developed partly in reaction against this majority culture. Because Islam grew to maturity within the conquered lands, it had to accommodate its non-Muslim subjects within the new socio-religious system. According to the *Shari'a* (the revealed law of Islam), Jews and Christians were awarded special, privileged status as 'People of the Book', who shared in God's revelation to mankind. In return for payment of what was part tribute and part religious tax (the *jizya*), Jews and Christians were granted the protection of the state (*amān* or *dhimma*) and were assured freedom of person, property, and worship. This is not to deny that the 'protected' non-Muslim subjects of Islam were treated as second-class citizens and suffered inequality before the law, penal taxation, and a variety of other discomforts, humiliations, and indignities. The legal settlement was sanctioned by religious law but, obviously, tended to vary from place to place and from time to time. None the less, the efficacy of the original mechanism for the incorporation of Jewish and Christian communities is amply demonstrated. The violent persecution of Christians by Muslims was extremely rare and was generally confined to individual or mob fanaticism, and to the punishment for gross and public blasphemy of a few individuals such as the martyrs of Cordoba in the 850s. Christian and Jewish communities thrived in almost all the Muslim conquests, in stark contrast to the failure of medieval Europe to incorporate permanently its subject communities of Muslims and Jews. The root of this contrast lies in the development of Muslim doctrine and in the reaction of Christendom to the challenge which it posed.

Islamic tradition teaches that Islam was not a new religion but the oldest of all religions, an aboriginal and natural (as opposed to prophetic) form of monotheism; the original and unadulterated religion of Abraham, from which both Judaism and Christianity had themselves developed: 'Abraham was neither a Jew nor a Christian, but he was of the pure faith who submitted to God (*muslim*)'. There are confirmations, independent of Islamic tradition, of the existence of this pre-Islamic Arab monotheism: as early as the fifth century, the Palestinian Christian historian Sozomenus sketched the outlines of a pre-Mosaic monotheism which, he said, some Arabs had rediscovered and still practised in his own day.

In time, according to Islamic tradition, mankind had strayed away from the religion of Abraham and a succession of prophets had been sent to recall them to the truth. Pre-eminent amongst these were Moses and Jesus, who were both true prophets, although the Jews and the Christians had perverted their respective revelations. Thus, Muhammad's mission was twofold: first, he restored the Arabs to the pure religion of their ancestor Abraham; second, he was the 'seal of the prophets', the vehicle for the last and greatest of God's revelations to all mankind. The divergent strands of the Near Eastern Monotheistic tradition were returned to their pure source: the Pentateuch of Moses and the Gospel of Jesus were reintegrated within the religion of Abraham by the Qur'ān of Muhammad.

In order to justify this claim, Islamic sacred history expanded the biography of Abraham. Genesis tells how, when Abraham had no sons by his wife Sarah, he fathered Ishmael upon his slave-girl Hagar. But God did eventually grant a son, Isaac, to Sarah, whereupon she had Hagar and Ishmael expelled from Abraham's household and abandoned in the desert, where they survived with divine assistance. From Sarah descend the tribes of Israel—the Jews; from Hagar the tribes of Ishmael—the Arabs. At this point, Islamic tradition picked up the story. Hagar and Ishmael were not abandoned by Abraham, but conducted by him to a barren valley (Mecca), where Gabriel opened for them a spring of water (the sacred well of Zamzam), and where Abraham and Ishmael founded a sanctuary (the Ka'ba) and established the rites of pilgrimage (*hajj*). Ishmael lived on in Mecca, the progenitor of the Arab race and the

Arabic language, and a prophet in his own right: the graves of Hagar and Ishmael lie within the sanctuary at Mecca. To this day, the *hajj* commemorates sites which are traditionally linked to episodes from the Islamic Abraham legend: for example, the pilgrims see the depression where father and son mixed the mortar for the building of the Ka'ba, and they throw pebbles at the *jamarāt* just as Abraham stoned the devil at God's command. Tradition transformed the Meccan environment into a specifically Islamic religious landscape: the Ka'ba was the navel of the world, the first spot to be created by God; Adam lived and died in Mecca and was buried within the sanctuary; on the Last Day, mankind will assemble at 'Arafāt to await judgement; and so forth.

The Islamicization of Mecca directly challenged the Judaeo-Christian religious landscape into which Islam was carried by the first conquests. For, according to early medieval Jewish and Christian legend, it was Jerusalem (not Mecca) that was the navel of the world, where Adam was created and buried. Again, while Islamic tradition teaches that Abraham prepared to sacrifice Ishmael at 'Arafāt, Judaeo-Christian tradition identifies Jerusalem as the site where Abraham prepared to sacrifice Isaac. And the Christian Day of Judgement was to take place in the valley of Jehosophat, not in the plain of 'Arafāt. Just as the Christians had transferred the sacred landmarks of Jewish Jerusalem from the Temple Mount to Golgotha, so the Muslims removed elements of the Judaeo-Christian religious landscape from Jerusalem to Mecca.

Exactly when these and other similar transfers occurred cannot now be determined with certainty. We have already seen that the Christian influence upon Muhammad at Mecca was slight. Islamic tradition suggests that the migration to Medina brought Muhammad and his followers into close contact with the influential Jewish communities of northern Hijāz and that, almost immediately, the Muslim community began to distinguish itself from its Jewish neighbours, by changing the direction of prayer away from Jerusalem towards

Mecca. This process of defining certain elements of Islamic doctrine and practice in reaction against the rites and beliefs of the Jews and the Christians accelerated after the conquest of Syria, Egypt, and Iraq.

In the Hijāz and the early conquests, Islam developed within a predominantly urban environment and the struggle of the minority Muslim community to maintain its sense of religious identity amongst the Judaeo-Christian majority is reflected in its early adoption of distinctive rites, practices, and architectural forms. A list of triads may be compiled to demonstrate the distinctive Islamic elements which rapidly emerged: Moses, Jesus, and Muhammad; Torah, Gospels, and Qur'ān; Hebrew, Greek (or Syriac or Latin), and Arabic; synagogue, church, and mosque; Saturday, Sunday, and Friday; horn, bell (or clapper), and muezzin; and so on.

This process is nowhere more evident than in the case of Jerusalem. The conquest of Jerusalem in 638 confronted the Muslims with a considerable challenge: how was the religious capital of Judaism and Christianity to be incorporated into the Islamic religious landscape? As we have seen, part of the answer lay, eventually, in the elevation of Mecca, but Jerusalem too had to be Islamicized. Soon after the conquest, the Muslims appropriated Mount Moriah and erected on the site of the Temple an Islamic sanctuary that was to rival both its Jewish predecessor and the Christian 'New Jerusalem' on Golgotha. Before 680, when the English pilgrim Arculf visited Jerusalem, the Muslims had built 'an oblong house of prayer, which they pieced together with upright planks and large beams over some ruined remains'. But this original form of the al-Aqsā Mosque was soon to be outshone by a far more splendid Muslim sanctuary: the Dome on the Rock, completed in 691–2 under the Umayyad caliph 'Abd al-Malik. The mosaic decoration of the interior, in which representations of jewellery appropriate to the Byzantine emperor and the Sassanid shah, and to Christ, the Virgin, and the saints, hang on the wall like trophies, symbolizes the military triumph of the Muslim state. Similarly, the Umayyad inscriptions proclaim the ascendancy and superiority of Islam over Judaism and Christianity. But the Dome on the Rock also stresses that the three faiths did share a common heritage, and invites the Jews and Christians to Islam. The location of the Dome on Mount Moriah may be an allusion to common Abrahamic roots, and the principal inscription of the interior accepts the Hebrew prophets and specifically Christ, among the forerunners of Islam. A later Muslim tradition identified the Rock as the point from which Muhammad ascended into heaven, where he was guided by the prophets who preceded him, including Abraham, Moses, and Jesus.

By the end of the seventh century, as the Islamic armies advanced beyond the Arab homelands, Islamic doctrine had grown to maturity and posed a major challenge to Christianity by its claim to be, at one and the same time, the aboriginal faith from which Judaism and Christianity had grown, and God's final revelation to all mankind, which superseded the earlier revelations of Moses and Christ. Similarly, Islam's total rejection of central Christian dogma, such as the divinity and resurrection of Christ and the Trinity, directly challenged Christian doctrine. But although Christians were urged to convert to Islam, and suffered varying fiscal and social penalties for not doing so, there was no general attempt to force Christians to convert: on the contrary, the Islamic socio-religious system was designed to accommodate subject communities of Christians. The doctrinal gauntlet was thrown down.

At no time did medieval Christendom unite in a concerted effort to meet this challenge. This is partly because the intensity of the threat varied according to the proximity in which the two communities lived. In certain areas and at certain times, Christians under Muslim rule were forced to engage in doctrinal debate because of the constant pressure maintained by Islam. Syrian Christians in the early ninth century were greeted by their Muslim masters not with any polite salutation but rather by the Islamic profession of faith—'there is no God but the One God, and Muhammad is the messenger of God'—a formula which, in stressing Islamic unitarianism, attacked the doctrine of the Trinity, and which, in acknowledging the prophethood of Muhammad, seemed to challenge the status of Christ.

In the East, some Christian communities immediately reacted to the perceived threat to Christian doctrine, and the earliest Oriental works of Christian apologetic and anti-Islamic polemic date from the seventh century. John of Damascus (*c*.675–*c*.750), who is in many ways the founder of the Christian tradition, ridiculed the Muslim claim to Abrahamic ancestry, by explaining that the Arabs were called 'Saracens' because they were 'empty of Sarah', and 'Hagarenes' because they were 'the bastard descendants of the slave-girl Hagar'. Similarly, he dismissed Islamic doctrine as no more than a hotchpotch, culled from the Old and New Testaments by the pseudo-prophet Muhammad, with assistance from an Arian monk. This aggressive approach reached a climax in the famous *Apology* attributed to al-Kindī, which probably dates from the early tenth century, in which Islam is portrayed as the law of Satan, and Muhammad as an idolatrous libertine.

Such abusive blustering by Christian writers cannot conceal Christian sensitivity to Muslim criticism. The doctrine of the Trinity was a constant butt for Muslim ridicule: the tenth-century Christian philosopher Yaḥyā ibn 'Adī was prompted to write his tract on the Unity and Trinity of God by the Muslim joke that Christians were innumerate—'with them, one is three and three is one'. Similarly, the Christians' reverence for the Cross and images in general exposed them to the accusation of idolatry: writing in *c*.725, Germanus of Constantinople instructed his readers to counter such charges by replying that the Muslims worshipped a stone called Chobar in the desert (i.e. the Ka'ba).

In contrast to this militant tradition, some Christian communities were carried along by a strong ecumenical current. *The Parable of the Pearl* by the Nestorian patriarch Timothy (*c*.728–823) is the earliest extant Christian work to acknowledge a

truth common to both Christianity and Islam. Far from accusing
the Muslims of idolatry, Timothy compares Muhammad to
Moses for his praiseworthy persecution of idolaters. It may be
that belief in a common truth was far more widespread than
the surviving written sources suggest. At the height of the
persecution of the Christians of Cordoba, a part of the Christian
community protested that the victims were not truly martyrs
because they had not been killed by pagans but by Muslims,
'men who worship God and acknowledge heavenly laws'. At
about the same time, Nicetas of Byzantium was prompted to
counter the opinion that Muslims worshipped the true God,
and, early in the next century, the patriarch Nicolas wrote to
the caliph that 'we have obtained the gift of our authorities [i.e.
the Qur'ān and the Gospels] from the same Source'. It may
have been as early as 717 that mosques were permitted within
the walls of Constantinople for the use of Muslim visitors and
prisoners of war. In the Christian West, this view is less well
known, but, in 1076, Pope Gregory VII wrote to the Hammādid
ruler al-Nāsir that 'we believe in and confess one God,
admittedly in a different way', and stressed the Abrahamic
roots of the two religions. This idea never seems to have taken
root in Western Europe, and had disappeared completely by
the First Crusade.

While it is true that the Christian communities which lived in
closest proximity to the Muslims led the polemic counter-
offensive against the doctrinal challenge posed by Islam, it is
also true that Islam's nearest Christian neighbours were best
able to appreciate the common ground shared by the two faiths
and—more important, perhaps—they had most to gain from
the establishment of a *modus vivendi*.

North-western Europe, although distant, was keenly aware
of the Muslim threat. As early as *c*.658, the Merovingian
chronicler Fredegar gave what may be the earliest extant
account in any language of the Arab conquests. During the
eighth century, a Latin version of Pseudo-Methodius' Syriac
Revelation, which dwelt upon the danger of Christians convert-

ing to Islam, circulated widely in Western Europe. Charlemagne even asked Alcuin to procure for him an anti-Muslim tract. By the mid-ninth century, under threat of the Muslim advance into the central Mediterranean and as news of the martyrs of Cordoba crossed the Pyrenees, north-western Europe seemed about to take up the doctrinal challenge. The military and the doctrinal threat were intimately linked in the minds of contemporaries. The Cordoban Paul Alvar claimed that the Muslims pretended to wage war 'as if by God's command', and a leading Carolingian theologian, Paschasius Radbertus (*c.*850), explicitly linked Muslim doctrine with an ambition for universal dominion. But as the military threat to Western Europe receded, and as cultural contacts with Byzantium declined, the short-lived interest of Latin Christendom in Islam was stifled beneath the weight of scriptural and patristic authority, to which the rise of Islam was no more significant than a marginal note to the books of Genesis or Revelation.

The Social Problem

The military successes of Western Christendom in the eleventh century, in Spain, in southern Italy and Sicily, and in the Near East, created a massive social problem for which Christianity was wholly unprepared. Western Christian society suddenly had to cope with the presence within its frontiers, not merely of the plethora of Greek and Oriental Christian sects and of a greatly increased Jewish community, but also of many tens of thousands of Muslims. Whereas, as we have seen, the Islamic socio-religious system had inbuilt mechanisms for the accommodation of Judaism and Christianity, Western Christian society, since the fourth century, had been perfecting its own machinery for the extermination of all internal heterodoxy. Only the Jewish communities of Western Europe had been permitted to remain, and these had been the victims of frequent persecutions, one of the most ferocious of which had immediately preceded the First Crusade. The accommodation of the

Jews in Western Christian society derives largely from the fact that Judaism could be located on a lower rung of the hierarchy of revelation which led to Christianity, in much the same way that Islam placed both Judaism and Christianity amongst its antecedents. In contrast, Christianity as a whole rejected Islam's claim to be the religion of Abraham and, instead, regarded it as a new and perverse mutation. The church, secular government, and the society at large all reacted differently to their new neighbours, but the ultimate inability of Western Christendom, as a whole, to incorporate its non-Catholic citizens, constitutes one of the most dismal failures in European history.

The attitude of Byzantium to its Muslim subjects was wholly different. Indeed, the principle of autonomous organization for minority communities was enshrined in Byzantine law and thence had been adopted by Islam. The long experience of Byzantium in dealing with its Arab neighbours, pagan, Christian, and finally Muslim, largely determined the nature of the relationship between Greek Christianity and Islam. In the lands won back from the Arabs during the tenth century, Byzantium induced Muslims to settle and successfully encouraged many to convert to Christianity. While the Greek church had a specific ritual which enabled Muslims to reject Islam and embrace Christianity, no similar rite is known from the West. In Norman Sicily, where the Greek and Latin churches existed side by side, only the Greek made any significant number of converts outside the closed and particular circle of the royal court. While Muslims or Muslim converts were fully integrated into Byzantine society, the non-Catholic subjects of Latin Christendom constituted an inferior class and were systematically exploited by their Catholic rulers.

For the most part, the Western church had shown an extra-ordinary lack of interest in the fate of Christian communities under Muslim rule. Late in the eighth century, Pope Hadrian I and Charlemagne did lend their support to a mission to succour the Christians of Spain and, in the 850s, news of the martyrs of Cordoba had prompted a modest response, but these were exceptional reactions. Moreover, when the church did take notice of Christian communities under Muslim rule, it showed itself peculiarly insensitive to their plight. When Gregory VII replied to the bishop of Carthage, who had been tortured for his refusal to accept uncanonical ordination by the Muslim ruler, the pope pointed out that the bishop would have done better had he attempted to convert his persecutors and suffered martyrdom at their hands. The absence of regular contacts between the Western church and Christian communities under Islam meant that the church never had the opportunity to observe the socio-legal mechanisms whereby Islam accommodated its Christian subjects. The only means, other than war, that the church could imagine for dealing with Muslims was conversion to Christianity. Before the eleventh century, however, although the Western church had sent many missions to the pagans of Northern and Eastern Europe, it had almost completely withheld from missionary activity in the Islamic world; nor did a single crusade have conversion of Muslims as its express aim. It was only when the Muslim community appeared within Christendom itself that the church perceived the problem.

Following the Christian advance in Spain, southern Italy, and Sicily, the church began to advocate the conversion of her new Muslim subjects. In 1088, when Urban II conferred the pallium upon the new archbishop of Toledo, he instructed him 'by word and example to convert, with God's grace, the infidels to the faith'. In 1170, the future Pope Gregory VIII, founder of the Spanish military Order of Santiago, specified that the conversion of Muslims was to be one of its principal objectives. In the thirteenth century, the religious revival within Christendom stimulated a new burst of missionary activity to Islam. Jacques of Vitry had developed his preaching technique under the influence of the European evangelical movement and had perfected it in a mission to the Albigensian heretics in 1213. It was therefore natural that, soon after his appointment to the bishopric of Acre in 1216, he should begin to preach, first to the Oriental Christian, and then to the Muslim subjects of the kingdom.

At the same time, the church dispatched the first organized missions to the Muslims outside Christendom. St Francis seems to have regarded his visit to the court of the Egyptian sultan al-Kāmil in 1218 as an extension of his mission from his fellow Christians to 'all peoples, races, tribes and tongues, all nations and all men of all countries, who are and who shall be'. Throughout the first half of the thirteenth century, the Franciscans, and the Dominicans too, pursued the missionary ideal in the Islamic world with equal enthusiasm and lack of success. As the number of Mendicant martyrs rose, so did the disillusion of the church with undefended missionary activity increase.

Even within Latin Christendom, Muslim communities proved extremely reluctant to convert. This was largely because Western rulers, unlike the Byzantines, did not actively encourage conversion during the twelfth century. There were, of course, exceptions to this trend, but practical considerations tended to persuade rulers to discourage mass conversion. Thus, Anselm was forbidden to convert the Saracen soldiers of Roger of Sicily, who, presumably, was seeking to exploit religious antagonism in employing Muslim troops against his Christian enemies. Again, the baptism of a Muslim slave could impose limits upon his master's rights and could lead to manumission, and, in Spain, even the Cistercian monasteries had to be repeatedly warned not to obstruct the baptism of their Muslim slaves. In the Crusader kingdom, it was even decreed that a slave could not be baptized in order 'to be freed from servitude'.

The attitude of Latin secular governments towards their Muslim subjects had encouraged social polarization by enforcing a sort of apartheid. In Sicily, in the Crusader States, and in Spain, Christian rulers had treated their Muslim subjects in roughly the same manner: the Muslim law and practices regarding subject communities of Christians were adapted to the needs of the new rulers. In return for payment of tribute, Muslims received the protection of the Christian state, and were promised freedom of person, property, and religion, together with certain other specified and variable freedoms and privileges. But this legal settlement did not work in Christendom as it had within Islam. The Muslim communities under the Crown of Aragon in the fourteenth century survived only because of the benevolent paternalism of the monarchs towards what they called their 'royal treasure'. The phrase is a significant one, for Christian governments regarded their Muslim subjects as a resource to be exploited. First and foremost, the Muslim population possessed the specialist skills and crafts upon which the economic prosperity of the conquests depended and, for this reason alone, it was strongly in the interests of the conquerors to maintain and to protect their Muslim subjects. But the Muslims also constituted a valuable fiscal resource: apart from the tribute, a variety of other taxes were levied exclusively from the Muslim community: upon ritual butchery and upon baths. The fiscal administration employed by the Christian conquerors was generally based upon the previous Muslim administration and tended to be staffed by Muslims or converts.

The paternalistic attitude of Christian rulers towards their Muslims was rarely shared by their Catholic subjects. In Norman Sicily, Muslims enjoyed their privileged status only in those areas where royal authority was strongest, in the major towns and on the royal domain. Elsewhere on the island, Muslim communities suffered from the increasing pressure of Latin immigration and colonization, combined with the advance of the hostile Latin church and the corresponding retreat of the comparatively sympathetic Greek church. Latin settlers strongly resented the privileged status of the indigenous Muslims and, wherever and whenever royal authority was weak, took the opportunity to drive them out and take over their possessions. Similarly, Latin lords resented the efficiency of the Arabic fiscal administration and its Muslim officers. During a baronial rebellion in 1161–2, Latin settlers in central Sicily massacred their Muslim neighbours and seized their lands, and, in Palermo, the royal *dīwān* or tax-office was sacked, its Arabic records burnt, and its Muslim officers slaughtered.

For the most part, subject Muslim communities reacted to

the royal policy of apartheid and to the persecution of the Catholic populace and the Latin church by closing their ranks and turning in on themselves. This process was encouraged by the church in the thirteenth and fourteenth centuries, when a series of papal decrees steadily restricted the social contacts which might legally take place between the two communities. Clement V (1305–14) even went so far as to decree that even the presence of Muslims on Christian soil amounted to 'an insult to the Creator'.

In Sicily and Spain, the marginalization of Muslim subject communities by the church and by secular government strengthened their own sense of cultural identity, and sometimes led them to revolt against their Christian masters. During the second half of the twelfth century, as the Muslim counter-crusade gained momentum in the East and as the Almohads advanced in the West, Muslim communities subject to the Normans began to rebel. In the 1150s, the Normans lost their North African possessions, and, in 1189, the Muslims of Sicily began the rebellion which was to drag on until 1246, and was to result in the expulsion of the Muslim community from the island by Frederick II. At about the same time, the kingdom of Valencia suffered a succession of Muslim rebellions, which began soon after the conquest and continued until 1276–7.

Thus, by the mid-thirteenth century, it was apparent that the missionary effort to the Islamic world had failed, and that the subject communities of Christendom were not going to convert but, on the contrary, were determined to resist and, on occasion, to rebel. The church reacted by linking Christian proselytism to the legitimate use of force. With regard to the Islamic world, Innocent IV (1243–54) decreed that, although Muslims must not be coerced into Christianity, the secular powers of Christendom could use force in order to ensure that the gospel was preached in Muslim lands. This does seem to have had a significant effect upon the late crusades in Spain and North Africa.

Within Christendom, the church renewed the missionary

effort, often with the support of secular government, and lent its full support to the suppression of Muslim rebellion. During the late 1190s, Pope Innocent III, who was then regent of Sicily for the young Frederick II, identified the Muslim rebels as the 'enemies of all Christendom', and offered a full crusading indulgence to any who might fight against them. And in 1221, Honorius III gave his full support to Frederick II in his campaign 'to exterminate completely from the island the Muslims of Sicily'. Similarly, during the 1276–7 revolt of the Valencian Muslims, Pope Gregory X handed over to King Peter III the crusade tithe originally intended for the Holy Land.

In Sicily and, later, in Spain, the secular authorities were ultimately forced to acknowledge their failure to incorporate their Muslim subjects into their kingdoms by expelling the entire Islamic community. Frederick II, after his suppression of the Muslim revolt, transported the rebels from Sicily to Lucera on the mainland, where they were maintained as a military colony until the early fourteenth century, when the Angevin kings encouraged their Catholic subjects and the papal inquisition to destroy the last sorry remnants of Muslim Sicily.

The church was just as eager to deal with spiritual rebellion amongst the subject Muslims. The papacy had secured the assistance of secular authority in the persecution of heterodoxy at the Fourth Lateran Council (1215), and with the establishment of the papal inquisition by Gregory IX (1231). The inquisition was not, of course, specifically aimed at the Muslims of Christendom but, none the less, it soon came to be used as an instrument for the persecution of Muslim apostates from Christianity. There was also a tendency to identify Muslims, and especially Muslim rebels, with Christian heterodoxy. In 1196, during the early years of the Muslim rebellion of Sicily, Joachim of Fiore warned that the Muslims were to ally with the Patarene heretics and persecute the church. Salimbene, who summarized Joachim's writings, had heard that the French Pastoreaux were led by evil men who were in league with the Muslims and who had raised funds in the name of Muhammad.

The excommunicant adult 'leaders' of the Children's Crusade were rumoured to have been in league with the Muslim rebels of Sicily. During their suppression, the Templars were occasionally accused of being crypto-Muslims. A band of French leper brigands was accused of having plotted with the Muslims. None of this is to be taken as the literal truth, but it demonstrates how easily a vague connection could be perceived between Christian heterodoxy and Islam.

The inquisition spread early to Aragon (1232) and, after the succession of Charles of Anjou, to the kingdom of Sicily in 1269: Pope Nicholas IV ordered that the inquisition be carried to Acre in 1290, just before the fall of the kingdom to the Muslims. In Castile, however, King Alfonso the Wise refused to permit the introduction of the inquisition, and it was not until 1478 that Ferdinand and Isabella allowed it into the kingdom. Its presence within a kingdom did not necessarily lead to the persecution of Muslims: thus, Muslims in the kingdom of Aragon seem to have fared very much better than those in Castile. None the less, the inquisition did play a major role in the final extermination of Islam from both the kingdom of Sicily in the early fourteenth century and from Spain in the fifteenth to seventeenth centuries.

A Common Heritage

Christianity and Islam both grew out of the same Near Eastern monotheistic tradition. From its very inception, Islam recognized and, indeed, emphasized this common heritage, but it did so only upon its own terms. Thus, Muslims acknowledged Jesus as a prophet, and even went so far as to accept the virgin birth, but absolutely rejected the divinity of Christ. In a similar way, Christianity recognized its relationship to Islam. It was common knowledge that the Arabs occupied a place in sacred history, and their claim to Abrahamic ancestry was accepted, but the significance which Christians gave to this heredity was very different from that given by Muslims. St Paul's interpretation of the Abraham legend was here put to good use (Gal. 4: 22–31). The 'sons of the slave-woman' Hagar were identified as the Muslims, whose inherent slavery was both spiritual and, within the borders of Christendom, physical. In contrast, the 'sons of the free woman' Sarah were the Christians who had been set free by their acceptance of Christ.

As we have seen, there was a current within the Christian tradition, stronger in Byzantium than in the West, which held that Christians and Muslims both worshipped the one true God. During the eleventh to thirteenth centuries, as Western Christendom came into closer contact with Islam, in Spain, Sicily, and—to a lesser extent—the Latin East, its appreciation of the nature of their common ideological heritage began to grow. Western scholars gradually produced a corpus of translations from the Arabic and studies of Islam. The most influential of these was the work of Peter the Venerable, abbot of Cluny, who sponsored the translation into Latin of the Qur'ān as part of a major project to study Islam, completed c.1143. These translations, and the commentaries which they provoked, constituted the principal source of informed Western knowledge of Islam until the sixteenth century. Western Europe's newly acquired knowledge was not used to develop the relationship between the two faiths, but instead, in so far as it was used at all, was selectively deployed by Christian missionaries in their assault against Islam. This, indeed, was the only use which even such intellectuals as Roger Bacon could conceive for the study of Arabic and Muslim doctrine.

At the same time that Western Christendom discovered and then tossed aside its common religious heritage with Islam, it had become acquainted with two other elements of their shared inheritance: the intellectual legacy of the Greek world and a common humanity.

Both Islam and Western Christianity, at crucial moments in their intellectual development, borrowed with almost frantic enthusiasm certain elements, both intellectual and material, from the culture of the other. It is no accident that this exchange coincided with the ebb and flow of the military conquests. Islam could borrow so heavily from Christendom because it had conquered much of Byzantium; Western Christendom was able to take so much from Islam because it was master of Spain and Sicily. This also helps to explain why the flow of ideas, at any given moment, was only in one direction. In the wake of the Muslim conquests, when Islam borrowed most heavily from Christendom, Christianity closed itself to Islam; in the aftermath of the Christian counter-offensive, when Christianity opened its mind to Islam, the Muslim world turned its back upon Christendom.

Neither culture borrowed wholesale from the other but, on the contrary, each was driven by specific internal needs and exercised considerable selectivity. During the ninth century, in 'Abbāsid Baghdad, the translation movement from Greek into Arabic was partly a response to a demand for new intellectual tools, created by the development of the schools of religious law and of grammar. Thus, for example, it was the Aristotelian philosophical corpus that was translated, while Homer was ignored. Similarly, Western Europe translated from the Arabic only those philosophical and scientific works which seemed to answer its own needs, and deliberately ignored works of theology, jurisprudence, history, geography, and fiction. Thus, in Latin Europe, Algazel was known exclusively as a commentator upon Greek metaphysics, from the translation of his minor treatise *The Intentions of the Philosophers*; while, in Islam, al-Ghazālī is still known as 'The Proof of Islam', whose great achievement was the reconciliation of Sūfī mysticism with official Islam.

The Greek learning which Islam acquired from Christendom and which, later, Christendom received from Islam, was to a greater or lesser extent transformed by the medium through which it had passed. What helped to make Greek metaphysics so very attractive to the Muslim philosophers of ninth-century Baghdad was that the Byzantine authors from whom they had their texts had already subtly transformed the originals, so that what had been metaphysical speculation now appeared to be a sort of 'natural theology'. Similarly, the corpus of Neo-Platonic thought which revitalized Augustinianism in the twelfth century, and inspired the great English and French Franciscan masters of the thirteenth, owed as much to Ibn Sīnā (Avicenna), and through him to al-Farābī, as it did to the Greek originals.

The contribution of Greek learning, transmitted through Islam, to the development of Christian philosophy, is so great that it cannot be quantified. It is therefore extraordinary that it did so little to improve the relationship between Christianity and Islam. In part, this is because Western Christian and Muslim intellectuals almost never got together. What separated them was, above all, a language barrier: only a few, very exceptional Western scholars knew Arabic and, as one of these, Roger Bacon, pointed out, Arabic was not taught in the Schools. Nor were foreign languages commonly studied by the Arabs. Translations tended to be the work of professional translators, not of the scholars themselves. Thus, an Arab scholar would not have been able to converse with Europe's greatest experts on Arabic philosophy, even if he could have made his way unmolested to Paris or to Bologna. Only at a few wholly exceptional points of contact, in Spain and Sicily, could Latin and Arab scholars meet, and there it was only the Latins who had anything to learn.

Language was not, however, the only barrier between Latin and Muslim scholars. Muslims showed a general disdain for the West, which had its origins in a typically Mediterranean contempt for northern barbarians. The eleventh-century intellectual historian, Sa'īd al-Andalusī, observed that, because Europeans lived in a cold climate, the growth of their brains was stunted, so they could not be expected to contribute to civilization. This attitude persisted into the twelfth and thirteenth centuries when, for the first time, Western scholars had attained an intellectual level at which dialogue would have been possible. When Frederick II posed his 'Sicilian Questions', inspired by Aristotelian metaphysics, to the Muslim world, the Spanish philosopher Ibn Sab'īn replied that they were silly questions (which they were not), and that he would answer only for the glory of Islam.

During the eleventh to thirteeth centuries, Latin Christendom developed a profound respect for aspects of Arab learning, which contrasted strongly with Muslim contempt for the Christian West. In Latin, a useful semantic distinction emerged between 'Arab', denoting race and language, and 'Saracen', denoting religion. Muslim scholars, such as Ibn Sīnā and al-Ghazālī, were detached from their Islamic roots and grafted onto the same non-religious tree of learning as had been Plato, Aristotle, and the scholars of the Classical past. In Dante's *Divine Comedy*, Muhammad is tortured in Hell, whilst, in Limbo, Ibn Sīnā and Ibn Rushd (Averroes) are permitted to spend all Eternity in pleasant discussion with the scholars of antiquity. Western artists portrayed Muslim scholars in the same garb as the Classical authors whom they had transmitted to the West: it was only during the Renaissance that Arab scholars began to be portrayed in contemporary Arab dress. But it was not always possible to separate Arab ideas from their Muslim context, and Europe's perception of Arab wisdom was still inevitably conditioned by religious currents. Ibn Rushd enjoyed great popularity in the West at the beginning of the thirteenth century, when he was welcomed as the great 'Commentator' upon Aristotle, but during the 1270s and, again, early in the fourteenth century, when the full impact of his ideas began to be felt, he was repeatedly condemned as an accursed infidel who had been inspired by Satan.

The intellectual transfer from Islam to Christendom was limited by the West's selectivity, and by the way in which it detached Classical learning and Arabic ideas from their Muslim environment. The West sought to dehumanize the Muslim scholars to which it owed so much, and to transform them into passive agents of transmission of Classical learning. At the same time, however, Western European society began to acknowledge that it did, after all, share a common humanity with the world of Islam.

The first mass encounter of Western Europe with its Muslim neighbours came in the second half of the eleventh century, during the Christian advance in Spain and Sicily and on the First Crusade. The earliest accounts reassure the West that its knights had found a worthy foe in the Saracen. The Norman chroniclers of southern Italy and Sicily, for example, contrast the treacherous Lombards and the weak, effeminate Byzantines, with the proud and warlike Muslims. Similarly, a south Italian chronicler of the First Crusade portrayed the Turks as the precise Muslim equivalent to the Franks: 'none could be found to equal them in strength, in courage or in the science of war', while the Turks themselves 'say they belong to the Frankish race and assert that no one, they and the Franks excepted, has the right to call himself a knight'. The *chansons de geste*, too, portray the Muslims as 'worthy of respect, a good enemy, difficult to conquer, a chance of glory, always numerous and their leaders notable for prowess'. This is a familiar topos, reinforcing man's need to believe that, in fighting and killing other men who are just as noble as he, he exhibits his most admirable and most human qualities.

In the wake of the Christian advance, it became generally known that Muslims could, and did, convert to Christianity. This was not just the passage from one religion to another, for being a Christian was one of the essential attributes of humanity: even to this day, throughout the Greek and Latin Mediterranean, 'Christian' means 'human being', or even just 'man', while to behave like a 'Turk' is to defy the conventions of human society. Thus, the realization that Muslims could convert to Christianity entailed a heightened awareness of a common humanity.

The theme of love between a Christian and a Muslim had a particular impact upon the popular imagination. Usually, it was a Saracen maiden who fell for a Christian knight and eventually accepted baptism for his sake, and this story is associated with some of the leaders of the First Crusade. But the reverse was also conceivable: it was rumoured that Frederick Barbarossa planned to marry his daughter to one of Saladin's sons.

Such themes found their way into some works of fiction, alongside appeals that common humanity be recognized and respected. In *Willehalm*, Wolfram von Eschenbach puts an appeal for toleration into the mouth of Gyburg, a beautiful Muslim girl who has converted for love. And many of the protagonists of Wolfram's *Parzival*, which largely derives from distant Oriental sources, are both Muslims and real characters, not just the crude caricatures of the *chansons de geste*.

Only very little Arabic fiction was known in Western Europe and, although the translations of such fantasies as *Kalīla wa-Dimna* and *Sinbad and the Seven Sages* may have had a considerable impact upon the European imagination, they can have done little to affect the West's perception of Islam. In contrast, Peter Alfonsi's collection of Arabic tales, the *Disciplina Clericalis*, which was immensely popular in the twelfth to fourteenth centuries and was even translated into the vernacular, showed ordinary men going about their daily business, and must have made Christian readers aware of what they had in common with its Muslim protagonists.

Yet, the dominant reaction of Western Christendom towards Islam remained violently xenophobic. The majority view was that Muslims were subhuman brutes, diabolically inspired, and unworthy of the rights and considerations due to mankind. Most Europeans do not seem to have perceived, still less to have been uncomfortable with this contradiction. Pope Gregory VII could write to a Muslim ruler that they worshipped the same God, but, to a Christian audience, he would refer to Muslims as 'pagans'. The popular image of Richard the Lionheart could reconcile his chivalry towards Saladin with the story that he had devoured with appetite roast head of Saracen, and then called out for more. Frederick II could maintain the appearance of an Arab monarch and could entertain at his court Muslim scholars and poets, whilst engaged in the systematic and violent extermination of the Muslim community of Sicily.

What lay behind this duality? The Christians of Western Europe generally accepted without question that Christianity was an essential component of their own humanity. At the same time, they refused to recognize, in Islam, a religious system which, no less than their own, conveyed humanity to its followers. It has been suggested that Christian exclusivity has its origins in the second- and third-century persecution of Christians and derives 'precisely from their pre-existing conviction that others always persecuted them'. Christian violence towards Muslims thus becomes an extension of Christian violence towards pagans and heretics. There may, indeed, be much that is valid within this hypothesis. A common trait of persecuted communities is that, once freed from persecution, they themselves persecute other, weaker communities. But why should Western Christendom have delayed seven centuries before taking so bloody a revenge for the persecution of the early church? Very different attitudes towards Muslims prevailed in Byzantium and in the Oriental churches, and so it would seem that violent xenophobia towards Muslims was not so much characteristic of medieval Christianity as of medieval Europe. The Latin church inevitably reflected the exclusivity and intolerance of European society, but it was not their cause.

Medieval Islam in the Modern World

One cannot but be struck by the way in which medieval Islam tolerated and cultivated the Christian and Jewish communities in its midst, whilst medieval Europe exploited, persecuted, and finally destroyed or expelled its Muslim (and Jewish) subjects. This contrast is all the more difficult to comprehend with the example of new radical Islam constantly before us. In part, our own distorted image of contemporary Islam is to blame. The new European stereotypes of the Muslim—the decadent and fabulously rich oil sheikh of the 1970s; the fanatic ayatollah, spattered with the blood of martyrs, of the 1980s—are no more representative of mundane reality than was the blood-thirsty and licentious pagan of medieval legend. And yet, the rise of radical fundamentalist Islam is bringing about a deep change in the relationship between Christianity and Islam, both within and beyond the boundaries of the Muslim world.

After the dismemberment of the Ottoman empire, all but four or five Muslim countries were engulfed by Christian imperial powers—Britain, France, Spain, Holland, and Russia— and old crusading wounds opened up anew. Muslim opponents of European political, cultural, and economic imperialism came to use 'crusader' as a synonym for 'imperialist', 'colonial', and even 'capitalist'. And, in a sense, they are justified in so doing: in 1920, when the French entered Damascus, their commander marched directly to Saladin's tomb, and declared: '*Nous revoilà, Saladin*'. Christian missions were actively supported by the colonial authorities, and indigenous Christian communities, such as the Maronites of Lebanon, were encouraged to assume a disproportionate role in the running of the colony.

Even after political independence, the cultural and economic expansionism of Europe and America continued to challenge and to undermine the traditional values and structures of Islamic society. Modernist regimes throughout the Muslim world, from Atatürk, to Nasser, to Jinnah, sought to model themselves upon the political systems of Europe, by introducing or con-solidating Western concepts such as the nation state and democracy, and by abolishing the socio-political pillars of Islamic society such as the *Sharī'a* and the Islamic educational system. The electronic media were employed as agents of modernization and they rapidly spread a yearning materialism that went hand in hand with the decay of traditional moral standards.

During the 1950s, the traditional conservatism which had always opposed modernism began to solidify into hard points of political resistance and, eventually, into open revolution.

The failure of capitalism to deliver the economic and social benefits that had been promised, combined with the spectacle of the manifest decadence and corruption of the Christian West, produced a profound popular disillusionment with the prevailing current of modernism. The intellectual leaders of the revolt, Maulana Maudoodi in India–Pakistan, Sayyid Qutb in Egypt, Sa'id Hawwa in Syria, began increasingly to employ the language of medieval theology to express their views. The modernist state, with its rejection of the *Sharī'a*, had returned to the corrupt paganism of pre-Islamic antiquity. The individual was called upon to make a personal renunciation of modern secular society, and to join in the *jihād* for the universal restoration of God's Law. The world was again divided between the *Dār al-Islām*, the 'abode of Islam', which was, in effect, limited to the small group of new radical Muslims, and the *Dār al-Harb*, 'the abode of war', which included not just the non-Muslim world, but also the secular modernist regimes.

This return to medieval Islam has involved a re-evaluation of the relationship between Islam and Christianity, of which the rejection of the West is the most obvious manifestation. Islam now spurns the society and values of Christian Europe and America as ungodly, unjust, decadent, and corrupt—exactly the components of medieval Europe's myths of Islam. But radical Islam has been concerned, above all else, to set its own house in order, and Christians within Islam have felt most strongly the wind of change. Some indigenous Christian communities, such as the Maronites of Lebanon, had been closely associated with European colonial rule, but everywhere the Christian middle class had thrown in its lot with the modernist regimes. The radical reaction against the West and modernism has inevitably brought with it a fierce backlash against their Christian supporters. In Lebanon, the *mujāhidūn* militia classified the Maronites as 'crusaders' and declared the *jihād* against them. In Egypt, radical Islam has made some use of anti-Coptic prejudice to further its own ends: the anti-Coptic riots of June 1981 set off the cycle of oppression and resistance which culminated in Sadat's assassination. In the Sudan, repeated efforts in the 1980s by the Muslim government to impose *Sharī'a* law upon the Christian south were amongst the causes of the civil war, which so exacerbated the terrible effects of famine and drought in north-east Africa. Everywhere the threat of a return to *Sharī'a* law, and the reimposition of 'protected people' status, in place of a tolerance predicated on the equality of all religions, is one which hangs heavily over the Christian communities of Islam.

In 1989, the opponents of Salman Rushdie's *Satanic Verses* reminded Europe that its Muslim citizens abide by values and laws very different from its own, and will use violence to ensure that they are respected. Once again, Europe is faced with the problem of how to incorporate its Muslim minorities into society. Unless Europe can abandon its medieval inheritance of exclusivity and intolerance, and unless Islam can break free from the medieval anachronisms advocated by its radical extremists, modern secularism is unlikely to succeed where medieval Christianity failed.

6

Christian Civilization
(1050–1400)

COLIN MORRIS

Christian Society in 1050

By about 1050, almost all of Western Europe was formally Christian. Many of the ancient provinces of the church had been lost to Islam, which controlled the whole of North Africa, Spain, Sicily, and much of western Asia, including the mother church of Jerusalem itself, but the main bulk of the continent was secure in its acceptance of Christianity. The older kingdoms had long been so, and more recently the rulers of Norway, Denmark, Poland, Hungary, and Russia had accepted baptism and established an ecclesiastical hierarchy. Within these wide boundaries, most people were baptized in childhood and knew no alternative pattern of worship. The religion into which they were thus admitted was cultic in character: that is, it valued above all the power of the church to win the blessing of God by its prayers. The ordinary affairs of men could only be upheld by the intervention of God: government depended on the king anointed in his name, justice was guaranteed by the ordeals which recorded a divine decision, and healing was bestowed by the power of the saints and the charms of healers. It was the task of monks and priests to pray, and of laymen to sustain them by their alms. Bishop Odo of Cambrai summarized this attitude when he said *c.*1113 that 'we pray in the sacrifice against the peril of fire for our homes, against drought or tempest for our crops, against sickness for our animals, and against other losses for everything else'. Prayer was the essential function of the priests. They possessed little ability to regulate the society around them, and the laity had little instruction about the requirements of the Christian faith. Social custom had long undergone a diffuse influence from the ceremonial of the church, but the real impact of the gospel upon such vital institutions as marriage and warfare was limited. Indeed, the bishops had largely lost control of the personnel and property of the churches, which it was supposed to be their primary task to regulate. Lay lords commonly received the tithe, the charge of one-tenth of produce which in principle provided the basic revenue of the clergy, and they treated the local churches as personal possessions, selling and leasing them, and charging for their services, in the same way as they did for the village mill or oven. The characteristic feature of church order in the first half of the eleventh century was what the German historians have called *Eigenkirchentum*, a word which can best be rendered as the 'privatization' of churches. The old discipline had been superseded by a system of private rights, some held by laymen and others by clergy, but all perceived as the personal possession of their holders. The best ordered and most learned institutions were the great monasteries such as Monte Cassino, Fleury, and Cluny. These represented an alternative way of life to that of secular society, and claimed to embody in their brotherhood the principles which had animated the apostolic community at Jerusalem in the first days of the church; but the influence which they enjoyed was the result of esteem for their ritual rather than their teaching, and they were themselves struggling to keep their lands and endowments free of the encroaching disorder around them.

The Building of Christendom

The distinctive feature of the next two centuries was a sustained attempt to apply the principles of the gospel and of canon law

Islamic territories

Byzantine empire

—— frontier of the Western empire

+ archbishoprics
(the very small archbishoprics of southern Italy
and the Alps are not shown)

0   200   400 km

0 50 100 150 200 250 miles

NORWAY

SWEDEN

Trondheim

IRELAND

SCOTLAND

WALES

York

ENGLAND

London

Canterbury

DENMARK

Hamburg

Bremen

WENDS

POMERANIA

SAXONY

Magdeburg

Goslar

Gniezno

POLAND

Rouen

NORMANDY

Reims

Cologne

LORRAINE

Mainz

Worms

Trier

BOHEMIA

Paris

Tours

Sens

FRANCE

Bourges

Cluny

SUABIA

Salzburg

AUSTRIA

Gran

HUNGARY

Kalocsa

Bordeaux

Compostella

SPANISH KINGDOMS

Auch

Toulouse

Narbonne

Lyons

BURGUNDY

Arles

Aix

LOMBARDY

Milan

Genoa

Venice

Ravenna

Pisa

Florence

Roma

Cordoba

CORSICA

SARDINIA

Palermo

SICILY

WESTERN CHRISTENDOM IN 1050

to contemporary society: initially, in the so-called Gregorian reform, to the discipline of the clergy, and subsequently to the life of the laity as well. In an earlier chapter Robert Markus stressed how the Christians in a newly converted Roman empire accepted the conventional standards of pagan society and its pattern of education. In the high Middle Ages, the picture was very different. While careful attention had to be paid to the demands of influential lay nobles, the initiative lay with the ecclesiastical hierarchy, whose authority and training fitted them to apply a programme of Christianization. The design was the formation of Christendom, not in the sense of the initial conversion of its constituent kingdoms, but of the conscious elaboration of a programme which was to bring mankind under the law of Christ. Many of the new assumptions and institutions were to survive until the French revolution and even into the modern world. To historians of earlier generations they appeared inevitable, and to Catholic historians they also appeared right. It is only in our own age, which has seen the collapse of Christendom, that it has become possible to perceive that many issues were hard fought, and might have been differently resolved; and that much which has come to be accepted as part of the Christian heritage was not necessarily an expression of the gospel. Some modern Christians, as well as modern agnostics, dismiss with impatience the whole idea of Christendom. It has, writes Peter Levi, 'been something of a ginger-bread palace for some time, and now the gilt is off the ginger-bread. Christendom was a provincial, western and insular parody of the great civilized Roman empire which still haunted the imagination'.

Social changes 1050–1200

The attempt at Christianization was based in part on laws which had been formulated by the Fathers and by Carolingian reformers. It was therefore not wholly new, but its impact on Western Europe was much more profound than that of previous attempts. The explanation for this is to be found in the social changes which were taking place in many parts of the continent in the eleventh and twelfth centuries. Marc Bloch has called them 'the age of the great clearances', in which forests were opened to settlement, marshes drained, and the wastes colonized. Along with this demographic growth in the countryside went the expansion of cities, some of them a response to a new pattern of international trade which led to the emergence of the communes of Flanders and Italy as major economic and political powers. Cathedral schools grew and offered an advanced curriculum unknown since the classical age, and the more out-standing ones such as Paris, Bologna, and Oxford were by 1200 establishing their position as universities. All these changes were facilitated by a great increase in the circulation of money. Historians have spoken of a 'renaissance' or a 'great thaw' around 1100, in which new economic forces heralded a new culture. The economic changes, to which the initiative of the churches contributed a great deal, had profound and contra-dictory effects. The clearance of the forests opened the way to new types of monasteries outside the network of dues and rents characteristic of manorial society; it also tempted them to add field to field in a vast display of entrepreneurial ambition. The new learning made possible the formulation of policies to regulate the ethics of the laity, and also provided material for dissidents to challenge accepted values. The immediate effect of the greater use of money was to precipitate a crisis among those who were disturbed by the sale of church rights and sacraments, but in the longer term it made possible the creation of great buildings and major international movements.

Local Centres

The most striking feature of the new Western Christendom was the extent of local enterprise. New ideas emerged from the cities, from great monasteries, from schools and universities, and from the courts of nobles, all of which had considerable ability to protect their own members from outside authority. Initially, the forces of control and integration were weak. The coherence of Western European culture did not depend (as in the former Roman empire) upon central direction, nor even upon regulation at a national level, for with a few exceptions royal government was ineffective and intermittent in its application. The local creative forces were not monitored at the level of national politics but shaped by the persuasive force of great international movements which began to emerge in this period.

The Papal Reform Movement

Beginning from 1050, new organizations and attitudes achieved international acceptance throughout Western Europe. The most obvious was the general recognition of the authority of the Roman church. In the early eleventh century this had been solidly rooted in the Roman earth. The popes were from the Roman aristocracy and rarely travelled far from the city, the cardinals (a term not unique to Rome) were clergy whose function was to conduct the liturgy in the great basilicas, and the councils were purely for the region of Rome itself. The shrines of the apostles and the antiquity of its foundation gave Rome primacy over the churches of the West, but it intervened rarely in affairs north of the Alps. In 1046 the Emperor Henry III, on the way to Rome for his imperial coronation, presided over the synod of Sutri, where the existing pope, Gregory VI, was removed on a charge of corruption, and two other claimants to the office were condemned. Henry appointed a German bishop in his place. The precedent was to be decisive, for, with just one important exception, there was to be no pope from the city of Rome itself for eighty years. The name of the new pope, Clement II (1046–7), suggests a conscious attempt to renew the apostolic spirit of the days of Clement I, the successor of St Peter. However this may be, the new policy was spectacularly advanced by another German pope, the charismatic Leo IX (1049–54), who toured Europe holding councils and proclaiming the judgement of God on sinners, terrifying his hearers into repentance. The campaign was specifically directed to the reform of the priesthood, especially its purification from simony (the purchase for money of ecclesiastical office and ordination) and from cohabitation with women. It was a radical attack on the existing order, for the payment of fees and clerical marriage were accepted social custom. We must be careful not to modernize the reformers' policy, which was not intended to provide better training for the clergy or even, in an ordinary sense, to make them better men. It was a cultic ideal: God would not be pleased by worship, above all by the sacrifice of the mass, if it were offered by hands defiled by money and women. With a practical realism characteristic of medieval men, it was recognized that there would be no release from either unless the clergy were separated into distinctive societies living outside the lay world, and the creation of such apostolic communities was one of the major aims of the reformers. The whole programme was directed to the shaping of ordinary clergy by monastic norms, and it is therefore not surprising that, while monk-popes have been rare in history, all the popes were monks for almost fifty years after 1073, and monastic advisers were very influential in the whole history of the papal reformers.

The Conflict of Empire and Papacy 1076–1122

The separation of clergy from laity inherent in this programme inevitably created tension with lay rulers, for whom control of patronage within the church was a customary right, and this was increased when the reformers formed connections with groups such as the Patarini at Milan, who adopted violent and revolutionary methods in challenging established order and the position of the traditional clergy. The conflict exploded in the pontificate of Gregory VII (1073–85). Gregory was a Roman who had been prominent in the papal reform movement from its earliest days, and from him it has drawn its name 'the Gregorian reform'. He had a profound sense that Peter was speaking in his person, and was a man of passionate rectitude— a friend once described him as 'holy Satan'. The Milan affair was allowed by both sides to escalate, and in 1076 the German bishops withdrew obedience from Gregory, who replied with a sentence of excommunication and deposition against the Emperor Henry IV. It was an unprecedented action, directed against the son of the ruler who had reformed the papacy in 1046. Henry's spectacular submission in a meeting at Canossa in 1077 opened the hope of reconciliation, but by 1080 it was clear that the breach was permanent. Gregory recognized Rudolf of Suabia, the leader of the German political opposition, as anti-king, and Henry appointed the distinguished Archbishop Wibert of Ravenna as Clement III—a name which significantly recalled the events of 1046. The wide range of issues between the two powers eventually was narrowed to the specific question of lay investiture. Emperors and kings claimed the right to appoint bishops by granting to them ring and staff, the insignia of their office, whereas the popes regarded this as the prerogative of the church. It was only in 1122, at the Concordat of Worms, that the long dispute was ended in a compromise, which involved the emperor's renunciation of his right to invest bishops, but left him in control of many of the other imperial rights over the German church. Although the Roman church was still far from exercising detailed supervision over Western Christendom, the events of 1046–1122 had made it a champion of reforming interests and given it an international status which could not be ignored.

The New Monastic Orders

During the same period the structure of monasticism was changing. The Rule of St Benedict had seen each abbey as independently governed by its abbot. The first group of monasteries to diverge decisively from this model was Cluny, where the 'gentle tyrant', Abbot Hugh of Sémur (1049–1109), subjected to the mother house not only new foundations, but also ancient abbeys which were put under his jurisdiction. In principle, the whole community was part of Cluny, with only one abbot at its head, and by the time of Hugh's death there were daughter houses in Spain, England, and northern Italy, as well as France. In a sense Cluny was the first monastic order, but its approach to an international structure was taken much further by the Cistercians. At its foundation in 1098 Cîteaux must have appeared no different from many experimental houses of the time, but it emerged as one of the most distinctive religious forces in the twelfth century. Its first daughter house was established in 1112; by 1153 there were 344 abbeys in the Cistercian Order, and 530 by 1200, from Norway to Portugal and from Ireland to the eastern Mediterranean. Its development was shaped in the early years by its able English Abbot Stephen Harding (1109–34) and the brilliant Bernard, abbot of the daughter house of Clairvaux (1115–53). The Cistercians insisted on literal obedience to the Benedictine Rule, and gave the status of abbey to all their houses; but to this they added a common constitution, the 'Charter of Charity', a machinery of supervision of daughter houses by their founder-abbey, and an annual general chapter which legislated for the whole order. The Cistercians represent the ultimate success-story among the new orders of the twelfth century, many of which spread widely, while observing common customs and having some form of central government. These orders include Fontevraud (founded by Robert of Arbrissel in 1101) and Savigny (founded 1112, united with the Cistercians 1147). Alongside these monastic departures were families of regular canons, who accepted the rather different Rule of St Augustine. They took many forms, and included the Premonstratensians (founded by Norbert of Xanten 1120), who were virtually monks in their way of life; canons in Austria and eastern Germany who for a time fulfilled the ideal of providing clerical communities for general pastoral oversight; and the Victorines, whose mother house had an impressive tradition of scholarship. Such regular canons were in contrast with the communities of canons who followed the old Carolingian life-style, which permitted private property; such 'secular' canons, as they came to be known, continued to form the bodies of clergy in most cathedrals. One feature restricted the effectiveness of the monastic orders: they were based on the principle of stability, by which a monk was supposed to remain in the same house throughout his life. To some limited extent the canons escaped from this restriction, and two major orders in the twelfth century were largely free of it: the Hospitallers (first general papal privilege 1113) and the Templars (1139). Both were founded for the service of pilgrims in the Holy Land, the first primarily for social and medical care and the second for defence, and both allowed for some transfer of members of the order as they were required.

The Crusades

Another force on the international scene was the crusade movement. In the course of the eleventh century, emergent powers in the western Mediterranean committed themselves to campaigns against Islam and used them to establish their moral and political authority. These forces included Pisa, the Normans of southern Italy, the rising monarchies of Christian Spain, and the French, who were showing an increasing interest in intervention in Spain and Italy; and the recovery of Spain and Sicily from Muslim rule was adopted as papal policy. When appeals were received from Constantinople and Jerusalem for protection against Turkish oppression, they were heard by Urban II, a French pope who already had close links with holy war in the western Mediterranean; and at the Council of Clermont in 1095 he proclaimed a great expedition for the relief of Jerusalem, which we know as the First Crusade. For several decades, the Western effort in the East was crowned with success. Jerusalem was captured in 1099, and by 1153 the whole Syrian coastline from Ascalon to Antioch was in Latin hands. It was only with the unification of Islam under Nureddin, and still more his successor Saladin, that Jerusalem was recovered for Muslim rule in 1187. Europeans expressed an increasing sense of common identity, which seems to have been forged particularly by the First Crusade. Its chroniclers use a terminology which, although it was not completely new, had been rare in the past; for the first time people were regularly describing themselves as 'westerners' or 'Christians' or as fellow members of *Christianitas*, a word which means both Christianity and Christendom and which came into common use at this time.

Authority and Splendour

The hierarchy was not shy about proclaiming the glory of God and the dignity of his ordained ministers. Triumphalism was the besetting temptation of the medieval church as secularism is that of the modern. It is most obvious to us in the splendour of the great buildings. At the beginning of our period, the finest were monastic churches, in particular Abbot Desiderius's new building at Monte Cassino (consecrated in a splendid ceremony in 1071) and Hugh's third church at Cluny (begun 1088 and completed about 1133), the largest church so far built for Christian worship. Neither of these survives, but there are many examples of the architectural campaign inaugurated by the Normans in England with the profits of their conquest in 1066. Another great wave was initiated after the rebuilding of St Denis by Abbot Suger (1122–51), where for the first time the pointed arch was consistently used in a structural way. The new 'Gothic' style, to use the modern term, was perfected in the cathedrals of northern France, such as Laon, Senlis, Notre Dame Paris, and Chartres, and from this region it spread to most parts of Western Europe. The churches provided a setting for worship, a processional space, and a home for the relics of the saints. Only fragments of the treasury of any great church remain from the Middle Ages, but there is enough to give a glimpse of the wealth which was once accumulated there. Precious metals were used in profusion for reliquaries and altar furnishings, service-books were magnificently written and bound, and the making of vestments was a major art form, especially in England, whose *opus anglicanum* was in demand all over the Continent.

The Growth of Papal Government in the Twelfth Century

By the end of the twelfth century the spiritual leadership which the popes had established was being developed into control over the affairs of the church. The first steps towards this had been taken long before, when Leo IX had brought northern reformers with him and appointed them as cardinal bishops to act as advisers. By 1130 the college of cardinals had emerged as administrative assistants of the popes, hearing judicial cases, representing the Roman church as legates, and taking the lead in the election of popes. Routine administration was in the hands of the papal curia or court, which had replaced the old urban administration of Rome with offices borrowed from the north, including the chamberlain who was responsible for finances and the chancellor in charge of the writing-office. With the appearance of a definitive collection of the old church law, the *Concordance of Discordant Canons* of Gratian (completed *c.*1140), there was a standard reference book for ecclesiastical tribunals. The following generation saw the rapid development of a system of appeals to Rome, with judges delegate hearing cases in their own countries by papal authority, and under Pope Alexander III (1159–81) the curia played an important part in standardizing the law by the issue of innumerable decretal letters for the guidance of judges in difficult cases. By the end of the century collections of these decretals were being made, pointing the way to the authoritative collection of Gregory IX (1226–39) which provided a sequel to Gratian and a definitive statement of the new canon law.

While the Roman church was expanding its influence among other churches, it was struggling to preserve its freedom of action against the empire. The Concordat of Worms had initiated a period of co-operation, but the brilliant Hohenstaufen emperor, Frederick I Barbarossa (1152–90), returned to a much more vigorous affirmation of imperial rights over the German church and over territories in Italy claimed by both empire and papacy. It was only with the alliance of the Lombard cities and the kingdom of Sicily that Alexander III was able to maintain himself in power against a series of imperialist anti-popes. The papacy was in even greater danger when the Emperor Henry VI succeeded in uniting Sicily to the empire and thus enforcing Hohenstaufen control throughout the whole peninsula. It was the death of Henry VI in 1197 which opened the way for the election of one of the youngest popes in the history of the church, a man of great ability who was able to lead the medieval papacy to its most impressive achievements.

Innocent III (1198–1216)

Lothar of Segni was the son of a noble Roman family, a Paris graduate and the author of a series of esteemed theological works. He was elected pope as Innocent III (1198–1216) at the age of 37. Innocent was famous for his skills as a judge—a contemporary satirist nicknamed him 'Solomon III'—but his greatest impact on papal thinking lay in the import of new ideas into canon law. For the exposition of papal rights in his letters Innocent drew from many sources: theology, rhetoric, and history were all laid under tribute. The pope was presented as vicar of Christ on earth and as Melchizedek, the Old Testament figure who was both king and priest; he was said to enjoy 'fullness of power', in contrast with the partial authority of all other bishops; and it was argued that the Roman church had shown its authority over the empire, which it had transferred from East to West. Innocent was not directly claiming to exercise the rights of the secular power, and accepted that kings

ITALY IN THE THIRTEENTH CENTURY

had a jurisdiction which was separate from that of the church. In practice, however, his policies involved intervention in political affairs on a scale which had not been seen in the past. The death of Henry VI had released the Roman church from the severe pressure to which he had been subjecting it, and had led to a disputed election to the empire. This freed Innocent's hands to demand the 'restitution' of papal rights in central Italy and Sicily, and thereby to become the founder of the Papal State in its later form; and to formulate an aggressive statement of the rights of the Roman church in the election of an emperor. Important decretal letters defined the right of the pope to intervene in secular causes 'by reason of sin' and 'on occasion' (*casualiter*). He actively cultivated the special relationship with those kingdoms which had in the past accepted the Roman church as overlord, and made an important addition to the list with the submission of John of England in 1214. All of this was ammunition for later canonists and popes, especially the outstanding lawyer Sinibald of Fieschi, who became pope as Innocent IV (1243–54). There were in fact few aspects of the life of Christendom which were not touched by the genius of Innocent III. One of his priorities was the crusading movement. After the Third Crusade (1189–92) had failed to recover Jerusalem, Innocent preached the Fourth, which diverted to Constantinople in the hope of securing Byzantine assistance and tragically ended in 1204 by storming the city and establishing a fragile Latin empire on the ruins of the Greek one. The Fifth Crusade was in an advanced state of preparation at Innocent's death. Equally important to him was the reform of the Western church, and to this end he brought to Rome ideas learned at Paris and made them the basis of a new ideal of pastoral ministry. Connected with reform was his determination to repress heresy and his encouragement of new movements such as those of Francis and Dominic. In many ways the culmination of the medieval papacy was the Fourth Lateran Council which assembled in November 1215 to deliberate upon all these and other matters. It was the largest ecumenical gathering the church had yet seen, with over 400 bishops and 800 abbots and other representative clergy. The council was dominated by two concerns which ran throughout the policy of Innocent III: crusade and reform. Its numerous decrees contained the plans for the Fifth Crusade, attempted a settlement of the disorders which had arisen from the Albigensian Crusade, and regulated the affairs of the Greek church, which had been subjected to Rome by the crusaders of 1204. Detailed provisions were made for the instruction and reform of the clergy, as well as the discipline of the laity (a matter to which we return later). Many of the decisions reflected the influence of Paris theology upon Innocent, for example in their strongly pastoral concerns and in such practical details as the abolition of the traditional ordeals and a revision of the law of marriage.

The Quest for Alternatives: The Monks

It would be a mistake to see the history of the medieval church as the simple assertion of authority by the hierarchy, restrained only by the resistance of lay powers whose customary position was threatened. It was the vocation of the monks to live the apostolic life in community, and therefore to pursue a radical alternative to the normal way of life of the laity and secular clergy. The new orders of the twelfth century represented this alternative in a much sharper form than the older monasticism. In Cluniac and Benedictine houses, the best-trained monks were those who had entered as boys, had been fully instructed in the complications of chant and ceremonial, and had seen secular society only from the cloister. The Cistercians and Premonstratensians, by contrast, were recruited from among adults, men who had lived in society and rejected its values. They conducted a polemic against the affluent society in the new cities: 'I will not dwell in cities,' declared Norbert of Xanten, 'but rather in deserts and uncultivated places'. Most of them were equally firm in their rejection of the new pattern of learning which was emerging in the growing schools (the future universities) and in their criticism of the violence of the aristocracy. This critique of contemporary society was, at least in part, shared by the leaders of the church, but monastic reformers went beyond the criticism of lay society to express their disquiet about the role of the church. Bernard of Clairvaux was acid about its wealth and display, and demanded (at least for monks) a strict simplicity of worship. When a Cistercian pupil of his became pope as Eugenius III (1145–53), Bernard dedicated to him a treatise *On Consideration*, which recommended guidelines for the conduct of the papal office and was particularly critical of the amount of judicial business which was already beginning to dominate the life of the curia. More was heard at Rome, he complained, of the laws of Justinian than of the law of Christ. The same complaint was made by a South German regular canon, Gerhoh of Reichersberg, who was sceptical about the compromise which had been made in the Concordat of Worms, was hostile to all individual ownership of ecclesiastical benefices, and complained that the title of the Roman curia (which was increasingly used as the standard term for the papal administration) was a secular one without precedent in the writings of former popes. Although in a different spirit, similar criticisms were heard from the humanists who had been trained in the schools. The greatest of all, John of Salisbury, commented at the Third Lateran Council in 1179 that there were too many new rules: 'What we need to do is to proclaim and strive for the keeping of the gospel'.

Popular Preaching

A different, and more serious, problem was presented by preachers who appealed widely to lay opinion. The rise of the cities now offered an audience for religious controversy, and the appeal had begun largely among radical supporters of the reforming papacy such as the Patarini at Milan, the Vallombrosan monks who at Florence accused the bishop of simony and secured his removal in 1068 after a sensational ordeal by fire, and the papalist preachers who attacked Henry IV publicly in the market places. These denunciations by Gregorian champions were naturally resented by the local clergy, and there was a scandalous episode at Cambrai in 1077 when a preacher named Ramihrd was lynched by the populace with the collusion of the bishop's officers. In Flanders and northern France around 1100 there was a great deal of popular preaching by hermits or itinerants such as Robert of Arbrissel and Vitalis of Savigny. They caused some anxiety to the bishops, who were eager to persuade them to settle with their followers in decent monastic stability, but there was little inclination to treat them as heretics and drive them outside the church. Indeed, around 1100 the word 'heresy' primarily meant simony, the 'simoniac heresy' against which so many reforming efforts were being directed; there was little sense of heresy as a false system of belief and virtually no machinery for investigating or combating it. That was to change, but only slowly.

The Rise of Heresy

In the first half of the twelfth century we can discover a small number of preachers who began to attack devotion to the crucifix and other images, to criticize infant baptism, and to reject the masses of corrupt priests, as well as protesting against the privileges of the clergy and the property of the church. Tanchelm of Antwerp received huge popular support with a message of this kind. Henry of Lausanne, a former monk, persuaded the people of Le Mans in 1116 to boycott their clergy, and subsequently went to preach in southern France, where Peter of Bruys was also active. It soon became necessary to turn some heavy artillery onto such preachers: the famous abbot of Cluny, Peter the Venerable, wrote a tract against Peter of Bruys about 1139, and a few years later Abbot Bernard of Clairvaux visited the south of France for a preaching campaign. Such 'heresiarchs' (this was the favourite term for them) may well be seen as extreme Gregorians, who had become convinced that the existing church was ineradicably soiled with the corruptions against which the papal reformers were campaigning. But in 1143 a group was discovered at Cologne which held to doctrines which, they said, had been faithfully preserved in Greece. They refused meat and all other products of intercourse, and observed a strict division between 'elect' and 'hearers'. They are the first clear evidence of influence from the dualist heretics of the Balkans, and the first known Cathars. Under a variety of names, they spread rapidly, and in the course of the 1160s we find them in many parts of northern Europe. They became firmly established in two regions: Languedoc, or southern France, where the heretics were usually called the Albigensians, and Lombardy. There the local nobility and the great cities were effectively independent of any higher political authority, and some of them were sympathetic to the Cathar cause or saw no advantage in persecuting them. Well before 1200 there were Cathar bishoprics, whose communities could freely meet for worship. The Cathars' beliefs echoed those which, long before, St Augustine had encountered among the Manichaeans. Matter was seen as inherently evil, the creation of the devil; the work of God was the universe of souls, and the path to salvation was their release from sinful flesh. It followed that the Catholic doctrine of the incarnation of Christ was a monstrous perversion, and the crucifixion an illusion, since the Saviour could not have been contaminated by participation in the material world. Sexual intercourse was inherently evil, as tending to continue the natural order, and so was the consumption of meat, milk, and eggs, which were the product of intercourse. The sacraments were rejected, and replaced by a simple act of admission called the *consolamentum*. Those who received it were enrolled in the ranks of the 'perfects' and were bound by the full rigours of the Cathar ethic. Their followers or 'hearers' were obliged only to support and reverence them and aimed to receive the *consolamentum* on their deathbed. It is difficult to determine how many people were influenced by Catharism: it may be that there was some element of 'reds under the bed', and that the situation was not as critical as some Catholics feared. But there were certainly reasons for alarm, and the church responded in two quite different ways.

The Reaction to Heresy: Poverty and Preaching

One of them was the development of a rival system of popular preaching. There were problems about this, because monks, the obvious candidates, were bound to their abbeys by the rule of stability. The life of poverty and preaching appealed increasingly to uneducated Catholics, but the hierarchy was worried about the problems of discipline which this implied. When Valdes, a rich merchant of Lyons, decided about 1174 to give away his goods and devote himself to the apostolic life, Alexander III at first showed considerable sympathy. Valdes' belief was orthodox, and his followers saw themselves as an answer to the Cathar menace; but they broke with the hierarchy over their insistence on preaching on the basis of vernacular translations of the Bible. The Waldensians eventually became a widespread movement, separate from the church, and survived until the Reformation. The fear of unauthorized preaching led the hierarchy to keep such groups at arm's length until Innocent III began a more liberal approach.

Dominicans and Franciscans

It was a crucial decision, because it enabled him to welcome and guide two men who were to have a major historical impact. Dominic, a Spanish regular canon, had encountered the Catharist heresy in southern France, and had created a small house of preachers to combat it. It was only in 1217, close to the end of his life, that he took the important decision to disperse this group, sending them to work in Paris and Bologna and insisting on a rigorous regime of poverty. Within a few years the Dominican Order, equipped with its highly sophisticated constitution of 1228, had houses in many parts of Europe and was leading the struggle against heresy. Even more spectacular in its spread was the Franciscan Order, the foundation of a man utterly unlike Dominic. Francis was a layman, born into a wealthy family of Assisi. A charismatic personality of tremendous charm, he devoted himself to a life of complete poverty and alternated his ministry between the crowded cities and his beloved hermitages. His devotion to the crucified Christ was intense, and culminated, shortly before his death in 1226, in his receiving the stigmata, the marks of the crucifixion on his hands and side. It is hard to imagine any more improbable founder of an order, for Francis had a talent for disorganization and was reluctant even to produce a rule. The attractive force of his personality created a vast literature of history and legend, whereas we know remarkably little about Dominic as a man; and it was this personality which inspired the foundation of a very numerous order. One of the first Franciscans about 1260 looked back over forty years of mission, and remarked, 'when I consider my own lowly state, and that of my companions who were sent with me to Germany, and when I consider the present state and glory of our order, I am astounded and praise the divine mercy in my heart'. Francis's ministry was not designed, as Dominic's was, for the fight against heresy, but it served the purpose well, with its commitment to popular teaching and its insistence on obedience to the pope and bishops. The little brothers or 'friars minor' were a much more varied order than Dominic's order of preachers. Numerically, the majority of its members were Italian, very many of them laymen, whereas in northern Europe it attracted scholars and theologians much more akin to the membership of the Dominicans.

The Reaction to Heresy: Crusades

The acquisition of an effective force of popular persuaders was important in combating heresy, but it was unlikely that persuasion would be enough, and the church sought also for means of coercion. As early as the Third Lateran Council in 1179 the possibility of directing a crusade against the Albigensian heretics of Languedoc had been envisaged, but it was only under Innocent III, after the failure of a series of preaching missions, that it was finally launched. In the summer of 1209 an army of northern French barons and bishops marched against the southern heretics and captured Béziers, where there was an appalling massacre, and Carcassonne. It was the beginning of a long and bitter war, as the northern invaders attempted to establish their dominance while the southerners (very many of whom were Catholic) fiercely defended their possessions. Partial peace was only restored in 1229. At this stage the struggle against heresy could hardly be regarded as a success. Little had been achieved in northern Italy, where the cities were resistant to ecclesiastical authority, and even in southern France it was difficult to discover leading Cathars and their sympathizers.

The Reaction to Heresy: Inquisition

Gregory IX therefore embarked on a new initiative. In 1231 he issued a general condemnation of heresy in his bull *Excommunicamus*, and followed it by a series of commissions of inquisition, given mostly to Dominican friars, in Germany, northern France, Languedoc, and Italy. The inquisition has come to occupy such a role in European demonology that we must be careful to keep it in proportion. It was not an institution, but a series of inquiries. In some countries these were so resented that they were not continued, and the surviving records indicate that the proportion of executions was not high. Action seems to have been concentrated on the 'perfects' among the Cathars, while the rank and file were more gently treated. Perhaps the most significant feature of these inquiries was the way the procedure suspended the normal rights of defendants, which in medieval law were very extensive. They were a response to an emergency, but a response which marked an important stage in the development from the easygoing ways of the past to a regime of repression. The same tightening of control was evident towards the Jews, who previously had lived on relatively comfortable terms in the towns of which they formed a part. The first major persecution came in the attacks on Jews in the Rhineland at the time of the First Crusade, and popular hostility grew steadily during the twelfth century. In the thirteenth, governments were joining in the repression: the Fourth Lateran Council required Jews to wear distinctive dress, Jewish books were burned, and official expulsions began—the Jews were banished from England in 1290 and were not to return until the seventeenth century.

Scholasticism

It is striking, however, that in the Middle Ages the exposition of doctrine was no longer, as in the past, primarily the responsibility of bishops or monks. They had been superseded as theologians by a new force in the church: the masters, who taught in the cathedral schools of the twelfth century and the universities of the thirteenth. For a long time, Paris was supreme as a centre of theology, although its character changed from one generation to another. The great Peter Abelard (d. 1142) covered wide ranges of doctrine, from the Trinity to the sacraments, in a style which was both speculative and humanist. By the time that Paris theology was dominated by Peter the Chanter (d. 1197), the emphasis was strongly pastoral, with a concentration on preaching and practical ethics. It was this form of theology which the young Innocent III took back from Paris to Rome, which shaped the pastoral reforms of the Fourth Lateran Council, and which attracted the Franciscans and Dominicans, in the first half of the thirteenth century, to make Paris their major training centre. No sooner had they settled there than the focus of theology began to change once more. The works of Aristotle on physics and metaphysics had been previously unknown in the Latin West. They arrived primarily through the Arab world, and with them were translated commentaries by Arabic Aristotelians, notably Averroes. The arrival of this material stimulated interest in natural science in the West, but it also had a dramatic impact upon theology, because Averroes had developed still further the materialistic basis of Aristotle's ideas. It was difficult to see how belief in the eternity of matter could be reconciled, for example, with the biblical view of creation. The conclusions of reason now seemed contrary to the teachings of faith, and some Christian Averroists adopted the conclusion that what was true in philosophy was not necessarily true in theology. The reconciliation between Catholic belief and the new learning was largely the work of two great Dominican thinkers, Albert the Great (d. 1280) and Thomas Aquinas (d. 1274). Much of Thomas's theology was traditional in character, but (as his biographer observed) he 'discovered new methods and employed new systems of proofs'. In particular he argued that, distinct from the supernatural order of grace, there was a natural order which could be studied by reason, but which itself pointed towards God: there were natural proofs of the existence of God, and natural grounds for ethics. The Thomist solution, however, was far from finding universal acceptance. Thomas was criticized in his own lifetime, and in the fourteenth century his philosophy was largely replaced in the schools by the teaching of the Franciscans Duns Scotus and William of Ockham. It was only in the post-Reformation period that Thomism began increasingly to be the accepted philosophy of the Catholic Church.

Personal Religion

The church of the earlier Middle Ages had placed weight, not on personal piety, but on the solemn offering of the liturgy. Even the Gregorian reform did not radically change this situation. It stressed above all the need for priests to have hands clean from women and money if they were to offer the mass acceptably to God. It did, however, have important implications for lay religion. The Gregorians looked to sympathizers among the laity to help them carry through their programme, and the very fact that they distinguished so sharply between clergy and laity raised questions about the proper function of lay people in the service of God. Moreover, in an increasingly diversified society, new lay groups were emerging and formulating customs to govern their behaviour. Lay religion in the twelfth century was above all a 'status' religion, prescribing the ethics and attitudes suitable for each rank in society. It is a curious misunderstanding of the medieval church that it is often thought to have been indifferent to social welfare. In fact, the quality of social thinking (although their ideas were naturally not the same as ours) compares very favourably with that in the modern church. One of its most important features was the careful definition of the law of marriage, which was seen as the sacrament which constituted the lay condition. While marriage was rejected for the priestly order, it was seen as the divinely appointed condition for the laity. Some of the characteristics of the new concept of marriage survived until our own century, including the prohibition of divorce and the insistence that marriage is a voluntary relationship which can be entered only by the consent of both parties. For each social rank an ethic was provided, including those whose activities in the past had been regarded as questionable. For the military classes there was a ceremony of admission to the order of knighthood and rules which the good knight should observe, including fidelity to his lord and protection of those in need. There was an increasing concern to provide norms for merchants; by the thirteenth century moralists were defining the circumstances in which loans might be made at interest, in spite of the clear biblical prohibitions of usury. The upper classes of the new cities were urged to provide hospitals, leper houses, and schools for their fellow citizens. Guilds took pride in sponsoring windows for the great churches with their emblems as vintners or butchers, although an offer from the prostitutes of Paris to provide a window dedicated to Mary Magdalen was firmly declined. This development was reflected in the emergence, late in the twelfth century, of sermons *ad status*, addressed specifically to knights, crusaders, merchants, housewives, and peasants. It was an approach which reflected the realities of contemporary society.

New Patterns of Devotion

At the same time new patterns of devotion were emerging. Among the Cistercians, we find a more intense devotion to the crucified Lord; Aelred of Rievaulx thought that the crucifix was the only appropriate decoration for a monastery church. There was a much greater output of lyrical hymns in the first person (a form of piety which had barely existed in the past), and a devotion to the Blessed Virgin, seen as a gracious lady and a loving mother. This more gentle and reflective religion can best be documented for monastic communities, but there are reasons for supposing that it also was influencing the lay nobles who were the patrons, and often the close relations, of the monks. The crucifix was becoming a prominent feature of church decoration, replacing the Christ in majesty which dominated earlier buildings, and it was a crucifix in a new style. The Lord was no longer shown, upright and majestic, clothed in purple and reigning from the tree: now, a dying man was offered for the loyalty and compassion of the beholders. And, although the matter is difficult to establish, it was probably in the twelfth century that a new position of prayer was widely adopted, kneeling with the hands together—the position of a man doing homage to his personal lord.

Most of these twelfth-century changes applied to the privileged classes. The thirteenth century showed a much greater awareness of the needs of the faithful as a whole. This was in part because of the ministry of the friars in bringing new devotions to the lower classes—Francis, for example, began the practice of making a Christmas crib to illustrate the story of the Nativity. But the concern spread beyond the friars, and had begun before they were really in existence. The programme of the Fourth Lateran Council in 1215 was an attempt to reconstruct the pastoral approach of the churches of the West and to bring some understanding of the faith to the majority of its members. Innocent III brought some of the ideas for his 'pastoral revolution', as it has been called, from his studies in Paris. They were centred above all upon preaching and the confessional. The decree *Omnis Utriusque Sexus* required that every adult Christian should make his or her confession and receive communion at least once each year. The implications were wide: for the first time there was a mechanism designed to take self-examination and counselling into every castle and village in Christendom. The council also approved a new creed, reflecting recent theological developments, intended to provide material for the teaching of the laity. A programme of this sort required a systematic attempt to improve the standard of the country clergy, for few of them had the skills to give advice in the confessional or to preach. Accordingly, there was a drive to improve the provision of clerical education, and a demand for the regular assembly of synods in which clergy could be briefed about their duties. In France and England energetic bishops produced synodal books or pamphlets for circulation among the clergy, with details of the sort of instruction which they should provide for their flocks. It must be said that much of this was very basic; a standard requirement was the Lord's Prayer, the apostles' creed, and the 'Hail Mary'. In the same way, we must not think of confession as providing counselling of an elevated kind, but rather as an organ of social control, which helped to ensure that the laity performed the duties appropriate to their station. Yet there were some bishops, like Robert Grosseteste of Lincoln (1235–53), who expected more of clergy and laity, and whose briefing covered a wide range of the basic features of the Christian faith; and, however elementary the standards which were being applied, it was important that a serious attempt was being made to train clergy for the effective instruction of the laity and not simply for the performance of certain ritual functions. The church was being pointed in a direction which it was to follow for many centuries.

Popular Religion

It is, however, another question how far this teaching reached the people for whom it was designed. It is a sad fact that little people leave no records, and we have only very limited information about the religious perceptions of ordinary people. Almost certainly, Christianization was more advanced in the cities than in the countryside. Town-dwellers could hear sermons, would receive the ministry of a house of friars and a substantial body of other clergy, and had the opportunity to join a professional or charitable guild; and we know that some laymen learnt from the friars a deep and genuine piety. While there were churches in every sizeable settlement in most of Western Europe, the country clergy would be few in number and, in spite of the efforts of the Fourth Lateran Council, were often ignorant and undisciplined. Moreover, in areas with a small population, villagers might be isolated: we hear of one hamlet where they only knew it was a saint's day when the old man who made it his hobby put his red shoes on. Ignorance of the formal content of the faith was general. It is far from certain that the faithful knew the three simple formularies enjoined by councils, and there were cases where the congregation had learned the 'Our Father' in Latin and did not know what it meant. It may also be unsafe to assume that ordinary laymen were regular attenders at weekly worship. We shall perhaps be closer to the truth if we cease to think in terms of Sunday worshippers with a good basic instruction in the modern manner, and see popular religion as a system of ceremonies and stories for great occasions.

Ceremonies and Stories

Certainly, the churches had marked out the local geography with a network of ceremonies. Processions (some of which were obligatory 'church parades' for the parishioners) went from parishes to the old mother church from which they had been founded. Rogationtide processions toured the fields, and on major festivals there were great processions through the cities, with guilds and heads of families taking part. In sickness a family would have recourse to the local saint's shrine, or travel even further afield. The ceremonial at one of the great shrines would have been immensely impressive. Participation in such processions and attendance at the ceremonies would occupy an important part of the religious activity of ordinary people. They would also know something of the Christian story. Writers in the past have often assumed that the imagination of medieval men was filled with a mixture of the gospel and surviving pagan legends left from a distant past, but we now recognize that the reality was far more complicated. The church generated its own legends, and Jacques le Goff has argued for the extensive reshaping of European folklore in the course of the twelfth century. A story of the taming of a fierce dragon by the gentleness of St Martha, for example, looks very like an adaptation of the 'Tarasque', the traditional dragon of Tarascon, to take account of the discovery of the body of the saint there in 1187. Sometimes there were startling confusions of motifs. An inquiry in the thirteenth century near Lyons into the cult of St Guinefort, who turned out to be no other than a holy greyhound, seems to reveal a combination of a Breton saint, a holy well, the custom of child exposure, and a classical legend (was this last a sermon illustration which had gone wrong?). Almost all the major Christian festivals had been complicated by legends and additional stories. The modern celebration of Christmas, with its three kings, deep midwinter, animals, gifts, and fir trees, preserves the flavour of this medieval mixture; but at that time all the great mysteries had suffered similar elaborations. For most people to be a Christian meant to participate in processions and ceremonies and to listen to the stories in their extended and mythical form.

Reaction

The first half of the thirteenth century was the golden age of papal power. Almost all the initiatives which went towards building up a Christian civilization, if they had not originated with the Roman church, had been shaped and approved by it. The crusades, pastoral reform, the friars, the inquisition, all bore the papal stamp. But the great experiment of a Christendom whose culture was directed by the clergy was showing signs of critical strain. If there was any one decision which brought the whole edifice into ruin, it was the concentration of the successors of Innocent III upon the conflict with the Hohenstaufen in Italy. Not that there was anything new in the defence of the papal political position: it had largely caused the conflict between Alexander III and Frederick Barbarossa, and Innocent III's policy of 'restitution' in the Papal State and his insistence upon papal rights in the empire and Sicily had affirmed the importance of these as a central concern of the Roman church. When Frederick II attempted to renew the union of Sicily and the empire, he was opposed by the popes with increasing violence. Gregory IX excommunicated him and from 1239 onwards extended crusading privileges to those who joined in fighting him, and redirected finances levied for the crusade to the struggle with the emperor. Innocent IV continued the policy, and even the death of Frederick in 1250 did not bring peace, for the popes continued to use the resources of the church to remove the viper brood of Hohenstaufen from the kingdom of Sicily; a policy which resulted in the conquest of the country by Charles of Anjou, of the Capetian royal family, in 1268 and an important step in the direction of a French supremacy in Italy. It was a disastrous misjudgement to give complete priority to the attack on the Hohenstaufen in papal policy, but we must also recognize that behind this error lay a deteriorating situation.

The old order was being challenged by the failure of the crusades, the failure of church reform, and the rise of the nation states.

The Failure of the Crusades

None of the expeditions to the East had succeeded in reversing the loss of Jerusalem, and the attacks on Egypt led by the legate Pelagius (1217–21) and King Louis IX of France (1249–50) continued the story of failure. The ignominious defeat of the expedition led by Louis, whom many contemporaries regarded as a saint, caused a particularly sharp reaction in the West, and gave rise to the conviction that God could not look after his own. The impression was confirmed when Louis died on his second crusade under the walls of Tunis. Louis's was the last major expedition to Asia, and in 1291 Acre, the last foothold in Syria, was lost to the Muslims. At much the same time, hopes which had been entertained of successes in the mission field opened in Asia by the creation of the Mongol empire proved illusory when the Mongol rulers adopted Islam, the religion of most of their subjects. The only real success of the crusading effort in the thirteenth century had been in 1229 when Frederick II, using diplomacy not war, had secured the cession of Jerusalem, although only on a transient basis, for the city was lost again in 1244. The failure of the crusades was ultimately due to military difficulties: it was impossible to achieve a decisive success against determined opposition at such an enormous distance. Public opinion, however, tended to blame the pope and the clergy. The Roman church appeared to be directing crusades almost everywhere except to Jerusalem: against the Albigensians, against the Greeks, and, worst of all, against the Hohenstaufen, at the very time when all available resources should have been made available to St Louis's expedition. Western Europeans did not give up the idea of crusading altogether, but significantly it was seen as a project which might be undertaken under the leadership of the expanding kingdom of France.

The Failure of Reform

A further failure was the weakening in the attempt to secure pastoral reform which had been spearheaded by the Fourth Lateran Council and the friars. To be sure, this achieved a good deal: the friars proved to be very popular preachers, and English and French bishops worked to raise the standard of the lower clergy and to provide themselves with efficient administrations. But success would have demanded the dedication of huge resources and a rigorous system of discipline. Medieval law was always kind to defendants; the general correction of abuses would have required emergency action, of the sort directed by the inquisition into heresy, applied on an enormous scale. In Germany, with a tradition of highly political bishops, and in southern and central Italy, where the small dioceses meant that there was in effect no level of administration with wide responsibilities, the secular church did little to support the efforts of the friars. In the event, the friars themselves produced serious problems for the papacy. Their preaching and counselling raised angry protests from local clergy about the invasion of their proper functions, as a series of conflicting papal decisions struggled to define the proper limits of the friars' ministry. The issues were only resolved by Boniface VIII's bull *Super Cathedram* in 1298, and by that time developments in the Franciscan Order were giving rise to still more acute difficulties. The radicals among them, influenced by the prophetic teaching of Abbot Joachim of Fiore (d. 1202), claimed that a truly spiritual church was now to supersede the existing one, and insisted on observing the rule of poverty with full rigour. At first the Roman curia sympathized with the moderate 'spirituals', but the situation changed when they claimed that Christ himself had renounced the use of all property. The implications of this doctrine for the pope, as the vicar of Christ, were alarming, and it was denounced as a heresy by John XXII in 1323. There followed a period of alienation between the papacy and the majority of Franciscans, whose leaders denounced the pope as a heretic and formed an alliance with his political opponents.

Papal Provisions

The original papal reforming policy also became entangled
with the need for the Roman church to exploit the resources of
the Western church as a whole. The problem of an international
government without visible means of support was a genuine
one; taxation was needed to sustain the crusade effort, and
appointments to provide for the staff of the curia. Popes
accordingly began to claim the right to appoint their own
nominees to profitable posts, especially as canons of cathedrals.
Such appointments or 'letters of provision', as they were called,
began to flow from Rome in great numbers. Reforming bishops
found that the resources of their own churches were being
deflected to maintain men who at best were absentee scholars
or administrators, and at worst were relatives of the pope and
cardinals. These were real difficulties in the way of reform, and
they were made far worse by the political conflict with the
Hohenstaufen. The political disorder in Germany and Italy
made pastoral improvement impossible, and Innocent IV, under
whom the conflict with Frederick II was at its height, resorted
to purely political (and scandalous) episcopal appointments in
Germany, and to an uncontrolled escalation in the numbers of
provisions. His great Council of Lyons in 1245, when compared
with the Fourth Lateran Council, is indicative of a great
change. It was devoted to measures against the Mongol threat
and, even more, to the conflict with the emperor; it enacted
some important judicial reforms, but no pastoral improvements at all. For the first time, in our whole period, the
Roman church had completely ceased to be an embodiment of
aspirations for reform.

National Monarchies

Behind these problems lay a still more intractable one. At first
sight the thirteenth century saw a great victory of the papacy
over the empire. The Hohenstaufen family was destroyed, the
union of Sicily with the empire cancelled, and imperial authority

virtually restricted to Germany, which itself had fragmented into a number of great lordships. The triumph was only apparent, and was undone by the rise of the nation state. It must not be supposed, of course, that royal power was a newcomer on the medieval scene. Emperors and kings had always been seen as having a God-given authority. In a limited number of regions, effective monarchies had restricted the power of the churches. The Norman kings of Sicily had acted as papal legates within their kingdom, and the power of English monarchs to control ecclesiastical affairs was impressive throughout most of the eleventh and twelfth centuries. The most striking clash between the English crown and the church was the quarrel between King Henry II and Thomas Becket, archbishop of Canterbury. Thomas had been a close companion of the king, and royal chancellor, but once he was appointed archbishop in 1162 he emerged as a fierce supporter of the privileges of the clergy. He resisted the attempts of the king to assert the power of the royal courts over the clergy and ecclesiastical rights, and in particular the claim that clergy found guilty by the bishop of major crimes should be handed to the lay power for punishment. The precise issues were technical, and could almost certainly have been resolved by sensible negotiation; but the two former friends had become bitter enemies, the one angry at insults to the majesty of the king, the other fearing the denial of the rights of God's servants. After the archbishop had been in exile in France for several years, he returned to Canterbury in 1170 on the basis of a patched-up peace, only to be murdered there by knights from the royal court. According to Henry, they had unfortunately misunderstood him. The episode caused an immediate sensation throughout Western Europe, and churches were dedicated to St Thomas everywhere from Iceland to Sicily. Murdering bishops was a crude and unsatisfactory method of securing royal control, and there are only a few cases in the period covered by this chapter, for more subtle methods were usually sufficient. The advantages to the church of royal favour and protection, along with the dangers of royal anger, were sufficient to enable strong kings to secure the loyalty of their bishops. It would be wrong, however, to think that the monarchies were becoming consciously secular institutions. They boasted of the holiness of their ancestors (Edward the Confessor, Charlemagne, Elizabeth of Hungary, and Louis IX of France were all elevated to the ranks of the saints), made much of their protection of the church against heretics and other enemies, and publicized the effectiveness of the healing touch of kings—a ceremony which probably became regular in the thirteenth century.

The Rise of the Nation States

Nevertheless the nations of 1300 were a far more formidable check on the rights of the church than those of 1150. There had been an immense improvement in the machinery of law and administration. More important still, the king was coming to be seen as in some sense the embodiment of the whole community. Nobles, knights, townsmen, and clergy formed part of representative assemblies, parliaments, or estates, which were perceived as speaking for the 'community of the realm'. All of this provided the monarchy with an income from taxation and means of legislation and control which had not existed in the past. The claims of the church were subject to regulation by statutes which had been considered by the whole community. A striking example is the series of statutes of provisors and *praemunire* enacted in England from 1351 onwards to prevent the papacy from making appointments to English benefices or from exercising any form of judicial authority. In practice, these laws were not much applied, but they were a significant means of control, and when the Tudor monarchy began its attack on Rome it found important weapons already in place. These governments were also willing to use the opportunities offered by critics of the papacy. Frederick II had already indicated an intention to return the papacy to an apostolic simplicity which it was not eager to embrace, but at that time the friars were, with few exceptions, firmly on the papal side. By the 1320s, we find the leading Franciscans, William of Ockham and Michael of Cesena, at the court of Louis of Bavaria and providing him with powerful propaganda against John XXII.

The Growth of Lay Authority

Although the kings of the fourteenth century still thought of their authority in religious terms, they were conscious of possessing power of government equally over clergy and laity. This was true also of the empire, in spite of its character as (by this time) a political white elephant. The tracts written in its support against the papacy, such as Dante's *De Monarchia* (*c.*1310) and the *Defensor Pacis* of Marsilius of Padua (1324), insisted on the power of a lay government in ecclesiastical matters, and have an important place in the evolution of modern political theory. Part of their argument was the denial that the pope or the clergy have any special claim to speak in the name of the church; as Marsilius put it, 'all Christ's faithful are churchmen'. In this sense the popes were right to connect such writers with the English theologian John Wyclif, whose attack on the hierarchy, developed especially between 1377 and his death in 1384, sounded the distinctive note of late medieval heresy. This increasingly lay character of government reflected the wider distribution of learning and administrative skills in society. It was now possible to form a government whose leading members were laymen, not to say anticlericals, such as the lawyers who surrounded Philip IV of France, and large areas of activity were steadily being transferred into lay hands. The Council of Vienne in 1311–12 ordered that experienced laymen should be appointed to the charge of hospitals; the fabric of the churches themselves was increasingly in the care of church-wardens; and private masses and guild commemorations reflected the demands of rich citizens. The civilization in which initiative and authority had been so much in the hands of the clergy was changing its character.

Philip IV and Boniface VIII

The crucial example of the new nation states was France. The power of the French monarchy had grown spectacularly in the course of the thirteenth century, and the change was all the more significant because the Capetians had been favourite sons and champions of the papacy. The papacy had achieved the defeat of the empire at the price of establishing the power of the Capetians in the Italian peninsula, thus creating a threat of French instead of imperial hegemony. In 1294 Boniface VIII was elected pope, an able and turbulent man who found compromise difficult. The decisive clash with Philip IV of France was more over principle than over a specific issue. A quarrel generated by the tactless Bishop Bernard Saisset of Pamiers escalated into a fierce conflict which culminated in the issue of the bull *Unam Sanctam* in 1302. This asserted the supremacy of the Roman church over mankind in a series of claims which individually had precedents, but taken together represented the high point of the assertion of papal monarchy. It was followed in 1303 by the excommunication of the king. Philip replied by sending his minister Nogaret to arrest Boniface at Anagni; and, although the pope was rescued by the townsmen, he died shortly afterwards.

The Avignon 'Captivity'

The pressure of the French king and the clumsy policy of Boniface had left the cardinals and the Papal State deeply divided. They led to the election in 1305 of a French pope, Clement V, and after him of a sequence of French popes who presided over a college of cardinals with a substantial majority of Frenchmen. These popes decided to wait under French protection until the imperial threat in Italy and the disorder in the Papal State had been overcome, but in practice this decision led to the lengthy establishment of the papacy at Avignon in southern France and the building there of the great papal palace as an administrative centre—the so-called Babylonian captivity of the popes. The Avignon papacy was by no means all bad. In some ways Avignon was a more rational centre for Western Christendom than distant Rome; an efficient administration was built up; and there were attempts at reform, especially under the Cistercian Pope Benedict XII (1334–42). But the loss of Italian revenues obliged the popes to be even more exacting in the levy of their spiritual income, and the French influence was deeply resented in Germany and England, especially after the outbreak of the Hundred Years War. Above all, Avignon inevitably appeared an exile to devout men and women who reverenced the Roman church as the see of Peter, and in 1377 the decision was made by Gregory XI to return to Rome.

The Beginning of the Great Schism

The problems of re-entry were great, but they were made insuperable by a series of misfortunes. Gregory died within a few months, and his death was followed by an irregular and disorderly conclave in which an Italian pope, Urban VI, was elected. Even so, the French king does not seem to have been looking for trouble, and it was Urban's rash and hostile behaviour which after a few months led the French majority among the cardinals to withdraw their obedience and elect Clement VII in his place. The papacy had returned to Rome only to become involved in the longest schism in its whole history.

7

The Late Medieval Church and its Reformation

1400–1600

PATRICK COLLINSON

Religion in Late Medieval Society

THE past is another country. Where, apart from libraries and archives, should the historian of late medieval religion travel in order to understand with that understanding which is sight, hearing, and sensation the meaning of the Christianity which we have lost, what it once meant to be religious? The answer must be 'nowhere'. But twentieth-century India might help. For, somewhat like Western Christendom on the eve of its greatest crisis, the confused world of Hinduism still embraces with immense generosity great extremes of theological and philosophical erudition, mystical refinement, and popular 'superstition', a range of supernatural explanations, compensations, and cures to ward off the slings and arrows of outrageous fortune.

Whatever may be the case in modern India, in early modern Europe these various forms of religion were not distributed according to a tidy social hierarchy. Luther's prince, the elector of Saxony Frederick the Wise, was at one and the same time patron of a modern university with a progressive faculty of theology and proud possessor of a vast collection of relics which, it was believed, contained the potency to reduce by many thousands of years the time spent by dead souls in purgatory. If that was a superstition it was not a superstition confined to the simple and illiterate. The elector's relic collection was served by a printed catalogue. In Ipswich in 1516 a young girl believed herself cured of epilepsy by an image of the Virgin and began to preach sermons in the middle of the night. 'A dowther', said her mother, 'ye must take hede to the grette clerkes and of ther sayyng.' But one 'great clerk', the abbot of Bury St Edmunds, came on foot across Suffolk to witness this marvel. The girl was not some peasant Bernadette but the daughter of the high sheriff of Essex and the event was described to the king of England by a high-ranking officer of the Holy Roman empire, retired. A few years later, a similar phenomenon in Kent became confused with high politics and the so-called 'Nun of Kent' and her aiders and abettors were executed not for 'superstition', nor even for 'heresy', but for the high treason of conspiring the king's death. Their weapon was not gunpowder but prophecy. 'Popular religion' is evidently a deceptive category which late medieval historians would be wise to abandon.

Unlike most modern and Western forms of Christianity, Hinduism and, for that matter, Islam, enfold everyone in a close-knit fabric of inheritance, relationship, and obligation from which there is no easy escape and to which there is no obvious alternative. This kind of religion is not confined to one day in the week, nor to a certain sacred place, nor to a select group of people, nor to a transient state of mind and feeling. Above all it is not associated with an almost unnatural niceness, a level of good behaviour not called for on all occasions and in itself considered 'religious'. The historian who has never visited Beirut or Belfast may find it hard to establish religious sympathy with a Richard III or a Henry VIII, who could hear mass before ordering the destruction of a political enemy. He might decide that they were both hypocrites. But would that be correct?

Henry VIII's marital and dynastic difficulties with his wife Catherine of Aragon may look like a problem of incompatibility compounded by Catherine's inability to provide her husband with a legitimate and viable male heir. But in the context of its time 'the king's great matter' was a religious problem. It was the pope, the spiritual head of Christendom, who ruled that Henry must honour his marriage, Henry's conscience which told him that he must disown it. The more practical, political implications of both positions were implicit, rarely explicit. Henry's conscience, which prevailed, dictated not only a divorce and a new marriage but a chain of unforeseen but logically connected religious changes which we call the English Reformation.

The German peasantry in 1525 had a number of grievances which projected them into insurrection and bloodshed. Historians are able to identify and analyse their material rationale and content. But if they are good historians they acknowledge not only that the great Peasants' War was articulated partly in religious terms but that these events, amounting to an early modern revolution of the common man, would not and perhaps could not have happened on such a scale without a high sense of religious legitimation. Nowadays we should have to look to the Gulf War between Iran and Iraq for a parallel. Martin Luther, a man of religion, took a rather original line in insisting that the cause of the peasants was in no way a religious cause.

The survival of unusually detailed parish records reveals that in South London in about 1600 almost everyone of an appropriate age received communion once a year, at the season of Easter, in striking contrast to the modern situation in which a smallish minority communicates in the Church of England. That was certainly a religious act but in a sense which we may find hard to penetrate. The communicants were registering their place on the electoral roll of the parish, asserting their responsibilities and claiming their rights, as well as responding instinctively and as of habit to the rhythm of the calendar. The cup of wine consumed at the communion was not absolutely different from the sociable drinking which in more mundane circumstances sealed a bargain or made peace after a quarrel. It was a good question, in church or in the alehouse, whether it was the cup which made peace between neighbours or whether a state of reconciliation had to exist before the cup could be shared. The historian can recognize all this. And yet he would be very unwise to conclude that Easter Communion in the early seventeenth century was not a 'religious' event as we understand religion, or that it excluded any sense of the sacred.

Reformation and Counter-Reformation

So in 1600 and in Southwark, where Shakespeare was living in lodgings, religious obligations were almost universally observed, a matter of routine, as they had been in 1400. John Donne would presently write that all coherence was gone but he exaggerated, or wrote with prophetic insight or from a wide angle. In Europe coherence had been lost. But within a single country, England, most people still shared one faith, the Catholic members of Donne's own family being rare exceptions to this rule. However, the obligations of religion were now different and fewer. In the intervening years, and especially after about 1520, almost every part of the elaborate fabric of traditional Christianity had come under critical scrutiny. Beliefs, practices, and institutions which had evolved as it were organically were now demolished or radically reconstructed, or given a new lease of life on a more deliberate and formal basis. This was the case not only in Protestant Europe but in those countries which remained Catholic in the sense of continuing in communion with Rome. Even continuity involved some discontinuity. The mere fact that Catholicism was now defined in contradistinction to other forms of belief deemed to be false distinguished it from the more diffuse and relaxed Catholicism of the past. In a reassuring but in many ways misleading piece of mental shorthand these great changes which subdivided and reconstructed Christendom are packaged in our history books as the Reformation and the Counter-Reformation, or Catholic Reformation.

Reformation and Counter-Reformation are not terms which

we can easily dispense with and yet they are deceptive, especially when preceded by the particularizing definite article. 'Reform' was a familiar word long before 1500, even a cliché, especially in the form 'reform of the Church in Head and members', meaning a hoped-for reform of pope, bishops, and other religious dignitaries and interests. *The* Reformation moved from talk and paper projects to action and event. Extensive changes now actually took place. Yet Martin Luther was not aware that he had inaugurated something called 'the Reformation' and no one spoke in that way of the Reformation before the seventeenth century. So it is meaningless, or at least unhistorical, to discuss whether this or that tendency or event was properly part of the Reformation, and just as mistaken to use Luther himself as some kind of standard by which to judge the validity and centrality of other reformers, would-be reformers, and stirrers. A leading historian of the German Reformation has recently described it (while regretting that we must continue to speak of 'it') as 'a complex extended historical process, going well beyond the endeavours of man or one tendency, and involving social, political and wider religious issues'. As for the Counter-Reformation, as a descriptive title for a whole epoch of church history, uniting a variety of events, personalities, and movements in a single cultural entity, this was a typical invention of the nineteenth-century synthetic mind, which also discovered the Renaissance and the Enlightenment. And yet to recognize the artificial nature of such concepts is not to deny meaningful connections between people, events, and movements, still less to pretend that the sixteenth century did not witness almost unprecedented disturbance in the ordering of Christian society.

It is not certain that major events require equally major causes but such causes are looked for, perhaps for emotional as well as intellectual reasons, and historians worth their salt are supposed to supply them. For more than a hundred years they have tried to account for the Reformation and, like historians of other super-events such as the French revolution or the First World War, they have grappled with a logical difficulty, not always with entire logical success. Because something happened was it bound to happen? Given the relation between causes and what are deemed to have been their consequences, could these causes have had other consequences? The philosophy of ultimacy and contingency converts into the historical language of long-term and short-term causes. Did one man, Martin Luther, begin the Reformation which otherwise would never have happened, by inventing a new theology or making an original protest against a particular piece of contemporary ecclesiastical practice? Thomas Carlyle, never one to underestimate the historical importance of the notable individual, thought so, pronouncing that if Luther had not stood his ground at the Diet of Worms, when called upon by the Holy Roman emperor to recant, there would have been no French revolution, no America, no modern freedom. Did Henry VIII's divorce cause the English Reformation, in the sense that without it no great alteration in English religion or church–state relations would have occurred, or was it merely the occasion or 'trigger' for changes which would have taken place in any case? Those sitting examinations have been asked that question in one form or another for generations, yet no one supposes that some candidate somewhere is about to discover the right answer, so laying to rest all further discussion.

Given the particular circumstances of the Reformation in England, the problem of long-term and short-term causes resembles an old historical chestnut which concerns the connection between high politics and underlying social and cultural circumstances or 'factors'. Are the causes of the First World War to be sought in the events in Sarajevo in July 1914, and more broadly at the level of great power diplomacy, or in the totality of European national cultures and their interaction? Similarly, the affairs of the church in the later Middle Ages were conducted at an advanced political and diplomatic level. As such they were defined in terms of particular contentious issues, such as the right to make ecclesiastical appointments, or to tax, or exercise jurisdiction; and also of structural problems which were constitutional and almost endemic. By nature these matters were adversarial and were pursued more or less aggressively, in litigation, diplomacy, even war. But attempts were also made to find acceptable solutions and consensual accommodations at a variety of levels, including those international summits known as general councils of the church. In so far as Reformation and Counter-Reformation amounted to a process of fragmentation, a series of painful but more or less orderly schisms legitimated at a high political level, they can be explained with reference to these processes. Historians will only have to argue, from their different ideological premises, whether the revolution of the Reformation could or could not have been avoided, by encouraging a liberal process of more gradual institutional and constitutional change. This is little different from discussing whether a Bloodless Revolution of 1688 in France would have forestalled the events of 1789.

But the Reformation was more than politics, more even than ecclesiastical politics. If it is to be explained pathologically, in terms of a *malaise*, then the *malaise* was more deep-seated, spiritual as well as institutional. If, on the contrary, it is understood as an episode of renewal and reconstruction, then it has to be described as a religious revival involving new teaching, new certainties, a new and transforming spirit which drew its strength from the very past which it repudiated. Negatively, the Reformation entailed various versions of anticlericalism, the urge to reduce the role in society of the clergy and to place limits on the space which priests and other religious persons occupied and the privileges and material rewards which they enjoyed, above all their capacity to overrule the laity. The other side of this coin was the assertion of the glorious liberty of the sons of God, all the sons, summed up in the figure identified by Luther as 'the Christian man' (and, in somewhat smaller print, the Christian woman).

Whether religious change in the sixteenth century is to be understood as a transformation imposed from above, by authority, or as a movement conveyed upwards by popular pressure for religious emancipation, is an issue keenly debated by historians of the English Reformation and available for discussion in relation to Reformation and Counter-Reformation in all parts of Europe. On the title-page of the first publicly authorized version of the Bible in English, engraved by Holbein, Henry VIII is shown handing out copies of the scriptures to an obedient and grateful people. But it was not the king who first put the New Testament into the hands of the young Chelmsford apprentice, William Maldon. He bought it with his own hard-earned pennies and hid it in his bed-straw. That he was able to buy a Testament at all was due to the self-appointed mission of a fugitive translator, William Tyndale, and to the merchants who sustained his efforts. The Counter-Reformation in a sense began with the conversion of Pope Paul III to some of its emergent principles and the pope's appointment of a commission of reforming cardinals who in 1537 presented the report *De Emendanda Ecclesia*. But the Catholic Reformation in the shape of its saints, martyrs, and missionaries could not be called to order as if from the menu of the cardinals' recommendations. However, it was later subjected to order, the order of the Council of Trent and of the authoritarian Catholic regimes of the seventeenth century.

Religion and High Politics

The question 'from above or from below?' cannot be tidily resolved. Both perceptions are equally valid and explanations of the Reformation and Counter-Reformation which focus on high politics and on underlying sentiments and conditions are both necessary, the essential fabric of the story consisting in multiple interactions between these higher and lower historical strata.

A recent study of the Wycliffite heresy of the Lollards in fifteenth-century England speaks of it as 'the premature reformation'. But at the level of higher ecclesiastical affairs the Reformation and Counter-Reformation of the sixteenth century may seem to have been overdue, delayed by events which should have happened earlier, as early as 1400. At that time the Western church was already in a state of turmoil and formal schism, the essence of which was not rival theologies or any principled rejection of the church's spiritual claims but the existence of two and, presently, three rival popes who between them divided the church into rival obediences. As would happen in the sixteenth century, these divisions were exploited politically. Already it was perceived that the logic of the situation might point towards as many popes as there were secular rulers, that is, to the emergence of a plurality of territorial and dynastic churches in which the stature of churchmen would be much reduced. The ecumenicity of the church in these circumstances would survive as no more than a pious fiction. The consequences of such a devolution for the integrity of the faith were likely to be no less grave. In central Europe, the divisive and even heretical movement which took its name from the Czech reformer Jan Hus proved impossible to suppress, a premature reformation indeed, containing most of the ingredients of what was to happen in neighbouring German lands in the sixteenth century. In England it was the orthodox vigilance of the new ruling house of Lancaster, not the church universal, which led to vigorous and largely successful countermeasures to curb the related Wycliffite heresy and to draw its political teeth.

In a satire written by an angry young man and future prince of the church, Pierre d'Ailly, the devil ('Leviathan') gloated over the impending ruin of the church and complained only about a few frogs who out of the depths of their mud croaked incessantly 'General Council, General Council!' D'Ailly was one of those frogs and they proved to have the answer. After the abortive Council of Pisa (1409), which only made matters worse, the Council of Constance (1414–18) succeeded in ending the Great Schism by enforcing the abdication of three rival popes and achieving the universal acceptance of a fourth, Martin V. Orthodoxy was also vindicated with the burning alive of

Hus on the authority of the council, regardless of the safe conduct which the Holy Roman emperor had issued and which had brought him to Constance.

However, the church was still far from discovering a final and comprehensive solution to the extensive crisis in its affairs of which the schism was no more than a superficial expression. A variety of sectional interests or 'members' of the whole, bishops, religious orders, universities, pulled against each other. 'Reform' tended to mean, for such is the nature of politics, reform of some other party or interest, in the sense of a reduction in its privileges and influence. Those members which were the nations of Europe, providing the formal basis of representation at Constance, were equally at odds. The English had arrived on the morning after, as it were, their improbable victory at Agincourt and in an understandably bullish mood. When the proctor for the king of France protested against their presence at the council as a distinct nation there were whistles and groans. An English spokesman, the dean of York, asked where the idea had come from that 'the glorious kingdom of England cannot be compared to the kingdom of France'. England should be recognized as several nations to France's one—'with all respect of course to the honour of that famous Gallican nation'.

There was also a philosophical crisis. The ideology which had prevailed at Constance was that a general council, truly representative of the entire church, had a greater authority than any of its members, not excluding the head himself. This doctrine challenged the principle of the papal plenitude of power by which the head was equivalent to the body: the pope, which is as much as to say, the church. Here was the groundwork for a political, Aristotelian constitution for the church: or for a kind of anarchy, a loss of coherence paralleled in theology by the threat to Thomist scholasticism posed by disintegrative Nominalism, which shared the same philosophical roots. Once having arisen from the philosophical resources of the fourteenth-century universities and law schools, 'Conciliarism' could not be disinvented. One of the decrees passed at Constance was a kind of Bill of Rights, placing the government of the church on a permanently conciliar basis and requiring the holding of general councils at regular intervals. But talking shops can behave irresponsibly, especially when dominated by academics. At the Council of Basle (1431–49) conciliarism took control and lost all sense of proportion. Pope and council enjoyed the expensive luxury of mutual anathemas. But at the end of that story it was the pope who was the pope, the council so much hot air.

The restored papacy emerged from this prolonged crisis apparently triumphant, its success celebrated in the Council of Ferrara–Florence (1438–47) which on the eve of the Turkish conquest of Constantinople achieved an abortive reunion with the Greek Church and even with certain exotic Abyssinian Christians from the land of Prester John. But the price was a measure of autonomy granted to what were now emerging as national churches, or to their secular rulers. The threat of a general council was now a political card to be played against a particular pope by a particular secular government in the ordinary course of power politics and for a defined purpose. Among those Europeans coming to maturity in the early sixteenth century, the young Henry VIII was somewhat exceptional in that enthusiasm for the papal office which earned him the title 'Defender of the Faith'; whereas his good and devout servant Thomas More was an old-fashioned conciliarist who cared more for the collective judgement of the whole church than for the dignity of the bishop of Rome.

The other side of the coin of political conciliarism was the progressive conversion of the papacy itself into an Italian principality which conducted its business not in the international language of Latin but in the local language and perceived its interests through the narrow and distorting lens of the unstable politics of the Italian peninsula, now descending into half a century of destructive Italian wars. Pope Leo X, a Medici from the Florence of Botticelli, a cardinal at the age of 13 and the patron of Michelangelo and Raphael, took a somewhat remote interest in the controversies in Germany stirred up by Martin

Luther and would perhaps not have noticed at all but for the threat they posed to the flow of cash to build his great cathedral of St Peter's. As the skies over Germany progressively darkened, through the 1520s and 1530s, it took many years of negotiation for the German–Dutch–Spanish Emperor Charles V to persuade Pope Paul III, born Alessandro Farnese, to refer the crisis to the general council which began its intermittent deliberations in the Alpine resort of Trent in 1545. Only slowly and pragmatically did Rome recognize in Trent not only a force for a limited reunification and consolidation of the threatened church but the means of restoring on altered terms the universality of the papal ascendancy. After the conclusion of Trent in 1563, with the content and agenda of Catholicism now redefined, it became the principal concern of a reformed papacy to persuade the Catholic powers of Europe to receive and implement its canons: a task involving a new round of diplomatic give and take.

The series of compromises which had ended the fifteenth-century conciliar crisis already indicated that at a high political level the overdue Reformation, when it came, would prove partly abortive. Unless there were special local and temporary circumstances working to the contrary, monarchical governments, and even as deeply anti-papal a republic as Venice, had no obvious interest in breaking off all formal relations with the Catholic Church and its central agencies of government in Rome. Most of the tangible advantages of schism were obtainable without it, as Francis I of France had proved in concluding a concordat with Leo X at Bologna in 1516. This was a pointer to the almost consistent policy of the French monarchy for centuries to come and it provides a model of the kind of church–state relations likely to prevail in a Europe dominated by ascendant monarchies. England was the most important of a handful of exceptions to this rule (which included the Scandinavian kingdoms and Scotland) and in the seventeenth century a tidal undercurrent tugged at the Stuart monarchy, threatening to pull even the British archipelago back into the harbour of Roman conformity and obedience. *Cujus regio, ejus religio*, the religion of the prince determines the religious allegiance of the state, the principle adapted at Augsburg in 1555 in the aftermath of the first round of religious wars, worked to the general advantage of Roman Catholicism. Only the geopolitical shift which progressively transferred wealth and power from the south and centre of Europe to its north-western shores, where Protestant regimes prevailed, left the two great confessions more or less evenly matched, with the advantage of the future favouring the maritime Protestant nations.

Fulfilment or Repudiation? The Reformation and its Late Medieval Sources

So far we have assumed that religious settlements, and religious deals, were made by popes and princes, and that it was at the same high political level that the ecclesiastical map of Europe was redrawn. But the stuff of these dealings was people, church property, religious beliefs and customs, all the concern of localized communities and ultimately of individuals, often as self-interested as their rulers but also anxious, credulous, devout.

Martin Luther as a parish priest, as well as monk and university professor, in the small Saxon town of Wittenberg found that the pastoral direction of his congregation was undermined when they crossed the river to foreign territory to buy certain pieces of parchment not obtainable at home. These were letters of indulgence bearing the name of the pope which, or so those purchasing them were told, not only relieved those in the land of the living from the temporal consequences of their sins but released the souls of their dead grandparents from purgatory, and all for a simple monetary transaction. That was where the shoe pinched and Luther protested in the Ninety-Five Theses of October 1517. At first he had no means of knowing that some of these funds were designed to service the debt of the large fee imposed by the pope on Margrave Albrecht of Brandenburg as the price of allowing him to combine the archbishopric of Mainz with the archbishopric of Magdeburg. Indeed it was to

Albrecht that Luther expressed his concern, as to his own pastor, professing to believe that the archbishop would repudiate the abuses perpetrated in his name if they were brought to his attention. 'It has gone abroad in your name, but doubtless without your knowledge . . . If agreeable to your grace, perhaps you would glance at my enclosed theses.' But Luther's anger at 'this wanton preaching of pardons' aroused an unexpected storm of public sympathy which the authorities in Germany and beyond, secular and spiritual, were unable to suppress, and this we call the Reformation.

The Concordat of Bologna determined how the interests of the Holy See and the French government were to be balanced in such matters as appointments to French bishoprics. But no concordat could ensure that all Frenchmen would continue to believe what, according to the church, they were supposed to believe. By 1560 more than half the nobility was Protestant and with the nobility much of the nation. It was no longer true, whatever Napoleon may have said later, that a Frenchman is a Catholic or he is nothing. This momentous and disturbing development was made up of many thousands of individual decisions to convert, as personal as the discovery of some country gentlewoman or the wife of a Lyons merchant that she found more spiritual satisfaction in reading her Bible and listening to Calvinist preachers than in the ministrations of the priest to whom she was bound to confess. It was through such women, to a great extent, that the Reformation established itself in the households of a supposedly male-dominated society. In France, England, and the Netherlands, hundreds of common people, women as well as men, were content to be burnt alive for their newly acquired Protestant beliefs. The Reformation had a cast of thousands. It was made in society, not imposed upon it.

How do historians account for its explosive force? In two almost contradictory ways. Either the Reformation arose in reaction to the corruption and spiritual impoverishment of the church and established religion or, more positively, from out of its rich spiritual resources. The contradiction existed in microcosm in Luther himself. His Ninety-Five Theses and the ever broadening stream of polemic and invective which subsequently flowed from his pen made a comprehensive indictment of a corrupt and corrupting religious system. The hungry sheep looked up and were not fed. 'Away, then, with those prophets who say to Christ's people, "Peace, peace!" when there is no peace' (Thesis 92). But this was the voice not of external criticism but of a conscience reared within the tradition which it denounced. If Luther condemned the church on the authority of what he read in the Bible, or in the writings of St Augustine, it was the church, in the persons of his teachers, spiritual directors, religious superiors, and employers, who had put these documents into his hands. (That is as much as to say Johann von Staupitz, to whom, Luther said, he owed his soul.) But it began earlier than that. Luther's deeply religious nature had been nurtured not only in the monastery and the university but in the social circle of his mother's family, the Lindemanns of Eisenach and from the sermons to which petty German bourgeois of that kind were regularly exposed. The young Luther was not told that there was peace when there was no peace. Nor were the citizens of Strasbourg flattered in their sins from the great pulpit which they set up in 1478 for their famous and fiery preacher Geiler von Kaisersberg, the German Savonarola. Luther was hardly a typical product of late medieval German Catholicism but he is recognizable as one of its authentic manifestations. He was also a looked-for and expected figure, since it was characteristic of a certain widespread mentality to hope for salvation by means of a great God-given *reformator*.

Explanations of the Reformation in terms of decadence, irreligion, and corruption are the more traditional and still infest indifferent textbooks. They reflect not only a predictable Protestant prejudice against Catholicism in all its works and ways but a simplistic reading of the literature of moral and anticlerical satire and complaint and of contemporary Protestant propaganda, as if these biased sources provide a realistic description of religious life on the eve of the Reformation.

Historians have no difficulty in drawing up an indictment of the evils of the unreformed church. Indeed, their work is done for them in such documents as the often-repeated *Gravamina* of the German nation (grievances referred to the imperial *Reichstag*), or in the copious and popular writings of the great Christian humanist Erasmus of Rotterdam, or, in early Tudor England, the speeches made to ecclesiastical assemblies by Dean John Colet of St Paul's or Chancellor Melton of York. The dice of ecclesiastical preferment carried rather few numbers between six and one. The church's priestly professional personnel included on the one hand such great possessioners as Albrecht of Mainz or the Englishman Thomas Wolsey, simultaneously archbishop of York, bishop of Lincoln, and abbot of St Albans, who was sufficiently contemptuous of the spiritual needs of his native town of Ipswich to appoint his bastard son Thomas Winter vicar of its leading parish church; and on the other, countless poorly beneficed and unbeneficed priests struggling for a meagre livelihood in an overcrowded ecclesiastical job market. Priests were supposed to be celibate and chaste but in many places, and especially in Switzerland and Wales, it was notorious that they were not. In mid-sixteenth-century Gloucestershire 168 out of 311 country clergy were unable to repeat the Ten Commandments and some could not say who composed the Lord's Prayer. What kind of instruction did the laity receive from such pastors? The records of visitations and church courts are a garner of cases of sexual incontinence and pastoral neglect from which incautious historians have cheerfully generalized. But like all criminal material these sources by their very nature are unrepresentative and testify as much to the energy of those conducting these investigations as to the enormity of the crimes detected.

The church is *semper reformanda*, always in need of improvement. Whether it was really more corrupt than in earlier generations or merely corrupt in the heightened moral perception of its critics, who represented a better educated and more demanding laity, is another question. 'Some say' was the anticlerical lawyer Christopher St Germain's way of introducing some new piece of incriminating scandal. Thomas More retorted that all his some says were of his own saying. Few of the complaints we hear in the early sixteenth century were new. Colet was anticipated by Chaucer and Langland. It is surely significant that except for England and Bohemia and certain remote Alpine valleys there was very little coherent heresy in the early sixteenth century. In that sense the church did not perceive itself to be in danger in Germany or in France. Luther claimed originality in attacking the church not in respect of its corrupt life, which many others had censured, not least that good Catholic Erasmus, but at the level of defective doctrine. His criticisms on that score were soon found by the church to be heretical but they were also, in the perspective of recent centuries, theologically unprecedented. If Erasmus could have foreseen what was about to happen to the religious economy which he attacked so remorselessly he might have exercised more restraint. Unlike the French and Russian revolutions, few could envisage the Reformation before it arrived.

A more sophisticated version of what might be called the pathological account of late medieval Catholicism is associated especially with the historian Jean Delumeau, who drew on the collective findings of a group of French historical sociologists of religion. In this perception, late medieval Europe, especially in its rural heartlands, remained a very superficially Christianized society, waiting not so much for a change of religious orientation as for its primary conversion to an informed, disciplined religion worthy of the name of Christianity. This was the task undertaken (with varying success) by both Reformation and Counter-Reformation movements. This thesis is doubtless too condescending to the intellectual and moral capacities of late medieval Europeans and probably exaggerates the strength in an at least nominally Christian society of irreligious forms of instrumental magic. But in so far as he recognizes in the reforming movements of the sixteenth century the climax of an impending Christian revival, Delumeau correctly acknowledges that Reformation and Counter-Reformation rested on a broad basis of long-standing reforming tendencies, that 'pre-Reform' which has always been part of the repertoire of French historians.

The perception that the Reformation was an event which occurred in a context of Catholic piety was Catholic in origin, part of a conspiratorial version of history which blamed Luther as a demon who devastated a garden in which all was loveliness before he burst on the scene. ('A wild boar', wrote Leo X in the bull *Exsurge Domini* (1520), 'has invaded thy vineyard.') But more recently the argument has been broadened by historians of other religious persuasions (and none) who appreciate the rich diversity of phenomena to which both Reformation and Counter-Reformation were legitimate heirs. In the words of William James's once famous title, Europe in about 1500 exhibited many 'varieties of religious experience', from mysticism to the crudely instrumental near-magic of popular cultic centres with their images and bleeding hosts, and from the Galilean Sunday School atmosphere of Erasmus's paraphrases and comments on the New Testament to the hectic and fearful apocalypticism which inspired both the peasant insurgent the Drummer of Niklaushausen and the greatest of the painters and engravers of the Northern Renaissance, Albrecht Dürer. Dürer also reflects an intense Christocentrism, not only in what profess to be portraits of Christ but in at least one of his self-portraits, anticipating the theology of Luther's lectures on the penitential Psalms: as in Christ, so in me. Dürer's older contemporary, Mathias Grünewald, suggests that the agonies of the dying Christ were a mirror for the sorrows of a society which was the victim as much of rampant and incurable disease as of social alienation.

Until recently, accounts of pre-Reformation religion have given prominence to the religion of the more striking and attractive of minorities. These included the form of Christianity characterized as 'the New Devotion' and practised in the Netherlands and north-east Germany by the Brethren (and Sisters) of the Common Life and their adherents and articulated in the phenomenonally successful *Imitation of Christ* of Thomas à Kempis (Kempen being a small town near Cologne). The conversion of the founder of the Jesuits, the Basque soldier Ignatius Loyola, was partly effected by devout literature in this tradition, which consequently flowed into the mainstream of the Counter-Reformation, part of a broader cultural influence reaching Spain and southern Europe from the advanced civilization of the late medieval Netherlands. Another very different minority tradition was the Bibliocentrism of the English craftsmen and yeoman farmers known to their detractors as 'Lollards'; and yet another the Bible study which infiltrated certain fashionable salons in the great Italian cities with a new and liberating enthusiasm for the Pauline theology of grace.

This was an age of many revivals, Pauline, Augustinian, even, among the Dominicans, Thomist. Some of the revivals were pulling in contrary directions. New cults arose centred on newly popular saints, such as the mother of the Virgin, St Anne, who was familiar to miners and metal workers, so that the young Luther, who came from this stock, cried 'Help me St Anna and I will become a monk' when caught in a thunderstorm. Images of St Anne's greater daughter, new and old, at Ipswich and Woolpit in Suffolk as powerfully as at Regensburg in South Germany, attracted excited devotion and worked miraculous cures. The Lollards were particularly hostile to such cults, denouncing Woolpit as 'Foulpit'. The self-discovery of the family which may have been a feature of late medieval civilization was reflected in a fascination with Christ's own kindred, the extended Holy Family. This is reflected in Leonardo da Vinci's 'Virgin of the Rocks' but also at Walsingham, where pilgrims supposed that they were visiting the Holy House of Nazareth itself, miraculously transported to Norfolk. (The Holy House was also claimed by Loreto, near Ancona.) Erasmus in his *Colloquies* laughed at Walsingham and much else in contemporary religiosity. His *Enchiridion Militis Christiani* ('Trusty Weapon of the Christian Soldier') which recommended an inward, Bible-centred piety of a very different kind, was soon immensely popular in literate lay society, in Spain as much as in the author's native Netherlands. Erasmus's 'philosophia Christi' has been regarded as the Christian Renaissance *par excellence* but it was far from summarizing the full extent of the Christian revival of the early sixteenth century.

More recent religious and social historians discount the historical importance of minority movements like the Lollards or the *Devotio Moderna* and make rather more of the positive connections between majority religion and what would happen in the sixteenth century. It now appears that it was a serious mistake to think of late medieval religion as a commodity provided by the clergy for lay people, which as customers they either understood or misunderstood, accepted or rejected. The centrality of the mass and of the priest as celebrant, supported by the arcane intellectual mystery of transubstantiation, makes this a pardonable error. But we now understand that mass priests were often the employees of the laity, particularly as associated in the mutual benefit societies which were guilds and fraternities. These fraternities (or confraternities) were also burial clubs and, since for late medieval Catholics a funeral was not the end of the matter, chantries to secure the singing of masses for the repose of the souls of dead members. It was even possible for the dead to join these societies. We are only beginning to have an adequate sense of the importance of this closely knotted network of fraternities of all shapes and kinds, from the *Scuole Grandi* which in Venice provided a safety net of social security to the petty guilds which maintained stocks of corn and wax to provide lights before the altars and images in remote fenland parishes in Cambridgeshire. Who built the soaring spires and generous naves and aisles which are the glory of the late medieval English parish church? The parishioners themselves.

In the Vercors of south-east France, lay fraternities counted for more than parishes. At the annual general meeting would-be pearly kings and queens (as it were) bid for their offices in wax, so supplying the constant demand for candles. Many of the ritual observances which were the stuff of late medieval popular religion were lay inventions or sustained by lay effort. If the clergy controlled, to some extent, the sacraments, the laity managed a mass of subsidiary rituals called 'sacramentals'. These events included processions at times of inclement weather, the Palm Sunday processions of an effigy of Christ on a wooden donkey drawn on a cart, the 'Palmesel', and, a week later, the strange ritual of burying and 'resurrecting' the same image. These activities were close to carnival, the mimetic language of popular celebration and protest.

The popular late medieval feast of Corpus Christi, celebrating the eucharist and devoting to the body of Christ transubstantiated in the host a higher form of the same respect which the fraternities rendered to the corpses of their own dead, was maintained by the generality of Christians, not simply by the clergy. In the towns especially there were Corpus Christi plays at midsummer, the climax of the festive year, in which the responsibility for providing pageants representing this or that episode of the biblical story was delegated to the various craft guilds. The language of these play cycles, where they still survive, suggests a homely and even bawdy familiarity linking the religious with the everyday, implying a distinctly underdeveloped sense of blasphemy. Preachers in Warwickshire told their congregations that if they had any reason to doubt what they had heard they should go to Coventry where they would see it all acted out on the stage. Seeing was believing. Images *were* the saints whom they represented as fully as the image on the modern television screen *is* the media personality, often fictitious, with whom the viewers identify.

It is not certain whether such 'religious' institutions, including the mystery plays, reflect the harmonious integration of the urban community or its threatened disintegration under the strains of economic contraction and inward immigration. To enter the world of the 'mysteries' is to sense a little of what has been called the 'social miracle' of late medieval Catholicism. But it was not a perfect miracle. Brotherhood implied otherhood and to the more orderly sixteenth-century mind voluntary fraternities were less helpful in maintaining a general social peace than parishes, compulsory units of cohabitation, in which people of all kinds were supposed to rub along, or face the consequences. Counter-Reformation Catholicism presently subjected lay religion to new forms of clerical dominance not previously known. In the mountains of the Lyonnais and the Vercors the fraternities were obliged to elect the parish priest as their president and to curtail the orgiastic abandon of their annual feasts. Voluntary support for what were properly lay and even anti-clerical activities fell away. In Protestant communities too a new clericalism arose in the person of the godly preacher and pastor, an austere and remote figure living in the bosom of his family and in his well-stocked study, emerging to denounce the sins of his congregation from the full height of the pulpit. George Herbert described the country parson as standing on a hill, looking out over his people.

The Old Religion Repudiated

We have now established that the lay assertiveness once directly attributed to the theology of the Reformation had deep roots which made the Reformation the fulfilment rather than simply a negation of pre-Reformation Catholic culture. However, we must face the awkward fact that the Reformation entailed the repudiation and even the physical destruction of the religious investment of the very recent past, and especially its exuberant imagery. Protestants discarded beliefs which were apparently at the heart of the everyday religion of the majority: especially belief in the sacrament of the altar and other prayers as efficacious for the dead. Late medieval religion has been called a religion practised by the living on behalf of the dead. But now it was taught that good works contributed nothing to salvation. If they could not help the living they could certainly do nothing for the dead. Symbols of the old religious values were assaulted in acts of iconoclasm, both public and lawful and private and riotous. The mind's eye too was corrected by that process of internal iconoclasm which replaced a religion of imagery with a faith sustained by the printed word of the Bible and the spoken word of the sermon. Now hearing, not seeing, was believing.

How could such a drastic religious revolution come about and so suddenly? For we must not think of the iconoclasts attacking what was old and 'medieval' but what was new and freshly painted. It would solve the problem if it could be shown that those who invented Protestantism had never believed in Catholicism. But the English Reformation had a much broader base than Lollardy. In the 1540s people on their deathbeds quite suddenly made no provision for the repose of their souls who would certainly have ordered their due share of requiem masses five or ten years before. Of course these testators knew that the practice was coming into official disfavour, was perhaps already illegal. But that is unlikely to have been the whole story. The compliance of the English people in the face of Henry VIII's injunctions is understandable: the rapidity of that compliance a remaining puzzle.

As late as 1518 the city of Regensburg became the centre of a highly successful new cult typical of the excitable, revivalist devotion of the time. The demolition of a synagogue in an episode of anti-Semitic violence and its replacement by a Christian chapel had been accompanied by a miracle when an injured workman was restored to health by an image of the Virgin. Within a few months the *Liebfrau* of Regensburg was attracting pilgrims by the thousand. In 1519–20 more than 12,000 tokens were sold to those who flocked to participate in this instant cult and in 1521 no less than 209 miraculous cures were recorded. But after a tense political struggle Regensburg embraced the Reform, the still new chapel was invaded by iconoclasts and in 1542 the famous miracle-working Virgin was destroyed. Such episodes have prompted the alluring if not literally exact aphorism that the image-breakers were the image-makers. In 1529 iconoclasts in Basle assaulted the great crucifix which had been brought out from the cathedral crying 'If you are God, defend yourself; if you are man then bleed', after which they burnt the image. That may take us as close to the mentality of image worship and image rejection as we are likely to get. As a perplexed John Donne would later write: 'To adore, or scorne an image, or protest, | May all be bad.'

A tempting if not entirely convincing solution to this problem argues that early sixteenth-century Europe was suffering not from too little religion but from too much. The apparent enthusiasm invested in religion brought not satisfaction and comfort but anxiety. Anxiety bred anxiety and soon religion became a burden. When the faithful were told that the heavy investment of their time and money in religious works designed to produce salvation was so much wasted effort perhaps there was relief like that experienced by the jogger who is told that his regular morning exercise is in fact bad for his health. What is the evidence for this? Dürer described Luther as the Christian man who had released him from great anxieties. Luther himself, looking back, described the punishing spiritual athleticism which had failed to bring peace. 'If ever a monk got to heaven through monkery, I should have been that man.'

But to extrapolate from Luther's experience to cover that of tens of thousands of more conventional Christians is unwise. Confession, which for a monk like Luther was a constant agony of conscience, was for most of his contemporaries a matter of occasional and conventional routine. There is no reason to suppose that the majority lived in that perpetual mood of morbid *angst* with which Jan Huizinga characterized and perhaps caricatured late medieval culture in *The Waning of the Middle Ages*. However, Erasmus told his many readers that their pious acts of external devotion, pilgrimages, vows, watchings, and fastings, were useless if the inner disposition was wanting; and that, given the inner disposition, perhaps nothing more was required. That was perhaps a message of liberating *glasnost* for a spiritually oppressed (albeit self-oppressed) society. One could have too much of a good thing. Yet it remains a puzzle that Frederick the Wise should have continued to back to the hilt Luther (whom he never met in the flesh) who taught that his expensive collection of relics consisted of so much worthless rubbish.

The New Religion: Protestant Confessions and Forms

Modern historians of the Reformation in their exploration of its social and cultural complexity have moved as far away from Carlyle's fixation on the heroic uniqueness of Martin Luther as it is possible to get. Yet it remains true that Luther invented Protestantism and probable that without him there would have been nothing like the Reformation with which these same historians have to contend. This remains the case even after we have conceded that Luther's individuality would have been speedily extinguished but for a set of uniquely favourable political circumstances; that Max Weber's important principle of 'elective affinity' suggests that what Luther was heard to be saying and why he was heard at all and with what consequences is historically at least as significant as the content of his message; and that Luther was only one of many preachers, publicists, and agitators who were causing excitement at this time, few of whom were card-carrying 'Lutherans'.

Luther's originality consisted in reducing Christianity to its essence, the essence which was the gospel (and especially the gospel according to St Paul), and bringing every other part of its doctrinal and organizational structure under the judgement of that single, simple principle, a process which may be described as psychologically existential and mentally dialectical. The effect was initially destructive and potentially anarchical. In Switzerland the partly independent reforming initiative taken from his pulpit in Zurich by Huldrych Zwingli lacked the profoundly subversive vision of Luther's version of the Gospel but outwardly and superficially involved a more devastatingly iconoclastic onslaught on familiar religious landmarks, in the name of a religion of word and spirit strongly opposed to flesh and sense as media of religious experience. All Europe contemplated the unacceptable implications of these negations in the great Peasants' War which engulfed much of south and central Germany between 1524 and 1526, with the radically millenarian reformer Thomas Müntzer playing a prominent part. Further alarm was caused by the bizarre rule of the fanatical 'saints' in the Westphalian city of Münster in 1533–5, the most violent episode in the history of the secondary and sectarian reformation of the so-called Anabaptists.

The remainder of the sixteenth century was spent in reconstructing new and alternative models of Christian order on the foundation of Luther's gospel or variant versions of it, a task undertaken by Luther himself but more effectively by his more practical and systematic colleague, Philip Melanchthon, a successor figure representing 'routinization' and replicated in the Swiss Reformation by Zwingli's son-in-law and successor, Heinrich Bullinger. Even the Anabaptists underwent routinization under the stabilizing leadership of a former Dutch priest, Menno Simons, who converted the shattered remains of a disorganized chiliastic movement into a law-abiding denomination ('Mennonites' or 'Baptists') differing from the established churches with which it coexisted and anticipating the situation of most churches in the modern world by its disconnection with the things of Caesar. But Protestantism as a credible alternative to Catholicism, churchly, ecumenical, and as capable of withstanding and undermining the political order of the state as of reinforcing it, was the creation above all of the French jurist and humanist turned reformer of Geneva, John Calvin. Calvin first broadened the theological basis of Protestantism in the more coherent, balanced divinity of his 'Institutes' (*Christianae Religionis Institutio*, first edition 1536, final and definitive edition 1559), and then matched this intellectual achievement with a working model of a church and community rightly reformed which was widely imitated and which earned from the Scottish reformer John Knox the admiring comment that in Geneva was the most perfect school of Christ to have been seen on earth since the days of the apostles.

What was the gospel of Christ, according to Luther and all subsequent Protestants? That man enjoys that acceptance with God called 'justification', the beginning and end of salvation, not through his own moral effort even in the smallest and slightest degree but entirely and only through the loving mercy of God made available in the merits of Christ and of his saving death on the Cross. This was not a process of gradual ethical improvement but an instantaneous transaction, somewhat like a marriage, in which Christ the bridegroom takes to himself an impoverished and wretched harlot and confers upon her all the riches which are his. The key to this transaction was faith, defined as a total and trustful commitment of the self to God, and in itself not a human achievement but the pure gift of God. 'Faith cometh by hearing and hearing by the word of God': *fides ex auditu*. Thereafter the justified Christian man, in himself and of his own nature a sinner but not seen as a sinner by God, brings forth those good works which consist in the love of God and neighbour, not slavishly to win any reward but gladly, that service which is perfect freedom.

The implications of what might appear, deceptively, a small shift in orthodox Augustinian theology, were almost limitless. The sacramental economy of the church together with the hierarchical priesthood, guardians of doctrine and of the souls of the church's members, was radically undermined, since in Luther's perception the mass and all other devotions were 'works' with a false motivation. There was no longer any rationale for monasticism. At Wittenberg Luther's house of Augustinian canons became his family home as he married off the local nuns and eventually took the last of them, Catherine von Bora, as his own wife: for clerical celibacy was no longer a virtue. It was not that sex and marriage were not in some sense sinful but that clergy were no different from other Christians and could not escape their shared involvement in the sinful things of this world which marriage symbolized. The distinction between clergy and laity now evaporated, leaving only a ministerial vocation, important but no worthier than any other honest calling. Presently the Catholic religious system in its entirety was integrated in Luther's mind and in Protestant propaganda as 'popery', a radical inversion and perversion of Christianity amounting to a false church, Babel.

Sacraments were not discarded but they were now closely linked with the divine word as a saving action directed by God towards man. With a distinctive insistence not shared by other reformers and specifically rejected by Zwingli and his successors in the leadership of the Swiss and south German reformations, Luther connected the fleshly incarnation of God the Son in the stable at Bethlehem with the sacrament of the Supper, where the bread and wine became in all reality the body and blood of Christ, a sacred mystery which Luther made no attempt to understand or express in the language of rational explanation but which was close to the heart of his piety. Here, and in a sense only here, could God and man come together.

The social and even political implications of this 'theology of the cross' in which God, a strange God, reveals and yet mysteriously conceals himself, in a baby in a manger, on a gallows, in bread and wine, were extensive. God is only to be found in the imperfect things of this world which are so many masks disguising his true benevolence. This was to condemn and secularize much that had been thought 'religious': mysticism, monasticism, virginity; and to endorse and sacralize much that was worldly: daily occupations however insignificant, marriage and parenthood, government, even war. This doctrine of vocation was at once conservative and revolutionary and it seems to account for much of the appeal which the new religion enjoyed, especially among artisans, entrepreneurs, and anyone who was capable of gaining some satisfaction from his occupation: unless that is Protestant and Weberian romanticism.

Where, according to Luther, was the church to be found? And also, in the taunt which Catholics hurled at Protestants, where was your church before Luther? The answer to both questions was: close to the gospel. Even a child knew that the church consists of those who hear their Master's voice, the sheep who respond to the shepherd's whistle. If the church in the shape of its public organization lacked the gospel, even set itself against the gospel, it was to be repudiated, even abandoned. But for Luther it was no solution to establish a brand new church and hang on it the sign 'Evangelical'. That would not be a 'true' church, any more than heaven could be created on earth. True Christians would always be rare birds. The church as a human structure was part of the *Weltliche Reich*, earthy. The first priority was to put the Gospel into the hands of Christians in the form of the Bible in an acceptable translation in their own language. Then everything would look after itself.

It will be seen why the word 'anarchy' has been used. Even Luther soon had to concede that a structure of parishes had to be maintained. A new German mass was composed, a greater and a smaller catechism, and a visitation was conducted to determine what people in rural Saxony knew about religion, with disturbing results. The needs of education and of charity had to be met. Education became the speciality of Melanchthon, known as *praeceptor Germaniae*. Melanchthon was also the prime author of a theological constitution for a Lutheran church, the Confession of Augsburg submitted to the emperor and the assembled princes at an imperial diet in 1530. Extensive powers in the fields of religion and morals were given to, or appropriated by, the secular authorities, princes, and self-governing cities. Soon it proved expedient to compel people to go to church and to punish deviants and heretics, even to kill them. This was not necessarily inconsistent with Luther's pristine teaching but it may have looked inconsistent, especially to deviants and heretics.

But it was the cities of south and central Germany and Switzerland which contributed most, both to the thorough eradication of the old order and to the construction of the new. The temperament of urban populations and the communal tensions and factions characteristic of urban life favoured a reform more iconoclastic than anything that Luther had cared to endorse, more radically opposed to sacraments and symbols, and especially to the symbol of the consecrated host. Almost universally the Reformation in the cities (and most of the great imperial cities and many smaller towns were involved) was demanded by popular agitation rather than imposed. But in the second stage, following the initial adoption of the Reform, magistrates and ministers combined, not always in perfect harmony, to construct new models of a Christian society to which conformity was demanded. These models built theologically upon the doctrines of election and predestination ('you have not chosen me but I have chosen you') which were implicit in Luther's gospel but not much taught by Lutheran preachers; biblically upon the collective experience of the covenanted people of God in the Old Testament, with which the baptized population of a 'godly' city like Zurich or Berne readily identified; but also, more pragmatically, on the inherited values of the urban commune, summed up in the title of the first publication of the greatest of the urban reformers, Martin Bucer of Strasbourg, that a man should not live for himself but for others, the common good (*Das yon selbs niemant, sonder anderen leben soll*, 1532).

Everyone, or everyone of the respectable rank of householder, was agreed that this desirable state of affairs was attainable by good government, or 'discipline'. But what kind of discipline? The name of an otherwise obscure Swiss physician, Thomas Erastus, has contributed our concept of 'Erastianism', the principle that where there are Christian magistrates there is no need of any other discipline. This doctrine was attractive to magistrates as diverse as Queen Elizabeth I of England and the republican syndics of Geneva, although most magistrates conceded a sphere of useful activity to the ministers of the church over and above their preaching, subject always to the ultimate arbitration of the magisterial sword. But what the later followers of Calvin came to regard as 'the discipline' in a special sense was the spiritual government of Christians by Christian officers, almost as if the church was a separate institution from the state and certainly a distinct jurisdiction. Specifically it was claimed that the ministers of the church and not the magistrates should determine the fitness of Christians to receive the Lord's Supper. According to Martin Bucer, the scriptural ministry was fourfold: pastors, teachers, elders, and deacons, discipline being the particular function of the eldership. Calvin adopted this scheme but declined to make discipline a distinct 'mark' or distinguishing feature of the church, restricting the marks of the church to two, gospel and sacraments. However Calvin's successor in the leadership of the Geneva Church Theodore Beza and other second-generation Calvinists made discipline, in the particular form we know as Presbyterianism, essential. Linked with the highly contentious matter of predestination, this provided the ongoing agenda for the Reformed Churches, leaving its variegated record in the confessions which sought to bring consensus out of potential confusion and conflict, the French and Belgic Confessions (1559 and 1561), the Heidelberg Catechism (1562), the English Thirty-nine Articles (1563), and the Articles of Dort (1619). As these documents imply, true doctrine was now at a premium, as much as it had been when the young church drew up the creeds; and for much the same reason, since it was necessary for the sake of unity to reconcile, or crush, intellectual differences. For this purpose heavy intellectual weapons came into play, above all a streamlined logical method tending towards a new and Protestant scholasticism. It was the beginning of a new age of orthodoxy, or of what a leading historian of French Protestantism called 'l'Établissement'.

By 1600 the Reformed Churches were widely established in Western Europe, from the Orkneys to the Pyrenees, and as far to the east as Hungary. By contrast the Evangelical or Lutheran Churches were geographically as well as politically and confessionally circumscribed and confined to the northern German states and Scandinavia, their own theological differences uneasily reconciled in the Formula of Concord (1577). (Not for nothing did Shakespeare speak of 'spleeny Lutherans'.) As early as the mid-sixteenth century and the reign of Edward VI it was becoming clear that English Protestantism would draw away from Lutheranism and towards the Reformed Churches, theologically, even liturgically and to some extent in polity and organization, at least in the aspirations of many, although the retention of bishops and other aspects of traditional ecclesiastical organization made the Church of England something of a case apart and hid the seeds of a future 'Anglicanism'. Under Elizabeth I and the early Stuart kings, but not with their consistent or wholehearted support, English Protestants identified strongly with 'the best reformed churches overseas', believing that their nation had been given a special and even unique role to play in the gathering apocalyptic drama of the age which we know as the age of the wars of religion.

The New Catholicism

Meanwhile, on the other side of a kind of Iron Curtain which had been descending since the earliest voices were raised against Luther to the definitive legislation of the Council of Trent and beyond, an alternative version of Christian civilization was taking shape, almost as different from medieval Christendom as Protestantism itself. In the textbooks the Counter-Reformation, in itself, as we have seen, a mere term of art, is neatly packaged as a sequence of more or less discrete topics or chapter headings: the Spanish and Italian reformers; the new religious orders and especially the Jesuits; the Roman inquisition and the *Index* of prohibited books; Trent; the Counter-Reformation popes and their achievement; missionary activity both in Europe and beyond, regaining Europe's heartland, gaining the crown of martyrdom in England, making new conquests for Christ in the Americas, Japan, and China; the political reimposition of Catholicism by a new generation of ardent Catholic rulers, notably the Habsburg Emperor Ferdinand II, product of a Jesuit education and hammer of the Protestants of Bohemia in the Thirty Years War; Counter-Reformation sanctity, the daunting spiritual uplands inhabited by St Teresa of Avila and St John of the Cross, the heroic work of clearing and cultivating undertaken by St Charles Borromeo and the great seventeenth-century French achievers, of many schools of devotion and conflicting theological tendencies; mannerist religious art.

Conventionally, and plausibly, the Counter-Reformation is seen to have moved from a hopeful and liberal eirenicism, a religious spirit not remote from Protestantism and prepared to come to terms with it, towards a more reactive repression. The early Italian Reform promised to be neither Protestant nor anti-Protestant but Evangelical. Cardinal Contarini, whose own religious experience in some ways resembled that of Luther, found that he could do business with the Protestants at the Conference of Ratisbon (or Regensburg) (1541). But in the event there was to be no fruitful meeting of minds, no reconciliation, either at Ratisbon or later at Trent. The general council which the French government hoped as late as 1561 might still find the elusive middle ground and heal Christendom's bleeding wounds merely confirmed its divisions and defined Catholicism as the religion of that portion of Western Christendom which anathematized the rest. The Counter-Reformation came to its maturity with the repression represented by the inquisition and the Index, notorious for the burning of the eclectic philosopher Giordano Bruno at Rome in 1600 (as Calvin was for the burning of the arch-heretic Servetus at Geneva in 1555) and for the condemnation in 1633 of Galileo's heliocentric universe. In the folk memory of modern European civilization Galileo's legendary words (as legendary as Luther's 'Here I stand' at Worms) 'Eppur si muove' ('but it does move all the same') have stood for the essentially progressive vitality of the forces against which Rome chose to set itself, the long-term sterility of the church of the Counter-Reformation as it degenerated into a kind of spiritual *ancien régime*.

But that is a very long perspective indeed. In a sense not only the Tridentine church but all the religious confessions and communities which were shaped or reshaped by the sustained episode of the Reformation and Counter-Reformation carried the genes of ultimate morbidity, for the end of all great enterprises of the human spirit is a measure of failure. But there were also seeds of future springs in the burnt-over country which, by the end of the seventeenth century, was Christian Europe. Pietism, evangelicalism, and neo-Catholicism in its liberal and ultra-montane forms would all arise from these ashes. A Galileo might say 'Eppur si muove!'

With the detachment of an age far gone in secularity it is the points of resemblance between the Reformation and the Counter-Reformation in the maturity of their respective establishments, not the differences, which impress. Both systems were didactic, even pedagogical, and both put the internalization of the Ten Commandments in the forefront of their educational efforts. The appropriate monument to this epoch of church history would be a vast pile of catechisms. Both backed up instruction with corrective, even coercive pastoral discipline, a force for order and deference so useful to secular governments that it is doubtful whether the emergence of the centralized authoritarian state would have been possible without it. Among other useful functions, it kept the number of illegitimate births at a very low figure. Both Catholic and Protestant churchmen were hostile to stage-plays, cruel sports, fairs, the drinking of toasts, dancing, ballads, disorderly funerals, Sabbath-breaking, the misuse of churchyards, blasphemy, gambling. Both, but especially the church of the Counter-Reformation, discouraged the spontaneity of lay initiatives, inducing a passive and deferential rather than ebullient religious spirit. Both Catholic and Protestant regimes gave, as they thought, honour to God by burning, on an unprecedented scale, those enemies of God, mostly female, who were believed to be witches and in league with Satan.

There were of course differences. Catholics burnt more witches than Protestants and achieved a higher rate of religious conformity and a lower illegitimate birth rate. There was also the irrepressible tendency of Protestantism to revert to type and reproduce new forms of autodidactic and dissenting religious enthusiasm. But that is another story.

8

Enlightenment: Secular and Christian
(1600–1800)

JOHN McMANNERS

THE two centuries preceding the French revolution were marked
by the growing secularization of West European society, culture,
and thought. It was not just a change from a 'Christian' to a
'secular' order. Indeed, Jean Delumeau has argued that medieval
life was 'Christian' only in so far as every secular passion and
inspiration had to be expressed in Christian forms; take away
compulsion, routine, impractical renunciation of the world,
magical beliefs, and fear of hell, and there was less true Christian
belief and conduct in medieval times than now. Not everyone
would agree with this austere limitation of religion to its inspirational essence, and perhaps the historian should stop short of
such a sweeping comparison of two eras, for how can he weigh
achievement against opportunity and judge the yearnings in the
souls of so many who have left no memorial? But it is reasonable
to say that a Christian civilization had arisen ahead of all possible
processes of individual conversion, and in its shelter, human
individuality and freedom had been evolving. Religion was on
its way to becoming a matter of intense personal decision: if
there was a single message and driving force behind Reformation
and Counter-Reformation, it was this. Secularization was the
inevitable counterpart, the opposite side of the coin, the reaction
of human nature to a demand almost too intense to bear. The

idea of Christianity as some huge galleon blown on to the rocks then pounded by the seas and plundered by coastal predators in an age of reason and materialism is mistaken. Christianity was itself evolving in ethos and doctrine, finding new emphases, new inspirations, appealing in new ways to new classes of people, even as the world changed around it—and, indeed, contributing to and forcing on that change. European life was being secularized; religion was becoming personalized, individualized: the two things went together, and were interdependent.

The fragmentation of the universal church into competing churches, and weariness with religious warfare, hastened on the secularization process. *Cujus regio, ejus religio*: politically speaking, and for practical men, this was how all the soul-searching, the shuddering fear of heresy, the striving for a godly society, the struggle to vindicate the majesty of God or the freewill of the creature had to end. Let the subject conform to the religion of his sovereign. The basis of the Peace of Augsburg in 1555, this cynical formula was reapplied in 1648 to bring the Thirty Years War to an end—the last war between European powers with religion as a major issue in the fighting. The Peace of Westphalia restored ecclesiastical property and control to the various parties—Catholic, Lutheran, and Calvinist—as in 1624 (in some places 1618), even if it meant chapters with canons of varying religious allegiances and, in one case, Catholic and Protestant bishops alternating in a diocese. A great deal of ecclesiastical property was secularized. A common phenomenon when godly men strive to bring religion back to orthodoxy or austerity is the enthusiastic co-operation of worldly entrepreneurs who serve the cause by confiscating the revenues that tempt to corruption.

No sooner had *cujus regio, ejus religio* been accepted than rulers found there was little profit in trying to enforce it. The duke of Hanover became a Catholic in 1651, the elector of Saxony in 1697 (to obtain the Polish throne), and the duke of Württemberg in 1733, but none of them was able to extract concessions for their new religion: the Lutheran establishment in their countries was too well organized. Even persecuting a small minority had its dangers. The Polish Diet laid disabilities on the 'dissidents' (Protestants and Eastern Orthodox) and powerful neighbours were glad of pretexts for intervention; the emperor tried to undermine the Calvinist nobles of Hungary, and they intrigued with the Turks. Absolutism was the order of the day, but so too was mercantilism, and persecution was a menace to peace and prosperity. The electors of Brandenburg were an example to Europe. Their own convictions were Calvinist, but they accepted the Lutheran domination in Prussia and protected Lutherans against the Calvinist majority in Cleves. In the build-up of the Prussian military and bureaucratic state the Lutheran clergy were useful collaborators, acting as army chaplains, teaching at the Cadet School in Berlin, and running the military orphanage in Potsdam, while pious laymen made the Civil Service their profession and were favoured in appointments by the government. The Hohenzollern rulers welcomed religious refugees into their territories, more especially if they brought new skills and worked hard, thus swelling the tax revenues.

Toleration, imposed in Brandenburg-Prussia by a crafty up-and-coming ruling family, sprang up spontaneously in Holland. The Northern provinces, separated from the Catholic South, had their early bout of rigorism, with the Synod of Dort in 1618 condemning 'Arminian' deviations from Calvinistic predestination. But in this least homogeneous state of Europe, which so soon had to fight for existence against the territorial ambitions of Louis XIV of France, ideological quarrels were too dangerous a luxury, while booming trade brought all classes into a co-operative venture in prosperity. 'It is the union of interests and not of opinions that gives peace to kingdoms', said an English Quaker, drawing the lesson from the Dutch example. 'Religion may possibly do more good in other places', said another Englishman, a diplomat in Holland, 'but it does less harm here.' By the end of the seventeenth century, religious

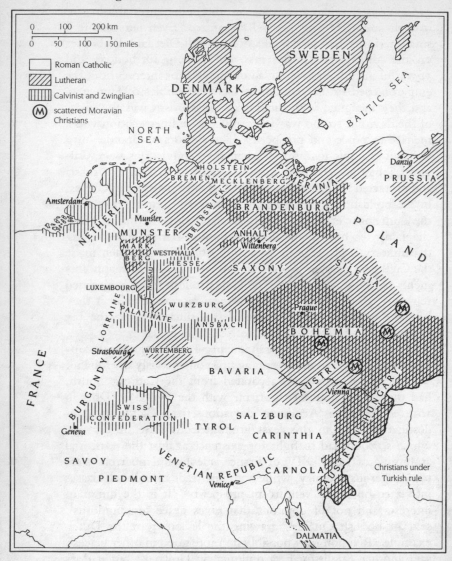

CENTRAL EUROPE AFTER THE REFORMATION, 1618

sects and inspirations of every kind found there the sort of refuge they had enjoyed briefly in England under Cromwell; even Socinians (who denied the divinity of Christ) and Roman Catholics were little troubled, while the arrival of Huguenot refugees from France made the country an international centre of debate and journalism, the capital of 'the republic of letters'.

In England—rising more securely to wealth and power—toleration came, as it came in Holland, from economic prudence and political necessity. The Restoration of 1660 was followed by measures penalizing dissent, for the memory of the Civil War was associated with the 'spawn of sects' and the rule of the 'Saints'. But the alarm of having a popish king on the throne in the person of James II and the respectability of the united Protestant revolution of 1688 which got rid of him made 'due tenderness to Dissenters' inevitable. Comprehension failed and a limited toleration was granted by Parliament. As for Scotland, presbyterian church government was established by law; when the monarch crossed the border, he was assumed to have changed his religious allegiance.

Events in France, meanwhile, formed a sinister contrast to those across the Channel; here, the case for toleration was proved by the effects of a monumental act of cruelty, Louis XIV's revocation of the Edict of Nantes and his unleashing of his licentious dragoons against Huguenots who would not conform to Catholicism. Whether he was motivated more by fear of hell than by a desire to win the Catholic princes of Germany, whether he was insensitive to cruelty or convinced himself the conversions came easily, must be left to the verdict of specialists in morbid psychology. Protestants take pride in the heroism of those who suffered—men who went to a living death on the galleys, women who were shorn and vanished into convents, refugees who abandoned everything and fled across the frontiers; they must note, too, another illustration of the universal truth that most people are not heroes, and how persecution succeeds. It all depends what 'success' means, of course. Cruelty weakened the force of religious dissent in the country and produced generations of unbelievers and anticlericals.

It was a commonplace assumption that religious diversity endangers national unity, and Louis XIV's grandiose resort to coercion was almost universally applauded in France. The clergy went along with the tide, many unenthusiastically. Some bishops allowed Calvinists to abjure in ambiguous terms, and two refused to allow the dragoons into their dioceses. But as one of these two, the bishop of Grenoble, told his clergy, 'I profited from the opportunity of the dragoons being in the vicinity to bring my diocesans back to the fold by kindness . . .'. The cruelties being on the king's conscience, the clergy used them. The pope condemned forced conversions—nearly three years after they had occurred. Churchmen did not believe in the right to persecute, but they were willing to reap their mission harvest on the margins of the secular power's ruthless drive for glory and national unity.

When Louis XIV was dead, Frenchmen could reflect on the economic advantages gained by their Protestant rivals by the recruitment of so many industrious refugees. This case, like the expulsion of 2,000 Protestants by the prince bishop of Salzburg in 1731, to the benefit of Prussia, was a stock example of the Enlightenment to prove the folly of persecution. But other arguments for toleration of a less self-interested kind were becoming current. 'We have just enough religion to make us hate, but not enough to make us love one another', said Dean Swift, in mordant criticism of the cause he served. It had to change; the true sense of the gospels was pressing against the panic fear of heresy that had caused so much evil. Persecution had been defended by biblical citations; this ended with Pierre Bayle's deadly commentary on 'Compel them to come in'; from henceforward, no isolated text could stand against the general sense of the gospels and natural decency. Christians came to terms with the existence of churches in the plural. The tremendous passions unleashed by the Reformation were being channelled into an insistence on individual conversion, a religion of the heart, deep and self-justifying, not dependent on the structure of routine conformity. In the creation of such internal conviction, force was irrelevant, counter-productive even. More and more, theologians accepted the idea of 'the invisible church', an intangible reality above and beyond the fragmented Christian bodies. The eighteenth century was the 'age of reason', and defenders of a reasonable Christianity thought of a church in terms of the collective allegiances of its members rather than as a divinely commissioned continuing organic unity—Locke's 'a voluntary society of men joining themselves together of their own accord to the public worshipping of God'.

If all believers belong to an invisible unity and if their allegiance to individual churches is a continuing act of will on their part, why cannot their wills reach out further, making their mystical unity into a visible reality? If intellectual argument could do it, there was a way ahead well-signposted. In the vein of Erasmus, Grotius in 1622, in an enormously influential book, had divided doctrines between those necessary to salvation and those which, however edifying, are optional. Others elaborated the idea. Ordinary people are not inferior to intellectuals in God's plan of salvation, yet the beliefs they can grasp are few and simple. As Dryden said (in 1682, three years before he was converted to Rome),

> Faith is not built on disquisitions vain,
> The things we must believe are few and plain.

Anglican churchmen, rejoicing in a form of church government they regarded as combining the best of both medieval and Reformation inspirations, conceded to continental Protestants that there was no divergence over essentials. 'Something which possesses divine authority may be lacking, at least in matters of outward governance, and yet salvation may remain unimpaired', wrote Bishop Lancelot Andrewes to a French Huguenot. In the second half of the seventeenth century, the ecumenical cause was promoted by indefatigable travellers—the Scot in Anglican orders, John Durie, Calixtus the German Lutheran, the Pole

Jablonski of the Bohemian Brethren; by utopian speculators—Comenius; by great savants—Leibniz; and ecclesiastical statesmen—Bossuet and Spinola, the general of the Franciscan Order. In the early eighteenth century the three chief theologians of Geneva led by Jean-Alphonse Turrettini were corresponding widely to try to hammer out a formula for Protestant unity, while Archbishop William Wake from Canterbury was in touch with Gallican scholars and Eastern Orthodox prelates. Realistically, Wake aimed, not at union, but at mutual recognition: each church was to declare each of the others 'a sound part of the Catholic Church and communicate with one another as such'. After so long a period of doctrinal dispute, it was natural to find the approach to unity through intellectual debate; but other ideas were in the air. The Philadelphian Society (founded in 1697 on the inspiration of a book with the charming title, *The Heavenly Cloud now Breaking*) was a meeting of Christians of every kind to exchange spiritual experiences, while the Deutsche Christentumsgesellschaft at Basle from 1756 onwards was the first international interchurch society, bringing Christians together in good works and mission enterprises.

As always, initiatives towards ecumenical understanding were the work of the few. Most Christians carried on in blinkered loyalty to their exclusive allegiances. There was an assumption—among worldly men and unbelievers as well as among Christians—that religious minorities ought to be allowed no more than the right to follow their consciences in worship; they were not to be allowed equal rights to proselytize or to enjoy public office. The anticlerical Emperor Joseph II's patent of toleration of 1781 for the Habsburg dominions did not include deists or atheists, minority churches were not allowed bells and steeples, their members had to pay dues to the Catholic clergy, while a Catholic wishing to convert to Protestantism had to submit to six weeks instruction in the Roman faith beforehand. The French toleration edict of 1787 did little more than allow Protestants to legalize their marriages and have sepulchres for their dead. In England at this time, in theory at any rate, it was essential to take the sacrament according to the rites of the Church of England to be eligible for public office, and even in 1829, when Roman Catholics were allowed to sit in parliament, it was only after taking an oath 'not to subvert the present church establishment as settled by law'. In no state of Europe were the members of religious minorities treated as completely equal before the French revolution.

In 1681, William Penn, the Quaker, received a land grant in the New World from Charles II. The charter for Pennsylvania, issued in 1701, went further than toleration; no one was 'at any time to be compelled to frequent or maintain any religious worship, place or ministry whatever, contrary to his or her mind'. It was a formula suited to a frontier society and it prevailed in the United States after they won their independence. In Europe, however, a state church was assumed to be a necessity. When the legislators of the French revolution sold off ecclesiastical property and banned monastic vows, they set up a new state church none the less, with clergy elected instead of being appointed by the Crown and patrons; when the old order was engulfed in the Terror, they tried official religions of 'Reason' and 'The Supreme Being'; when Napoleon imposed his dictatorship, he 'restored the altars' by a new concordat with the papacy, which carried on as the basis of an ecclesiastical establishment all through the nineteenth century. The argument underlying the unquestioned acceptance of the necessity of official religion was Swift's: 'We need religion as we need our dinner, wickedness makes Christianity indispensable and there's an end of it'. By exercising pastoral care, preaching moral conduct, denouncing immorality and, more positively, leading in charitable and educational work, the clergy would tame human wickedness sufficiently to maintain public order; in addition, they would intercede with God on behalf of the nation and represent the divine presence in public ceremonies. But why should there not be a diversity of Christian organizations acting as a pluralistic framework to guarantee the morality of society? The idea was discussed in England during the Puritan revolution, and was subjected to powerful vituperation by Thomas Edwards, the Puritan and Presbyterian divine, in his *Reasons against the Independent Government of Particular Congregations* (1641). But in fact, writes Michael Watts, 'only once . . . did men who rejected the principle of a national church appear to come near to controlling the destinies of the nation', this was in the Barebones Parliament of 1653—the proposal to abolish tithe failed and the moderates wound up proceedings and surrendered power to Cromwell.

Hooker, the judicious apologist of the Elizabethan settlement, had described the Anglican Church as all-inclusive: 'there is not any man a member of the Commonwealth who is not also of the Church of England'. Even in an age when dissent was freely allowed, here was an ideal which a state church needed to recognize; it was meant to be an institution with which the great majority could identify. There was a particular difficulty if the established church was Calvinist, for to the Lutheran preaching of the word and administration of the sacraments as marks of the church, Calvinists added 'discipline'. In Holland, this led to the distinction between the *liefhebbers* and the *lidmaten*; the former came to sermons, the latter had placed themselves entirely 'under the sweet yoke of our chief shepherd Jesus Christ'. The States of Holland wanting a genuine national church, proposed to end this distinction, and to admit all to the Lord's table. This was never achieved; the Reformed Church clung to the spirit of the war against Philip II, and the sense of being the chosen people. In Massachusetts, the 'gathered church' had a membership limited to the 'visible saints' who covenanted with one another, giving evidence of 'saving grace'. It was impossible to go on with so many excluded—hence, the 'half-way covenant' and, finally, property qualifications for voting as against church membership.

The concept of the elect recognizing one another and confederating was one suited for struggles of survival against hostile armies or adverse conditions, but not for a theology of peaceful growth—and certainly not for the age of reason. For Anglicans, there was a difficulty of a different kind in the development of an ecclesiology of the establishment. The high church emphasis on the body of Christ, the church of the apostles and Fathers adapted to a particular nation did not entirely answer the question: why this particular church as against the other variants? Locke's 'voluntary society' might be the answer here, and this was the view taken, in a notorious sermon, by Benjamin Hoadly, bishop of Bangor, in 1717, for which he was trounced, wittily and unfairly, by William Law the high churchman. Christ left no authority to represent him, his kingdom not being of this world, said Hoadly, and the church is the gathering of those willingly submitting themselves to him. William Warburton, in his *Alliance between Church and State* (1736), drew the reasonable conclusion: as a matter of 'civic utility', the state sets up as the established church the religious body with the most numerous membership. This was in the logic of the situation in which Presbyterianism was established in Scotland and Anglicanism in England. What if the majority is lost, or if all Christians collectively are reduced to a minority? At the time, the prospect was unthinkable.

'Let every soul be subject to the higher powers . . . the powers that be are ordained by God'. St Paul's dictum was standard doctrine. There was, running underground, another current of thought in Christianity, millenarian, anarchistic, utopian, yearning for the overthrow of secular dominion and a return to the freedom of a sinless Eden. During the Civil War and Commonwealth in England, these ideas had broken to the surface as half-religious, half-secular aspirations. To the Ranters, sin was an invention of priests and rulers to keep men in subjection; Levellers and Diggers dreamt of a new heaven and new earth, instantly attainable by the casting out of covetousness. But this spectacle of 'the world turned upside down' by radical ideas, like that of the wars of religion on the Continent, made moderate men cleave to the authority of the secular power, the power ordained by God which alone could keep the peace. This argument from fear of anarchy underlay so much of the seventeenth-century sycophantic rhetoric about the Divine Right of Kings. 'Ye are gods', said Bossuet of kings, but he was citing Psalm 82: 'Ye are gods . . . nevertheless ye shall die like men and fall like one of the princes'. 'Oh gods of flesh and blood, gods of dust and mud,' he thunders on, 'all that is godlike and continuous is your authority.' A particular ruler is just a transient mortal under God's judgement. Stripped of the loyal trappings of personal allegiance, the Christian's duty came down to simple non-resistance. 'Absolute submission', said the university of Oxford in 1683; prayer is the only weapon against a wicked ruler, said the Lutheran Veit von Seckendorff two years later.

The matter was put to the test in that very year 1685, when Louis XIV's persecution of the Huguenots reached its climax and the Roman Catholic James II ascended the English throne. Among the Calvinist refugees in Holland, Bayle continued to insist on the standard doctrine of submission; Jurieu, by contrast, proclaimed the sovereignty of the people. Anglican divines justified getting rid of their popish monarch by switching from Divine Right to 'providential election'; besides, James had 'abdicated' by flight. Even so, some bishops who had refused to obey James II also refused to take the oath of loyalty to his successor, in contrast to Bishop Compton of London, who turned out for the Protestant cause in buff coat and jackboots with sword and pistols. A hundred years later, when a very different revolution in France violently overturned the old regime and the monarchy, theologians had to consider the desperate casuistry of the obligation to take the successive revolutionary oaths. The romantic trappings of loyalty dropped away and the bedrock principle was revealed: a *de facto* government has to be obeyed. It was bitter for the French Catholic royalists to accept that the 'powers that be' could include a revolutionary assembly, as it was even more bitter for German and Russian Christians to accept the Pauline text under Hitler and Stalin.

'The alliance of church and state' was a cliché of political theory and ecclesiology common to all the countries of Europe in the eighteenth century. It was an unequal alliance. When Warburton published his book, lay control was dominant and encroaching. At the Restoration of 1660, the English clergy had abandoned their power of taxing themselves; the Prayer Book of 1662 passed Parliament by only six votes, with the House insisting on its right to debate future changes; in 1717, the Whig government suspended the Convocation of Canterbury's authority to conduct business. The Crown's power to appoint bishops became part of the duke of Newcastle's patronage network, and the votes of the prelates in the Lords were expected to be available to the government. Traditionally powerful, the Lutheran pastors of Sweden and the Calvinist ministers of Geneva fell more and more under the control, even if exercised by collaboration, of local notables and lay magistrates. The Lutheran clergy of Germany tended to be subservient to secular rulers; with authority in their churches divided among super-intendents, consistories, and abbots of cloisters, and the social origins of pastors being undistinguished, this was not surprising, though recently historians have become interested in the clerical writers who stood against the 'cameralist' and absolutist lawyers. In France, the Gallican church was accustomed to claim inde-pendence in its own sphere. 'Within the alliance of temporal and spiritual, each power is sovereign and absolute in what concerns it', said the Assembly of Clergy in 1765. But the Gallican lawyers were speaking for the lay establishment every-where when they added the gloss: 'it is not the business of ministers of the church to fix the boundaries God has placed between the two powers'. In the last resort, the will of the state must prevail. The magistrates of the Parlement of Paris made this clear in the mid-eighteenth century, when they took ruthless action against clergy who obeyed the archbishop's order to refuse the last sacraments to dying Jansenists—granted, the sacraments were in the sphere of the clergy, but citizens had their rights and could not be subjected to public defamation. In all the countries of Catholic Europe (more especially in Venice), the church was pinned down by the lawyers of the state; the

role of ecclesiastical courts and the right of ecclesiastical institutions to acquire property were circumscribed; Roman bulls
and briefs could not be published without consent, and where
papal approval for collation to benefices was required, it had to
be given automatically. The Catholic crowns used their cardinals
and power of veto to ensure the election of compliant popes; it
took six months' conclave and the exhausting of every intrigue
before the one effective candidate of the eighteenth century,
Benedict XIV, was elected in 1740. In spite of papal protests,
the Jesuits were expelled from Portugal, Spain, and France and
finally, in 1773, Clement XIV was obliged to suppress the
Jesuit Order altogether.

While the Catholic sovereigns tyrannized over popes, their
control of the church at home was not what it seemed. They
appointed the bishops and had the patronage of the great
monasteries, but the aristocracy expected to have these vast
revenues for their younger sons. Only once between 1715 and
1789 was a commoner appointed to rule one of the 130 dioceses
of France (and that was 30 parishes lost in wild mountains). In
Spain, Portugal, and Naples, the rich sees were reserved for
nobles, and in Germany, where chapters elected, their choice
fell almost invariably on aristocrats—in 1730, the two branches
of the Wittelsbach family held the two great sees of Cologne
and Mainz and nine minor bishoprics. Indefensible in principle,
this aristocratic monopoly was inevitable in practice. A commoner would not carry the authority to defend his clergy and
people against local nobles and officials. The aristocratic upper
clergy of France, meeting in their quinquennial assemblies to
vote their own taxation were—along with the magistrates of
the Parlements—a bulwark of a peculiar oligarchical liberty
against absolutism. Normally, they used their leverage to protect
ecclesiastical privileges, but in their remonstrance of 15 June
1788 to the king they rose above self-interest to call for liberty
for the whole nation. Their peculiar rights, they said, were 'the
remains of the old national franchises', and they asked for the
summoning of the Estates General to vote taxes on behalf of

all: 'human nature will begin to regain its dignity, and the people will begin to count for something'. Their manifesto was a notable contribution to the Enlightenment.

In the secularization of European thought, the decisive change came about at the end of the seventeenth century and the beginning of the eighteenth, 'la crise de la conscience européenne', in Hazard's famous phrase. By 1778, the year of the deaths of Voltaire and Rousseau, all the stock arguments against Christianity had been invented except, perhaps, 'science versus religion', a gambit as yet undetected behind the 'Wisdom of God manifest in the Works of Creation' theme which had inspired John Ray, Robert Boyle, and Isaac Newton. Age-old anticlerical envies were taken over by economic theorists attacking ecclesiastical wealth and monastic idleness; from sceptics of the Italian Renaissance, French *libertins* of the seventeenth century, and English Deists of the early eighteenth came doubts about the Bible and revelation; the arguments from miracle and prophecy were seen to be inconclusive; geographical discoveries allied to an education founded on the classics encouraged the development of the comparative study of religions, with slanted praise of pagan philosophers, Chinese sages, and noble savages. 'It is come, I know not how,' wrote Bishop Butler in 1736, 'to be taken for granted by many persons, that Christianity is now at length discovered to be fictitious'.

Some of the replies of Christian apologists had philosophical cogency, like Butler's own picture of a universe where all is mysterious and 'probability is the guide of life'. But how could the scriptures be validated? It was an especially worrying question for Protestants, with Catholics on the one hand proclaiming the authority of the church as the only warrant for accepting the Bible and sects on the other saying much the same about the 'inner light'. As the Quaker Samuel Fisher argued in his *The Rustics Alarm to the Rabbies* (1660), neither the text nor the canon was certain in this 'bulk of heterogeneous writings'. John Bunyan reflected that the Turks had a book to prove their belief in Muhammad—what if Christ and the Bible 'should be but a I think so too?' Richard Simon, the French Oratorian laid the foundation for the critical study of the Old Testament (1678), not without a sidelong glance at the uncertainty he was sowing among Protestants, but as yet he had no successors. Fundamentalist interpretation of the Bible was a millstone around the neck of the defenders of revelation. One has only to look at Dom Calmet's commentaries, Voltaire's handy index for scriptural references to God's vindictiveness, to see how hopeless was the task of explaining contradictions and cruelties on fundamentalist presuppositions. The ridicule heaped upon the Bible by the writers of the Enlightenment did Christians a great service by compelling them to begin the process of tracing the evolution of a lofty idea of God from crude primitive origins, as against their static picture, indiscriminately compiled, of a timeless tyrant.

The Enlightenment did a further service to Christianity by ridiculing hell, the ironies of Voltaire and Diderot clinching the case already advanced by innovative Christian thinkers. Throughout the seventeenth century, Christian writers on the fringes of orthodoxy—Platonists, chiliasts, patristic scholars rediscovering Origen's universalism, liberal Anglicans, Protestant mystics—denounced the idea of eternal punishment as incompatible with the love of God. Archbishop Tillotson, unable to break free from fundamentalist exegesis, took refuge in the thought that the biblical texts about hell were contrived by God as salutary threats which he had no intention of enforcing. Pierre Poiret, Protestant theologian and mystic (1682), John Locke, Anglican philosopher (1695), and Pierre Cuppé, a French *curé* (1698), proclaimed God's willingness to save all men of goodwill, be they pagans, heretics, or unbelievers. Only those who adamantly used their free will to resist divine grace would miss salvation, said Poiret, but it would not be God who punished them: lost in the darkness, their lives would disintegrate in meaninglessness. Their arguments were brought to a universalist conclusion in 1731 by Marie Huber, a Protestant who took purgatory more seriously than the

Catholics, for everyone would go there, even the devils, and finally be cleansed and reach beatitude to the degree of which they are capable. She makes the decisive point that scriptural references must not be interpreted to go against the verities which are at the source of all religion. Rousseau went to the heart of the matter when he wrote the deathbed scene of his heroine Julie; she knows no fear of awakening for she goes to sleep in the bosom of a loving Father. Jean-Jacques Rousseau, sentimental deist and publicist of genius, systematized the ideas of thinkers on the liberal fringes of Protestantism into the broad principles which were to revolutionize Christian thought in the coming century: 'the necessity of qualifying all doctrine by the paramount assertion that God is love; the rule of interpreting all scripture in the light of God's nature and not as a quarry of information, even about spiritual things; the acceptance of the limitation of our knowledge of God to what is morally necessary—light enough to live by'. These principles conform to Locke's 'reasonableness of Christianity' as well as looking forward to Schleiermacher's definition of religion (at the end of the century), as our response to God's saving love, the feeling of 'absolute dependence'.

When the Enlightenment attacked superstition often enough it was with clerical support. Both Reformation and Counter-Reformation had worked for an educated clergy, produced by the universities of England and Germany and the seminaries of Catholic countries set up on the orders of the Council of Trent, and the social status of the clergy was enhanced as their incomes improved with the rising yield of tithe. The eighteenth century, as readers of Fielding, Goldsmith, and Parson Woodforde and of the innumerable anecdotes about 'le bon curé' in France will recognize, was the golden age of the parish priest, the leader of a coherent local community in the last decades before general religious conformity broke down. In a sense, in his community the priest represented tradition and the past; but he was also one of the chief instruments of social change. The old community religion of processions, carnivals, pilgrimages, Corpus Christi pageants, bonfires on St John's eve, saints with healing powers, and sacred shrines and springs has been evoked recently in brilliant historical studies touched with nostalgia; those were the days before we came of age and discovered loneliness. The reforming clergy of the seventeenth and eighteenth centuries showed scant respect for these old observances. In the areas of peasant Europe where the iconoclasm and austerity of the Reformation had not destroyed them, the Catholic clergy purged away everything regarded as a pagan survival, frivolous, superstitious, or promoting too great a familiarity between the sexes. Many a venerable image was pulled out of its niche in church and buried (such was the canonical rule) in the churchyard. Festivals cherished by modern folklorists and praised by sociologists as affirmations of social solidarity were banned by bishops or broken up by muscular parish priests. 'Abbots of misrule' and prank-playing choir boys were censured; men of refined piety shook their heads when hooded flagellants stalked the streets and sombre confraternities of Penitents attended public executions. New confraternities, for strictly religious ends, were organized by the clergy—for the adoration of the Holy Sacrament, for maintaining the parish church, for praying for the souls of the departed.

A precondition for the continuing influence of the Enlightenment was the growing literacy of the population, progress being remarkably rapid in Sweden, England, Holland, and in certain parts of France, especially in the north. Though literacy helped on the process of secularization it was, in fact, a creation of the churches, in parish schools in Protestant lands and in the schools run by the religious orders which the Counter-Reformation had created in Catholic Europe. Unlike Voltaire, the clergy did not think it dangerous to educate the poor; they wanted them to be able to read simple devotional literature. Protestants had catechisms modelled on those of Luther and Calvin and the Heidelberg Catechism of 1563; in the eighteenth century the Swedish version was possessed by one in every five households, and the ministers came round from door to door testing the families on their knowledge of it. Roman Catholic catechisms followed those of Canisius (1555) and Bellarmine (1597) and borrowed surreptitiously from Protestant ones, while bishops allowed scope to the ingenuity of their canon theologians to devise locally relevant items, as well as issuing translations into the local patois. Between 1670 and 1685, twenty diocesan catechisms were published in France, the most famous being the severe, Jansenistical work of 'the three Henrys' (the three bishops composing it); there were three versions, one of 27 pages for children, one of 93 pages for preparation for First Communion, and a compendium of 382 pages for adults. The universal availability of the Bible—albeit still too expensive for most families to possess a copy—had an enormous effect on the life of Protestant Europe. Arise Evans in 1653 described how he had come to London in 1629 and made the great discovery: 'Afor I looked upon the Scripture as a history of things that passed in other countries, pertaining to other persons; but now I looked upon it as a mystery to be opened at this time, belonging also to us'. Family religious exercises were facilitated, unattached preachers and liturgical innovators could follow their inspirations, the search for God by lonely individuals was made easier, while elevated, forceful, and poetic turns of phrase became part of the vocabulary of every man. Translations kept appearing—the Swedish church produced a Finnish version in 1642 which fixed the language. England was particularly fortunate in its Authorized (King James) Bible (1611). The translators did not refer to all the manuscripts and their Hebrew was shaky, their use of Tyndale and Coverdale's versions meant the language was old-fashioned even in their own day, and their book did not win immediate acceptance— even Archbishop Laud used the familiar Genevan Bible when preaching. Yet, through a blend of propitious circumstance and genius, they produced one of the seminal works of English literature and life. The dim lust for intelligibility of reforming clergy of our own generation has not yet succeeded in obliterating its cadences from our national consciousness. Unfortunately for Catholic Europe, reaction against Protestantism drove Rome to cleave to the Vulgate and discourage the laity from Bible study; not until 1752 did the Holy Office sanction translations, and then only if an orthodox commentary accompanied them. Up to that date, there had been German, French, and Polish translations, widely read in spite of Roman prohibitions; thereafter, Italian and Spanish translations appeared, and by the end of 1800 there were no less than 71 Catholic vernacular bibles.

Both Catholics and Protestants published a vast deal of other religious literature—on prayer, the devotional life, moral conduct, and preparation for death. It is in the nature of the genre—written to speak to a particular generation—that its vogue is ephemeral, though St Francis de Sales's *Introduction à la vie dévote* and Bunyan's *Pilgrim's Progress* are immortal. All the while, the secularizing process was under way: while the volume of book production at least doubled in the eighteenth century, the proportion devoted to strictly religious topics declined. Even so, a great deal of secular moralistic writing, not directly Christian, but inclining the Christian way, was becoming fashionable: the transition from *Pilgrim's Progress* to *Robinson Crusoe* does not take the reader outside the great tradition. It was an illustration of the way the world was moving: religion more intense for more people than ever before, yet the framework of life for everyone being remorselessly secularized, and the secular order taking over so many of the emotions and preoccupations which had once been purely religious.

As in thought and literature, so in the arts: the arts were escaping from ecclesiastical control, yet were being put to ecclesiastical use with a sophistication and brilliance never equalled. The once great 'Christian' civilization of the West was in decline, but autumn is a mellow season, in some ways, the most beautiful. This was 'the last great building age of Christianity'. The mental inhibitions which had constrained the artist to distinguish between styles suitable for churches and those for palaces and theatres were breaking down and, as baroque moved into rococo, it might have seemed there was more secular splendour than spirituality in the gilt and vivid colours of Fischer von Erlach and the brothers Asam, in the ecclesiastical art of southern Germany. Yet the great baroque churches of Italy were designed to express the Counter-Reformation's apostolic drive, magnificent settings for the celebration of the mass in the full view of the worshippers, just as Wren's London churches were built with a Protestant concern for preaching and the seating of the poor. For the Middle Ages, the symbol of sanctity was miracle: for the seventeenth century, ecstasy, hauntingly exemplified in portrayal of abandonment and union with the divine, reaching a supreme height of both spirituality and eroticism in Bernini's St Teresa. The medieval cathedrals soared upwards reaching for infinity: the ceilings of the Gesù, S. Pantaleo, and S. Ignazio at Rome show a luminous eternity reaching down to draw us into the celestial hierarchy. The austerity of Catholicism was expressed in the sombre saints of Zurbarán and the pale nuns of Philippe de Champaigne, but artists were turning more to tenderness and hope, neglecting even the sufferings of Christ for the Annunciation, the Immaculate Conception, and the Nativity, with their favourite saint as Mary Magdalen, who had sinned much, but had loved more. The musical talent once concentrated into masses was diversifying into oratorio, cantata, and opera, but the age that runs from Purcell to J. S. Bach and Handel produced some of the greatest religious music the world has known, as moving, though more sophisticated and diversified, as the work of the sixteenth-century masters of counterpoint, Palestrina, Lassus, Victoria, and Byrd. It was, too, the age of the hymn, the ideal means of expression of a religious conviction intensely personal, yet collectively held. Metrical versions of the psalms, sombre inspiration to Cromwell's Ironsides and French Huguenot Camisards as they moved into battle, and the resort of persecuted exiles by the waters of Babylon, were inadequate to express the relationship of the believer to Christ and the sense of joy and assurance which was at the heart of the religious revival in Protestant lands. Biblical fundamentalists were reluctant to venture beyond them, though fortunately there was Matthew 26: 30 to warrant poetic invention in connection with the Lord's Supper. The great Lutheran tradition of hymnology, which began with Luther himself and reached the heights of emotional self-revelation in Paul Gerhardt's songs of hope amid a lifetime of suffering, came to its climax in eighteenth-century England with Isaac Watts, Philip Doddridge, and Charles Wesley. In their vast production, there are lapses into bathos and harsh theology, but their great hymns that have entered into the Anglo-Saxon heritage of worship are variations on the theme of the joy springing from the healing touch of Christ: 'When I Survey the Wondrous Cross', 'Hark the Glad Sound! the Saviour comes', 'Rejoice the Lord is King', 'Love Divine All Loves Excelling'. So embedded are they, and many others like them, in the Christian consciousness, and so inextricably do words and music fuse, that it is only with difficulty that one can break through to consider the men who wrote them. Thomas Ken, who sacrificed his bishopric for conscience sake, accompanied himself on his lute as he sang his morning and evening hymns; of them, says Gordon Rupp, 'once . . . got by heart, neither dawn nor dusk can ever be the same again'. 'Hark my Soul it is the Lord' and 'God Moves in a Mysterious Way', songs of quiet confidence, were written by William Cowper as he sank gently into his private world of madness. 'How Sweet the Name of Jesus Sounds' was by John Newton, converted captain of a slave ship; 'Rock of Ages Cleft for Me' was by Augustus Toplady, a rabid Calvinist; it seems that there are times when men can draw on some subconscious force of enormous evocative power far beyond their individual capacity. This is poetry of a peculiar kind, highly personal yet expressing a collective experience, simple, but subtle in psychological implications, pent with emotion geared to practical action, of its age yet timeless, an instrument of the new Christianity of personal commitment which was evolving in an increasingly secularized society.

Am I saved? The question became insistent once the old cadres of routine conformity broke and so many folk observances half-implying a corporate salvation were banished—and once the Reformation had rendered impossible, for both Catholics and Protestants, a simple doctrine of salvation by works.

The iron law of predestination did not provide an answer, except to the very naïve ('I, Joseph Jostyn of Cranham, yeoman, bequeath my soul to God, believing myself to be "one of the number of the Elect"', November 1642). Even as predestinarian doctrines were being solemnly reaffirmed at the Synod of Dort, they were being rejected by most Protestants. Calvinists took refuge in 'covenant' and 'gathered churches' to find comfort, and struggled with William Perkin's paradoxical praise of uncertainty as an essential component of assurance. Oddly, it was in the Roman church in France that Augustinian doctrines in their strictness lingered longest. The story is a strange one, not least because good men were constrained to express their deepest convictions with casuistical craft to avoid falling foul of the two authorities they accepted as—almost—infallible: Rome and Versailles. Theologically, Jansenism was a movement of return to Augustinian and predestinarian doctrines, beginning with the posthumous publication of a book by Jansenius, bishop of Ypres, in 1640. To students of the history of ideas, it may appear as an attempt to assimilate some of the virtues of Calvinism into Catholicism, just as the rival Jesuits were trying to assimilate the humanism of the Renaissance. In secular history, it is the story of a party in the French church persecuted by the Jesuits and defended by Pascal's savage ironies, of cynical French statesmen trapping the papacy into forthright condemnations of non-existent propositions and ambiguous condemnations of unexceptional ones, of a cause which in the eighteenth century became an excuse for the Parlement of Paris to feud with the Crown and for the lower clergy to demand their rights as against the bishops, and of a spirituality which ran to seed in the fantasies of the convulsionists. Yet beneath the confusion and scandal there was a tide of puritanical piety which transformed so many lives. The sophisticated simplicity of the dedicated life at Port Royal, Pascal's night of fire and the meeting with the God of Abraham, of Isaac, and of Jacob, the works of logic and of grammar, the translation of the New Testament, the cold ethereal beauty of the paintings of Philippe de Champaigne, the plays of Racine, the *Pensées* of Pascal—these are some of the finest things in the seventeenth century. There was also a movement for austerity in the confessional, for liturgical reform, for lay participation in the leadership of worship, for a more serious role for women, which was influential in Italy as well as France.

In the political struggles of the eighteenth century, the persecuted Jansenists stood for liberty. The bull *Unigenitus* (1713), devised against them, was deviously drafted. It censured 101 propositions, some the actual words of scripture, in a book by the aged and pious Quesnel, who was condemned unheard and roundly declared 'a crafty hypocrite'. It included statements which the author had amended or withdrawn in subsequent editions, and it applied to all the propositions twenty-four adjectives, some damning, some trivial, without discrimination. How could a Christian give honest acceptance to such a farrago? asked the Jansenists. Against the bull, they claimed to be 'witnesses to the truth': 'il ne suffit pas d'être Catholique pour être sauvé, il faut encore rendre témoignage à la vérité'. Here was an issue where a puritanical religious faction fought alongside the magistrates of the Parlement of Paris and the sceptical writers of the Enlightenment, filling the century with tumult.

Whether a man had an Augustinian theory of grace or an Arminian one, in strict logic, there could be no certainty of salvation. In *Pilgrim's Progress*, there is a side path to hell at the very gates of heaven, and the vast Catholic literature on preparation for dying admitted the possibility of failure at the end, even for dedicated believers. Catholic devotional literature talked of a balance of fear and confidence (the small point of fear always remaining necessary to keep pride at bay). Mystics of the school of Quietism took the heroic path of 'pure love', the deliberate renunciation of all hope of reward, the acceptance of damnation out of disinterested devotion to God, an extreme device of pious reflection that was outlawed when Rome condemned Fénelon in 1699. Thereafter, a new refinement of Quietism reached perfection in Père de Caussade's 'abandonment to Divine Providence'. Say 'Thy will be done' to everything, to Cross or to happiness equally, and ask no questions of our loving Master. 'Souls that walk in light sing the canticles of light; those that walk in darkness sing the songs of darkness. Both must be allowed to sing to the end the part allotted to them by God in his motet . . . every drop of divinely ordained bitterness must be allowed to flow freely'. All this writing, some crude, some rich in psychological insight, was moving away from the gospel of fear towards the rediscovery of the great Christian belief that annihilates every doctrine which wavers from it and is all that matters at the hour of death: the love of God shown and offered in his Son. George Fox broke out of his despair when he heard the voice, 'There is one, even Christ Jesus, that can speak to thy condition', and he went on to develop the theme of the continuing presence of Christ in his doctrine of the 'inner light'. But the language more effectively carrying on to guide and purify the central Christian tradition was that of friendship. The French Calvinist Pierre du Moulin spoke of Christ as 'our eternal friend: and it is a law of friendship that friends support one another'. This was in one of those vast treatises beloved by the seventeenth century. To a wider audience, the poets of the age expressed their rejoicing in the certainty. George Herbert heard the voice calling 'child', and replied, 'My Lord'. Baxter, separated from his earthly companions, found solace in 'my best and surest friend'—'who shall divide me from thy love?', and Henry Vaughan, the royalist soldier, experienced the same assurance:

> He is thy gracious friend
> And (O my soul awake!)
> Did in pure love descend
> To die here for my sake.

By the eighteenth century, Lutheran orthodoxy, dominated by the Faculty of Theology of Wittenberg, seemed lost in a new scholasticism of subtleties about 'ubiquity'. But these fine-drawn controversies at least had the merit of keeping Lutheran thought Christocentric. 'Lo, I am with you always, even to the end of the world'—the key text of ubiquity—what did that imply for the individual believer? As an answer, there arose the movement of renewal that became known as 'Pietism', a movement returning to the yearning for the 'gracious friend' who 'died here for my sake'. Johan Arndt (d. 1621) changed Luther's 'justification' to 'sanctification': Christ dwells in the believer and brings him to a life of holiness. It was, said Francke, a 'new birth', but not an instantaneous creation; rather, a life progressively conformed to the will of God, with the Cross borne daily, though always with joy. Spener's *Pia Desideria* (1675) proposed the means to disseminate the new piety: the formation of groups of dedicated laymen within the existing ecclesiastical organization. Forty years later, the Pietist ideal found embodiment on a bigger scale, in the life of the Christian community established by the Bohemian Brethren (a late medieval sect from Bohemia and Poland, later known as 'Moravian Brethren'), on the estates of Count Zinzendorf in Saxony. This astonishingly happy community (arranged marriages and decisions of policy by lot notwithstanding) exemplified the simple gospel of love to which Zinzendorf reduced all theology. It was 'heart religion'. 'As soon as a truth becomes a system', he said, 'one does not possess it'. We cannot know God in himself, but only through the Son, and the Son we know essentially by feeling. Zinzendorf did not hesitate to use erotic language about the divine love, and to dwell obsessively on the sufferings of Christ: all religion was reduced to 'we love him because he first loved us'. There was no fear, for perfect love casts out fear. Death would be a joyful incident: 'going home'.

Am I saved? For Zinzendorf, the question had no meaning: lovers do not ask questions. This same discovery of the God of love converted George Whitefield and Howel Harris, the Calvinist evangelists, in 1735. 'Abba, Father!' wrote Harris, 'I knew that I was his child and that he loved and heard me. . . . Christ died for me, and all my sins were laid on him.' Harris went on to found the Calvinist Methodists in Wales, and Whitefield to preach over the Protestant world, with no less than thirteen journeys to America. A different Pauline text, though with the same force, ended John Wesley's quest for certainty, in the meeting with the Son 'who loved me and gave himself for me'. It was on 24 May 1738, just before 10 p.m.: 'I felt my heart strangely warmed. I felt I did trust in Christ, Christ alone for salvation, and an assurance was given me that he had taken away my sins, even mine'. The two great evangelists, Whitefield and Wesley, could not join forces, for the 'horrible decrees' of predestinarian theology stood between them, and while Whitefield's charismatic preaching rolled on unsystematically, Wesley was a genius at organization. So unsure himself in personal relationships, especially with women, Wesley nevertheless saw Christianity as essentially a system of personal relationships linking believers together, 'watching over one another in love', on their way to Christian perfection, the 'pure and spotless . . . new creation' celebrated in his brother Charles's hymn. 'The gospel of Christ', said John, 'knows no religion but social, no holiness but social holiness.' In his organization, the laity were in control, and there was scope for everyone's talents, including women, who could lead worship and preach. But the movement was not built on startling conversions, as its preachers sometimes implied. It imitated the methods and drew on the personnel of the multitude of religious societies for meditation and mutual edification which were proliferating in England, not least within the established church, from the end of the seventeenth century, and it appealed to the hard-working and respectable families of tradesmen and artisans who wanted to find in their religion a deeper sense of 'belonging'. Even so, Wesley's preachers struck out into the spiritual wastelands where industrial development and mining were creating a new class estranged from religious observances, and among them the 'chapel' became a unique civilizing influence.

And who would convert high society? Not Wesley's movement; William Wilberforce, a rich young Member of Parliament, was to thank God he had not become 'a bigoted despised Methodist'. When, in 1785, he was converted from 'mere nominal Christianity', he was convinced of his vocation to the great: 'there was needed some reformer of the nation's morals and who should raise his voice in the high places of the land'. One of the dilemmas Christians have always faced is the question of giving special consideration to converting the influential— the method of the Jesuits, changing the world by acting as confessors and educators to the ruling class. Purists who regret Wilberforce's concentration on the élite may reflect that their reservations were shared at the time by ship and plantation owners who feared legislative action against the slave-trade.

Christian preachers demanded individual commitment, a demand addressed to all men and women, whatever their work, whatever their intelligence and education. This involved the creation of what was—almost—a new type of spirituality, a spirituality for every day and for ordinary people. The secret way of the mystics—the progress from dryness to quietness to the death of the senses, abandonment, and, finally, union, the way of St Teresa and St John of the Cross, could not be for everyone. Nor was the great renunciation of the world and the flesh, the clerical and monastic vocation. In the seventeenth century, books of Catholic devotion proliferated addressed to those 'in the world'; the lip-service paid to the monastic life as the highest continued, but with a less convincing sound. For both Catholics and Protestants, pious authors prescribed strict routines of prayer for the laity, fitted into the interstices of daily work; generally with offerings of thanks and petitions for guidance in the morning, with grace before meals, and medi-tation on death at night. Family prayers became a common practice in respectable households. As a regulator of individual spiritual progress, Catholics had the confessor, the 'director', and the seventeenth century saw the development of a literature of casuistry. Pascal's attack on examples of marginal brinkmanship and disputes about 'Probabalism' give an unjust picture of this sort of writing. Some of its deviousness (as in the books of Jesuits in Marseilles and Lyons legitimizing loans at interest) was intellectual gymnastics justifying common sense against outmoded 'rigorism'; most of the argument was high-minded and necessary.

The Protestant alternative to the confessional was self-examination, sometimes extending to continuous assessment in the keeping of a solemn diary—'to give a strict account on that great day to the high Lord of all our wayes, and of all his wayes towards us', as John Beadle recorded in 1656. His contemporary, the countess of Warwick, left 40,000 pages of prayers and thanksgivings, while in Germany, Ludwig Kleinhempel, master coppersmith and pious Lutheran, recorded his life of submission to God amid domestic tragedy and civil war. Sometimes an account would be published for edification, as the Quakers published deathbed testimonies and journals, including that of George Fox. Richard Baxter did so himself, 'that young Christians may be warned by the mistakes and failings of my unriper times'—his crimes consisting of stealing fruit and reading 'romances, fables and old tales'. The Pietists of the next century collected and edited 'Histories of the Reborn' and 'Biographies of Holy Souls', including the confessions of peasants and maid-servants. These were lives ordinary Christians could imitate; the official saints and the heroes of the Reformation seemed to move in a non-attainable stratosphere.

One of the characteristics of the new everyday spirituality was the acceptance of my station and its duties—and, indeed, its pleasures, provided they were innocent. St Francis de Sales was the originator of this humane attitude to enjoyment, his austerity being tempered by a sense of proportion and an insight into the enervating effects of excessive scrupulosity. The *honnête homme*, he says, accepts the honours of the world as an adventurer from Peru, laden with silver, may include curious monkeys and parrots in his cargo. The point was stretched further, perhaps with too much indulgence to purple and fine linen, when Archbishop Tillotson argued that Dives was condemned for not helping Lazarus, not for his luxurious life-style. The formula of James Archer, the famous English Catholic preacher of the 1780s was safer: sanctity was compatible 'with a cheerful enjoyment of our situation in the world'. Having said this, a man must do his duty. 'All your employments, my brethren, are properly religious exercises', Archer went on, and a saint is 'one who discharges the duties of his station'. A Protestant would have said rather that it was possible to 'glorify God' in a secular vocation (words which Kepler had used when he had abandoned the study of theology for that of astronomy). Indeed, Protestant divines worked out a systematic theory of vocation, with no hesitation about the profit motive. The tradesman, said an English clerical writer in 1684, was 'to serve God in his calling and drive it as far as it will go'. A man must choose the most gainful way, if lawful, when God shows it, held Richard Baxter. But the reason why the 'gainful' way is right is important. God wishes us to act as his 'stewards'. A Christian is not free to do what he wills with his own; this, says Baxter, is 'an atheistical misconceit'—there is 'no absolute propriety but God's'. And there was another proviso, sometimes not so clearly stated: no worldly pursuit ought to become obsessive. A man must not fail to observe Sunday, and his daily routines of prayer. The chief work of devotion for English Catholics in the eighteenth century, Challoner's *Garden of the Soul* (1740), went further; it taught the gospel of work, but not with 'over great eagerness'; the soul must also seek 'calmness and peace'.

All honest work, however menial, was a fulfilment of God's vocation:

> Who sweeps a room as for thy laws
> Makes that and the action fine.

A cynic might reflect that George Herbert had half a dozen servants to sweep his rectory: there was a certain complacency about the rightness of the hierarchical social order. Only in strange sects and fantastic utopias were echoes of the primitive

Christian experiment in social equality heard. But preachers were under an obligation (more so in an age which took the Old Testament prophets so seriously) to denounce social evils, and theologians would become pamphleteers against usurers and rack-renting landlords. The preaching of hell fire, which seems so un-Christian now in its use of the weapon of fear, was often most concerned with the proclamation of the ultimate equality. Death 'comes equally to us all', said Donne, 'and makes us all equal when it comes'. 'More servants than masters, more tenants than landlords, will inherit the kingdom of heaven', said Bunyan.

The heart of the new lay spirituality was the family. The pre-Reformation presupposition that sexual activity was sinful unless directed towards the conception of children was swept away. Calvin urged husband and wife to use this remedy against concupiscence 'joyfully', and the Jesuit Sanchez at the beginning of the seventeenth century put 'mutual comfort' on a level with procreation as the purpose of sexuality. Over the centuries during which the vast majority had lived on the verge of subsistence not far removed in physical condition from animals, the church had continually recalled Christians to reverence the mystery of human love in the forms of the Blessed Virgin and the Holy Child. Improvements in agriculture, technology, and communications were now raising the general standard of living, and those who were lifted above the brutal poverty of mere existence broke through to new possibilities of expressing the devotion and affection bound up with the sexual drive. Counter-Reformation devotion rediscovered the Christmas crib, and Christian art turned to the Nativity scene in the stable, infinitely tender by candlelight, as if rejoicing that its inwardness would now be recognized in purely human terms. That indeed was happening. The pressure of the confessional upon domestic conduct, the Puritan doctrine of the wife as 'helpmeet', the role of the clergy as arbitrators with families to save children from loveless marriages, together with the more favourable conditions of living, helped to transform the position of women; they contributed more to social and economic life, and there was a beginning of elementary contraception to release them from the tyranny of continual child-bearing. In Protestantism, they won a fuller share in church life. In the Anglican and Lutheran Churches, the parson's wife became an established and influential figure; in the Nonconformist sects women were allowed to lead worship and preach—as Fox said, 'may not the Spirit of Christ speak in the female as in the male?' In the Roman church, they took over the expanding education for girls and the work of hospitals; St Francis de Sales needed Jeanne de Chantal to found the order of the Visitation, and St Vincent de Paul needed Louise de Marillac to establish the Sisters of Charity. As women rose to consideration, their children accompanied them. Once treated as little adults incapable of fulfilling adult obligation, they came to be regarded as complete personalities in their own right. Rousseau was to be the theorist of the new sentiment, but it was found in devotional manuals before him, notably in Jeremy Taylor's *Holy Living and Holy Dying*.

Socially, the Christianity of the day was a non-revolutionary faith. It was to bring its adherents over the dark river into God's other kingdom, rather than to change the structure of this transitory world. 'As a traveller expects not the same conveniences at an inn as he hath at home', said *The Whole Duty of Man* (1658), an enormously influential book of devotion, 'so thou hast reason to be content with whatever entertainment thou findest here, knowing thou art upon thy journey to a place of infinite happiness.' But acceptance of social evils was counter-balanced by the obligations of charity. Sometimes it was a generosity tied up with the deferential observance of religious practices by its recipients, and principally directed towards the *pauvres honteux*, the *poveri vergognosi*, the 'deserving poor', rather than the shiftless and idle, yet it was remarkable how universally the obligation was accepted and how numerous were the initiatives to fulfil it. From huge institutions like the Albergo dei Poveri at Genoa and the Hôtel Dieu at Paris down to tiny three-bed hospitals in villages, from orders expert in surgery to others specializing in ransoming slaves from the Barbary corsairs, Catholic Europe was covered with a network of organizations to help the poor and sick, with parish priests and committees of devout ladies organizing outdoor relief. The worldly bishops who adorned French towns with their palace building would run up huge debts to feed the population of their dioceses in time of famine—they discovered their Christian vocation in times of crisis. In Protestant Europe, voluntary societies arose to fill the gap left by the abolition of the religious orders. Pious laymen, reinforced towards the end of the eighteenth century by some of the less pious who were afraid of revolution, were astonishingly active. The list of societies— something like a hundred—to which Wilberforce subscribed indicates the scope of the movement: the Society for the Propagation of the Gospel (running now for a century), the Church Missionary Society, the new British and Foreign Bible Society, societies for suppressing vice, for prosecuting blasphemy, for promoting the welfare of soldiers and sailors, setting up orphanages, lying-in homes for poor women, and refuges for vagrants, and others more specific in nature to aid 'climbing boys', French refugees, Irish serving girls, debtors, and 'criminal poor children'—and still more specifically, 'the City of London Truss Society for the Relief of the Ruptured Poor'. In our time and in our favoured fifth of the globe, it is difficult to do justice to this paternalistic and piecemeal generosity. We can be critical of its shortcomings, for the gospel ideal of charity has now been taken over by the secularized society; the welfare state performs the duties to the poor and disinherited which once made Christianity appear indispensable. In so far as Christianity permeates society, it ensures its own 'decline' in terms of statistical allegiance and obvious practical relevance. In religion, nothing fails like success.

The Expansion of Christianity
(1500–1800)

JOHN McMANNERS

By the year 1800, Christianity girdled the globe from China to Peru. Yet three hundred years earlier, it had been the religion of Europe alone, hemmed in on the east by militant Islam, to the south by the desert, to the north by barren tundra, and to the west by the great ocean. Islam ruled in the land where Christ had been born and crucified. It had swept away the Christian communities of the North African coast, and its pressures were driving the Monophysite Copts of Egypt to convert to the Prophet; the sister Coptic church in Ethiopia survived only because of its wild remoteness in the mountains. In the Sudan, where Christianity had once been dominant, the faith of the Qur'ān now prevailed. The Jacobites and the far-flung Nestorian church which had extended into China, Central Asia, Persia, and India had been overwhelmed by the destruction wrought by the hordes of Tamerlane in the second half of the fourteenth century; a few communities survived scattered along the trade routes. But there was an exception. Hidden away in the far south of India in the midst of a vast Hindu population, the Nestorian 'Church of St Thomas' remained, worshipping with a liturgy in the Syriac tongue, and obtaining its bishops by precarious contacts with Chaldean patriarchs in Mesopotamia. Ignorant of the existence of the pope and of theological quarrels, and proud to remember its origins from the first generation of the apostles, it was there to greet the

Portuguese when they landed at Cragnagore in 1500. The old Roman dream of a Christian–Mongol alliance against Islam was dead; the Mongols gravitated to the advanced Islamic culture which they met as their invasions rolled westwards from Central Asia. The Ottoman Turks, rising as the Mongol power declined, in 1453 took Constantinople; the Eastern empire, Europe's bastion, crumbled. Turkish warlords and janizaries occupied Greece and the Balkans, Muslim sultans lorded it over the patriarchs of the Orthodox Church within their dominions, and negotiated proudly with the Christian sovereigns of Europe, even with the papacy. The future seemed to lie with the Crescent rather than the Cross.

In 1492, Columbus crossed the Atlantic and reached the islands he called the 'West Indies'. It was the beginning of the great Spanish colonial adventure. Five years later, Vasco da Gama cast anchor at Calicut in India, inaugurating the Portuguese trading empire in the east. Western Europe was beginning its break out to dominate the world. Why did it happen? Improvements in navigation, ship construction, and naval gunnery, and the familiarity of fishermen with the heavy Atlantic seas, had created the possibility, and there was an intense curiosity about the unknown regions of the globe, helped by the rediscovery of the geographical writings of Ptolemy and by Pope Pius II's *Historia Rerum Ubique Gestarum*, which declared Africa to be circumnavigable. There was a desire for a share in the lucrative trade in spices and silks which was monopolized by Venice and Genoa, and taxed by the Muslims. But the stupendous events of European expansion have seemed to need a more dramatic explanation: there was an inner dynamism in the West European psyche, perhaps arising from Christianity, and there was, too, the true religious motive in its simplicity, the desire to take the gospel to new peoples. The argument needs careful statement. For long, Portugal and Spain had fought the Muslims; Portugal had overwhelmed them first, but continued to war against them in Morocco, and the last Moorish

Legend:

Christian Europe

expansion by Russia 1490–1600, reached Tobolsk by 1600

voyage of discovery

scattered Christian communities outside Europe (arrow indicates general direction)

Ottoman expansion 1490–1600

Iceland (held by Denmark)

NORWAY

DENMARK

IRELAND

SCOTLAND

ENGLAND

HANSEATIC LEAGUE

NETHER-LANDS

THE EMPIRE

BO

FRANCE

SWISS CONFEDERATION

SAVOY

GENOA

VE

PORTUGAL

SPAIN

Lisbon

Vasco da Gama to India (1497)

Palos

Cadiz

Granada

Columbus to America (1492)

CORSICA (held by Genoa)

PAPAL STATES

SARDINIA

NA

SICIL

MUSLIM SULTANATES

MEDIT

| 0 | 200 | 400 | 600 km |

| 0 | 100 | 200 | 300 | 400 miles |

1530

CHRISTIAN EUROPE IN 1490 ON THE EVE OF THE EXPANSION

SWEDEN

MUSCOVY

KHANATE
OF KAZAN

✠ Nestorian groups
in Asia

TEUTONIC ORDER

LITHUANIA

KHANATE
OF
ASTRAKHAN

POLAND

...MIA

KHANATE
OF THE
CRIMEA

CASPIAN
SEA

Vienna
Turkish seige
1529

HUNGARY

MOLDAVIA

BLACK SEA

OTTOMAN   EMPIRE

Constantinople

Mosul

SAFAVID
PERSIA

1570

CYPRUS
(held by
Venice)

...RANEAN   SEA

CRETE
(held by
Venice)

✠ in
South India

Alexandria   1517

✠ in
Egypt

✠ in
Ethiopia

fortress in Spain, Granada, was not taken until 1492, the year
of Columbus (it was the year too when the Jews were expelled
from Spain, revealing a new strain of rigidity and intolerance in
Spanish Catholicism). One crusade was over and now, in the
adventures overseas, a new crusade against the heathen could
begin. As in all the 'crusades', the Christian motive was
tied to material aspirations. In Spain, the knights who had
warred against the Moors had seized fiefs for themselves in the
reclaimed territories; now they could carve out new domains in
America—studies of the social composition of the *conquistadores*
show them to have been, most often, *caballeros* and *hidalgos*,
hard-up sons of noble or would-be noble families with their
fortunes to make. By rounding Africa, the Portuguese took the
Islamic forces in the rear. They found the trade down the East
African coast to Mozambique, to India, and further eastwards,
was run by Arabs and Muslim Gujaratis; to cut off their ships,
as well as to outface them as infidels, Albuquerque seized Goa
as an Indian base (1510), then Ormuz on the Persian Gulf and
Malacca commanding the Malay Straits.

Yet the crudeness of crusading self-interest does not detract
from the genuineness of the zeal to spread the Christian faith—
the self-interest and the zeal coexisted without contemporaries
being conscious of their incompatibility. Prince Henry the
Navigator, who inspired the Portuguese voyages, had as his
objectives (solemnly affirmed for him in a papal bull) to spread
Christianity and to join forces with fellow Christians—a reference to the hope of finding the mysterious kingdom of Prester
John, a legendary Christian king in Ethiopia or Asia. When
Vasco da Gama landed at Calicut, he said his quest was for
fellow Christians and for spices. The official policy of the
Spanish Crown put the conversion of the native population
as first priority. The royal letter of 1523 to Cortés forbade
oppression, so the Indians would be won to Christianity by
kindness. The grim events of the overthrow of the Aztec civilization were at variance with this pious hope and the teaching
of the gospels, yet Cortés's crusading zeal was sincere. He

exhorted his men to seek 'fame' and emulate the ancient Romans, but he also called on them to show the courage of soldiers of Christ and had them pray to St Peter and St James before battle; on his first landing on the Yucatán coast he destroyed idols and had mass celebrated at a Christian altar. Without the peculiar force of religious certainty, it is hard to see how the *conquistadores* could have triumphed; steel blades, thirteen muskets, sixteen horses, and intrigues with dissatisfied tribes are hardly sufficient explanation. To understand the mentality of the early sixteenth century one has to come to terms with men who insisted on the preliminary baptism of the Indian women they took as their concubines. Bernal Diaz del Castillo, that literate soldier of fortune, summed up his reasons for going to the Indies: 'to serve God and His Majesty, to give light to those who were in darkness, and to grow rich, as all men desire to do'. It was axiomatic to him that unbelievers were in darkness; converting them was to serve God, and there was no reason why he should not enrich himself on the way.

A whole new world was opening for exploitation—and evangelism—yet, human nature being what it is, the two Iberian powers might have quarrelled over their respective spheres of influence. In 1493, Pope Alexander VI averted the danger by drawing a line down the map of the Atlantic, awarding discoveries to the west to Spain, and to the east to Portugal. The same pope completed the policies of his predecessors in granting the two Catholic sovereigns the extensive powers over the church which were necessary if overseas evangelism was to be effective (the Portuguese *padroado*, the Spanish *patronato*). He also ruled the American Indians to be capable of making their own decision to accept the faith, as against those who held them to be sub-human. These wise and apostolic decisions came from an immoral, machiavellian pope who has made the name of Borgia synonymous with Renaissance criminality.

Fortunately, Rome did not remain the Rome of the Borgias; under the shock of Luther's revolt the Catholic Church was to reform itself. Indeed, the Spanish church was already

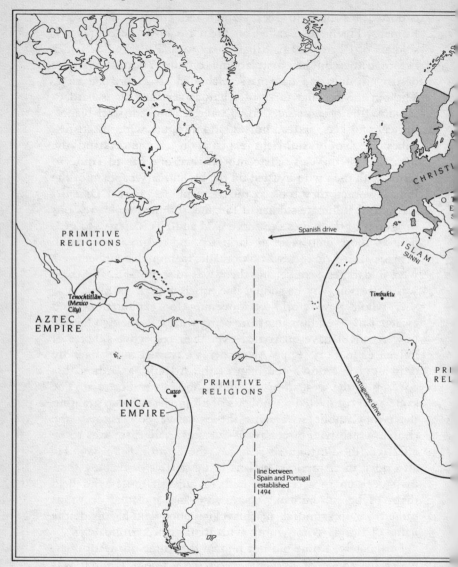

PRIMITIVE
RELIGIONS

Spanish drive

CHRISTI

OT
E

ISLAM
SUNNI

Timbuktu

Tenochtitlan
(Mexico
City)

AZTEC
EMPIRE

PRIMITIVE
RELIGIONS

Cuzco

INCA
EMPIRE

Portuguese drive

PRI
REL

line between
Spain and Portugal
established
1494

THE WORLD IN 1500: ORGANIZED STATES AND RELIGIONS

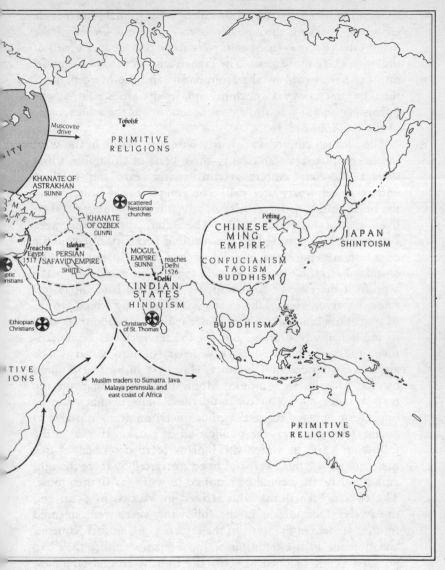

Muscovite drive

Tobolsk

PRIMITIVE
RELIGIONS

KHANATE OF
ASTRAKHAN
SUNNI

scattered Nestorian
churches

KHANATE
OF OZBEK
SUNNI

Ispahan

PERSIAN
SAFAVID EMPIRE
SHIITE

reaches
Egypt
1517

MOGUL
EMPIRE
SUNNI

reaches
Delhi
1526

Delhi

INDIAN
STATES

HINDUISM

Peking

CHINESE
MING
EMPIRE

CONFUCIANISM
TAOISM
BUDDHISM

JAPAN
SHINTOISM

Coptic
Christians

Ethiopian
Christians

Christians
of St. Thomas

BUDDHISM

TIVE
IONS

Muslim traders to Sumatra, Java,
Malaya peninsula, and
east coast of Africa

PRIMITIVE
RELIGIONS

transformed, before Columbus sailed, by Cardinal Ximénez de Cisneros, working through his own Franciscan Order of the Strict Observance—friars who were to be the advance guard of the missionary movement. The Franciscans were to be followed into the new world by the Dominicans and the Mercedarians, then by the newer Capuchins and Jesuits. In so far as the Spanish conquest was also a conversion, it was the achievement of the religious orders.

The Spanish empire was swiftly won: the seizure of the West Indies completed within twenty-three years of Columbus's first voyage, the Aztec empire overthrown six years later, the Inca empire fifteen years later still. The conquest was brutal, with the brash uncalculating cruelty of adventurers fighting for their lives against enormous odds. Thereafter, the Indians were systematically oppressed by the seeming necessity of economic circumstance; once the initial loot had been shared out, the *conquistadores*, their successors, and the Crown could only make a profit if there was a labour supply to till the land and, later, mine the silver. Hence, the *encomienda* system, by which groups of Indian households were to render tribute and labour services to individual adventurers. But for the intervention of church-men, the system would have degenerated into slavery. The alarm was sounded on Christmas Day 1511 in Santo Domingo by the Dominican António Montesinos, preaching on the text 'a voice crying in the wilderness'. His denunciation of oppression enraged the settlers, but the Dominicans appealed to Spain. The result was the publication of a colonial code in the following year, in which the Indians were described as free men, not slaves; they were not to be converted by force though, ambiguously, they could be required to work, as all men must. The twelve Franciscans who arrived in Mexico in 1524, and the twelve Dominicans in the following year, were splendid figures, austere in the spirit of the reforms of Cardinal Ximénez and humane in the tradition of the Erasmus studies they had pursued. They planned to settle the Indians around churches, protect them from oppression by racial segregation, and convert them by colourful ceremonies and pious example—a design flatly opposed to the interests of the *encomenderos*. Zumárraga, first bishop of Mexico, was prepared to back the friars, even by the use of interdict. The Spanish government, not loath to increase the powers of the central administration, was persuaded, and in 1542 published laws reforming the whole system: the control of Indian households was to revert to the Crown on the deaths of the present *encomenderos* (later, after various revolts, changed to a term of two lives). Forced labour was to end; the Indians were to pay tribute and nothing more.

These laws were the result of pressure by the church. In 1537, in a bull solicited by the Dominicans of Hispaniola, Pope Paul III affirmed the right of the Indians to liberty and to property. Two years later, the great Dominican jurist Vitoria, one of the founders of international law, lectured at Salamanca on the legitimacy of the Spanish conquest. There was no right to wage war on a nation because it was inferior in civilization, or idolatrous, or to convert its people. Force could only be used against an aggressor state, or one that refused entry to peaceful Christian missionaries. Thus, he conceded, the Spaniards had a theoretical justification for their invasion, but they 'had far exceeded what is allowed by human and divine law'. How far they had exceeded just bounds was proclaimed in lurid detail by another Dominican, Bartolomé de Las Casas, the son of one of the adventurers with the second voyage of Columbus and the first priest to be ordained in America. He had studied at the university of Salamanca, then returned to Hispaniola to manage his estates; conscience-stricken at the plight of the Indians, he sought ordination and devoted himself to their cause. In matters practical, he failed: his naïve belief in the inherent virtue of the Indians was demonstrably mistaken; his efforts to found a colonial establishment using free labour were disastrous; when, at the age of 70, he accepted a bishopric in the New World, his liberal ideas made it impossible for him to control his diocese. Yet he succeeded in his propaganda. His journeys to and fro between the Indies and Spain, and his dialectical skill in refuting the Aristotelian proposition that some men are naturally slaves, were a continual reminder to the official conscience of Spain's Christian responsibility to the Indians.

Though the native populations of Spanish America were not enslaved, theirs was a tragic fate all the same. Their numbers rapidly declined—from ill-treatment, epidemics, and despair. An enquiry in the areas of Quito, Lima, and Charcas between 1582 and 1586 reported the Indians as giving a reason for their decline which sounds paradoxical to our ears—'freedom'. Their undemanding communal routines of subsistence agriculture had been broken; with their old world destroyed, they had lost the will to live. Only the Franciscan ideal of protected Christian communities could have rescued them, and this was swept aside by economic pressures. The Crown, drawing an increasing proportion of its revenue from the colonial empire, more especially from the *quinto*, the silver tax, wished to push on the development of cattle ranches and the exploitation of deeper mines. Hence, the system of drafting labour began. The government fixed a tariff of wages, then the headman of each village had to send relays of short-term labour to the mines and other projects (including the building of the splendid baroque churches). Indians who found permanent work on the great estates soon fell into debt and became peons, free in their persons but not free to move. Christian influence had forced the guarantee of the principle that the Indians were human beings and free; free, but exploited, they were doomed to be the mass of poor labourers at the base of the social pyramid.

Like the conquest, the conversion was rapid. The Crown took its responsibilities seriously and pushed on the organization of the framework of religion. By the mid-sixteenth century there were eight dioceses in the Antilles, eight in Mexico, and three in South America. The religious orders had poured in their missionaries; by then, there were 200 Dominicans, 200 Augustinians, and still more Franciscans. The old-established civilizations came over *en masse* to the religion of the conquerors.

Force was not used, except in the sense that the Spaniards felt obliged to get rid of the visible signs of paganism. Bishop Zumárraga in 1531 boasted he had presided over the demolition of 500 temples and 26,000 idols. The missionaries used intelligent techniques, concentrating on the education of the children, organizing young men into bands with 'captains' responsible for leading in church attendance, and in their teaching using the affinities with Christianity which they discovered in the stories of the old defeated gods. By the end of the sixteenth century, the 7,000,000 Indians of the Spanish empire were, in name at least, Christians. Where we have statistics of conversions (Pedro de Gante, a relative of the Emperor Charles V, who had joined the missionaries, told of baptizing 14,000 with the help of a single companion in one day), it is evident no serious preliminary instruction had been possible. Nor was it easy to develop Christian awareness after the formal admission, for the social and family structures were inimical to moral upbringing. The Spaniards were ruled by racial prejudice in social relationships but not in sexual ones: there were multitudes of irregular unions and unstable pseudo-families with children of mixed blood of debatable social status.

The decision of the Council of Lima in 1552 to withhold the eucharist from the Indians is deplored today as racial prejudice; at the time it was a recognition of the superficiality of the conversion. Less certainly so was the recommendation of the Council of Mexico in 1555 not to ordain Indians, mestizos, or mulattos. The restriction must have seemed realistic, Bishop Zumárraga's college at Tlateloleo having failed, none of the students being attracted to the life of celibacy. Yet, if the conversion was to become a reality, the first requisite was a native priesthood. Pope Gregory XIV recognized the fact in 1576 by specifically allowing the ordination of half-castes and illegitimate sons. Even so, at the end of the century, there were few Indians or mestizos in the ministry of the church. The more was the pity, for by then, much to the dismay of the regulars, the parishes of the settled areas had been taken over by secular priests, most of them unadventurous and some idle and worldly.

Upon the mass of superficially converted believers, a religious cadre of overwhelming magnificence was imposed. To impress the simple, ceremonies were conducted with a splendour unknown in Europe. The huge walled enclosures with only an arcade to house the sacrament gave way to stone churches, built in the varying Spanish regional styles, with exotic influences showing in the decoration—Aztec skulls and masks among the angels; monkeys, macaws, and coconut palms in riotous colour as a background to scriptural stories. The missionary orders were still producing heroic figures, like Pedro Claver, Jesuit and Spanish aristocrat, who through the first half of the seventeenth century ministered to the Negroes in the slave ships arriving at Cartagena. Most of the friars were still on the frontiers, pushing out into the wilderness. By 1630 they had penetrated deep into South America, into the swamps of the Gran Chaco and beyond, and northwards to California, Florida, and Texas. We catch the occasional glimpse of them—wandering barefoot with cross and breviary, preaching, skull in hand, reciting doctrine in rhymes, singing psalms to their own violin accompaniment, providing seeds for new crops, teaching new ways to build houses and bridges, and dying alone of sickness or savage cruelties.

The papal division of the world between Spain and Portugal (revised by the two powers themselves in 1494) allowed the Portuguese a foothold in America (Brazil) and, since the world is round, did not exclude Spain from the east, provided the approach was by way of the Pacific Ocean. In 1561–2, a Spanish expedition from America seized the Philippines. Five Augustinian friars accompanied the invasion, and the orders from Philip II forbade violence and injustice. The natives were primitive in their culture and offered little resistance to Spanish arms or to Spanish religion. The pattern of events followed that in America, but in a lower key. The religious orders moved in, and there were mass conversions, something over half a million people baptized in thirty years. The *encomienda* system was introduced and began to degenerate into slavery. Salazar, a Dominican who had served in America and had gone to Spain to fight for the Indians, became bishop of Manila in 1581, and intervened decisively for justice, while the Augustinians complained at home and obtained a declaration from Pope Gregory XIV that the Filipino people ought to be compensated for their losses in the conquest. The rule that Christian protest can alleviate misery but not turn back great economic processes was validated, but this time in a fashion favourable to the natives. Chinese junks began to ply to Manila to exchange silks and porcelain for American silver; levies on this entrepôt trade gave the government its revenue, and the Spanish settlers began to seek wealth in trade rather than in exacting tribute and labour services in the countryside. By the early seventeenth century, Spanish rule was firmly established, and less oppressively than in America. The church had covered the islands with its institutions, and fully half the population was converted. As ever, with success came relaxation. Some of the friars succumbed to the temptations of rule over simple peoples and became exacting, the orders feuded with each other and with the bishop—all this a sure proof that Christianity was safely dominant.

The Spanish empire was one of settlement and dominion, with Catholicism at the heart of the Spanish way of life which was exported. In Brazil, the Portuguese had an opportunity to emulate the imperialism of the Spaniards—thanks to the line of division which awarded them a slice of South American territory—though in lands where vast areas were closed to settlement by the tropical climate and dense forests, and whose inhabitants were shy and savage tribesmen who died off quickly if they were forced to do labour service. This did not prevent their enslavement. A sinister feature of Portuguese expansion inland was the activity of the *bandeiras*, raiding slavers with their Indian auxiliaries. The Jesuits on the Spanish side of the frontier had to drill their converts into militia forces to ward off these intruders. In the end it was the importing of stronger African slaves which made it possible for Portuguese entrepreneurs to create a multitude of sugar plantations (with their labour-intensive refining processes). By the end of the seventeenth century, the sugar fleets sailing to Europe contained as many ships annually as the flotillas that plied between the Indies and Spain. It was a lucrative trade for a poor country, and idealistic opposition to the way in which labour was obtained was not likely to be effective. With slavery more blatant than in the Spanish possessions, and the natives lacking organized patterns of existence which might have formed the underlying structure for mass conversions, Christianity progressed more slowly than in Mexico and Peru, though the wealth accruing from sugar and slavery found expression in the mingled piety and ostentation which built the ornate mannerist churches of Sao Salvador (Bahia). To preserve the indigenous peoples from ill-treatment, the Jesuits of Brazil followed the policy invented by the Spanish Franciscans, and organized their converts into villages around churches (*doutrinas*); the civil government prohibited the incursions of slavers into these communities, and extended protection to runaway slaves who took refuge in the Jesuit compounds. Official protection, in fact, often proved illusory. The Portuguese settlers, many with dubious backgrounds, and ministered to by secular priests who were rejects from home, had largely forsaken the exercise of religion; regulations against their material interests, issued by distant governors and recommended by unworldly friars, were disregarded. António de Vieira, Jesuit missionary, intellectual, and court preacher, who travelled between Brazil and Lisbon throughout the second half of the seventeenth century, recorded the continuing history of cruelty and exploitation—and did something to alleviate it, by his passionate denunciations; he was the Las Casas of the conquest of Brazil.

The Portuguese lacked the manpower and military strength to build an empire of settlement of the Spanish kind. Besides, the papal award had given them, for their principal sphere of expansion, the East, where conditions were entirely different from those in America. Here, in India and beyond, they built up an empire of a very different kind, one which was commercial; embattled and ruthless, but holding ports essentially for trading purposes. The clergy had a difficult task ministering to the traders, officials, soldiers, married settlers (*casados*), and the native and half-caste levies, a hard and motley crew, given to licence and corruption. Cruelty and bad faith characterized the relations of the indigenous people and the new arrivals, on both sides. The slave-trade played its part in debasing human relationships, in the East, as in Brazil. From Mozambique, the Portuguese exported African slaves to Goa and beyond; Dominicans and Augustinians tried to convert them on the journey, but were powerless to stop the traffic.

Missions to the peoples of Asia were difficult, not least because the Portuguese were hated, and because so many of them were poor advertisements for the religion they professed. Missionary enterprise was disrupted by warfare: skirmishes with Turkish galleys from Egypt or the fleet of the Javanese state of Japara, attacks on Malacca by the sultans of Achin, risings in the Moluccas; in 1570 Goa itself was under siege for ten months by the neighbouring sultans. As the government at Lisbon ran into debt, the salaries of the clergy fell into arrears and many had to maintain themselves by secular activities. And, above all, unlike the Spaniards in America and the Philippines, the Portuguese were confronted by proud and ancient civilizations, and higher religions. Islam, Hinduism, Buddhism, and Confucianism had their philosophical arguments, sacred writings, mystical traditions, holy men, and preachers; they were accustomed to absorbing other faiths and were already there, with access to the seats of power.

In India, there was a mass conversion, Spanish-American

style, when the Paravas, fishers of the Coromandel coast were baptized, all 10,000 of them, in 1534, thus gaining Portuguese protection from raiders from the north. There were predictable conversions in the areas around Portuguese bases—Cochin, Madras, Madurai, and, notably, Goa, a fortified town of churches and monasteries. Here, some converts were won by Franciscan preaching, others—the sick and the poor—by the generous treatment they received in the hospital and the great Misericordia; many more because of marriage or employment as servants or slaves. Higher on the social scale, there might be more sophisticated calculation. The first Brahman to be baptized (1548) had fallen on hard times; the young raja of Tanor, secretly admitted as a Christian in the following year, was shortly to ask for special privileges in the pepper trade.

Once these conversions within the narrow confines of Portuguese power were in train, how else could progress be made? The Jesuits proposed an answer. In 1542, a Basque nobleman who had been a friend of Loyola in the University of Paris arrived—Francis Xavier. With him, the crude formula of a crusade against unbelievers was transmuted into the idea of an intellectual and moral battle for the control of men's minds. After an apprenticeship teaching simple litanies to the Paravas, he went on adventurous journeys to the furthest horizons, to Ceylon and Japan, until in 1552 he died on an island off Canton while awaiting permission to enter China. In Japan, Xavier worked out his scheme for adapting Christianity to absorb what was best in Japanese culture, the key to success being to win individual *daimyos* (the 250 territorial lords who wielded the real political power) by appealing to their cult of honour. This supple policy was confirmed by Alessandri Valignano, visitor of the Jesuit establishments in the east, when he came to Japan in 1579. All local customs not directly in contradiction to Christianity were to be accepted—for example, the Jesuit fathers were to adopt the status of Zen priests and strictly observe Japanese etiquette. Whether as a result of these policies or not, twenty-two years later there was a flourishing church in

Japan: there were 250 Japanese catechists, three having just been ordained, and 300,000 believers, some belonging to high-ranking families, with an especially strong Christian community in the booming port of Nagasaki.

Valignano hoped to follow similar tactics in China, the proud, closed empire which normally accepted Westerners only as traders or to offer tribute, and he set two members of his order to study Chinese language and culture, and await their opportunity. An invitation to Peking came in 1600, and Matteo Ricci went to the imperial court, where he was welcomed for his skill at clock-repairing and map-making, his scientific knowledge, and his learning in the Chinese tradition. In the ten years before he died he worked out an accommodation between Christianity and the intellectual modes of China. He wore the robes of a Confucian scholar and approved of Confucian rites and ancestor worship, on the ground they were purely civil ceremonies; he interpreted the Chinese classics in ways that served missionary purposes, suggesting that the references to 'Heaven' and 'the Sovereign on High' were evidence of an early monotheism which had since been lost. Recent work on Chinese sources has suggested that Ricci's presentation of Christianity was difficult to understand in terms of Chinese philosophy; even so, at his death there were about 2,000 converts, some of high rank, and the Jesuit mission was in high favour.

In India, in 1580, a similar opportunity of putting Christian propagandists into the entourage of a mighty ruler had occurred, for Akbar, the Mogul emperor, sent for Jesuit fathers to debate before him. A deputation and two later ones were sent and made some converts, and Father Jerome Xavier, a great-nephew of Francis, wrote works of Christian apologetics in Persian, the language of the court. But the hopes of converting the emperor were illusory. Akbar, a philosopher king, was engaged in dilettante experiments to create a new religion, synthesized from his own Muslim faith and Hindu, Parsee, and Christian beliefs and practices, with himself vaguely recognized as a semi-divinity; his suggestion that a Jesuit with a Bible and a mullah with a Qur'ān should compete for a miracle by walking through a fire was, presumably, an example of his irony. His successor Jahangir (1605–27) took Christianity more seriously, and showed signs of devotion to Christ and the Virgin. Thereafter, orthodox Muslim rulers took over the Mogul throne, and Christians were subjected to harassment ranging from violence to differential taxation.

In 1605, Roberto de Nobili arrived in India to carry the Jesuit policy of religious adaptation to its logical extreme. For the next 37 years in Madurai he lived the life of an Indian sannyasi (holy man), dressed in ochre robes, wearing no leather, eating no meat, learning classical Tamil and Sanskrit, and striving to get behind the Sanskrit to the forbidden world of the Veda; he refused all contact with fellow Europeans, and debated solely with the Brahmans. St Paul had been willing to 'become all things to all men' if perchance he 'could win some of them'. Would this have included accepting the caste system? Inevitably, Christians, the Jesuits included, were divided about the answer. But one thing was sure: without the acceptance of the Chinese rites and the Hindu caste structure, there could be no Christian breakthrough among the upper classes of either country.

About 1630, the far eastern scene had been reconnoitred. At the cost of his life, the Jesuit Bento de Goes had travelled from India to China disguised as a Persian trader, but taking a name proclaiming his allegiance, 'Abdullah Isai', the servant of God. His five-year journey in 1602–7 across the roof of the world proved there was no kingdom of Prester John and no Cathay but China. Franciscans, Dominicans, and Jesuits had pushed into Burma and Siam in the wake of Portuguese mercenaries who took service with local kings. From Portuguese Malacca and Spanish Manila the friars went to Cambodia and Cochin China, and adventured through the network of the powerful Islamic presence in the Malay archipelago. Of the Jesuits, Antonio de Andrade had crossed vertiginous gulfs on rope-bridges and arches of snow to enter Tibet, and built the first

Christian church there in 1626. Five years later, Francisco de Azevede was drinking buttered tea with the king of Ladak, a scruffy figure with a necklace of skulls who nevertheless gave him a skeletal horse and two yaks' tails as a present. By contrast, other members of the order were deep in sophisticated liaison with the imperial court of China. Around the coasts of India there were solidly established communities of Christians, and in Ceylon, where the Portuguese had successfully intervened in wars between rival kingdoms, the Franciscans had 80 establishments and the Jesuits 16. The Church of St Thomas was now incorporated in the Roman communion. The archbishop of Goa had packed the Synod of Udayamperur (1599) with a crowd of hurriedly ordained priests, and in proceedings in Portuguese which they ill understood, those guileless Christians had voted the abolition of their ancient church. The dictatorial bluff worked at the time, though in the end it brought bitterness and schism.

For Christianity there were hopeful streaks of light in the eastern sky—except in Japan. Here, a terrible truth was revealed: if force can sponsor conversions, it can also undo them. Christianity and the Christian *daimyo* had benefited from the political instability of the country, and from the links between the Jesuits and Portuguese trade. The situation changed when Tokugawa Kyasu unified Japan in 1600, and when Dutch and then English traders established bases there. The Japanese were aware of the conflicts between Catholic and Protestant, Jesuit and Franciscan; perhaps many were suspicious of the inherent European will for domination—in any case, it is clear that Christianity was regarded as a threat to the long-term stability of the Tokugawa regime. In 1614 and 1616 edicts were issued prohibiting Christian worship. A grim persecution was unleashed, with cruelties rivalling the worst excesses of the warfare in Europe between Catholics and Protestants. Sixty-two missionaries and 2,000 Japanese converts perished by torture—buried alive or crucified on the shore as the tide came in. By 1639, no active missionary was left, and those Christians who had not perished had left the country or gone underground; henceforward, Japanese contacts with the rest of the world were to be rigidly controlled and circumscribed until the mid-nineteenth century. Meanwhile, the power base of the Catholic missionary efforts was crumbling. Portugal was in decline. The Dutch were sending their high and heavy-gunned ships to cut the monsoon trade routes, and their fortresses were being erected on the Indian coast and in the Spice Islands. Having fought for their existence against Spain, they hated the Roman religion and sought to extirpate it wherever they triumphed. Spain, with its Atlantic lifeline under threat from England and Holland, was in no place to take over Portuguese responsibilities. The Roman missionary effort now had no weapons save the strategy of insinuation of Ricci and Nobili, and the courage of its martyrs.

Under worthy and unworthy popes alike, the papacy had unerringly condemned the enslavement of conquered unbelieving races. To maintain this principle, to fill the void left by the decline of Spain and Portugal, to provide central direction to missionary activity, and to enhance its own authority, in 1622 Rome set up the Congregation for the Propagation of the Faith, commonly known as 'Propaganda' to direct missionary work. The cardinals of the new establishment showed astonishing insight. In addition to the obvious decisions to create more bishoprics, find more secular clergy, and exercise more control, they recognized the two principles on which the future of enlightened Christian missionary work was to depend. Firstly, an indigenous clergy must be recruited in every country: it was the only way to find the numbers required, and to have priests who could effectively go 'underground' to keep the faith alive in times of persecution. Secondly, the customs of the various peoples must be respected except when they were offensive to religion and morals and, even then, change must be gradual. 'It is in the nature of men to love above everything else their own country and its ways'.

Respect for these principles had been lacking in the Spanish colonial adventure: perhaps they might prevail in the new conquests being made by the French in Canada. The Recollects arrived in 1615, the Jesuits ten years later, the Sulpicians and the priests of the seminary of the Missions Étrangères following. Marie de l'Incarnation brought Ursuline nuns in 1639 to set up schools for children of settlers and Indians, and hospital sisters came from Anjou. But Propaganda's ideal of preserving local customs and ordaining native clergy was, in this case, unrealistic. The Indians were cruel and treacherous, their only virtue courage; their perpetual tribal warfare was exacerbated by the wars between England and France in which they were used as auxiliaries. The French had the Hurons, and the English the Iroquois confederation; it was when the Iroquois finally hunted down the Hurons in 1649 that the two Jesuit fathers Jean de Brébeuf and Gabriel Lalemant met their unbelievably cruel martyrdom. It was impossible to settle the Indians in villages as the Jesuits desired, partly because of their own vagrant nature, and partly because the French presence itself was not so much an agricultural settlement as a vast fur-trapping organization coupled with a strategic drive up the Great Lakes turning southwards towards the Mississippi—an advance with the Jesuits as the inevitable reconnaissance party. Brandy for furs: it was in the interests of the colony to corrupt the Indians. Threats of excommunication by two successive bishops of Quebec—two fearless, authoritarian aristocrats—fell on deaf ears. With few secular priests (only 70 in 1700), they could exercise little control over morals, whether of the drunken *coureurs des bois* or of the dissolute social set at Quebec and Montreal which unconvincingly aped the salons of Paris. But austere with the old seventeenth-century virtues, the churchmen of Canada carried on to be the backbone of French national pride after their country was surrendered to Britain after the Seven Years War in 1763.

It was too late for Propaganda to hope to exercise control in Spanish America. The Crown was jealous of its rights, and the tendency of the age was to intensify secular control. In the eighteenth century, 'mortmain' legislation prevented the colonial church from enlarging its property, and in 1734 the religious orders were prohibited from establishing new conventual houses. In the latter part of the century, there was an outburst of periodical literature in the cities, and the ideas of the Enlightenment seconded the anticlericalism implicit in the government's erastian policies. The pressure of circumstances, however, was fortifying Propaganda's ideal of an indigenous clergy. From an early date, the creoles (*criollos*, pure-blooded Spaniards born in the New World) had competed bitterly with Spaniards born in Spain (*peninsulares*) for the choice of clerical positions, and rising in wealth, and with an improved education from the expanding American seminaries, were becoming more insistent. And in any case, fewer Spaniards were willing to emigrate. It was the policy of the bishops to put secular priests into parishes and push the friars (who were recalcitrant to diocesan discipline) out to the frontiers. More and more priests born in America were ordained and, since the number of creole volunteers did not suffice to fill the humbler pastoral posts, first mestizos, then later, full-blooded Indians, were appointed. The progress—limited, though significant so far as principle was concerned—towards the formation of a native clergy may be inferred from a royal ordinance of 1768: at least a quarter of the students admitted to seminaries were to be mestizos or Indians.

The great era of church-building continued. After the Peruvian earthquake of 1650, the cathedrals of Lima and Cuzco rose again in exuberant splendour; in the eighteenth century, the 'ultra baroque' style produced masterpieces in Mexico that outvie the achievements of Europe—like the church of Santa Prisca at Taxco whose towers and dome dominate the mountain approaches. Turning their backs on all this splendour and on the genial torpor of the parishes, the religious orders continued to push out into the wilderness—the Jesuits into California, Arizona, and Texas, followed by the soldiers setting up *presidos*, the blockhouses to hold the line, among the Mojos and Chiquitos of what is now Bolivia, and the fierce Arauncians of southern Chile; the Franciscans in Central America; the Capuchins at the mouth of the Orinoco, in Venezuela, Trinidad, and Guiana. They were encountering peoples too rudimentary in their civilization for Propaganda's ideal of the preservation of the native culture to be relevant. There was a way—the now almost forgotten plan of the friars who had followed the first *conquistadores*: authoritarian, clerical, and defiant of progress. Heroically, the Jesuits put it into effect with the primitive tribes of the Guaranis in the vast forests of Paraguay. A single Jesuit with a splendid church building would have a village of Guaranis around him; they would have to work the church lands for so many hours, and cultivate their own in the rest of their time. They were taught handicrafts, and brought to a simple level of literacy, and to a far from simple level of musical performance. Europeans were excluded, and the Jesuits formed a militia to defend their communities against Portuguese slave raiders. It was a venture which fascinated the writers of the Enlightenment, who were torn between admiration of a realized utopia of 'noble savages' and condemnation of Jesuit paternalism. The Indians retained their sense of community together with Christian religious practice and the more elementary amenities of European civilization. But theirs was a static and vulnerable world. There were no ordinations or vocations to the religious life, and only token self-government. When the Catholic crowns destroyed the Jesuit Order, the Guaranis were left as children, helpless before the exploiters and slavers.

'It is in the nature of men to love above everything else their own country and what belongs to it.' In India and China, the Jesuits were showing due regard for the warning of Propaganda. In the fashion of Nobili, the Portuguese aristocrat Britto, the Frenchman La Fontaine, and, later, at the beginning of the eighteenth century, the Italian Beschi lived as sannyasi in various places in southern India, winning the ear of local rulers, and gaining a certain fame as poets in the local languages (La Fontaine in Telugu, Beschi in Tamil). Of Beschi, high in the favour of the raja of Tanjore, it was said he appeared only in state among the great ones, yet he ended his days ministering to the poor Paravas of the Fishery Coast. Britto, falling foul of the prince of Marawa, met a martyr's death. Brahmans were being converted—only a few of them, but the fact was significant, for the higher castes were regarded as the great hope for vocations to the priesthood. In China, though the other religious orders were active, it was the Jesuits who held the key to the future, from their position of influence at the imperial court in Peking. Here, they had survived a change of dynasty, and risen again to high favour as in the days of Ricci. When the Fleming Jesuit Verbiest, director of the Bureau of Astronomy and Mandarin of the Sixth Order died in 1688, the emperor's guards marched behind images of the Blessed Virgin and the child Jesus in his funeral cortège. In 1692, there was a dramatic success, for the great Emperor Kang Xi (K'ang Hsi) issued an edict tolerating Christian worship; since the Christians do not excite sedition or teach dangerous doctrines, he said, they were not to be opposed.

Rome recognized the importance of the Indian and Chinese missions, imaginatively, by the episcopal consecration of two natives; Matthaeus de Castro, a Brahman from Goa, was sent back from the papal court to India in 1658 as vicar apostolic of Bijapur, and Luo Wenzzo (Lô Wen-Tsao), of a Chinese peasant family, who had been converted by Franciscans and educated in Manila, was named, in 1674, as vicar apostolic of northern China. Neither appointment had much immediate effect. Portuguese hostility ensured the delay of Luo's consecration for eleven years, and deprived Castro of recognition altogether. But the symbolic importance of the Roman initiative was enormous. The principle of native clergy was well established— there were numerous secular priests under the archbishop of Goa of Eurasian or high-caste Hindu descent; the appointment of native bishops could have been the beginning of Indian and Chinese churches free from the handicap of European associations (other than allegiance to Rome) and progressively becoming independent of Portuguese official protection. On one condition: the respect of local customs, as Propaganda had prescribed.

There are, of course, customs and customs, and the integrity of Christian doctrine has to be preserved. Not everyone, even in Jesuit circles, was happy with the concessions being made, especially where the Indian caste system was concerned. Some complaints against Nobili's system were contrived and insensitive—objections to wives wearing the *tali* around their necks instead of a wedding ring on the finger, or to the sacred tuft on the shaven head of the Brahmans. The *punal*, the sacred thread worn on the left shoulder might be admissible as a badge of distinction, though strictly it was a sign of merit in a previous existence. But separating the castes at the communion table was the point when concession was betraying principle, and even the later Jesuit device of dividing walls and separate doors fell short of edifying. No such argument, however, could be advanced against the Chinese rites: it was folly to treat the Indian and Chinese situations as equally dangerous.

By the beginning of the eighteenth century, there was a massing of forces against the Jesuits. Envy of their success had led other religious orders to denounce their methods as devious compromises. In Europe, where they were specializing as confessors to the great, their enemies made accusations of easygoing standards in matters of conscience, and Rome had condemned certain propositions of 'relaxed' morality. 'Tutiorism' (taking the safest way) was the Roman line now, rather than allowing the penitent to look around for options among those arguably justifiable. By analogy, the Jesuits in the mission field ought not to be allowed to take risks with the purity of doctrine. The Jansenists of France, harassed by the Jesuits, had struck back by sponsoring the condemnation of the 'Chinese Rites' by the Sorbonne, and one of the first to seek audience with Pope Clement XI after his election in 1700 was Cardinal de Noailles, archbishop of Paris, urging him to maintain his predecessors' pronouncements against Jansenism and, as a counter-balance, to censure the Chinese Rites of the Jesuits. A primary rule of Roman policy was to ensure the authority of the pope; perhaps, as the possibility of the emergence of peculiarly Indian or Chinese versions of Christianity drew nearer, they began to look less attractive because they might be inclined towards independence. Whatever the reasons, by 1701, Rome had decided to abandon the earlier vision of Propaganda and bring to an end the Jesuit adventure in the East. Charles Maillard de Tournon was sent out as legate to make the announcements. Proud, insecure, and in ill health, he proceeded brusquely and unimaginatively. At Pondicherry in 1704, he issued a wholesale condemnation of Nobili's policies, then went on to Nanking to publish an equally comprehensive denunciation of Ricci's. The effect in China was devastating. The emperor was angry. He had accepted a document in which the Jesuits set forth their view of the honours paid to Confucius and the ancestors as purely civil. Now someone called the Pope had forbidden these rites; the vicar apostolic of Fukien, who had accompanied Tournon to Peking, could not read Chinese yet presumed to call the emperor and his people atheists. An imperial decree expelled all missionaries who did not accept the *modus vivendi* established of old by Ricci. In 1742 and 1744, Pope Benedict XIV issued bulls confirming the judgements of Tournon. The hope of a great new church in China, tolerated by power and enriched by borrowings from Confucianism and the old wisdom of the country was destroyed. Though the Jesuits hung on in Peking, the story of the rest of the century is one of intermittent persecution and steady decline.

Everything seemed to conspire to bring Catholic expansion in the East to an end. An exception was the Philippines, and another was South Vietnam, where the Jesuit system of native catechists had struck deep roots, and where the French *Société des Missions Étrangères* had taken over with extensive resources. Elsewhere, the horizons were darkening. In 1773, under ruthless pressure from the Catholic crowns, the pope abolished the Jesuit Order; the greatest of all the missionary orders was silenced. Two decades later, the French revolution brought disorder and war to Catholic Europe. The Capuchins had been driven out of Tibet, China was hostile, Japan was closed. In Ceylon, Dutch hostility and a Buddhist revival reduced Catholic numbers; in India the Muslim sultans of Mysore destroyed Christian churches. Yet, if Catholics were small and endangered minorities, in absolute terms their numbers were significant— possibly 1,000,000 in India, 500,000 in Ceylon, 250,000 in South Vietnam, and 250,000 in China. Catechisms, handbooks of devotion, and liturgical books had been translated into the major languages and many dialects. A tradition of heroism and martyrdom remained as an inspiration to vocations and an incentive to generosity among the faithful in Europe. There was a foundation for the vast nineteenth-century missionary campaign to build on.

'Go ye into all the world and preach the gospel to every creature.' Protestants were late in accepting the obligation, thus incurring the censures of Roman controversialists. A few of their divines ventured excuses: the command was mandatory only on the first apostles; the end of the world was approaching; or (for hard-line Calvinists) predestination would take care of everything. These arguments won little credence. If there had been a unique divine incursion into history, the Pauline question remained: 'How shall they hear without a preacher?' In fact, the reason why the Protestant churches were not sending out preachers had nothing to do with doctrine or interpretations of scriptural texts. They were absorbed in white-hot arguments and battles for existence against Rome and against each other, and in any case, the heathen were not accessible for evangelism until England and Holland moved from buccaneering to commerce, and from commerce to empire. Rejecting the concept of the monastic life, the Protestants did not possess a task force like the Franciscans and Jesuits to do missionary exploration.

True, there were a few adventurers; there were Swedes who went northwards to the Lapps, a group of French Huguenots who in the mid-sixteenth century set up a mission station in Brazil, and a lonely eccentric Peter Heyling, a Lutheran law student of Lübeck, who went to Egypt in 1633 and on to Abyssinia, where he perished.

These were exceptional cases. Even so, when trade, warfare, or emigration brought them into contact with other races, Protestants did attempt to propagate their faith. From the start, the Dutch East India Company accepted the obligation—in a dour, unidealistic, but practical fashion. Wherever Dutch control was established, Catholics and adherents of other religions were harassed. Every station had its chaplain, trained at the Company's seminary at Leiden; they were encouraged to draw in natives by the offer of a bonus to salary for every duly certified conversion. These conversions were to uncompromisingly biblical Christianity; significantly, the first Bible translation into a south-east Asian language came from the Dutch, the New Testament in Malay in 1688.

The formal recognition of the missionary obligation in England was embodied in the charters granted by the Crown for overseas ventures, that to Sir Humphrey Gilbert in 1583 including the patriotic conceit: 'it seeming probable that God hath reserved these Gentiles to be introduced into Christian civility by the English nation'. James I's charter to Virginia spoke of taking the gospel to such 'as yet live in darkness', and Charles I's to Massachusetts, in charming phraseology, required the colonists to 'win and invite' the natives to Christianity. In 1698, the East India Company was ordered to appoint chaplains who would have to learn Portuguese (the lingua franca of the East), so they could teach the servants of the Company. In their principal trading stations in India, the English communities built churches (Madras 1680, Calcutta 1709)—that of St Thomas in Bombay, consecrated in 1718, was a huge building so there would be room for the natives to enter and 'observe the purity and gravity of our devotions'. In New England, genuine efforts were made to comply with the pious exhortations of the charter of Charles I. In 1644, the General Court of Massachusetts ordered the sending of missionaries to the Indians, and five years later the Society for the Propagation of the Gospel in New England was founded, with collections for its support levied in London by order of the Long Parliament. As the Franciscans and Jesuits had found, the only way to win and keep Indian converts was to settle them in villages. This was the policy of pastor John Eliot, who gathered tribesmen into his 'Praying Towns', into which the heads of households entered by subscribing to a solemn covenant.

Lacking sea-borne contact with the distant mission fields, Germany, it seemed, would contribute little to Protestant effort—that is, until Pietism, the great movement of spiritual renewal, arose within Lutheranism. In 1706, at the invitation of the king of Denmark, two Pietist missionaries from the University of Halle went to Tranquebar, the Danish trading station in south-east India. In 1730, Count Zinzendorf, who presided over a Pietistic community on his estates in Saxony, attended the coronation of Christian VI at Copenhagen; here, he met Eskimo and Negro Christians, which inspired him to send emissaries from his Moravian Brethren to the slaves in the Danish West Indies and to join Hans Egede, the lonely Norwegian missionary in Greenland. Thereafter, the Moravians wandered the world, expounding the New Testament to pious groups in England and America and evangelizing the heathen wherever they could gain a foothold. Some of them were simple men, who could preach only by example. Others were intellectuals, like Bartholomew Ziegenbalg, who worked in India from 1706 to 1729, translating the New Testament, Luther's Catechism, and hymns into Tamil, and Christian Friedrich Schwartz, one of his successors, who in a long ministry from 1746 to 1798 preached and wrote in half a dozen languages, became prime minister of the raja of Tanjore and, in spite of holding that high office, won a reputation for sanctity among the Hindu population. The English SPCK financed the

German Lutherans to expand their mission outside the Danish territory, and the East India Company accepted its pastors as chaplains; throughout the century, without benefit of Anglican orders, they celebrated the services of the Book of Common Prayer in English and, in their own translation, in Tamil. By 1800, the German–Danish–English mission had 20,000 converts, mainly Pariahs and half-caste Portuguese, a modest flock by comparison with the 300,000 in Ceylon under Dutch ministers, though won by more Christian methods. Free from the competitive itch to promote the interests of a single church, nation, or religious order, the Pietistic missionaries recaptured something of the spirit of the first apostles, resolved—in the Pauline phrase—'to preach Christ and him crucified' without doctrinal insistence or confessional boastings, recommending their belief by providing translations of the New Testament, sympathetic to local customs yet unconditionally offering European education; their system was a blueprint for the highest missionary ideals of the future.

If Christianity was to become the universal religion, viable to all and challenging all, it would have to cease to be identified exclusively with European civilization. This was still a distant, almost unthinkable prospect. It was to be long before the generality of European Christians reached a sympathetic understanding of other cultures, let alone encouraged them to remake Christianity in their own image. True, thanks to the writers of the Enlightenment and, later, those of German romanticism, the eighteenth century was drawn sympathetically to the old civilizations of India and China, but evangelical piety, utilitarianism, and the cult of technological progress and education combined to darken the picture into one of stagnation and worse—the cruelties of suttee and female infanticide as against the insights of the *Bhagavadgita*. As Europe raced on to an unparalleled military, technological, and economic domination, it was difficult to see the world apart from the ingrained conviction of European superiority, though the concept of 'trusteeship', which was to mitigate the exercise of raw power in British India, was arising. But one thing could be done towards removing the reproach of Europe's heartless triumphalism: the repudiation of slavery by enlightened Christian thinkers had to be made a reality.

The evil trade had expanded, so that, in the second half of the eighteenth century, a yearly average of 60,000 Negroes made the terrible middle passage of the Atlantic in the stinking holds of English, French, and Portuguese slave ships. The commerce was defended by bluff arguments which had a certain cogency—it saved African prisoners who would otherwise be massacred, or victims of famine who would die anyway. Those who despaired of preventing the injustice took refuge (not unworthily, sometimes heroically) in trying to convert the slaves and improve their lot. Hence, some unpleasant paradoxes: rosaries and crucifixes among the merchandise the slave-traders took to the African coasts; the SPG in 1712 accepting a legacy of plantation slaves and treating them well but not freeing them; the slaves of Cape Colony, more numerous than the settlers, remaining unbaptized because the pastors ruled that baptism automatically conferred freedom. From the mid-eighteenth century, Methodists and Moravians worked among the slaves and, more dangerously, the outlawed runaways, of the West Indies. The evangelists were strangely contrasting figures: Nathaniel Gilbert a converted planter, John Baxter a shipwright, Thomas Coke an Oxford graduate and Anglican clergyman, George Liele the freed Negro Baptist from the United States. Their news got back to England to swell the tide of Christian anger. Thomas Clarkson, the Quaker, did the research on conditions in the slave ships which led to parliamentary regulations in 1788. In 1787, the evangelical banker Henry Thornton presided over the company which founded Sierra Leone to be a refuge for emancipated slaves and a demonstration of how Africa could become a commercial client of Europe rather than a reservoir of forced labour. The stage was set for the decisive intervention of the evangelical conscience, demanding freedom for every man to make his lonely peace with God, and Wilberforce's dynamic leadership, ruthlessly exercising leverage among the greatest of the land.

The way was being cleared for the dramatic take-off of Christian expansion in the next hundred years, Latourette's 'great century'. The reproach of the slave-trade was being progressively lifted from the Christian nations, and the full drive of Protestant initiative was being harnessed by the foundation of missionary societies—dominated by laymen, often inter-denominational in ethos, the Protestant equivalent of the Roman religious orders, but rooted in the life of the churches and chapels where the money was raised. The Anglican SPG had been active in America from 1701; in 1792 came the Baptist Missionary Society, the Church Missionary Society seven years later, the British and Foreign Bible Society in 1804. Then in America, following local societies for work among the Indians, the American Board of Commissioners for Foreign Missions (1810), and the American Baptist Missionary Board (1814). Thereafter societies innumerable, whose names alone would fill a volume.

The rise of American societies was significant. The United States was to be the predominant missionary force of the future, self-righteous and recklessly generous, naïve yet alive with enterprise and business know-how. In the light of what the future was to bring, the cruel and heroic story of conquest and mission all over the globe is, arguably, less important in Christian history than the widening of the Christian-European power base as the frontier moved westwards in near-empty North America, eastwards through the wastes of Siberia, and southwards into the vast sea-girt continent of Australasia. Almost unnoticed, the power of the tsars of Moscow had crept towards the Pacific shore, with the Russian Orthodox Church absorbing strange tribesmen and staking the claim to be the church of the future in vast empty lands. Peter the Great, dragging his people into civilization by the methods of barbarism, kept the Russian Orthodox Church in subjection, but used it as an instrument to settle and give rudimentary education to the scattered Siberian tribes. The monks who went out as missionaries were able to call on military escorts and were allowed to offer exemption from taxation and military service as rewards for conversion. Statistics were rarely recorded, but Luke Konashevitch, metropolitan of Kazan, kept a running tally showing how half a million Tchermisses and other peoples of the middle Volga had been brought into the fold in 1741–62, success on a scale which indicates the inevitable superficiality of the Christianizing process. So far, there was a parallel with the earlier work of the Spaniards in South America; similarly, both Spanish Catholicism and Russian Orthodoxy had their heroes of the mission field. There was Philoteus, metropolitan of Tobolsk under Peter the Great, yearning to go back to the peace of his monastery, yet active in his diocese and sending his missionaries to the Pacific coast and his ecclesiastical envoys to the imperial court of China; there was Cyril Suchanov the lay evangelist who wandered in absolute poverty with the nomadic Tungus tribe until, at last, in 1776 he managed to settle some of them around a church building; there were the martyrs of Kamchatka where, against a background of volcanoes and permanent frost, monks attempted to convert stone-age natives and—more difficult still—the brutalized inhabitants of the Russian penal colony. Fur traders and adventurers and missionaries went ahead, to be followed by agricultural settlers. In the mid-seventeenth century the Russian population of Siberia had been 70,000; in the 1780s it was a million—with secular priests to minister in its scattered parishes.

By then, in the Southern Sea, a great continent—perhaps destined one day to be as significant in the world as the Russian Siberian wilderness has become—was opening to Anglo-Saxon enterprise. The first convict fleet reached New South Wales in 1788. The single Church of England chaplain on board was there as an afterthought, at the insistence of William Wilberforce, but the penal settlements had their routine Christian observances, with stone churches built by convict labour (at Port Arthur in Tasmania with a convict architect). From these grim beginnings, a new nation arose. As free settlers poured in, the idea of a church establishment faded away, but the newcomers nostalgically looked back to the various religious denominations they had belonged to in England, Scotland, or Ireland, and Christianity remained an integral part of their civilization.

Meanwhile, the North American continent was being taken over by Anglo-Saxon civilization, a new world into which the surplus population of nineteenth-century Europe would surge and continue to multiply. In the first half of the eighteenth century, Quakers, German Anabaptists, Swiss Mennonites, Scottish and Scottish–Irish Presbyterians, Calvinist Baptists, and Arminian Baptists flourished in Rhode Island, New York, New Jersey, Pennsylvania, and Delaware. Here, religious liberty and pluralism prevailed—the pattern of the American future. New England Puritanism evolved towards liberalism, and the Anglican establishment in Virginia, Maryland, and the Carolinas was on the way to becoming a denomination, gaining in vitality as it did so. After 1720, German immigrants moved in, chiefly Lutheran. The harshness of frontier life and the lack of structured ecclesiastical organization threatened routine conformity, but the 'Great Awakening' turned the tide, a surge of revivalist movements which Richard Hofstadter has called 'a second and milder Reformation'. As 'the noise among the dry bones waxed louder and louder', the denominationalist idea was spread, each church taking itself to be a distinctive member of a larger whole, creating a sense of American religious unity above the mosaic of confessional diversity. America had become a nation, and it was to be a religious nation, the future heartland of Christian missionary endeavour.

The Jesuit vision of a new Christianity arising in India and China, annexing the wisdom and insights of those ancient civilizations, had failed. But in the vast empty lands of the West, in North America, inspirations always implicit in Christianity had free play, creating something new, an idiosyncratic mutation—a Christianity diverse, fissiparous, and inventive, not held in check by the state or beholden to it, not taking orders from Rome or supervised from Europe, enjoying freedom and extending freedom to others, thriving on democratic systems of church government, the voluntary principle, and lay leadership. There were those in eighteenth-century America who glimpsed the future and—as ever with millennial dreams—saw it in impossibly utopian terms, free of the tarnishing which the world and the passage of generations brings to every human enthusiasm. In the mid-century, Jonathan Edwards, the Calvinistic doyen of the Awakening, reflected on the vista opening up ahead:

America has received the religion of the old continent, the church of ancient times had been there, and Christ is from thence: but that there may have been an equality, and inasmuch as that continent has crucified Christ, they shall not have the honor of communicating religion in its most glorious state to us, but we to them. . . . When God is about to turn the earth into a Paradise, he does not begin his work where there is some good growth already, but in a wilderness where . . . nothing is to be seen but dry sand and barren rocks; that the light may shine out of darkness, and the world replenished from emptiness, and the earth watered by springs from a droughty desert.

CHRISTIANITY
SINCE 1800

10

Great Britain and Europe

OWEN CHADWICK

The Partial Loss of European Dominance in Christianity

DURING the modern period Christianity in Europe was transformed. It lost a large part of its predominance in the Christianity of the world. Christians from Europe settled overseas and converted indigenous populations to Christianity, or developed for the better the churches of indigenous populations which were of long standing. Then Europe lost its own self-confidence as the bearer of Christianity to these other worlds. It came under attack first for its doctrines, on the ground that they were untrue, and then for its morals, on the ground that they were either weak or less than the highest. And it encountered persecution in some countries of Europe. Europeans found, in fact, that Europe was a more barbarian continent than they supposed, and were not so sure that it was so good to export all its beliefs, practices, morals, and customs to the countries of the other continents. At first the expansive effort of Christianity was extraordinary, and throughout the period it never ceased to be extraordinary because of what happened in Africa and Latin America. But in Europe it slowly lost confidence, and feared that it might be losing its homeland, and felt more against the contemporary world, with sometimes remarkable consequences in the churches.

The wars of religion, and then the Enlightenment, and then the French revolution, taught Europe the hard lesson of toleration. Throughout the nineteenth century the various

European countries were dismantling the social disadvantages attached to professing a faith which was not the majority faith of the community. In Catholic countries, though slowly, Protestants were given freedom, and then Jews and then atheists. In Protestant countries, though less slowly, Roman Catholics were given freedom, and then Jews and then atheists. In England and Ireland the Roman Catholics were given an equality of citizenship by the Roman Catholic Emancipation Act of 1829. In France the freedoms established by the French revolution were never lost, despite the desire of some very conservative Catholics to go back upon them. Belgium, Switzerland, Holland, and western Germany were also strongly influenced by the Napoleonic ordering of society.

Countries where nationality and religion were still closely mingled found it far more difficult to concede toleration because dissent from the prevailing religion was suspected as dissent from the accepted order of society. Despite several liberal epochs in Spain of the nineteenth century, when Protestant churches could form and when a George Borrow could travel round distributing Bibles, the underlying attitude of the ordinary Spaniard remained intolerant into the twentieth century. For reasons mainly of national loyalty, Poles found it difficult to give equality to their large Jewish population, for the circumstances of Poland under tsarist rule made the Catholic faith a dissent from the tsar and therefore a sign of Polish nationality.

The real coming of toleration, for atheism or for any sort of religion, was the biggest single difference between 1800 and 1914. It was in part not yet true of Spain and Portugal, for all their waves of liberalism. Curious survivals of intolerance remained, like the exclusion of the Jesuits from Switzerland, a ban not lifted until 1973. Nor was it true of Russia. But over almost all Europe toleration and equality had come. That was the greatest possible gain to Christendom and presented it with its greatest challenge: under these conditions of freedom could it any longer be called Christendom? In the long run it meant that if people were going to be Christians they must consciously make this choice. That led to sincerity and to higher standards in the pastoral care of the churches. Simultaneously it diminished the Christian moral influence in society because people no longer took for granted everything about Christianity, even its moral standards.

The Evangelicals

The Pietist or evangelical movement in Western European Protestantism was at its strongest during the first thirty or forty years of the nineteenth century, it conditioned the earnestness of what in England was called the Victorian ethos. It was very biblical; puritan in behaviour; and dedicated to the propagation of the gospel both at home and abroad. Most of the successful Protestant missions to Africa or India or China during the nineteenth century were evangelical in their inspiration, whether they came from Britain or Germany or Holland or Switzerland. In the middle years of the nineteenth century they attained for a moment the leadership of the churches in England and Lutheran Germany, for during the 1850s both the British government, with Palmerston as prime minister, and the Prussian government under a conservative king Frederick William IV, favoured them for higher church posts. Evangelical missions were for a time surprisingly successful in Spain and Portugal and Italy, though in a very small way. But their public influence in Europe (not their public influence overseas) declined during the second half of the century. This was something to do with their inability, at first, to tackle the difficult intellectual problems over the Bible, or religion and science; something to do with the way in which so many of their best people went to Africa or India or China and left fewer possible leaders for the home front; and something to do with the way in which their ideas were taken up into high church movements. The leaders of the Oxford Movement in Britain, which was high church and Anglican, mostly came from evangelical families, and their piety had an evangelical root, for all its Catholic-sounding language. This was less true in Germany, where high church Lutheranism looked back towards a return to an older Lutheran tradition distinct from Pietism. The power of the evangelical movement in Scotland split the church there in 1843; the divided bodies were reunited in 1929.

The Decline of Faith

In 1914, as compared with 1800, a lot more people in Europe refused to profess Christianity. Why? No one is yet sure, and the argument is in progress.

1. Medical science improved. Death among the young grew less common. Anaesthetics made suffering easier to bear. The impact of mortality was blunted. We have no evidence that this affected the need for religion. It is a guess. And the need for religion—not necessarily the need for orthodox religion— remained very strong. Observation of its persistent strength led to the frequent conviction that the religious instinct was part of the constitution of humanity.

2. People moved out of villages into towns. A people's religion was often associated in feeling with a rural environment. Many Christian heroes of the nineteenth century were still rural heroes: a John Keble as a parish priest in southern England, a Curé d'Ars in a tiny French parish. After their country church, when peasants moved into the city, their town church felt irrelevant to their lives. This theory is based upon a statistic. It is certain that fewer people per cent went to church in towns. The bigger the town the smaller the proportion. Was it the move from country to town? Or the nature of the city? Or the nature of work in the city? Or the removal of city dwellers from the natural sources of their well-being like fresh streams and cornfields and milk-bearing cows? Or the inability of churches to supply enough places of worship and a sufficiency of pastoral care in the city? This last cannot be the right explanation. In previous ages, and in modern Africa or India, a shortage of pastors did nothing whatever to stem human need for religion.

3. The coming of toleration made the churches, and all the non-churches, compete for the allegiance of the public. Instead of expecting the people to come to church because they wanted it as much as they wanted the local school or bakery, the churches had a suspicion that the people did not feel the need of them, and therefore went out in campaigns to persuade them— missions, evangelism, soap-box oratory. Toleration meant, not only Christian ideas, but anticlerical ideas, anti-Christian ideas, put before the public. Some minds were unsettled by the conflict of ideas. Christian practice and morality rested upon customs and language handed down from parents to children. Mostly these had been accepted unquestioningly. When religion was in the market-place acceptance could hardly be so automatic. The pushing of religion out into the market-place was given a sudden impetus—during the 1860s by the coming of national newspapers, which by the 1890s were reaching a mass audience; during the 1930s by radio; and during the 1950s by the coming of television, which at last took the market-place into everyone's home, so that they need no longer move out of their armchairs to shop at its booths.

4. The study of the Bible proved that it contained historical legend. Far fewer people in 1914, as compared with 1800, believed in the story of Noah's Ark, though everyone taught it to their children as they taught the story of Father Christmas. As a religious belief, Noah's Ark was not relevant. But the Bible and its authority were not irrelevant. It seemed less important to many Christians of 1914 to know the Bible thoroughly, than it had seemed to most Protestant Christians in 1800; and this happened even though by 1914 many more Europeans had learnt to read and so were able to read the Bible for themselves.

Science and Religion

The Christian churches had been teaching that the Bible was history in all its parts. That was not true. The discovery could hardly avoid lessening their authority in society at large. It did not weaken it nearly as much as might have been expected because the historicity of Noah was wholly unimportant to religion and the same applied to much else. Just as the value of St George as a symbol was in no whit diminished by the persons who pretended that he was a pork-butcher or that he did not exist, because the symbol was far more important than the narrative evidence on which it was built, the shaking of biblical narratives appears to have had less impact upon the religion of general society. Except among a limited circle of intellectuals, religion was much more likely to be shaken by a social fact like the movement of population than by intellectual facts such as the discoveries about evolution towards which Darwin's *Origin of Species* (1859) pointed the way.

But the churches went on serving the needs of the people. The dead must be buried, with affection and with hope. Some brides and bridegrooms wished their marriage to be a self-dedication, and others for it to be a liturgical occasion and thus rather splendid. Some of them wanted their children to grow up as moral and honourable beings and were sure that the morality taught by the Christian church was the true safeguard of character. Some of them had that innate sense of a trans-cendent world which appears to be the natural and not inculcated property of a large number within the human race. That is, they needed to worship God and the church offered them the way. Many had moral convictions which for them would never not be associated with religious language and practice. And some, though only a few and more rarefied souls, believed that they had a direct and overwhelming experience of the divine in their lives which made all argument about God a triviality and an irrelevance.

It is still a question whether the conflict between science and religion, which raged between about 1840 and 1939, had any effect upon religion. Was science taken to prove mechanical purpose in the universe—for a theory of mechanical purpose was undoubtedly incompatible with religion? None of the best scientists said so. Mechanical purpose could not be extracted from science but was a theory imported into science from outside it. The German scientist Haeckel, who was also a crude publicist, told Christians that they were fools because science had proved that there was no God. But Haeckel would only be believed by other persons who had themselves formed the desire to believe that God was a figment of the human imagination.

The symbol 'Evolution' deprived Europeans of the feeling that they knew about their origins, and thereby gave them the vague anxiety which comes to every person who is ignorant of birth or early life or past.

An illustration of the consequences might be taken from the successive rites of ordination in the Church of England.

1662–1927: 'Do you unfeignedly believe all the canonical Scriptures of the Old and New Testament?'

1928–1980: 'Do you unfeignedly believe all the canonical Scriptures of the Old and the New Testament, as given by God to convey to us in many parts and divers manners the revelation of himself which is fulfilled in our Lord Jesus Christ?'

1980–   : 'Do you accept the Holy Scriptures as revealing all things necessary for eternal salvation through faith in Jesus Christ?'

So lately as 1928 they unfeignedly believed. From 1980 they only accepted. Even in 1928 they believed in the Old Testament as well as the New Testament, though they saved intellectual integrity by acknowledging that the revelation came through these Testaments 'in many parts and divers manners'. From 1980 they did not need to profess that the revelation came to them through the Old Testament as well as the New Testament. Progressively, the formulas allowed a larger liberty to minds which felt themselves to be truly Christian but nevertheless had doubts about the way in which a revelation of God came to them through the Bible.

The formula of 1980 has a further interest for this problem. In the consecration of bishops it added a statement of the historic unchanging creed—'This Church is part of the one holy catholic and apostolic Church, worshipping the one true God, Father, Son and Holy Spirit. It professes the faith uniquely revealed in the holy Scriptures and set forth in the catholic creeds, which faith the Church is called upon to proclaim afresh in each generation . . .'.

It is observable how little had changed. The church was still in the context of the historic doctrines, from the doctrine of the Holy Trinity to all the doctrines mentioned in the catholic creeds, including the virgin birth of Christ and the resurrection of the body. So far as a restatement of the words of Christian doctrine was concerned, Darwin need never have written. And the illustration has this importance, because this is not a small and obscure sect keeping itself unspotted from the world but a church with a strong liberal tradition of thought and a willingness to try to meet the culture of the day and the truths (if any) established by scientific or historical discovery. It looks in retrospect as though the age of the conflict between science and religion had less impact upon the Christian churches (taken as worshipping, liturgical, and moral bodies) than some people thought at the time.

The Conservative Nature of the Creed

The meaning of words is in the upper intelligence. The association of words is an affair of association in the heart. Therefore words still continue to be used in worship even when their meaning cannot be accepted in its old sense. The apostles' creed is a catholic creed from very early in Christian history. It contains a profession of faith in the resurrection of the body. How many Christians of 1980 believed in the resurrection of the body in the sense in which many of their forefathers of 1800 believed? The question has no possible answer, but it is also impossible not to postulate a very large change of opinion. The Middle Ages understood the clause literally. By the twentieth century (and before) it was only tolerable because anyone who used it turned it into a piece of metaphor or allegory or poetry, a profession of hope in personal survival and a declaration that a 'survival' by merging into an infinite world of spirit was an idea not adequate to express the Christian hope.

The phrase could not be dropped because it was in the apostles' creed and the creed was canonized. During the nineteenth century several leaders of the Lutheran churches, German or Danish, tried to drop it from use, whether at ordination or confirmation. The Lutherans were conservative. In 1845 they dismissed from office a Königsberg pastor, Julius Rupp, because he preached not against the apostles' creed, but against the language of the Athanasian creed, a creed with less catholic authority. Two other Lutheran pastors were ejected from their offices because they refused to use the apostles' creed. The Prussian general synod of 1846 sanctioned the use of a paraphrased creed which did not mention the virgin birth or the descent into hell or the resurrection of the body. The creed is known as the creed of Nitzsch after the theologian who was its chief drafter. Intended to bring peace in the churches, it caused nothing but fierce controversy. In the Berlin of the 1870s this argument, between liberals and conservatives, flared up again. It reached its climax in the Schrempf case. Christoph Schrempf was a Württemberg pastor who was ejected because he refused to use the apostles' creed. A group of students appealed to the great Berlin theologian Harnack who argued that the apostles' creed ought to be respected but should not be compulsorily used in the liturgy; and indeed said that an instructed modern Christian must take offence at the creed if he studied the Bible and church history. This utterance caused a bitter argument involving important men on both sides. No one ever made peace in this battle; and even in 1924 there were cases in the more conservative Lutheran churches of pastors being dismissed because they refused to say the apostles' creed. The apostles' creed was so canonized that none of the proposed paraphrases, any more than that of Nitzsch, succeeded in being accepted by the churches.

The Tension over Biblical Criticism

All the churches were troubled by division over this matter of the truth of the Bible and the consequences of the discoveries of science and history.

The Free Church of Scotland, which separated from the established Church of Scotland in 1843 on a point of principle (the Free Church refused, the established church accepted, the right of state to back the legal rights of patrons against the decision of the church authority)—the split is known as the Disruption—ejected from his post at Aberdeen (1881) a young but eminent Old Testament scholar, William Robertson Smith, because he not only accepted but contributed to the discovery of the truth about the development of the Old Testament and the early religion of the Semitic peoples, and summarized these opinions in the *Encyclopaedia Britannica*.

In every denomination some tension of this sort could be found. But far the most serious tension could be found in the largest of the churches, that of the Roman Catholics. It was serious because authority in that church was strong and particularly conservative; and also because, for a variety of political reasons, the higher education of Catholics was in poor shape through most of the nineteenth century; the religious orders, who had once produced great scholars, were now much needed for pastoral care; and therefore the tension between Catholic scholars and the authorities of their church came late; and because late, more anguished, and with more consequence in creating the sense of gulf between the church and the normal educated world of Europe.

In 1907 Pius X (1903–14), who was a simple godly person with no real understanding of intellectual problems, and who came to fear that traitors were secretly working away inside the church to dissolve the apostolic gospel, issued the encyclical *Pascendi*. This created an umbrella picture of a movement called 'modernism' which was posing as Christian but was falling away into agnosticism. None of the Catholic scholars of the time accepted that the portrait in the encyclical fitted their faces. Most of the church accepted the encyclical easily. A few scholars left the church, of whom the most celebrated was the Anglo-Irish Jesuit George Tyrrell, and the most senior a Frenchman who was bishop of Tarentaise. Apparently authority had won; and indeed there were many Christians in Europe, not only Catholic, who were glad that the pope came out so mightily for the old truths and the old paths.

But, underneath, this was one of the big disasters in the churches since 1800. The pope had not only stopped scholars who were becoming agnostics. He blighted the prospects of scholars who were not. And the succeeding six years saw something very unpleasant, in the dismissal on inadequate grounds, often on rumour, of teachers in seminaries, or even canons and parish priests. Some of the leading Catholics of the middle of the twentieth century had passed through a phase, usually short, when they were under suspicion for being tainted with 'modernism' (for example, the future Pope John XXIII). John Henry Newman was of all the English Catholics of the nineteenth century the mind who stood most openly for adherence to the true faith with acceptance of the justified conclusions of science and history where they were mature, and in 1879 was made a cardinal. Fifteen years after his death in 1890 he fell under a black cloud, as a sort of modernist before the time of modernism, and only recovered his deserved reputation slowly, after the Second World War.

This ecclesiastical backwardness was ending even before Pope Pius X died in 1914. But it had grave consequences. At a vital moment in the relations between the churches and the world's mentality, their largest and most powerful body adopted a public posture which the world could and did represent as obscurantism. That was bound to have effects upon other churches.

The natural sciences acquired prestige as a mode of enquiry into truth. To move forward here a little and there a little, by a long series of practical experiments, seemed to be the way to find reality. The natural sciences became far more prominent as instruments of education and took many more hours in the syllabuses of schools. Therefore religious men became conscious of the inadequacy of the words which they used. When they thought about it religious men had always known that their words were not adequate to the mystery which they sought to describe. Now they began to have a deeper sense of that inadequacy; or, that truth was more difficult to find than their fathers supposed.

The Text of the Bible

In this connection the history of the text of the Bible had religious consequences. In 1800 the Roman Catholic Church was still saying that St Jerome's Latin Vulgate was the authentic version from which religious truth was to be taken. The Germans were using some form of Luther's Bible. British Protestants were all using the King James version of 1611, though most of them used it in editions omitting the Apocrypha, which stout Protestants had come to think ought not to be printed within the same covers as the Old and New Testaments. Children were taught to read with it, families had a large copy as a family Bible, presents were made of it at confirmation or baptism; in England its stories and poetry were quite as much a part of British culture as Shakespeare, indeed even more, for its phrases were known to very simple and hardly educated people. In Germany and Britain scholars were aware that these sacred translations, often beloved of the people, did not always represent the original; for the text history had shown them that already. But by 1800 the Old Testament was beginning to be a moral problem to Christians; the portrait of Jehovah which it contained was sometimes seen to be primitive and not in accord with the ordinary ethical standard of that age. In England the novelist Thackeray started sitting loose to Christianity because he could not bear what he found in the Old Testament, and he was far from being the only one. In Germany in 1818 the

Church of the Palatinate tried to make a definition that the New Testament alone was 'the norm of faith', but was prevented from carrying this through by the conservative Lutherans of Bavaria. To such moral difficulties the historians' study of the Old Testament came as heartfelt relief, because they showed how the idea of God developed through the Hebrew centuries until its fruition in the New Testament.

Meanwhile greater knowledge of the history of the text produced, inevitably, a demand that the accepted translations of the Bible be amended. This affected religion as well as learning. For example, the Lutherans and Anglicans and Roman Catholics had always used the text of Job 19: 25 and following as evidence for the resurrection ('though after my skin worms destroy this body yet in my flesh shall I see God': King James version). Students were sure that, whatever the verse meant— which was uncertain as the Hebrew is not intelligible—it could not mean what the old versions said. Yet it was hallowed in popular devotion, especially at funerals. The received versions of the Old Testament were all based on the Jewish Massoretic text. The earliest translation of the Bible, namely the Greek Septuagint, proved that another Hebrew version existed. The quest for the authentic text was given extraordinary advances, first when a hoard of manuscripts was found in Cairo (1890, the Cairo Geniza), and then after 1947 when the Dead Sea Scrolls discovered at Qumran were found to contain versions of parts of the Old Testament, and when the scholar Kahle also used old Hebrew manuscripts from the library at Leningrad. Britain had since 1628 possessed a great Bible manuscript, the Codex Alexandrinus, so called because formerly it belonged to the Patriarch of Alexandria. During the nineteenth century the Vatican, under a certain amount of pressure from inside as well as outside, released to scholars the Codex Vaticanus which it had owned since at least 1475. Then the German Lutheran Konstantin Tischendorf discovered (1844 and 1859) the Codex Sinaiticus in the monastery of St Catherine on Mount Sinai; and, by a route not quite consistent with honour, the manuscript came to the Russian Tsar and was sold by the Communists to the British Museum in 1933. These three manuscripts were better than anything hitherto known; Vaticanus and Sinaiticus were both of the fourth century, Alexandrinus a little later. In the last third of the nineteenth century scholars seemed to be building assured modern translations upon the basis of these three texts; an epoch represented by the edition of the New Testament by the Cambridge scholars B. F. Westcott and F. J. A. Hort (1881), which rested on Vaticanus and Sinaiticus, and for three decades appeared to be the final settlement of most of the New Testament problems of text. But then they began to discover the evidence of the papyri fragments, most of the third or fourth century. Not many of these were important. But enough of them, put with other new manuscript evidence, shattered the assurance that the solution had been found. The most important were papyri collected in 1930–1 by the Englishman Chester Beatty and known after his name. There were twelve papyrus codices with substantial fragments of the gospels, Acts, the epistles of Paul, and the Apocalypse. These papyri were a century or a century and a half older than any previously known text of the New Testament. In 1947 the discovery of the Dead Sea Scrolls at Qumran added a little more information and rather more unsettlement.

When all was taken together, not a lot of difference was made to the religious use of the Bible. It was still possible for the pastor to read publicly in church, or for the private soul to read in personal devotion, Luther's Bible or the King James version. Because by its nature religious devotion is conservative of familiar words, that was done very often. The King James version continued into the last quarter of the twentieth century to be sold in more copies than any other translation.

All this forced a demand for new translations, reliable according to the texts as the best scholars now understood them, and in modern versions. In the German and English traditions the famous passages of the Bible were deeply embedded in the culture and language of the people. They rapidly ceased to be so; the old Bibles which were enshrined were thought by the young to be out of date, and the new versions were not, at least not as yet, part of anyone's literature or culture. There was the compensation that the new translations were doing better what the Reformation had wanted, making the text of the Bible understood by the ordinary person in the ordinary pew. But for a time the devotional and literary loss, and consequent loss in the influence of the text among those not specially biblical by nature, was grave.

A meeting of the German church (*Kirchentag*) in Stuttgart in 1857, decided to revise the Bible of Luther. It was not completed properly till 1912. Naturally it was at once out of date, and revision began again, to be finished in 1956; a further revision was completed in 1970–5. The Germans had a particular difficulty in that they could not totally accept 'modern German' because that must take them too far from Luther's Bible which the people would not do without. In England the Revised Version of 1881–5 was very conservative. During the period after the Second World War the people's English began to be influenced by American idiom; and therefore a translation into 'modern English' needed to depart much more widely from the English of the King James version, and of necessity used colloquialisms and paraphrases. The most important versions were the New English Bible (because it had a sort of official status and very scholarly translators) and popular versions like the Good News Bible. By this time translators perceived a new need: to speak in an English which would be understood not only by people of British descent but by immigrants for whom English was a second language. Naturally this need made more for the virtue of clarity than for memorable poetry. No doubt by devotional use some of these translations became loved by worshippers. But it is safe to say that none of them acquired the affection felt by many for the King James version during the first half of the nineteenth century. In the Europe of 1980 the Bible was a much less authoritative book than in the Europe of 1800. Even denominational schools taught far less of its contents.

For Roman Catholics the problem was at once easier and more complex. It was easier because their devotional tradition depended less on copies of the Bible and more on extracts from the Bible inserted into the service-books. It was more complex because the Council of Trent sanctified the Vulgate Latin translation of St Jerome, which ran into continual trouble from the new discoveries over the original texts. For a long time, therefore, Catholic scholars made no attempt to compete with the Protestants in creating accurate translations. Not until the hand of the Curia began to relax on biblical work, soon after the Second World War, did serious scholarly ventures begin. Much the most important was the Herder Bible, published in 1965, which was then worked over to become the Jerusalem Bible the following year. This was the first Catholic version ever to be used by a lot of Catholics and yet not depend on the Vulgate text, and the first Catholic version ever to be used in preference by some Protestants. The Catholic translators had an aim opposite to that of the Protestants. The Protestants wanted to spread out the single Bible translation into a lot of new translations. The Catholics, not having a type to which they could revert, struggled to bring the various efforts at translation into a single form. To this end the Catholic bishops in Germany, Austria, Luxemburg, and Switzerland sanctioned a scholarly version (1979–80).

Pilgrimage

If modern transport had effects in the government of churches, and their ecumenical relations, it also increased pilgrimage. The new age of mass travel was the new age of mass pilgrimage. Pilgrimage and tourism were often hard to distinguish. Far more people could visit the historic goals of pilgrimage, Rome and Jerusalem. For the first time large numbers of Protestants were able to go on pilgrimage to these two cities of Christian origins, or hire a travel firm to take them 'in the steps of St Paul'. The old goals of Catholic pilgrimage apart from Rome had declined in the eighteenth century. With the coming of the railways some of them began to recover. Le Puy, an ancient pilgrimage site, had 300,000 pilgrims in 1853. Einsiedeln in Switzerland, another old site, had 150,000 pilgrims a year during the first decade of the twentieth century. The Holy House at Loreto in North Italy had never quite lost its drawing-power. Compostela in north-east Spain maintained itself but never quite recovered the numbers of an earlier age despite better access.

Certain old shrines, defunct for decades or centuries, were consciously revived. Rocamadour was recreated as a shrine by an intelligent bishop of Cahors, though it never recaptured its old drawing-power. Walsingham in Norfolk, destroyed at the Reformation, began to revive as a goal of pilgrimage about 1897 and by 1934 attracted Anglicans as well as Roman Catholics. More interest was paid to certain places because of relics—Trier because of Christ's garment, the Holy Shroud at Turin (which was tested scientifically in 1988 and proved not to be genuine). One city became a modern place of pilgrimage which it never was before: Assisi, because knowledge of St Francis, spread from 1860, proved to be magnetic to both Catholics and Protestants.

As in past centuries new shrines came into existence, usually from some rural vision after which miracles happened. The icon of the Virgin on the island of Tenos in the Aegean was found early in the nineteenth century after the dream of a nun and soon became the chief centre of pilgrimage in the Greek world. At La Salette near Grenoble (1846), Lourdes (1858), Ilaca in Croatia (1865), Philippsdorf in Bohemia (1871), Knock in Ireland (1879), Fatima in Portugal (1917), modern shrines were created as a direct result of visions, in almost all cases by children, which then were followed by healings. Parish priests would be sceptical, agnostics would mock, bishops would enquire, and occasionally the people's cult was ruled illicit; but in all the cases mentioned the church after hesitation sanctioned the people's cult. Among them Lourdes grew to be the big new shrine of the modern age; so that Pope Leo XIII even built 'a grotto of Lourdes' in the Vatican gardens. In the centenary year 1958 Lourdes attracted six million pilgrims. Bernadette Soubirous, the child of 14 who saw the visions of the Virgin, was worthy of the strange vocation in which she afterwards found herself, and was canonized in 1933.

The Attacks upon the Church

The most astonishing feature of the twentieth century was the reversion to an age of persecution of Christianity. In 1800 Europe identified itself with Christendom. Christianity assumed that Europe would make a nominal profession of the faith; and that the cult of reason among the French revolutionaries was a passing aberration.

The free market in ideas which the age of toleration produced during the nineteenth century naturally threw up a lot of anti-Christian ideas, not so much on the plea that Christianity was untrue as on the axiom that its morals were bad for society. This criticism came in two chief forms: first, that religion preaches resignation to the will of God, and therefore makes the poor and the destitute passive under the oppression of the middle or upper classes when they ought to be encouraged to rise and throw off their yoke; and this was characteristic of the thought of the German Jew Karl Marx (d. 1882) in his quest for the radical reform of society. He saw Christianity as opium, a form of drug to keep the wretched in their place.

The second chief criticism was the opposite: that Christianity was bad for society because it protected the weak. The world needs strong peoples to give it proper leadership and government, and is so designed that some peoples are by nature stronger than others, and Christianity preaches that all are equally children of God and therefore leads society towards weakness and decadence and degeneration. This criticism of Christianity took various forms; the most famous because the most shocking was in the teaching of Nietzsche (d. 1900); son of a German Lutheran pastor, he had a brilliant academic career followed by mental disturbance. He wished to overturn the values of Christian society. He believed democracy to be fatal to society and attributed most of its faults to the Christian values beneath it. But much more influential, from the point of view of future persecution of the churches, were theorists of race. Houston Stewart Chamberlain (d. 1927) was an Englishman of naval and military families who married a German and was influenced by the Germanic race-religiosity of the composer Richard Wagner, and finally naturalized as a German during the First World War. His book *The Foundations of the Nineteenth Century* (original German 1899, English version 1911) held up the Germans (meaning all the Germanic peoples) as the destined leaders of humanity and its culture. He rejected churches but had a religious sense of destiny about the 'Germans' as the chosen people. He would not allow Christ to be a Jew.

But the first idea to take effect in a form of persecution was the notion that democracy is insecure if it does not suppress Catholicism. This doctrine was a paradox: democracy stood for liberty and tolerance and human rights, but the French revolution showed that this belief in liberty and tolerance ended when churches were (rightly or wrongly) believed to be enemies of the revolution. In Belgium and Spain and to some extent in Switzerland, in Germany, in a different way in Italy, and above all in France, the coming liberal democracy felt itself to be fighting for its rights against a reactionary church whose bishops were supported by obedient religious orders and by an even more reactionary Pope. In all these countries the nineteenth-century church was associated with a conservatism in politics and a repudiation of liberalism. The worst fights came over who was to control education, in which the Catholic religious orders had always taken a very prominent part. Once the question of church or anti-church was political, the church became useful to the democrats as a scapegoat. They could unify their radical parties, who had otherwise much to quarrel about, by being totally and unitedly opposed to any form of surviving church power in the state.

Amid the revolutionary ferments of the mid-century, the church was in grievous trouble.

In Spain in 1846 thirty-eight out of fifty-nine dioceses had no bishop; monasteries and even church buildings were often to be found lying empty and looted; the priests were in a state of impoverishment.

In Italy, two years later, Pope Pius IX fled in disguise from the city of Rome after a mob fired upon his palace and killed a monsignor standing near him at a window; the Jesuits quietly evacuated the city to avoid riots against them.

In Switzerland during 1847 it came to actual war between the Protestant cantons and the Catholic cantons, the so-called 'Sonderbund War', the last ostensibly religious war in Europe, which seemed like an anachronism, a harking back to the seventeenth century.

In Germany the major change of the nineteenth century was the passing of German leadership from the historical Catholic power Austria to Prussia, the chief of the Protestant states, which in 1871 united all Germany except Austria under its headship. This made another big change in the Christian feel of Europe. Before Napoleon Bonaparte the balance of power in Europe still lay, as always since the Reformation, just with the Catholics—the great powers, Austria, France, and Spain, set against Britain and the Protestants of North Germany. The fall of Napoleon left Spain no longer a great power, France rather weaker, Britain stronger, North German Protestantism much stronger, Russia, a non-Roman Catholic power, much stronger. The balance of power in Europe henceforth was decisively Protestant until after 1918, when states began to be unable to call themselves, with conviction, either Protestant or Catholic; except for Italy, where Mussolini and Pope Pius XI agreed (by the Lateran Treaty, 1929) it to be a Catholic country. (The Lateran Treaty was altered by agreement in 1984, ending the provision that Roman Catholicism is the state religion of Italy and the special place of Rome as a 'sacred city'.)

Therefore the new Protestant rulers of Germany saw the Catholics, who were mainly in Bavaria and the Rhineland or in occupied Poland, as a peril to the unity of the new Germany. From 1871 till 1880 Bismarck the German chancellor carried on an ever more menacing campaign to keep Catholics out of public life (the so-called *Kulturkampf* 'struggle over culture'), a misleading name because it sought to imply that Protestants had 'culture' and Catholics did not. The main onslaught was confined to Prussia. He expelled the Jesuits, and later other religious orders, brought education under state control, including the training of the clergy, and imprisoned or drove out bishops or clergy who resisted. Such a form of half-hearted persecution was impossible to prolong in a state which accepted the rights of democratic citizens; and between ten and fifteen years after it started most of the anti-Catholic measures were quietly revoked.

But the strangest of these illiberal acts of liberal governments appeared in France. After the overthrow of the dictator Louis Napoleon by the Germans in 1870, the French steadily developed the first example in Western Europe (except perhaps for Belgium) of a true and stable modern democratic state, committed to liberalism, toleration, and human rights. But the church was much associated with the fallen dictatorship in the minds of democrats. They felt that democracy was insecure and that the church was not reconciled to it. Pope Leo XIII in 1892 tried to make the French church publicly reconcile itself to the new republic, but could not make most of the Catholics desert their loyalty to the old monarchy or to the Bonapartist cause. Therefore the French parliaments successively passed measures aimed at weakening the church. Then, by a sad accident of history, the Dreyfus case (1894–1906), in which a Jewish officer was accused, mainly on forged evidence, of handing military secrets to Germany, divided Frenchmen in such a way that the Catholic Church, or a lot of its more articulate pamphleteers, seemed to be on the side of the army, which came to be more on trial than Dreyfus, and not a few of them were tarnished with anti-Semitic language. The ill-feeling aroused by the Dreyfus case against the French Catholic Church was bitter, and it fuelled the already existing anticlerical campaign. In 1903 an ex-ordinand who hated the church, Emile Combes, became prime minister. He closed or secularized some thousands of Catholic schools, expelled some 20,000 monks and nuns, allowed the French president to visit the king of Italy without also visiting the pope, recalled the French ambassador from the Vatican, and proposed a bill to disestablish the church. The government of Combes fell in 1905 when his anticlericalism proved too radical even for the Socialists who believed in liberty. But his successor carried through the bill in an improved form. It nationalized all church property and allowed the clergy to use most of the buildings under state control. Because France was a democracy such a form of republican anticlericalism could not last long, since it contradicted the principles of liberty and human rights, and twenty years later it was only a memory. But it was the most marked moment of the mood found in Spain and Portugal and Switzerland and Prussia, where liberal governments were so insecure that they contradicted their own principles by refusing to tolerate fully a church which stated its opposition to liberalism.

It is not easy to tell how far this sort of attack strengthened the church. In Germany the attack of the *Kulturkampf* greatly strengthened Catholic self-consciousness and militancy. In France the anticlerical campaign had much the same effect. Yet in France, and also in Spain, a battle being fought over some people's deepest and most religious feelings divided the soul of the nation and left problems of identity with religion which lasted much longer than the legal effects of the anticlerical legislation.

The Christian Social Movement

Between about 1860 and 1930 (or later) was the age of struggle between classes. The great Socialist parties of Europe were founded then; in most cases, except in Britain, with an anti-Christian or at least an anti-church bias. The churches at first disliked them; partly because they denounced churches as agents of capitalist oppression, partly because they preached class war which Christians could not accept as moral, and sometimes because some of them preached the need for revolution which most Christians regarded as unjustified violence. The Prussian church government of 1878 sanctioned the law that made the Socialist party illegal.

Therefore in several churches were founded groups of Christian Socialists who wanted to show Christians that Socialists had justice on their side and wanted to show Socialists that Christianity was not part of the system of oppression of the working class as they supposed. The earliest of these reconcilers were French or German during the 1840s. But the name 'Christian Socialist' was put on the map by the English theologian Frederick Denison Maurice and the novelist Charles Kingsley (during five years, 1848–53). The question was whether the church's only duty is to convert individuals and leave politics to the politicians, or whether if society is unjust it is the duty of churchmen to change society. One of Maurice's disciples Charles Gore made a mild form of Christian Socialism weighty within English Christianity and captured William Temple (who was to be archbishop of Canterbury 1942–4) and was afterwards to be influential in emergent Africa.

In Germany Adolf Stöcker started a Christian-Socialist party but it was stained by anti-semitism and soon faded away. In Switzerland two Christian thinkers, Kutter and Ragaz, founded (1903–6) an international League of Religious Socialists, which put forward Socialism as a new revelation to the church like the Reformation. They were under the influence of a German pastor who was the first really important Christian Socialist in Protestant Germany, Christoph Blumhardt (Social-Democrat MP in Württemberg 1900–6).

In the Roman Catholic Church the German Bishop Ketteler of Mainz (1867 and after) tried to move his church towards sympathy with Socialism or rather its better ideals. Pope Pius IX condemned Socialism in the Syllabus of Errors (1864) and

372 Great Britain and Europe

his successor Leo XIII repeated the condemnation. Nevertheless in 1891 Leo XIII issued the encyclical *Rerum Novarum* which allowed a great deal of latitude to Catholic minds who wanted to baptize Socialist ideals. It was important in that steady lessening of tension between the churches and the Socialist European parties (apart from the Socialist left in its Communist forms) which marked the first thirty years of the twentieth century.

Christianity and National Socialism

But now came a more ominous form of attack upon the churches, and not only the Catholic Church. The rising nationalists of central Europe found Christian principles hard to reconcile with their needs. They despised the desire for peace they identified in them, the internationalism, the rejection of racialism, the preference for non-resistance and allowance of force only as a last resort or as police-action, the conviction that every human being of whatever race or culture is equally a child of God. The Marxists did not like Christianity because it was against revolution (except as a last resort), and because churches therefore seemed to Marxists to be one pillar of middle-class society. The racialists did not like Christianity because it was against international war (except as a last resort) and because Christian influence was therefore thrown against the rise of the nations which were said to be on the side of the best human destiny. When Adolf Hitler wrote his *Mein Kampf* (1923 in prison, published in 1925 and 1927) he found in Houston Stewart Chamberlain ideas which well expressed a justification for the nationalist and anti-Semitic doctrines about which he was already fanatical. Jesus was no Semite and the churches had corrupted his influence and Judaized his message. Hitler himself had been baptized an Austrian Roman Catholic. From his late teens he hated Roman Catholic priests and despised Protestant pastors.

In 1914 no one could suppose that such doctrines were

anything but the eccentric notions of a few cranks. The idea that they would overturn Christendom was unthinkable. But the First World War shattered this confidence. No one had thought it possible that so-called Christian nations would kill and go on killing until millions were dead and the European leadership of the world was wounded irretrievably. And as a direct consequence of that war these two different anti-Christian doctrines—religion as the opium of the people, and religion as the false bulwark against nationalist ideals—took hold of the two most powerful military nations in the world.

From 1917 a Marxist government seized power in Russia and over the next three decades tried to strangle Russian Christianity. From 1933 a violently nationalist government ruled Germany. For two or three years the Nazi party tried to harness the German churches, both Catholic and Protestant, to the service of nationalism, to the sense of vocation in a nation, to self-sacrifice for a national cause, to the belief in a chosen people, to the putting of the Jews out of national life. In this endeavour it had some success. These appeals to self-sacrifice and destiny fitted some aspects of Christianity, and the compromises of weak leaders did the rest. Even as late as 1939 some churchmen, and a few Nazis, hoped for the marriage between nationalism and Christianity. But by 1937 Hitler himself had lost all faith that the churches could be of any use to German destiny. Among Protestants the so-called Confessing Church was founded in 1934 to resist Nazification of the churches. Its real leader was the Lutheran pastor Martin Niemöller, whom Hitler put into a concentration camp in 1937 and never released. A lot of its thought rested upon the strong biblical ideas of the Swiss professor of divinity Karl Barth. Its most inspiring meeting, the synod of Barmen of May 1934, had long consequences in the history of Christianity in central Europe.

Among Catholics the resistance was headed by a few stalwart bishops and priests, appealing to Catholic tradition and trying to get the help of Pope Pius XI from outside. After an air of compromise when the pope (July 1933) made a concordat with

Hitler which was very favourable to Catholicism and which Hitler had no intention of observing, the help of the Pope was at last given in March 1937, when the encyclical *Mit brennender Sorge* ('with a burning anxiety') was smuggled into Germany and read from most Catholic pulpits. It told all Europe of the evil pressures of the Nazis on schools, justice, publications, monasteries, and nunneries.

The church resistance to Nazification was divided and often weak. But by 1937 it was enough to convince Hitler that Christianity was worse than useless, an obstruction to the national mission to rule the world. He determined to destroy the churches after he had beaten Russia in war and made himself the ruler of Europe. Meanwhile a running persecution (petty for most Christians but cruel or demonic for individuals) was carried out by local Nazi bosses against the churches, varying very much according to the personality of the boss. In 1938 Hitler occupied Austria and the pressure started on the strong Catholic Church of Austria.

There were quite a lot of actual martyrdoms. Only one Catholic bishop of Germany was expelled, by organized Nazi mobs, from his see. A significant number of priests or Protestant pastors or church officers were murdered in concentration camps. (And this does not include the numerous Polish clergy murdered after the German–Polish war of 1939.) The Catholic dean of the cathedral at Berlin, Lichtenberg, who protested from his pulpit against the persecution of the Jews, died on the way to a concentration camp and no doubt would never have come out alive. Such incidents were in hindsight too rare for Christian comfort. In the Russian persecution under Stalin it was difficult for Christian congregations even to meet. There was nothing like that in Nazi Germany. The churches were able to continue their ways of worship even though a policeman would be sitting under the pulpit taking notes on the sermon. But the better parts of the churches succeeded in remaining a focus of Christian philosophy and ethic and therefore a body of passive resistance to the immoralities of the regime. In one area they had a striking success ethically. In 1940–1 Hitler sanctioned a programme for euthanasia of incurables. Its only legal basis was the chancellor's decree and it was to be kept secret. Nazi managers widened its application, and death certificates that were obviously fabricated began to appear; the secrecy could not be kept; the people were disturbed. Strong protests by churchmen, especially Count Galen, the Catholic bishop of Münster, and the Protestant pastor von Bodelschwingh, persuaded Hitler that he was unwise and the programme was stopped. There was no comparable protest about the Jewish pogrom though a good deal of effort went into saving individual Jews.

Catholic Action

During the last quarter of the nineteenth century the Catholic parishes, like the Protestant, built all kinds of parish organizations—youth clubs especially, but mothers' unions, savings banks, nursing associations, meetings for prayer, and later cinematograph centres. In the first decade of the twentieth century these various organizations began to be called, first in Italy, Catholic Action. The phrase came to mean, first that all such organizations were a united instrument subject to the leadership of the pope and the bishops; and secondly, that they were instruments of lay evangelism—that is, the church was asking lay men and women to do work for society which earlier days expected the priests to do. Pope Pius XI defined Catholic Action (1922) as 'the participation of the laity in the apostolate of the church's hierarchy'.

This movement took various forms in different countries. Its commonest constituent was the youth movement; and in Belgium the priest Joseph Cardijn built up the Jocists (Jeunesse Ouvrière Chrétienne), a very successful youth movement which was copied in other countries. But the biggest problem was its relation to politics. Most concordats between church and state during the decades between the two World Wars made some provision for it. Dictators did not like church youth movements. Mussolini was determined to make Italian youth Fascist and his interference with Catholic Action caused the pope to denounce him in an encyclical of 1931, but he more or less got his way. In Germany, where Catholic Action under that name was never strong, Hitler suppressed all youth movements apart from the Hitler Youth. After the Second World War Catholic Action was prominent in the effort to keep the Communists out of power in Italy and suffered for a time from this political reputation. During the 1950s and 1960s there came to be tension between the young people running the clubs, who were forward-looking, and some members of the hierarchy who believed that Catholic Action was founded for obedience.

An institution which was part of this same movement to enlist the lay people in the apostolate under the hierarchy was Opus Dei. This was founded by a Spanish priest in Madrid in 1928. The events of the Spanish Civil War and its aftermath gave it a slant to the political right in church and state and its leaders were usually found on that wing. Rome approved of it in 1950, and it ran the Catholic University of Pamplona and some other educational institutions.

The Right of Resistance

The persecution under Hitler had an unexpected consequence. Everyone agreed that Christian resistance to an immoral government must be passive, in the sense of trying to refuse to do immoral acts even if government commanded them. But could Christians, committed by the New Testament to a strong doctrine of the state and the moral duty of obedience, engage in active resistance? If the only way of stopping vile injustice was to conspire against the tyrant, could a Christian be a conspirator? This debate had hardly happened in Christendom since the debates on tyrannicide towards the end of the sixteenth century. Many, perhaps most, continued to hold that they could not. But some high authorities took the contrary view. In Germany one of Pastor Niemöller's disciples, Dietrich Bonhoeffer, who happened to be closely related to some of the leading lay conspirators against Hitler, became convinced that he had to take part and was executed for his (marginal) part in the conspiracy. A Jesuit Father Delp suffered the same fate. The opinion was given its highest authority early in 1940, when Pope Pius XII secretly allowed himself to be used as a channel of communication between the German conspirators against Hitler and the British government; his justification being that this might save very many lives.

But the opinion remained controversial. It was to become extremely important in Christian debates because young liberation movements in Southern Africa or Latin America appealed to these European precedents to justify a Christian resort to force against a military dictatorship. In this area there were difficult debates between the African or Asian or Latin American church leaders and some of their European colleagues.

The German and Russian persecutions were not the only persecutions in Europe of that age. The worst was in Spain from 1936, when Communists or Anarchists, trying to resist General Franco, murdered large numbers of innocent monks and nuns and priests. In a civil war, it is never possible to identify who starts the murder; still, it was significant that the troops of the extreme left when out of proper control should select these good people for some of their principal victims. To murder a nun, who had done no one any harm and perhaps had done some people much good, requires a certain obsession, comparable with the Nazi obsession over Jews; and just as the Nazi attitude could partly (but only partly) be explained in the context of the long history of European anti-Semitism, so the Spanish Anarchist murder of nuns could only be explained within the tortuous history of European anticlericalism and of the more bizarre dregs thrown up by Marxism. In some forms of modern persecution Christians were more liable to ill-treatment because they did some good and professed to do some good.

The Links between Church and State

These new attitudes of hostility to Christianity were not necessarily anything to do with the process of separating churches from their states which went on steadily in Europe throughout the period. Democracy meant the equality of everyone before the law; therefore everyone must have an equal right to practise his or her religion or irreligion. Meanwhile the ructions of various societies, and the new political formations of Europe, caused emigrations and mixed communities and created modern societies which were no longer of one religion or one denomination. A country might still be largely of one denomination—as with Catholics in Spain, Portugal, Italy, parts of South Germany, Belgium, Poland; or with a leadership of honour to one denomination, as with the Presbyterians in Scotland, the Anglicans in England, the Lutherans in Sweden, Norway, and Denmark, the Reformed in Holland and northern Switzerland, the Lutherans in North-West Germany—all countries where other denominations might be numerous but where history and folk-tradition still kept the established church in a primacy of honour. But even where a denomination had a large majority or had historic support, the age saw a steady whittling away of its special rights.

The French act of disestablishment of 1905–6 was rare in being entangled with bitter hostility to the church. A more common form of disestablishment occurred when a monarchy was overthrown. When Kaiser Wilhelm II was removed in the German revolution of 1918 all the German churches lost their established status, but only nominally. The successor governments in Germany continued to retain an influence over the choice of church leaders. The revolution preserved what used to be regarded as the chief feature of an established church, the right to tax the citizens for its maintenance. The German church tax exists in West Germany to this day. Hitler never abolished it (though in private he grumbled and planned to do so at the end of the war) and it was only abolished in East Germany by the Communist regime after 1945. In England tax for the church was abolished in 1868; in Ireland in 1833. In Switzerland the cantons raised taxes for the churches; a proposal to separate church and state was voted down in a referendum of 1980. In the surviving monarchies the constitution preserved various forms within the old establishment; such as the necessity for the sovereign to be of the old established religion, as in Spain or Britain or Sweden or Belgium; or the presence of representatives of the old established church in an upper house of parliament, as in Britain to this day or Austria-Hungary till the revolution of 1918. Not only in the monarchies but elsewhere, constitutions quite often preserved, though never without controversy, the duty of state schools to teach the Christian religion to those who did not refuse on conscientious grounds to attend such classes.

In this process of prising a historic church apart from its state government, there was no necessary hostility to religion, though it might be present, as with France or Spain or Italy. Many of its proponents were devout members of an established church who simply wished for equality and justice, and the removal of the sense of grievance in a state, or to free the church from those state interventions—veto on church legislation or publication, nomination of chief pastors, or veto on the names of those proposed—which they believed to be anachronistic, and for their church to feel free in its pastoral endeavours.

But all over Europe traces of the old system of Crown nomination for bishops continued to be found. States regarded the leaders of the church as important in the moulding of public opinion. In all the Communist states of Eastern Europe after 1945 it became impossible to choose a bishop who was not acceptable to the government of the state. In France and Spain there continued to be negotiation between the governments and the pope. In England the sovereign, which in this case meant mostly the prime minister, nominated the bishops of the Church of England (from about 1922 always choosing from a list approved by the archbishops, until 1977 when the

Crown agreed a system under which the list was reduced to two names proposed by a committee of the General Synod of the church). From country to country it varied; whether this weakening of state authority in the churches was due to the weakening of state authority in democracies and it was simply one among a number of features of that process, or whether the state felt embarrassed, when its leaders were of every sort of Christian denomination or none, in choosing high clergymen; or whether the state thought that churches, being weaker as political pressure-groups nowadays, were less important to the state and could be allowed more say over the choice of their own leaders. Where the government was not a democracy, this last point of view was never taken. In autocratic or politburo states, government always controlled or influenced the choices. But then they also controlled a lot of other choices, like the choice of leaders of trade unions.

The Ecumenical Movement

The only successful union between churches before the coming of modern transport was the Prussian union, between Lutheran and Reformed, in 1817; an example followed in a few other German states. These were state-directed unions, which most churchmen in Prussia, but by no means all, accepted.

When modern transport threw the world together, and modern politics or ease of transfer made for vast movements of populations, the divisions of Christians came to feel more troublesome. The church of Rome was not at first interested. It wanted other churches to accept the authority of the pope and therefore did not feel it right to take part in negotiations which implied that it was one of several churches. The Eastern church was not at first interested because its ideal was the acceptance by other churches of the Eastern teaching on doctrine and way of worship. But this was already affected during the nineteenth century by the perception of some Roman Catholics and some Eastern Orthodox that some Protestants were gaining a deeper apprehension of catholicity and sympathy for its ways. Dr Pusey (the professor of Hebrew at Oxford University) and the high Anglican churchmen in England, disciples of the Oxford Movement, a movement of high churchmanship which Newman, Keble, and Pusey founded in 1833 (and which was also known as the Tractarian Movement because its first public papers were tracts), talked much of Catholic unity and met much sympathy from some liberal-minded Roman Catholics. In 1871 German and then Swiss professors who could not bring themselves to accept the decision of the Vatican Council of 1870 that the Pope is infallible when he speaks *ex cathedra* on faith and morals even without the formal agreement of the church, formed the Old Catholic Church; that is, Catholic without this 'new' doctrine of the Vatican Council, and consequently in disobedience to the pope. Naturally the Eastern church, and the high Anglicans, looked for a time with much optimism on this rebellion. They hoped that it might pave the way for a wider Catholicism which could go back behind the Council of Trent and that the churches might agree on adherence to the faith of the early centuries of Christendom. To this end the first examples of the modern 'ecumenical conference' were held in Bonn in 1874 and 1875 under the presidency of Döllinger, professor of church history at Munich and the leader of the refusal to accept the Vatican decrees. These were small affairs—some fifty or so members, many of them interested laymen. Their results in practice were very small; but they started a process of mutual understanding; and as one of their results the Anglicans followed an American example and laid down the Lambeth Quadrilateral (1888), that is, the basic conditions under which Anglicans could consider reunion: the Old and New Testaments as containing all things necessary to salvation; the apostles' creed and Nicene creed; the two sacraments of baptism and the Lord's Supper; and the historic episcopate, locally adapted to the needs of the different nations. When a church could lay down such a document it was clear that a search for an international Christian unity had begun.

Meanwhile two quite different strands were to create the modern ecumenical movement. From 1846 various Protestant bodies united in the Evangelical Alliance which had the conscious intention of joining Protestants in resistance to Catholicism. It never had much influence. But it was the first sign of a movement which did not so much aim at the unity of the Christian church as the unity of the Protestant churches.

Secondly, the needs of the mission field, especially in Africa and India, led to much greater co-operation between the various churches. This was important; it became the chief way in which the African and Indian and later Latin American churches started to influence European Christendom. These non-European churches did not see why their Christian relationships should be complicated by traditional European postures which had little to do with them. Therefore the missionary expansion of the church became the chief channel for injecting into Europe the ecumenical ideal and creating an organization to foster that ideal. A World Missionary Conference at Edinburgh in 1910 led to the creation of a Faith and Order movement at Lausanne in 1927 and finally to the creation of the World Council of Churches at Amsterdam in 1948. They encouraged a lot of talk and negotiation between the leaders of the various Christian denominations. At the meeting in Delhi (1961) they were joined for the first time officially by the Russian Orthodox, and by official 'observers' from the Roman Catholic Church.

Therefore, without exception, all the main successes of the movement happened outside Europe. And as the headquarters of the movement in Geneva gained more authority as a voice of Christian influence through the world, it led to tension between some European churches and the organization, which from about 1960 was largely led by the interests of the non-European churches who were in a post-colonial situation. In European Christendom the ecumenical movement, as an organization though not as a mood, was far more influential in the 1950s than it grew to be in the 1980s. This was not mainly due to the tension between European churches and non-European, but to the perception of many that the high hopes and optimism of the earlier days of the movement had not led to quick results. There was also a difference of emphasis. In 1950 the prime task of the movement was seen to be theological and its secretary was an eminent Dutch theologian Visser t'Hooft. By 1980 the stress of the movement itself lay in ethics, liberation, and what the older churches could do for the newer; and its West Indian secretary, Philip Potter, was rather a man of ethical and political leadership than a man concerned directly with the task in theology.

Nevertheless the ecumenical mood had consequences in the European churches. They were far readier to share their altars with each other, and even their church buildings, and to co-operate in common social ventures.

This difference was most marked in the Roman Catholic Church. Since the Counter-Reformation Rome taught that it alone was the church; non-Roman Christians could only be part of it if their baptism was Catholic, and the denominations to which they belonged were not churches. In the nineteenth century, when Catholicism was centralizing itself ever more in Rome, Pope Pius IX admitted that men might be saved outside the church by reason of 'invincible ignorance' of the true faith. This was a large concession of charity in the tradition of thought. But it made no difference to the strict feeling that the church could not co-operate in any way with any other church lest it mislead them into thinking that they also were recognized as such. To this there was a partial exception in the Eastern Orthodox churches who received a reluctant recognition as a deficient part of the Catholic Church. It made no difference to the attitude to the Anglicans, whose ministerial orders Pope Leo XIII condemned as null and void in a bull of 1896 (*Apostolicae Curae*), nor to any of the Protestant denominations. When the ecumenical movement grew strong, Pope Pius XI formally refused to take part (1928), lest participation imply a recognition that the Roman Catholic Church was but one of a number of denominations. The same encyclical forbad Roman Catholics to take part in conferences with non-Roman Catholics.

All this began to change after the Second World War. But it was the accession of Pope John XXIII in 1958 which began to transform the atmosphere. Part of his object in summoning the Second Vatican Council was to heal the separations in East and West, and he continued to recognize the Protestants of the West as brothers. An encyclical of 1959 greeted non-Catholics as 'separated brethren and sons'. In 1960 the pope set up a Secretariat for Christian Unity. In the same year he received Archbishop Fisher of Canterbury. In 1961 he allowed Roman Catholic observers to attend the meeting of the World Council at Delhi. His successor Paul VI carried this new and far more charitable attitude much further. In 1965 he and the Patriarch of Constantinople Athenagoras agreed a joint declaration deploring the mutual excommunications of 1054 which had stained their past histories as churches. In 1967 he met the Patriarch again, the year after he had met Archbishop Ramsey of Canterbury. The doctrine that Roman Catholics cannot share in worship with other Christians was finally killed by the Polish Pope John Paul II when in 1982 he went to Canterbury Cathedral with the Anglican Archbishop Runcie of Canterbury. They were not however able to receive the sacrament together.

All this was part of the coming out of the papacy towards the world. The effect of the nineteenth-century onslaughts upon the church was to drive the papal office in upon itself; to elevate the walls of the Vatican higher and higher; to make it a sanctuary instead of a capital; to force the papacy to stand strong against all the world, an attitude symbolized by the name 'the prisoner of the Vatican', which applied to the pope from 1870 because the Italians had deprived him of his historical papal states, until Mussolini settled the problem in 1929 (the Lateran Treaty) by creating the state of Vatican City, only a little more than 100 acres but an independent sovereignty.

From 1929 the pope possessed again a measure of real

political independence and slowly began to act more confidently towards the world. This was delayed because the incense of the sanctuary hung about the popes who had grown up in the atmosphere of Rome after 1870. This was specially true of Pope Pius XII, pope from 1939 to 1958; a truly hieratic pope, a man of much prayer, rather remote personally. His reign was the climax of the process by which the old ruler of a central Italian state, weighty in European politics, was converted by the loss of his state into a purely spiritual leader. The final symbol of this change came in 1978, when Pope John Paul I refused to be crowned as a sovereign.

But from 1958, with the coming of John XXIII, the papacy moved out towards the world. The stiffness was softened, the ritual simplified, the minds more open, the hearts more charitable. Simultaneously popes began to move out of their palace as hardly since the Middle Ages. This was made possible by the arrival of modern international airlines. Paul VI was the first pope to make a pilgrimage to Jerusalem and the Holy Land. He went to Bombay for a eucharistic congress, and to New York to talk to the United Nations. He said his prayers at the Portuguese shrine to the Blessed Virgin at Fatima. He visited the church in Uganda, and in the Far East. It was a wholly new type of papacy, which used the speed of modern transport to go out to meet the world. When John Paul II became pope in 1978 the pope's main work and mission lay in travelling; to turn the person and office of the pope into an instrument of world evangelism.

Naturally this coming out from behind high walls carried physical risks. Paul VI just escaped an attempt to murder him when he visited Manila. In 1981 John Paul II was shot in the stomach while riding in a jeep in St Peter's Square and was badly wounded. In Portugal the year after there was another attempt to assassinate him. A story was put about that John Paul I was murdered (1978) to stop his reforming programme. The story had no foundation in fact but was another sign of the risks of the new papacy.

Changes to Christian Burial

The development of urban society entailed drastic alterations in certain of the customs and moral judgements of the European churches.

First, the Christian custom of burial was dramatically altered. The pressure upon urban cemeteries grew until cremation seemed the obvious way to meet a great practical difficulty. Cremation needed machinery, and such machinery was not available till about 1873. The practice began about 1875, amid much suspicion and criticism. From its earliest days historic Christianity practised burial of the body, with its face towards the east in expectation of the general resurrection. From this traditional viewpoint the modern canon law of the Roman Catholic Church (codified in 1917) condemned cremation and demanded burial, except in cases of necessity as in time of plague; and anyone who asked for cremation, or ordered it in the will, was not permitted church burial. But in 1963 the Congregation of the Holy Office allowed cremation and later a form of service was provided and in 1983 a new canon allowed it, while still preferring burial. The Protestants started with the same repugnance to a change of custom; but their churches never ruled against the practice formally, and little by little the health and practical reasons which moved the population generally, moved also the churches to accept cremation as a Christian way of burial. The Church of England formally recognized this in its prayer book of 1928.

From the anthropological point of view this was an enormous change of habit. It is impossible at present to find that it made the slightest difference to Christian attitudes to reverence for the human body or to the doctrine of the resurrection. It has been suggested that the consequent decline of the churchyard had subconscious religious consequences in the minds of the people. But churchyards declined far more because of the people's mobility, which took them away from their ancestors alive or dead, than because the remains of a body were now in a different form. In its early days cremation was strongly promoted by free-thinkers who had the naïve feeling that this would destroy the doctrine of the resurrection. It appeared to have no such consequences. In some cases reverence for the human body was more evident in burning than in burial.

Divorce

In industrial society the family was just as important to the growth of the children and the health of the adults but it was no longer an economic unit as in the old rural economy. The urban world valued freedom of choice and hesitated to choose marriages for its daughters. From the eighteenth century the laws of marriage in the European states slowly freed themselves from accepting biblical or theological grounds as the basis of their regulation, and relied only upon the 'law of nature' or pastoral expediency. This meant a growing recognition that there might be other grounds for divorce apart from adultery. This was easy for the descendants of the German Reformation to accept because from the earliest years some of the Reformers had acknowledged the possibility of the breakdown of a marriage. Similarly the Easterners had long admitted divorce for various grounds in their tradition. It was not at all easy for Western Catholics to accept, nor for the Anglicans. The popes had steadily condemned all possibility of divorce unless the marriage was unconsummated. A marriage could be nullified but a full marriage could not be ended.

As the European states of the nineteenth century widened the grounds of divorce (Britain from 1857), the divorce rate naturally grew. At first it did not grow fast because of the lack of opportunities for independence for women, especially if they had children. But with the coming of the twentieth century, and the steady rise in feminine employment, this difficulty in the way of divorce diminished until almost the only force keeping an unhappy couple together was the needs of the children. Therefore the rate of divorce suddenly began to grow in a way which alarmed all the churches, which stood for the sanctity of the family and its life and were well aware what damage easy divorce could do.

But the problem of the churches was not so much the fight against an inevitable social movement, partly conditioned by economics. They were happy to change from the idea of a patriarchal family to the idea of a partnership of free persons. They kept saying that they believed in the sanctity of marriage and the home. Pope Pius XI issued the encyclical of 1930, *Casti Connubii*, which retained the idea of the man as the head of the family: 'the primacy of the husband, the ready subjection of the wife', but the encyclical then faced the modern world by saying that she keeps her liberty as a human being and is not to obey her husband when he asks what is not according to right reason or compatible with her dignity as a wife. The churches continued to demand that the bride and bridegroom should promise solemnly to remain with each other till death; though the Church of England (from 1928) allowed brides, if they wished, to refrain from promising to obey their husbands. The problem of the churches was the discipline of those who despite everything were divorced, and then remarried. Were they to go on treating the remarriage as a form of adultery? Were they to readmit to the sacraments and to church privileges those who were divorced and remarried? Were they to allow a couple to remarry in church, and if they did must they exact a promise for the second time to remain with each other till death? As the number of divorces mounted, it became clear that the churches did more for the home and the family if they were not rigid about most of these questions. They did not want to seem thus to weaken their mission to proclaim the lasting nature of marriage and the stability of the home. But they faced facts. Honour and affection proved to be too complex to be treated by automatic rules.

This pastoral difficulty produced tension in the churches. In 1969 both the West German Protestant churches and the Church of England recognized the total breakdown of marriage as a ground for divorce. Both churches were, for several decades, pastoral and flexible about the admission to communion of the remarried. By the late 1970s they began to be flexible, at least in certain circumstances, about the possibility that the divorced might be permitted to remarry in church. This was not true of the church of Rome; within which, however, much debate upon these questions continued.

Contraception

Since the eighteenth century, if not before, Christians had practised various primitive forms of birth control other than abstention from intercourse. By the later nineteenth century these were becoming more reliable and more freely available. By the middle twentieth century they were both reliable (almost totally) and available. Since the chief barrier to indiscriminate sexual intercourse had always been the coming of an unwanted child, with social consequences for both parents, the churches were therefore faced with a new moral problem which could weaken the sanctity of the home and of the faithful marriage.

The first question was whether the churches would accept contraception at all. The first purpose of marriage, in traditional Christian doctrine, was that children might be brought up in the fear of the Lord; and an exercise of sexual intercourse which prevented the coming of the child seemed to be corrupting to the purposes of marriage. This attitude was quickly altered among the Protestant churches. The ground for this ease of change lay in a different emphasis upon the nature and purposes of marriage, which had always been seen, not only as a way of producing babies, but as a mutual form of affection; and it took very little time for Protestant moralists to accept that family planning could allow this purpose of marriage to be fruitful and could also help many families in a variety of social conditions. They also became aware that the problems of Africa and India would be far more easily coped with if methods of family planning were available. In Britain, for example, a proposal to condemn contraception at the Anglican Lambeth Conference of 1930 was rejected. The Lambeth Conference of 1958 accepted that the practice of family planning, with artificial methods, in certain circumstances is right and Christian. In 1967 a commission of Roman Catholic theologians recommended by a majority to the pope that he should take the same view. But Paul VI rejected the recommendation and issued the encyclical *Humanae Vitae* which maintained the old view that the only method of birth control is by abstention at fertile times. This encyclical the 1968 Lambeth Conference took the unusual step of rejecting formally on behalf of the Anglicans. It became clear during the 1970s that many Roman Catholics in Europe took no notice of *Humanae Vitae*. But its view remained the formal discipline of the Roman Catholic Church. Some Catholics argued that its language taught that what it said was difficult and therefore that couples who felt unable to obey were not to be denied the sacraments of the church. The people exercised their right to follow their consciences.

Abortion

Humanae Vitae also condemned abortion, even for urgent reasons of health. The church had from its earliest days condemned abortion, but the rights of doctors to save life were long recognized. Until 1967 English law allowed it only to save a mother's life but in that year an Act allowed it for a wider variety of reasons concerning the good of the mother or the coming child or even of the other children in the family. Medical science had made abortion easily available and safe, and mothers were getting rid of unwanted children: the churches had to take an attitude. They divided. Those who accepted *Humanae Vitae* or were near to it regarded all abortion, except in extreme circumstances of danger to the mother, as a form of murder, and the churches stood for the sacredness of human life. Those who thought the civil law rational accepted it as the best for all parties and were not prepared to condemn abortion in the earlier stages of pregnancy—provided (it was a big proviso) the sacredness of human life was maintained. This division was not along Catholic–Protestant lines, though most Catholics were on the side of the conservative view and most Protestants probably accepted the regulation by the state.

The ability, due to modern medicine, to have sexual inter-course without children inevitably produced in Europe far freer attitudes to sexual intercourse. The churches had always taught that the sex act must be kept within marriage and that all other forms of intercourse were wrong. All churches continued to teach that doctrine. But they were confronted by quite a lot of their younger people who could not see the point of it. Since the young thought that they were not going to produce children they could not see why they should not live together and have intercourse. The practice of living together as man and wife before marriage, and then marrying when a child began to come, became far more widespread than ever before in Europe. The churches did not like it. They saw that it weakened the home and family. While they continued to condemn it, pastor-ally they were gentle to it when it happened. But this was a fact contributing during the later twentieth century to one form of alienation between the younger generation of Europeans and the churches.

The Ministry of Women

Industrial society changed the place of women in the economy. They had been workers on a smallholding or farm within a family context. Now they were individual workers in mills, if they had work. But a lot of them did not. They were thrust back into the home. The female had to occupy herself with house and children while the male was away at the office or factory. Of course many women were much sought after in industries like textiles; and during the nineteenth and early twentieth century many women were in domestic service. Christian thinkers were for the first time arguing on theological grounds the equality of the two sexes in the design of creation and that the work of God was to be found in the partnership between their differences. Protestantism, having abolished nuns, had less place for the ministerial vocation of women. But in the revival movements of Germany and England in the early nineteenth century several women were leaders.

Urban society produced the need for nuns which the Protestants did not possess. Therefore from the 1840s, in both England and Germany, groups of women came together—at first amid a small amount of popular opposition—to serve the needs which nuns served, in nursing, education, or the care of the old. In England from 1842 they were called nuns and were inspired by the Oxford Movement and were sometimes directed by its leader Dr Pusey. In Germany they were called deaconesses, an order founded first by Theodor Fliedner in Kaiserswerth in 1836. Soon there were also deaconesses in England. In the Roman Catholic Church there was at the same time or soon after a great flowering of little orders of nuns, specially dedicated to such social needs. Meanwhile the nursing profession became a far more disciplined and caring body of women, with Florence Nightingale as the model and guide after her experiences ministering to the wounded of the Crimean war. Although a Protestant she was much influenced by her knowledge of the Catholic sisters of St Vincent de Paul. The Protestant groups did not invariably give the leadership to women in the way that nuns were subject to a mother superior. Fliedner, for example, insisted that his societies of deaconesses must be organized by men. But simultaneously other groups of nursing sisters in Protestantism were fully led by women; perhaps the earliest was formed by Amalie Sieveking at Hamburg in 1832. She refused an invitation to join with Fliedner because she feared that male control would diminish her work.

Meanwhile all over Europe, though faster in the Protestant countries than in Catholic, education for women was developing. By 1900 it was clear that in European society women had less paid employment than men if they were uneducated, and still less if they were educated, as then they were hardly supposed to want work. In some places, for example in Germany as early as 1848, trade unions conducted a bitter struggle against female workers. The women's movement began.

The woman active in her profession or trade did not quite correspond to the portrait of a woman in most of the Christian books. The churches stood as ever for the home and family, to which the woman was of necessity the high priestess. If all women decided to have full-time careers (supposing that were ever possible) the churches shuddered for the consequences to children and homes. They were slow to recognize that some women were never going to have families; that other women were going to have one child or two and needed something to do when the children grew up. They were still slower to recognize the new conditions provided by the flood of contraceptive practice and the invention of so many labour-saving devices within the home. And they were equally slow to recognize that in a now educated female sex they had a huge pastoral resource which was not then used adequately.

In the churches the aggressiveness of some leaders of the women's movement built up resistance. They objected to the old use of the word 'man' as a common noun to mean both sexes, which (if accepted) affected all prayer books. They were suspicious of some presentations of Christianity which stressed the Fatherhood of God. There began to be some curious liturgies couched in feminist language, especially in the United States of America.

But the real controversy arose over the question whether women could be priests. The more free Protestant churches had long accepted women as their preachers and ministers. Towards the end of the nineteenth century this already began to affect more traditional Protestant denominations like the Congregationalists. With a host of well-educated women now for the first time in history at their disposal, all churches wanted them to take their share of responsibility in the work of their church, in teaching, election of church officers, administration. The Catholic Church was already able to use women, as nuns, in many areas and so was slower to feel the need to extend opportunities to other educated women. But the number of nuns declined relative to Catholic populations, and even in Catholicism women began more and more to be used in the same way.

On the one hand women were deaconesses, and church officers. They were often accustomed to teach, and sometimes better educated than the men, and full of devotion, and with access to nearly all the formerly male professions—except the higher ranks of the clergy. At the same time the number of males coming forward for ordination in the traditional churches declined; partly because they had other opportunities; partly because the intellectual unsettlements of the age made men a little less ready to commit themselves to so public a profession, Christian though they believed themselves to be; partly because the inflation of the twentieth century in Europe was very serious in its effect upon the old endowments of churches and made it more difficult for them to pay enough priests a living wage; and in the Roman Catholic Church because the insistence on celibacy did not fit the sexual mores of twentieth-century Europe. It was obvious that in these conditions some women would feel a vocation to the priesthood.

A few famous Catholics—as for example the delightful French Carmelite saint Thérèse of Lisieux (d. 1897, aged only 24)—believed that women should be allowed to be priests. But for nearly all the Roman Catholic Church, and all the Eastern Church, and some Anglicans, and some other Protestants, this idea was too great a breach with apostolic tradition to countenance. Therefore it would affect the better ecumenical mood of the age and damage relations between churches, adding to Protestantism a new 'heresy' in the eyes of Catholics.

The Second World War produced many cases where in concentration camps conditions would not allow the canonical way of taking services—for example, in eastern camps there might be neither bread nor wine, and imprisoned clergy asked themselves whether they could celebrate a sacrament with rice and juice for want of the proper elements. One of these crises of extreme war conditions affected the question of women dramatically. Bishop Hall of Hong Kong (which Japanese forces occupied) had a deaconess, Florence Li, in Macao. In the effort to get sacraments to his people he ordained her as a priest. She happened to be the best sort of Christian minister. After the war she obeyed a request to retire from her priesthood, and suffered for a time in the Cultural Revolution of China. The precedent was weighty. In 1971 it was the next bishop of Hong Kong who ordained the first Anglican women to the priesthood. Thereafter several Anglican Churches across the world accepted women as priests. In the Church of England, some were keenly aware of a probable breach in its new and happy relations with the church of Rome and the East; other members believed the act a breach of apostolic order which would never be possible unless a General Council of the whole church were so to decide. But it was accepted by a two-thirds majority of the General Synod in November 1992.

11

North America

MARTIN MARTY

'W E are a religious people'. Thus wrote a rather secular-minded Justice William O. Douglas in a Supreme Court decision in 1952. He was thus characterizing the citizens of the United States, a people often thought of as worldly, materialistic, and secular-minded.

'We are a religious people'. This was how most Americans thought of themselves, even at the end of the twentieth century whose spirit, at least in the Western world, was usually characterized as secular. When an opinion poll surveyor came by any time in the second half of the century, they told him the same kind of thing. Well over nine out of ten of them said they believed in God, whatever they meant by God, and there was no reason to doubt them who doubted not God. Seven out of ten claimed to be voluntarily on the rolls of religious organizations; six out of ten could be found there; four out of ten claimed to have been at worship the previous weekend. Whatever was in their hearts, their heads and bodies suggested that they were enthusiastically at home with Justice Douglas's characterization that they were a religious people.

The story in Canada, the spatially enormous but much more lightly populated nation to the north of the United States was similar. True, the indicators in opinion polls in every case were slightly lower than they were in the United States. In this respect Canada seemed to have more in common with the sentiments and practices of Western European peoples, yet the percentages of people affirming religious faith and carrying out practices was still much higher than in any nation in Europe. Again, against all odds in a secular era, Canadians had remained and were 'a religious people'.

The sheer amount of religion, if one can speak of a pattern of belief and behaviour in quantitative terms, in both nations was impressive, surprising. The polities of the two societies were different. In the United States since before 1800 there had been serious efforts, issuing from the Constitution and its First Amendment, to prevent establishment of all religion or even privileging of a particular one. Members of civil society progressively withdrew their support from religious institutions. The churches received tax exemption for their properties, and that was a huge boon. They did not receive subsidy, however. Canada was a bit more generous, following the European model, and making it possible for there to be state funding support for the elementary schools of various religions. Yet in both nations there was reliance chiefly on what came to be called 'the voluntary system'. Religion was to be a private affair; in theory it should have waned. Yet it tended to prosper and, periodically and in selective ways, was of public consequence.

The American Way of Being Religious

That North Americans were religious peoples seemed indisputable. *How* they were so was a complex issue for observers to make sense of and analyse. Most of the observers, especially the travellers from Europe who were used to coming from, say, a Catholic or Lutheran, an Anglican or Reformed society, noted that citizens were preoccupied with the significant religious question of 'the one and the many'. This theme came to be near the heart of these travellers' accounts, just as it characterized the plot of domestic treatises by social scientists and theologians in the two nations.

A moment's attention to the reasons for this preoccupation will make the telling of a complex story and the choice of its highlights much simpler. Why the preoccupation with 'the one'? By this is meant the impulse that religious people ordinarily have to want to grasp life as a whole, to see a single and final purpose or system of meaning or set of symbols by which an individual and, she or he hopes, 'the world' or at least a society, can live and be organized. To believe in one God in one way and then to find my neighbour disbelieving, or believing in another God or in another way, and still being a fine, moral, functioning member of society—this can be a challenge to the grip I have on my faith. I, a believer, want all to be 'one'.

What is more, especially in the United States, there have been popular demands for expression of 'oneness' in what might be called a political sense. This is less concern for a personal hold on ultimate truth and more interest in the good of what philosophers of old called 'the human city'. Many citizens believed that a functioning society had or needed to have, in a very broad sense, a common religion. In 1749 one of the American founders, practical-minded Benjamin Franklin, had urged the development of what he called a 'Publick Religion', one that, to be sure, favoured Christianity but still one that bore its own distinctive stamp. In 1955 Jewish sociologist Will Herberg spoke of a 'civic faith'; in 1963 historian Sidney E. Mead wrote of 'the religion of the republic'; in 1967 another sociologist, Robert N. Bellah, observed and urged upon a diverse people a single 'civil religion'.

The common or civil faith, which was to be 'one', tolerant and ill-defined as it must be, was supposed to serve as a kind of cement for a society that might otherwise fall apart, a lubrication for the nation's processes. Earlier covenants, for example the famed Mayflower Compact of New England's Plymouth Colony in 1620, conventionally began something like 'In the name of God, Amen'. In 1787 the drafters of the United States constitution began without divine reference their consistently godless constitution, 'We the people of the United States'. By 1800 citizens were shown to be hard at work finding a *consensus juris*, some sort of agreement that stood behind law and the support of law. They joined the national founders in saying that, for such a consensus to develop and prosper and receive support, there must be a people characterized by 'civic virtue'. This virtue derived from a moral system. Most of the founders went one step further and argued that such a moral system was finally grounded in a deep if broad and diffuse religion or religious outlook.

Canada, it must be noted, as a bi-religious society, 'Protestant' everywhere except in 'Catholic' Quebec, was less preoccupied with a religiously grounded consensus. British political scientist Bernard Crick explicitly cited Canada as a nation that, like most of those in Europe, no longer had, if it ever possessed, such a consensus. He also could not find much of one in the United States, but he did agree that United States citizens thought they had one, and wanted to see it develop healthily.

The Many Ways of Being Religious in North America

Here is where 'the many' comes in, and with it a certain irony. For this largely Christian nation, with all its interest in 'the one', exemplified to the world the richest and wildest anarchy of denominations. The *Yearbook of the American and Canadian Churches* in the late 1980s gave statistics and other specifics for the United States on well over 200 separate contending denominations, most of them Christian, each of them somehow suggesting that they possessed the truth and were valid if not superior agents for promoting private faith and public weal. If it took 219 bodies to house the 142,172,138 members of reporting denominations—and many, particularly among racial minorities and the poor, did not report—so the much smaller Canadian population displayed 85 denominations with 16,476,866 members. Gordon J. Melton's *The Encyclopedia of American Religions* included small, occult, non-Christian, and ephemeral groups and came up with over 1,200 examples, each of them potentially causing disarray in the minds of those who sought 'the one' in the face of such a 'many'.

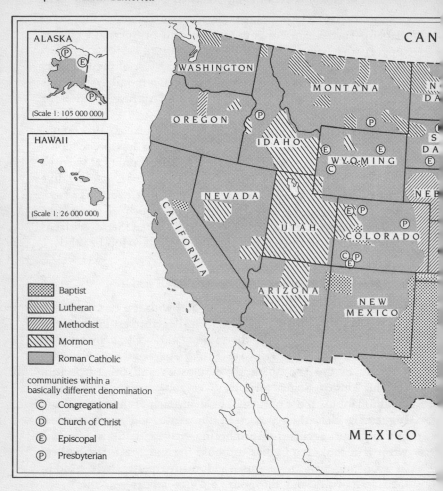

ALASKA

(Scale 1: 105 000 000)

HAWAII

(Scale 1: 26 000 000)

Baptist

Lutheran

Methodist

Mormon

Roman Catholic

communities within a
basically different denomination

Ⓒ Congregational

Ⓓ Church of Christ

Ⓔ Episcopal

Ⓟ Presbyterian

CAN

WASHINGTON

MONTANA

N
DA

OREGON

IDAHO

I
S
DA
Ⓔ

Ⓔ

Ⓔ WYOMING

Ⓒ

NEE

NEVADA

CALIFORNIA

UTAH

Ⓔ Ⓟ

COLORADO

Ⓟ

Ⓒ Ⓟ
Ⓔ

ARIZONA

NEW
MEXICO

MEXICO

**DISTRIBUTION OF MAIN CHRISTIAN
DENOMINATIONS IN THE UNITED STATES OF
AMERICA, 1980**

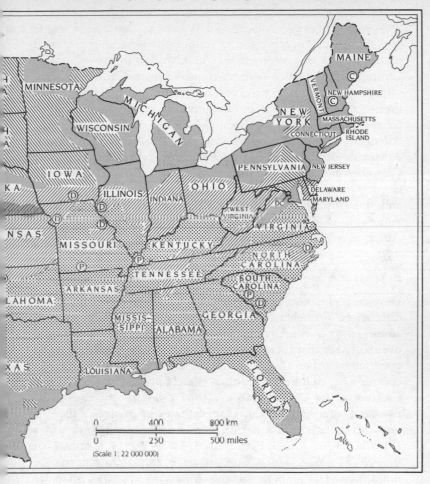

MINNESOTA

WISCONSIN

MICHIGAN

MAINE

©C

VERMONT

NEW HAMPSHIRE

©C

NEW
YORK

MASSACHUSETTS

CONNECTICUT

RHODE
ISLAND

IOWA

©D

ILLINOIS

©D

INDIANA

OHIO

PENNSYLVANIA

NEW JERSEY

DELAWARE

MARYLAND

WEST
VIRGINIA

DC

©D

©D

MISSOURI

KENTUCKY

VIRGINIA

©P

©P

TENNESSEE

NORTH
CAROLINA

©D

NSAS

ARKANSAS

SOUTH
CAROLINA

©P

©D

LAHOMA

MISSIS-
SIPPI

ALABAMA

GEORGIA

XAS

LOUISIANA

FLORIDA

0   400   800 km

0   250   500 miles

(Scale 1: 22 000 000)

How tell the story of Christianity in North America after 1800 in such diverse societies? It is hard to conceive a single plot that brings together the 53 million member (in the United States) or 10 million member (in Canada) Roman Catholic Church with the seven-congregationed Amana Church Society, which is exclusively in rural Iowa. The eye falls on the first few listings of United States bodies and sees an array of ethnic or other-national vestiges: African Methodist Episcopal Church, Albanian Orthodox Archdiocese in America (vying with Albanian Orthodox Diocese of America), American Baptist Churches in the USA, American Carpatho-Russian Orthodox Greek Old Catholic Church, the Anglican Orthodox Church, and the Antiochian Orthodox Churches of the East, North American Diocese, and the Armenian Apostolic Church of America. What can they all have in common?

Believers at Home in their Environment

Despite the apparent anarchy and disarray and the very profound differences in beliefs, appearances, and behaviour patterns among their various constituencies, members of most would ordinarily say that there is also something very American about their religion. For all their differences, they have something in common, something more than merely sharing a place called Canada or the United States, a time called the nineteenth or twentieth centuries. In the United States in particular there is not only 'religion in America' but 'American religion', and a Christianity of a particular stamp. Third-World members of the World Council of Churches have something specific in mind when they speak of the American churches that are members. When African Christians confer with Afro-American Christians, they are aware of differences from their fellow-believers. When evangelicals from the poor nations meet with evangelicals from the United States, they make clear that they share one Lord and one faith, but they have no difficulty discerning certain characteristics among the American evangelical churches from which came missionaries to convert their own churches. They are very American, expressers, somehow, of the 'one'.

The longer one observes American religion, the more clear it becomes that, however much Christians believe in a revelation that comes from a different moment in history, roughly 2,000 years ago, and a redemptive story that derives from a different place, now called Israel, most citizens, particularly in the United States, somehow conceive of their own natural and cultural environment as somehow revelatory and redemptive. They speak of 'this nation under God', despite the many gods or interpretations of God they must have in mind and even though they assure full legal and citizen status to non-believers in any God. Some of them talk, in terms at once jocular and reverent, of the most barren American landscapes, their own, as 'God's country'. Most of them assent to the notion that the United States is somehow a covenanted nation, called into being by a provident God, guided by such a God, impelled into a 'mission', and inspired by a 'destiny' under God. Such outlooks might well have been expected in medieval Christendom, when one faith under one custodianship, the Roman pope, and in a way for a time in one empire, created a 'one', but not in the 200 churches and 2,000 religious societies in modern, religiously free, pluralistic North America. In all these respects, then, American Christianity lends itself well to the theme that unites the stories in this book: there is an especially vivid dialogue with the context surrounding Christianity. The historian must keep an eye on the impact of the social environment on the churches and, in turn, of the churches on the social environment.

Immigration and Innovation

Why so many religions in the United States and Canadian 'many'? The first great answer, and one that unfolded much more after 1800 than before, is 'immigration', most of it voluntarily from Europe but also, under the forced conditions of the slave-trade which continued well into the nineteeth century, from Africa. The immigrants brought along different and competing faiths that had nothing to do with each other or which encouraged hostility against each other, depending upon whether they were from Ireland, Scotland, or England, from Germany, France, or Scandinavia, or, later, upon whether they came from Albania or Antioch or Armenia.

In the colonial era the immigrant plot was already diverse, but still containable, and the citizen of 1800 could still see some coherence, a shorter list for any *Yearbook* or *Encyclopedia* if any had then existed. From 1492 in the hemisphere, or 1565 on what was to become United States soil, there had been an original Roman Catholic monopoly. In 1607 Anglicans challenged that and after 1620 and 1630 Puritans in New England set up their own distinctive colonies. Soon there were Dutch and Swedish and any number of other colonial intrusions on any 'one' notion that British colonists might have had.

In 1800 there were approximately five million white citizens of the United States; almost all of them were of Protestant provenance. Roman Catholics there numbered in the tens of thousands, and most of the North American Catholics were sequestered in Quebec. The United States was, then, not only a Christian society in general, but a Protestant society in particular, though with ever fewer vestigial legal establishments of religion. (New Hampshire kept its vestigial establishment until 1818, Connecticut until 1819, and after Massachusetts 'fell' into legal pluralism in 1833 there were no more such legal support systems or privilegings of any religion or, officially, of any one religion.) And the people, immigrant peoples whose ways did not match the faith and outlook and practice of earlier settlers, kept coming. In the course of the centuries a Jewish community of five to six million developed to complicate the picture of the United States as a Christian nation.

Meanwhile, the 'many' kept growing because, beyond immigration there was inventiveness and innovation. An observer might almost conclude that, on the American and Canadian landscape, if there was some ecological niche unfilled, some discernible human need unmet, this environment would find someone who could reveal a new redemptive pattern. Mother Ann Lee had brought, and developed, the Shakers, a kind of post-Christian or post-orthodox communal faith. Joseph Smith, a New York farm boy, saw two angelic personages who revealed to him some gold plates on which were written a book of revelation about North America—and he founded in 1830 the Church of Jesus Christ of Latter-day Saints, the Mormons. A century and a half later it had almost four million American adherents, and had spread around the world. William Miller and Ellen Gould White founded and refounded (officially in 1863) the millennium-minded Seventh-day Adventists, who attracted two-thirds of a million members. Charles Taze Russell patented a Zion's Watch Tower Tract Society in 1881: after a century these Jehovah's Witnesses claimed almost three-quarters of a million active, very active, members in the United States. Late in the nineteenth century Mary Baker Eddy, experiencing and discerning a need for connecting religion and health, founded the Church of Christ, Scientist, a group that does not disclose statistics but which attracted hundreds of thousands. Each of these groups and scores more kept enriching the 'many' that came along earlier with the baggage of immigrants.

Constant Changes in Denominational Power

For all the differences, there was a search for homogeneity, and the plot of American Christianity around 1800 showed citizens preoccupied with a call for religious 'sameness' in an extremely diverse society. It is the United States plot, then, that will provide the connecting in this narrative, while the Canadian story will receive proportionately less notice (the numbers and world influence being significantly smaller in that northern nation), notice of a comparative sort where plausible and a distinctive character where valid.

A first glimpse at Canada, however, will illustrate the major problem in both countries. The church leadership had to retain and exploit the loyalties of East Coast people as the West opened, and then win the Westerners. Canada's circumstance was somewhat distinctive because French Catholic Quebec lay as a virtual nation separating the Protestant Maritimes and what was to become a Protestant Western Canada. During the westward moves, Canada saw conflict between the two kinds of Christians in part as a reaction against an imagined 'papal aggression', the charge itself echoing one heard in mid-century England. Canada, as we shall see, was not to have a monopoly on Catholic–Protestant tensions. When Protestants took their mind off these, they often effectively helped church the west-ward bound. Methodism was best poised to prosper and serve in this respect, and did so for decades. Canadian Christians failed as much as their counterparts in the United States were to do when it came to converting Native Americans *en masse* to Christianity.

In the new United States of 1800, not much had occurred to alter the population mix revealed in a census of 1790. At that time, 83.5 per cent of the white population (blacks and Native Americans were not citizens) were of English stock. The Scots and Germans came next, with 6.7 per cent and 5.6 per cent, followed by tiny percentages of Dutch (2), Irish (1.6) and 'all others' (0.6). This meant that English was the language of the overwhelming majority, and churches of English pro-venance helped promote a 'sameness' that was to be lost a century later as non-English-speaking arrivals predominated among immigrants.

If English people and the English language promoted homo-geneity, churches began to test colonial unities, and power shifts among them were occurring. While it is impossible to know how many adherents each church had, we can know how many local churches represented each communion. In the decade of the nation's birth, Congregationalists were first, with about 750; Presbyterians had almost 500 congregations.

Anglicans, heirs of colonial establishment in the southern colonies, were impressive with over 400 parishes. But something portentous occurred in the 1780s: the upstart Baptists overtook the Anglicans and were approaching 500 churches. Lutherans and German and Dutch Reformed trailed, but they were growing, and with them came non-English churches. As for Roman Catholicism, it lagged, with fewer than sixty congregations in all the colonies. None were in New England or the deeper South; most were in Maryland and southern Pennsylvania.

How different things began to be twenty years later, in 1800, where our story begins. Now there were estimates of memberships, and Baptists had come into first place, ready to take off for a century-long competition with Methodism; eventually they were to become the largest Protestant group, especially in the South. The Congregationalists were second, but lost place a year or two later, and they experienced such slow growth that group after group overtook the original Puritan cluster. Meanwhile, as if out of nowhere, came the Methodists; by 1820 they overtook the Baptists and remained first in numbers of adherents until around 1920. Presbyterians and Lutherans approximated each other's growth until around 1900, when European immigration helped Lutherans begin their growth to more than double the size of the Presbyterians, while Episcopalians, heirs of the colonial Anglicans, kept losing place throughout the century, as the Disciples of Christ, a new movement, appeared on the scene and was organized in 1827. Within a few years the Disciples of Christ overtook these Episcopalians.

Statistics and lines on graphs can be lifeless and bloodless, but they reflect a lively though not quite bloody competition. Whoever wishes to find an explanation for the shift in power and the relative loss by the 'colonial big three' to the 'frontier big three', from Congregational–Presbyterian–Episcopal dominance to Baptist–Methodist–Disciples of Christ predominance, can find much of the clue in one word: revivalism. While mass revivalism and local renewals have remained a standard part of the plot in both United States and Canadian religion, evangelistic endeavours in the early nineteenth century played an almost unimaginably large part in the shifting of power among Christians.

Congregationalism Pioneers

The story of revivalism demands a moment's preliminary glance at the colonial heritage. Congregationalism was chiefly a religion of the northern United States, and remained so; to this day its offspring (the result of a merger in 1957 with historically German-speaking Evangelical and Reformed churches) the United Church of Christ is hardly represented in the South. Congregationalism went where Yankees went, from New England through New York and then to town after town in Ohio, Indiana, Illinois, and the Upper Midwest tier of states. The Congregationalists made up élites in this period. They organized new towns on ordered New England models, and planted 'First Church' at the downtown crossroads. They established fine liberal arts colleges and brought culture to the western lands that opened during the years of frontier settlement.

Congregationalism was not universally opposed to revivalism. Indeed, the greatest of American native preachers of conversion (and theologians), Yale graduate Jonathan Edwards, who preached revivals at Northampton, Massachusetts, in the 1730s and 1740s, was Congregational Puritan to the core. In 1801 Congregationalism entered a Plan of Union with its kin, Presbyterianism. The Plan broke down in 1837, however, because Presbyterians more effectively preached conversion and Congregationalists felt they got the worst of the bargain.

Congregationalism's great legacy to the United States was not revival but a style of church leadership, theology, and concepts of world mission. This Puritan movement, by stressing the autonomy of local churches, helped give impetus to its rebellious, indeed schismatic, offspring, the Baptists, a style of initiating ready-to-go churches on frontiers that Congregational élites themselves could not or would not master. Theologically, the 'Edwardsean' line lived on and was transformed. In the nineteenth century, under preachers like William Ellery Channing, a liberal wing took shape as a Unitarian denomination. This was a rational-minded church movement, organized in 1815, that made less of the supernatural, the miraculous, or the divinity of Christ and preached the benevolence of one God and the moral conscience of humans. Harvard College was its intellectual focus, Boston its centre.

The majority of Congregationalists remained Trinitarian and proclaimed the deity of Christ. But they were embarrassed by or in rebellion themselves against many of their inherited Calvinist–Puritan themes. Particularly, under the leadership of clerics like Yale's Nathaniel William Taylor (1786–1858), they worked to soften the 'decrees', the proclamation that a predestining God determined the salvation or damnation of individuals. In practice such proclamation was long compromised, for Congregationalist revival preachers had had to adapt. If people were to express their will by acts of repentance and conversion to God in Christ, they seemed to have more control of their destiny than older Calvinism had allowed. Taylor, contending with Unitarians, gave away much: he had to depart from older Congregational theology and admit that in the fall of the human race not all elements of human volition, response, or free agency had disappeared.

Congregational theology was to produce, at mid-century, one of the giants of United States Christian thought in the form of the pastor of Hartford, Connecticut, Horace Bushnell (1802–76). Bushnell, who feared the rough and tumble of the frontier, as he expressed it in *Barbarism the First Danger*, also opposed Catholicism as a threat to national 'sameness' and 'oneness'. But he was best known for his critique of revivalism for its emotional wrenching of converts. Instead he proclaimed a gentler *Christian Nurture*, which left great room for natural human dignity and saw the human growing through stages of grace and morality without such wrenching.

Another style blended old and new in New England religion.

Congregationalist, sometime Presbyterian, Lyman Beecher (1776–1863) was as representative as any. This doughty New England pastor who contended with Unitarians, helped redefine Puritan theology, and moved West to help found a seminary in Cincinnati (only to lose out when abolitionist-minded students and faculty left it for more congenial Oberlin College in Ohio), reflected a kind of busy-bee reformist attitude. Like Bushnell he feared the barbarian and infidel as much as the slave-holder and the Catholic, and on all fronts found reason to preach revival and advance to the frontier to head off the enemies he described there.

Congregationalism, before it began its decline, left another legacy to North American religion: the impetus towards world mission. Some have seen in this effort to work overseas a sign of defeat since it had failed to convert the Native American at its own backyard. Still others see it as an imperial attempt to reclaim a kingdom as it lost its own in New England. Whatever the motives, Congregationalists organized in the 1810s, and in the 1820s began to send agents for Christ and America to the Sandwich Islands and 'into all the world'. They took with them ideas, models, and agencies of education, healing, and. 'civilizing'. In due course they saw their place as missionaries outpaced by other groups, but they started it all. Their place in the historic 'mainstream' was secure.

Episcopalianism and Presbyterianism

The Episcopalians in the South had suffered because most of their clergy were loyalists in the War of Independence, and their parishes were in sad decline in Virginia and the Carolinas. Some thought that this form of Christianity would die in America. Yet under the leadership of Samuel Seabury its first bishop (after 1784) and other pioneer bishops, this Anglican offspring also moved West genteelly and without revivalism as an instrument. It remained a church of educated élites and often attracted or produced people of wealth and influence. They assured it a status beyond that suggested by the numbers of its adherents and were thinly spread throughout the nation. Their arguments over the historic episcopate, over 'High' and 'Low' church styles, and similar issues, preoccupied them for much of the nineteenth century and were of little interest beyond their communion.

The Presbyterians represented higher drama. Heirs of Scottish–Irish immigrations in the eighteenth century, they were not established but were powerful in Pennsylvania and New Jersey. Poorer migrants settled in a backwoods corridor along a 500 mile strip along the Appalachian mountains, and were poised to move across those mountains when the passes and trails opened at the turn of the century. This they did. While Presbyterians perpetuated Scottish doctrinal controversies and promoted the idea of 'an educated ministry', using Princeton Seminary as their base, they were more ready than their colonial rivals to encourage revivalism. They clearly profited from the Plan of Union between 1801 and 1837, and planted not only their versions of First Church and fine colleges, but also back-country leaders who brought social control to many American frontier settlements.

Out of churches like the Congregational and Presbyterian came lay and clerical leadership to fashion what some historians have called an 'errand of mercy'. This was the American link in a connection of agencies that had branches in both England and America. These set out to do mission work, spread the Bible and evangelical tracts, establish Sunday schools, and engage in moral reform. They thus recognized that they could win back in the ethos what they had lost in law. They could not be officially established, but they could fashion a reformist and evangelical Protestant empire, and they did. Much of their impetus came from a peculiar twist that they gave to millennial thought. Called 'post-millennial' because they taught that Christ would return and begin to rule *after* his agents and churches had won many converts and made the world attractive by reform, they contributed to American homogeneity through this voluntary 'errand'. This contribution was matched later on by frontier denominations.

Frontier Denominations

The frontier denominations, Baptist, Methodist, and Disciples of Christ, help set the scene for the whole century. The Baptists were not heirs of European Anabaptism but splits off colonial Congregationalism. They were, in the main, active Calvinists who wanted to set high standards for church membership. They concluded that infant baptism lowered these, that adult 'believers' baptism was necessary for discipleship. Aggressive, they began to make a mark far beyond Rhode Island, their original New England home (where Brown University was their intellectual centre). By 1800 they were active on the frontier in Virginia and helped lead the transappalachian moves, especially into the South. While northern Baptists turned moderate and found company with Congregationalists, southern Baptists cherished biblical conservatism which helped them devise literalist support for slavery in the Cotton Kingdom. Because of their belief in local autonomy, Baptists were positioned so that they could produce ordained ministers, educated or not, 'on the spot', as it were. They did not possess theological unity; some repudiated Calvinism. Not all favoured organization for evangelization and mission. Yet most of them evangelized and carried on mission. They surged.

Methodism, the legacy of founder John Wesley in England, came with a very different theology and polity, but was at least as successful at revivalism and frontier mastery. Francis Asbury was the main agent, a Wesleyan missionary who helped Methodism recover from the Tory imagery with which Wesley had left it. Methodism was 'Arminian', not Calvinist. It stressed the human striving for perfection, the vast scope of God's saving act in Christ and benevolence towards all people, and views of great human potential. This meant that God was not the sole agent in conversion. The human also co-operated and received credit from God for doing so. It was also organized 'episcopally', with bishops to represent the well-being of the church. The Wesleyans and Asburyites produced networks for conversion, care, and mission; they anticipated an impressive variety of circumstances and met great numbers of needs on the frontier. Preachers of emotional revival to large gatherings, they also produced order and agencies of social control, especially through the mid-South, north of the Baptist empire.

The Disciples of Christ was a 'primitive' movement that sought Christian simplicity. Some Presbyterian and some Baptist elements went into the mix produced by Thomas Campbell and his son Alexander, the latter an immigrant from Scotland in 1809. Independent movements led by Walter Scott, a genius simplifier, worked other parts of the frontier. These people, some of whom wanted their party simply to be known as 'Christians', and others who preferred the name 'Disciples of Christ' proclaimed that they would speak where the New Testament spoke and be silent about what it was silent. They would not be a church among the churches, a denomination, but a movement towards true and final Christian unity. Ironically, but inevitably, they became another set of churches, another denomination.

America's Religious Diversity Grows

One can only glance at some other church trends in the period. Roman Catholicism remained small at first, dependent upon priests and missionaries from Europe, but Catholicism also prospered as its members helped people the frontier in the West. Historians of our time have discerned that Catholics also learned and adopted revivalist styles similar to those of Protestants. They were not able to attract many people of Protestant stock, to whom they appeared to be a massive menace, an agency of an anti-Republican if not demonic foreign power, the pope. They did have to attract the energies and loyalties of the dispersed flow of immigrants, many of whom were religiously apathetic when they arrived: Irish in East Coast cities like Boston, German in Ohio, Indiana, and on the Midwestern frontier. The great population increase among Catholics occurred after the Irish potato famines and European revolutions of the 1840s.

Catholic growth provoked reaction among Protestants. One party called itself the 'Know-Nothings' and others came to be called the 'Nativists' towards mid-century. Their virulent anti-Catholicism was respectable in wide cultural circles then, but in a more tolerant century to come has been seen as a mark of shame. In the 1840s, however, the reaction seemed reasonable to them, for Catholics were a threat to American 'one-ness', the Protestant-based dream of homogeneity. Their new immigrant population was poor, crowded into slums, hard-drinking, unruly, undemocratic—or so, at least, thought their enemies. These Catholic immigrants were politically adept and began to develop what all critics saw as ominous and corrupt political machines in great cities: they might one day run America! They were attracting a few notable converts from Protestantism, such as layman and publicist Orestes Brownson or Isaac Hecker, the founder of the Paulists, a religious order which set out to commend Catholicism to America.

They had to be stopped, if American institutions were to prevail and 'oneness' endure as an ideal. That is why the Lyman Beechers and Horace Bushnells fought Catholicism as a barbarism. That is why mobs burned a convent school in Charlestown near Boston in 1834 and attacked Irish crowds, killing some people in Philadelphia in 1844. That is why there was a market for scandalous books like Maria Monk's *Awful Disclosures of the Hotel Dieu Nunnery of Montreal*. All this bewildered Catholics for they felt at home with Republican institutions in America. They paid no heed to the *Syllabus of Errors* of 1864 in which Pope Pius IX promulgated reactionary, anti-modern, and anti-democratic notions. While all this controversy was occurring, around mid-century, Catholicism became the largest Christian group in America.

Other European groups like the Lutherans built on their small colonial foundations and by the 1830s and 1840s were prospering from immigrations into the Midwest, to Missouri, Iowa, Wisconsin, and the like. They were generally acceptable theologically to the dominant Protestants around them; after all, Martin Luther was the pioneer Protestant. Culturally, however, they were misfits. Some, like Catholics, started foreign-language-speaking parochial schools alongside the common or public schools. They drank beer in increasingly temperance-minded Anglo-Protestant America. They kept to themselves and fought over who was most orthodox in seventeenth-century German Lutheran credal senses. Few of them favoured revival-ism, but they, too, borrowed revivalist techniques and provided havens for new immigrants in emerging cities like Chicago, Milwaukee, and St Louis, or in remote frontier settlements.

It is hard to determine how much of a threat to the dream of a single kingdom, 'redeemer nation' or empire, the small new religious movements were. Certainly the communes in frontier forests or on the plains were challenges to the meaning-systems of conventional Plan of Union type evangelical Protestants. Some were led by agnostics like Robert Owen, who purchased the land and buildings of a defunct German Protestant com-munity at New Harmony, Indiana, and tried a non- or anti-Christian Socialist experiment. 'Backwoods Utopias' developed under such auspices or under what others regarded as heretical Christian ventures. At Oneida, New York, maverick cleric John Humphrey Noyes promoted ideas that the scandalized orthodox called 'free love', and they opposed that just as they scorned the Shakers. Statistically these were small endeavours. The conventional gave them publicity beyond their numbers, seeing in them challenges to ideals of the family as it was then ordinarily constituted or 'early capitalist' economy and ordinary behaviour.

More of an intellectual challenge came from the Unitarian left and from independent sources that generated movements like Transcendentalism among the Boston élites and others.

Giants like Henry David Thoreau and Ralph Waldo Emerson spoke of divinity in terms far different from those associated with the God of the Bible or the static deity, the 'Being' of orthodox theology. 'Forget historical Christianity' urged the Transcendentalists, as they described 'Oversoul' (in Emerson's terms), the divinity in nature and the flux of human interaction, or in forms of piety that bypassed church worship, sacraments, and dogma. They were of the proper old stock, but they rebelled against the old 'oneness' and, in promoting a new 'one', contributed to the many.

There were other complicators. Throughout the nineteenth century the Native Americans or Indians were not regarded as citizens constitutionally. They were, in a sense, problems or objects, to be warred against, 'removed' or 'reservated' in segregated badlands of the great West, or converted and civilized, or forgotten. While some Protestant and Catholic missioners kept trying to be humane, some of them as agents of the government under President Ulysses S. Grant's post-Civil War Indian policy, many wearied. There were relatively few or complete conversions. Indians who cherished, or would fuse with Christianity, their ancient beliefs about spirit, nature, and tribe, were dismissed as heathen, pagans, and barbarians. They represented 'the many' on American soil, but wholly as negative images with no positive potential.

Similarly, blacks complicated the picture. Most of them were slaves, property of other humans (most of them Protestant Christian), largely in the American South but, it was feared, soon also in the American West. As the Cotton Kingdom developed after 1800, slavery grew instead of declining. The anti-slavery societies which had once dotted the South began to wane and abolition came to be a northern minority cause, often of people who worked with Christian impetus but found Christian churches to be laggard or opposed to their efforts. So abolitionists and anti-abolitionists and North and South further sundered ideas of seamless oneness.

From a distance an observer might have thought that the

development of black churches would lead to convergence, not disunity. After all, when slavemasters began to care for the souls of the blacks (or sought to control them through religion) as well as when minority freedmen organized churches of their own, they matched the two main Christian forms in the South, Methodist and Baptist. Richard Allen, the Philadelphia freedman who helped form the African Methodist Episcopal Church, like most of his colleagues, was a conventionally orthodox Methodist in doctrine, an enthusiast for Methodist revivalism and organization alike. White mainstream Methodists encouraged such separate organization and generally welcomed Methodist revivals among slaves on plantations. But they preferred to have white revivalists or white supervision and discouraged the rise of literacy among slaves.

At the same time, the other great southern complex, the Baptists, also saw the development of a black counterpart set of churches. These Baptist groups could form by a kind of spontaneous combustion, just as white congregations did, and the growth of tiny Baptist churches among blacks was impressive. Yet, while some white Baptists engaged in acts of charity toward them, there were certainly no contacts that implied parity, communion, or human intimacy. A black Methodist–Baptist empire grew up alongside the white ones, and the attitudes of whites helped create the very 'manyness' they professed to want to discourage.

The Conflict between North and South

Reference to differing policies in North and South shows once again a strain on the idea of a single 'redeemer nation' or 'righteous empire'. Even northern gradualists, who did not want to interfere or be aggressive abolitionists, opposed slavery ever more vocally. They lived at some distance from the Carolinas or wherever else slave revolts led by messianic-minded blacks like Nat Turner were threats to public complacency and peace. So they did not react to these with desires for more repressive measures, as southerners did, but with more keenness to see slavery end. They had more flexible views of biblical interpretation and found ways to explain away biblical permissions for slavery. They saw southern church leaders, including the most sophisticated Presbyterian theologians like Robert Lewis Dabney, nurture elaborate and firm biblical and Calvinist defences of slavery and eventually of secession from the union. Such southern theologians also provided rationales for resisting racial integration during postwar Reconstruction and for generations to come.

As distrust and rancour between northern and southern branches of denominations erupted into aggressive language and policy, churches began to split. The Presbyterians had done so already in 1837, in schisms complicated by more than racial issues, schisms that lasted until the 1980s. Methodists divided in convention at Louisville, Kentucky, in 1845, and could not come completely together until 1939. A Southern Baptist Convention was born in 1845 at Augusta, Georgia. By then differences between northern and southern Baptists had grown so wide that there was no hope of reunion after the Civil War. The Southern Baptist Convention became the dominant, almost (unofficially) established church of the South, and grew in the second half of the twentieth century to be the largest Protestant denomination in the United States. Episcopalians found their bonds strained, but did not formally break.

The Civil War is a kind of mid-point in American history. The old 'oneness' was broken on sectional lines in the bloody war in 1861–5, precisely between peoples who had once together dreamed of a homogeneous place where the ways and words and works of Christ would prevail among the nations. Curiously and ironically, President Abraham Lincoln during and at the end of the war, though no church member himself (and thus unique among United States presidents), invoked biblical and specifically Christian language in an effort to judge both sides and to work for reconciliation. American professors of 'civil religion' regularly turn to his rhetoric to hear evocations of what might be or might have been or could become a common soul, part of a common story. He invoked notions of 'transcendent justice' that saw the almighty if mysterious God having his own purposes beyond that of earthly partisans. All this while himself holding to the idea of the Union with a passion that some have compared to religious mysticism.

Canadian Confederation

While the United States had been coming apart in the 1860s, Canada came together, bloodlessly and without drama, in an act of Confederation that took place in 1867. In the midst of intense Protestant–Catholic rivalry and conflict during the 1850s, economic and political interests promoted a unity of the Canadian provinces. Both Catholics and Protestants in the main fell into line and supported the move. Canadians have never associated their act of Confederation with religious meaning as United States people have done to their War of Independence and constitution-drafting. It is usually suggested that while in the United States the concern has been over 'the many' and 'the one', Canada has had to be too preoccupied with 'twoness', with Catholic and Protestant interpretations, to come up with a coherent and compelling myth.

In the years after Confederation Canada, a land more vast than the United States but with a small population, began to develop its western provinces, but without an ideology that impelled people to convert barbarians on the frontier. The land was simply settled by churched and churching people. Yet there were enthusiastic bodies, most notably the Methodists, who combined revivalism with semi-rural versions of a 'social gospel', an effort at economic reform. This movement became stronger in the eastern cities, where Anglicanism and the other traditional Protestant churches faced the problems of slums, poverty, and crowding that went with urban growth.

Catholicism remained strongest, with over 40 per cent of Canadians being members in the 1890s. Three out of four of

these were French Canadians, most of whose leaders were
strong supporters of conservative policies. Most notable among
these was Elzéar Taschereau (1820–98) of Quebec, who intervened in some United States Catholic disputes against the progressives there. He developed his conservative theological and
moderately liberal social outlook over against strongly 'ultra-
montane' or papalist parties that dominated late nineteenth-
century Catholicism. Taschereau won out in Canada as his
party did not in the United States.

An Era of Religious Prosperity

Between the Civil War and the end of the First World War,
Christianity prospered along with America at large. This
prosperity strikes European observers as curious, for these
were the years of urbanization, industrialization, and the great
formation of corporate life, organized labour, and modern
universities. In Europe such a period saw the emptying of
churches, the loss of the allegiance of organized labour, and
the development of anti-Christian (Marxist, Nietzschean,
Darwinian, Freudian, and other 'god-killing') ideologies. On
any screen of prophetic images after the Enlightenment there
should have been the reflection of a landscape devoid of new
church steeples. Who, sceptics asked, would still believe in
God, still fill the churches?

Instead, as cities grew, so did the churches. The immigrants
from eastern and southern Europe, joining the earlier arriving
(and still coming) Irish and Germans, were attracted to urban
Catholic parishes. Penny-a-week contributions by labourers
helped build giant city churches. These became centres not
only of devotional and liturgical lives but also of credit unions,
some labour organization, social existence (which encouraged
marriage of Catholic to Catholic), parochial education, a kind
of enveloping set of religious symbols in an environment that
did little to provide welcome or support for Catholics.

Under the leadership of men like Cardinal James Gibbons

(1843–1921) of Baltimore, Catholicism came to be a force in pluralist America. On one hand, he kept demonstrating how loyal Catholics were. He supported the Spanish–American War effort in 1898, even though that war had little moral justification and could be seen to be waged against Catholic powers by Protestant imperialists. Gibbons became a confidant of presidents, regularly portrayed in public at their side. It was hard to see Catholics as disloyal when he and his hierarchical colleagues urged Catholics into the First World War in 1917.

At the same time, Gibbons spoke up for labour. Protestantism tended to be middle class and rural, hostile to labour organization as a violation of 'natural law' and God's intended way of encouraging individualism. Catholics were seen as untrustworthy because in Europe labour was usually hostile to the church, and early organization in America almost necessarily took on quasi Masonic 'brotherhood' and 'lodge' character, to be condemned with all secret orders. Yet Gibbons prevented conservative hierarchs from getting the pioneering Knights of Labor condemned. As this fraternity which anticipated the functions of labour unions declined, to be replaced by the American Federation of Labor and other more open groups, labourers found that they could be faithful to church and union.

Leaders like Gibbons, while nurturing Catholic institutions like parochial schools and colleges which seemed to segregate or did segregate Catholic children from public life, also worked to help them enter the mainstream. While such leaders were orthodox and criticized the few theologically adaptive modernists in their midst, they resented Vatican attempts to depict modernism as an actual threat or a large presence in the American churches. And Gibbons and colleagues of his stripe mediated between a Vatican that suspected 'Americanist' heresies, which would result from over-adaptation to non-Catholic environments, as these were portrayed to Rome by zealous American Catholic intransigents, and 'Americanizers' who might have strayed. By the time the Vatican in 1908 redefined American Catholicism as being no longer under the Congregation for the Propagation of the Faith and hence no longer a 'mission', the church in North America was a mature, ethnically divided, doctrinally united, vital participant in the world church and a powerful if mistrusted agent in American political life.

Urban and industrial America brought another major Christian voice or cluster of voices to the scene. Eastern Orthodoxy was almost unknown in the United States until the end of the nineteenth century. The earliest presences were Russian Orthodox missionaries in Alaska, which the United States purchased in 1867. While most Christians came overland from the East, other Orthodox, almost all of them Russian, came in the ensuing decades by sea to the West Coast, to Seattle and San Francisco. Then, from the Atlantic crossings, Russians, Greeks, and any number of other Orthodox peoples settled the coal-mining country of Pennsylvania or helped populate steel mill cities like Gary, Indiana.

Jurisdictional battles between Russians and Greeks, between laity and clergy, marked much of the early life of Orthodoxy in America. Because the new immigrants often held to their European languages, settled in rather tight enclaves, and often experienced harassment or scorn from the older Protestant stock, Orthodoxy did not come to be well known by non-Orthodox until after the Second World War, when some saw it as a 'fourth American faith' alongside Protestantism, Catholicism, and Judaism.

Black churches prospered in the era of segregation during and after Reconstruction. Most of them were still in the rural South, but around the First World War the industrial North beckoned workers to mills and factories, or even to a change of venue for their poverty in unemployment. Wherever blacks were or went, the Methodist and Baptist churches accompanied them. Some black churches in the North took over huge buildings abandoned by whites who left areas that were being favoured by new Negro arrivals. Others improvised with 'storefront' churches where entrepreneurial ministers who could gather a flock did so. Meanwhile, sometimes under the benefaction of northern Christian charities, there developed a network of colleges and universities to train black élites. A middle class began to develop. In that case as in others, the church was still the centre of community life for many, the professional and vocational outlet for black males when they were denied access to many other professions. The militant black élitist and eventual Communist W. E. B. DuBois later spoke of the African Methodist Episcopal Church as the most impressive achievement of black organizers in nineteenth-century America.

White Protestants, however, did little to build bonds with these churches, and racially there were at least two Americas or Christianities. Doctrinal and practical similarity counted for little. At the turn of the century anthropologists, sociologists, and historians began to adopt and apply European-invented explicitly racist theories to prove the inferiority of blacks and to legitimate their segregation. The United States Supreme Court in *Plessy* v. *Ferguson* in 1894 allowed for 'separate but equal' facilities for blacks and thus promoted 'Jim Crow' segregation models. Critics noted that the Sunday Protestant worship hour was the most segregated time of the week. Indeed, the once righteous churches of the North, after proclaiming triumph over the evils of slavery and the South, came during the next century to adopt southern styles of regard for blacks and their churches, and there was little positive contact even within denominational families.

Through it all, however, the old white Protestant groups still held most political, cultural, and religious power throughout America, not only in the South. While religious statistics are necessarily imprecise, even early in the twentieth century when the United States census still included religious data, one can get some sense of the general shape of power. Roman Catholics were first, with 10,658,066 adult members, in the 1906 census. Methodists and Baptists towered, with the loyalties of well over five million members each—to say nothing of unreckoned, uncountable black Baptists. Well below them but strong were the evenly matched Presbyterians and Lutherans, with almost two millions each. Lutherans were profiting from continuing immigration as Presbyterians were not. The Disciples of Christ were the fifth largest denomination, followed by Episcopalians, Congregationalists, and Latter-day Saints, with Reformed and Quakers remaining small.

Protestantism endeavoured to continue as a strong presence in the industrial city, and in selective ways did so. As a rural, middle-class, and later suburban church, Protestantism through its journals and sermons conventionally spoke of the workforce as 'they', not 'we'. The immigrant was to be feared as Catholic or Socialist or Anarchist. Sporadic efforts to convert people of non-Protestant stock were not productive and were soon allowed to be forgotten. Yet Protestants did not by any means simply abandon the modern world, its corporate life, urban population, or thought patterns.

As for corporate life, here was a whole new field. Clerical leaders like Lyman's son Henry Ward Beecher and a generation of 'princes of the pulpit' preached that God was in league with money. Whereas a generation earlier believers were enjoined to be suspicious of the rich or of riches, if they had wealth, and to be content with humble status, now they were to get rich under God's blessing. The process of rising into and through the middle class was itself a sign not only of God's blessing but of divinely favoured human achievement. It produced a call to stewardship of wealth.

In this generation, then, the Protestant critique of worldliness was muted in fashionable churches. The immensely wealthy entrepreneurs and corporate leaders—the Rockefellers and Drews, the Fisks and McCormicks and Vanderbilts, were church members and generous donors. Many of them endowed seminaries, colleges, universities, charities. Under their influence and tutelage, of course, it became difficult for clergy or lay prophets to call into question the ruthless acquisition of wealth, even ill-gotten gain.

The Social Gospel and Liberalism

Some Protestants tried, however, to bring the new capitalist corporate order under what they saw as a word of divine judgement. Among Episcopalians like W. D. P. Bliss and Vida Scudder, this meant kinship with British Anglican Christian Socialists. They would reconceive the social order. Among mainstream American Protestants this meant a 'social gospel'. Leaders like Baptist seminary professor Walter Rauschenbusch, Ohio Congregationalist preacher Washington Gladden, and Wisconsin lay economist Richard Ely, argued that the corporate or business order had to be and could be 'Christianized'. Few were Socialists and none of note favoured Marxism or violent revolution. They were often vague about the reorganization of power in post-capitalist America, and not many labour leaders or Socialists turned to these mild progressives.

The social gospellers, however, were of considerable influence as critics of Social Darwinism, a kind of justification for the 'survival of the fittest' notion in economics. They were for involving the churches in support for more government intervention in 'trust-busting' and general social welfare work. They worked to address slum problems, issues of poverty. Some began 'institutional churches', which attempted to deal with social and recreational and not only spiritual needs of the urban poor. Walter Rauschenbusch in 1907 wrote *Christianity and the Social Crisis* and found a considerable following. In 1908 the Methodists formulated a Social Creed. That year Protestants also formed a Federal Council of Churches. This agency not only breathed the spirit of practical Christian ecumenism or church co-operation towards reunion. It concentrated on a social vision, to the neglect of explicit evangelism.

The social gospel had its blind spots. The problems of black America hardly ever found notice by its leaders, except in so far as blacks shared general negative effects from poverty during industrialization. While Christians, and, sometimes, restless critics of Christianity, were working for women's rights and women's suffrage, which came to be assured through a Constitutional Amendment in 1917, the social gospel males not only did not speak up for women's rights. Many of them advocated the Victorian Home model of domesticity which called for women to stay at home and make their contribution to America and Christianity through domestic faithfulness. Instead, social gospellers joined forces with more conservative Protestants to promote temperance and then, in a Constitutional Amendment in 1919, the prohibition of alcoholic beverages.

The social gospel was to suffer set-back around and after the First World War. It is hard to see how many converts it had in middle-class Protestantism. In so far as it was based on a metaphysics of progress and the endeavour to 'bring in the Kingdom', it lost out when the horrendous futility of the First World War came to obscure if not destroy signs of human progress. Post-war prosperity doomed much of the social gospel programme as America went for 'normalcy' and a new legitimation of competition.

Concurrently with this social adjustment, many leaders in progressive Protestant denominations also experimented with theological adaptation to modernity. The movements were called 'liberalism' and, in more extreme form, 'modernism', and came from the tradition of Horace Bushnell, which stressed the immanence of God. But now two new factors entered. For one, what was called the higher criticism of the Bible, suddenly arrived in the 1880s as an import from Germany and, to a lesser extent, from England. This meant that scholars began to subject the Bible to scrutiny as they would any other ancient book. They found within it a different history from that propounded by the literalists. They called the authorship of many books into question and saw strata of development in the texts. What would such historical and literary examination do to the authority of a divinely, verbally inspired book? After all, that book had also helped promote American oneness and sameness. What would failure to employ such scientific examination do to people of intelligence? Leaders like University of Chicago founder William Rainey Harper, a Yale Semitics professor in his earlier years, feared this might lead to loss of faith among literate people. They would, they must, be 'scientific' about Bible study.

Similarly, the challenge of evolution was also something that liberals picked up. Darwin's *Origin of Species*, published in 1859, did not lead to immediate, massive, unthinking resistance in America, as many accounts suggest. Cultural lag played its part, but within a generation educated Americans were well aware of its findings, its argument. What cushioned the shock was the fact that through the nineteenth century the dominant evolutionary school was not Darwinian but neo-Lamarckian. This meant that evolution could be, as Henry Ward Beecher called it, 'God's way of doing things'. There was room for the argument for divine design in evolution. Only when Darwinian 'natural selection' prevailed in the scientific community, as it eventually did, with its observance of accidental, arbitrary, almost anarchic processes at work, did moderate conservatives feel forced to depart from the evolutionary vision.

The liberals saw their vision as promoting oneness. They tended to be Anglo-Saxons who believed in their racial superiority and thought they could use it to unify the nation and set a guide for all humanity. They were for Christian ecumenism or unity, desiring to overcome sectarian diversity in one church. Their vision of divine immanence brought God and world together as radically transcendent views did not. The social gospel, they thought, drew on simple pre-modern models of integrated human life that, projected in the future, could help overcome competition and division. Meanwhile, evolution, in which they believed, was an inevitable force which over the aeons drew disparate phenomena into ever greater measures of unity. Christians should adapt their forms of life to advance this process. Roman Catholics might believe mild versions of all these and then be chased from them by Vatican condemnations of modernism in 1907. Such condemnations came, and were effective, even if this meant that Catholic intellectual life was discouraged and creativity thwarted for the next half-century to come.

Conservative Reactions in Protestantism

Protestants had no Vatican authority to counter liberalism or modernism. They had to fight over their republic, their churches, the spoils. A reactionary party began to form. First, under revivalists like Dwight L. Moody, their evangelists began to spread a new import from John Darby and British Plymouth Brethren. This was a complex of pre-millennial views to counter the older liberal post-millennialism. Pre-millennialism saw the world not as getting better, as producing the Kingdom of God on earth. It was getting worse, and would do so until Christ came again for his thousand-year rule. Christians would do well to evangelize, to convert others quickly. There was little point in reforming social institutions.

Second, in the face of biblical criticism, the reactionaries began to draw on seventeenth-century European Protestant formulations and to fuse them with some current scientific or philosophical views. They chose Princeton's enduring if challenged hold on Scottish Common Sense Realism. This 'what you see and what you feel is what you get' philosophy, fused with Francis Bacon's inductivism, led to some common sense approaches to the Bible, based on syllogism. The Bible is God's word. God being perfect cannot err. Therefore the Bible cannot err. It cannot err either in matters of geography, history, and science. It offers an alternative account to evolution's. But one must believe, as liberals did not, in an errorless Bible, one which in its original manuscripts could not be in error.

In the tumult of the times, as such intransigents began in the second decade of the twentieth century to publish pamphlets called *The Fundamentals*, they found that the notion of inerrancy was a fine definer of parties. It was also a good weapon in intradenominational warfare. The party that claimed it could always make the other side sound less sure, less authoritative, more ambiguous. In a world of sudden change, religion was to be a bulwark, a fortress, a sure rock. Inerrancy seemed to supply that, never mind how much inerrantists fought with each other on so many points, without assurance or an agreed upon theology issuing from their first point.

After the First World War was the moment to strike. The heirs of *The Fundamentals*, which had been rather moderate, turned militant. They formed a World Christian Fundamentalist Association in 1919 and saw a Baptist leader among them, Curtis Lee Laws, ask that the whole movement henceforth be 'Fundamentalist', in an editorial which appeared in July 1920. Militant, often rough-mannered though not always unintellectual, they possessed in Princeton Presbyterian J. Gresham Machen a mind of intelligence; also, in a progressive leader, one-time almost-pacifist Secretary of State (in 1914) and three-time Democratic presidential candidate William Jennings Bryan, they had a doughty warrior against evolution.

By 1925 the stage was set for intradenominational battles, chiefly in northern Baptist and Presbyterian circles. Fundamentalists wanted to purge the major seminaries and mission boards of liberals and modernists, for they, it was argued, were poisoning the clergy and the mission fields. In that year in Tennessee, Bryan defended anti-evolution views in the famed Scopes Trial. While his side technically won the case, all but the most fanatic partisan of the movement felt that he had disgraced the Fundamentalist cause, because his arguments seemed ill-founded, his positions obscurantist. Having lost in denominational struggles, Fundamentalists went off to found Bible schools, publishing agencies, small and frequently re-splitting denominations and radio evangelist networks.

Canadian Protestantism saw conflicting trends also during the 1920s. For one thing, its mainstream churches, Methodist, Presbyterian, and Congregational, succeeded in merging in 1925 into a United Church of Canada, though the union came with expressions of regret that Anglicans were not part of it and that some 784 Presbyterian congregations had refused to enter the merger. Protestant Canada was responding to a unitive idea, the concept of 'a national church'. This 'national church', minus Anglicanism and some small groups, included 600,000 members in almost 5,000 formerly Methodist, almost 4,000 Presbyterian, and only 166 Congregationalist local churches. The social gospel that had arisen before the First World War days was a part of the expression of the UCC, but it was to be eclipsed in Canada for reasons similar to those that shadowed it in the United States.

Canada also had its militant fundamentalism. The Reverend T. T. Shields, a Toronto belligerent, attacked leading Baptist institutions including McMaster University, and won quite a following for his protest against Baptist activities. In Western Canada, layman William Aberhart was similarly disruptive of mainstream Protestantism and contributed to the rise of a Bible institute movement and, curiously, a radical populist economic outlook and political movement.

New Debates in the 1920s and 1930s

Meanwhile, in the United States, the non-Fundamentalists tended to avert their gaze from these reactionary trends. They had other things to face. First was the set of spiritual distractions which many felt was blighting a prosperous and materialist culture in the 1920s. Protestants put energies into trying to prevent repeal of the Prohibition amendment, but lost in 1933. In 1928 they united to oppose the first plausible Catholic presidential candidate, Alfred E. Smith, and he lost. They saw the rebirth of a radically right-wing Protestant-based Ku Klux Klan which indiscriminately promoted prejudice against Jews, blacks, and Catholics.

In the Great Depression, which began in 1929 but whose full impact was felt around 1933, during the new presidency of Franklin Delano Roosevelt, they acquired a new agenda. Roman Catholics divided loyalties between two schools of social thought. One, headed by Monsignor John J. Ryan, 'the Right Reverend New Dealer', used papal encyclicals and natural law teaching to support progressive legislation. The other, the millions of followers of radio preacher Father Francis Coughlin, were attracted for a time to a kind of Fascist and eventually anti-Semitic populism.

Meanwhile, mainstream Protestant leaders were torn between the pacifism that developed in reaction to the First World War and the vision of 'realism' that led top theologian Reinhold Niebuhr to break with pacifists and agitate for readiness to meet the demonic challenge of Adolf Hitler. During the war years most supported the military effort and the moral cause against the Axis. This convergence of enemies produced a more or less united America, whose unity summoned more than Christian energies and was often 'civilly religious' in its oneness-motifs.

Canada also had to debate the coming of the Second World War, which it entered in 1939. There, too, debates over pacifism raged, but only in Quebec was there a religious complication in respect to the war effort. There were oppositions to the military draft, but the archbishop of Quebec, Cardinal Villeneuve, came to the support of the government and spoke up in the interest of Canadian unity—a unity that would be tested after the war during movements of Quebecois or Francophonic and Catholic separatism. During the war itself, as Canadians tired of participation, the French Catholics in Quebec grew increasingly restless and strained at the unity they had earlier assented to.

Post-war Canadian Christianity for a time experienced a boom that was to mirror and match one that emerged in the United States. An influx of European immigrants meant a new mission for church people who helped resettle them. The suburban building boom in cities like Toronto and Montreal and, in the west, Edmonton or Vancouver, gave new opportunities for church expansion and Canadian families participated in these activities with vigour. Through it the United Church of Canada retained its dominance outside Quebec, but the popularity of revivalist crusades among more evangelical sects and believers was a harbinger of the arrival of a mature Canadian evangelicalism, more moderate than the fundamentalism of the T. T. Shields era. Canadian Catholicism profited, as did Protestantism, from many of the trends mentioned.

'Manyness': American Pluralism after the Second World War

In the United States after the Second World War and during the early years of the cold war there were signs that 'oneness' would have it over 'manyness'. President Dwight Eisenhower after 1952 was a figurehead leader for a 'religious revival' in an 'era of good feeling'. His 'crusade against atheistic Communism' attracted moderate Protestants as much as right-wing conservatives and historically anti-Communist Catholics. Protestants and Orthodox Americans helped form a World Council of Churches in 1948, to advance ecumenism, and hosted the WCC at Evanston, Illinois, in 1954. They translated the old Federal Council of Churches to a more encompassing National Council of Churches in 1951. Beyond Christianity, agencies like the National Conference of Christians and Jews promoted interfaith amity. Denominations set their houses in order, as various Presbyterian, Lutheran, and other historically divided bodies clarified their intentions and outlines. In 1960 a Consultation on Church Union, called for by Presbyterian Eugene Carson Blake and Episcopal Bishop James C. Pike, offered the promise of eventual merger of mainstream white Protestant and some leading black denominations. All the while much Christian leadership supported the United Nations and other secular symbols of human concord and convergence, of a diffuse 'oneness', if you will. In 1960 the election of Roman Catholic John F. Kennedy showed that Christians of non-Catholic stripe had overcome old suspicions and hostilities.

Encouraged by these signs of unity, Will Herberg wrote his famed *Protestant–Catholic–Jew* in 1955. In it he envisioned a three-faith model of 'oneness', in which in three separate large clusters most Americans supported a single American Way of Life ethos and religion. The calling of the Second Vatican Council (1962–5) by Pope John XXIII gave stimulus to Christian unity, especially in America, where there was much hunger for it. President Kennedy's appeal to idealism, as in the formation of the Peace Corps, often motivated Christians to see an emergent world-changing possibility. As black Baptist Martin Luther King and other Christian leaders came to the forefront, integration-minded Christians belatedly joined them and with still another kind of idealism promoted racial oneness on religious grounds.

Then, suddenly, 'manyness' prevailed. In the late 1960s, as the Vietnam War intensified, the cities burned in racial and sometimes nihilist protest, students dissented and often turned to violence, the convergent and coherent models were obscured. Blacks who had promoted integration now in anger promoted 'black power' and often argued for separatism. Afro-American Christians followed the pioneering example of a Detroit Protestant, the Reverend Albert Cleage, who called his church the 'Shrine of the Black Madonna' and employed anti-white imagery. Millions of Americans of Hispanic Catholic background organized Hispanic rights movements that did not blend in with the older Catholic ethnic groups. Native Americans promoted consciousness movements. So did militant women. Many of them, on Christian grounds, began to reread the biblical tradition and the kind of American story we have told here. Where, they asked, were women? Why were they not ordained? Why, since they outnumbered men, did they not receive notice when journalists or historians wrote the modern Christian chronicles?

America underwent considerable moral and political change. United States Supreme Court decisions in 1962 and 1963 proscribed school prayer. It was ever harder for public schools to serve as the educational institution which initiated the young into the generalized civil religion, one that had Christian reminiscence and accent. As more women entered the work-force and a new sexual ethos came to prevail there were challenges to the conventional family. Some Christian marriages resulted in divorce along with others. The invention of the birth control pill encouraged new casual sexual mores that countered historic Christian restraints.

Many thought that the only basis for a renewed and newly moral America would have to be found outside the channels of 'oneness', of the American civil or Christian or even Judaeo-Christian religions. 'New religions', often of occult, oriental, or revived ancient form challenged Christianity as people entertained Zen Buddhism, Nichiren Shoshu, Transcendental Meditation, Yoga, and a thousand variants. Statistically they may not have been large, but they did call into question the homogenizers of American life. Catholic dissent after Vatican II showed how authority could be called into question in the church with the most intact and enforceable unitive system. The crisis of authority in United States Catholicism was accompanied in Quebec by a decline in mass attendance and other church activity that in some ways matched European declines and some began to speak, as the Catholic leadership in France did, of ministering in a 'pagan' land.

In the midst of all these forces, most Americans were aware in the 1970s and 1980s of the reappearance of a long-submerged, often neglected Christian cohort. The Fundamentalists, who seemed to have slunk away in disgrace in 1925, had reorganized, as had their more moderate evangelical rivals, in 1942 and 1943. After the Second World War, the presence of evangelists like Billy Graham and healers like Oral Roberts showed the enduring power of conservative Protestantism. Alongside these Fundamentalists and Evangelicals were a 'Third Force', Pentecostalists. They had arisen at the turn of the century on Wesleyan soil where perfectionist-minded people had spread a movement called 'Holiness'. Blacks and whites, most of them poor and southern, claimed that the Holy Spirit spoke to them directly in unknown tongues and helped them interpret and heal. Now in the 1970s they had come out of cultural isolation and into the middle class.

Before long this triad of forces learned to use the television that Catholics and mainstream Protestants had endeavoured to put to work, but which they generally used so ineffectively. The brand of Christianity that called for and allowed for instant conversion, that put people to work evangelizing and subsidizing evangelism, and whose devotees craved entertainment denied them in merely worldly settings, learned how to project Christian symbols and to gather large audiences. These audiences were easily mobilized into critical social forces. Many of them kept the dream of 'oneness' alive by nostalgically calling for a return to the simple pre-pluralist America that remained as a myth if not an available reality.

What came to be a 'New Christian Right' organized itself to oppose abortion, to support an amendment to the United States Constitution which allowed for or even called for prayer in public schools, to legislate against pornography, to support a strong military establishment, to promote the state of Israel (for reasons connected with biblical prophecy and the Second Coming). In the candidacy of President Jimmy Carter in 1976 they were to find a leader who spoke the 'Born Again' language favoured by evangelicals, but his policies frustrated them. In Ronald Reagan in 1980 and 1984 they found a more congenial evoker of the 'oneness' theme, now often coded as 'Judaeo-Christian' but led by Fundamentalists, Pentecostalists, and Evangelicals.

At the time of the bicentennial of the United States Constitution in 1987 American Christians had a good opportunity to see what had become of the old evangelical Protestant homogenizing notions. It was clear that 'manyness', diversity, and pluralism were growing daily. Asians were a strong non-Christian presence. Private religion prospered. The Judaeo-Christian theme had popular appeal but was hard to enact. Pluralist-minded people put their energies into showing how they thought America could generate 'civil virtue' and a *consensus juris* that would support their laws and public fabric. However publics would determine their future attitudes and policies, it was clear that Christianity would remain somehow the dominant force. Millions of people who followed in the path of Jesus Christ and the tradition of the church would lead others in supporting Justice Douglas's word. Still: 'We are a religious people . . .'.

12

Latin America

FREDRICK B. PIKE

Ethnic and Sociological Background

THE manifestations of Christianity (meaning, for all practical purposes, Roman Catholicism) in late eighteenth-century Latin America are diverse and complex, almost beyond description. Not surprisingly, then, when the independence movement erupted early in the nineteenth century, Christianity proved a divisive rather than a unifying force. A few of the factors contributing to divisiveness must be sketched before turning to the crucial independence era and its immediate aftermath.

Part of Latin America's religious diversity within its one faith arose out of regional differences shaped by geography and contrasting patterns of Iberian conquest and colonial settlement. Ethnic and social determinants contributed even more to shaping the various forms of religious life that undermine the validity of all sweeping generalizations—even of the generalizations that abound in this essay.

Indian, black, and mixed-blood lower sectors, comprising more than 80 per cent of the population towards the end of the colonial period, were second-class Catholics. Although the Portuguese in Brazil tended to be more lax in this regard than Spaniards in their part of the New World, the non-white castes in general were denied ordination into the priesthood, while Indians often required special dispensation to receive the sacrament of the eucharist. For underlings in what has been termed a 'pigmentocracy', with whites at the tip of a social pyramid, and even for white women and children, religious life often seemed to issue out of priest-ridden authoritarianism.

In sharp contrast stood upper-sector male adults, comprising mainly creoles (whites of pure European extraction born in the New World and constituting some 15 per cent of the Spanish American population of about sixteen million and perhaps no more than 10 per cent of the three million or so Brazilians towards the end of the eighteenth century). These élites—whose claims to whiteness often belied extremely swarthy complexions—saw salvation largely as a private affair between them and God. However, salvation might require the services of judiciously selected 'lawyers' to plead the layman's cause with God. Generally heading the list of such pleaders was the Virgin Mary, one of whose titles was 'lawyer of sinners'. Reliance upon the powers of advocates accredited for supernatural practice led many upper-sector males to ignore the church's officially proclaimed rules of right conduct.

Besides the virgin, salvation-seekers—both the socially powerful and the humble—could call on the assistance of saints by the dozen. Upper-sector males, however, tended to acknowledge only grudgingly the need for bishops and priests to plead their cause with God. Aided by their own intercessors, by their powers of reason, and by mystical approaches of their individual selection, creole male élites appeared to believe they could attend to matters of salvation with only minimal intervention by the tonsured ranks. In this belief lay the ultimate justification for anticlericalism. Worldly considerations also nourished anticlericalism. Often creole élites found themselves seriously in debt to the clergy, the only licit practitioners of banking functions. Not surprisingly, their debt spawned resentment against the creditors.

Their personal anticlericalism notwithstanding, creole males acknowledged a useful and even essential priestly role. The priests were needed to bring salvation to Indians, blacks, and mixed-bloods, as well as to women and children of every social status. All of these, because they were assumed to lack full powers of reason, must live in spiritual dependence upon the moral instruction and grace doled out to them by those who specialized in doing God's work in a hierarchical and functionally structured society.

The clergy insisted that even as in matters of supernatural security the humble must acknowledge dependence on a specially elevated caste, so also in matters of temporal security the masses must accept dependence on groups whose power derived largely from circumstances of birth. For all their anticlericalism, then, upper-sector men found comfort in the clergy's teaching that in matters heavenly and earthly, dependence was equally essential for the masses. Also socially useful was the insistence of most clergymen that for the vast majority of God's children, heavenly joys issued out of earthly suffering and abnegation.

Tensions, then, existed between lay élites and clergy; but means of mediation arose out of the recognition by the former of the latter's spiritual and social utility. By the late eighteenth century, however, new tensions appeared, often unaccompanied by new means of mediation. What is more, these often pitted not just religious against laity, but clergymen against clergymen.

Fostered by various Spanish- and Portuguese-based societies hoping to stimulate economic and social reform, the spirit of enterprise began to filter into Latin America. Most New World clerics reacted in dismay to ideas of progress based on individual enterprise and the quest of personal profit. They equated any stimulus to economic liberalism with an assault on the church's traditional attempt to regulate the economy in line with scholasticism's social justice philosophy. Beyond this, they warned that social tranquillity depended upon maintenance of the vast paternalistic apparatus staffed and financed by the church, and upon the continuing infusion into the masses of other-worldly attitudes.

Surprisingly, an influential minority of the Latin American clergy went along with the spirit of economic liberalism. Almost to a man, however, they balked at Crown-imposed innovations that threatened ecclesiastical wealth. Such an innovation surfaced in 1804 with the consolidation issue that focused on New Spain (Mexico), Guatemala, and Nueva Granada (Colombia, Venezuela, and Ecuador). For decades and even centuries the church had collected annual interest payments of some 5 per cent on loans to owners of agricultural estates. Suddenly in 1804 the financially hard pressed Spanish Crown ordered debtor landowners to amortize their loans by paying the full amount due, not to the church, but to the Crown, which in turn would deliver annual interest payments to the church of 3 rather than 5 per cent. In rapid succession came various other royal decrees that threatened the church's financial base. While some of these decrees, including the consolidation edict, were subsequently suspended, the clergy came to regard the unpredictable Crown with a new suspiciousness which in the next twenty years developed into acceptance of the idea of independence, and in some cases into an active role in fomenting and supporting the independence struggle.

The Struggle for Independence

The Napoleonic invasion of Portugal in 1807 led rather directly to Brazilian independence. Fleeing Napoleon's armies, the Portuguese royal family found sanctuary in Brazil, where they remained until recalled to Lisbon in 1821. Returning to Portugal, King John VI left his son Pedro in Brazil. In 1822 this son proclaimed Brazil's independence and began his rule over the new domain as Emperor Pedro I. In consequence, a legitimate monarch presided over church–state relations in the early independence period that witnessed an attempt to resolve some of the conflicts that had festered for decades. In Spain, on the other hand, the Napoleonic invasion of 1808 produced no overseas flight by the royal family. As Spaniards took up massive guerrilla resistance against the French invaders, Spanish Americans began to exercise the rights of self-government pending the restoration of legitimate authority in the peninsula. With Ferdinand VII restored to the Spanish throne in 1814, many

New World colonials decided, for a complex multiplicity of reasons, to continue along the paths of self-government, thereby entering into the overt phase of their quest for independence.

The wars for independence introduced new elements of divisiveness among the Spanish American clergy. Spanish-born bishops and priests lent overwhelming support to the motherland, but many of the native-born clergy favoured independence. The number of creole pro-independence clergy swelled as anticlerical liberals gained the upper hand in the civil struggles that erupted in Spain during the decade following Ferdinand's 1814 restoration. Previously alarmed by measures such as the 1804 consolidation decrees, the clergy responded in outrage to the stridently anticlerical features of the Spanish constitution of 1812 suspended in 1814 but reapplied in 1820 after a liberal coup.

By 1824 the independence movement, overwhelmingly supported in its final stages by an understaffed, unorganized, and undisciplined creole clergy, had triumphed in Spanish America. Almost at once the clergy fell into dispute with the new civilian rulers.

In the Iberian world, church conflict with secular authority was no new phenomenon. Within the context of the traditional religio-political system, however, the Crown had always enjoyed sufficient legitimacy to effect final resolution of church–state contention. In the new setting of republicanism, churchmen refused to accept the legitimacy of civilian rulers who made decisions inimical to church interests, and they set out to establish a new type of religio-political system in which final authority in all matters involving issues of morality—the parameters of which the clergy reserved the right to define—would be exercised by the church. On the other hand, many civilian rulers in the new republics objected to any religious influence in temporal affairs; and even those rulers who accepted the clergy's temporal influence demanded the right to demarcate the social uses of religion and, in many instances, to control the internal structures of the church.

Locked at the very outset of independence into struggle with civilian rulers, Spanish American churchmen also confronted serious internal division. Some had responded to the circumstances that produced the independence movement in a purely practical manner, concerning themselves with protecting and expanding the church's political, social, and economic powers, and adducing theological—and therefore uncompromisable—arguments deriving ostensibly from revelation and from the medieval Scholastic tradition to justify their stance. The world of the future, as they envisioned it, would be very much like the world of the past, for basic human nature could not be reformed. Within the new context of independent republics, however, churchmen would enjoy enhanced importance as the guarantors of stability, as the only specialists possessing the skills to keep the depravity of human nature in check.

Perceptions of a New Age

Other clergymen looked upon independence as the dawn of a new age in which humanity would achieve previously undreamt of degrees of perfection. (Historians have not yet studied how women religious personnel regarded the situation.) Some of these veritable post-millennialists took up theories first voiced by sixteenth-century missionaries who responded ecstatically to the opportunity to Christianize (or re-Christianize) the New World's native inhabitants. According to these theories, the apostle St Thomas (associated in Mexico with the Indian deity Quetzalcoatl and in Peru with Viracocha, among other legendary pre-Inca culture-bearer deities) had appeared among the Indians not long after Christ's crucifixion, and initiated the New World's first age of Christianity. (In some theories, St Brendan replaced or supplemented St Thomas.) Subsequently, the work of Christianization had been facilitated by various apparitions of the Virgin.

Considerably embellishing sixteenth-century hypotheses, certain clergymen and even devout laymen of the independence era postulated the splendours of a flourishing native American Christian culture that had been snuffed out at the time of conquest by an Iberian variant of Christianity vitiated by greed, individualism, and materialism. With independence achieved, the moment had arrived when a new generation, building on the perfections of pre-conquest Christianity, could usher in a truly golden age. Behind the new faith in a new earth occupied by a new humanity lay not only millenarian currents of medieval Catholic thought and popular religion but also various occult and esoteric influences, some perhaps even relating to the mystical visions of the Cabala and Islamic Sufism. Expectations of miraculous deliverance from worldly suffering associated with African faiths, absorbed along with various ingredients of aboriginal mysticism and apocalypticism into Latin America's unique form of Catholicism, contributed also to the super-natural and suprarational expectations that infused early post-independence religious thought.

New World millennialists, trusting in the singularly favoured past and future of their *sui generis* brand of Christianity, might well have wondered about the need for ties with Rome, which they tended to view as the authority centre for a corrupted form of Catholicism. Even Latin American clergymen relatively unaffected by millennialist enthusiasm based on myths of pre-conquest Christianization looked forward to a new era of progress and human perfection arising out of the expansion of liberty both in the religious and secular spheres. Pre-eminent among the many Latin American clergymen who believed that liberty would propel humanity toward a utopian existence stood Peru's Francisco de Paula González Vigil (1792–1875).

Beginning his public life as the defender of political liberalism, federalism, and parliamentary supremacy, Father Vigil by the mid-1830s was already preoccupied by the authoritarianism that lay at the core of the Catholic Church. In particular, he fretted over the alleged innovations through which popes and the curia had gradually come to claim absolute power in religious matters over national political authorities and bishops, contrary—so he charged—to the initial spirit of Christianity. In 1836, after having served for a time in Peru's national congress, Vigil began to work on what became a celebrated eight-volume defence of the authority of governments and bishops against the 'pretensions' of the Roman curia. (The work was completed in 1856.) Informed by 1850 as to the contents of the ongoing work, Pope Pius IX is reported to have said: 'How is it that even in the land of St Rose [of Lima] they persecute me? Well, to the Index with this diabolical work'.

Father Vigil figured among numerous priests whose attitudes found expression in the words Willa Cather, in her celebrated novel *Death Comes for the Archbishop* (1927), attributed to New Mexico's real-life priest José Antonio Martínez in the 1850s: 'We pay a filial respect to the person of the Holy Father, but Rome has no authority here . . . The Church the . . . [Spanish] Fathers planted here was cut off; this is the second growth, and it is indigenous'.

Contributing to such attitudes of autonomy was the fact that Rome's authority over the Catholic Church in Latin America actually constituted an innovation. Since the earliest days of conquest both the Spanish and Portuguese crowns enjoyed such sweeping powers of patronage that for all practical effects the Catholic Church in the colonies lay under the control of Madrid and Lisbon, not of Rome. The vital question after independence was, could Rome—especially after having overtly supported Spain during the wars of independence—establish authority over the purportedly Roman Catholic Church in Latin America?

Ultimately, the chaos that enveloped most of Spanish—if not Portuguese—America in the decades following independence convinced the overwhelming majority of the clergy that their church had to supply a backbone for societies that had become invertebrate, and that the church itself could remain a rock of stability only by retaining a hierarchical structure based on ties to Rome, a citadel of authority, tradition, and charisma mercifully isolated from Latin American chaos.

The escape of Christianity from the control of Rome stands

as one of the great might-have-beens in the nineteenth-century history of at least several Latin American republics. Rome met the challenge, but it was a close call. Not until the 1970s, with millennialist hopes and liberation enthusiasms peaking once again, would Rome face another challenge even remotely approximating the seriousness of the 1820–50 crisis.

The Church under Siege

In Latin America, Rome had very little of a hierarchical structure to build upon as it sought to establish authority over post-independence Christianity. Most of the European-born prelates left their posts in the course of the independence struggle, generally returning to Spain. A contest ensued—and lasted for many years—between Rome and Latin America's national governments (both in Rio de Janeiro and in the capitals of the Spanish-speaking republics) over whether the Vatican or the new civil authorities had the right to appoint prelates. The result in many Spanish American republics was that, for a time at least, most bishoprics lay empty. Without bishops to ordain priests and maintain discipline, church activities ground virtually to a halt. All the while, the dwindling number of clergy acquired a steadily deteriorating reputation both for learning and personal morality. Moreover, between 1826 and the early 1830s, many Spanish American governments suppressed the religious orders, thereby compounding the church's problems.

Vulnerable and already wounded, the Catholic Church confronted national governments over a broad array of issues that included taxation policy. Despite the clergy's denunciations, new civilian powerholders abandoned colonial tradition that had called on the state to collect tithes for the church. At the same time separate church law courts, provided for by the ecclesiastical *fuero* (a charter of privileges) of colonial times, came in for attack. Moreover, the church's wealth and land holdings evoked mounting criticism not only from the laity but even, in the 1820s and 1830s, from a fair number of the clergy.

The issues of appointment to ecclesiastical office, of taxation, of clerical law courts, and of church property, had already been fought out in various parts of Europe, from the eleventh century. In Spanish America and also to some degree in Brazil, vexatious problems that Europeans had settled for themselves over the centuries appeared for the first time only after independence. In some countries, resolution of the issues came through civil wars, which intemperate churchpersons often described as holy wars.

With the powers, pretensions, and aspirations of the Catholic Church already under siege, Herman Allen, the first United States diplomatic representative in Chile, misread the situation when he reported in 1824: 'Priests [enjoy] complete Supremacy, in State as well as Church'. Allen referred also to the excessive number of 'these miserable beings', who caused their countrymen to waste, in 'ridiculous ceremonies', time that could have been used productively. In his observations, Allen reflected the prevailing attitudes of his countrymen toward the ostensibly priest-ridden countries to the south. To the ill-disguised United States animus, Latin Americans eventually responded by rallying in defence of their traditional culture and contrasting its virtues with the alleged vices of North America's Protestant and capitalist ethos.

However, in the initial decades after independence, many of Latin America's nominal and even a few devout Catholics, sometimes on their own and sometimes in league with their Protestant northern neighbours, joined in assailing virtually every aspect of the Catholic Church's temporal power. Those Latin Americans critical of Catholicism's secular influence, who harked back knowingly or not to pre-independence Enlightenment regalists, proudly called themselves liberals. At first, they tended to identify with many aspects of United States culture as they embarked on the quest for material progress and took up arms against their allegedly obscurantist and clerically dominated foes, the conservatives.

In truth, regional, family, ethnic, and social animosities often lay more at the heart of liberal–conservative rivalry and warfare than ideology. In so far as ideology mattered, anticlericalism lay at the heart of the liberals' stance. They urged that religion be confined to the private realm as society underwent secularization. Professing an avid interest in progress, they demanded elimination of the paternalistic apparatus, traditionally controlled by the church, that heretofore allegedly had stifled the spirit of self-reliance and economic freedom on which progress rested. Liberals railed also against the number of religious holidays and fiestas that wasted both time and economic resources, and they attacked the corporatist basis of colonial society that fostered a communal, rather than an individualistic, spirit among members of the various components into which society was structured. At the same time, they spoke of the need to liberate land from the dead hand of the church, ostensibly in the interest of greater productivity but actually as often as not to sate the land hunger of aspiring liberal élites. Challenging the church's monopoly over national education, liberals demanded state controlled instruction. Frequently aligned with Freemasonry, they urged religious toleration and denounced the 'theocratic state'. According to them, the theocratic state was one that accepted, even to a minimal degree, the interpenetration of religion and politics. They further defined it as one in which the state lacked control over the church, even in its internal workings.

In their ideological stance conservatives presented a mirror image of liberals, and so the particulars of their position need not be detailed. It should be noted, though, that in contrast to liberals who anathematized the theocratic state, conservatives of many Latin American republics condemned the 'atheistic state'. By their definition, this was one in which religion and politics were not mutually interfused, with the clergy enjoying the right to resolve all issues of morality, to define the scope of morality, and to set the tone of politics and secular life.

At the outset of the independence movement, many of the clergy sided with liberalism rather than conservatism, Father Vigil being by no means atypical in this respect. However, by the 1850s (and considerably earlier in Mexico and a few other republics), the clergy had rallied around the banner of conservatism. They acted out of dismay over the political chaos that they attributed to the excesses of liberalism and out of the need for an ally in Rome as they battled to escape control of church affairs by anticlericals. The *rapprochement* with Rome did not at first serve to check the advance of liberalism. Indeed, in the period between the 1850s and the 1890s the liberal position came to prevail in most of Latin America.

The wave of liberalism first crested in Mexico during the wars of 'La Reforma' in the 1850s, in consequence of which the liberals achieved the full scope of their anticlerical programme, even as they abandoned most of their stated economic and social goals. From Mexico, the liberal wave spread southward, enveloping most of Central and much of South America, although being turned back in Colombia where conservatives gained the upper hand in the 1880s. Yet precisely at the time when liberalism's blatant anticlericalism seemed almost irresistible, the Catholic Church entered upon the regeneration that would permit it not only to survive but to emerge in the twentieth century as an institution of spiritual vitality and, in some republics, of considerable temporal power.

Based largely on intellectual élitism, liberalism had turned a hostile eye towards all elements of popular religion, dismissing them as rank superstition. Given its disdain toward the animating beliefs and myths of the popular elements, liberalism was fated, despite its lip-service to liberty, to develop an authoritarian streak as it sought to uplift and reform the masses. In Pius IX, liberals confronted a populist pope who could appeal to the people over—and beneath—the heads of intellectuals and political élites. Drawing inspiration from the vision of Bernadette at Lourdes in 1858, Pius IX rallied to his cause the forces of popular religion, not only in Latin Europe but in Latin America as well. Although it was not apparent at the time, the church turned the corner in its struggle with Latin American liberalism during Pius IX's pontificate (1846–78).

In sixteenth-century Europe the Catholic Church had resisted the Reformation in part by aligning itself with popular religiosity as it authenticated miracles of the Virgin and saints and sanctioned worship at innumerable local shrines. In analogous manner, the papacy revitalized mid-nineteenth-century Latin American Catholicism by encouraging enthusiasm for the Virgin's miracles and for other popular beliefs that the liberals, in their disdain for popular culture, had dismissed as irrational. Enthusiasm, of course, could accomplish only so much, and once it had been fanned Pius IX moved to establish centralized authority over the slack structure of the Latin American church. Sending armies of foreign priests to reactivate parishes and seminaries, the pope forged a church whose leaders and flocks began, almost for the first time in some republics, to turn their eyes across the sea and mountains to Rome. While the veritable invasion of French, Spanish, and other priests helped the church re-establish an institutional structure, the chauvinism of many of the newcomers created cultural clashes, a phenomenon that reappeared in the 1950s and 1960s when a new wave of foreign priests, preponderantly from North America but also from West Germany and other parts of Europe, arrived to 'save' the church in Latin America.

The Feminine Principle in Catholicism

In basing his appeal on the Virgin rather than the dynamo, to draw on that dichotomy made famous by Henry Adams (one of America's most eminent intellectuals and a grandson of his country's sixth president), Pius IX dealt a blow in Latin America to the spirit of modernity that he had blanketly attacked in his 1864 *Syllabus of Errors*. Thereby he strengthened Catholicism's identification with forces inimical to material progress. It may be, though, that only by drawing on the Virgin's mystique could Pius have enabled Catholicism to hold its own with liberalism. At the same time, the pope may unwittingly have breathed new life into the female-centred aspects of Latin American Catholicism and even indirectly have encouraged unorthodox ideas about the Trinity. These developments require a word of explanation.

Traditionally important for salvation in Iberian Catholicism was the intercession of wives and mothers, expected—at least among males of the élite caste—to be pure, pious, and scarcely creaturely. Despite the Catholic Church's rigid patriarchalism, religion came almost to be, *de facto*, matriarchal, resting on the mediating power of saintly women—the Virgin and those on earth who sought to approximate her model—to save errant males. Moreover, many of the most widely venerated saints colonial Latin America had produced were women who, like St Rose of Lima, functioned outside cloistered life as third-order affiliates of various convents. These pious women (*beatas*) ministered both to the spiritual needs of society's humble sectors and, through charitable work, to their temporal requirements.

The cult of the female in the supernatural order contrasted sharply with the cult of manliness (*machismo*) in secular life that stressed male domination over women. The dialectical tensions between the contradictory cults explain many features both of Latin America's Catholicism and of its social mores.

However much the male dominated on earth, in matters of heaven and its attainment the female retained a certain pre-eminence. And, standing above all other women was, of course, the Virgin, the 'lawyer of sinners'. Indeed, in Latin American Catholicism the Virgin's importance was such that she came, always unofficially, to be seen as a member of a quaternity that challenged the Trinity stipulated by orthodox theology. For Latin American Christianity the consequences of the unorthodox quaternity have been so vast that the background to the phenomenon must be briefly explored.

Pre-conquest Indian religions always included the worship of goddesses. Aztecs and their forerunners, for example, had worshipped various earth-mother deities, among whom figured Tonantzín, on the site of whose temple sixteenth-century Spaniards would build the shrine to the Virgin Mary in her guise as the Lady of Guadalupe. Incas and their forerunners had worshipped earth goddesses among whom Pacha Mama was pre-eminent. Invariably, the goddesses, associated generally with fertility, had been especially revered by the lower social strata in the hierarchically structured pre-conquest cultures. Those who tilled the soil prayed and sacrificed to Tonantzín and Pacha Mama, while privileged sectors focused their worship on sky gods thought to control not only earthly functions, along with lesser female deities, but also the cosmos.

With the arrival of Spaniards and Portuguese, the powers attributed to native earth mothers were transferred not only to the Virgin but to a more-or-less androgynous Christ prefigured in the 'Jesus-as-mother' cult of the Middle Ages, about which Carolyne Walker Bynum published a justly celebrated essay in 1982. The sorrowful mother–suffering Christ archetype came to be the favoured role model of the masses, reduced to a fatalistic acceptance of earthly privation and powerlessness. Complementing the Father and the Mother–Son symbol (which is influenced by the aboriginal tendency, still alive in Latin America, to unite feminine and masculine opposites in religious thought and symbols) was the Holy Spirit. However, only in periods of popular millennialist frenzy, which surfaced about as frequently in colonial and nineteenth-century Latin America as in medieval Europe, did the Holy Spirit, as the agent of ushering in an era of heaven on earth, assume prominence in the unorthodox quaternity that influenced both popular and élite religion.

Completing the quaternity was an aggressive and assertive role model of special significance to upper-sector males: an archetypal Santiago (St James)—either Santiago himself or some similar warrior saint, such as St Michael. Medieval Spaniards had sometimes considered Santiago, who manifested his sanctity by killing Moors, more important to Christianity than Christ himself. Spanish conquerors transferred his cult to the New World, where it proved strong enough to elevate the warrior-saint type into a *de facto* presence in an unorthodox quaternity. Like the non-privileged sectors, upper social echelons found occasional use for the Holy Spirit. For the privileged, the Holy

Spirit stood for the mystical approach to salvation, the divine presence within that could bring exalted states of being.

Neither the resigned, suffering, dependent goddess– androgynous Christ who served as the role model for the masses nor the militant saint dedicated to quixotic adventurism attracted Latin American liberals. Here were models appropriate only to the pre-modern society that liberals hoped to transcend. Some nineteenth-century liberals perceived in the unique quaternity a pathology so threatening that they turned to Protestantism in quest of theological justification for robust bourgeois values.

Attitudes on Charity and Poverty

Returning now to the chronological flow of events following Pius IX's pontificate, our story resumes with the changing conditions under which conservatives and liberals waged their debate over charity. Traditionally, the iconography of St Martin of Tours had always loomed large in Latin American Catholicism. St Martin, the symbol of charity who cut his cloak with his sword and gave half the garment to a beggar, lent supernatural sanction to the church's stress on charity as the only proper solution to social problems. Liberals, and many of the late nineteenth-century positivists who assumed liberalism's mantle, rejected charity as inimical to progress and called upon all people, from the lowliest to the mightiest, to take up the virtues associated with what Max Weber (1881–1961) would christen the Protestant ethic. However, positivists tended to lose their nerve around the turn of the century. Frightened by the appearance of Anarchist and Socialist doctrines and by the labour strife spawned by the abuses of incipient capitalist modernization, positivists returned to the mainstream Iberian tradition by accepting the spirit of St Martin. Still unresolved, though, was the issue of whether church or state should dispense charity.

A sprinkling at least of liberals and positivists actually welcomed the charitable work that Catholic Action, called into being by the Vatican in an attempt to mobilize well-to-do sectors of the laity in catechizing and succouring the poor, initiated at the beginning of the twentieth century. Some even applauded the hostility to the spirit of individualistic capitalism that pervaded papal encyclicals from Leo XIII's *Rerum Novarum* (1891) to Pius XI's *Quadragesimo Anno* (1931). And a good number of them accepted the labour organizations that the church established in the years preceding and following the First World War as less of a menace than the secular labour movement whose leaders generally professed Anarchist or Socialist credos.

As the twentieth century began, Latin American intellectuals fell under the sway of European thinkers who proclaimed the mission of writers, painters, architects, and composers to lead humanity toward higher stages of consciousness and to liberate the masses from the life-limiting restraints of materialism. Jeremy Bentham, Auguste Comte, and Herbert Spencer passed out of vogue in Latin America, and the new cultural heroes came to include Ernest Renan, Henri Bergson, and a good sprinkling of gurus of esoteric cults.

Since late medieval times, one of the Iberian world's greatest obstacles to the so-called modern spirit has been an ongoing dedication to the aristocratic ethic according to which 'las letras dan nobleza'—letters, or culture, confer nobility. To *belles-lettres* as the means to confer noble status, Latin American intellectuals at the turn of the century added the full panoply of art and humanistic culture, as well as spiritualism or the esoteric arts. Many intellectuals sought progress, but they equated it with enhanced states of being. Adequate conditions of material well-being would somehow follow automatically, they assumed, in the wake of enhanced states of mind and spirit. All the while Latin America's new intellectual élites—in whose purview rights of political leadership derived from cultural attainments but never from mere economic accomplishments—assumed that political stability would result from the willingness of heretofore culturally starved masses to appreciate the non-material rewards that their artistic and cultural superiors knew how to confer— even as social stability in an earlier age had been guaranteed by priests who doled out redeeming grace. In hindsight, the vision of social tranquillity in a non-materialistic society ruled by spiritually and aesthetically sensitive élites seems ridiculous. But the vision was no more absurd than the expectations that inspired a broad cross-section of Europe's turn-of-the-century intelligentsia and ultimately helped lead not a few of them into the myth-haunted realms of Communist and Fascist movements.

Latin America's reaction against positivism and the whole bourgeois ethic derived much of its initial impetus from lapsed Catholics satisfied that humanism, perhaps with an added sprinkling of some of the esoteric or spiritualist concepts so much in vogue throughout the Western world at the turn of the twentieth century, offered adequate means for attaining moral discipline and spiritual enlightenment. Then, roughly between 1910 and 1930, with the situation differing considerably from country to country, a new pattern emerged. Increasingly the leaders of the spiritual reaction against utilitarian and mechanistic culture began to return to the Catholic Church, persuaded that defence of the higher values upon which social hierarchy depended required the theological and organizational discipline, as well as the whole myth-and-symbol apparatus, of Roman Catholicism.

Medieval Catholicism's aristocratic ethic, which in the Old and New Iberian Worlds endured well into the twentieth century, insisted that nobility derived not only from letters but also from arms: 'Las letras y las armas dan nobleza.' In turn-of-the-century Latin America not only Bergson, Neoplatonists, symbolists, and spiritualist gurus were in vogue. Also very much the man of the hour was Friedrich Nietzsche. In his disdain for 'effeminate' bourgeois values, Nietzsche helped provide intellectual justification for the ambitions of the military and to popularize a secularized version of the Santiago myth. Then, in an early twentieth-century development that Nietzsche would certainly have condemned, militarism and clericalism came together, at least in some Latin American countries, in defence of the higher, heroic virtues of the Christian knight.

While many sources of disagreement existed, among them the fact that the military paid more attention than the clergy thought justifiable to constructing a powerful industrial complex as a basis of martial strength, officers and priests generally shared a common dislike of bourgeois liberalism and the one-man, one-vote variety of democracy. Both groups dismissed liberal democracy as an inorganic contrivance that destroyed the corporative divisions natural to society. Their version of corporative social philosophy assumed that conflicts among the body politic's organic components could be mediated and harmonized only by a religio-political power whose legitimacy rested ultimately on theological-ideological purity and infallibility.

Catholicism, Politics, and Revolutionary Ferment

Encouraged by a new-found acceptance in many Latin American countries by the time of the First World War, church leaders found it possible to abide by the Vatican insistence, voiced with particular urgency by Pope Leo XIII (1878–1903), that they avoid direct affiliation with specific political groups while endeavouring to set the general tone of social and political morality. Chastened by earlier attempts to associate their interests exclusively with conservative parties, only to see those parties more often than not bested by anticlerical liberals, the Latin American clergy inclined to hedge political bets by not identifying with any one party. Except for Mexico—a unique case discussed below—the policy of avoiding direct political entanglement (a policy sometimes followed more in theory than in practice by an episcopate bound to Rome only by a very loose leash) worked moderately well, and by the 1920s and 1930s in much of Latin America the church had begun to regain some of the temporal influence swept away by the liberal-positivist successes of the preceding century. However, just as the tide appeared to be running in its favour, the church encountered a fresh adversary in Marxism-Leninism.

On the whole, those Latin American Marxists who wielded the most intellectual influence were not card-carrying Communists. Indeed, so far as the Comintern was concerned, they were outright heretics; for they seemed consistently more interested in 'superstructure' than 'base'. In ideas, and the force of the spirit, rather than in economic processes, they found—or imagined they found—the power to change the world. Inclined towards a mystical, almost spiritualist approach, they resonated to some of the ideas that emerged from the Frankfurt school, from Antonio Gramsci, and from the Russian symbolist turned Communist, Anatoli Lunacharsky. Preaching a myth not unlike that of the incarnation, they urged men—for there was little feminism in early Latin American Marxism—of superior spiritual gifts to descend among and awaken the latent spirituality of the masses, of the *Volk*, and thereby unleash the energy needed to destroy the old, materialistic order. Out of the destruction of the old would issue a new era in which humans moved toward higher stages of consciousness and spiritual development, and in which economic problems would disappear before the liberated forces of mind-energy and will.

As their new adversaries, Latin American Catholics did not confront a hard core of dedicated materialists. Instead, they faced militant idealists who traded in a secularized version of the same sort of death-and-regeneration myths that the Catholic clergy had long sought to monopolize. Marxism's most potent weapon against Christianity in Latin America was not its use of scientific economics but its ability to compose variations on themes of Christian myth and to tap some of the vitality of popular religion. In a way, Marxism-Leninism was old hat, for often in the past such myths had been taken over by purportedly prophetic lay leaders of the millenarian movements that issued periodically out of Latin America's marginalized sectors.

Erupting in 1910, the Mexican revolution had quickly taken on the characteristics of a religious movement. In it, an original element of Anarchist apocalyptism soon combined with romantic Marxian utopianism, the occultism of symbolical Masonry, and other sources of esotericism, and the expectations of miraculous deliverance that often produce millennialist paroxysms. Extolling the Indian as the symbol of all who had been most oppressed in the old order but who would soon be exalted as the world turned upside down, the revolution countered traditional religion's stress on heavenly rewards for suffering with the vision of an earthly paradise. All the while, many revolutionary leaders traded on Christian symbolism and imagery as they harped on death and regeneration and on irrigating the soil with the blood of martyrs. An exalted, organic society would issue from the divine earth, rendered freshly fecund; and humans, with a new, collective, egalitarian consciousness, indifferent to material ambitions, would comprise the new society.

Such was the mystique of the revolution. In actual practice, those who thrived best on its upheavals were simply men on the make. The visionaries became the losers. Among the latter, Emiliano Zapata was the most fascinating apostle of doomed dreams. At least as portrayed by his myth, which flowered after his assassination in 1919, Zapata was for the Mexican masses a new kind of Christ figure, patterned more along the lines of the militant Santiago than the androgynous Jesus-as-mother figure. Unwilling to settle for charity, Zapata, a genuine agrarian millennialist, demanded land and liberty for his peasant followers, and did not hesitate to attack the entire established order to obtain these objectives.

By the end of the 1930s the revolution's apocalyptic fervour had played itself out, and Mexico's leaders had begun to forge an accommodation with the old religion, although inherent tensions between the two different eschatologies still persisted half a century later. Meantime, however, in lands to the south fresh manifestations of secularized religious frenzy appeared. Populist leaders invoked new variations on the incarnation myth as they spoke of their destiny to descend into the masses, into their very minds and hearts, and to awaken their energies by holding up to them the vision of the new society that could be fashioned through the miraculous powers of faith, and through the action or praxis that faith could inspire. In the 1930s the boldest proponent of a new society resting on a new religion was Peru's Víctor Raúl Haya de la Torre. Finding his inspiration in the early Mexican revolution, in Anarchism, in social gospel Protestantism, and the Book of Revelation, in Anatoli Lunacharsky's interpretation of the Bolshevik revolution and in Romain Rolland's brand of spiritualism, in symbolic Masonry and pre-conquest Inca religious beliefs, in Heraclitus and Pythagoras and other exemplars of esoteric enlightenment, and in hazy concepts of raising consciousness to the fourth dimension purportedly deriving from Albert Einstein, Haya de la Torre proclaimed that only his religio-political movement could bring redemption to Peru.

His uncanny populist-revivalist skills in declaiming what he unabashedly termed a new religion came close to making Haya de la Torre president of his republic. In Colombia Jorge Eliécer Gaitán, until his assassination in 1948, dealt successfully in some of the new strains of unorthodox religious populism that had become *au courant* in much of Latin America; so did Juan José Arévalo who became president of Guatemala in the mid-1940s. In many ways, though, Juan Domingo Perón during his first stint as president of Argentina (1946–55) proved the most adept practitioner of a brand of political populism that found inspiration in religious mythology and also in esoteric traditions that stressed the reconciliation of opposites in harmony. Thus, in his movement's philosophy that he called *justicialismo*, Perón stressed that he would usher in a new era by blending materialism and spirituality, individualism and collectivism. With this accomplished, the Peaceable Kingdom would be at hand. Seemingly more successful than Peru's Haya de la Torre, in that he served twice as Argentina's president, Perón ultimately was done in by the sheer hucksterism that vitiated his revivalism.

Aiding Perón as he turned a religious mystique to political purposes, and thereby estranged the traditional church (he was excommunicated in 1955), was his wife, Eva Duarte de Perón. Drawing on the mythology of the Virgin, and of Mary Magdalen, to picture herself as a larger-than-life, succouring mother of the poor, 'Evita' demonstrated her purported sanctity through social work, in the tradition of a long line of notable colonial *beatas* whose passion for charity had helped earn them sainthood. Evita became the most successful of 'supermadre' types into which several ambitious Latin American politicians tried to convert their wives, or daughters. Evita also assumed the role of great mediatrix between the humble and her husband, the lord of the national domain allegedly endowed with godlike qualities.

Little wonder that as late as 1982 a prominent Peronist proclaimed, 'We're more than an ideology, we're a religion'. Little wonder, too, that in the 1970s 'Third World Priests' pursuing visions of heaven on earth hailed *justicialismo* as pointing the way toward their goal, and mourned the passing of President Perón when he died in office in 1974, ignoring the fact that he had started his country off on a precipitous road towards chaos. Little wonder, finally, that in 1986 the Vatican document 'Instruction on Christian Freedom and Liberation' contained these words: 'It would be criminal to take the energies of the popular piety and misdirect them toward a purely earthly plan of liberation'. Marxism was but one of the forces confronting the traditional church that did precisely this in twentieth-century Latin America.

Since the 1940s an increasing number of clergy and Catholic laity began to focus attention on ameliorating the social and economic adversity that the poor confronted on this earth, thereby challenging the other-worldly orientation historically associated with Iberian Catholicism. This trend acquired momentum after 1953, the year in which a Catholic-Action-sponsored survey revealed that while 90 per cent of Latin Americans had been baptized in the church, only 15 per cent practised their faith. Moreover, industrial workers and professional classes were almost completely non-practising. Shocked to discover that theirs was in some respects a minority church, the Catholic clergy intensified efforts aimed at winning the working classes. Perhaps some of the clergy overlooked the degree to which the vast majority of Latin Americans remained Catholic in their own way, if not in the way prescribed by Rome. Even while living in concubinage and contributing to high national percentages of illegitimate births, they periodically performed private devotions of their own choice that, in their own estimation at least, re-linked them to the church. In this way the masses had assimilated the religious style once claimed as a prerequisite of upper-class status.

Catholicism's social reformist stance contributed to the emergence of a strong Christian Democratic movement in the 1950s and 1960s. Initially under the influence of French philosopher Jacques Maritain and far less free-market oriented than their namesake parties in Europe, Latin America's Christian Democrats criticized individualistic capitalism as inevitably leading to economic injustice. While avoiding any formal connection with the church's hierarchy, Christian Democrats urged implementation of programmes inspired by the Vatican's social encyclicals. In their view social justice demanded state intervention in the social and economic spheres; it demanded also a communitarian society based on principles of distributive justice and organized organically or corporatively into various functional associations, each enjoying some degree of popular participation and self-direction. Christian Democrats, however, carefully avoided the Fascist model of authoritarian corporatism that had appealed to a fair number of Catholic lay leaders and clergy during the 1920s and 1930s.

Actually, many critics of Catholic corporatism had assumed incorrectly that any form of corporatism had ties to Fascism. Fascism's defeat and well-merited disgrace in the aftermath of the Second World War brought, in a specious guilt-by-association line of reasoning, repudiation of innovative corporatist thought in Catholic circles that could conceivably have fostered viable alternatives to liberal capitalism. Catholic corporatism, surviving only as one anaemic component of Christian Democracy because of its alleged Fascist connection, is another of the great might-have-beens in the history of Latin American Christianity.

Origins and Development of Liberation Theology

By the 1960s many Catholic thinkers found the gradual reformism and harmonization of class interests generally favoured by Christian Democracy entirely too tame an approach to Latin American ills. Resembling in many ways certain sixteenth-century missionary millennialists who extolled Indians in the newly discovered lands as the only humans uncontaminated by the greed, materialism, and corruption of a decadent age, certain radical Catholic reformers in Latin America praised the region's poor as uniquely undefiled by the vices of bourgeois capitalism. In this, they echoed the tenets of the 'social gospel' movement in turn-of-the-twentieth-century Britain and North America. At the same time, they brought a new intensity to Iberian Catholicism's traditional distrust of capitalism.

According to many among the new breed of Catholic thinkers, lay and clerical, social and economic problems sprang not from inevitable human flaws or from deficiencies of economic resources. Nature, whether of humans or of the physical environment, was not at fault. Instead, problems arose out of the structural inequities of prevailing systems of international capitalism. In Latin America and the so-called Third World in general, economic underdevelopment and social inequities stemmed above all from dependence on the predatory capitalist structure of the developed world. However incomplete and biased its diagnoses, dependency analysis represented an understandable reaction to the one-sided viewpoint prevalent in the developed world that attributed all third-world problems to internal short-comings that included lack of character, inherent economic myopia and political corruption, and even racial inferiority.

Expounded particularly by Marxian-influenced intellectuals, dependency analysis basked in cult status during the 1960s and 1970s, enshrined as official dogma by an international counter-culture whose disciples took over strategic teaching posts in many of the world's leading universities. To these universities came a new generation of Latin American clergy, ready to study not only theology but economics, sociology, and political science, these last three being the disciplines most influenced by dependency theory. Many of the clergy wedded theology to these three disciplines as they attached the seal of divinely sanctioned approval to dependency analysis.

Strictly out of the Latin American experience of recent years came another source of inspiration for an emerging radicalized clergy. Many priests, brothers, and sisters had witnessed at first hand the success of populist politicians in eliciting frenzied mass support through religiously inspired mythology, symbolism, and pageantry. There was no reason why these populists, whose opportunism in the manipulation of religious imagery was often patent, should remain unchallenged in energizing the masses. Nor was there any reason why Fidel Castro and Ernesto 'Che' Guevara, who unleashed in Cuba a new wave of populist millennialism as the 1960s began, should be allowed to monopolize the use of mythological archetypes that sprang certainly as much from Christianity as from Marxism-Leninism. Instead, the clergy would mobilize the masses in consciousness-raising crusades promising rich moral rewards and the ultimate transformation of social and economic structures. Thereby they would banish alienation and restore human warmth, community, and economic security. At the same time the clergy might reacquire some of the temporal powers surrendered in the past century to liberal secularizers.

Latin America, it has been said, can be understood only by those aware of the intellectual baggage bequeathed by Dante, St Thomas Aquinas, and Machiavelli. To this trio it may be necessary to add Plotinus. Only by taking into account the abiding presence of ideas that at least behave as if they derived from the Neoplatonism that Plotinus helped father in the third century AD can one account for the Latin American propensity to assume that will, consciousness, and mind-energy can always triumph over matter—or the illusion of matter. Somewhere along the way, Amerindian cosmology and magic may have lent Plotinus a helping hand in Latin America, together with Old World mysticism and magic of diverse origins; but one cannot know for certain about such murky matters.

Out of Latin America in that singularly optimistic decade of the 1960s came a new theology, soon designated theology of liberation. In it are elements of mystical Marxism, dependency analysis, an apocalyptic world-view extending back to pre-Columbian times, and the utopianism, often verging on post-millennialism, of twentieth-century populist movements steeped in religious mythology. Present, in addition, is a residue of Henri Bergson's concepts of creative evolution and the *élan vital* (postulating the predominance of the spiritual or mental over material determinants) that enjoyed tremendous vogue in early twentieth-century Latin America. Liberation theology may also be seen as the product of one of those cyclical eras of religious enthusiasm when Latin Americans accept the Holy Spirit's pre-eminent place in the Trinity (or quaternity) as an agent for inspiring the perfect society on earth. Undergirding all these aspects, though, is a strain of Neoplatonism which renders liberation theology ahistorical. Ultimately, this theology rests on the faith that history can be transcended through the creation of a new human, called into existence by consciousness raised to a higher power. Through higher consciousness the new human can overcome the imperfections of material life that have in turn sprung from the false consciousness of previous generations.

At its peak at the outset of the 1980s, liberation theology, buttressed by a wide-ranging endeavour of churchmen and women to initiate social reform and possibly even revolution, helped trigger a new kind of religious war in Latin America. On one hand stood purported defenders of traditional religion.

They saw the sorrowful mother–man of sorrows as the only suitable icon for the lower classes, reserved to upper sectors the role model of militant saints, and called upon St Martin's imagery in urging charity as the means to social tranquillity. Countering those who traded on the symbols of religious traditionalism, new cadres of militants downgraded role models of suffering, dispensed with saints of charity, and transformed Christ into a warrior bent upon annihilating the established social order. Beneficiaries and defenders of that order found in religious traditionalism alleged justification for their actions as they moved to terrorize radical priests and nuns into quiescence, in the process killing hundreds of them. In March 1980, El Salvador's Archbishop Oscar A. Romero, a militant and somewhat naïve spokesman of the poor, was assassinated as he celebrated mass. This was the most striking incident in the struggle to define the proper uses of religion.

Catholicism, Human Rights, and Sexuality

Despite the Vatican's growing distrust in the 1970s of revolutionary theology and actions, the vicious attacks on religious personnel prodded Rome into increasingly outspoken condemnation of the methods by which authoritarian regimes defended the status quo. Thereby Rome repudiated the ties between authoritarian militarism and clericalism. Increasingly, the Vatican backed its bishops as they defended their clergy. This pattern began in the 1960s as Brazilian prelates not only defended their radicalized clergy but often launched their own denunciations of military autocrats. From Brazil the pattern spread to Argentina, Chile, and Uruguay in the 1970s.

Meantime, a revolution from above had begun within the Catholic Church, and in ways not always anticipated it interacted with the far less cautious revolution initiated by Latin America's radicalized clergy. One of the main features of the 'new opening' proclaimed by Pope John XXIII as he summoned the Second Vatican Council (1962–5) was concern for universal human rights. Subsequent popes were cautious towards new openings, but they were given little alternative to supporting civil rights when events in Latin America acquired a momentum of their own. However much the post-John XXIII Vatican may have disliked a radicalized clergy, it disliked even more persecution of the clergy by civilian governments and paragovernmental organizations. Continually forced into defending a revolutionary clergy's human rights, the Vatican had little choice but to assert the human rights of revolutionary lay persons as well.

In the past, citizenship in the eyes of Latin American prelates and theologians, generally reflecting but sometimes going beyond Vatican teachings, had depended upon churchmanship; and all of those persons out of line with church teachings had been considered beyond the pale and not fully entitled to civil safeguards. Only in the 1960s did the old inquisitorial spirit of reserving basic rights of humanity to those in the good graces of the clergy give way to a comprehensive concern with the rights of all persons, not in the light of their Catholic orthodoxy but of their humanity. A century prior to this, the clergy had been dubious about the human rights of liberals; but now many of them began to assert the rights of Marxist-Leninists, Jews, and other erstwhile pariahs. This momentous change, still bitterly resisted by certain traditionalists, came about partly because the clergy themselves had begun to act in a manner that branded them as unorthodox by old standards.

More fundamentally, the change represented the church's response, originating in Europe and the United States, to the world-wide trend towards individualism. In line with this trend, persons are valued because of their individual humanity rather than because of the organizations and institutions, sacred or secular, to which they belong. Tension between the private and organizational or collective basis of evaluation remains unresolved; and the very presence of tension suggests that a veritable sea change may well be in the making.

At the same time as it championed human rights the Catholic

Church in the 1980s manifested a chilling authoritarianism, especially on issues falling under the broad umbrella of sexuality. How Latin Americans, accustomed—at least in the case of males—to a wide degree of religious voluntarism, respond remains to be seen. In view of Latin America's estimated 40 million abandoned children (in a total population of some 390 millions in the mid-1980s, up from approximately 61 million in 1900), and population increases that swamp gains in economic productivity and doom ever increasing numbers to unemployment or under-employment, the faithful are coming to ignore the church's opposition to all methods of birth control except the so-called natural or rhythm method. In this respect, Latin American women have begun to exercise the voluntarism heretofore confined largely to males on issues involving sexuality. Furthermore, in view of the worsening shortage of priests (the 1960 average of one priest to every 5,500 Catholics is projected to become one to 6,680 by the year 2000), issues such as clerical celibacy have provoked debate and could even stoke the fires of schism. And, should Rome ever seriously consider the ordination of women to the priesthood, Latin American males, culturally indoctrinated in the values of *machismo*, might respond in horror. No one can be certain, though. To the ordination of women Latin American males could conceivably respond with a shrug of the shoulders, accustomed as they have been to regarding religion as a woman's affair.

Base Communities

To keep the faith alive and vital in an age of chronic scarcity of priests (likely to worsen despite an unexpected upsurge in vocations in many Latin American countries during the late 1980s), some bishops and clergy began in the post-Vatican II era to encourage formation of ecclesial base communities (CEBs)— small groups of Catholics, numbering from ten to twenty, who gather once a week or so for religious services (such as Bible reading) and discussion of religious and social matters. Combining do-it-yourself pastoralism with social consciousness-raising, the CEBs are supervised through occasional visits by priests, but remain most of the time under the care of lay assistants. By the early 1980s, some estimates placed the number of Latin Americans participating in CEBs at close to three million, with about two-thirds of them in Brazil.

Despite accounts of some enthusiasts who equate them with genuine ecclesial democracy, the CEBs are usually the products and agents of clerical authority (except in post-1979 Nicaragua under Sandinista rule, where the base communities contributed to the emergence of a partially schismatic 'Church of the People'). What is more, the effectiveness of episcopal power, not only in regard to CEBs but to the entire gamut of church activities, has been on a steady upswing since the 1955 formation of the Conference of Latin American Bishops (CELAM). Since the 1950s, moreover, Rome has established more efficient control mechanisms for co-ordinating the activities of the Latin American episcopate.

Especially effective in strengthening papal power lines since 1979 have been the shrewdly conceived and meticulously planned Latin American visits of Pope John Paul II, in the course of which he has expanded on Pius IX's populist legacy by exercising at first hand his personal magnetism over the masses. Unlike John XXIII who only twenty years earlier had exercised his charisma from Rome in the cause of renewal, which always implies a certain reversion to chaos, John Paul II has applied his charisma, sometimes on the spot, in the cause of restoration of order.

Tightened hierarchical authority as well as populist mobilization of the masses, effected in part through CEBs that permit some semblance of religious participation while providing new nests of community, have prepared the Catholic Church to meet new threats both from within and from without. Since the Second World War Catholicism's great external nemesis, Protestantism, has begun seriously to assert itself; and many new initiatives that the Catholic Church has undertaken in

Latin America must be seen as a response to the Protestant challenge.

Protestantism

Protestant churches, often encouraged by liberal rulers (including Brazil's Emperor Pedro II, Venezuela's Antonio Guzmán Blanco, and Guatemala's Justo Rufino Barrios) began to appear with some frequency in the second half of the nineteenth century. For many decades, though, Protestantism made little impact on the overall religious landscape. A century later the situation had changed dramatically, and since the 1960s the most significant development in Latin American Christianity has been the rise of Protestant influence. Ultimately, Catholicism and Protestantism may function together in relative harmony; and harmony on the sacred level could conceivably filter down to the political terrain and moderate the holy-war characteristics of party struggles that have stifled the spirit of secular compromise. This, at least, is the optimistic scenario for the future of Latin America's interacting religion and politics. Less far-fetched, perhaps, are pessimistic scenarios, ranging all the way to a worst-case one in which religious rivalry feeds secular violence on a scale approximating that of Ireland and the Middle East.

Latin Americans in the 1960s witnessed a considerable splintering of Protestant churches established decades earlier by, among others, Lutheran, Presbyterian, Methodist, Baptist, Moravian, Christian Science, and Brethren of Christ missionaries. Many of the proliferating splinter groups set up evangelical churches. At the same time a wave of new missionaries, especially from the United States, led by Seventh Day Adventists, Mormons, and a broad assortment of evangelicals, won masses of converts, often from the rural and urban poor, especially in Chile, Brazil, and Guatemala. Rejecting the structuralist approach of some of Catholicism's most zealous social-reform advocates, the new wave of Protestant missionaries stressed personal reform based on the individual's eradication of sinfulness.

Fundamentalists and evangelicals, with their stern views on personal morality (contrasting with the relaxed approach to individual virtue that has characterized Iberian Catholicism), with their welcoming of public declarations of faith in moments of born-again enthusiasm, and with their sing-along choruses, satisfied certain spiritual needs long undernourished in Latin America. The Vatican 'Instruction' issued in 1986 surmised that Protestant fundamentalist groups prospered in Latin America because they provided 'human warmth, care and support in small close-knit communities' in addition to 'a style of prayer and preaching close to the cultural traits and aspirations of the people'. Whatever the reasons, Latin Americans who since the mid-twentieth century have turned to Protestantism seem to prefer those forms of it that are furthest removed from traditional Catholicism.

Between 1960 and 1985, the number of Puerto Rican Protestants increased from approximately 20 to some 30 per cent of the island's population. Perhaps this was to be expected, given the overweening influence of the United States in its dependency. However, similar Protestant gains appeared elsewhere in the Caribbean, and extended, on a reduced scale, into Brazil and all the way down to the southern cone countries. By the mid-1980s, with about one of every five citizens of El Salvador a Protestant, the evangelical movement had won influence and respectability not only among the country's poor, but among the military officers, businessmen, and university students, many of whom believed their new faiths provided firmer bastions of anti-Communism than Catholicism with its numerous leftist-leaning clergy. Also by the mid-1980s, various Protestant denominations and Mormons claimed over 20 per cent of the Guatemalan populace, while fundamentalist groups reported an annual growth rate of some 15 per cent. In the early 1980s a Guatemalan president who belonged to a Protestant sect called 'The Word' proclaimed that only a purer form of Christianity than Catholicism could resolve society's problems through emphasis on individual probity.

The Protestant expansion into Latin America has benefited from huge infusions of capital from United States churches, many of whose members are convinced that only fundamentalism can stem the Communist tide and introduce the type of ethics necessary for economic development and for evolution toward democracy. In many of its guises, the Protestant crusade challenges Iberian Catholicism's traditional rejection of the values of individualistic capitalism; it extols the self-control and sublimation thought to underlie entrepreneurial success as well as political stability; and it denounces the initiative-inhibiting influences of paternalism and of economic interventionism by the state. Tired of being regarded as pariahs within Catholicism's value system, with its newly stressed preferential option for the poor, many a successful Latin American entrepreneur has turned to faiths that hail the dedicated businessman as a social hero whose temporal triumphs result from his religious convictions. Undoubtedly this factor has contributed to the remarkable upsurge of Protestant conversions in Mexico during the 1980s. Also involved is the fact that Mexico's one-party system, gradually shedding the virulent anticlericalism that characterized official policy for two generations after the 1910 revolution, has entered in recent years into peaceful collaboration with the Catholic Church. With church and state lumped together in a system that has incurred increasing resentment and that seems impotent in the face of a worsening social and economic crisis, many Mexicans manifest their dissatisfaction with the status quo by converting to Protestantism.

All in all, the Protestant incursion threatens not just Latin America's old religion but all of the social and economic structures rooted in the values of that religion. Indeed, the Marxist-Leninist panacea that appeared after the First World War may actually have posed less of a challenge to the old order than the panacea that some Latin Americans first began to perceive in Protestantism not long after the Second World War.

Opus Dei

In a way, Protestantism's spread in contemporary Latin America represents a new development in the cultural clash between Roman Catholic traditionalism and United States religious, economic, and social values that has been under way for a century and a half—a clash revealed already in the 1824 remarks of Herman Allen quoted earlier in this essay. Except in the Opus Dei approach, originating in Spain in 1928 but acquiring real impact only after the Second World War, Catholicism in the Iberian world has generally used religion as a justification for poverty rather than as a spur for economic advance. Its rich iconography has been bereft of elements that could be used to extol and sanctify the businessman. Here is one reason why many nineteenth-century Latin Americans drawn to the business life grew indifferent if not hostile to the traditional faith and enrolled in local liberal parties and Masonic lodges. With the surge of Protestantism in the late twentieth century Latin Americans have another alternative. In years to come, however, the Protestant alternative could face a mounting challenge from the Opus Dei, with its attempt to replace the Christian knight role model with that of the godly businessman who subordinates individualistic acquisitiveness to the service of a higher social and religious calling. Clearly Pope John Paul II regards the future role of Opus Dei with high hopes. Indeed, he has made Opus Dei a personal prelature.

Both Opus Dei and many of its Protestant rivals turn their principal attention toward the upper social strata. Among the struggling masses, however, certain Protestant denominations have won impressive numbers of converts. Unpersuaded by activist priests who promise heaven on earth, society's underlings have begun to turn to those Protestant denominations that stress glorification in the next world. Just as within the old faith so also within the new, two sets of role models can be found: one for those hopeful about the here and now, another for those who have given up hope in it. Opus Dei is Catholicism's new stimulus to the hopeful.

Religious Pluralism

Throughout the nineteenth century and well into the twentieth, many Catholic leaders and thinkers believed their church was the one institution with enough broadly recognized charisma (grace, sanctity, divine approbation) to mediate among the various political, economic, and ideological factions that battled each other in civil society. At first the clergy hoped to exercise their influence over society from within governments that welcomed the penetration of politics by religion. Then, as anticlerical liberalism swept to victory in much of Latin America, the clergy aspired to an all-pervasive moral authority to be wielded from outside the political structure.

Even when Latin America had only one major Christian religion, the Catholic Church's ambition to exercise a society-wide mediating power lacked a sense of reality, given the degree to which church leaders, both on the spot and across the sea, differed among themselves on fundamental issues of social and even moral philosophy. With the appearance of religious pluralism, the claims of the Roman Catholic clergy to a prophetic, mediating role in society have lost all possibility of realization; for Latin American Christians no longer recognize only one church as the font of charisma.

Secularization and Resacralization

Early in the nineteenth century, Latin American liberals set out to desacralize the public arena. Toward the end of the century, buttressed by cadres of positivists, they seemed within reach of their objective. Since then, the mass-based political parties that drew on religious imagery, the unabated strength of popular religions, the lingering influence of pre-Columbian and African religions, the mystical side of Marxism, and the revitalization of Catholicism have contributed to the resacralization of society. Most recently, Protestantism has lent new momentum to resacralization.

There is another side to the story. Secularization in the twentieth century has chalked up its share of triumphs. For millions of Latin Americans the most cherished shrine, where they perform the rituals most meaningful to them, has become the shopping mall. And the only soil that thousands revere as somehow linked to what is transcendent lies beneath the foreign banks where they have deposited their gains. Religious wars, moreover, have given way to struggles for control of the narcotics trade. The new generation of narcotics tycoons growing rich over the decline of United States society seems to have even less interest in Christian teachings than did the nineteenth-century Latin American tycoons who provided some of the raw materials facilitating the rise of that society. All the while, below the level of triumphant secularism the majority of Latin Americans remain on the edge of economic catastrophe, enduring the circumstances that in the past have encouraged fatalistic other-worldliness punctuated by periodic outbursts of millennialism.

It is hazardous to predict the future pattern of interaction between the two Latin Americas, the one inhabited by some of the most unprincipled pursuers of mammon in all the annals of uninhibited greed, the other by superfluous masses reduced to the problematic pursuit of survival—for already Latin America has more people than can possibly be absorbed by its agencies of socialization and its economic structures, and at 1985 rates of increase the population will double in thirty years. It requires little prescience to discern that Christianity will both influence and be influenced by the ways in which the two Latin Americas interact. Finally, if historical precedent can be counted on for guidance, it may be safe to predict that Christianity will help to mitigate while at the same time remaining a part of the social problem that torments Latin America.

13

Africa

PETER HINCHLIFF

UNTIL after the Second World War histories of Africa had a tendency to treat the continent as though it were simply a setting for the actions of white men (and a few white women). This was because they were written, for the most part by people of European stock who had been taught that history should be based on parliamentary reports, Civil Service minutes, and the private correspondence of those who possessed power and influence. The policies of European or colonial governments, which could be researched in archives, were what had made history. Influential persons had been Europeans. And this created the impression that Africa had no history of its own. History had come from outside and if some of it happened in Africa that was almost coincidental.

Modern historians have attempted to correct this attitude by using African as well as European sources, oral tradition as well as documents. They treat white exploration, commerce, and colonialism as an episode in a much longer history. We now know a good deal about the rise and fall of African kingdoms. There was, for instance, a great empire of Ghana, centre of an elaborate trading network, as early as the tenth century. On the other side of the continent Christian Nubian kingdoms, with a written language preserved in brick-built monasteries, survived until the fifteenth century. By that time walled Hausa 'cities', with a flourishing Islamic civilization, had begun to appear in West Africa. Further to the south nomadic herders of cattle gradually spread outwards from the Congo, settling and merging with earlier inhabitants.

It follows that there could be no 'typical' African society. Even where sheer distance prevented contact with the literate cultures of Islam and Christianity, there were indigenous civilizations like that whose people built the stone structures of Zimbabwe in the fifteenth century and whose successors survived until the nineteenth. The growth and decline of such societies, moreover, implies shifts of power and, often, the actual geographical movement of peoples. The last of the Zimbabwean states was destroyed by Ngoni invaders from the south, who were themselves driven by the explosive effects of Shaka's creation of the Zulu kingdom (*c.*1820). This welding into a military empire of half a hundred semi-independent clans, based on the hutted village or homestead called a 'kraal', was well known in Europe. Its effects had been noted and recorded by missionaries and others. But most of the story of Africa was simply unappreciated by the outside world. There was a tendency to assume that what Europeans found when they arrived was what had always been there.

The resentment bred by a colonial understanding of history has affected the modern determination to correct earlier distortions. Inevitably it has produced distortions of its own. One may, for instance, be told that the colonial administration in Algeria strenuously attempted to replace the 'indigenous' Arabic with its own 'foreign' language. And strictly, of course, Arabic is no more indigenous to Africa than French. In spite of such blemishes, however, the new approach is preferable to the older alternative, which was as absurd as a history of Britain that treated the Roman occupation as the only episode of any importance.

It remains true, however, that much of what happened in Africa in the nineteenth and early twentieth centuries was due to the intervention of Europeans in particular. And missions, along with colonialism, trade, and exploration, were one of the principal factors in the European penetration of Africa.

Inevitably, therefore, part of the history of Christianity in Africa since 1800 is an account of the white missionaries who imported their religion: only part of it is an account of Christianity among African people themselves. Any fairly detailed chronology of events in African history for the period up to 1900 will contain a large number of 'missionary' items, even if the chronicle is primarily a secular one. After that date such events will be far less prominent.

The reason why Christianity was inevitably an aspect of European penetration hardly needs to be explained. The nineteenth century was the great period of commercial and colonial expansion from Europe. Europe was also a centre of contemporary missionary enterprise. There was a widespread conviction that Christians had an almost crushing responsibility for the inhabitants of the non-Christian world. When the evangelical Henry Martyn, on his way to India, chanced to be present at the British capture of the Cape in 1806, he wrote in his diary: 'I prayed that . . . England whilst she sent the thunder of her arms to distant regions of the globe, might not remain proud and ungodly at home; but might show herself great indeed, by sending forth the ministers of her church to diffuse the gospel of peace.' This was not mere pious sentiment. Martyn, who had spent the day ministering to the dying, had been deeply distressed by his first experience of battle and by the arrogance of the British troops. He, like other missionaries, believed that Britain's vocation was not to conquer but to convert. No one can read the letters of such men without becoming aware of their courage, their selflessness, and their religious devotion. Unattractive, foolish, and immoral missionaries were exceptions in what was, by and large, an impressive body. But missionaries were human, with human failings, and their motives were not pure and unmixed. There was, for instance, a strong—but fairly harmless—sense of romantic adventure about the enterprise. When the founders of the London Missionary Society announced the list of places to which they intended to send agents the exotic music of the names seems more important than any strategic consideration—'Tahiti, Africa, Tartary, Astrachan, Surat, Calabar, Bengal, Coromandel and Sumatra'.

More serious, however, was the unconscious arrogance that some missionaries displayed. The very existence of their enterprise depended on the conviction that they possessed something better than that which already existed in the areas to which they went. The consequent temptation to arrogance all too easily spilled over into a belief that all things European were better than anything African, that any white man, however unimportant and uneducated, was better than the most powerful African ruler. Hence, for instance, the eagerness of missionaries to 'convert' the ancient Christian kingdom of Ethiopia. Coptic Christianity no doubt seemed barbaric and superstitious, but it was unquestionably arrogant to treat Ethiopia as a 'heathen land'.

For Christianity was not new to the continent of Africa. Cyprian's Carthage and Augustine's Hippo had left no heirs but there were ancient churches in Egypt as well as in Abyssinia and when European explorers first tried to circumnavigate the Cape of Good Hope the Christian Nubian kingdoms still existed to the north. In 1862 the Emperor Theodore of Ethiopia wrote to Queen Victoria proposing an alliance of Christian sovereigns against the threat of Islam. For Ethiopia this was as serious as the Turkish menace had been to the Christians of sixteenth-century Europe. But European attitudes to Ethiopian religion had already been clearly demonstrated. Within the previous twenty-five years the Church Missionary Society had maintained a German (J. L. Krapf) there and the Vatican had created the vicariate of Abyssinia. Theodore himself was not, indeed, the most balanced of rulers. Clerks in the British Foreign Office were probably amused by the presumption of this uncivilized chieftain. There were other issues in international politics which the British government thought more pressing. But the whole story, culminating in the invasion of Abyssinia by a British army, is somehow characteristic of Europe's inability to take Africa, and African Christianity, seriously.

In part this was due to an unavoidable ignorance. It was hardly possible for missionaries to know anything about the places to which they were being sent. Often no other European had been there before them. There was no one to teach them the language and customs of the people. In the early part of the century maps of Africa were mostly guesses interspersed with empty spaces. It is not surprising, then, that about 1830 a Wesleyan missionary at the Cape should discover that his society did not really know where one of its stations was. Part of the importance of David Livingstone in missionary history is that he possessed the scientific knowledge and the equipment to chart his discoveries fairly accurately. Yet when Livingstone himself was engaged, in the early 1860s, in establishing the Universities' Mission to Central Africa he failed to grasp the fact that the whole of the region was in a state of flux. The slave-trade, which had only recently penetrated the area, had created uncertainty and panic. There was a fierce local power struggle. Livingstone and the missionaries, though reluctantly prepared to use arms to free the slaves, may actually have chosen to support the side that had done most slaving.

This ignorance extended into matters of religion also. Since early missionaries could not know the language, they had to depend on interpreters whose own linguistic competence might be small and who might lack any knowledge of Christianity. What kind of gospel the missionaries were heard to preach can only be guessed at. And their own incomprehension must have been just as great. Robert Moffat, the great pioneer missionary with whom Livingstone served his apprenticeship and whose daughter he married, was able to say that none of the people among whom he had worked for twenty years, had any religion of their own.

Such ignorance was relative, of course. The missionaries were less ignorant than most Europeans. They laid the ground-work for anthropological, geographical, and linguistic studies. Missionary societies were often better informed about conditions and events in Africa than the Colonial Office in Whitehall. Dr

John Philip of the London Missionary Society, struggling in the 1820s and 1830s for the rights of the aboriginal inhabitants of southern Africa, was again and again proved to be more accurate in his information than other Europeans, official or unofficial.

Christianity was not, therefore, the worst aspect of the European irruption into African history but it has attracted a great deal of unfavourable attention—perhaps because of a feeling that missionaries should have behaved better than anyone else. It was fashionable among historians in the 1960s and 1970s to treat missionaries as the principal agents of colonialism and Christianity is still often labelled as the religion of the white imperialists in a way in which Islam is never thought of as the religion of the most active slave-traders.

For this there are many reasons, not least the fact that Christianity so often appeared to be *officially* linked with the spread of European domination in a way in which Islam was never identifiably a part of the trade in slaves. It is true, of course, that many generalizations about the part played by missionaries in the colonization of Africa are simplistic. 'The missionaries' were not a homogeneous body. Their attitudes to colonialism varied enormously. Their reasons for supporting it, when they did, were equally varied. They confronted a genuine dilemma. European penetration of Africa could not be prevented. It often seemed, and was sometimes objectively the case, that the intervention of a European power was to be preferred to uncontrolled private enterprise or to what already existed in Africa. And one European power could seem preferable to another, not simply for nationalistic reasons.

Missionary involvement in secular European rivalry in Africa stretches back behind the high imperialism of the late nineteenth century, through the era when free trade was the orthodox doctrine, into the mercantilist period. As early as 1764 British trading interests in Senegal and the Gambia told the Society for the Propagation of the Gospel that the appointment of a French-speaking Protestant clergyman in West Africa 'would be the best step which could be taken to Secure our Possession of the Place which we look upon as in a very Dangerous situation upon any future Rupture with the French'. Similar sentiments, *mutatis mutandis*, would have been characteristic of the French themselves, whose church and state were allied in a belief that they possessed a civilizing mission to the savage world.

But the motive was not always nationalistic. When Krapf left Ethiopia in the 1840s he became a missionary in East Africa. In principle deeply opposed to European intervention and, as a German, having little chauvinistic reason to support British colonialism, he came to do so because he feared the spread of Islam and the imperial ambitions of Roman Catholic France.

A generation later, in the late 1870s, the clash of interests foreseen by Krapf came to a head in the kingdom of Buganda (now part of Uganda). The Church Missionary Society was the first Christian body to reach the country but a few years later there also appeared on the scene the 'White Fathers' (Pères Blancs) founded by Archbishop Lavigerie in Algiers in 1868. This was a community of secular priests and laymen solemnly bound to lifelong missionary work in Africa but not, in the strict sense, a monastic order. If the CMS missionaries conceived of themselves as bringing the truth of English evangelical religion, the White Fathers were equally convinced that to be civilized was to be French and Catholic. That tradition had persisted in spite of the secularization of French society and government. Neither party understood the complex rivalry of Bugandan politics. Islam was also making headway in the country and events to the north, where the English Protestant General Gordon was embroiled in an even more complex political and religious struggle, exacerbated the internal Bugandan situation.

The various Bugandan parties allied themselves with the different in-coming religions, Islam as well as rival kinds of Christianity. Successive kabakas (rulers), like any medieval European monarch, had to thread their way through a complicated dance, playing magnate off against magnate, allying themselves now with the CMS, now with the White Fathers, sometimes choosing Islam so as to avoid either Christian party. In the process they earned—and often deserved—a reputation for cruel duplicity. Martyrdoms, coups, and civil war followed. By 1889 it looked as though the Catholics were in control but in the following year Captain Lugard of the British East Africa Company (a chartered corporation founded by Glasgow businessmen interested in commercial profit, missions, and the destruction of the slave-trade) intervened in Bugandan affairs. The effect of this campaign by the armed forces of a British commercial institution was to leave the Protestant (and pro-British) faction in control by the beginning of 1892. It is significant that the Vatican itself decided that the Roman Catholic mission in Buganda could only be continued if the French connection was severed. It was therefore taken over by the Mill Hill Fathers (mission priests trained at St Joseph's College, Mill Hill, in London). Herbert Vaughan, the founder of the college had recently become archbishop of Westminster and his 'English' Roman Catholic missionaries were able to work in Buganda where the White Fathers would no longer have been acceptable. The centralizing authority of the Vatican, sometimes thought to be a handicap to Roman Catholic missionaries, could thus on occasion be a considerable advantage. No other Christian body would have had that ability to exchange a politically acceptable for a politically unacceptable group of missionaries.

Even so radical a champion of the people of Africa as John Philip had been willing to support European rule on the ground that it might prevent something worse. When, in 1834 and 1835, there was an outbreak of war along the eastern frontier of the Cape, Philip consistently identified the colonists' greed for African land as the cause of the trouble. A Wesleyan missionary called Shrewsbury took the opposite view, advocating a policy of 'extermination', though he used the term in its strict etymological sense of 'driving back beyond the frontier'. Nevertheless Shrewsbury's society disowned him and Philip went back to England to give evidence against the colonists. But even he could not bring himself to argue for the abandonment of newly won colonial territory. He did not wish land to be alienated from its previous users but he believed that British rule would be better than that of the chiefs and would provide an opportunity for the growth of missions.

Missionaries did not simply regard local rulers as tyrants. It was often, and this is where 'civilization' came into the picture, that questions of tribal law raised moral issues. Mission stations sometimes served as places of refuge for Africans charged with crimes by their own rulers. If they were escaped slaves or accused of witchcraft, missionaries felt that they could not hand them back for punishment. Tension between the chief and the mission was bound to result and, under such circumstances, missionaries often expressed a desire for the protection of a European government.

The mixture of motives at work is well illustrated by the story of the beginnings of Rhodesia in the last two decades of the century. The London Missionary Society's agents have been accused of persuading the Matabele king Lobengula to grant Rhodes's British South Africa Company the necessary concession to mine for gold. One of them, Charles Helm, a colonial of German extraction, is sometimes said to have been 'bought' by the company. In fact, Helm's own correspondence with the LMS shows that he was chiefly motivated by the fear that, if Rhodes did not obtain the sole concession, Lobengula's territory would be taken over by the same kind of 'riff-raff' which had swamped the Kimberley diamond fields in the early days.

But Helm was not the only missionary to support Rhodes's venture. Bishop Knight Bruce, an Eton and Oxford Anglican high churchman, having once denounced Rhodes as unscrupulous, dangerous, and immoral, became his friend and ally. And a Jesuit missionary, Father Prestage, ardent supporter of Irish home rule though he was, recorded in his diary a tacit approval of the crushing of Lobengula's power. Just as Helm thought the company more desirable than the 'riff-raff', Prestage thought it would be preferable to Lobengula's oppression of the Mashona. In spite of their different backgrounds and for very different reasons, all these men believed European rule to be for the good of the people of Africa.

There was, in fact, a kind of inevitability about colonial expansion, even when the governments of Europe and the individuals caught up in the process were reluctant to encourage it. In the middle of the century a Wesleyan missionary called Thomas Jenkins had established himself as an influential adviser to the Mpondo ruler beyond the eastern frontier of the Cape Colony. For a long time Jenkins helped to maintain peace on the frontier and prevented the subjugation of the independent people. But in the final crisis, when the colonists seemed determined to take possession of Mpondo territory, Jenkins stood aside. Divided loyalties would not allow him to oppose colonial expansion. It seemed that contact between Europeans and Africans was bound to lead to the loss of the latter's independence. Moreover, the individuals who were the actual points of contact, whatever their motives and in spite of their principles, seemed unable in the last resort to discover any way out of that inevitability.

It is not surprising, then, that when it became fashionable in the 1860s to use the concept of 'evolution' to explain developments in areas which had little or nothing to do with biology, there were those who sought to account for this inevitability in terms of 'the survival of the fittest'. In 1865 Bishop J. W. Colenso of Natal, one of the most perceptive of nineteenth-century missionaries, thought it necessary to deliver a paper to the Marylebone Literary Institute in reply to pseudo-Darwinian notions. His unnamed opponent evidently believed that missions were not only undesirable but actually destructive, arguing that the presence of a 'superior' race alongside an 'inferior' one was bound to cause the disappearance of the one less fit to survive. The bishop accepted the likely truth of Darwin's biological hypothesis and showed very clearly that he actually understood what it meant, a rare thing among missionaries.

But he insisted that it had been misapplied in this case and he concluded his paper by arguing that Africa had as much to contribute to Christianity as Christianity to Africa.

It was his recognition that Africa possessed its own important history and culture which marked Colenso out from most other missionaries. It also helped to make him a highly controversial figure. Almost from the first moment of his arrival in Africa in 1854 he had argued that polygamists should be allowed to become Christians. Polygamy, he maintained, was not a symptom of a gross and pagan sexuality but an integral part of African society. To attack it would be to undermine the stability of the social structure. Since Colenso's theology of the atonement led him to insist that all human beings were already redeemed, he conceived of his mission less in terms of the *conversion* of individuals and more in terms of Christianizing the whole culture and people.

In translating the Bible Colenso insisted on using the traditional Zulu name for God rather than the neologism used by most missionaries. He became acutely aware of the difficulty of trying to defend some of the Old Testament narratives. It seemed to him to be absurd to insist that God had made the world in seven days or demanded the massacre of the Amalekites at the same time as one was urging one's hearers to abandon their own legends and their warlike traditions. So he immersed himself in the work of the German biblical critics and produced his own five-volume *Pentateuch and the Book of Joshua, Critically Examined*. His technique was to demonstrate (for he was a well-known mathematician) the arithmetical impossibility of some of the biblical stories. But the real purpose of the work was to show that the Old Testament could not be literally true and that the absurdities and the immoralities need not, therefore, be regarded as an essential part of the faith. His latter years, after he had been excommunicated for his opinions, were devoted to championing African rights against the colonial government in Natal.

The bishop had reopened a good many of the well-worn

missionary debates. Was the missionary's function to sow the
seed as widely as possible or to build up a small, carefully
tested group of converts? Should he strive for individual conversions or, like early missionaries in Europe, persuade a ruler
to bring his whole people into the Church? Most Christian
denominations in Africa tended to employ the techniques that
one would expect to find chiefly among evangelicals. Though
every missionary saw advantages in obtaining the protection of
a chief, very few aimed openly at mass conversions. Evangelical
revivalist techniques used in Europe were adapted for Africa
and even missionaries influenced by the Oxford Movement did
not, for instance, devise methods based on theories about reserve
in communicating religious truth. While Roman Catholics were,
perhaps, less tied to the belief that men and women ought to
become Christians as a result of an individual, 'felt' conversion,
they were no less concerned than most Protestants to build up,
slowly and painfully, a community of demonstrably faithful
converts.

For this reason missionaries tended to regard the nomadic
behaviour of some of the African peoples as a hindrance to
their work. It became their object to create settlements where
their converts could live together, under Christian discipline.
Missionary settlements became typical of official African Christianity. Sometimes they were places of refuge for freed slaves.
Sometimes, as in East Africa, they became almost autonomous
states. And every denomination developed them. In southern
Africa the Moravians were the first to introduce the mission
settlement but the most elaborate example was to be the Roman
Catholic station at Marianhill in Natal, consciously modelled
on the monastic missions of early medieval Europe. Inevitably,
the use of such settlements implied that new Christians were
being converted out of their own society and into a new and
self-contained world with its own small-holdings, workshops,
schools, and stores. Even Colenso created such settlements,
including one which contained his 'kaffir Harrow' for the sons
of chiefs.

These settlements were instrumental in propagating a European way of life as well as Christian faith. In the second and third quarters of the nineteenth century, when there was an alliance of free trade and humanitarian interests and when anti-slavery was a great rallying cry, a great deal of missionary thinking seems to have assumed that the Christian religion, like the exports of industrial Europe, would make its way in Africa by its sheer evident superiority over local products. Though there was less openly acknowledged desire for colonialism in this period, civilization was simply equated with European civilization. The Victorian missionaries' determination to put their converts into clothes has been laughed at for generations as an example of narrow prudishness. In fact, it probably followed from notions of what constituted civilized behaviour rather than from sexual obsession. In precisely the same spirit, missionaries also preferred their converts to live in rectangular rather than circular houses. And they could be deeply shocked when relatively 'civilized' people continued to use clicks and other 'barbaric' sounds instead of 'proper' consonants.

The effect of what might be called the 'Free Trade' approach to missions was, in other words, to make Christianity a Europeanizing agency. The missions tended to preserve in almost every detail the form Christianity had acquired in Europe. Even Henry Venn, the remarkable secretary of the Church Missionary Society from 1841 to 1872, who devised a missionary strategy which looked forward to the creation of 'a self-supporting, self-governing, self-propagating Church', took it for granted that the new indigenous Christian community would use the seventeenth-century English Book of Common Prayer.

The zenith of Venn's programme was the appointment of Samuel Adjayi Crowther as the first black Anglican bishop, responsible for 'all West Africa beyond the dominions of the British crown' in 1865. Crowther had been born a Yoruba and when quite young was taken as a slave. After being liberated, he was educated in Sierra Leone and at the CMS college in

Islington. He was first sent to work in Sierra Leone, then in Abeokuta in the south-western corner of modern Nigeria. Later he accompanied the famous Niger expedition and became a member of the Niger mission where he was in every sense a good and effective missionary.

Crowther's career shows just how impenetrable European assumptions were, even among those most sympathetic to Africa. It seems to have been taken for granted that someone who was black, even though he had long been separated from his own people and culture, was the ideal person to convert Africans, regardless of the part of the continent from which they came. Africa was a single unit in the European imagination. In actuality, however, because Sierra Leone was used as a refuge for liberated slaves, it had become a very cosmopolitan, Anglicized, un-African place. Someone educated there and in England, consecrated on the authority of the British Crown, given an honorary doctorate by the University of Oxford, was not really an indigenous figure simply because he was black. Crowther's great achievement, in fact, was the way in which he managed to surmount the difficulties of being almost as much a stranger in his own country as if he had been an Englishman.

Gradually most Christian missions in Africa began to use their converts as agents in spreading the gospel. Training institutions were set up. Africans were ordained. Regulations were devised to define their status. There were many heroic people, like the martyred Bernard Mizeki in what is now Zimbabwe, who were sent by the churches to work a very long way from where they had been born. But perhaps the most remarkable thing of all was that Christianity often spread through the activities of converts who had no sort of official standing. In the second half of the nineteenth century, for instance, the Methodists in the Transvaal suddenly discovered that there was a whole community of 'Wesleyans' about whom they had known nothing but which owed its existence to unofficial missionaries.

African converts also played their part in the 'civilizing' of Africa, which was considered so integral to the missionary task. The black Christians of Sierra Leone were prominent in the process. They spread south and east from Freetown, taking their Christianity and their Europeanized way of life with them. In Abeokuta in the 1860s, for instance, they ran an industrial institution on behalf of a missionary society, and induced the local people to take up the cleaning and pressing of raw cotton. A printing-press was established, too, and a local newspaper founded. The missionary in charge described all this to his society in language that evokes an idyllic picture of local notables reclining with their morning paper while the people engage in useful labour in the cotton fields.

The reality was sometimes rather different. Sierra Leonean Christians often exploited the people to whom they went. The local rulers were well able to distinguish between the benefits of commerce and the disadvantages of Christian intrusions into their lives. And the missionaries themselves, from naïvety or honesty, reported that the chiefs complained about European influence, saying, 'Who do they think they are, coming here to rob us of our wives and slaves and destroy all the customs of our fathers by force?'

The alliance between Christianity and commerce, often alleged to have destroyed African resistance to colonialism, began as part of the campaign against the slave-trade in which Christians were prominent. Doubt has recently been cast on the purity of the motives of even such leading figures as William Wilberforce, but it is clear that nineteenth-century opinion was genuinely turning against the trade in human beings. In 1800 there were an estimated 800,000 negro slaves in Spanish America and about 300,000 in Jamaica. By 1850 25,000 people were exported annually to South America through Mozambique alone. From West Africa the volume of trade was enormous and, as is well-known, the conditions under which the slaves were shipped across the Atlantic were appalling.

European governments began to take action. In 1807 Britain

made the trade illegal, followed in 1814 by Holland. In the following year Sierra Leone, which had already been established by English evangelical interests as a refuge for liberated slaves, was made a crown colony and the Navy was directed to maintain a patrol off the coast of West Africa. Two years later Portugal, with a moral enthusiasm modified by pragmatic considerations, restricted trading in slaves to areas south of the Equator. In 1824 Britain declared slave-dealing to be a form of piracy, which provided a pretext for her to use the Navy to prevent nationals of other European countries from transporting slaves at sea. The Protestant nations had begun to think of themselves as far more whole-hearted than Catholic Europe in their determination to root out the trade.

In British territories emancipation came in 1833 and its enforcement was at least partly the cause of the emigration of some white colonists of Dutch descent from the Cape into the interior. The Portuguese continued to be ambivalent in their approach. The imperial government in Lisbon forbad slavery but the colonial administration in Mozambique suspended the decree, on the ground of 'absolute necessity'. It was, however, becoming more difficult for Catholic countries to condone slavery. Pope Gregory XVI condemned it in the bull *In Supremo* in 1839. In 1845 France mounted an expedition against slave-traders in West Africa and three years later slavery was forbidden in all French colonies, though it was not until 1864 that Napoleon III formally made the slave-trade illegal.

In the meantime in Britain Thomas Fowell Buxton had succeeded to the mantle of Wilberforce as the almost official leader of the anti-slavery movement. Buxton embodied in his own person the alliance of humanitarian, evangelical, and free trade enthusiasms, which was so marked a feature of the middle of the century. Supporting Philip's campaign for the rights of the aboriginal people in the Cape Colony, Buxton had said that all they asked for was 'the power of bringing their labour to a fair market'. The free trade gospel of a Christian philanthropist could not have been better put. The same gospel was preached in Buxton's *The Slave Trade*, published in 1838 and subsequently republished with an addendum, as *The Slave Trade and its Remedy*. This work argued that attempts to stamp out the trade had failed because they had used force rather than the natural resources of Africa. What was needed was the establishment of settlements, protected by Britain, where those resources could be developed until Africa was able to bring to the international market goods other than human beings. Then slavery would be eradicated and religion established in Africa. The Africa Civilization Society was formed in 1839 to further these aims. It sponsored an expedition up the Niger river in the early 1840s, with some government support. The aims of the expedition were grandiose in the extreme. Virtually every possible kind of 'civilizing' venture was listed, including paper-making and printing, but the real purpose was to establish model farms which would serve to inform local agriculture. Malaria killed 40 of the 143 Europeans involved in the enterprise and the whole project was soon abandoned.

The first annual meeting of the Civilization Society, was graced by the presence of Prince Albert, Sir Robert Peel, Lord Shaftesbury, Mr Gladstone, and the French ambassador, Guizot, about to become Louis Philippe's foreign minister. Among the less exalted members of the audience was the young David Livingstone who was to become, in his heyday, the best known exponent of Buxton's strategy. He was always arguing that commerce and Christianity, in that order, were what were needed in Africa if slavery were ever to be eliminated. In his own mind at least, the principal reason for his journeys of exploration was to open up the continent to precisely the kind of commercial and missionary settlements that Buxton had envisaged.

Livingstone was not an advocate of colonialism. He told Lord John Russell that white inhabitants of the proposed settlements should possess no more than 'squatters' rights'. But ironically Livingstone's dramatic death in 1873 made him, almost overnight, an heroic figure in the popular imagination and rendered his ideas extremely influential. It also came on the very eve of the high imperial era. In the new climate of opinion the belief in the power of an alliance between commerce and Christianity changed shape. Livingstone's ideas were used as justification for the chartered companies such as that which sent Lugard into Buganda. These companies were by no means always commercially successful but they became a powerful factor in the scramble for Africa in which Europe proceeded to indulge.

Though imperialism was much more openly espoused than before, there were variations among European powers as to the proper policies to be adopted. Britain preferred to rule through local authorities wherever possible. France espoused direct rule, more in keeping with the traditional policy of *mission civilisatrice*. The best of imperial theories maintained that the European powers were in Africa to act as guardians of the undeveloped indigenous population. Whatever hypocrisy, conscious or unconscious, may have been hidden under these theories, they did impose restraints upon their exponents. But some Europeans exploited Africa quite openly and unashamedly. To missionaries it often seemed that, given the apparent inevitability of colonization, they had a duty to support the imperial power whose policies they judged to be the most enlightened. And it also seemed clear that the presence of a European government was preferable to uncontrolled commercial enterprise. Leopold of Belgium ruled the Congo as a piece of private property not as a Belgian colony. That the Congo was widely reputed to be the most brutally exploited part of Africa seemed to prove that governments would accept restraints that individuals could ignore with impunity.

In the last quarter of the century missionary thinking seems almost to have mirrored its political counterpart. By the 1870s there was a sense of disillusionment among many missionaries. In part, this was because the number of converts had not increased at the rate which had been anticipated. All missionary agencies, Catholic as well as Protestant, depended on voluntary giving and—to maintain this—needed to be able to advertise concrete successes. But there was also a feeling that Africans had not displayed the necessary characteristics for leadership. What this really meant was that they had not become sufficiently Europeanized. Again and again missionary organizations expressed disappointment at the quality of indigenous leaders. What happened to Bishop Crowther in West Africa was only a spectacular example of a more general tendency. His Niger church broke up amid accusations of nepotism and indiscipline. Though, in fact, the trouble had been caused at least as much by a change of outlook on the part of English missionaries, it was argued that the experiment had failed. The same kind of disappointment existed elsewhere and it became the prevalent missionary view that the church in Africa would have to remain under white control for the foreseeable future. Guardianship became the dominant note in missionary as in imperial thinking.

Yet, ironically, the European sense of superiority in the proud epoch of imperialism and idealism proved tolerant of African culture and traditions. In West Africa, which on the whole was evangelized in the 1840s and 1850s, Christianity remained very foreign in appearance. A convert of a British missionary would be likely to be baptized Albert after the prince consort and given as his 'surname' the name of some Englishman revered in the missionary enterprise. In East Africa, which was for the most part evangelized at the end of the century, this Europeanizing tendency was much less obvious. Frank Weston, the bishop of Zanzibar for the Universities' Mission to Central Africa, encouraged the development of a local liturgy. Some missionaries went further and advocated the use in the eucharist of a drink brewed from bananas. African names were no longer thought of as necessarily pagan. And all this was symptomatic of a deeper change. The assumption was that since these people were really like children, who needed to be protected and guided by the wisdom of Europeans, it was less disastrous if they developed their own way of doing things. In a sense, the apartheid ideology, developed in South Africa with the tacit blessing of the Dutch Reformed Church, is no more than an extreme form of this thinking. It is based on the premiss that each culture ought to be separate from every other and allowed to develop on its own lines, in tune with its own cultural traditions. Thus a separate church for each racial group would not only be necessary but an expression of the divine will.

It may seem strange that, burdened with this European sense of superiority, Christianity made any headway at all. Yet it seems that Africa welcomed it. The coastal fringe of West Africa and the Cape of Good Hope at the southernmost tip of the continent were the earliest centres for Christian missions, which then gradually penetrated into the interior, more effectively in the south where the climate was hospitable and Islam less powerful. In the 1870s and 1880s new endeavours took Christianity into central Africa from both the east and west coasts so that by 1900 it had penetrated into most parts of the continent. By that date there were some two million Roman Catholics in that part of Africa which stretches southward from the River Congo. By the middle of the twentieth century Christians formed between a third and a half of the entire population of most countries of sub-Saharan Africa.

Some parts of the continent—Sierra Leone, the Cape, and, curiously enough, the Congo, where colonial brutality was so appallingly obvious—seem to have attracted a particularly large number of different missions. The existence of so many denominations was a potential problem. Sometimes, at least among Protestants, relations were quite easy. At the Cape in the middle of the nineteenth century, for instance, Dr Philip of the London Missionary Society seems to have acted as a sort of unofficial co-ordinator, arranging for the Paris Evangelical Missionary Society to go to Botswana, the Rhenish Mission to Namaqualand, and the American Board of Commissioners for Foreign Missions to Zululand. But there was often very sharp rivalry, even between missions that were not divided by obvious theological differences. Letters from missionaries to their headquarters are full of complaints about the activities of other denominations. In some parts of the continent there were official or unofficial agreements to divide the country between rival brands of Christianity. Often, once the scramble for Africa had begun, a change in the sphere of influence of a European nation also involved a change in the sphere of influence of a Christian mission.

Such difficulties—and not, of course, in Africa alone—led to the international missionary conference in Edinburgh in 1910. It was a significant landmark in the history of ecumenism but it revealed very clearly that missions continued to be led and directed by expatriates. There were hardly any representatives of indigenous Christianity from any part of the world. Precisely the same aspects of missionary Christianity were manifested in the so-called Kikuyu controversy. Missionaries of the Church Missionary Society met with representatives of Protestant bodies on the Church of Scotland station at Kikuyu in 1913 to try and devise a formula for creating a federation of Christians in the British East Africa Protectorate. They were motivated partly by a desire to present a united front against Islam and Roman Catholicism but they were also very conscious of the fact that a divided Christendom raised doubts among their converts.

But the proposal was typical of the attitudes implicit in the Edinburgh conference in that it was essentially an initiative by an expatriate leadership for the benefit of an indigenous rank and file. The missionaries themselves would have remained members of their own denominations 'at home'. The new federation would be too poor and too small to support itself financially so it would need to retain very close organizational links with the missionary agencies that were bringing it into being. But it was hoped that it would provide the framework for a united East African Church. What made Kikuyu notorious was the opposition of the Anglo-Catholic bishop of Zanzibar, Frank Weston, who attacked the scheme because it was 'pan-protestant'. It was this aspect of the affair which attracted public attention. But Weston had not only encouraged an

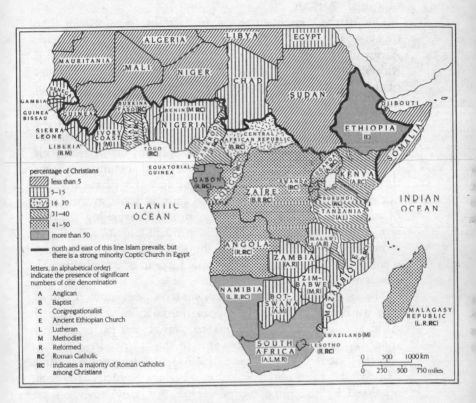

percentage of Christians

- ⧄ less than 5
- ⊟ 5–15
- 16–20
- ⧄ 31–40
- 41–50
- more than 50

— north and east of this line Islam prevails, but there is a strong minority Coptic Church in Egypt

letters, (in alphabetical order) indicate the presence of significant numbers of one denomination

- A   Anglican
- B   Baptist
- C   Congregationalist
- E   Ancient Ethiopian Church
- L   Lutheran
- M   Methodist
- R   Reformed
- RC Roman Catholic
- **RC** indicates a majority of Roman Catholics among Christians

CHRISTIANITY IN CONTEMPORARY AFRICA

indigenous liturgy in his diocese, he had also developed a system which gave African clergy independent pastoral responsibility and a voice in synodical government. It seemed to him absurd to try and design a church for Africa without the presence of a single African.

One of the consequences of the fact that missionaries (like everyone else) took it for granted that the West should shape Africa in its own image, was the emergence of what is called 'Ethiopianism'—new, separate, distinctively African varieties of the Christian religion. The term 'Ethiopianism' appears to have been a label used by whites for black churches and religious movements though occasionally the word 'Ethiopia' or its derivatives appears in the names of the black churches themselves. In neither case does the term imply any connection with the country of Abyssinia or Ethiopia. Since that country was, in the late nineteenth century, one of the very few parts of Africa not ruled by European powers and since it was also the home of an ancient African Christianity, it is not surprising that the term embodies longings for an independent Christian Africa. It is interesting that the name of the last emperor of Abyssinia seems to have something of the same force in twentieth-century Rastafarianism.

Though the causes of Ethiopianism have been much debated, it is usually agreed that European domination, which denied Africans opportunities of leadership, was at least partly responsible. But it is also clear that some of the independent African churches came into existence because of a regrowth within Christianity of traditional cultural values, which had been repressed by the missionaries. There was almost always an element of protest in the origins of these churches, even to the extent of upholding polygamy as a way of asserting their African character.

But there were other strands that went to make up independent African Christianity. A charismatic or prophetic element was often present, too. In West Africa towards the end of the nineteenth century Garrick Braid, an Anglican who never entirely broke with his own church, was known to his followers as Elijah II, a clear indication of the central place occupied by his own prophetic role. In the same period 'Prophet Harris', an almost illiterate but dynamic evangelist, became a one-man revivalist mission from Liberia to the Ivory Coast. The same features may be seen in the Church of the Lord (Aladura) which, nearly a hundred years later, has become one of the most important of independent African churches. It has its roots in a number of different indigenous religious movements—healing, visionary, and revivalist. Its founder, Josiah Olunowo Oshitelu, was a first-generation Nigerian Christian. He was baptized in 1914 and, while being trained as an Anglican catechist in 1925, received a vision in which he was called to become a prophet.

Like many independent churches, the Aladura church uses many of the vestments and titles familiar to 'catholic' Christianity. Its beliefs reveal a blend of the standard tenets of Christian creeds with much that clearly derives from what is traditionally African. In what has been the conventional way of categorizing these movements—'Ethiopian' for those which are more 'orthodox' and westernized, 'Zionist' for the much more decidedly indigenous (some would say syncretistic) bodies—it belongs in the second group. Indeed, prophetism is generally more likely to exist among Zionists than among Ethiopians.

Understandably it has been in South Africa, where white political domination has been most intransigent, that both types have multiplied most rapidly. In the last quarter of the nineteenth century Methodism was the parent body from which the majority of the secessions took place, probably because Methodism had relied more heavily on 'native agents' in the work of evangelism. Such were the Tembu National Church founded in 1884 and the Ethiopian Church created by Mangena Mokoni in 1892. Almost all denominations have been affected but Roman Catholicism least of all, which has led some theorists to suggest that the phenomenon is merely a manifestation of the fissiparous tendency of Protestantism.

The earliest movements were Ethiopian rather than Zionist. Their thinking and practice showed few indigenous features. When the leadership of Mokoni's church was taken over by James Dwane and it eventually united with the Anglican Church as a semi-autonomous 'Order of Ethiopia', there was much discussion about valid ordination and episcopal succession, in very conventional terms. And, at first, the new denominations were very small. In 1904 it was reckoned that there were only three independent churches in southern Africa, with a combined membership of about 25,000. But their existence was already regarded as ominous. J. T. Jabavu, a prominent Christian layman and a leader of African opinion, condemned Ethiopianism as a kind of suicidal madness. White missionaries regarded it as an unmitigated evil and the first meeting of the South African General Missionary Conference in 1904 condemned 'the low morals, lack of discipline and mistrust of the white man' manifested by 'Ethiopians'.

So worrying was this new religious movement that in 1903 the four British colonies in southern Africa (the Cape, Natal, the Transvaal, and the Orange River Colony) had appointed a joint commission to investigate, among other things, the political significance of Ethiopianism. The commission's conclusion was that the Ethiopian threat was not a very serious one. But in the same year in which the report was published there appeared on the scene the first Zionist movement in southern Africa. In its origin the new movement was not notably African. It was derived from American Pentecostalism through the influence of a missionary of the Dutch Reformed Church, but its charismatic character seems to have released something truly indigenous. One of its leaders, Paul Mabilitsa, became a prophet on the West African pattern and, like many of the outstanding figures of prophetism, was suspected of politically subversive behaviour. The Zionists were thought to have played a large part in the Zulu rebellion of 1906 but the truth probably was that, if there were Zionist rebels, it was because they were frustrated, resentful members of the Zulu nation rather than because they were Zionists.

Nor was it only in the south that indigenous Christianity appeared to be linked with political frustration. Similar threats, real or imagined, were reported elsewhere on the continent. In Nyasaland John Chilembwe had been converted to Christianity by a vigorous and idiosyncratic missionary, John Booth, who combined a conservative, fundamentalist theology with radical political opinions that made him one of the harshest critics of the British administration. Chilembwe became an evangelist of the same type. His preaching was at first fairly conventional, though not without overtones which were militantly nationalist. By 1915 there was open rebellion, with atrocities on both sides.

In spite of widespread suspicion among whites, obvious and extreme politico-religious movements were rare. Nevertheless the number of independent African churches continued to grow. Many of them came into existence because of a belief that expatriate missionaries were unwilling to relinquish control. An agent of the Berlin Society in the Transvaal, for instance, helped to create a secession church in Sekukuniland, maintaining that missionaries were as repressive of African independence as any colonial government. Almost the first act of the new church was the expulsion of its founder: the point he had been making had clearly been taken.

In southern Africa alone the number of these independent churches rose from three in 1904 to one hundred and thirty in 1925, though some of them were very small. The South African census of 1946 revealed that the membership had risen to over a million and there were then thought to be 1,300 churches. By the 1960s it was estimated that there were well over 2,000. In the rest of the continent the independent churches have probably not proliferated to quite the same extent but surveys clearly show that their existence is a feature of Christianity all over Africa. Some of the antagonism between these movements and the churches which originated in Europe seems to have waned.

The World Council of Churches recognizes the *Église de Jésus Christ par le Prophète Simon Kimbangu,* founded in the Belgian Congo in the 1920s. The significance of this recognition must not be over-emphasized since the World Council has always refused to act as a judge of orthodoxy. It was a fundamental tenet of the World Conference Movement before the Great War of 1914–18 that churches would only be excluded by their own decision. The World Council which evolved from the movement retained that principle, declaring itself at its foundation in 1948 simply to be a fellowship of churches 'accepting Jesus Christ as God and Saviour'. Nevertheless, recognition of this African church is a far cry from the accusations of 'Messianism' levelled against Kimbanguists as recently as the 1950s.

Kimbanguists were also regarded as politically subversive by the Belgian colonial authorities and the element of political protest has always been present among the independent African churches. But the Christian mission in Africa has also always contained radical and outspoken critics of colonialism as well as its tacit supporters. In South Africa, as is well known, there has been a succession of heroic protesters against apartheid. Among the best known have been black laymen like Albert Luthuli as well as expatriate clergymen like Trevor Huddleston. And this protest goes back to the very creation of the Union of South Africa in 1910. Since the constitution of the new dominion was to include a clause which entrenched a colour bar, leaders of Anglican, Methodist, Baptist, Presbyterian, and other denominations in southern Africa delivered a formal protest against the Bill before it came to the Westminster parliament. But British liberals were more concerned to achieve reconciliation with the Afrikaners defeated in the Boer War. The protest failed. The archbishop of Canterbury told the House of Lords that, if the British would trust their former enemies, black South Africans would gradually acquire greater political rights in the future.

The episode is instructive. Because of their dilemma over colonialism the churches have often been ambivalent in their attitudes to European government in Africa. From time to time individuals have expressed vigorous misgivings about some aspects of 'pacification' and imperialism. Occasionally a missionary order or a society or a denomination has taken an official stand against activities which seemed demonstrably to be contrary to the good of the local people. But for the most part such protests achieved little, perhaps because they were seldom concerted. Individual missionaries, for instance, who protested openly against Lugard's administration of Nigeria were dealt with as sharply by their own societies as by the government. Lugard himself dismissed missionaries' complaints as arising from their jealousy of the influence and prestige of the government's district officers. In Nyasaland missionaries objected strongly to H. H. Johnston's sometimes harsh methods of collecting taxes but were happy enough to train the clerks who kept the administration running.

European missionaries were plainly convinced that, in the long run, some forms of colonial government could be shown to be for the good of the people of Africa. Roman Catholics, who already received privileged treatment in Portuguese and Belgian territories, were enthusiastic in co-operating with British colonial administration. In 1927 the Vatican created a new post of Visitor Apostolic to Catholic Missions in British African Colonies. Arthur Hinsley, who went from the English College in Rome to occupy this office, was an ardent advocate of co-operation with the colonial authorities, particularly in matters of education. He believed that British policies offered a genuine opportunity for progress towards the eventual emergence of an independent people capable of governing themselves.

Most churches and missionary societies had come to accept the *fact* of colonial government, however much they might criticize certain aspects of its policies or the manner in which they were put into effect. Colonialism existed and it was not, after all, wholly unreasonable to argue that it was better than some of the possible alternatives. Individual missionaries believed, as did most of their contemporaries in Europe, that white rule had done much for Africa. They were often amongst the most outspoken critics when white administrators behaved badly. But often, at least tacitly, they shared the general European assumption that Africa was unlikely to produce its own leaders for some time to come.

On the other hand, there is no evidence of a missionary conspiracy to keep Africa in subjection to Europe. There was surprisingly little contact, for instance, between the British Colonial Office and the missionary societies. The register of incoming daily correspondence at the Colonial Office for 1890, at the height of the imperial era, contains very few entries indeed relating to missionary affairs. There are one or two letters from the London Missionary Society about the 'liquor traffic' in the Pacific and several from the Wesleyan Missionary Society about marriage regulations in West Africa. A Norwegian mission applied for permission to open a station in Zululand and the Society for the Propagation of the Gospel wrote about a Bill to reduce grants to the Church of England in Mauritius. All in all, there is probably more correspondence from chambers of commerce in such seaports as Manchester and Plymouth than there is from the missionary organizations. There is no evidence at all to suggest that the societies were urging the maintenance and extension of British colonial authority for the sake of any advantage that they themselves might hope to gain from it. In other words, white missionaries were willing to accept European rule in Africa because they shared the general outlook of their contemporaries rather than because they planned a deliberate strategy of destroying African independence in order to reduce resistance to the gospel. It was simply a version of the paternalism which was such a feature of all European attitudes to Africa.

African Christianity, however, needed to escape from paternalism as well as from more open forms of repression. It is noteworthy that there were far fewer independent Christian church movements in Tanganyika than anywhere else in Africa. The most probable explanation is that the outbreak of the First

World War removed the German missionaries from the scene at a crucial moment, leaving African Christians free to run their own ecclesiastical affairs. On the other hand prophetism has sometimes taken a form which has seemed to express a desire for a specifically African Christ. Isaiah Shembe's Nazareth Movement in South Africa is a case in point. Shembe, who died about 1960 and was succeeded as leader of the movement by his son, is spoken of in language which suggests a quasi-divine figure. His birth was miraculous and his origins mysterious. He was born of the Spirit: he was Spirit. He was not of the world but of heaven. He was a servant sent by God, we are told, and through him we know that God is not beyond the ocean but here among us. Language of this kind has led some scholars to label such movements 'Messianic' to distinguish them from Ethiopian and Zionist churches. They are thought to be an expression of a desire for a Christianity independent of white control.

It had been widely prophesied that when colonialism went, Christianity would go with it. It was argued that it was 'merely the symbol of a passing phenomenon of the colonial era, gaining what strength it had from its prestige as the religion of the foreign rulers'. In the event, when independence came Christianity did not disappear: it survived and flourished. There were those, of course, who argued that this was merely evidence of the truth of the gospel. There were others who maintained that it was simply a consequence of the fact that the churches had provided the only education available in Africa and the new leaders had, therefore, necessarily been educated in missionary establishments. Perhaps the most sophisticated theory suggested that it happened because Africa possessed nothing like the powerful cultural and religious traditions which served as vehicles for resistance to colonialism in other parts of the world. Tribal traditions and animistic religion were simply incapable of providing an alternative to Western culture and government. And, in any case, colonialism had often destroyed tribal unity, either by dividing former groupings or by submerging them in larger, artificially delimited territories. So it has been argued that Christianity, itself part of the colonial intrusion, sometimes provided the means of creating a national consciousness to replace it.

This theory, if true, implies that Christianity had genuinely become part of an indigenous African way of life. There is a good deal of evidence to support such a view. It was not only the Ethiopian and Zionist forms of Christianity which acquired a genuinely African flavour; the mainstream originally European denominations did the same. Their leadership has become black. They have become more African in art and music. Even their theology has acquired a distinctly African style and it has been difficult for Europeans, sometimes, to distinguish between it and the theology of more syncretistic bodies. On occasion this has caused problems within a world-wide church. Emmanuel Milingo, Roman Catholic archbishop of Lusaka in Zambia from 1969 until he was compelled to resign in 1982, came—like many of the independent church leaders—to perceive the ministry of healing as central to his work and self-understanding. Among the complaints made against him, not always justly, was the charge that he mixed pagan African traditions quite unacceptably with Christianity.

Curiously, the churches' relations with the governments of independent Africa have been much the same as those of the missionaries with colonial governments. Sometimes churchmen have been accused of being active agents of independence, in the same manner that missionaries have been accused of being agents of imperialism: in Angola in the 1950s and 1960s black Roman Catholic dignitaries were charged with acts of subversive nationalist politics. Most often Christian leaders have accepted the givenness of government and protested against its injustices and excesses, as was the case with Archbishop Luwum in Idi Amin's Uganda. And sometimes the same religious movements have been similarly perceived, by independent as by colonial governments. The followers of the prophetess Alice Lenshina continued to be repressed, as a threat to law and order, by the government of Zambia as by that of the Central African Federation before it collapsed in 1963.

The Christian denominations which originated in Europe transported their particular traditions to Africa and, in a sense, forced them upon Africans. Africa took its revenge by making Christianity its own. The election of Desmond Tutu as Anglican archbishop of Cape Town is perhaps symbolic of this, for the churches have always found it most difficult to become indigenous in those parts of Africa which were colonies of European settlement. The existence of a white settler Christianity has made the emergence of black leadership particularly slow. Nowhere was this more obvious than in South Africa, where the overwhelming majority of Anglicans are black but where there had never been a black bishop until the second half of the twentieth century. Tutu has been called both 'radical' and 'moderate'. In truth he is neither. His theology bears little resemblance to the liberation theology which has emerged in Latin America. It is closer to the Anglo-Catholic 'Christian socialism' of men like Charles Gore. And though Tutu has been courageously opposed to violence, 'moderate'—with its implications of neutrality—is hardly an apt description of his style. He has an unwavering determination that his people shall achieve justice. His sense of humour, his patience, and even his physical movements, are inescapably African.

And yet Africa's relationship with Christianity is, perhaps, still somewhat uneasy. This shows up most clearly in matters relating to marriage, women, and the family. It has been commonplace for a long time to say that religious communities and a celibate priesthood have no appeal in Africa because the traditional importance of the ancestors makes it so desirable to possess descendants. For the same reason, the response of African Roman Catholics to *Humanae Vitae* has been very mixed. For every sophisticate arguing in favour of limiting the population increase, there have been a far larger number of simple people who have felt that large families were highly desirable. And one would find something of the same kind of division of opinion over polygamy. Vigorously condemned by missionaries but permitted by many of the independent movements, it received sympathetic treatment by the African Anglican bishops at the Lambeth Conference of 1988. But there was an immediate reaction from those who said that if the bishops had been women their sympathy would have been much more limited. In fact, women have been enormously important in the process of making Christianity at home in Africa. Indeed the Christianizing of modern Africa has sometimes been represented as the black woman's search for God. Women's organizations, in striking and colourful uniforms, have been a prominent feature in all the churches. There have been some famous women prophets, healers, and leaders among the independent movements. But, on the whole, the leadership of the 'mainstream' churches has remained male.

Christianity and Islam continue to compete for religious dominance in Africa and, perhaps, the rivalry has become more intense in recent years. Nevertheless, Africa is now, in one sense, the centre of the Christian world. This is certainly true if one measures importance in terms of the proportion of active Christians to the population as a whole. Africa has been very receptive to Christianity, but it has made Christianity decidedly its own. Nor is the result merely a quaint throw-back to a primitive culture. It is very much engaged with the modern Africa and its place in the world of the twentieth century. The influence of Christian social thought on the political ideas of Léopold Senghor of Senegal, Kenneth Kaunda of Zambia, and Julius Nyerere of Tanzania is evidence of its contribution to the new Africa. The All Africa Conference of Churches was born out of the same pan-Africanism which led to the creation of the Organization for African Unity in the political field. That pan-Africanism is not a nostalgia for something that belongs to a past age. It frankly recognizes that Africa has little power in international affairs but is determined that it shall live on equal terms with the rest of the world.

The first assembly of the AACC was held in 1963. Four

years later its general secretary, S. H. Amissah, spoke of Africa as 'throwing away the shackles of old domination and entering upon a new life of hope, dignity and confidence in a world still dominated by economic forces and frustrated by racial tensions' and looking forward to the discovery of a new basis for 'a truly enriching, useful and satisfying life'. He was expressing an opinion which is widespread among the leaders of modern African Christianity. They believe they have a vocation to contribute a sense of value to the people of the continent, who are determined to be taken seriously by the West without being swamped by Western materialism.

14

Asia

KENNETH AND HELEN BALLHATCHET

THE history of Christianity in Asia during the nineteenth century and much of the twentieth was dominated by the growth of missionary activity. This activity built on what had gone before, but there were two new factors. One of these was the emergence of Protestant missions as a significant force; the other was the development in the West of military, technological, and commercial capabilities which were clearly superior to anything in Asia. Missionary activity itself was profoundly affected by this new Western dominance. In addition, we must note a factor which, although not new in the nineteenth century, gradually grew in importance throughout our period. This is the contribution of Asian Christians themselves to the development of Christianity.

The similar structures and processes which we can detect in the history of Christianity in the different countries of Asia mainly resulted from the presence and interaction of these three factors. The wide-ranging activities of missionaries meant that everywhere Christianity brought change. Missionaries did more than preach the gospel. Especially under colonial regimes missionary pressure helped to push governments into social reforms. Missionaries also exerted a social influence in many of their activities. By working for the neglected in society—the outcasts, the lepers, the blind—they encouraged the idea that all men, and women, were equal in the sight of God, and had equal rights to sympathy and help. Missionaries did much to promote Western medicine and Western-style education for both sexes. Graduates of missionary colleges, whether Christians or not, often went on to become social reformers, nationalists, and even revolutionary leaders.

Moreover, despite the great number of different missionary bodies, we can discern clear, and related, patterns in the attitudes of missionaries to what they were doing and how they should do it. At one extreme there were those who thought it the task of the missionary to save souls that would otherwise be condemned to eternal punishment: other activities could only be justified if they had a direct effect in producing conversions. At the other extreme there were those who saw the missionary as working indirectly, aiming at the gradual Christianization of society as a whole through the propagation of humanitarian ideas. This school of thought was associated with 'liberal' Christians who did not believe in the eternal damnation of the unconverted. They tended to identify Western society with Christianity, and therefore greeted signs of Westernization as steps towards Christianization. Their influence grew as time went on. Most missionaries, however, seem to have stood in practice, if not in principle, somewhere between these two extremes. Many were content, without overmuch reflection, to see themselves as obeying the divine command to go through the world, preaching, teaching, and healing the sick. A continuing problem within this context was whether missionaries should concentrate on élites or lower classes: towards the end of the nineteenth century a variant of the latter strategy was that of mass conversion.

These differences were related to the general question of the relationship between Christianity and other religions. Logically there were three possibilities—to condemn other religions as the work of the Devil, to approach them tolerantly as merely the result of human error, or to grant them limited approval as imperfect expressions of religious truth, as God's way of preparing humanity for Christianity. Those who saw other religions as satanic tended to see themselves as teaching something completely new and as having no need to study the religious beliefs of those to whom they were speaking. Non-Christian societies were considered inherently evil, and if converts were denationalized that was all for the best. They should certainly refrain from all heathen practices. On the other hand, those who saw good in other religions, springing either from human sincerity or from divine prompting, emphasized the need to study them, and some were even prepared to see converts retain such devotional practices as were compatible with Christian ideas. With the possible exception of some of the recent advocates of religious dialogue, however, all missionaries, whatever their attitude to other religions, have ultimately been committed to replacing them with Christianity.

The effects of Western dominance were various. Missionaries were seldom conscious agents of imperialism, but many saw a providential link between the material superiority of the West and the moral superiority of Christianity, which also seemed self-evident to them. Missionaries were generally willing to accept help from Western powers in gaining access to hostile countries, and in providing protection for themselves and their converts in time of need.

Western power also affected Asian attitudes to Christianity and to conversion. If there was resentment at Western diplomatic, military, or commercial intervention, there was also resentment at parallel attempts at religious interference. On the other hand, many converts were no doubt initially attracted to Christianity because of the protection and employment which missionaries could provide, or because they saw the Christian message as the key to technological and military development.

Asian churches were for a long time subject to the dominance of Western missionary bodies, with a high degree of financial dependence and few Asian Christians in influential positions. The personal relationships between missionaries and Asian clergy and laity were sometimes strained. Moreover, at times of political tension with the West, Asian Christians were often accused of a lack of patriotism, and some found it difficult to reconcile their sense of national identity with their allegiance to a seemingly Western religion. Such strains often led to the growth of indigenous Christian groups hostile to 'Western' forms of Christianity. In some countries, only the expulsion of missionaries by anti-Western governments gave mainstream churches independence. However, missionary bodies gradually became more sensitive to questions of autonomy. Even so, the 'Western' nature of Christianity and the tendency of Christian minorities to be isolated from majority society are still often seen as problems by Asian churches. The search for authentically 'Asian' forms of Christianity involved not only art, architecture, and the liturgy but also the breaking down of 'Western' denominational barriers, and attempts to write Christian theology in 'Asian' terms.

South and South-East Asia

How far did missionaries serve imperialism or benefit from it? The establishment of British dominance in India and Sri Lanka was accompanied by much missionary activity on the part of various Protestant societies drawing their inspiration from the evangelical revival. Nor did the British authorities welcome such activity. Indeed, historians have portrayed the East India Company as hostile to missions for political reasons. But this is misleading. True, the Court of Directors resisted the free entry of missionaries until 1813, when a sustained evangelical campaign procured the insertion in the Act renewing the Company's Charter of a clause allowing anyone who was denied permission to enter British India the right of appeal to the Board of Control, which was headed by a government minister. But in practice the Company's Indian governments proved sympathetic to missionaries who were politically useful. When the revolutionary and Napoleonic wars interrupted communications between Rome and India the Company provided subventions to the Roman Catholic Vicars Apostolic in Bombay and Verapoli. In fact, Roman Catholic missionaries were regularly used by the Company as military chaplains: during the first half of the nineteenth century nearly half the British troops in India were Irish Roman Catholics. Similarly, English Baptist missionaries who settled in Danish territory at Srirampur were soon allowed into the British territories in Bengal: a scholar with the linguistic attainments of the Baptist missionary William Carey was useful in the training of the Company's officials.

The Court of Directors had some reason for caution. Protestant missionaries denounced Hinduism and Islam as devilish, sometimes taking to the streets to do so. Such tactlessness, many officials thought, would cause disorder, and in 1806 a mutiny at Vellore, in South India, was blamed on proselytizing zeal. Roman Catholic missionaries had a similarly negative attitude towards Hinduism and Islam, but in the early years of the century they were too preoccupied with the spiritual needs of Indian Catholics to have time or opportunity to seek converts. When Catholic priests increased in numbers they then seemed to devote more attention to converting Protestants than Hindus—to the irritation of Protestant missionaries. This procedure seems to have been based on the notion that Protestants as heretics were doomed to Hell, whereas virtuous pagans were merely dispatched to Limbo, where they might be comfortable enough, though precluded from beatitude.

The mutiny and revolt in northern India in 1857 revived fears of the political danger of missionary activities, but most conversions were in fact in the South, and these fears were short-lived. Thereafter the government evinced little concern, until the growth of nationalism in the twentieth century attracted the warm support of missionaries such as C. F. Andrews and Verrier Elwin. In general, the authorities welcomed the services of missionaries, both Protestant and Roman Catholic, as teachers in schools and colleges and as doctors and nurses in hospitals. And missionaries found that their understanding of the procedures and values of the British administration helped them to protect the interests of converts in trouble with the law or with their Hindu or Muslim neighbours. This was also true of British territories elsewhere, in Sri

Lanka, Burma, and Malaysia. In Indo-China, however, the French authorities did not welcome Protestant missions, and favoured Roman Catholics to such an extent that many held influential positions. Again, in Indonesia the Dutch authorities were unsympathetic to Roman Catholicism until the twentieth century, when a more tolerant policy prompted a surge of Catholic missionary activity. Missionaries were also affected by the fortunes of war. During the Second World War, Roman Catholic missions in India and Sri Lanka suffered because German and Italian priests were interned, but in South-East Asia Protestant missions suffered because their missionaries were mostly British or American, whereas the Japanese authorities tolerated the presence of French, German, and Italian missionaries, who were mostly Roman Catholic. The case of Indonesia was a little different in that the Dutch authorities expelled German missionaries, who were mostly Protestant, at the beginning of the war, and the Japanese authorities subsequently interned Dutch missionaries, both Protestant and Catholic. The end of colonial rule brought a new situation, and in various countries the entry of foreign missionaries was prohibited or restricted, but by this time the growth of local clergy enabled most churches to replace them smoothly. Roman Catholics continued to hold influential positions in Vietnam after independence, but with the general imposition of Communist rule the position of Catholics became far from agreeable.

The varied activities of missionaries were periodically challenged, within the Protestant churches, by those who wanted to concentrate on preaching the gospel in order to convert the heathen. Before the end of the nineteenth century some Protestant missionaries, such as William Miller of Madras Christian College, argued that their task was not so much to convert Hindus as to permeate Hindu society with Christian values through influencing the élite who were taking to Western education. This prompted criticism from radical Nonconformist missionaries sensitive to the arguments of Hugh Price Hughes in England to the effect that Methodism was becoming middle-class and was in danger of losing its roots among the working classes. In India such missionaries criticized Miller and his colleagues for preparing high-caste Hindus for lucrative careers instead of helping low-caste converts to overcome their social and economic difficulties.

Many Protestant missionaries in India concerned themselves with social questions. Early in the nineteenth century they denounced such customs as the burning of widows and the killing of girl babies, until the government made them criminal offences. Caste was an enduring problem both for Protestants and for Catholics. From the 1830s the Anglican Bishop Wilson opposed its persistence among converts, and his example was generally followed by other Protestant denominations, with the exception of the Lutherans. Roman Catholic missionaries, however, were less united in their attitude to caste among Christians. Although the French missionaries in South India were generally agreed that caste should be respected, most Irish missionaries opposed it, while Italian missionaries were divided on the matter.

Caste had been a fundamental issue in the controversy over the observance of Malabar rites, which was associated with the controversy over Chinese rites. De Tournon's settlement had been broadly ratified by Pope Benedict XIV, who ruled in 1744 that Catholics of high and low birth should hear mass and take communion together in the same church at the same time. The Jesuits in South India solved the problem by erecting little walls in their churches and by providing different entrances to separate the high from the low castes. They were then able to claim that they observed the precepts of Benedict XIV, but their opponents thought this Jesuitical in the pejorative sense of the term. After the suppression of the Jesuits as a religious order, their successors appealed for a ruling from Rome, and the Sacred Congregation *de Propaganda Fide* stated in 1778 that such practices were allowable for the time being, provided that missionaries did their best to eradicate caste feelings.

However, in the nineteenth century the problem became more complex. Until then, Catholic missionaries tried to avoid offending high castes, and when Indians were selected for ordination as priests they were mostly Brahmans or Eurasians, especially from Goa. But the rising expectations accompanying socio-economic change led various low-caste leaders to demand that young men of their own caste should be admitted to seminaries and trained as priests. In the area now known as Kerala it was argued on behalf of the Mukkuvan, or Fisher, caste that St Peter himself, the first pope, had been a fisherman, and this point was duly relayed to Rome, where it had a powerful impact. Propaganda Fide ruled in 1836 that half a dozen low-caste youths should be selected for training, sent to a seminary in the more tolerant atmosphere of Bombay, and after ordination be appointed to predominantly low-caste parishes in Kerala. But it proved difficult to implement such policies. One Irish bishop and one Italian archbishop who successively proposed to accept low-caste candidates for ordination were each accused of sexual immorality and recalled to Rome. The evidence came from high-caste priests, and its validity was secretly doubted in Rome, but it was accepted in the Holy Office investigations that the usefulness of such prelates in the mission field had been destroyed by these accusations, whatever their truth or falsity.

The existence of a rival jurisdiction operating under the Portuguese *padroado* in virtual independence of Rome enabled dissatisfied congregations to transfer their allegiance from one to the other. In Kerala many low-caste congregations transferred their allegiance from the Italian Carmelite bishop under Propaganda Fide to the archbishop of Goa under the *padroado*. On the other hand, in Bombay several high-caste congregations transferred their allegiance to the archbishop of Goa from the Italian Carmelite archbishop, who there proved sympathetic to low-caste ambitions. After the Jesuits returned to South India in the 1830s they did their best to maintain caste *punctilio*, seeing themselves as the heirs of Nobili. Their colleagues of the Missions Étrangères were equally determined to do so. But they were gradually forced to accept that times had changed. Although they hoped to convert Brahmans they had to recognize that most Indian Christians were non-Brahmans: some were high-status Vellalas, a dominant agricultural caste, but many more were low-status Nadars, or toddy-tappers, and more still were Paravas. Indeed, the whole of the Parava caste of Tamil Nadu were Catholics. Traditionally fishermen like the Mukkuvans of Kerala, some had taken to trade and prospered exceedingly, as had some Nadars. There were demands not only for low-caste priests but also for low-caste altar servers, and for more schools, the surest means of upward mobility. Those who found the Jesuits' rigidity distasteful turned to priests operating under the rival *padroado* jurisdiction of Mailapur. And there were many areas of life in which the Jesuits seemed rigid. By the 1880s they were forwarding complaints to Rome that Goanese priests were so lax that they were expanding their schools by employing Protestant schoolmistresses. In fact there were a number of priests of lower caste by the end of the century. One reason why a general seminary was then established at Kandy, in Sri Lanka, rather than in India, was the expectation that caste feelings were less likely to flourish there. It was placed under the direction of Belgian Jesuits, who had had long experience in Bengal, where they were less rigid in deference to caste than their French brethren in South India and less hostile to Goanese priests associated with the *padroado*.

In 1902 the Apostolic Delegate pointed out that although Nobili had made such efforts to convert some Brahmans, none of their descendants remained in the Catholic Church whereas there were many Catholic descendants of the lower castes converted by St Francis Xavier. By this time some Jesuits had succeeded in converting whole groups of low-caste peasants, and in the twentieth century both Protestant and Catholic missionaries developed the technique of conversion as a mass movement. This was much criticized by higher-caste Hindus, notably Mahatma Gandhi, on the ground that such converts were motivated by material considerations. But advocates of mass conversion argued that a mixture of motives might influence many converts without affecting the genuineness of their conversion, and that a desire for a fuller life for themselves and their families was not an ignoble motive, especially on the part of the lowest castes who were treated as untouchable and forbidden to enter Hindu temples.

There was little in the preaching of the early Protestant missionaries to appeal to the educated. Their emphasis upon the miraculous did not impress Hindus familiar with the many accounts of supernatural wonders in their own devotional literature, while Muslims thought that such notions were superstitious. The frequent reference which evangelicals and Nonconformists made to salvation through the blood of Christ seemed distasteful to Hindus, and the notion of atonement through the sacrifice of a sinless victim seemed unjust. But Christ's personality and ethical teachings aroused interest among many educated Hindus, who found the New Testament much more congenial than the Old. In 1820 Ram Mohan Roy, a Bengali Brahman and a distinguished religious reformer, published a selection of Christ's ethical teachings entitled *The Precepts of Jesus, the Guide to Peace and Happiness*. He was friendly with some of the early Baptist missionaries in Bengal, and they had great hopes of converting him. In fact, however, he converted one of them to Unitarianism: this was the Reverend William Adam, who was thereafter known in Calcutta as 'the second fallen Adam'.

By the 1850s Protestant missionaries in Bengal had become troubled by the small number of conversions, and at a conference in Calcutta they formally resolved to be more tactful in their preaching—praising whatever they could in the religious life and conduct of Hindus and Muslims and avoiding wholesale denunciation. Such tendencies led to the strategy elaborated by J. N. Farquhar, of portraying Hinduism as leading towards Christianity, and as being fulfilled in it. To treat other religions as a divinely inspired preparation for the gospel had been the advice of Tertullian in the third century AD, but it had long since been forgotten or ignored. The 'fulfilment theory' gained widespread acceptance among Protestant missionaries in India, and also at the Protestant World Missionary Conference at Edinburgh in 1910.

Farquhar had in fact been anticipated by some Indian theologians. As early as 1875 Krishna Mohan Banerjea, a Bengali Brahman who became an Anglican clergyman, argued that the Aryan ancestors of the Hindus had been aware of such doctrines as that of a propitiatory blood sacrifice, that Hinduism pointed towards Christianity, and that Hindus could be converted without deserting their cultural heritage. Towards the end of the nineteenth century other Indian Christians urged that Christianity in India should assume an Indian form. Brahmabandhab Upadhyay, a Roman Catholic, wore the robes of a Hindu holy man, and thought it possible to be both a Hindu and a Christian. A Brahman himself, he argued in his journal *Sophia* that the caste system was beneficial and that Christian doctrines should be formulated in Indian terminology, but the Apostolic Delegate forbade Catholics to read it.

When the Salvation Army came to India in the 1880s its officers wore an Indian style of uniform, some took Indian names, and great use was made of Indian music. This troubled many British officials, but had little perceptible effect on Indians. There were many other attempts to clothe Christianity in Indian dress. In 1887 Kali Charan Banerjea founded the Calcutta Christo Samaj, with no liturgy and no distinction between priests and laity, but it only lasted for seven years. A National Church was founded in Madras in 1886, and scattered congregations survived in South India until the 1920s. The Hindu *ashram*—a community of monks under a teacher—attracted interest, and a Christian *ashram* was founded in 1917 by Narayan Vaman Tilak, a Maratha Christian of Brahman origin who wrote religious poetry. Others followed, notably Christa Seva Sangh under the Anglican Jack Winslow in Pune. There were suggestions that Vedic or other Hindu texts might take the place of the Old Testament in a Christian liturgy suited to India, and there were similar proposals in other parts of Asia. But such tendencies were checked by Hendrik Kraemer.

The Dutch Church in Indonesia had no intention of being influenced by other religions, and it was confronted by a resurgent and intolerant Islam. In this context, Kraemer propounded in Barthian style the thesis that Christianity was fundamentally different from all other religions, which were of merely human origin, and his *Christian Message in a Non-Christian World* turned much Protestant opinion in a conservative direction when the International Missionary Conference was held at Tambaram, near Madras, in 1938. On the other hand, Caodaism, a synthesis of Buddhism, Taoism, and Roman Catholicism, flourished in Vietnam from its foundation in the 1920s, in spite of official disapproval, and after the Second World War it developed a military wing opposed first to French and subsequently to Communist authority. It has been severely repressed by the present regime.

The attainment of Indian independence in 1947 reinforced the view that Christianity should lose its 'Western' aspects, and especially the denominational divisions which had come with Western missionaries. Anglicans, Methodists, and some other denominations joined in the Church of South India in 1947, and in 1970 a Protestant Church of North India and a Protestant Church of Pakistan were founded. In the Roman Catholic Church the *padroado* had remained, in spite of efforts to settle the jurisdictional problem when an ecclesiastical hierarchy was established in 1886, but Indian independence made the continuance of Portuguese ecclesiastical authority seem anachronistic, and the *padroado* duly ended. However, the problem was not merely one of ecclesiastical law. When the last Portuguese bishop of Cochin retired in 1952 the hostility of high and low castes there was such that the diocese was divided into two, with a bishop of appropriate caste at the head of each. There remained some suspicion of Christianity as a foreign religion, and in 1956 a committee appointed by the Madhya

Pradesh government criticized the Christian churches as anti-national and subject to American influence. In the ensuing controversy much evidence was presented to the effect that Christianity in India had become authentically Indian. There was also much Hindu criticism of attempts to make converts.

In this situation many of the clergy turned to the idea of dialogue as a technique of sharing religious ideas, and various Indian theologians, especially the Roman Catholic Raimundo Panikkar, studied the sophisticated metaphysical texts of post-Vedic Hinduism to show that Christianity was compatible with many of its ideas and values, developing the notion of fulfilment in more scholarly ways than had previously been achieved. However, the process of dialogue was criticized as mainly of interest to theologians, and as one-sided, since most Hindus, however scholarly, were convinced that they had nothing to learn from other religions. More Christian *ashrams* were founded, both Protestant and Roman Catholic, and there were further attempts to devise liturgies of an Indian type. However, these experiments were criticized as of interest mainly to priests and a minority of the élite, whereas most people preferred the liturgy to which they were accustomed, which encouraged them to feel that their religion was different from Hinduism rather than in danger of being absorbed by it.

As a consequence of the growth of Protestant missionary activity since the late eighteenth century, Protestant numbers in India have increased, although Roman Catholics remain in the majority. In 1971, of 14 million Christians there 8 million were Roman Catholics. In accounting for the relative strength of Catholicism one may note the longer history of its missions. One may bear in mind also the comments of the Abbé Dubois, a missionary with long experience of Mysore in the early years of the nineteenth century, who pointed to the similarity between Catholic and Hindu devotional practices—processions, holy water, images, the ringing of bells, fasts with strict rules, feasts with much splendour—and, one may add, the mystery associated with a liturgy in a sacred language. Much of this has been discarded as a consequence of the Second Vatican Council, and the results for Catholic Christianity have yet to be seen. In Pakistan, where missionaries confronted the more austere devotional practices of Islam, of one million Christians in the 1970s only 280,000 were Roman Catholics.

In the maritime provinces of Sri Lanka, the Roman Catholic Church took root under Portuguese rule, the Dutch Reformed Church under Dutch rule, and Anglican and Nonconformist Churches under British rule. Converts came especially from the Karawa fisher caste and from the Salagama cinnamon caste. Their commercial contacts with the Portuguese and Dutch opened the way to Western education and administrative careers, but ordination as Buddhist monks was reserved to members of the dominant Goyigama caste, whose stronghold was in the independent mountain kingdom of Kandy. The British conquest of Kandy in 1815 and subsequent unification of the country did not change this situation. The reaction of some upwardly mobile members of the Karawa and Salagama castes, in the late eighteenth and early nineteenth century, was to form new orders of monks based on ordination in Thailand. Others were converted to Christianity, and members of those castes have played a leading part in the Roman Catholic and Protestant churches.

At first Buddhist monks in Sri Lanka looked sympathetically upon Christian missionaries as engaged in meritorious activity: they allowed missionaries to use their prayer halls, and some helped translate the Bible. They were shocked when missionaries refused to allow them in return to use churches and school halls, and they were antagonized by the bitterness of evangelical and Nonconformist attacks on Buddhism. This was the context of the Buddhist revival during the second half of the nineteenth century, in which Karawas were especially prominent and when recourse was had to some of the techniques associated with Christianity, such as the publication of religious tracts and the formation of the Young Men's Buddhist Association on the lines of the YMCA. After independence successive governments under Buddhist influence placed restrictions on missionaries, but the various churches had developed strong local roots. By the 1970s, of one million Christians in Sri Lanka, 879,000 were Roman Catholics. One reason for this disproportion is no doubt the long history of the Catholic Church there, from the coming of the Portuguese in the sixteenth century.

In Thailand, on the other hand, in spite of the efforts of the Missions Étrangères since the seventeenth century, there were relatively few Christians: there had been no European power to stand behind the missionaries. In Burma, where British rule lasted for barely a century, the Buddhists, who formed the majority of the population, showed little inclination to change their faith, and Roman Catholic and Protestant missionaries made most converts among the Karen and Shan tribes. After independence this situation provoked some official suspicion of Christianity as encouraging such minorities in their separate identity. Similarly, the Muslim majority in Malaya proved impervious to missionary endeavours, but the Chinese minority provided many converts. In Indonesia also, Christianity appealed not to the Muslim majority but to minorities such as the Chinese commercial community in the towns and the inhabitants of the islands of Flores and Timor, where Christianity began with the coming of the Portuguese.

The Philippines is the only country in Asia with a predominantly Christian population. Although many people are not in fact practising Christians, church attendance is relatively high and religious life in the islands is vigorous and colourful. Christianity is also capable of exerting a decisive influence on political affairs: this was made clear, for example, by the events leading to the end of the Marcos regime in 1986.

At the beginning of the nineteenth century, the Philippines had already been a primarily Christian country for about two hundred years, although Muslim communities existed in the south, and there were some remote mountainous areas which had not yet been successfully evangelized. Pre-Christian beliefs and practices had not entirely disappeared, however, and a distinctively Filipino 'folk' Catholicism had emerged, in which such elements were fully integrated. This was, and is, especially evident in the Filipino versions of the elaborate rituals of Spanish Catholicism, such as the spectacular processions with their life-size images of holy figures. Moreover, in some areas which received little if any direct evangelization, pre-Christian elements, particularly those connected with illness and death, were able to preserve a separate identity. Ordinary Christians from such areas saw no objection to consulting both official and 'folk' religious specialists if the need arose.

While Christianity at a popular level was deeply Filipino, the same could not be said of its institutional structure. In fact, opposition to Spanish domination of the church, and in particular to the wealth and corruption of the religious orders, played an important part in the gradual build-up of nationalist feeling in the nineteenth century. The complex three-way relationship which existed between the episcopate, the Spanish government, and the powerful religious orders, had acted against the development of a strong indigenous clergy. Very few Filipinos were able to join the orders, and even in the less privileged secular priesthood they tended to have low status. Filipinos in general were thought to be unsuitable, because the level of seminary education was not high, and, in the case of the orders, because they did not want to share their political power with those whose loyalty to Spain was suspect. This situation caused much bitterness, particularly among the growing number of educated Filipino clergy, but attempts to gain a position of equality were greeted with accusations of rebellion. From mid-century, such priests did, in fact, become increasingly open to moves for more general political reform. When the abortive Cavite mutiny of 1872 led to a general round-up of leading Filipino reformists, on very flimsy evidence, a significant number were priests, and three of these, including the young and active José Burgos, were executed. Although the Filipino clergy did not play a leading role in the more radical nationalist movement which now developed, their support remained, and the three executed priests became national heroes.

When the Philippine revolution broke out in 1896, the

hierarchy supported Spain, but after annexation by the United States in 1898 it threw in its lot with the Americans, primarily because of the anticlerical attitude of the revolutionaries. The following decade brought radical changes to Roman Catholicism in the Philippines, with legal separation of church and state, the gradual withdrawal of the Spanish religious orders, and the arrival of many non-Spanish Roman Catholic clergy. Spanish bishops were gradually replaced, but by Americans rather than Filipinos. Resentment against the church remained, and it now had to face competition from both the nationalist Iglesia Filipina Independiente, and from American Protestant missionaries.

The Iglesia Filipina Independiente began to take shape in 1899, when Gregorio Aglipay, a Filipino priest, responded to a call from leaders of the revolution to form an organization to take over church affairs now that Spanish rule had ended. Aglipay hoped for recognition from Rome but was urged to accept leadership of a completely independent church, and did so in 1902. It is estimated that he was followed by nearly a quarter of all Catholics in the Philippines, but many equally patriotic Filipinos and Filipino clergy were not willing to give up their allegiance to Rome. Under the influence of Isabelo de los Reyes, a patriotic Filipino lawyer and journalist who had been exiled by the Spanish, the official theology of the new church developed decidedly Unitarian leanings and close links were formed with the American Unitarian Association in the 1930s. In terms of outward liturgical form, however, little changed, and the same could probably be said of the beliefs of most ordinary members. The new church faced many difficulties, primarily arising from a lack of finance and the low educational level of most of its clergy. Its membership figures failed to keep pace with the growth in population. It was meeting strong opposition from a Roman Catholic Church which was gradually regaining equilibrium, and in which Filipino priests were coming to play an increasingly prominent role. In addition, the leaders of the new church became involved in political activities, and the formation of the Republican Party.

With the exception of the Episcopal Church, which worked among the remote non-Christian tribes and the Muslim communities, the Protestant denominations concentrated on evangelizing among Roman Catholics. They were also involved in much health, education, and general social work. For this reason, Protestantism had greater influence on society than actual numbers of converts would suggest. Various splits occurred within the denominations as independent churches were formed by Filipinos anxious for control over their own religious affairs. This encouraged the missionary societies themselves to hand over power voluntarily to legitimate Filipino sister denominations. Interest was also shown in co-operation and even unity by groups of mainstream denominations and separate groups of indigenous churches.

Churches which have been called only 'quasi-Christian' also came into being. The most important of these was the Iglesia ni Cristo, formed in 1914 by Felix Manalo, who had before then had contacts with various Christian bodies, including the Seventh-day Adventists. He believed himself to be the angel 'having the seal of the living God' of Revelation 7: 2 and taught that the Iglesia ni Cristo was the only true church, and that there was no salvation outside it. Tightly organized and with aggressive recruiting methods, it has grown particularly rapidly since the Second World War.

The Second World War affected Christianity in the Philippines along with everything else. Lives were lost and property damaged. In addition, the Japanese occupiers tried to exert religious control, just as they were doing in Korea and in Japan itself. This led to a certain amount of animosity immediately after the war between those Protestant denominations which had been willing to co-operate and those which had refused.

In 1946, the Philippines gained independence. Christianity has continued to play a very important role in the country. The Roman Catholic Church has been plagued by a shortage of male vocations and still depends on foreign clergy, most of them members of religious orders. The Protestant denominations are under Filipino control, but foreign financial help is still very important. There has also been an influx of fundamentalist missionary groups. Since the war, the Iglesia Filipina Independiente has rejected its Unitarian past, at the expense of a minor schism, and developed very close links, including an intercommunion agreement, with the Philippine Episcopal Church. Relations between the Roman Catholic Church and other Christian groups in the Philippines have also become much closer.

The most important issue facing Christianity in the Philippines today is the question of political involvement. Although the Vatican urged a position of neutrality, from the mid-1970s the Catholic hierarchy, later joined by the Protestant National Council of Churches, began to emphasize the wider social implications of faith and criticize the excesses of the Marcos regime. Matters came to a head with the 1986 election, when Cardinal Sin, the Catholic Bishops' Conference of the Philippines, and the Catholic Radio Veritas played a crucial and unprecedented role in mobilizing domestic and world opinion against Marcos on moral grounds and then calling for peaceful resistance against a fraudulent victory. The resulting 'bloodless revolution' was widely interpreted as the fruit of divine intervention.

Divisions exist, however. 'Conservative' and 'progressive' Christians united in order to oppose Marcos, but while the fundamentally anti-Communist majority probably hope that this will prevent an eventual violent left-wing revolution, a vocal minority sees radical left-wing policies as the only solution to the basic social inequalities of the present system. Whatever the future brings, Christianity in the Philippines will be expected to retain a moral voice in political affairs.

East Asia

China, Japan, and Korea have a broadly similar religious background, particularly as regards the close relationship between

Confucianism and the state. At the beginning of our period, Roman Catholic Christianity had been rejected by the government in all three countries, for political rather than religious reasons, and Christian communities were being persecuted. When the Western powers began to try to develop Western-style diplomatic and commercial links with East Asia in the early nineteenth century, this was accompanied by a general reawakening of missionary interest, from the new Protestant missionary societies as well as from the Roman Catholics. Christianity was about to make a fresh appearance, still as the alien religion of the West, but as the religion of a West which now had undeniable commercial, technological, and military superiority; a West which was to be feared, but from which there was also clearly much to learn. This new situation inevitably influenced both the missionaries and those who listened to them, but in ways which differed significantly according to the balance of power.

In all three countries, restrictions on Christianity and on evangelizing were only lifted gradually, as a result of religious toleration clauses in 'unequal' treaties unwillingly signed with Western countries, and prolonged diplomatic pressure, particularly from France. Missionaries accepted this situation and even saw in it the workings of divine providence, although they were aware that the Western powers, and Western merchants, did not always act in a 'Christian' manner.

In China, Christianity had a complex and ambivalent relationship with the Western powers. It would be wrong to say that the Christian message itself had no appeal. This is clear, for example, in the, admittedly distorted, influence of 'Messianic' evangelical ideas on the ideology of the Taiping rebellion of 1850–64, and from the recent evidence of the survival, and even growth, of Christianity in mainland China since 1949. Even so, there is some truth behind the 'rice Christian' stereotype. The hope of Western protection and material help must have exerted at least an initial influence on poor and uneducated converts, who formed the great majority, and was clearly exploited by some missionaries, in particular the French Roman Catholics. On the other hand, the very fact of Western power, and its use to support missionaries and Chinese Christians in local disputes, enhanced the disruptive and subversive reputation of Christianity. It also made equal relationships between missionaries and Chinese Christians difficult. Western power made wide-scale missionary activity possible, but Christianity was vulnerable in periods of strong nationalist feeling as seen in the Boxer Uprising of 1900, in the 1920s, and under Communist rule. In the long term, the growth of a nationally accepted and independent Christianity was clearly impeded by its association with the West.

In Japan, Western economic and political encroachment never reached the level which it did in China, and relationships between missionaries and local officials were generally more harmonious. Missionaries saw a positive connection between Japan's desire for material 'Westernization' and the prospects for Christianity, and consequently welcomed the achievements of the new Meiji government (formed in 1868). However, they soon had to contend with rational and scientific arguments against Christianity of Western origin. As time went on, the increasing imbalance between Japan's success at adapting Western technology and its relative indifference to Christianity challenged their optimism. Even so, writers, the pioneers of Socialism, and even those trying to reform Buddhism, all received some Christian influence. In Japan, too, however, the Western connection of Christianity was a mixed blessing, and Christians were always having to battle against the stigma of disloyalty.

Korea provides a fascinating contrast both with China and Japan, and with the rest of Asia, since it came under the domination of non-Christian countries, first China and then Japan, rather than experiencing the direct threat of Western imperialism. Although Western missionaries tried as far as possible to remain politically neutral in their relationship with the Japanese, Christianity became identified with anti-Japanese feeling and actually became an expression of patriotism rather than the reverse. It is surely significant that today Christianity is much stronger in Korea than in any other Asian country, with the exception of the Philippines.

Christianity in China had been undergoing intermittent persecutions since the early eighteenth century, but it had not died out, and Roman Catholic missionaries had never been completely expelled. When missionaries again gained easy access to the country as a result of clauses in treaties of 1844, 1858, and 1860, one of the Catholic priorities was to re-establish their control over the surviving Christian communities, which remained sources of Catholic strength. Protestant missionaries only arrived on the Chinese mainland in real numbers after 1844, although the first had come in 1807. Like their Roman Catholic contemporaries, few showed any interest in Chinese culture or in the type of approach developed by Ricci in the late sixteenth and early seventeenth centuries, but special mention should be made of James Legge, whose pioneering translations of the Chinese classics are still highly regarded today.

Both Catholics and Protestants became involved in setting up schools and hospitals, and in famine relief. The primary justification for such secular work was that it opened the way for evangelization, although the evidence for this was slight. However, some Protestant missionaries clearly saw the social reform of China as part of their task, and even as an essential preliminary to successful evangelization. In the 1890s, a small group of these, including the British Baptist missionary Timothy Richard, managed to make contact with members of the scholarly élite who were interested in reforming China on Western lines. The influence at court of this reforming party was very short-lived, however.

Early in his career, Richard decided that adopting Chinese dress and other customs would help him to make contact with the Chinese. In this he was similar to another British missionary who provides a complete contrast to him in most other respects, Hudson Taylor, the founder of the China Inland Mission.

Together they provide a nice illustration of the two extremes in attitude referred to at the beginning of this chapter. While Taylor's hard-line approach to ancestor worship, and to Chinese culture in general, doubtless antagonized many Chinese, his message was clearly defined and his methods clearly focused to one end. Richard was just as committed to producing a Christian China. His softer attitude to Chinese culture and his interest in secular reform made him a more acceptable figure, but also meant that the Christian core of his message could be ignored. Both made a decided impact on the missionary community, and Taylor produced many converts, but neither produced a Christian China.

Interest in reforming China on Western lines increased during the early twentieth century, and this encouraged positive interest in Christianity. The abolition of the Confucian-based examination system in 1905 increased the popularity of Western-style education and Protestants in particular made great efforts, especially at the secondary and university level. Hopes for a new, strong, and Christian China ran high, and were focused mainly on Sun Yat-sen, who was missionary-educated, a baptized (if somewhat wayward) Christian, and greatly influenced by the 'social gospel' movement. Several who joined with him in trying to overthrow Imperial rule were from similar backgrounds. Chiang Kai-shek, who took over effective leadership of the Kuomintang on Sun Yat-sen's death in 1925, showed a favourable attitude to Christianity even when it was deeply unpopular, and he was baptized in 1930, although it may be that he was partly motivated by the boost this gave to his reputation in the West.

Despite the growing interest in Christianity, particularly in the decade following the 1911 revolution, it was now competing with the much wider stream of foreign ideas entering China, and which educated Chinese encountered abroad. Social Darwinism, Socialism, and eventually Marxism-Leninism, presented paths of development which challenged Christianity as well as Confucianism. Matters came to a head in the 1920s when groups such as the Anti-Christian League were formed and radicals and nationalists denounced Christianity for being irrational, an obstacle to change, and in league with Western imperialism. Missionaries and Chinese Christians tried to answer these attacks, and to distance themselves from imperialism, but when the disturbances died down it was because of action taken by Chiang Kai-shek, not because the trend away from Christian solutions to China's problems had been reversed.

There were related conflicts within Christianity itself, primarily over the desire for a self-supporting and autonomous Chinese Christianity with its roots in Chinese culture and, in the case of Protestantism, free from Western denominational divisions. Progress was made in this direction by both Protestants and Roman Catholics, the crucial impetus coming from above, partly from missionaries but largely from Western-educated Chinese Christians who had been influenced by liberal theology, such as Wu Yao-tsung (Y. T. Wu), and from outside, from the Vatican and from the International Missionary Council. On the other hand, at a grass-roots level, independent Christian movements of a strong 'fundamentalist' and Pentecostalist flavour began to appear. Among them were the Family of Jesus with its emphasis on mutual co-operation, and the Little Flock, founded by Watchman Nee in 1926, which was less overtly Pentecostalist and tended to attract more educated members.

Christians suffered from the Japanese invasion of China in the same way as the rest of the population. Church property was destroyed, and educational work disrupted, but Christians took part in relief work, and were able to channel outside aid into China. When the war ended, they were ready to help in the work of reconstruction, and missionary reinforcements arrived. Civil war broke out, however, and the Communist success in 1949 transformed the situation. While ostensibly allowing freedom of religious belief, the Communists were naturally suspicious of the links between Christianity in China and foreign imperialism, particularly in view of the anti-Communist stance of both the Vatican and the United States.

As international tension increased during 1950–1, foreign missionaries left, were expelled, and even imprisoned. Meanwhile, the mainstream Protestant Chinese leaders, disillusioned by the corruption of the Nationalists, and optimistic about the possibility of real change, tried to come to terms with the government. A 'Christian Manifesto' was produced which Protestants were encouraged to sign, and in 1951 the Three-Self (self-support, self-government, self-propagation) Patriotic Movement was established, with Wu Yao-tsung as elected chairman. Prominent Christians had to undergo re-education, and those who took a hard line, in particular members of indigenous groups such as the Family of Jesus and the Little Flock, were harshly treated. By 1952 all Protestant ties with foreign organizations had been severed; from 1958, during the Great Leap Forward, steps were taken to encourage the unification of the various denominations.

The position of Catholics was somewhat more complicated, since complete separation from the Vatican was required. There was a Patriotic Association, similar to the Three-Self Movement, but it took much longer to attract members. Priests and lay people were harassed and arrested, particularly in Shanghai, with its long tradition of Catholicism, which proved a centre of resistance. The real split with the Vatican did not come until 1958, when the first bishops were elected by local priests, and consecrated despite Vatican opposition. The status of such bishops is still a delicate question.

Restrictions on Christian activity gradually increased, and in 1966 the Cultural Revolution began. All religions were a target. Churches were closed or used for other purposes, Bibles burnt, priests and ministers sent to work-camps for re-education. No public worship was possible; outside China it was thought that organized Christianity must have died. Yet the faith was kept, and even spread, through the efforts of ordinary Christians who formed 'house congregations' and met to worship secretly in each other's homes. This became clear as the religious situation began to thaw, particularly after 1979, when public worship again became possible. No one knows what the future will bring, and there is evidence of a division between 'official' and 'underground' groups, particularly in the case of the Catholics. However, the vitality of a Christianity of which Chinese Christians themselves at last have control is beyond dispute.

Missionaries had been completely driven from Japan in the early part of the seventeenth century. They only began to re-enter after the treaties of 1857 and 1858 and even then had no permission actually to evangelize. In 1865, a group of 'hidden' Christians made contact with Roman Catholic priests at Nagasaki, and it was estimated that, in the Nagasaki area alone, as many as 20,000 believers had survived over 200 years of intermittent persecution and continuous danger in isolated rural communities. Tragically, when the authorities became aware of the situation, a new wave of persecutions started, and only ceased in 1873, as a result of strong diplomatic pressure. The beliefs and practices of the hidden communities had inevitably wandered from the path of orthodoxy, and the attention of the Roman Catholic missionaries was initially focused on the task of bringing them back to the fold. Many of the groups preferred to remain outside the church rather than change the practices which they had preserved at such cost. After 1873 there were few practical restrictions on the activities of missionaries and Christians, although they were apt to be regarded with suspicion at times of national tension.

The most notable feature of early Protestant Christianity in Japan was the conversion of a significant group of educated Japanese ex-*samurai* who emphasized the importance of self-support and independence. Missionaries played a much less prominent role than in China; as time went on they came under increasing criticism for being arrogant, badly educated, and old-fashioned and narrow in their theological views. The most famous of the early Japanese Protestant leaders is undoubtedly Uchimura Kanzo, who started the Non-Church Movement. This sees the traditional church structure of Christianity as a Western accretion, and rejects all formal religious institutions in favour of loosely organized Bible-study groups based on the more familiar Asian teacher–pupil relationship. A complex figure, Uchimura won national attention for his moral stand on political issues, particularly in the 1890s and early 1900s. He is most admired in Japan today for the forthright way in which he struggled with the problem of being both a patriotic Japanese and a good Christian.

From the early twentieth century, Christianity in Japan gradually became less important in rural areas and developed the association with the urban salaried middle class which it still has today. Despite this, Christians displayed concern for those who had suffered rather than flourished as a result of Japan's successful industrialization and Kagawa Toyohiko achieved national, and even more international, acclaim for his work among such people. Christian educational institutions were competing against a better equipped, cheaper, public education system, and tended to lack academic prestige. Christianity itself was popular among students in the 1910s and 1920s, however, and Christian educational establishments remained very important for women.

During this time, Japan was emerging as a world power and beginning to penetrate the rest of Asia, both economically and militarily. Reflecting the desire of their members to be good Japanese as well as good Christians, the mainstream churches tended to accept what was happening and interpret it in as favourable a light as possible. Powerful elements in the Nihon Kirisuto Kumiai Kyokai (Japan Congregational Church) welcomed the Japanese annexation of Korea in 1910 and sent missionaries to the Koreans in order to provide them with spiritual as well as political leadership. Individual Christians, such as Kashiwagi Gien of the Kumiai Kyokai and, later on, Yanaihara Tadao of the Non-Church movement, were more sceptical and openly criticized the actions of the government, but they were very much in the minority.

As time went on, government pressure on all religious bodies increased, and attendance at Shinto shrines became an important part of public life. In 1936, Propaganda Fide officially accepted the government's claim that Shinto and its rites were patriotic rather than religious. Once the nation was clearly committed to all-out war with China in 1937, almost everyone closed ranks, or retreated into silence. As a result of the Religious Bodies Law of 1939 and even greater government pressure, ties with foreign missionary organizations were cut, and most of the Protestant church bodies decided that their best chance of survival lay in joining forces and gaining recognition as a religious body from the Department of Education. Thus in 1941 the Nihon Kirisuto Kyodan was formed. Those churches which did not join were subject to much harassment until the end of the war, as were the fundamentalist and millenarian Holiness churches, even though they had joined. The Catholic Church also applied for recognition and was successful, in spite of the fact that its Japanese leadership refused to separate from Rome.

The atomic bomb dropped on Nagasaki in 1945 devastated the country's oldest centre of Christianity; in general, Christians and Christian property suffered from the effects of a disastrous war along with the rest of the country. With the end of the war missionaries returned, many of them representing new fundamentalist groups, and financial aid poured in from Christian sources. The reaction against the old order and enthusiasm for reform and democracy was accompanied by new interest in Christianity, although this gradually waned. Some Protestant churches split off from the Kyodan, but it remained the biggest Protestant body. As Japanese Christians tried to come to terms with their complicity in the events leading up to the war, they became determined not to let anything like that happen again. They are active in the peace movement, and are always on the alert to oppose government involvement with Shinto, particularly the participation of members of the Cabinet in rituals for the war dead at the Yasukuni shrine. In present-day Japan there are prominent Christian writers such as Endo Shusaku, Bibles sell well, Christmas is a successful commercial festival, and many of the 'new' religions which have shown such spectacular growth since the war reveal traces of Christian influence. Yet Christianity itself still tends to be seen as an alien, Western religion, glamorous for that reason, but also beyond the spiritual reach of the average Japanese.

In the case of Korea, Roman Catholic Christianity only really began to enter, through China, in the late eighteenth century, and there was virtually no Western missionary presence until the mid-1840s, but it was quickly able to attract converts from all ranks of society. Its appeal, particularly to members of the élite, made it an object of government suspicion, however, and there were several severe outbreaks of persecution, the first occurring in 1801. Protestant Christianity began to enter Korea in a similarly indirect and clandestine way from the 1870s, but concerted missionary efforts only became possible when the Western powers, this time preceded by Japan in 1876, started to sign treaties with Korea in the 1880s; even then the situation remained somewhat precarious, with Roman Catholic missionaries taking a fairly aggressive attitude and their Protestant counterparts being more cautious, until the beginning of the next decade. Important features of this early stage of Christianity in Korea are the emphasis of both Roman Catholics and Protestants on the use of native Korean script, which made Christianity accessible to ordinary Koreans, and the Protestant concentration on encouraging self-support and self-propagation by individual Korean Christians rather than on building formal church organizations.

Korean interest in Christianity only really began to grow after Japan's victory in the Sino-Japanese War in 1895, which led to increasing Japanese influence in Korean affairs. Christianity was associated with the new influx of Western ideas and interest in modernization, but also exerted a strong spiritual appeal, particularly in times of national despair and hardship, as is shown by the revival movement of 1907. In addition, it became identified with patriotic anti-Japanese feeling. After annexation in 1910 this tendency increased, since church groups were virtually the only independent bodies with national organizations and international ties. Christians were accordingly regarded with great suspicion and formed the majority of the over 150 intellectuals arrested and tortured for allegedly conspiring against Japanese rule in 1911. Even so, they played a prominent part in popular anti-Japanese protests, notably the March 1st movement of 1919. Persecution became even greater in the 1930s, when the question of Christian attendance at Shinto shrines became an issue. Great bravery was shown, but eventually all the Christian bodies had to accept the official line that Shinto observances were non-religious expressions of loyalty to the Japanese state, or cease to exist.

For Korea, the end of the Second World War meant an end to Japanese domination, but the beginning of fresh political strife. Christianity was affected both by the partition of North and South, and, in the case of Protestantism, by internal difficulties, as ministers who had been imprisoned for refusing to worship at Shinto shrines were released and criticized those who had compromised. There were also institutional divisions between those who supported the world-wide ecumenical movement and those who regarded it as both politically and theologically unsound. The Korean War (1950–3) brought huge influxes of refugees to the South, many of whom were Christian, since the Communists took a hard-line attitude to both Korean Christians and foreign missionaries, regarding them as spies. Public church worship is not allowed in North Korea at present, but there is evidence that Christianity is surviving underground through the bravery of ordinary Korean Christians, with a household church movement similar to that of mainland China. In the South, various interesting developments have occurred. As in Japan, new religious movements have emerged which show traces of Christian influence. The most famous in the West is the Unification Church of Moon Sun Myung, who may well see himself as sent to complete the task which Christ left unfinished on his death.

The first two Presidents of South Korea were prominent Christians. After the military takeover of 1961 mainstream

Christianity grew increasingly politicized, the impetus for this coming from liberal Protestants; from the mid-1970s it became a major centre of opposition activity. Linked to this has been the development of a Korean equivalent to the liberation theology of Latin America, *minjung* theology, in which the historical experience of the Korean people is closely identified with the experience of the Israelites as revealed in the Old Testament. Christianity seems to have become an accepted part of national life.

In Asia, Christianity encountered ancient and sophisticated civilizations with differing religio-philosophical traditions, and interacted with them in a variety of ways. It may appear that the human effort and suffering, the amounts of money expended, have not been commensurate with the small numerical results. But Christianity in Asia has exerted an influence out of proportion to the actual numbers of believers, just as Asian Christians have made their own contribution to the development of Christianity as a world religion, through their writings and through their active participation in international Christian movements, particularly those of an ecumenical nature. The diverse experience of Christianity in Asia is also important because of the questions which it poses. It leads us to examine the causes and effects of missionary activity, in particular its links with Western imperialism. It also leads us to ponder the nature of Christianity itself, its social and economic implications, as we see its challenge to structures and processes different from those of the West, and the significance of its claim to be a unique and universal revelation which transcends the boundaries of Western civilization.

15

The Orthodox Churches of
Eastern Europe

SERGEI HACKEL

THE Orthodox Church would normally insist that all bishops
have equal, if different, responsibilities. In the words of St
Cyprian, 'the episcopate is a single whole, in which each bishop
enjoys full possession'. Nevertheless, in the eighteenth and
nineteenth centuries the Orthodox world possessed two pivotal
points of particular importance.

One had an ancient claim on the loyalties of the faithful, and
even those who were formally beyond its boundaries nurtured
a residual awe for what it represented or should seek to represent.
Constantinople had long ceased to be the capital of the Christian
empire. But its patriarchal see was still the keeper of its sacred
heritage. More than this, the patriarchate, even the city itself,
were often seen as the earnest of a Christian empire yet to be
revived. Greek proponents of the 'Great Idea' and Russian
Panslavists were at one at least in this, that each sought validation for their various plans by laying claim to the city of the
world's desire. 'For this holy city is the pride, the support, the
sanctification and the glory of the whole inhabited world': such
were the proud words of the Byzantine patriarch of 1400, such
remained the sentiments of nineteenth-century dreamers, regardless of the much-changed circumstances. 'Athens is the capital of
the kingdom', announced Ioannis Kolettis to the Greek National
Assembly in 1844; 'Constantinople is the great capital, the
City, the dream and home of all Greeks'.

No comparable dignity could be claimed by the other major centre of the day, St Petersburg. It was a parvenu among capitals, an early eighteenth-century foundation, and almost entirely secular in its orientation at that. Indeed its very foundation by Peter the Great involved the spurning of an earlier tradition in accordance with which Moscow, the former capital of Russia, had claimed not only to equal, but to supersede, Constantine's city, his New and Second Rome. In keeping with Moscow's fifteenth-century status and vocation as the Third (and final) Rome—the Second having fallen inwardly by temporary/temporizing union with Rome (1439), even before succumbing outwardly to the onslaught of Islam (1453)—the Russian church had achieved patriarchal status by the end of the century to follow (1589), a rare privilege at that time. But the same emperor who removed the country's capital to St Petersburg also left the patriarchal throne vacant (1700–21) before expressly abolishing the Russian patriarchate itself (1721). Dark rumours circulated among his people to the effect that the emperor was the Antichrist himself, and that the last days were to be expected. For this was certainly more than a change in nomenclature. The Russian church administration was to be directed by an attenuated synod, so constituted as to be under close and constant government control. Such proposals for the reconsideration and reform of church–state relations as were repeatedly put forward by individual churchmen throughout the two centuries of the synod's existence were to be ignored and relegated to the archives.

It was particularly galling that the synod's principal Civil Servant and supervisor was to be a layman who might not even be Orthodox by faith. Peter's original instructions required no more than he be 'a good man . . . to be chosen from among the officers': he was to be 'our eye and personal representative for the affairs of state'. Significantly, his title *Oberprokuror* was borrowed from the German language and the Protestant milieu. Not surprisingly, 'Peter listened to no part of what I told him more attentively', noted an Anglican divine in 1698, 'than when

I explained the authority that the Christian Emperours [*sic*] assumed in the matters of religion and the supremacy of our Kings'. Such supremacy of kings was much in keeping with the Russian ruler's plans.

Thus the kind of spiritual, even administrative, autonomy which the patriarch of Constantinople might enjoy within the confines of the Islamic Ottoman empire—his role as administrator of the Christian population or *millet* was clearly defined and generally respected—was not conceded, in an overtly Christian society, to the synod of the Russian church.

Nevertheless, Christian and Orthodox this society could still claim to be, and justifiably so. The majority of the population were long to remain largely unaffected by that Westernization and secularization of the upper and managerial classes over which Peter had presided. Furthermore, from coronations downwards, the formal Orthodoxy of public life was safeguarded at all levels of society.

For long Russia was alone in her public and overt adherence to Orthodoxy. She was thus a point of reference and a source of strength for subjugated nations who sought comparable opportunities and status. Hence the involvement of St Petersburg, or at least the expectation of it, when such nations made their move towards political and ecclesiastical independence; not least because of the antagonism which in any case existed between the Russian and the Ottoman empires. For it was principally against the hegemony of the Constantinople patriarchate that would-be or fledgling independent churches needed to react. Moreover, the search for ecclesiastical self-determination was not unrelated to an anti-Ottoman or anti-Muslim stance adopted by the citizens of various emergent nations. There was usually no question of doubting the orthodoxy of the patriarchate of Constantinople, although the pronounced Calvinism of a seventeenth-century patriarch like Cyril Loukaris was not easily forgotten. But any patriarch was inevitably in the favour of the sultan, who alone could confirm or countermand his election. This favour was gained at considerable expense. For the patriarch was expected to pave the way to his throne by offering the sultan a munificent *peshkesh*, and the patriarchate as a whole was required to make additional contributions to the Ottoman treasury year by year. In return, the patriarch was entrusted with the oversight of all the sultan's Christian subjects. He was effectively their ethnarch, virtually vicegerent to the Islamic Porte. Paradoxically, his potential power was greater than before the Turkish conquest. But Christians as well as Muslims thus had every reason to expect a degree of conformism, if not passivity, on his part. It may well have been Patriarch Gregory V who in 1798 issued (albeit under the name of Anthimos, patriarch of Jerusalem) a document which would have fully confirmed them in such expectations. Under the title *Paternal Exhortation* it urged wholehearted acceptance of Turkish rule, with all its benefits for Christians: it was clearly God's will that things should be so ordered. By contrast, any striving for political emancipation was 'an incitement of the devil, a deadly poison, destined to push the people into disorder and destruction'.

New Kingdoms, Independent Churches

However, many were ready for such disorder and, if need be, destruction. In particular, a secularized Greek intelligentsia, impressed by the precedent of the French revolution, and guided more by reading of the *philosophes* than of the Fathers, were already at work preparing the ground for nationalistic uprisings. The Orthodox Church was not central to such plans. Nevertheless, this was the church to which the mass of the Greek population belonged: and their evident faith, upheld though it was largely by unsophisticated participation in the age-old liturgical round, could hardly be ignored. Thus, despite their condescension, even the intellectuals were eventually to concede (in the words of the first Greek Constitution) that 'the religion of the state is the Eastern Orthodox Church of Christ'. Nevertheless, a 'religion of the state' required that new structures should accompany new boundaries; and their nature was to be debated over several decades.

In the case of neighbouring Serbia new structures were less evidently needed than in Greece since the patriarch of Constantinople had earlier recognized the separate or at least the individual status of the church in Serbian lands: an autonomous archdiocese of Peć had been suppressed only as recently as 1766, and Constantinople still accorded the local church at least some dignity by exercising its authority locally by means of an intermediary, an exarch, albeit a Greek. It was therefore the more natural for the patriarchate eventually to go further, if only under pressure from the Serbs. In due course it countenanced the gradual replacement of Greek by Serbian bishops; it accepted also the autonomy of the national church in the newly liberated Serbian kingdom. Formal autonomy, granted in 1832, was to be confirmed and extended in 1879 by the granting of full autocephaly; by 1920 the Serbian church had regained its patriarchal status, formerly accorded as early as 1346.

But for Greece there was no such precedent, and the successful revolt against the Turks of 1821 left church and state uncertain as to their respective roles and status. The fact that one of the Greek bishops, Germanos of Old Patras, had enthusiastically blessed the Greek uprising at the onset (25 March 1821) and had thereby helped to unleash a holy war, was not to gain the church a satisfactory, let alone a dominant, role in the new order of things. Constantinople, for its part, was also cautious about the abrupt and untoward demands of the Greek separatists. Had not its patriarch been hanged in April 1821 in direct reprisal for the Greek revolt? The memory of his execution was never to be erased.

Only in 1852 did the Greeks determine what the new pattern of church–state relations should be. But it was significant that the carefully devised concessions of Constantinople's patriarchal council, granting autocephaly even to the Greeks, were to be revised unilaterally and without further consultation by the parliament of Greece. For the 'freedom' now gained by the new Holy Synod of the Church of Greece ultimately involved subservience to one secular authority rather than to another. In this respect the Greek authorities turned consciously to St

Petersburg for their model. Here too were Peter the Great's Lutheran norms of church–state relations to prevail, and this despite the fact that an earlier proposal (1833) that Greek church administration should be framed 'according to the example of the Russian Church' had met with widespread disfavour among the local bishops. Here, as in St Petersburg, was a royal commissioner appointed (in effect, an *Oberprokuror*), with full authority—nominally, the king's—to validate or countermand the decisions of the Holy Synod. Even at this late stage there could be found a bishop who urged that 'we are Greek before we are Russian'. But his plea went unheeded in legislative circles. In any case, Constantinople itself had acknowledged the propriety of the Russian pattern in its time. Heterodox in origin it might have been, but not inimical to Orthodoxy for that reason. Thus Patriarch Jeremias of Constantinople not only 'confirmed, ratified and declared' his recognition of the Russian Holy Synod almost as soon as he learned of its foundation (1723), but apostrophized it somewhat curiously as 'our holy brother in Christ'.

The Russian pattern of church administration, in its essentials, was to be retained in Greece down to modern times. However it was to be less rigorously followed by other newly emergent churches in the course of the nineteenth century. Not that any one of them rejected the idea of a governing synod, or doubted that its every decision would require the assent of the relevant secular authorities before coming into force. Yet the equivalent of a procurator-general was less in evidence. Thus the state's minister of religion, who necessarily attended the sessions of the Romanian synod after 1885 (the year of that synod's formal institution), was expected to act more as an observer than as a scrutator or a censor; while the Bulgarian synod (established 1870) included no such figure at all, and that, paradoxically enough, on the advice of Russian Civil Servants.

All in all, a common adherence to the Orthodox faith signally failed to bring about uniformity in administrative practice among the churches of the Balkans. Nor did their Russian patron ever learn judiciously to reconcile the support given to one with the concomitant disillusion engendered in another. Such disillusion, in its turn, could lead to conflict. Thus, the establishment of a Russian-sponsored Greater Bulgaria in 1877–8 raised the fraught question of whether Macedonia fell into the orbit of Greek, Serbian, or Bulgarian church administrations. The resulting fractionalism would lead at times to Macedonian irregulars attacking not only their Turkish overlords, but also their own co-religionists. For those who had never abandoned their allegiance to the patriarch of Constantinople, nor indeed had cause to do so, were deemed to be no less supporters of the sultan's rule than he. Even the controversial establishment of a separate Macedonian Orthodox Church within the confines of the Serbian patriarchate almost a century later (1959) was not to bring a resolution of the problems shared and aggravated by the Orthodox of the several states involved. Secession from Constantinople indeed might bring cultural or even spiritual gains. But stability was harder to attain, and mutual toleration beyond the grasp of many.

Nationalism and its Limits

The independence accorded by the patriarchate of Constantinople, however reluctantly, to the churches of Greece, Serbia or Romania, was long to be withheld from the Bulgarian church. In effect, this meant ignoring a *fait accompli* not only at the time, but for the succeeding three-quarters of a century (1870–1945). In part this was due to the Bulgarians' peculiar approach to the question of their church independence and jurisdiction. It was argued that a Bulgarian church should take responsibility for Bulgarian Christians far beyond the confines of their native land, indeed wherever they might be located. Even in Constantinople itself there should be a separate Bulgarian exarch. None of this proved acceptable to the city's ancient patriarchate. But, aware of Bulgarian aspirations, and in the vain hope of averting a Bulgarian nationalist uprising (all the less welcome since it would attract powerful support from Russia), it was the Muslim sultan who took the initiative in February 1870 of issuing a *firman* to bring the proposed exarchate into being. Here was no question (yet) of a state seeking independence from the Porte and therefore (as in the case of Greece) independence also from that church administration which the Porte approved. Rather was it the assertion of an ethnic claim to separate development, such as Sts Cyril and Methodius might well have approved a thousand years before. Certainly, if (as was then argued) it is the prerogative of great nations 'to render glory to God in their own languages', Slavonic was to be preferred to Greek, if not modern Bulgarian to either. But all this was to be promptly defined as 'phyletism' (excessive nationalism, even tribalism, within the church) and roundly condemned by the patriarchate of Constantinople at a specially convened council of 1872. At the same time the Bulgarian exarchate was declared to be schismatic.

Whatever the justice of these condemnations, the patriarchate could well have found further symptoms of the same phyletism. Some of it, indeed, may be said to have emanated from the patriarchate itself. For no body of people offered it more constant or munificent support than the specifically Greek élite of Constantinople, the proud residents of the Phanar, the Phanariots. This could not but sway the patriarchate's cultural policies in favour of those factors which would lead in God's good time, so it was believed, to the revival of a Byzantine—for them this also meant Hellenic—realm. Its hallmarks were to be Greek language and Greek learning; Greek scholars and Greek hierarchs would be required for these to be purveyed throughout the Orthodox world. Thus, while the rising tide of modern nationalism would favour a promotion of Hellenism in the Greek-speaking milieu, the same tide would run counter to it in areas where Serbian, Bulgarian, or Romanian culture was in the ascendant, with legitimate claims to be no less, if otherwise, Orthodox.

It was therefore not surprising that the first Serbian insurrection against the Turks in 1804 was to be followed by the expulsion from the kingdom of Greek parish clergy. Too long had the latter been seen to dominate and exploit the indigenous population. All the readier were Serbs prepared to tolerate some losses in the field of education, which formerly was sponsored and promoted almost exclusively by Greeks. Some degree of the resulting or anticipated Hellenization might have been justified if the Orthodox populations of the Balkans and Asia Minor were ready to form a single spiritual and administrative entity once the Turks were altogether overthrown, as was the expectation of a Rigas Velestinlis (1797). But the reality was quite other.

Constantinople Regained

In any case, Greeks were not alone in yearning for Constantinople to become a Christian capital once more. Already in 1774 at the treaty of Kuçuk Kainarci, Catherine II had gained, or believed she had gained, the right for Russia to protect the Christian subjects of the sultan. The Russian ruler could thus be seen as a fellow patron of the patriarch's *millet*, and Catherine could dream of ruling a Christian, Russian-sponsored empire in the sultan's place. At least her grandson was named Constantine against the day. Belief in the support of Russia, sometimes justified, often over-optimistic, motivated uprisings against Ottoman suzerainty in the Morea (1770), in the Romanian (Moldavian and Wallachian) provinces (1806), or in the Greek world (1821). But plans for the specifically Russian conquest of Constantinople itself were not to be forgotten. Indeed, Russian armies engaged in the liberation of Bulgaria from the Turks (1877–8) were poised to take the city. What for the armies would have appeared as a major diplomatic and commercial prize was seen by the Muscovite Panslavists, the vociferous promoters of the war, as nothing other than a sacred city. Thus Dostoevsky could exclaim in his *Diary of a Writer*, 'Constantinople must be ours, conquered by the Russians from the

Turks, and it must remain ours in perpetuity'. Russia, as 'leader of the Orthodox world, its patron and protector' could claim this 'as a moral right'.

It was hardly for reasons such as these that the Western allies in 1915 offered Constantinople secretly to the Russians as a prize once the Great War should be successfully concluded. In the event, Russia left the war too early. In any case the Russian realm was now to propagate an entirely different and secular orthodoxy to the outside world and in the process to abandon any of its former claims to be the spiritual centre of the Eastern world. It was therefore without any support from the Russians, and in pursuit of an entirely Hellenic 'Great Idea', that another attempt was to be made in 1919–22 to restore former Byzantine territory in Asia Minor, potentially Constantinople itself, to the kingdom of the Greeks and thus, by extension, to Orthodoxy as well. But the ill-advised incursion into the Turkish mainland of the Greek armies at the behest of Venizelos and King Constantine was to bring unmitigated disaster on the military and civilian front alike. When these forces, together with the local Greek population, were driven ruthlessly into the sea at Smyrna in September 1922, the formerly Byzantine base in Asia Minor on which the Greeks had so fervently hoped to build (or recreate) 'their' empire was finally demolished. The martyrdom of the city's bishop, Chrysostom, emphasized the fragility of the patriarchate's new position. In a Constantinople which the former allies of the First World War had not surrendered to the Greeks when they might still have been expected so to do (an appeal to this effect had been rejected by them earlier that year), the patriarch was left with a drastically reduced flock and little of his former standing.

In the Orthodox world he remained 'first among equals' and as the eventual convenor of a projected Great and Holy Council of the Orthodox Church in the latter part of the twentieth century he could still be expected to play a role of some importance. In the Christian world at large he could also make a weighty contribution and the ecumenical movement has been the richer for it. But he was no longer a potentate. More and more could he be seen essentially as the undemanding *servus servorum Dei* (servant of the servants of God). Only the extension of his jurisdiction via the Greek diaspora in other parts of the world like the United States of America or Australia was to provide a new application for his Byzantine designation *oikoumenikou*, universal.

The 'equals' among whom the patriarch of Constantinople takes precedence were formerly few. But their number has increased in modern times. Many, if by no means all, emerged or re-emerged as the result of the nationalisms and frontier changes of the nineteenth and twentieth centuries. Thus to the ancient patriarchates of Alexandria, Antioch, and Jerusalem were once more added Georgia (1917), Serbia (1920), and, eventually, Bulgaria (1953). Russia also regained her patriarchate in 1917, although her church had no need to re-emerge from an ethnically alien church administration. By contrast, the Romanian church as such was an entirely new creation, formed out of the Wallachian, Moldavian, and Transylvanian eparchies of the Constantinople patriarchate (recognized as an autocephalous body in 1885, granted patriarchal status in 1925). In addition to Greece, independent archbishoprics were established in Finland (1924), Poland (1924), and Czechoslovakia (1947). An Albanian Orthodox Church also emerged briefly and was granted autocephaly in 1937. But all religious bodies and activities without distinction were prohibited by the local state authorities thirty years later, and this church was forced to withdraw into the shadows.

The Russian Foreign Office and the Church

In the course of the nineteenth century Russian plans to further the cause of Orthodoxy in the Balkans or the Middle East were by no means limited to the re-establishment of a Christian empire at Constantinople. Like the abortive (and misguided) plans for Constantinople, these were kept within the bounds of

Russian foreign policy. Not that the latter necessarily defined all their ends or determined all their detail. Thus the Orthodox Palestine Society pursued a laudable charitable programme, which involved the foundation and maintenance of schools and hospitals for the Arab population of the Holy Land. But the addition of the designation 'Imperial' to the society's name in 1885 seemed only to confirm what many of the Greek hierarchy in the Middle East had long suspected: that apparently worthy missionary activities were also, if not mainly, aimed at asserting Russian dominance in areas of diplomatic importance for the tsar's establishment. For political reasons, the Orthodox in the Holy Land and Syria were thus divided in their assessment and support of such work. The suspicions of the Greek élite in the region seemed to be confirmed in 1899 when, for the first time ever, it was not one of their number who was elected patriarch of Antioch, but an Arab with the backing of the Russian church. This could be seen as a rebuff to Constantinople, however indirect. Russian support for the Bulgarian declaration of independence from the patriarchate of Constantinople likewise courted the latter's displeasure. In this case the involvement of the Russian Foreign Office was undisguised: it was the Russian ambassador to the Porte, the Panslavist Nikolai Ignat'ev, who most of all determined his country's policy in this regard, rather than any churchman. Less obviously, if less effectively, Russian Civil Servants also offered support to the Serbian Orthodox Church. Thus the russophile metropolitan of Serbia, Mihailo, received regular subsidies for his church at Ignat'ev's instigation. Ignat'ev spoke of him as 'our most trustworthy ally': he consistently supported the metropolitan for fifteen years against various enemies and intrigues. For his part Mihailo saw himself as the spokesman of 'the southern Slavs who seek their salvation only in Russia and expect from her sincere paternal aid'. His deposition at the behest of the Serbian ruler in 1881 marked a low ebb in Russo–Serb relations in the aftermath of the Serbo–Turkish war, just as his restoration eight years later indicated that these relations had taken a turn for the better. In either case, foreign policy concerns were to the fore. Even when it was the ecclesiastical arm of the government which gave moral and financial support to central European Orthodox like the harried Old Ruthenian Adolf Dobrianskii in the 1870s, this was as much a device to gain a Russian foothold in Hungarian lands as to counteract Catholic or Uniate influences there. In other words, the aims or activities of church and state were not easily to be distinguished; and it is not surprising to find the longest-serving procurator-general of the Russian synod, Konstantin Pobedonostsev, referring with warm approval to Dobrianskii's conviction that 'the Orthodox faith is the principal guardian of national values'.

Westernization Reassessed

This was in 1875. But the idea had already become a familiar one in educated Russian circles some decades before, not least as the result of slavophile influence. Earlier generations, by contrast, failed to perceive the importance, even the existence, of the link between such factors as these. The previous century had witnessed the ever-increasing Westernization of the ruling classes. Even in the church milieu, where popular piety might have been expected to provide an effective earth for newly generated currents, there was a ready acceptance, hasty and ill-considered, of Western norms, theological, pedagogical, musical, and iconographical. The old ways were no longer sacrosanct. Those who adhered to them despite the changing fashions—the peasantry, the vast majority of the population—were treated with condescension or despised. Some, like the stalwart Old Believers, were peripheralized and persecuted. Only in the aftermath of the romantic movement were there Russian intellectuals who repented of their eighteenth-century heritage and sought enlightenment beyond the limits provided or prompted by the age of reason. Hence their reversion to the well-tried ways of the unsophisticated Orthodox around them. The organic and integral nature of the popular religion was found to be self-validating. The very simplicity of the people's faith made its adherents all the sounder as custodians of tradition. For custodians they were, insisted the slavophile theologian Aleksei Khomiakov: tradition is 'guarded by the totality, by the whole people of the Church, which is the Body of Christ'. It depends ultimately neither on the hierarchical order, nor on academic theologians, least of all on procurators-general. Indeed, the whole idea of authority is turned on its head. For 'the Church is not authority; rather is it the truth'. Thus 'it would be unfair to suppose that the Church requires enforced unity or enforced obedience. On the contrary, it rejects either. In matters of faith, enforced unity is a falsehood, while enforced obedience is death.' Khomiakov's tentatively delineated concept of catholic conciliarity (he coined the term *sobornost'* for it) was to receive ever wider acceptance by the turn of the century. But in his lifetime he was little heeded.

This was due in no small part to Khomiakov's initiative in departing from the then prevailing modes of discourse. Both in the Russian and the Greek academies of the preceding period, undiscriminating traditionalism was too often tempered by dependence on intellectual models borrowed from the West, not least because the Catholic or Protestant milieux had long provided would-be scholars with their education or at least their books. Issues which arose in Western disputes and debates were naïvely deemed to be of equal relevance to theologians of the Christian East. Hence the incongruous teaching of their course in the Latin language with which Russian seminarians had been burdened throughout the eighteenth century. Even more incongruous was the related study of scholastic thought. Increasingly, the West was perceived to be culturally superior. Such studies were intended to liberate the Orthodox from their 'benighted' state.

Much of this had resulted from Ukrainian Westernizing influence on and within the Russian church. This antedated the formal incorporation of the formerly Polish-dominated Ukraine into the Muscovite realm (1654), but it was confirmed and furthered by it. Additional confirmation was to follow in the 1680s with the assimilation of the Kievan (Ukrainian) metropolia—formerly under the jurisdiction of Constantinople—into the patriarchate of Moscow.

Comparable Westernizing tendencies were to be observed in the Greek-speaking world. Many an aspiring theologian would still proceed to Venice or to Florence for his studies, as had his forebears since the fifteenth century, often abandoning his Orthodox allegiance for the purpose. In due course such travellers would bring back not only scholastic, but rationalist texts, and would promote their study. Hence the improbable appearance, late in the eighteenth century, of Locke or Leibniz on the syllabus of the Athonite Academy, at the heart of the Orthodox monastic world. Here also were taught the philosophers of ancient Greece, not only, and not principally, the Fathers of the church. On Athos, at least, it could not be expected to last. Outraged traditionalists were to set the academy on fire, and its ruins were never to be used again. But elsewhere the appetite for materials to which the Christian East had only partial and occasional access still persisted. The Renaissance, the Reformation, and the Counter-Reformation, not to mention the Enlightenment, each had its epicentre elsewhere. Hence that allegedly benighted state which only Westernized education might be expected to dispel.

The Hesychast Revival

Such assumptions could not be fought by fire alone, nor by further innovation. Instead, the undervalued patterns of the past were to attract attention. Thus it was felt that if the arid and Westernizing manuals of the Russian theological schools were to be displaced, the classics of patristic thought must be allowed to exercise their influence. To this end, a fresh and augmented body of translations was required, and it was one of Khomiakov's fellow slavophiles, Ivan Kireevskii, who was to dedicate the years of his maturity to the unfashionable task. He worked as the member of a team, for the publication of the new patristic library had been undertaken by his neighbours in Kaluga, the monks of Optina pustyn'. The publishers were as important as the publications. For their reintegration of scholarship with traditional spirituality was to leave a lasting imprint on the Russian Orthodox Church, and their living witness, in Kireevskii's opinion, was 'more important than any books or ideas'.

The monastic community at Optino was in the forefront of a revival in mystical, hesychastic prayer, the prayer of the heart. This in turn was closely associated with the practice of spiritual guidance. For the fruit of prayer was not to be cherished and secreted away. Rather did the great mid-nineteenth-century elders of Optino—Leonid Nagolkin, Makarii Ivanov, and Amvrosii Grenkov—make themselves available to a continuous stream of pilgrims and enquirers. In this they emulated the great Serafim of Sarov, formerly a hermit, who had responded no less generously to the needs of the secular world in the immediately preceding years.

This hesychast revival was not unique to Optino, nor was it limited to Russia. To a remarkable degree, indeed, it overstepped linguistic, ethnic, and political frontiers. Far-removed from St Petersburg and Constantinople (though not thereby proof against the intrigues of one or the other) was a different focal point of the Orthodox world, the monastic 'republic' of Mount Athos. The monks of its many communities were certainly of various nationalities and backgrounds. Indeed, this had led at times to unseemly tensions and troubles, not least between Greeks and Russians. Yet at the same time, the juxtaposition of local or national trends on the Holy Mountain could also lead to their interplay and cross-fertilization.

Thus, while a Greek like the erudite Nikodemos of Dionysiou might assemble and publish a seminal collection of spiritual writings in the *Philokalia* (1782), the influence of this book depended equally on a Ukrainian with Moldavian connections who lived out its precepts and propagated them. Such was the *starets* Paisii Velichkovskii. The texts assembled by the one and in due course (1793) translated into Slavonic by the other, provided the framework for a dedicated life of inner prayer. But it was, above all, the personal example of the saintly Paisii and of his disciples which validated the framework and commended it to others. Paisii's influence radiated initially from Athos itself, then from the Moldavian community at Neamţ, to which the *starets* had transferred his work. From Neamţ the Paisian teachings penetrated to Optino, there to flourish. They penetrated equally to other Russian centres, such as the monasteries at Valaamo or Vysha. It was at Vysha that the remarkable Bishop Feofan Govorov lived out the last thirty years of his life as a recluse, committed to perpetual prayer, yet involved also in a wide-ranging pastoral role by means of correspondence. But the new hesychasm made its impact not only on monastics. Equally affected were individual seekers of authentic prayer who were 'in the world', the kind of unsophisticated layman whose involvement in the Jesus Prayer is vividly, perhaps too vividly, described in *The Way of a Pilgrim* (1884). At least one of the Optino elders (Amvrosii) gave this work his approval. But in any case it had its own momentum, and was to bring the teachings of the *Philokalia* far beyond the boundaries of the Russian, even of the Orthodox, world.

Unfortunately, it was the very practice of the Jesus Prayer (the ceaseless repetition and assimilation of the words 'Lord Jesus Christ, Son of God, be merciful to me a sinner') which was to provoke such a controversy on Athos as to involve not only the ecclesiastical authorities of Constantinople and St Petersburg, but even the armed forces of the Russian empire. For commitment to the prayer led at least some Russian Athonites to make incautious claims as to its nature and effects. The name of Jesus was itself divine, it was argued: hence invocation of it brought about communion with God, who is present in his Name. But was this 'onomatoxy' (praise of the Name) or, as critics of the teaching maintained, 'onomatolatry' (idolization of it)? When condemnation of the teaching by both the patriarch of Constantinople (1912) and by the Holy Synod at St Petersburg (1913) failed to still the intense debate among the Russian monks of Athos, the Russian government decided on extreme measures. The formerly Turkish territory of Athos had been ceded to Greece in 1912. Nevertheless, it was a Russian gunboat which was now sent to the peninsula. Thus were 833 monks forcibly deported to their homeland. It was a clumsy way to deal with a theological problem. Moreover, the problem itself remained unresolved. But that a government should concern itself at all with such matters provides an intriguing reflection on Russian church–state relations in the last days of the empire. Within the next four years the might of the abruptly secularized state was to be otherwise directed, and without even a residual thought of offering the church support. For the days of the empire were numbered.

Resources, Aspirations, and Potential of the Russian Church

Previously Russian missionary efforts, often unobtrusively, had kept pace with the political and economic expansion of the Russian realm. At the same time, they sought not to be narrowly or chauvinistically Russian. The Siberian Altai mission involved pioneer translations in one of the local languages, Telengut. Elsewhere, Chuvash, Tatar, Tungus, or Yakut were similarly used. Diplomacy and trade also caused missions to be established far afield. In the New World, there was an Alaskan diocese with its own language, Aleut. In the Far East, there were Orthodox missions in China, Korea, and Japan. Alone of the Orthodox states, Russia had the resources and the outreach for such activities, which themselves dispel the familiar misapprehension that Orthodoxy finds no place for missionary work. But in the days to come, the 'home' missions were to be run down, the foreign missions left to regulate their own affairs.

Even in the early years of the twentieth century, the close links between church and state, which previously had been conducive to missionary activity, were being subjected to critical scrutiny as never before. In the missionary, educational, social, and cultural spheres, the powerful support (in some respects, the virtual monopoly) which the church had enjoyed for so long was being questioned and eroded, not least as the result of the political unrest of 1904–5. But this also involved the prospect of new freedoms and renewed vitality. The church was seeking autonomy *vis-à-vis* the state. Above all, it sought the diminution, if not abolition, of the procurator-general's role. Thus it made preparations for the convocation of a Russian church council. Unlike the recently inaugurated state Duma this was to be invested with ample legislative powers. Rarely had the term *sobornost'* been so widely used: it was held to provide a yardstick for the reforms proposed. The seeds nurtured by the slavophiles in their time seemed ready to bear fruit, and this time, it was hoped, at every level of church life. The canonization in 1905 of that most numinous of nineteenth-century hesychasts, Serafim of Sarov, provided the incipient revival with an additional catalyst and patron. And while some argued that the tsar should preside at the forthcoming council, like the Byzantine emperors of old, it was equally possible for Vladimir, the bishop of Ekaterinburg, to propose that the president's place should be set aside for some venerable *starets*: the community at Optino was mentioned as a likely source.

The inner, even administrative, freedom which had eluded the Russian church for so long seemed near to realization in the summer of 1917. The council, over the convocation of which the last tsar had hesitated to the end, was at last in session. It urged that the life of the national church be restructured. It restored the office of patriarch. Equally important, it endeavoured to provide the appropriate conditions for the operation of that much-debated spirit of conciliarity, *sobornost'*. Consequently, even the patriarch was to be subordinate to the council which had elected him. For 'the supreme authority in the Russian Orthodox Church—legislative, administrative, disciplinary and supervisory—shall be vested in the Local Council, periodically convoked, and consisting of bishops, clergy and laity'.

However, the work of this first council of the post-synodal period, which began in the permissive days of the 1917 provisional government, was soon to be curtailed by the ever-increasing hostility and brutality of the new Bolshevik establishment. In the event, few of its rulings were ever implemented. What was announced merely as 'the separation of church from state and school from church' in Lenin's decree of 23 January 1918 was soon to involve subjugation of church to state, and on terms dictated by the latter. In so far as the state espoused the cause of militant atheism, a paradoxical and ominous situation prevailed.

Persecution and Purgation

Thus was inaugurated a new period in the history of the Russian church, indeed of Christendom at large, a period of deprivation, persecution, and (unprecedented in its scope) martyrdom. Optino was but one of the numerous monasteries closed in the first decade of Soviet rule. Like the great northern monastery at Solovki, it was to house a forced labour camp. At the outset of the Second World War, not a single monastery or convent remained open out of the thousand or more with which the Soviet period began. At the same time, the mass closure and destruction of churches, the arrest and liquidation of churchmen, reduced the visible presence of the former state church to a handful of bishops, a pitifully diminished body of clerics, and hardly a hundred places of worship. In vain did the residual body of bishops attempt to negotiate some agreement with the state authorities in 1927. The resulting agreement, the work of Metropolitan Sergii Stragorodskii, posed as many questions as it answered, and it antagonized many. In the end (as an earlier version of the same agreement had anticipated) it hardly proved possible 'to reconcile that which is irreconcilable', to ignore 'the contradictions which exist between our Orthodox people and the communists who govern our Union'.

Nevertheless, the enforced silence of the church, its lack of public life, veiled a retirement into its inner depths. Disorganized, rent by schisms, often underground, the church experienced a purgation which may be said to have aligned it with Isaiah's Man of Sorrows as never before. These decades gave rise to remarkable individuals. Some few, like the modest metropolitan of Petrograd, Veniamin, were to receive a show trial (1922). Most were to disappear without trace. But the steadfastness of the average and anonymous church members deserves to be noted above all. In their many millions they were to answer the (unconstitutional) Soviet census question of 1937 as to whether they believed in God or no with an unswerving (and to the state authorities, disconcerting) 'yes', thereby risking their freedom and their lives. Thus, at the height of the anti-religious campaign and in the midst of the Great Terror, spoke the majority of the population.

The anti-religious campaign itself involved a concerted assault not only on religious institutions, but also on inherited behavioural and conceptual norms. The Russian past was under judgement, and much of Russian culture at a discount. In the process, both in law and practice, religion was designated as nothing other than a cult. But while Christian icons could be burned on public bonfires, the state proposed its rival icons and its rival cult.

Only at the approach of war was fresh consideration given to the role of Russian history and its application to the present day. But it was not until the outbreak of hostilities in 1941 that the church was to benefit from this. For the needs of the moment dictated that the war be waged on patriotic, rather than on party grounds. A full-blooded patriotism could not but involve the church, the well-tried patron of defensive Russian wars throughout the ages. A pointer in this direction was provided by the author of the controversial 1927 declaration on church–state relations. While Stalin kept silent, Metropolitan Sergii, possibly on his own initiative, issued a patriotic address on the very day that enemy troops broached the Soviet frontier. Thus he set the pattern for the future.

The state found itself able to draw on unexpected support and hitherto disregarded resources. Within two years Stalin had concluded an oral (or at least unpublished) concordat with the church. After a lapse of almost two decades a new patriarch (the same Sergii) was ushered into office, plans for theological schools were approved, a limited number of church publications issued or projected. Meanwhile, on both sides of the front, churches were being reopened in great numbers. In the German zone of occupation, moreover, monasteries were again at work. The believers who answered the 1937 census were coming into their own.

Not that all restrictions on the practice of religion were to be removed: rather were state controls less punitively applied to the newly extended spectrum of church life. Nevertheless, there was no disguising the fact that the antecedent persecution had failed in its objectives. Against that background, and within the stated limits, believers had some reason to be grateful.

Orthodoxy in the Post-War World

However, the background was not shared by the Orthodox of Eastern Europe, and their experience of new, post-war limitations was correspondingly less sanguine. Previously the Orthodox churches of the region had lived with the support of the establishment. In Romania and Bulgaria, indeed, the clergy even received their stipends from the state. Such support had not always saved them from depredations at their patron's hands. It was a nominally Orthodox state, after all, which had closed the minor monasteries of Greece in 1833 and confiscated their landholdings. It was no less an Orthodox state which went even further in 1863, when all monasteries and monastic lands without exception were sequestered (if only for some years, and with the specific aim of combatting Phanariot influence) by the ruler of Wallachia and Moldavia. Nor did the official (albeit residual) Orthodoxy of late twentieth-century Greece prevent the country's government from proceeding with comparable claims on behalf of landless farmers in 1987. Nevertheless, in Greece and Romania, as in Bulgaria and Serbia/ Yugoslavia, the church had been allowed, had been expected, to play a part in public life which was commensurate to its popular support.

But as the war drew to its close the situation was to change. Communist governments came to power throughout the region, Greece (in the aftermath of a bitter civil war) alone excepted. This brought restrictive legislation for the church, with Soviet precedent in mind; and with it, marked peripheralization of church life. There were years of intensified repression, notably 1948–53. Only in due course did the requirements of Bulgarian or Romanian nationalism once more make themselves felt and provide at least some basis for a *modus vivendi*. For the Orthodox Church is 'the traditional religion of the Bulgarian people and is linked with its history', according to legislation issued in 1949. Moreover, as the Romanian Communist Party leader Petru Groza declared in 1948, 'the Church is an institution of constant benefit to the nation'. In Groza's judgement, 'she is part of the state and, as such, seeks to remain in tune with the spirit of the age'. But this was prescriptive, rather than descriptive; it was to bring burdens, rather than relief. For the officially promoted spirit of the age would expect the church on occasion to heed the demands of the nation in preference to its own.

Participation in the life of the state in the early 1950s could therefore mean that the Romanian Orthodox Church was required to assimilate the local Eastern-rite Catholic Church when the latter was abruptly outlawed by the state. Any Orthodox who protested followed their recalcitrant Eastern-rite compatriots to the labour camps. A comparable situation obtained over the border in the USSR. Only in Bulgaria were Eastern-rite Catholics eventually allowed to retain something of their public life. The question did not arise in the same way in Yugoslavia as in Romania or the USSR, mainly for lack of a sizeable Catholic Eastern-rite community. Persecution rather than assimilation was the order of the day. In any case, the federal and multinational structure of the Yugoslav state would have inhibited the official promotion of any one religious body. Thus was avoided any danger of a gruesome reversal and re-enactment of the wartime policies of the Fascist state of Croatia, which had involved the forced conversion of Orthodox Serbs to Catholicism and the slaughter of all who resisted. Some 350,000 had died in the process.

The Orthodox of Bulgaria and Romania were to experience renewed pressure and persecution in the period of Nikita Khrushchev's ascendancy. But foremost among those affected by the latter's reversion to some of the Soviet Communist Party's pre-war policies were members of the Russian Orthodox Church in the USSR itself. Here the number of reopened churches was drastically reduced to a half of the post-war figure, leaving less than 7,500. At the same time, the number of theological schools (of which there had been ten) was halved, and out of 69 monastic houses hardly a dozen and a half remained open. An attitude of bitterness and scorn was officially encouraged not only to religion (the Constitution allowed anti-religious propaganda), but also to religious people.

'The Gates of Hell Shall Not Prevail'

Yet again the church remained essentially unshaken. 'We Christians know how we should live', stated the patriarch of Moscow, Aleksii, in 1960, 'and our love cannot be diminished by any circumstances whatsoever'. Church life was not tolerated unless it was concerned with cult. But this gave worship exceptional dignity and power. Guidance in the traditional ways of prayer continued to be sought. The republication of the *Philokalia* in a new Romanian edition (1946–   ) or in Greek (1957–63) could not be expected to affect the Russian reader, for there were political as well as linguistic frontiers for the volumes to surmount. But there were still *startsy* to be found, and their writings were passed eagerly from hand to hand. At the same time, church life involved more than a retreat into pietism.

Against the background of the Khrushchev years was engendered a vigorous movement of church intelligentsia, anxious at the very least to ensure the state's compliance with the existing laws on church–state relations, but also in due course to move beyond them. The seminal documents in this regard were prepared in 1965 by two young priests, Gleb Iakunin and Nikolai Eshliman. These were to pave the way for others in the years to come.

After numerous set-backs (Iakunin was later sentenced to seven years in labour camps and several more of penal exile), the unexpected flexibility of the Soviet authorities in the first years of Gorbachev's administration, coinciding as it does with the celebration of the millennium of Russian Christianity, has afforded the church intelligentsia—indeed, the church at large—fresh opportunities and new perspectives. Sooner or later, it is hoped, the church may be allowed once more to organize the education of its youth; sooner or later, engage in social and charitable works. The revolution of 1917 undermined a long-established, albeit (as the pre-revolutionary Metropolitan Antonii of St Petersburg continually urged) insufficiently developed tradition in either field; the Soviet legislation of 1929 expressly countermanded it. Petru Groza's Romanian concept of a church which is of 'constant benefit to the life of the nation' might eventually come nearer to realization, regardless of local Marxist qualms. These have hitherto required subservience, rather than independent collaboration. But 'authentic separation between church and state' has been urged in at least one public statement by a distinguished Russian scholar, Dimitrii Likhachev (1987). The adjective 'authentic' provides a wry commentary on the Communist Party's practice since 1918. But it could also help to prompt revision of it. Meanwhile the Russian church council of the millenary year (1988) has begun to test the ground with vigour and determination.

To what degree such putative developments in the USSR might influence Bulgaria or Romania will remain to be seen. Neither is any longer a unit in a monolithic empire such as

Stalin planned; the former Yugoslavia even less so, and since earlier times.

Indeed, the era of empires could be said to have passed altogether. Formerly, the Russian empire, with its established church, had attempted to support a variety of Orthodox causes and communities beyond its borders. The Austro-Hungarian empire tended to counter this by favouring Catholic or Catholic Eastern-rite initiatives and bodies, especially where Western and Eastern churches overlapped. For its part, the Muslim Ottoman empire, alien as it was to either, provided constitutional safeguards and guidelines for its Orthodox *millet*, while striving to ensure the latter's administrative balance. But little of this survived into the 1920s. By that time the ecclesiastical map of Orthodox Eastern Europe had been largely redrawn to include the new national churches of the Balkans. There was no longer talk of a *millet* in a secularized Turkey, nor was there anything other than a residual Christian population out of which to form one. As for the largest and most powerful of Orthodox churches, the Russian, it had been deprived of its former glory, status, and support. Worse, it was eventually required to play the role of an established church in the context of a regime which preferred to utilize religion cynically on the international stage, while seeking to discredit and uproot it in its home environment.

All or any of these changes could have proved divisive. Yet whatever happened at the level of administration, the Orthodox churches have remained steadfastly at one in liturgy and dogma. It is precisely in these areas that they have been able to make their distinct contribution in the ecumenical movement of the twentieth century, some patriarchates (like Constantinople) from the very outset, others (like Moscow) from the 1960s, arguing (as did Georges Florovsky at the 1954 assembly of the World Council of Churches) for Christendom to counteract its age-long fragmentation by recourse to 'retraditioning'—a dynamic *anamnesis* or recollection, for which the Orthodox might help to set the pattern. In this sphere, as in others, such coherence as the Orthodox can display on essentials tends to outweigh and counteract the pragmatic and potentially disruptive forces among the multifarious, even at times phyletically inclined, jurisdictions. For it is a sacred coherence which speaks of an unforced, even unconscious faithfulness to patristic tradition. It antedates the modern jurisdictions, and it should outlast them.

In any case, it is not administrations of one kind or another which have preserved the Orthodox against the challenges of militant atheism, or the disestablishment and despoliation which were its concomitants. Neither have they proved a bulwark against secularization of one kind or another. Least of all could it be argued that its future survival is likely to depend on the restitution, whether by Greek administrators or by Russian, of any fabled city whatsoever.

Postscript

The speed with which the communist power structures of the USSR and Eastern Europe were dismantled could easily distract observers from the residual side effects of the *ancien régime*, which were manifold, pernicious, and profound. They were the less obvious also since their impact was diffused in the minds of those millions who flocked to the Orthodox church once all restrictions on membership were removed, possibly seeking the panacea which Marxism had so signally failed to provide. Such an influx of neophytes could not have been anticipated, with the result that baptism was rarely matched with appropriate preparation. Nor did the church attempt to determine whether the newcomers were not simply replacing one 'safe' ideology with another. At the same time even well-established members were ill-prepared for the role which their previously marginalized church was now allowed to play in public life. At a time of poverty and disarray, the Orthodox churches of Russia and Eastern Europe were suddenly required to address a wide range of tasks in the field of politics and education, charity and social welfare. With a certain trepidation it was recalled that the very term for Christian charity (*miloserdie*) had been virtually expunged from Russian usage in the Soviet period.

Rehabilitation for the church meant restitution of sacred artefacts, buildings, and institutions which had been sequestered by the state in previous decades. In Albania this involved much more: until 1991, no religious body could function in any way whatever, even in the privacy of the home.

Most of the government ministries which had formerly exercised control over religious affairs were abolished. Russia dispensed with her most recent *Oberprokuror* in 1991. In the process, however, certain safeguards were removed. Thus, the Orthodox found themselves subjected to missionary pressures from the West as never before. The Russian church authorities complained bitterly, and paid particular attention to alleged machinations by the Roman Catholic world. At an unprecedented convocation of Orthodox church leaders at the Phanar, which was chaired by the Patriarch of Constantinople, the plaint was modified, but upheld (1991).

However, there were would-be reformers in church circles who sought to rid the community not only of state supervisors, but also of their ecclesiastical appointees. In Romania and Bulgaria, for example, attempts were made to replace the church leadership, but they failed to clear the air. The problem of alleged collaborators with the former atheist régime haunts the Russian church as well, and seasoned dissidents like Gleb Iakunin secure it much attention in the press. There are those who anticipate the public resolution of the problem by joining rival (in effect, schismatic) bodies. Russia, Bulgaria, and Ukraine each have Orthodox schisms of their own.

But Ukrainians also have another reason for their schism. The new Ukrainian frontiers have impelled a sizeable proportion of Orthodox believers to establish an independent (self-validating) patriarchate of Kiev, thus segregating themselves from fellow-Orthodox, who are less forthright and precipitate in asserting their separateness from the Moscow patriarchate. In either case, the decisions of the 1680s are being set at naught. Nationalism, if not phyletism, is once more at work. Latvians, Estonians, and Belorussians, more moderate though they are, likewise moved towards autonomy in keeping with new borders.

Not that new borders are required to stimulate endemic phyletism, as is demonstrated in the case of Serbia. I suggested earlier that 'a gruesome reversal and re-enactment' of the war-time policies of Ustashi Croatia vis-à-vis the Serbs was not to be foreseen. The judgement was premature, and it was wrong. To make things worse, the supposed defence of Orthodox values by the Serbs has also come to mean retribution against the descendants of one-time Muslim masters of the country, as in Bosnia. In vain did the gathered leaders of the Orthodox churches appeal against 'the exploitation of religious sentiment for political and national reasons' when they met at the Phanar.

In the days of communist pressure and persecution, the enforced interiorization of Orthodox church life in Russia and Eastern Europe seemed to promise concomitant purgation. This would have been a fruit of inestimable value to bring to any future Great and Holy Council of the Orthodox Church, indeed to Christendom at large. For the present, in the flurry and disorientation of the quinquennium since 1988, such a fruit is less in evidence than anyone might once have wished. Least of all does phyletism speak of such purgation.

Troubles are compounded by the fact that many a patriarch or leading bishop is unduly anxious for his church to be a dominant, if not established one, in the belief that history has groomed it for that role, even the history of the recent past.

Only a careful study of that past could act as a corrective. In Russia, the long-delayed canonization (1992) of at least three martyrs of the post-1917 period (Veniamin of Petrograd among them) could provide the necessary stimulus for it. Such a study might also bring churchmen once more to consider a concept which last attracted some attention on the very eve of the Bolshevik seizure of power, when it still seemed possible to envisage 'a free church in a free state'.

CHRISTIANITY TODAY AND TOMORROW

16

What Christians Believe

MAURICE WILES

'QUOT homines, tot sententiae': there are as many opinions as there are people. It is tempting to adapt the old adage and say that there are as many beliefs as there are Christians. In one sense that is true. For belief is a personal matter, and each of us believes in his or her own unique way. But belief is also a communal matter. We do not invent or develop our beliefs on our own. We draw upon the beliefs of the community to which we belong for both the substance and the form of our believing. So the phrase 'What Christians believe' could be filled out in two very different ways—either by pen-pictures of the immensely varied forms of belief held by different Christians in different parts of the world or by a summary account of that common stock of beliefs on which all draw in such diverse ways. The former approach, skilfully pursued by Ninian Smart in the opening chapters of his book, *The Phenomenon of Christianity*, calls for a more diffuse treatment than a single article allows; the latter runs the risk of unduly formalizing the rich variety of belief as it is lived and practised, but the risk must be run. The common stock of beliefs must not be identified simply with the formularies of the official creeds. Allowance must even here be made for the broad variation of ways in which those formularies are understood. And that is something which has not only changed through the course of history, not only something that differs between Christian confessions, but increasingly also something that differs greatly within all the main Christian confessions. How to depict so complex a canvas? The underlying Trinitarian shape of Christian belief, illustrated by the three-clause structure of the most widely accepted creeds (the apostles' and the Nicene creeds), is so all-pervasive that it offers the most natural structure for our reflection.

Christians believe in God. But what do they mean by 'God'? Two streams, already beginning to merge before the Christian era, have come together to feed distinctively Christian belief in God. On the one hand, he is the God of Abraham, of Isaac, and of Jacob; he is the God of the biblical story and it is there that we can learn the meaning of the word, there that we can read his character. He calls Abraham to follow him and be the father of a special people; he calls Moses to rescue that people from slavery in Egypt and lead them to their own promised land. He is a God with a purpose in history, who is grieved by the failures of his people to live up to that purpose but never abandons them. He continues to pursue his purpose through acts of mercy and of judgement, until its culmination in the coming of his Son, his supreme act of mercy and judgement in the death and resurrection of Jesus. But he is also the supreme reality sought by the reflective mind, particularly as that search was carried on in the Platonic tradition of Greek thought. He is the ultimate, changeless reality that lies behind and gives reality to the transient phenomena of the world of the senses. His divinity lies in his self-existent completeness and perfection, his need of nothing from outside of himself, his freedom from the passions of our human, historical existence. Formal Christian doctrines of God have moulded together these two streams of belief as best they have been able. The two have been uneasy bedfellows. Few Christians have desired to do wholly without either. But the inevitable tensions between them have given rise to very divergent conformations of belief.

The tension at the heart of Christian belief in God can be put another way. 'I believe in God the Father almighty, maker of heaven and earth . . .'. So the apostles' creed begins. And that for some is the starting-point of their belief in God—God the ultimate source of the mysterious existence of our world and of ourselves. But that, others object, is to start Christian belief on the wrong foot. They insist that Christian belief in God is, from start to finish, belief in the triune God, God as Father, Son, and Holy Spirit. It is in the culminating action and self-revelation of God in the death of the Son on the cross that the starting-point and key to all properly Christian belief in God is to be found. Again, it is not normally a matter of direct opposition. The former approach was not intending to deny the crucial significance of the Cross for our understanding of God, and the latter has no wish to repudiate the conviction that God is creator. But the chosen point of departure can make a big difference to the form of the final picture.

No Christian picture of God can be final. Both streams have stressed the inadequacy of human language for such a task. 'To whom will you compare me that I should be like him?', says the Hebrew prophet, speaking in the person of God (Isaiah 40: 25); 'God can in no way be described', says Plato. So the continued existence of the tensions and the failures of our verbal formulations are not matters for surprise or for despair. Despite them, Christians believe that the ultimacy of transcendence and the generosity of self-giving to the point of death and godforsakenness are both proper evocations of the God whom they worship.

The conviction that the person of Christ, and above all his death on the Cross, are determinative of Christian belief in God poses a second problem. Not only does it stand in tension with the idea of God's changeless perfection; it does not fit easily either with the fact that it was the man, Jesus of Nazareth, who died on the Cross. Christians, as I said earlier, echoing the start of the Epistle to the Hebrews, see the culminating action and self-revelation of God in the death of his Son on the Cross. But that death was the death of a real man. That is an equally basic Christian belief. The combination of these two beliefs (which I have just described as a 'problem', as indeed it is for the intellect) constitutes the cardinal Christian affirmation of the incarnation, of God's coming to the world in the person of Jesus Christ. Christ is both divine and human, God and man. Formal statements of belief have insisted that both halves of that affirmation are to be taken with equal and full seriousness. Jesus, it is true, is not to be identified with God without qualification; he is the Son not the Father. But he is not some lesser, junior, second-order God. The Son is God in the same full sense that the Father is God. So, since there is only one God, in speaking of Father and Son we are speaking of some distinction within the being of God that does not undermine that fundamental unity nor imply any lower level of divinity in the case of the Son. What Christ is and does, is what God is and does. But that does not make Christ any the less human. He was tempted as we are, like us in everything except sin. He is the model not only of what it is to be God, but of what it is to be truly human also. Yet in this case too, it is questionable how far it has been possible to hold these two convictions together by way either of reasoned explanation or of imaginative depiction. In the experience of faith one aspect seems inevitably to have dominated the other. In the past Christ has often been apprehended primarily as God on earth, his humanity becoming little more than the outward envelope of that divine reality. Today, the culturally conditioned particularity of his human person is more readily grasped, with the divine reality so indirectly present as to be in danger of disappearing from view. But neither reasoned explanation nor imaginative depiction are, in the short run at least, indispensable to belief. Christ as the symbol of God's self-identification with our human lot in the extremity of its degradation, and also of his power to transform it, is the heart of what Christians believe.

This transformation is not something that takes place at a distance, as it were, either in space or time. If we were to speak in terms of belief in God simply as Father and Son, that could easily be misunderstood to imply that we know God only as transcendent source and as decisively active at a moment in past history. But Christians believe in God who is Father, Son, and

Holy Spirit. Belief in God as Holy Spirit gives expression to the conviction that God is continually and dynamically active within the world of his creation. This aspect of Christian belief in God has its specific intellectual formulation too. He is spoken of as a third 'person' of the Godhead, in the same qualified sense of the word 'person' that is intended with respect to the Father and the Son. And attempts have been made to define the eternal relation of this third person with the Father and the Son. The differing outcomes of those attempts (whether he is said to proceed from the Father or from both the Father and the Son) remain a point of division between Eastern and Western Christians to this day. But if it be true in general, as I have argued, that Christian belief, for all its struggle to find reasoned and coherent expression, is always more than its formulation in intellectual terms, nowhere is that more true than in the case of the Holy Spirit. One might even say that belief in the Holy Spirit *is* belief in God as transcending the rational dimension, not in a way that removes him from the realm of human reason but in a way that shows him to be too fundamental to all human experience to be fully apprehended by it. That with which the individual has to do in the deepest moments of his experience—be they the ecstasies of the mystic or experiences of a more ordinary kind—is God; that with which the church has to do in the distinctive moments of its corporate life is God. We may misunderstand and misuse those experiences, but in them God is present, God in the same full sense in which the Father and the Son are God. For God is no absentee landlord; he is present reality.

The dangers of misunderstanding and misuse of this conviction of God's immediate presence to the believer are real and serious, as a book like William James's *Varieties of Religious Experience* vividly illustrates. But the system of Christian belief has a built-in corrective against such distortions. It is one and the same God whom we know as Father, Son, and Holy Spirit. So the intimations of all the varied sources of our faith in God need to be combined in mutual self-correction. Different emphases will characterize the believing of the philosophically minded believer and the charismatic Christian given to speaking in tongues. But neither has a right to claim a monopoly of Christian truth. There is for the Christian one God; and what may be known of God in the creative work of the Father, the redemptive activity of the Son, and the transforming power of the Spirit must agree together as complementary aspects of a properly Christian faith in God.

I have just spoken of creation, redemption, and transformation as linked respectively to Father, Son, and Holy Spirit (as does the Anglican catechism, except that it uses the word 'sanctification' for its third term). But the work of God is not divided up in that kind of way. So the linking of particular aspects of God's activity with particular persons of the Trinity represents an aid to human understanding rather than any fundamental difference between the three persons of the Godhead. Up to this point in my reflections on the threefold pattern of Christian belief in Father, Son, and Holy Spirit, I have been considering its implications for the nature and being of the God in whom Christians believe. But now the allied triad of creation, redemption, and sanctification can serve as a framework for reflection on Christian belief about how God is at work in our human world.

That world only exists because of God. It did not just happen; it did not create itself. However far back and in however great detail the scientist can describe its emergence and development, the question remains of how it is that there is anything at all. The Christian affirmation is that God created the world out of nothing. When Christians try to imagine what that affirmation might mean, they inevitably tend to envisage that 'nothing' as a pre-existing emptiness out of which the world derives. But that is not the real intention of the belief. It is intended to insist rather that the fact that the world exists at all and continues to exist is because God wills it to exist. God does not create a world because he needs it; creation is a matter of his free choice, or, perhaps better, the spontaneous overflow of his goodness. So the fact *that* the world is, is due wholly and solely to God.

But *how* the world is, is not wholly dependent on God in the same way. There have been Christians who have suggested that everything that happens in the world is predetermined by God. But the main line of Christian belief has affirmed the freedom of human beings. In creating a human world, God has not only created something other than himself but has created something with a genuine measure of independence over against himself. This is part of what is meant by saying that men and women have been created in the image of God. Although as creatures they are of a totally different level of being from the self-existent God, they do have an affinity with God. They, too, in their own way, are creators; by their decisions and their actions they contribute to the course that the continuing process of the world's creation is taking.

But if men and women made in the image of God are seen as the central feature of God's creation, it is the whole world, inanimate as well as animate, that is his creation. To call something a 'creation' can have a commendatory or a depreciative intention. And this applies to Christian evaluation of the physical world. It is a created order—not God, and not therefore of supreme or ultimate worth. At its best, this has given Christians a sense of freedom or detachment in relation to the vicissitudes of our physical existence; at its worst, it has led to a fear and hatred of it. The 'world' and the 'flesh' have been joined with the devil as the enemies of a truly Christian way of life. But they are created by God, and that means that the world and the body cannot be intrinsically evil. As creations of the good God, they must themselves be good and capable of reflecting and expressing God's goodness. It is not our physical environment or our physical nature as such that are at fault; it is with our abuse of them or our ascription to them of a falsely absolute value that the trouble lies. In themselves they are to be welcomed and enjoyed as God's good gifts to us.

This conviction about the fundamental goodness of creation

was more easily held in times when it seemed possible to ascribe every aspect of disorder in nature to human sin. The fall of Adam was an invaluable explanatory tool. God's original creation, the garden of Eden, was a paradise of delight. Adam's sin was the cause not only of the sins of future generations, but was responsible also for the bringing of pain and travail into the production of food and the bearing of children. Even then the explanation was not without its problems. Behind the fall of Adam lay the supra-human fall of Satan—the inexplicable choice of evil within the higher, angelic order of God's creation. But today it is even more self-evidently impossible to tie up disorder in nature so comprehensively with human sinfulness. The mythological character of the story of Adam's fall means that it functions for Christians today as a vivid portrayal of the human condition as we experience it and not as an explanation of how human sinfulness has arisen. The surd element in evil, which cannot be fully integrated into the Christian belief about God's good creation, stands out sharply.

But the *explanation* of evil has never been at the centre of Christian belief. Christianity is a religion of *redemption*. Sin is an enemy to be conquered, not an anomaly to be explained. Satan is its vivid personification, and the heart of Christian belief is that this enemy has been conquered by Jesus Christ. The origin of sin is a theoretical question, the conquest of it a practical one. And whatever answer can or cannot be given to the former, Christians believe that in Christ God has acted decisively in the world to put right what has gone wrong. A practical problem calls for a solution in action. So it is the action of God that is the heart of the answer. The story of the incarnation tells of God's coming in a new and specific relation to the world by living the life of a man, Jesus of Nazareth; the story of the Cross tells of his acceptance of the evil and the pain inflicted on him by human sinfulness even to the point of death; the story of the resurrection tells of his triumph over those forces of evil and over death. It is the power of that story, understood as something that God has done for humankind and for each individual within it, that has been the effective heart of the Christian message and of Christian belief.

But the distinction between theoretical and practical issues is never absolute. The story of a death died for us cries out for some account of how it is 'for us'. Christians have not defined their doctrine of atonement with the same measure of precision as their doctrine of Christ's person. But many varied images and explanations have coloured their beliefs about it. Christ's death was a sacrifice to do away with sin, a ransom to set free the devil's prisoners, a substitutionary bearing of the punishment which guilty men and women would otherwise have had to undergo. Such forms of belief are still widely held, though for many, moral sensitivity about what they appear to imply about God has led to a stress on the fact that they are not precise descriptions of the way God deals with us but only very imperfect human pictures of it.

I have spoken of these redemptive beliefs as grounded in the story of the incarnation, crucifixion, and resurrection of Christ. It is as story that Christians read about them in the gospels and hear about them as those gospels are read in the public worship of the church. They are not stories in the sense of sheer fictions; but nor are they precise historical accounts. They are varied interpretations of things that happened. The interpretation and the happening are bound up together in these foundational Christian beliefs. The crucifixion is a victory over Satan and an execution under Pontius Pilate. Christian belief about the death of Christ involves both categories. But there is scope for a great deal of variety of emphasis. It is what is told in the story that matters. But for some what matters most is that it happened in human history as the story tells it; for others what matters most is the story to which the history gave rise, the story with its evocative power and symbolic truth.

So Christians believe that Christ's coming, death, and resurrection (however understood) are of decisive significance in relation to the sin and evil that deface the world and thwart God's purpose for it. But they have always had to come to terms with the fact that that decisive significance is not very evident. Sin and evil continue to flourish. However the decisive significance of Christ's coming is understood, it is certainly one that has to be apprehended and worked out in every aspect of our human life. And here too Christians believe that God is at work. The sanctifying or transforming work of the Holy Spirit is the essential complement to the work of creation and redemption. But where do Christians believe that work is to be found and how do they believe it to be effective in the lives of individuals and of communities?

The story of the giving of the Holy Spirit on the day of Pentecost, recounted in the second chapter of the Acts of the Apostles, is also spoken of as the birthday of the church. And the church has traditionally been seen as the place where the Spirit is primarily at work. At times it has been believed that it is only in the church that the Holy Spirit is to be found and Christian salvation received. But more often Christians have spoken of the Spirit also at work in the far wider range of God's creative activity. The church is then seen as the sphere in which the Spirit is present in a fully personal way, bringing to fruition the fundamental purpose of creation—the union of created human lives with the uncreated life of God himself.

On one important aspect of this belief, Christians have been sharply divided. Where is the church to be found? What constitutes the church? Roman Catholics have sought to give an answer in terms of union with the See of Rome; a broader catholic tradition has given a defining role to a duly authorized episcopal ministry; Protestants have put their emphasis on the faith of believers. In the past these differing beliefs have been held so firmly and exclusively that each category has wanted to deny the title of Christian to the others. Today the differences of emphasis remain, but in an ecumenical atmosphere of mutual acknowledgement and not repudiation.

The most distinctive feature of the church's life for almost all Christians is its sacramental character, particularly the place ascribed to the two dominical sacraments of baptism and eucharist. Baptism marks a person's entry into membership of the church and symbolizes the need of every person for forgiveness and renewal. Because it happens only once in a person's life and, for most Christians, at a time of life when they have no awareness of what is happening, it does not figure so strongly in their belief pattern as it has sometimes done in a pioneering, missionary situation. It is the regularly repeated sacrament of Holy Communion that plays the more important role in the faith and life of most Christian believers. Despite the difference of their symbolisms, the fundamental meaning structure of the two sacraments is essentially the same. Each ties together the realms of creation, redemption, and transformation, and makes them effective in the life of the believer. A sacrament by definition embodies a positive evaluation of the created order; it uses some aspect of the physical world in a manner designed to convey a religious meaning and a spiritual power. Both baptism and eucharist recall in action the death of Christ and make it effective in the life of the participating worshipper. How past history, present experience, and eternal meaning are brought together in the sacramental action has been variously understood. The competing understandings have often been set in violent opposition to one another—and sometimes still are. But at the heart of the most contradictory theorizings is a common conviction: that in the eucharist the eternal love of God, decisively expressed in the crucifixion and resurrection of Jesus, is brought into special and transforming relation with the lives of the believing worshippers.

The institutional character of the church and the physical character of the sacraments are a feature of the Christian conviction that religion is not a form of escapism from the ordinary practicalities of life. But that same fact of their social, physical, and historical nature has made Christians the more inclined to claim to be able to define and control precisely where the power of the Spirit is at work. At worst, the sacrament of the eucharist has been used as an instrument of priestly power, exploiting and encouraging superstitions or magical beliefs. At best, it has fed the lives of saints, uniting in a single ritual the two commands of love of God and love of neighbour. The devotion of the high mass takes the believer out of him- or herself in the spirit of adoration; the shared bread and wine commits him or her to a faith which seeks to share the world's resources with every other child of God.

But Christianity is marked not only by a tension between the calls of contemplation and action, between worship and service. Christians are aware also of a tension between present and future. The Spirit is not only a spirit of presence, but a spirit of promise. It speaks not only of a presence of God, effecting transformation (however incomplete) of human life as it is experienced now; it speaks also of a radical transformation of the world in the future, bringing it into proper conformity with the will and purpose of God. That hope is set before the Christian in a host of differing images. The heavenly city is presented sometimes as a transformed world, sometimes as a place of escape from this doomed and irredeemable order. The second coming of Christ is sometimes depicted as a coming to rule on this earth for a millennium, sometimes as a coming to snatch away the faithful to be with him on clouds of glory. And so that hope functions for some as a spur to reforming zeal in relation to the social and political conditions of their times, and for others as a reason for accepting and tolerating those conditions as no more than secondary and transient realities.

This sketch of what I have called the common stock of Christian beliefs has inevitably offered a picture that is too old-fashioned, too uniform, and too static to do justice to the complex pattern of what Christians believe today—let alone tomorrow.

It is too old-fashioned because the common stock of beliefs on which Christians depend and from which they draw at any given time comes from past tradition, from the way in which Christians have articulated their beliefs in the past. But it would be impossible to read the earlier chapters on the history of Christianity in this volume without being struck by the many ways in which what Christians believe has changed and continues to change. One example out of many is the belief in hell. For much of Christian history the condemnation of unbelievers and evil-doers to the eternal torments of hell has not only been a formal item of Christian belief but a powerful and vividly portrayed aspect of the way in which the church has sought to ensure conformity of belief and reformation of life. But today it is questionable how many Christians, outside the most conservative of Christian circles, hold to that belief in anything like the same sense. Some, who would still hold to a division after death between the saved and the unsaved, prefer to speak of annihilation by exclusion from God's presence rather than of torment. Others would hold to some form of universalist belief, according to which God's purpose will ultimately be achieved in every person. Yet others again, while remaining firmly within the Christian fold, would declare themselves agnostic about any form of post-mortem existence and understand any talk of hell as a poetic evocation of the horror of alienation from the way of God in the present. Many other examples could be given of beliefs which have at one time been a cardinal element in Christian teaching, but which have now been largely set on one side or transformed out of all recognition.

The example I have given is an example not only of how any summary of the common stock of beliefs is likely to sound old-fashioned, because it must fail to do justice to the phenomenon of change through history; it can also serve as an example of how any such account is bound to appear too uniform, by failing to do justice to the variety of belief among contemporary Christians. But that variety is not simply a matter of differences in relation to particular items of belief. It is a matter also of different emphases, different overall conformations of the whole system of belief. Differences in the choice of what serves as the guiding symbol in one's overall pattern of belief can affect the whole character of how a Christian believes. For some Christians and some Christian communities it has been the incarnation that has been the central co-ordinating symbol; for others it has been the crucifixion. The former tends towards a more world-affirming style of belief. God has not only created our world; he has entered right into it and brought to it a new dimension of value. Grace perfects nature. The latter has tended in the past to emphasize God's judgement on human sin, and has lent itself to a more pessimistic evaluation of the world and of human life within it. Today that same stress on the crucifixion as the primary key to truly Christian belief in God is more inclined to see in it an answer to suffering. The crucifixion is God's way of sharing in the suffering and injustice of the world, and of moving forward the day of its elimination, of which the resurrection is the foretaste and the promise. None of those approaches need deny the leading affirmations of the other. But which is seen as the leading one, in terms of which the other is understood, is highly significant for the overall character of what is believed.

But this variety among Christians takes another form as well. It is not only a matter of different particular beliefs and different overall conformations of belief. It is a matter also of how those beliefs are understood to be true. A full-blooded literalism, according to which God actually has a right hand at which the Son sits, has never been part of the common stock of Christian belief—however much artistic portrayal may have seemed to suggest it. But there is, none the less, a wide divergence in the degree to which Christians understand their beliefs to be of a symbolic or poetic nature. At one extreme are those for whom the language is not to be understood in any 'objective' or 'realistic' way. Our beliefs about God are not beliefs about some entity, distinguishable from the entities which constitute the world of our ordinary knowledge; they are a form of speech designed to order our corporate and spiritual lives, in a way appropriate to the depth of relationship and experience which this world makes possible. At the other extreme are those who, while falling short of pure literalism, apprehend their beliefs about God as factual in a way closely allied to that of our day-to-day, commonsense beliefs. God is not physical, but he is a person—as we are; the Father is not a male progenitor, but there is that about him which corresponds to masculinity and makes the language of Fatherhood not just valuable for the rich associations it has acquired in a long spiritual tradition but the proper way to speak of God to the exclusion of the language of Motherhood—and makes a male priesthood acceptable but not a female one. Between these equally unsatisfactory extremes lies a whole range of ways of believing, ways which affirm that there is a reality other than ourselves at the heart of what our beliefs as Christians are about, but which acknowledge also that the forms that those beliefs have taken are the utterly inadequate attempts of human language to express an ultimately inexpressible mystery.

But our picture has also been too static. If change has always been a characteristic of Christian beliefs, the pace of change has quickened—as it has for social life and for our understanding of the world in other ways. The growth of historical knowledge has affected the way in which Christians understand the Bible, the primary source of distinctively Christian beliefs, to have been written; the growth of scientific knowledge has affected the way in which it seems possible to understand God's action in the world; a deeper sociological awareness has made us more sensitive to the ways in which specifically Western and patriarchal attitudes have moulded Christian beliefs. These new forms of understanding have already affected what Christians believe. But the long-term implications for Christian belief of, for example, feminism or a changed attitude to other religious traditions are by no means clear. For some the impact such developments have already had is seen as a form of betrayal. The rallying-call is to a greater faithfulness to past tradition, to some form of that 'common stock of belief' that I have been trying to describe. Perhaps that way will find itself at home in a future, post-Enlightenment culture. But it seems more likely to lead in the direction of a Christian ghetto, Christian belief as a minority option clearly seen to be incompatible with the main stream of human understanding of the world. For others the need for further change in the forms of Christian belief seems self-evident, however uncertain they may be of the precise direction in which it may lead. For them what Christians believe today remains a crucial guide to life and truth, but it has a necessary provisionality about it. What such people hold is perhaps less a clear-cut system of belief than a conviction that the resources of scripture and the Christian tradition will continue to inform a way of believing in God through Jesus Christ which will be consistent with our changing understanding of the world.

17

New Images of Christian Community

BRYAN WILSON

Christianity in the Context of Secularization

THE sense of what constitutes the Christian community has
undergone persistent and continuous change over the centuries,
but at no time more dramatically than in the twentieth century.
Current changes in the image of the Christian church are in
large part a consequence of the extensive secularization of
modern social systems. Secularization is here taken to be not
merely a change in popular consciousness (although that is also
implied) but, more fundamentally, a radical reorganization of
the structure of society. It is a process in which the major areas
of social organization (economy, government, defence, law,
education, health maintenance, and recreation) become differentiated and autonomous, and in which organized religion has
finally relinquished the last remnants of the presidency that
once it enjoyed over the whole gamut of social affairs. Inevitably, as society has been rationalized, and as what counts
as worthwhile knowledge has become increasingly empirical,
so the consciousness of individuals has also changed, and their
forms of sociation have undergone transformation, but most
conspicuously Christianity has lost its erstwhile functions of
legitimating authority and polity; of informing and super-
intending justice and the law; of providing the basis for education; and of reinforcing social control. Social support for religion
has declined and the Christian constituency has generally

dwindled in most Western countries. Where it has declined less dramatically, that, it may be plausibly argued, is because there the churches still fulfil social functions (other, that is, than the transmission of religious knowledge and occasions for worship) that are manifestly significant to still sizeable sections of the population, for example, in serving as a surrogate for genuine community in such highly mobile societies as the United States. Some societies have so evolved in organization and culture that the church has been left as an almost alien enclave, virtually reduced to the status of a sect: in others, where its public and institutional presence remains more in evidence, religious and devotional concerns have often been supplanted and in consequence eviscerated by concern for purely organizational goals such as the interests of its personnel in the matter of training, placement, status, and remuneration; the maintenance of fabric; and the concern for routine efficiency characteristic in bureaucratic structures.

The diminishing significance of religion for the operation of the social system, and changed dispositions with regard to the supernatural, have powerfully demanded the adjustment of the institutional expressions of Christianity. The institutional church had evolved as an agency in many respects envisaged and experienced in the way in which that other abstraction, the state, was understood and experienced. It represented religion as an official, established, objective, and thoroughly legitimated social phenomenon. This form had evolved over centuries, and the church had taken on the character of a complex, virtually autonomous, social sub-system, with its own impressive plant, its elaborate structure of procedures, an internal hierarchy of command, and with a professional personnel ministering to a clientele that was sharply differentiated from it. 'The Church', in the way in which that concept was commonly perceived, had come to mean the clergy. It had come to legitimize itself specifically in transcendent terms, and to claim (never with complete success, of course) the monopoly of access to things supernatural. The rapid acceleration of the processes of rationalization and secularization had the effect, markedly in the early decades of the twentieth century, and even more emphatically after the Second World War, of rendering this institutional structure increasingly hollow.

The institutionalized forms of the church differed according to the historical relationship of church and state: thus it took on a different character in Britain and Scandinavia, with their established state churches, from that found in France and Belgium, where the state emerged as the secular arm, in some respects parallel to, and in other respects almost in rivalry with, if not in opposition to, the church. In many ways, the latent potential for institutionalization was most fully evident in those countries where the church was separate from the state and where it claimed a certain autonomy in relation to it, if not a transcendence which put it beyond the claims of mere secular polity. This aspect of what, by the end of the nineteenth century, to a greater or lesser degree, and in more or less explicit form, the church had become in most parts of Christendom was exemplified in France by the integralist conception of (Catholic) Christianity and in Belgium by the process of 'pillarization'—the development of alternative Christian systems of schools, universities, hospitals, trade unions, social welfare agencies, and the mass media, among other agencies, which rivalled those of the secular state.

Integralism was both a political philosophy with respect to the role of the church in society, and a practical justification for the church's institutional structure. All areas of social life were to be fully impregnated with Christian values, and the church's demands were to be imprinted on all relationships and evident in conduct of every kind. The functions that were, at least incipiently, becoming specialized in other institutions were, as fully as possible, to be retained under the aegis of the church, and their retention (or even reappropriation) was an objective to be vigorously pursued. In no field was the policy more earnestly promoted than in education. The church also had its own conception of work relationships, the 'containment' of the burgeoning pattern of capitalist economic practice, and increasingly spread its self-conscious pursuit of cultural hegemony to such areas as medical care. The church was ready to take charge of large areas of civic activity, and, at the very least, to protect its own faithful within a deliberately constructed Christian subculture. If the church could not control, as once in a less organized and less conscious fashion it did, all of these social activities throughout the whole of society, then it would at least provide facilities, with appropriate Christian commitment, alternative to those being organized in the secular state. After all, the clergy conceived of the church as the guardian of mankind in the interim, until natural law was restored in the truly perfect society under God's justice: until then, the church would offer the near-perfect Christian society as an alternative to the civic society of the secular state.

Perhaps this policy was most clearly illustrated in Belgium, where, following the vigorous condemnation of contemporary liberalism by Pope Pius IX, the church sought by 'pillarization' to embrace its members in what almost amounted to an alternative Christian society, rejecting civil provision, almost like a state within a state. It created (as elsewhere in Europe) its own political party to promote its interests and the moral philosophy that lay behind them. The Catholic, Socialist, and Liberal 'pillars' became recognized as triplicated (or sometimes merely duplicated) facilities that together constituted the now dominant mode in which human society was organized—the nation state.

Even in this vigorous attempt to reassert control over social and cultural concerns, there is already an indication of retreat, and of the dominance of secular agencies that forced the church to accept a new and more constricted image of itself. In seeking to encompass these various, increasingly autonomous, institutional orders under its own auspices, the church was pushed into new patterns of co-ordinated and deliberative action. In this process the church was implicitly redefining itself, and doing so explicitly in relation to, and contradistinction from, the non-church secular society. Those who accepted the embrace of the Catholic subculture of the newly emerging 'pillarized' institutions did so as a matter of personal choice. The principle of voluntarism was apparent, and the church was now tacitly acknowledging the growing strength of the organized secular civil alternative to church organization and Christian culture.

This process was most pronounced in those European societies in which, from at least the time of the French revolution, anticlericalism had a rooted tradition. Even so, elsewhere, although concealed by the partnership of church and state in those countries with officially established churches, the secularization of the civil society was also steadily imposing on the church the character of a subculture, albeit sometimes of an officially protected subculture integrated at various points with governmental, cultural, and social élites. In European Protestant countries, however, 'dissent' had long been tolerated, and although, at least in Britain, diminishing in vigour towards the end of the nineteenth century, it had already provided a conscious and at times conspicuous alternative to official religion. Toleration of dissent (and a married clergy, perhaps) may have preserved Protestant countries from the rampant anticlericalism evident in Catholic Europe. For a time, that toleration may have helped to keep political and cultural contention within Christian parameters. In the long run, however, the issues that had caused division receded into diminished significance; the vigour of dissenting churches declined; and secular concerns of a more technical (and less ideological) variety made divergent positions within Christianity of little relevance. If the dissenting communities had always been distinctive and separate subcultures, they now lost some of their distinctiveness, while Christianity in general, coming to terms with its relaxing grasp on the centres of political and social power, was steadily forced to recognize its own much reduced place within society at large.

Religion and Secularization in the New World

In many respects, Christianity in North America presents a different picture. In a constitutionally secular society such as the United States, the church never enjoyed formal access to government, and had a more restricted role in regard to differentiated social institutions (such as education). Religion was always a voluntary concern, and the absence of the long history of religious coercion or religious obligation, such as had prevailed in Europe, has coloured the image of the churches in that country. In America, choice in matters of religion was a charter freedom, and this in itself reduced the pretensions of the European churches (Catholic and Protestant) with their triumphalist claims to transcend the state or their Erastian assumption of being co-terminous with it, just as it elevated the status of every minor sect. All were denominations, that unique image of church organization that was the American contribution to the structural forms of Christianity. Just as men were equal so, apparently, were their religions. Whereas in European societies, religious diversity (dissent) was regarded as a threat to social cohesion, in America, tolerance of such diversity was a prerequisite condition for it. The denomination became the dominant model of the Christian community. Diversity itself was almost a virtue, but claims to superiority or pre-eminence such as had been automatic assumptions for Catholicism or for state churches in Europe were, in this context, neither realistic nor tolerable. To a considerable degree the same may be said of Australia where early assumptions of an Anglican ascendancy had to be modified in the face of the growing numbers of Scottish (Presbyterian), Irish (Catholic), and Methodist immigrants.

The requirement of toleration, and the fact that denominations were transplanted to an American context far removed from the circumstances in which they had originally developed and in which they had, in contention with other variants of Christian faith, often struggled to establish their distinctive identity, had its own effect on the self-images and other-images that gradually evolved. Denominational distinctiveness was more quickly eroded, at least for the majority, and American Protestant churches steadily assimilated to a certain cultural norm. They became voluntary associations with different brand-names but with diminished differences in ideological commitment (certain fundamentalist bodies excepted). An increasing incidence of interdenominational migration occurred even of the ministerial personnel, who moved not on grounds of changed theological conviction but for such considerations as a better pension scheme or, for example, to avoid the Methodist requirement of periodic transfer from one congregation to another—all of which indicates the relatively hollow character of denominational distinctiveness. The theological contention and historical circumstance that had brought many of these denominations into being were eroded, but the separate movements for the most part persisted as self-perpetuating organizational structures.

What has been plausibly suggested as a distinction in the experience of churches in the United States and in Europe is that whereas, in Europe, secularization has been a process gradually eliminating religious influence within the wider society, in the United States, which began as a formally secular society, the process has largely led to an evacuation of theological, worshipful, and spiritual orientations within the churches—a process of internal secularization. These two patterns of structural secularization appear to have had dissimilar consequences for church attendance and the use of churches for sacramental rites. Although decline is virtually universal for all such indicators (baptism, confirmation, church membership, communion) throughout Christendom, the rates of decline vary from one society to another. What is evident is that 'going to church' or 'having a child confirmed' are not unitary acts—the cultural meaning of such an action differs from one society to another. With its reduced religious content, the act of church-going in the United States may fulfil other functions for the proportionately greater percentage of American church-goers than does church-going in, say, Sweden: the same point might be made about confirmation, a general custom in Sweden but much less frequent in other Protestant countries.

The process of secularization in this century has, in various manifestations, been evident to churchmen, even if they have been more aware of declining church attendance than of the decline in the significance of religion for the operation of the social system. The Christian community has responded to this change in its circumstances in various ways. Social conditions have changed more rapidly than at any previous period in history, and the inherited institutions of religion have been rendered steadily more impotent. The churches have increasingly lacked the manpower, the resources, the leadership skills, and even the clear sense of purpose to be able to sustain, much less revitalize, their organization and activity. Excepting those situations, as in Northern Ireland and Poland, in which religion has become a surrogate expression of ethnic or national identity, the public collectivist representation of religion has become less and less congenial to modern publics, as both the state and the nation have today become more readily challenged as primary points of reference for individual identity. The self-confidence and assurance of corporate social agglomerates of this kind have dwindled, and there has been a widening acknowledgement of individual human rights (publicly proclaimed by the United Nations, the Council of Europe, the Strasburg Court, the Helsinki Accord, and in a wide variety of legislation in particular countries). Such expressions of individualism, and the recognition of the primacy of individual conscience, have shifted the locale of personal identity not only from race, nation, statehood, but also from religious affiliation. Religion has undergone perhaps more challenge than these other categories, in that race and nationhood are involuntary affiliations, and statehood can be changed only with some difficulty: religious attachments are, however, a matter of will and are easily surrendered.

If there is less will to be automatically identified with a church into which the individual has been born, and more emphasis, influenced in part by the American model, on personal choice, there has also been a marked erosion of the moral basis of contemporary society. Whereas traditional societies were 'held together' by a shared consciousness of what constituted right behaviour, modern societies, with their emphasis on heightened individual freedom, increasingly open government, and ever more explicit democracy, rely on the integrative agencies of bureaucracy, fiscal control, the web of shared indebtedness, and such technical phenomena, more than on the cohesive bonds of moral consensus. Religion played a vital part in the maintenance of that old-style moral cohesion: it has no role in the maintenance of organizational integration. Once personal choice becomes the criterion for individual action, as it has in politics, consumerism, entertainment, and religion, so the last constraints on individual faith disappear, and the functions of corporate worship—worship as an act of community—also vanish. It is in this sense that one may refer to the received institutions of Christianity as having become hollow. Such structures no longer represent acceptable images of what faith and religious life might be, even if, for some indeterminate transitional period, they may survive as structural remnants of the role of Christian faith as once it functioned for society.

Church Responses to Social Change

The responses of the churches to the changed social milieux in which they have had to operate have been diverse, some more consciously adaptive than others. In addition to these institutional responses there have also been the responses of individuals in seeking new forms of religious expression adequate to meet their felt needs in the new systems and patterns of relationship that modern society imposes. The most obvious adaptations are those that have occurred at the liturgical level, in the shift from formalism and objectivism to an emphasis on informal styles of worship, symbolized in the shift from Latin to the vernacular in Catholicism and from language dignified with the patina of antiquity to the banalities of colloquial usage in Anglicanism. The cultivation of informality, subjectivism, and increased participation, and the partial rejection of the high cultural tradition which for centuries had marked the relation of the church to the arts, represented, no less in music than in language, the adoption of the demotic in the pursuit of relevance and congruence in a society which, in its forms and in its assumptions, had grown away from religion. Liturgical change was, of course, accompanied by theological legitimation or rationalization. The conscious limitation of the claims made for the clergy in the Catholic and Anglo-Catholic traditions represented a new interpretation of the priesthood and of ministry: the laity were to be brought in and acknowledged to have faculties that, at least in practice, had long been but scantly recognized. Structural changes in churches—not always aesthetically well-accommodated to the fabric of ancient buildings—gave visual effect to these transformations, and were intended to reduce the distance between the laity and the priest, between the secular and the sacred.

Such processes of change may have caught something of the currents at work in the wider society, in which democracy, participation, informality, open access, and equal eligibility were all evident demands: they may also have been a surrender to trends in developed societies that were temporary and the logical conclusion of which might have been, or might yet be, the relegation of spiritual issues (and the culture which had so well accommodated them) as epiphenomenal concerns. That the churches have lost an initiative of their own is also evident in another response to religious decline—the attempt to rationalize their operation and to streamline their organization on the lines common to business corporations. Advocacy of such a course was most conspicuous in the report on *The Deployment and the Payment of the Clergy* (the Paul Report) in the

Church of England in 1964: the spirit of rationalized structures is no less evident in team ministries, the management of corporate finance, and increasingly representative decision-making bodies. The church of Rome has also faced pressure, not least from some bishops, to extend participation in its synods to the laity and in particular to women, and slowly that church, too, responds.

Efforts to come to terms with the changing shape and structure of modern society and with the aspirations of its citizens were also evident in the later stages of integralist policies on the continent of Europe. These endeavours in the Roman church have regularly brought into action priests who have sought to integrate with the people, sometimes in ways which eventually met with the disapproval of the hierarchy. The worker-priest movement and the other experiments promoted at grass-roots level were eventually controlled from the centre. Catholic Action had been an earlier endeavour along not dissimilar lines. But social involvement, conjoining spiritual perspectives and activist material goals, has recurrently jeopardized the primacy of the spiritual in favour of more tangible ends that might be achieved only by political, and perhaps eventually only by militant and revolutionary, means. At a much later stage, liberation theology, as a blend of Catholicism and Marxism found a cadre of recruits among priests whose vision of what the church might do had either been soured or had been appropriated by political ideology. Those priests whose conception of religion has come to be cast in terms of active amelioration of the conditions of the oppressed or the destitute have always been likely to use the church, with its well-established and well-legitimated collective structure, to mobilize a following prompted less by spiritual than by practical goals.

Another conscious response of the churches to the changing character of society has been manifested in ecumenicalism. The ecumenist goal has proved to have enormous attraction for the churches. It can be readily represented as a direct expression of the will of God: division in the church can be stigmatized, however belatedly, as a scandal. Thus, ecumenism had supreme legitimation. Beyond this, it was clearly the case that the causes of the divisions among churches were often lost in theological controversies known only to historians. The circumstances in which separate congregations found need for independence had long since disappeared. What persisted, rather than the seriously held theological beliefs that had differentiated one church from another, were ecclesiastical polities of radically different forms. Ecumenical effort might need theological justification, but what was more difficult was the amendment of existing patterns of church organization and religious practice to accommodate union. The need, however, was apparent. With diminishing congregations, surplus plant, increased maintenance costs, and the vague conviction that divisions among Christians acted as a deterrent to prospective converts, the union of churches appeared more and more desirable. It was understandably easiest to take steps to attain that goal in the mission field, where Christian divisions were often locally irrelevant, and were overshadowed by the differences between Christians and non-Christians. The Church of South India, formed in 1947, succeeded in unifying churches that had three distinctive patterns of ecclesiastical polity—episcopal, presbyterian, and congregational. It retained some measure of internal diversity, but effected a union that became an inspiration for churches elsewhere. The idea of organic union, and even of inter-communion, sometimes met resistance, however, and even theologically less troubled mergers, such as those of the United Church in Canada, the Uniting Church in Australia, and the United Reformed Church in England, encountered difficulties with church polity. The plan for nine denominations to unite (the Church of Christ Uniting) in the United States in the 1970s met strong opposition which, after fifteen years, may have been resolved by the less radical concept of 'covenanting'. In Britain, Anglican–Methodist proposals were rejected, and talks between Anglicans and Presbyterians foundered, while the protracted process of conversation between Anglicans and Catholics has proceeded very cautiously and with strong consciousness of severely disputed issues still to be tackled.

Ecumenical union appears to have emerged in large part as a response to the diminishing influence of the churches, perceived particularly by the clergy. The laity were rarely the moving spirits, and sometimes resented the idea of abandoning old patterns of worship, ingrained habits, and cherished systems of faith and order. Only more recently and at local level has there been evidence of a strong ecumenical tide among the laity, and this as the distinctiveness of denominational commitment has been steadily eroded. Ecumenical effort, whether denominational or local, has not, however, fulfilled some of the expectations of its prime movers. There has been little recognition by outsiders that the church had now 'put its house in order', that there was now a clearer call to Christian duty, and that the impediments to faith had somehow been spirited away. The evidence shows no patterns of new growth among united denominations in Western countries, and in some cases union appears to have had no effect whatsoever in reversing or even retarding the continuing process of decline in church membership.

The growing together of Christian churches, despite all the difficulties of effecting actual union, was almost an inevitability. As old doctrinal or organizational principles became irrelevant to modern problems they ceased to be the touchstones for denominational identity. As modern societies came to function with diminished regard for religion, private individuals also ceased to reinforce their own identity in specifically religious terms: Baptist or Methodist, and eventually Anglican or even Roman Catholic, became labels with diminishing differentiation. The major Protestant denominations came to make common cause in establishing councils of churches at national level, and eventually at world level. Those councils have not always been uncontroversial among Christians but the disputation about them has centred less specifically on any threat they might be supposed to pose to denominational autonomy than on the quasi-political role which they, and the World Council in particular, have at times assumed. Co-operative ventures at denominational level have been promoted especially by ministries specializing in such areas as industry, prisons, hospitals, counselling, therapy, or youth work: the more specialized ministries become, the more relevant to them become technical and professional norms and the less relevant are distinctive denominational prescriptions.

At local level, ecumenicity has had its most practical effects, in the rapid increase in shared activities, in the exchange of pulpits, and intercommunion. Sometimes under economic constraint, but more readily because the differences between them have seemed to matter less, different denominations have come to use the same facilities, and, especially in North America, there has been a growth of community churches described as 'interdenominational' or 'non-denominational'. The very early murmurings of ecumenism, which found expression in such organizations as the YMCA and the Student Christian Movement, have been followed only rather slowly by the merging of actual denominations, where the hardening of the organizational arteries retarded the flexibility of institutional responses. The ecumenizing churches might, however, heed the eventual fate of the YMCA—now considerably secularized—and the SCM, which has fallen victim to fringe groups and extremists that have caused its decay.

Extra-ecclesial Revitalization

Other currents in religious life and other images of the church and of worship, arising at the grass roots, have had their effect not only on interdenominational endeavours but also on patterns of religious participation. The most conspicuous of these currents has been the Charismatic Renewal movement, the beginning of which can be traced back to an Episcopalian church in Van Nuys, California, in 1958. All the central ideas and practices of this movement go back to an earlier time, however, and illustrate the way in which initially sectarian (if not outright heretical) tendencies have, in more recent times, moved towards the centre of Christian life. For centuries, the Christian churches taught that the gifts of the Holy Spirit, referred to in 1 Corinthians, had been gifts limited in their operation to the apostolic age, and subsequent manifestations of what claimed to be those gifts (and most conspicuously of glossolalia) were condemned. Glossolalia has been a not uncommon occurrence in Christian history, but always as an extreme and castigated phenomenon until, beginning in 1900, the modern Pentecostalist sects emerged. Those claiming to exercise the gifts of the Spirit were generally extruded from the mainstream churches and a congeries of Pentecostal bodies sprang up throughout the Christian world, beginning in America but spreading rapidly to Scandinavia, Russia, the Protestant countries of northern Europe, and eventually to India, Africa, and Latin America. Until 1958, the Spirit gifts were tacitly if not overtly rejected by the major denominations.

The claims of those at Van Nuys were quickly taken up across America in churches of all the major denominations, and the movement known as Charismatic Renewal spread throughout the Christian world. It appears to have a particular appeal in Catholic churches, and in the 1960s rallies of American Catholics, including many priests and nuns, were organized to celebrate the gifts of the Spirit. Church authorities appear to have been taken off guard by this sudden resurgence of ecstatic Christianity, but in place of the earlier condemnation of the theory and practice of this type of charismatic manifestation, they were initially silent and subsequently tolerant of the Charismatic Renewal movement, which eventually received the endorsement of some prominent clergymen, including the then archbishop of Michelen, Belgium. The manifestations occurred typically in prayer meetings that were interdenominational and quite informal. Not infrequently, strong local leaders emerged who imposed a measure of discipline on ecstatic utterance, but such leaders were not always or even usually clergy. The movement had a strong lay spirit and gave opportunity for spontaneous participation. Without permanent or separate premises of its own, it represented a movement within the churches rather than a division from them.

None the less, the impulses and the implications of Charismatic Renewal were largely anti-structural and anti-ecclesiastical. In place of liturgy there was ecstasy; in place of institutionalized authority there was inspirational utterance; in place of collective acts there was opportunity for individual and even atomistic behaviour. If the Holy Spirit is likely to speak through any individual, then the need for a clergy becomes less evident. The movement reflected the secular currents of the period of its emergence, with the demands, for example among beatniks, hippies, encounter groups, and others, for spontaneity, immediacy, personal freedom of expression, and the elevation of experience above intellect. Like those young people's movements, it broke out of the bounds of conventional activity, and although the Spirit manifestations generally needed a social context for their appearance, charismatic behaviour was in itself none the less a manifestation of highly individuated, implicitly privatized, impulses. If it was held to be a deepening of spiritual experience, that in itself only underlined the apparent inadequacy and emptiness of older, ritualistic, and institutionalized forms of Christianity. As a rapidly spreading enthusiasm, Charismatic Renewal probably did more in a few years to promote a certain type of ecumenical practice than had been achieved in decades by the formal proceedings of church assemblies and committees.

The natural home for charismatic manifestations was in informal and unstructured contexts—the prayer meeting rather than the cathedral. This deinstitutionalized image of the church was associated with the demand for the removal of constraints on spirituality. The old forms, often less well understood, appeared to many to be inadequate, if not archaic and otiose: it was as if, in religion as in so many other social activities, the expectation that worshippers would conform to regulated norms was superseded by the demand of the 1960s and 1970s that people should 'do their own thing' and should 'let it all hang out', as the colloquial slogans of the time suggested. The clergy, as authority figures, were in part the butt of these trends, even though some clergy were themselves involved in the search for new and informal patterns of worship. Similar demands for opportunities for greater participation and the elimination of authority symbols and status differences might be detected in the 'underground church' as it developed in Italy, and the 'house church' movement occurring principally among free church groups in Britain. That such new organizations sometimes themselves evolved new authority structures and new routines that superseded old rituals is only an evidence of the force of institutionalizing tendencies and the difficulty with which currents of enthusiasm can be sustained.

Nor should it be supposed that in as complex a phenomenon as religion any current of thought can go unchallenged or unrivalled. In the very period in which new emphasis was being given to individualism, there persisted movements, many of them arising before the Second World War, which sought to introduce new communal experience of religion. The development even within Protestant churches of groups that emulated the religious orders of Catholicism cannot be ignored. At Taizé in France, Grandchamp in Switzerland, Iona in Scotland, Lee Abbey in England, and the ecumenical Sisterhood of Mary at Darmstadt in Germany, new experiments in communal religious life survived the war years and for some time thereafter flourished and spread. Although these groups were necessarily composed of very small numbers, they had a symbolic significance within the churches, and at retreats, such as those organized at Taizé and Iona, larger numbers were drawn into the sphere of influence of these new, but in some ways recollective representations of the church. The vigour of enthusiasm for the life of religious, within Catholicism as well as among the more recently developed Protestant imitators, appeared to reach a peak in the early 1960s and then waned.

Religious orders have, of course, arisen and declined in earlier periods of Christian history, but the decline of almost all the long-established orders during the later 1960s and early 1970s was perhaps unprecedented, and accompanied the slackening vigour of communal endeavours begun as enthusiastic inter-war or early post-war experiments. Later, at the fringe of Christianity or beyond it, another wave of communitarianism occurred attracting younger people into less stable communal organizations.

Perhaps as a development of the hippy communities in California, these later varieties of experiment in communal religious living were embarked upon in the early 1970s. The Jesus movement in the western United States was a congeries of often short-lived communities, many of them of ex-hippies, who became targets for local evangelists and were 'redeemed'. The new communities did not last long and established no regular religious life, whilst some of their offshoots evolved distinctly antinomian tendencies, conspicuously so in the case of the Children of God (later renamed the Family of Love). But the attraction of communal life and even of communitarian principles persisted in various forms, and the Bugbrooke, notionally Baptist, community, is a British example of the recurrent if controversial experiments in communitarianism which have occurred in Western countries. The Unification Church, which shares a considerable part of the Christian heritage, evidences the strong appeal for young people from many countries of self-sacrifice and shared effort, even though the church's leaders explicitly indicate that, for most of the movement's votaries, the near-monastic lifestyle is for only a limited number of years. Beyond the fringes of Christendom, the same type of appeal to communal living is found in Hindu, Buddhist, and Islamic new movements that have had more appeal for significant numbers of young people than have the traditional monastic orders of the Christian church.

Communal experimentation, as a counter-current to the dominant force of privatization in religion, can affect only relatively few people, and the main effort of the churches has been to reinforce their appeal and popular commitment to established forms of church allegiance by other methods. The great rally or the newly designated league of renewal has been a not uncommon if, in general, a not particularly successful device by which the churches have sought to reinstitute faith. Among the more open endeavours of this kind are the secular institutes within Roman Catholicism, which encouraged a measure of dedication intended to be parallel to that of monastic orders among lay people committed to a life of prayer. Each institute has a central house under a director: in France one with a contemplative vocation is loosely attached to the Carmelites; in Britain the Grail Society concentrates on summer schools and study, as well as on retreats; others are constituted among particular professions and have special concerns—with the sick, the elderly, or with prostitutes. Although a nineteenth-century movement, the institutes received official recognition only after the Second World War. Organized in a different way but with not dissimilar aims in seeking to strengthen faith and to act as a leaven is the *Kirchentag* created in Germany in 1950 as a movement bringing together often hundreds of thousands of Lutherans to rededicate themselves to the spiritual ideals of their church. The development of Evangelical Academies in Germany, designed as conference centres more than as retreats, is another example of a way in which a changed image of the church has been projected in a mass society, where the old parochial principle has less relevance. More ephemeral projects, that have sought to propel church people to recommit themselves as much as to attract outsiders, have come and gone, often leaving little permanent effect: the Sword of the Spirit movement promoted in wartime England among Roman Catholics was one such effort. Within the mainline churches these campaigns to promote rededication or remoralization have been mounted from time to time, even though experience has shown that they are of only temporary significance.

The archetypical project to regalvanize the church in

Protestant countries has been the revival campaign, and although more characteristic and perhaps more effective in the nineteenth century than in the twentieth, this type of exercise has by no means died out. As a method it has often been suspect in the eyes of orthodox churchmen, who have seen it as producing conversions in the heat of artificial emotion by crude methods, and by preaching a version of Christianity that was unduly simple and perhaps unbalanced. None the less, the much publicized campaigns of the past four decades, with celebrated preachers such as Billy Graham, have received the endorsement of many of the leaders of the church, even though such induced revivals of faith appear, in most cases, to have effects of very limited duration. The evidence suggests that the revivalist is often preaching to believers, many of whom 'go forward' not so much to be converted as to rededicate themselves. The majority are perhaps already church-goers and many are members of evangelical and fundamentalist organizations in which the tenor of ordinary Sunday worship and of the many week-night meetings retains much of the atmosphere of revival meetings.

The great rally is, however, a way of introducing excitement into a message that for many may have palled by repetition. When the entertainment industry encourages novelty and constant changes of fashion, the staid and even rhythms of established Christian practice are, in many respects, at a disadvantage being out of keeping with the spirit of contemporary society. The rally, the revival, the pilgrimage, serve as horizons in an otherwise unduly bland experience, and may be for some the way in which religious interest can be revitalized. Such events, too, are a commentary on the perceived or half-perceived limitations of the parochial system—of religion organized in terms of static geography. Such organization might suit static communities, long settled in agricultural pursuits or extractive industries, but in an increasingly mobile society, where the daytime distribution of population differs markedly from the night-time distribution, parochial assumptions are less and less warranted. If people are on the move, or are used to moving over considerable distances for the supply of their needs (to suburban supermarkets for food; as commuters to work or school; to strange cities for their higher education; and to 'other', sometimes far distant places for their recreation, whether on a diurnal, hebdomadal, or annual basis), then religion organized in static facilities may be at a disadvantage. In such a social context, religion may need other agencies and other modes of organization if it is to maintain support. The revival was one early attempt to cope with a dispersed, mobile, and unsettled population. The modern rally—so effectively used by Jehovah's Witnesses—may be such another. The appeal of the pilgrimage as a form of religious tourism, which appears often to develop around shrines of dubious authenticity and without the sanction of the church, is perhaps an indication of the changed image of the faith. What is implicit in all such endeavours is the sense that parochial organization, and beyond it, the hierarchic structure of command related principally to geographic terrain, may be a lingering remnant of feudalism which fails to meet contemporary needs and the expectations of what the church should be and where and how faith should be organized and expressed.

Christianity and Technological Change

The traditional patterns of authority had assumed the superiority of age over youth, of men over women, of the more civilized over the less developed, but technological and social change, which has occurred at unprecedented speed since the Second World War, sets a premium on youth and puts age at a discount. Being untrained, or trained in an earlier and now obsolete technology, older persons are easily defined as 'has-beens': in technical concerns, long experience, once thought of as in itself a prerequisite of wisdom, becomes a distinct handicap. Although the premises on which such attitudes rest have less application in the moral and spiritual sphere than in perhaps any other, so pervasive is the influence of science and technology in contemporary life that even those areas in which they have least relevance are unlikely to be untouched by their influence, or the influence of the social relationships which technology increasingly predicates. That the image of the Christian community prevailing in modern society should increasingly be divested of dependence on patterns of authority evolved in former times is entirely unsurprising. Sacerdotalism appears not only less desirable and less plausible, but becomes, for economic reasons, less sustainable in a society in which labour becomes so expensive that it is economically supportable only when mixed with increasing capital.

The economic effects of technical advance combine with the enhanced demand for democratic structures to render priestly authority subject to radical re-interpretation. The old imagery of a flock under a shepherd becomes anachronistic in an age when priests, far from having their one-time monopoly of learning, are often much less well-educated (and perhaps for modern life less relevantly educated) than many of those to whom they are expected to minister. In many of the areas in which the priest was at one time the best available guide (social care, marital harmony, work relations, moral dilemmas) there have grown up supposedly expert bodies of professionals to replace his amateur ministrations. The values that the priest was once expected to represent and to express are challenged, and alternative and more powerful communicators now voice different values which often contradict and sometimes oppose those values traditionally reposited in the church. In those areas in which religious are still engaged as auxiliaries, as they are extensively, for example, in the school systems of France and Belgium, and in Catholic hospitals and old people's homes, their specific religious commitment invariably succumbs to the insistent demands for professional standards. Catholic hospitals and Catholic schools become less and less differentiated in their organization, style, and values from those of the secular state. The experience throughout the Western world has been of a diminished labour force of the spiritually inspired and their replacement by professionally trained counterparts.

The modern image of the Christian community, as evidenced by new developments both within the mainstream denominations and by the character of sectarian and non-Christian religious movements outside them, accords a diminished place to the clergy. The shift to lay control, to something first expressed as a priesthood of all believers, has been a long-term shift, with successive denominations—Lutherans, Baptists, Methodists, Salvationists, and Pentecostals—according ever larger roles to lay men and also to lay women. That the same current should in recent decades have also become increasingly manifest in the major churches, Catholic and Protestant, was to be expected: the process reflects dominant currents in secular society which religious agencies are ill-equipped to resist. Participation has become a powerful demand and, although lay participation within the Roman Catholic synods is as yet no more than a token concession, the pressure for its increase is vigorous and unlikely to be unsuccessful. Nor is participation confined to organizational decision-making. It is increasingly conceded in liturgical and sacramental concerns. If, as some advanced theologians have urged, there is no priest but Christ, then a multiplicity of ministries, with various talents and degrees of training, become increasingly relevant and opportune.

In general, religion does not appear to be an activity susceptible to much technical improvement. The church has had very limited recourse to the benefits of science and technology. The nineteenth-century antagonism of science and religion may no longer provide vigorous debate or interest, but technical means appear to be largely alien to the spiritual quest. One may note, in passing, the attempt at reconciliation of these spheres in the emergence of Christian Science and its various imitators which offer therapy as a pragmatic justification of a faith which purports to be as demonstrable as the natural sciences. And one may, albeit passing beyond the Christian community as such, note the deliberate and much-vaunted development of 'religious technology' in the Scientology movement, which with the use of technical means claims to have replaced the unsystematic, random, and subjective process of confession of sins by an objective, reliable, and standardized pattern of therapy. In the history of Christianity these instances are almost incidental items, but they are also straws in the wind indicating one process of adaptation to what is a powerful secular current. There is one other exception to the general neglect of technology, albeit of a somewhat different order, but with a more profound influence on the way in which the Christian faith is perceived.

Christianity, and Protestant Christianity in particular, depends for its effectiveness on adequate means of verbal communication. Whilst participation in collective ritual has been the primeval means of incorporating the individual in a spiritual experience and in the sanctified community of the saved, progressive individuation in advancing societies has rendered repetitive and regular collective ritual much less compelling. Since the Reformation, Christianity has come to rely more heavily on the communication of beliefs, on the rhetoric of the preached word, and the dissemination of intellectually communicated specific values (in contrast to the unconscious assumption of folk mores and collective sentiments). Modern media of communication do not facilitate the experience of incorporation into the community of the saved, but they do very powerfully reinforce the spoken word and achieve its instantaneous and simultaneous diffusion. The Protestant tradition acquired a new technique with which to disseminate Christian teachings, and, first in radio and subsequently in television, a new alliance has been formed between technical means and spiritual ends.

That the means can come radically to affect the ends in any social activity, and that this has been so in the development of radio and, more significantly, television presentations of Christianity, is apparent, but the real import of what has become termed 'televangelism', at least within North America, is a changed conception of Christian community. For many practising Christians, television has become the agency through which religious and spiritual values are communicated. By this means, as vast audiences are simultaneously reached, the geographic captivity of the churches is ended, localism is transcended, diversity is diminished, and the illusion is created that the minister and the viewer are uniquely in communication. Although the evangelists who use this medium usually build up a large organizational infrastructure, the contours of which may or may not become evident to the viewing public, the image of the Christian community which is projected is very often of a simple relationship between viewer and televised preacher. He is projected in quasi-charismatic manner, often acclaimed as a healer or miracle-worker, and his message is couched in emotional and sometimes crude terms. The claim is often made that there are millions of others heeding and responding to the message, but the individual or couple watching the television screen are isolated, their faith unsupported by an active participating community. If participation has become a powerful demand within Christian organizations, the 'electronic church', so-called, eliminates all but the most passive reception of a message. It represents another of those counter-currents in contemporary society in which dominant trends appear to stimulate alternative responses.

The electronic church makes its explicit commitment to 'old time religion', to that type of individualistic Protestantism familiar to its audiences from Sunday-School days, but it promotes the further privatization of faith. The image of the Christian community ceases to be that of a corporate body of the faithful, and becomes a dispersed constituency of individuals. They may survive without church structures as a self-selected population who proclaim themselves as Christians without, however, needing to subscribe to any particular body of dogma or to participate in any particular corporate acts of worship. Privatization of religion is in effect a solvent of shared Christian faith, which is replaced by private beliefs which need not be declared, but which are to be taken in good faith as indeed Christian. Even within the churches, the variant and subjective interpretations of belief need be neither challenged nor exposed: the private individual can make his claims and need not divulge his sources. There is an implicit relativism in the emergence of privatized religion, in which diverse conceptions of truth are equally tolerated, no matter how uninformed or uninstructed, the full extent of which can be seen when the vigorous evangelical Baptist televangelist, Jerry Falwell, can call on Catholics, Protestants, Jews, Mormons, and all Americans to unite on moral principles, and can say, 'God hears the cry of any sincere person who calls on him'. The supreme right of individuals to arrive at and choose their own beliefs independent of all formal religious agencies has recently been shown to be the opinion of the majority of Americans.

A Change of Face; a New Complexion; a Lower Profile

It is entirely appropriate to the dialectic pattern of religious change that privatization, which has gone on alongside the internal secularization of the churches in the United States, should also encounter opposition. A radically different movement has also attained prominence in the United States in the 1970s and 1980s, namely the evangelical revival, which incorporates those of a fundamentalist position and other conservative Christians. In the nineteenth century, this type of religiosity was one of the dominant strands within American Protestantism: it has survived and now, in considerable measure, has been relaunched as almost a fashionable ideal of Christian community. In its extreme form it accepts the inerrance of scripture, belief in the sufficiency of Christ's death and resurrection for the salvation of the individual soul, and the eventual, and perhaps imminent, second advent. The strong commitment to personal holiness and social morality provide the basis for the claim of 'born-again' Christians and for their allegiance to the 'moral majority'. This evangelical tradition, at times almost confined to sectarian forms of Christianity and to the Southern Baptists, has undergone a resurgence within other denominations, and it is now apparent that the old denominational images of the Christian community are seriously compromised by the divisions of evangelicals and liberals within their own churches. The countervailing fashionability of privatized religion and the absence of cohesive denominational ideologies prevent these older forms of religious organizations splitting asunder on doctrinal issues. Powerful as the new evangelicalism may be, it has not tended to induce schism: the formal structure of denominations is no longer sufficiently cohesive for schism to become the consequence of ideological divergences. In effect, however, within the same mainline denominations there are wide differences of belief within individual churches, and even more emphatic, differences between churches within the same denomination. Such divergences can be found within the Church of England, and among English Baptists, but they are more common in North American denominations. The evidence there is that it is the conservative churches which are growing, perhaps because these churches are relatively strict and demand strong commitment at a time when the looseness of moral commitment and the uncertainty of belief characterize so-called 'liberal Protestantism'.

Conservative reaction to the trends of modern times—against moral change; against secularization; against the growing diffuseness and uncertainty about beliefs within the churches themselves—is not confined to the doctrinally dissipated Protestant denominations. It occurs in Catholicism, as the persistence of the small but vigorous movement for the Tridentine mass indicates, and as the growth and spread of Opus Dei implies. Even a church so strongly committed to authoritarianism as the Roman church cannot impose uniformity of belief and practice. Similar evidences can also be seen in the growth of a variety of sectarian movements. The Assemblies of God, a loosely federated Pentecostal body, has experienced spectacular growth in the United States and even in some supposedly Catholic countries. In Brazil and Chile, and to some extent in Italy and Portugal, this movement and other Pentecostal churches have made serious inroads into a formerly at least nominally Catholic population. Other movements committed to similarly conservative and sectarian ideals have also proved increasingly attractive. The Church of Jesus Christ of Latter-day Saints and the Seventh-day Adventist Church have experienced rapid growth, particularly in the Third World, and although there is evidence to suggest that its membership is subject to some considerable turnover, the Watchtower movement (Jehovah's Witnesses) also continues to attract new adherents.

One paradox in the present situation, which affects all missionary religious organizations, from the Roman Catholic Church to the newer international sects, is the adaptation of Christianity to the needs and demands of Third World populations. Differential population growth and the decline in support for the mainline denominations in western countries, ensures for the Roman Catholic Church, just as differential success in proselytizing produces a similar result for the Seventh-day Adventists, and to a not much less extent for the Mormons, that the complexion of the Christian community will change. There will be more Christians in the Third World and fewer in the West, and sooner or later the demand for greater participation in the authority structure of the relevant organizations will become irresistible.

The cultural assumptions and expectations of Third World Christians differ from those of Westerners and become increasingly insistent. The Roman Catholic Church, after early resistance, finally accepted the new model of spiritual household communities of the Jamaa movement in Zaïre in the 1960s, but the hierarchy has remained generally wary of such movements. The so-called basic communities (*communidades eclesias de base*) in Brazil and elsewhere in Latin America (but with some parallel organizations in, for example, Holland and Italy) are sometimes explicitly critical of church orthodoxy. In style, they stand in sharp contrast to the traditional parish, emphasizing democratic lay participation, promoting the gospel rather than traditional liturgy and doctrine. Growing mainly among the poor, some of them operate primarily as prayer groups; in others, radical priests have sought to engage in 'consciousness-raising' to stimulate social and even political action. Thus far, these groups remain, somewhat uneasily, within the church, but there are others which grow up at the fringe of Christian orthodoxy in their accommodation of indigenous Third World cultures. The World Council of Churches has recognized movements that espouse beliefs that many Western Christians would find alien—the importance accorded to its prophet by the *Église de Jésus-Christ sur la Terre par le Prophète Simon Kimbangu* in Zaïre, for example; or the encouragement given to lay leaders in The Church of the Lord (Aladura) in West Africa to issue to individual worshippers revelatory warnings of ailment, accident, or baleful witchcraft, and to prescribe techniques by which they might be avoided (the worshipper might be told to sprinkle holy water round his room and, standing naked at midnight, to recite a particular psalm three times). The Roman Catholic Church has been less accommodating to such demands than the World Council, refusing full participation to polygamists for example, and so precipitating the emergence of separatist movements like the Mario Legio movement in Kenya; and, in another instance, relieving the archbishop of Lusaka of his post because of his persistent use of traditional healing methods in his ministry.

Third World Christians often seek to conserve indigenous values, but these do not always conflict with traditional Christian ideals, and where they converge, Third World churches may represent a conservative influence within Christianity. Thus, in the Seventh-day Adventist Church, the incipient liberalism being voiced by some Adventists in the United States is effectively checked, in such matters as the admission of women to a larger role in church affairs, by the resistance of the numerically increasingly dominant Third World membership. Third World conservatism reinforces the established position of the Roman Catholic authorities on the issue of the ordination of women— although Third World Catholics might exert a different influence on the question of clerical celibacy. The strong advocacy of liberation theology by some Catholic clergy in Latin America appears not significantly to alter the picture: some of the clergy at the periphery seek to exert a revolutionary influence against a conservative centre, but Catholic lay support for this intellectual radicalism is not, as yet, impressive.

The images of the Christian community that obtain in contemporary society are undergoing rapid and radical transformation. Religion itself is coming to occupy a different place, and in many respects a lesser place, in the experience of individuals as in the operation of social systems. Religious authority, both in the sense of the claims of Christian teaching, and the power, status, and influence of Christian leaders, has diminished. The priesthood, as the normal agency of orthodoxy and orthopraxy, is faced with transformation as the assault is made on priestly celibacy in the Roman church, and the demand for women priests arises there and in the Church of England. The struggle over both issues may well be overtaken by other developments: the institution of a multiplicity of ministries, and the economic need (since religion commands a diminishing proportion of the world's wealth) for a less costly labour force, which may impose greater reliance on lay men and women. As priestly roles have been eroded and reduced to the narrowly sacramental with a margin of amateur caring functions, and as many of their former functions have been taken over by technically expert agencies, the priesthood itself becomes marginal to society's organization. Christian moral precepts that were mandatory only a decade or two ago are now relegated or even abandoned: in the new permissive age, 'sin' becomes an unfashionable, perhaps anachronistic concept. The great institutional church buildings have been becoming increasingly difficult to maintain and some are surplus to requirement. In consequence of these changes, the new model of the Christian community is likely to be much less structured by authority relationships and moral consensus, and much less typically accommodated in visible edifices intended to impress upon all the objective reality of the church and its stability and permanence.

The search for community, for fellowship, for psychic therapy, and the elation of the human spirit are, of course, unlikely to disappear, and from these elements new forms of association are likely to emerge. As modern societies become more heterogeneous in cultural origin and ethnic mixture, it seems likely, if they are to hold together, that the specific and distinctive cultural and religious inheritance of indigenous populations will become more muted and more accommodating to other, formerly alien, manifestations of these human aspirations. The new images of community are less likely to be so explicitly Christian since that emphasis excludes increasing proportions of modern populations. No doubt some such models will persist, but in the nature of contemporary pluralism, which relativizes all religious claims, such communities will either use increasingly empty symbols, or will themselves become more explicitly sectarian. Religion in diverse forms will doubtless find continuing expression, and its ceremonial and legitimating role (for public events, national celebrations, and solemn occasions of state) will not, or will not quickly, disappear, but the conception of Christian community, under the diverse pressures of the mass media, new technologies, increased social and geographic mobility, the privatization of beliefs, and the deinstitutionalization of moral codes, is destined to further change and perhaps more rapid change than has been evident even in the very recent past.

18

The Christian Conscience

BASIL MITCHELL

THE challenges to the Christian conscience in the modern period have generally been felt to be of a different order from any previously encountered. Three aspects have to be considered: first of all, the developments in the world at large that pose the problems, almost all of them associated with the growth of science and technology; next, the spiritual and intellectual resources from which the Christian conscience might hope to address them; and finally, the situation, or rather the contrasting situations, in which the churches find themselves in relation to the world which sets the problems.

The Situation of the Churches

To begin with the last of these. Our own age has seen the culmination of 'the triumph of the West' in which 'Western' culture, especially but not only its science and technology, came very largely to dominate the world. That culture was Christian in the minimal sense that it had been developed in the Christian countries of Western Europe and North America, and, perhaps, in the somewhat stronger sense that two of its characteristic features, scientific enquiry and liberal democracy, had originated within the matrix of a Christian world-view.

This modern Western outlook had, however, a very strong tendency to call in question constituted authority of any kind, and all Western societies have become increasingly secularized. Whatever the formal relationship may be between the Christian church and a particular nation state, the churches no longer retain the capacity to determine social and political policy. They can only expect, like the British monarch, 'to be consulted, to encourage and to warn'. The churches were, for the most part, slow to recognize this situation, so that revolt against imposed authority in general has taken the form of revolt against religious authority in particular. It was not until the Second Vatican Council (1962–5) that the Roman Catholic Church revised its political theory so as to take account of the new situation, and, indeed, to endorse it. In *The Declaration on Religious Freedom*, promulgated in 1965, it finally abandoned the traditional doctrine that 'error has no rights' and embraced a more liberal theory based upon the rights of the person, and the individual's duty to follow his conscience. This momentous decision brought the Roman Catholic Church into line with the mainstream Protestant churches and allowed Catholics, in principle as well as in practice, to participate fully and without reservations in the decision-making processes of democratic societies.

It remains, nevertheless, a controversial question what the relationship ought to be between Christian moral thinking and the laws and customs of society at large. Granted that in modern Western societies legal systems no longer embody Christian principles just because they are Christian, there is disagreement as to how far such principles may be appealed to in the public debates that influence law and social policy. At one extreme are those who regard all such appeals as inappropriate to a 'secular' or 'pluralist' society. In the United States they may claim the authority of the constitutional separation of church and state. At the other extreme are those who argue that in varying degrees the countries of the Western world are still essentially Christian, and there should be at least a presumption in favour of Christianity.

However this issue may be resolved in particular cases, it is clear that the social and political problems facing these countries are not, and are not generally thought of as, problems for the

Christian conscience alone. Both the Christian churches as institutions and individual Christians have to confront problems which they are not called upon to resolve on their own. Even the Roman Catholic Church which, throughout its history, has tended to conceive of morality as a system of laws, natural and divine, mediated by the church, is increasingly unable to make that conception effective even among its own members.

It will be apparent that, in attempting to describe the situation in which the churches have to operate in Western societies, we have already uncovered one of the contemporary challenges to the Christian conscience. For the relationship between church and society is a question about which Christians profoundly disagree. In all the mainstream denominations there is a tension between people of a conservative temper who want, so far as possible, to maintain and strengthen a Christian ethos in society and liberals who accept the concept of a 'pluralist' society with more or less enthusiasm. These competing approaches go with rival political philosophies. The conservatives think of the institutions of society as contributing to a common good upon which the well-being of individuals and their freedom ultimately depends; the liberals place their emphasis upon individual and group autonomy, which presupposes, as they see it, comparatively little in the way of shared values in society as a whole.

This systematic disagreement illustrates a further aspect of the situation. The Christian conscience is far from being entirely homogeneous. Indeed, it is tempting to argue that, so great are the differences between the moral judgements of contemporary Christians on this and other matters of importance, that it is a misnomer to talk of 'the Christian conscience' at all. The 'acids of modernity' which have eaten away at the customary foundations of society have eroded no less effectively the Christian ethical tradition itself (which was, in any case, varied and fragmented from the beginning).

Whether this conclusion ought to be drawn we must leave for the moment. It is enough for the time being to note that, within contemporary Christianity, there are markedly different approaches to the problems facing the Christian conscience and, in consequence, differing conceptions of what the problems are. Indeed, to talk of 'problems' is to acknowledge this. A state of affairs is a problem only to the extent that it is felt to be unusual or abnormal and such that something ought to be done about it. Conservative thinkers see the decline of the formal authority and public influence of the churches in Western societies as a problem, to be thought of in terms of decay or disintegration; whereas liberals, viewing the same process as a natural and healthy development, find a problem only in the reluctance of the churches to adapt themselves to it.

The Challenge of 'Modernity'

It is impossible, therefore, to analyse the problems facing Christianity today without looking at the challenge of ideas—ideas which, on the face of it, stand in opposition to Christianity as traditionally understood, but which cannot be readily discounted. They must be accommodated into Christian belief itself or deliberately rejected.

Ever since the Enlightenment Christianity has been subjected to a moral and intellectual critique which, although not unknown before it, was greatly intensified by it. In one way or another this critique is associated with the growth of modern science. It has been plausibly argued that two things were necessary for the development of science, belief in the world as an intelligible order and the conviction that this order could not be discerned by speculative reason alone but had to be discovered by painstaking observation and experiment. Both of these were provided by Christianity which held that the world was created by God, and, since man has no direct access to the divine plan, he must find it out for himself. But science as it advanced seemed to threaten this Christian scheme of things in two different ways. It offered explanations of events within the natural world that were, in principle, complete and appeared to leave no room for divine agency; and it provided a paradigm of reason which dispensed with appeals to divine revelation and ecclesiastical authority. Confronted by these challenges Christian doctrine began a long retreat, in which the question to be decided was how much territory to yield to the advancing sciences. Attempts to construct a rational theology of a quasi-scientific kind were for the most part intellectually thin and spiritually unsustaining and were increasingly vulnerable to sceptical limitations upon the scope of reason. This sceptical tendency was not wholly out of line with traditional strands in Lutheran theology, with its central emphasis on justification by faith alone, and there began to develop on the continent of Europe, and especially in Germany, a conception of theology which was content to leave reason and objective reality to the sciences and to base religious faith upon the emotions, the imagination, and the will. While liberal Protestants endeavoured to share the disputed territory somewhat uneasily with the scientists, and romantic theologians surrendered whole areas of it in return for a licence to explore the rest without hindrance, the dominant theology of the Roman Catholic Church withdrew to its traditional strongholds and allowed the invading armies of scientific rationalism to flow past unchallenged. With its basically Aristotelian philosophy it made virtually no attempt to grapple with modern science. Similarly, conservative Protestants took refuge in their own fortresses of biblical fundamentalism, particularly in the United States.

The effects upon ethics of these developments were bound to be momentous. In particular, the fundamental assumption, shared by Christians with the pagan philosophers of antiquity, that morality was derived from the very nature of things, more especially human nature, was steadily eroded, except in Roman Catholic moral theology where it ossified in neothomist isolation from the main stream of modern thought. The nature of things, as studied by the sciences and manipulated by technology, was not capable of yielding moral insights except of a crudely cost/benefit kind. The moral significance of persons, in particular, tended to be dissolved: either they were exhaustively definable in scientific terms and human decisions were, like other natural events, in principle predictable; or their freedom was vindicated in terms of the radical subjectivity of individual choices.

The process of erosion advanced very much more slowly and attained less extreme forms in Britain and North America than on the continent of Europe. Partly because of an ingrained pragmatism and partly because of the more rapid advance of technology the appeal of utilitarian attitudes was much stronger, and the effective alternative to this was not, as on the continent, a strain of subjectivism or even nihilism, but rather a Christian ethic increasingly cut off from its roots in the Christian tradition. The Victorian period in England was characterized by agonizing doubts about the validity of Christian doctrine, together with a generally unshaken confidence in the deliverances of the traditional Christian conscience.

In the United States, where utilitarianism was even more at home than in Britain, there remained as a live alternative to it a simple, if selective, appeal to scripture as an authority for moral choices. The intellectual tendencies we have mentioned as operative in Europe were, until comparatively recently, very much less influential in the United States, where they served to dilute rather than to erode the native strains of Protestantism.

There was, however, one influence which, if not peculiarly American, did develop with particular rapidity in that country and remains very strong in it, namely relativism. The social sciences and their therapeutic applications affected the middle classes from the turn of the century and encouraged people to think of 'moralities' in the plural as reflecting the needs or preferences of particular individuals or groups. The *de facto* pluralism of American society contributed to this, together with a liberal interpretation of the Constitution as entirely neutral between value systems. All these tendencies were accentuated by conditions in a highly mobile society in which public and private life were more and more separated—the state of affairs known to sociologists as 'privatization'.

These conditions were not, of course, peculiar to the United

States, but manifested themselves to some extent in all Western industrialized countries. They represented a large part of that 'modernity' which more traditional societies came to experience as an alien importation threatening their inherited way of life. Christianity itself inevitably incurred some degree of guilt by association as having exercised a formative role in the early stages of this destabilizing process.

It could be said that the main predicament facing the Christian conscience in the modern period is that of defining its attitude to this entire phenomenon of modernity. And since the developments which constitute modernity are to a very considerable extent intellectual ones, the predicament requires not simply a decision as to how to address what is happening in the world, but even more a decision as to how the Christian conscience is now to define itself in the face of the intellectual challenges. Are Christians to identify Christian values, the ones they ought to uphold, with the values formulated by Christian thinkers in the past, and Christian institutions with what have passed as such in earlier periods—notwithstanding their inevitable limitations—or are they to associate themselves with some at least of the features of modernity, and if so, which? The intellectual culture in Western societies since the Enlightenment has been largely a revolt against Christianity with its unified vision of the world and its idea of an objective moral order founded upon the creative purposes of God. The dominant theme of this revolt has been individual autonomy and the rejection of authority; and the church remains a potent symbol of authority even though its actual political power has long been in decline.

The situation we have been describing is that of the church in Western industrial societies. There are, however, other societies in which the position is dramatically different. Chief among these are the Socialist countries of Eastern Europe whose governments have been officially Marxist and atheist and where the churches have been subjected to strict regulation and, from time to time, actual persecution. Here the churches are free of responsibility for the official social and political order and are able often to provide the focus for an impassioned reassertion of the inherited values of the national society. Here there need be no conflict between the authority of the church and the liberal demands of political freedom and human rights. In the USSR itself the national church has made an accommodation with the state, by which it effectively forfeits any political role in order to preserve as far as possible intact its devotional life and its institutional existence. In the entire Soviet bloc until very recently there have been fewer dilemmas for the corporate Christian conscience (although there have been grievous trials for individuals), because the freedom has been lacking which in more liberal societies both creates problems and offers some possibility of solving them. The situation has now changed dramatically. Marxism has largely discredited itself and the churches are looked to as providing the inspiration for a more open society.

In Latin America, by contrast, the situation is reversed. A long history of authoritarian regimes enjoying in the past the tacit support of the Roman Catholic Church, itself established in the first instance with the help of military conquest, makes liberal democracy an uncertain growth and gives Marxism a moral advantage. Here, then, it is possible for Christians to argue that the failure of Marxist regimes elsewhere to acknowledge human rights is not irreparable and that, in any case, the rights that matter to the poor and oppressed are not those championed by the proponents of bourgeois capitalism. From the standpoint of 'liberation theology' what passes for Christian ethics in the liberal West is a bourgeois sham. Similar attitudes are often expressed by the religious leaders of other Third World countries, especially African ones. The Christian churches are apt to appear as the agents of a cultural imperialism which seeks to impose an alien way of life upon the older indigenous culture. Thus, for example, in the World Council of Churches, representatives of mainstream Western churches are accustomed to find themselves in the dock, arraigned as at best an irrelevance, at the worst an aberration.

Finally there remains a further challenge which has always existed potentially, but which has become insistent only recently, that of the other world religions, intensified in many Western countries by the presence of immigrants who profess them and do not wish to be assimilated. This challenge has been reinforced, at a more intellectual level, by the appeal of, especially, Hindu and Buddhist philosophies of life to certain sections of the intelligentsia, offering as they do (at least in the forms in which they are available in the West) a type of spirituality and an ascetic discipline free from the dogmatism and the institutional demands of traditional Christianity.

Problems for the Christian Conscience

Given the variety of situations in which the Christian churches find themselves and the different problems they face, let us make some attempt to consider the more significant challenges to the Christian conscience and to examine the resources available within Christianity to meet them. If it is right to associate these challenges particularly with the advent of modernity, deriving from the impact of science and technology upon our world and our world-view, there is warrant for giving a certain priority to the experience of the Christian West, because it is there that the impulses of modernity have been strongest and its challenges most keenly felt.

As the twentieth century nears its end, the intellectual scene is becoming clearer. The nineteenth-century conception of a scientific world-view, in which all occurrences were in principle predictable, is effectively obsolete. Contemporary work in the history of science has done much to discredit the legendary story of the development of science as a continuous struggle against religious obscurantism. At the same time, studies in the philosophy of science stress the role of models and metaphors in scientific reasoning, so that the dichotomy which has dominated the modern mind between science, as dealing with matters of objective fact, and religion and morality, as concerned with the expression of emotion or with existential decision, becomes steadily less plausible. Meanwhile, the objectivity of the natural sciences, whose intellectual authority has for so long been unchallenged, is beginning to be called in question by some trends in the sociology of knowledge. Hence the natural scientists are, for the first time, beginning to experience some of the intellectual pressures that have affected theologians throughout the modern period. There are signs of a developing community of interest. Both need to vindicate the capacity of the human mind to understand the world against the attacks of sceptical or relativizing critics and the strategies available to each are broadly similar. Thus, appeal by theologians to a realm of subjectivity which has no place for truth or explanation becomes a steadily less tempting option, and the long retreat of Christian doctrine could well be at an end.

These issues remain controversial, and one feature of modernity that is certain to endure is the need to live with controversy. However, a position may be open to controversy and yet worthy of acceptance; and it may be widely influential without being uniformly imposed. The capacity of any world-view to survive in the West will depend on its being able to maintain this tension between confidence and criticism, which Christianity has known traditionally as the problem of faith and reason.

A consequence of these developments is that one of the most pervasive themes of modernity, that morality can only be a human invention with no authority but that of the individual or the corporate will, although still taken largely for granted by the intelligentsia, lacks the manifest intellectual authority claimed for it. Serious attempts to grapple with the moral challenges of the contemporary world find people exploring the implications for ethics of what is known about human nature, and man's place in the natural order, in a manner that makes Christian teaching about these matters once more clearly relevant.

Nevertheless, the challenges to Christianity in the Western world remain formidable. The intellectual tendencies to which we have referred were closely involved with social changes which are still operative. In those generally prosperous countries in which modern technology has brought palpable benefits to the majority of the population only comparatively recently, it is natural for people to want to enjoy them freely and the release they bring from inherited constraints. Hence an emphasis upon individual self-fulfilment and self-expression. But there are signs that the resulting fragmentation leads to loss of community; and communities cannot be rebuilt through merely contractual relationships between atomized individuals. There is a felt need for shared values and common institutions, together with a general reluctance to accept the sort of authority that secured them in the past.

Meanwhile, the churches themselves are affected by the tendencies which they seek to confront, and this presents them with a dilemma. In so far as they reconcile themselves to pluralism and the intellectual and moral attitudes that go with it, they fail to address the underlying *malaise* of rootlessness; yet a simple assertion of traditional authority is unacceptable in principle and unable in practice to match the seriousness and complexity of the problems that face the modern world.

History, moreover, has left the Christian churches in the West in an equivocal position with responsibilities, which they cannot easily disown, for a civilization which Christianity helped to form but which never was, and is not now, adequately Christian. The churches as institutions do not stand over against it in prophetic purity but are embedded in it and compromised by it. Many of their more active members earnestly wish that they could free themselves from this incubus and return to the catacombs. They must often envy the church in Poland or in Latin America or, indeed, in South Africa, where the responsibilities are less diffuse and less ambiguous, the issues more clear cut, and the lines of conflict more sharply drawn. But if and when those battles are won and a greater measure of freedom is achieved for those now suffering oppression, the problems they will then face will be essentially the same as those which now confront the West. Doubtless their present hardships are more difficult to endure, but their problems are not more difficult to resolve.

The time has come to consider what are the problems for the Christian conscience today and what are the resources within the Christian tradition from which to meet them. It has already been said that for the most part they derive from the development in modern times of science and technology. This is obviously true of the problem of modern war and nuclear weapons.

War and Nuclear Weapons

Whether it was legitimate for a Christian to engage in war was a problem for the Christian conscience from the start. What has made it so severe in modern times is the scale and indiscriminate character of the weapons available and their incalculable destructiveness. This would not constitute a problem if control of war were not thought to be attainable; and it would not be a problem for the Christian conscience if the Christian churches or individual Christians could disclaim responsibility for national policies. The development in modern times of the organized bureaucratic state, ultimately answerable to an electorate of all competent adults, has brought the conduct of war and the aim of limiting or abolishing war within the boundaries of possibility and, therefore, within the domain of active moral concern.

The dilemma posed by nuclear weapons is terrifyingly simple. The damage they do is on so vast a scale that it necessarily involves non-combatants, and moreover the ill effects extend to deaths from radioactivity many years later. To some they represent the ultimate expression of the evil of war as such, and thus reinforce the case for absolute pacifism, based upon the teaching of Jesus in the Sermon on the Mount. To others, who, with the majority of Christians through the ages, have accepted the need for war under certain conditions (although with increasing anxiety as 'conventional' weapons become ever more destructive), the totally indiscriminate nature of nuclear weapons places them in a different category and renders their use wholly illegitimate. However—and here lies the dilemma—the very enormity of the disaster that would attend their use makes it a matter of supreme, and it would seem overriding, importance that they should not in fact be used, and this introduces an inescapable element of political calculation. A potential enemy who possessed such weapons might not scruple to use them if confident that they would not be used against him. The safer plan, then, might be one of 'mutually assured destruction' in which neither party was prepared to start hostilities so long as there remained the possibility that the other might retaliate with nuclear weapons. The 'logic of deterrence' entailed that peace was more likely to be kept if the parties together maintained a threat to use the weapons rather than if one party did not.

Many Christians, and they include a majority of those of them actually exercising political power, have accepted this reasoning, albeit often with the greatest compunction; many have strenuously resisted it. No issue in modern times has divided Christians more bitterly. Nevertheless, there is a large measure of agreement among Christian thinkers as to the principles that are relevant to this debate. They are those of the traditional doctrine of the Just War, especially the principle of non-combatant immunity and the principle of proportion, namely that the harm done by the methods used in war must not exceed the good to be achieved. Only convinced pacifists, on the one side, and convinced 'realists', on the other, have denied that these were the proper principles to apply. But those who accept them have differed sharply on how they should be applied to the present case. 'Unilateralists' have argued that it is unconditionally wrong to use nuclear weapons because they are indiscriminate and their effects out of all proportion, and, following from this, that it is also absolutely wrong to deploy them and to threaten to use them. Their opponents have, for the most part, conceded that it would be wrong to use them, but argued that it would not be wrong to threaten to use them, if the intention was to deter a potential enemy and if the probable effect of the threat was to make nuclear war itself less likely. The difference in moral discrimination dictated a radical difference in policy, the one side urging unilateral nuclear disarmament, even if the result were to be the overthrow by force or threat of force of liberal democratic governments, the other favouring disarmament by negotiation under the shield of nuclear deterrence.

The dispute illustrates two strains or tensions within the contemporary Christian conscience. One has to do with the role of consequences in resolving ethical problems. The other concerns the extent to which Christians have a duty to maintain and defend the modern liberal state with its commitment to fundamental human rights. Christian thinkers are not as a rule utilitarians—they do not believe that the rightness or wrongness of actions depends solely upon their consequences—but they differ as to how far consequences are relevant, and why. Those who regard the use of nuclear weapons, and the threat to use them, as unconditionally wrong and who are prepared to accept any consequences, no matter what they might be, rather than be guilty of this sin, will not have to consider consequences at all. But those who feel constrained to take account of possible consequences have in mind not only the chances of nuclear war itself, or of the sufferings consequent upon invasion, but also the potential moral hazards involved in such outcomes. In particular, they would argue, political decisions inevitably involve some weighing of the moral as well as other costs of any projected course of action. It is necessary, therefore, to consider how far the freedoms and other values of Western societies are worth defending—what weight they ought to have in the balance—and how far the overthrow of democratic governments would expose people to the risk of moral corruption as well as to the loss of freedom and prosperity. Although Christianity has coexisted with authoritarian regimes in the past, and has served to legitimate them, the liberal democratic state owes its existence very largely to Christianity in its Protestant forms and rests upon certain values of freedom and the worth of persons which are authentically, if not exclusively, Christian.

The Social and Political Order

Most Christians in the West would continue to believe that freedom of conscience, freedom of expression, the right of political dissent, and a large measure of economic freedom, are both good in themselves and the practically necessary conditions of a worthwhile society. But a vigorous minority of Christian thinkers incline to share the view of those liberation theologians who, in their struggle against authoritarian regimes in Latin America, have adopted a Marxist critique of 'bourgeois capitalism'. From this standpoint the 'human rights' which Western governments are committed to defend and which Marxist regimes are accused of violating, are of interest chiefly to the well-to-do, and have little to offer the poor and oppressed. These people lack the basic necessities of life without which they scarcely can exist as persons and are in no position to avail themselves of the opportunities which the liberal society claims to offer them. The critique, although most fully developed in Latin America, is readily applicable to the world scene. With the solitary exceptions of the former USSR and Japan, economic power, together with military power, is vested overwhelmingly in the Western industrialized countries, many of which until recently possessed colonial empires. The ills of the Third World are attributed to the workings of a world market which serves the interests of the holders of economic power and is at the same time associated with an individualist, 'consumerist' philosophy which represents a constant threat to traditional indigenous cultures. Christianity can also be seen as part of this threat, since it came with the colonial power and still has its historic centres in Europe.

Hence the Christian conscience is concerned, perplexed, and divided by problems of the social and political order, both national and international. The demands of individual charity are accepted and obeyed in all kinds of voluntary organizations, and this is a Christian impulse which finds a ready response in the secular world, but the underlying problems of poverty and hunger are seen ultimately to require political and economic solutions, about which agreement is hard to achieve. It has always been a problem for Christianity how to accommodate itself to the political order, and the differences of the past have been accentuated and extended in modern times by the sheer complexity of the issues and the varying situations of Christians in relation to them. There are those—particularly evangelical Protestants—whose primary concern is the salvation of individual souls and who wish so far as possible to keep religion and politics apart. Their political influence tends to be strongly conservative, especially in the United States where the traditional values of the society are individualistic. There are others of a more liberal temper whose Christian vision is a predominantly social one, the bringing of the Kingdom of God, and who tend to see the existing structures of society as essentially hostile to this vision so that their instincts are anti-authoritarian. Yet others are equally insistent upon the duty of Christians to seek the common good, but are more deeply impressed by the reality of sin and correspondingly more concerned to defend such elements of Christian culture as are represented by the existing values and institutions in nominally Christian societies. This is often the case with the social thinking of the Roman Catholic Church.

Divergencies between these trends in explicitly Christian thought are deepened by their affinities with secular movements, whether openly acknowledged or not. The commercial inspiration of much American evangelism is notorious; the social philosophy of liberal progressive Christians as influenced by liberation theology has Marxist overtones; and the more traditional thinking of moderate reformers, including that of the Second Vatican Council, owes much to the mainstream Western democratic tradition. If this is an awkward predicament, it is also an inescapable one. Christianity cannot be a purely private matter, and, as soon as its implications for the wider society begin to be worked out in practice, allowances must be made for differing situations, and accommodations reached with rival schools of thought, not all of which can be dismissed out of hand as inherently anti-Christian. In particular, the 'secular thought' of societies with a long history of Christian influence may sometimes turn out to have been more authentically Christian than what has been officially received as Christian teaching. Like the 'braids' of a river, they leave the main stream when its waters are held up and feed back into it later.

The Environment

The problems of war, especially nuclear war, and of the social and economic order, are, as we have seen, largely the product of modern science and technology. Until comparatively recently the development of science and technology themselves was almost universally regarded as good. It was a duty laid upon man to be a steward over nature and this, it was assumed, implied a responsibility to comprehend the workings of nature and to use the knowledge thus attained for human purposes, so long as these were morally legitimate. To free human beings from poverty, and from the back-breaking labour and disease that went with it, was a purpose that needed no justification. Protests were directed not against this aim, but against distortions and unintended ill effects of particular means employed to attain it. The impetus to control nature and to use her in the best interests of man was strongest in Protestant forms of Christianity, especially in the United States, where a whole continent had required to be subdued and made fruitful, and where it was reckoned a grievous sin to be idle and unproductive. Given the immensity of the task it could scarcely have been otherwise.

The transition from this situation and the attendant attitudes to one in which, for the majority, affluence was taken for granted, and there was more emphasis on consumption than production, provoked something of a moral crisis. Not only could it be condemned in terms of the traditional 'work ethic' as involving waste and profligacy, but it evoked in some quarters an altogether new response. This was the ecological movement which viewed the history of Western technology as an aggressive assault by man upon the natural world in pursuit of his own exclusive interests, narrowly conceived. In a milder form the environmental movement sought to restrain the excesses of technological exploitation, to control pollution, and inhibit waste; but there was also increasingly, at any rate among the more articulate, a revolt against the entire philosophy which had, since the seventeenth century, underlain the growth of science and technology. This went hand in hand with the theoretical critique of the cognitive status of science, to which reference has already been made. The claims of natural science to provide an objective account of the way things actually are—to give knowledge of the 'real world'—were contested, and alternative ways of conceiving the world and acting in it were allowed equal legitimacy. Hence alternative medicine and alternative lifestyles were canvassed, together with a spiritual appeal to the oneness of man and nature. The mainstream churches, which had striven during the modern period—often with great difficulty—to effect an accommodation with the scientific world-view and the technological society, found themselves challenged in the name of spiritual values which, in the eyes of some, were more at home in Buddhism and in Hinduism than in Christianity.

The problems raised by the environment are genuine ones and have challenged Christians to revive and review neglected teachings about man's responsibility for the created order. The more extreme positions are, however, unlikely to predominate for two reasons. One is that, in spite of protestations to the contrary, they reflect too narrowly the interests of the West— and, indeed, of leisured classes in the West. In the developing world, the older imperatives retain their force: people need to be fed, diseases eliminated, lives extended; and, although technologies need often to be modified, they must be effectively exploited. The other is that only scientific explanation and experience, sensitively developed and administered, are competent to analyse the problems and find appropriate remedies. The moral problems raised by science and technology are not likely to be resolved except within the ambit of a world-view which can contain science without being eroded by it.

Medicine and Biological Research

The achievements of scientific medicine in the modern period have been dramatic. Many of the 'killer' diseases have been eliminated or effectively controlled and the expectation of life substantially extended. As a consequence, the practice of medicine has encountered a whole new range of ethical problems engendered in part by the greater expectations people now have. Sufferings and handicaps that were once thought to be an inevitable part of the human condition are now less readily accepted and people increasingly expect to be able to control every aspect of their lives. Technology itself exerts its own pressure: what can be done should be done. Scientific medicine, in spite of its achievements, attracts two kinds of criticism. It places too much power in the hands of the medical experts and, because of specialization, it fails to consider the patient as a whole person. Some of the critics, especially in the United States, in effect challenge the status of the medical profession as such in the name of the autonomy of the individual. The more the practice of medicine comes to be seen as a matter of applying the discoveries of the chemical and biological sciences, which are in principle available to all, the more evident it seems to such critics that it should provide whatever individuals want, without reference to the constraints traditionally imposed upon it by the ethics of the profession. The logic of such a claim is to transfer responsibility entirely to the patient (more appropriately thought of as 'client'). Decisions about abortion would be made by the pregnant woman, about euthanasia by the patient (perhaps through a 'living will') or, in the case of incompetents, by an appropriate surrogate. Decisions about research on embryos would be made by the donors. The law would have a limited role in protecting the interests of society. 'Medical ethics' as a concern of the medical profession would be squeezed between a high doctrine of patient autonomy on the one hand and the requirements of the law on the other.

The other criticism of scientific medicine tends, by contrast, to reinforce the traditional conception of medicine as the art of healing with its own internal standards. By emphasizing the needs of the whole person it presupposes an objective norm of health and sets constraints upon the uses to which medical technology may be put. It invests the profession of medicine with a special moral responsibility, to be shared with the patient but not wholly surrendered to him. Closely associated with this conception of medicine is the adherence of the wider society in Western countries to the principle of the sanctity of life. The former was accepted into Christianity from the ancient Greeks; the latter entered the culture of the Western world with Christianity itself. Together they represent a continuing insistence upon morality as flowing from the nature of things rather than as a construction of the human mind.

Hence the Christian churches themselves agree in opposing the extreme libertarian position which has some claim to be the characteristically modern one. They cannot locate questions of life and death within a private domain of individual preference; they are inescapably matters of shared ethical concern and as such cannot be decided simply to suit the wishes of individuals.

There are, however, differences among Christians as to what the principle of the sanctity of life actually requires in particular instances. Is abortion, at no matter what stage of pregnancy, tantamount to murder; or may the claims of the foetus be overridden in the interests of the mother's health or the broader interests of the family? Granted that life is a good to be held in trust from God and the necessary condition of all other goods, at what stage, if any, may it properly be judged, and by whom, that the burdens it imposes override the duty of prolonging it?

The question of the status of the embryo is involved also in the debate about the limits of biological research. No Christian church regards it as a matter of indifference whether the life of an embryo is terminated, but the official Roman Catholic position that the embryo deserves at all stages the full protection afforded to any human being is not shared by the mainstream Protestant churches. They think rather of the embryo as potentially a person and worthy of respect, and a degree of protection, as such.

These issues continue to be the subject of serious debate in Western countries and in others influenced by them, and it is largely taken for granted that the Christian conscience has an essential contribution to make to the debate. This is, perhaps, least true in relation to abortion, where, especially in the United States, the dispute has become highly polarized. The contrast between 'pro choice' and 'pro life' is in some ways excessively simplistic, but it does bring out the extent to which, on this issue, modernity is in conflict with the older Christian culture.

Sexual Ethics

The traditional assumption that there are limits to acceptable sexual behaviour is now widely challenged. In this area more than any other there has in the modern period been a revolt against Christian conceptions, both in literature and in life.

Partly it was a revolt against widespread hypocrisy, against double standards for men and women, and against the subordination of marriage to the interests of property. Often it was a plea for a more deeply personal conception of erotic love, involving its own more flexible and sensitive sexual ethic, in which what mattered was the authenticity of the love expressed. Increasingly, however, the constraints even of this conception were abandoned and sexual activity came to be regarded as a mode of self-expression which should be subject to no constraints except those freely accepted by the partners. The only moral principles involved were those admitted to be relevant in any other realm of human behaviour—the avoidance of exploitation and deception. Within this strongly individualistic framework, freedom to express one's sexual preferences is claimed as an important human right. In line with this tendency the century has witnessed in all Western advanced countries a progressive liberalization of the law and a tacit abandonment of traditional sexual ethics.

In this whole area the church has experienced in a particularly acute form the dilemmas which proceed from its close, but equivocal, association with the culture of the past in Europe and America. It distrusts many, if not most, of the new individualistic tendencies, which it regards as destroying or distorting certain fundamental human relationships, but it is not able, for the most part, to defend a purely conservative position. There is too much, for example, that is doubtfully Christian in the institution of marriage as accepted in Europe until recent times, especially in its subordination of women and its close association with property rights; and the treatment of 'deviants' in the past has been too harsh and hypocritical to be contemplated with an easy conscience. Hence there is an urgent need for a rethinking of attitudes towards sex and the family which will distinguish what is essential in traditional Christian teaching and apply it in a defensible way to the modern situation.

The task is to articulate the relevant principles and to get them accepted, and the two requirements affect one another.

Principles may be carefully articulated and ably presented but fail to persuade because they simply do not accord with experience. And an attractive new doctrine which expresses what many people are ready to hear and receive may lack firm intellectual and spiritual foundations.

The first has been the fate of the official Roman Catholic teaching on contraception as set out definitively in *Humanae Vitae*. The argument employed a version of natural law theory which stigmatized as unnatural, and therefore illicit, any interference with the procreative function of sexual intercourse. Hence a married couple who employed a contraceptive device (including 'the pill') in order to enjoy intercourse without its being 'open to procreation' were committing a sinful act, even if their intention was to have a family of manageable size and to rear and educate their children as well as possible. If contraception was sinful in this way, so, by the same or parallel reasoning, were homosexual intercourse, artificial insemination by donor, surrogate motherhood, and *in vitro* fertilization. Opposition to *Humanae Vitae*, both among Catholic and non-Catholic Christians, tended to focus on the 'mechanical' and 'impersonal' nature of the criteria involved. Could matters of physiological detail be so crucial in a relationship as intensely personal as marriage? The alternative approach was to emphasize the personal aspect of sexuality in general and, the 'unitive' function of marriage—'the mutual society, help and comfort that the one ought to have of the other'. In this way the actual experience of the faithful in their married lives could be brought effectively into the reckoning.

This appeal to personal experience endorsed one of the leading themes of the modern period, going back at least to the beginnings of the romantic movement, and it is hard not to acknowledge it as a permanent advance in human awareness. The problem for Christian ethics is that its secular manifestations have been increasingly in terms of purely individual self-fulfilment and self-expression. Exclusive reliance upon the personal could easily become dangerously subjective. Not only could non-procreative relationships between men and women in marriage be justified by this criterion, but also between men and women outside marriage, and between people of the same sex. In Europe and America the churches were faced by insistent demands, even within their own active membership, for acceptance of 'homosexual equality'.

To admit all these claims would not only be to abandon the 'conventional morality' of the recent past, but also to jettison what had been the consistent and continuous contention of Christian moralists since the earliest days of the church: that morality was not simply a human invention but was founded upon certain fundamental constants of human nature. Whether this conviction was articulated, as in the Roman Catholic Church, in terms of natural law, or, as in most of the Protestant churches, in terms of divinely instituted orders of creation, it stood fast against the characteristically modern conception of morality as the expression, ultimately, of individual preferences. It is because of this underlying issue that the Roman Catholic Church has agonized for so long and, to the outside world, so inexplicably, about contraception. Unless the line was held here, it was hard to see where else it was to be held; and, if it was not held at all, then a great part of what had been received from the past as essential to Christianity, including religious authority, was felt to be in jeopardy. And not only in the sexual realm, for the principles that Christians appealed to in relation to war, the social and political order, the protection of the environment, the limits of medical and scientific research and practice, all presupposed that God in creation had ordained the proper ends of human life and in so doing had imposed certain constraints upon the means for achieving them. The sexual realm itself, which is regarded by many modern thinkers as confined to an area of purely private behaviour, affects a great deal more than is apparent at first sight. The institution of the family, in particular, is deeply involved in the formation of individual character and in the maintenance of an ordered society, and it is not only from a specifically Christian standpoint that its breakdown would give cause for alarm. Some of the trends which to many modern thinkers represent a welcome liberalization of society, through a loosening of the bonds of a family-based 'conventional' morality, may carry untoward penalties in the way of personal insecurity and social disintegration.

The predicament of the Roman Catholic Church in relation to contraception illustrates in an extreme form the dilemma of the Christian conscience in the modern world. There has in Western countries been a widespread rejection of traditional Christian standards, chiefly but not exclusively in the realm of sexual behaviour. This revolt has been associated with secular philosophies which stress personal authenticity and individual self-expression. That these philosophies are inadequate to the whole range of moral problems which beset the modern world is increasingly apparent to many reflective people. The churches, therefore, have an obligation, which non-believers expect them to acknowledge, to maintain and strengthen the Christian ethical tradition. It is a resource that the modern world cannot do without. But the churches are liable, in this situation, to adopt one or other of two alternatives, neither of which is satisfactory. The first is to reassert without qualification the ethical prescriptions which have been accepted in the recent past, without considering whether the underlying principles require fresh applications in the light of current knowledge, and to assert them, moreover, in an authoritative manner. This reinforces the modernist revolt which has fed upon the continuing repudiation of just this stereotype. The second alternative is to embrace the typical modern world-view in one or other of its forms and interpret the Christian ethical tradition in terms of it. The first, conservative, approach fails as a rule to address itself to the problems in their full context and is insufficiently sensitive to the possibility that, because of the ossification of conventional teaching, genuinely Christian insights have sometimes had to flow through secular channels. The second, liberal, approach, fails in a different way to address the problems, because it identifies itself too closely with the very attitudes that have been largely responsible for creating them. What is needed is conservatives who are prepared to be critical of the tradition and liberals who are prepared to be critical of contemporary fashions.

There is, in any case, little likelihood of formal agreement between Christian thinkers, placed in very different situations and owning very different histories. At an earlier stage we raised the question whether the differences between Christians at diverse times and places have not been so extensive as to cast doubt on the very identity of Christianity as a system of belief and grounds for action. Yet Christians of all ages agree in seeking 'the mind of Christ' and the guidance of the Holy Spirit. They agree in looking for inspiration in the Bible, especially the New Testament, and the life and teaching of Jesus. There they find the commandment to love one another and an appeal to God's purposes in creation, illustrated in part by moral precepts drawn from Jewish and Graeco-Roman culture. As the Christian tradition develops, it exerts its own authority, formal or informal, upon the consciences of Christians, which are formed by it but not wholly determined by it, as they respond also to new developments of thought and experience. The ethical insights gained through this process have to be applied by different people to differing situations, in which the deliverances of conscience are sometimes unambiguous, but in which, inevitably, accommodations are often made and compromises sought which leave sincere Christians opposed to one another.

Sometimes in retrospect we may feel bound to judge that the Christian conscience was corrupted or diluted or diverted from its proper course; or, more simply, that it failed altogether to make itself felt. In making such judgements we implicitly acknowledge its continuing identity.

19

The Future of Christianity

JOHN TAYLOR

THERE is arrogance and folly in adding this epilogue, and many Christians would say that taking thought for the morrow bespeaks a lack of faith. The alternative is to end like *1066 and All That*: 'America became top nation and history came to a .' But there is no full stop. This generation is in some measure creating the circumstances of the next, so it is mere fecklessness not to look ahead, even in the certainty of being taken by surprise. For the story of Christianity has been, and will always be, a series of impromptu responses to events. That thought should not disconcert the followers of one who, it is said, was born into the makeshift improvisations of people coping with an emergency. Christian life is by nature reactive. This does not mean it is adrift. Its mandate stands; but it obeys only by responding to eventualities.

To approach the matter of the future by this method does, of course, beg a fundamental question. For there are many who firmly deny that the *form* of a religion—its thought, action, and organization—can properly be affected by the vicissitudes of politics and economics or the expansion of human knowledge, and regard those who countenance such adaptations in the same way as Marxists have condemned their revisionists. To such Christians religion is a self-contained subculture, pursuing an autonomous belief-system and way of life derived from a divine revelation and, consequently, independent of the history of a world which impinges only inasmuch as it promotes or restricts religious freedom. But historical investigation lends little support to the notion that influence can be confined to a one-way flow. A religion, like every other system of ideas or body of tradition, stands in a context of exchange, affecting and being affected by its historical and social situation. This truth is implicit in the biblical understanding of revelation. But this is not the place to pursue that argument, for, as H. G. Wells observed, 'It is on the whole more convenient to keep history and theology apart.'

The Prospect for Humanity

Any forecast of the next fifty years must assume, however cautiously, that history will not come to the ultimate full stop of nuclear catastrophe. That hope, however, cannot wisely be based upon the ending of the Cold War between the Western allies and the Soviet Union, nor even upon the mutual scaling down of their nuclear arsenals. Nuclear weapons are a fact, and it would be arrogance amounting to madness for those nations that possess them to suppose that they can forever prevent others from doing so. The security of the world cannot be preserved by an unending series of 'Gulf wars' against each state in turn that dares to assume the right to its quota of weapons of mass destruction. The liberation of Eastern Europe and the impending break-up of the Soviet Union have created a vast area of instability and a power vacuum of immense potential danger. Political and religious fanaticism is on the increase everywhere. Never before have the patient skills of detached conciliation been so necessary to the peace of the world. They are skills in which Christianity, in the light of the Gospel, should be well versed, but in which, in the light of its history, it can claim no expertise. Yet, if they are to have any future, all religions, including Christianity, will have to put peace and justice high on their agenda.

There are other dangers, hardly less grave, that could threaten human life as a whole within the next century. On the strength of falling oil prices, beef and cereal 'mountains', and a successful manipulation of markets, the richer nations have been able to dismiss for the present the apocalyptic predictions of the Club of Rome and the Brandt Commission. It seems probable that new discoveries may provide the means for averting the cumulative threats of population explosions and diminishing food or resources. But AIDS and acid rain point to other possibilities of global catastrophe inherent in the very vigour, if not ruthlessness, of human advance. And it remains to be seen whether *nationally* based political systems can apply the remedies with enough conviction to deal with *global* emergencies. Industrial capitalism will almost certainly continue to change its shape with the greater dominance of multinational consortiums, the emergence of economic blocs additional to those we now have, and that high technology of data analysis, communication, and 'intelligent' machines, loosely called the post-industrial revolution. The economy of the self-contained nation state will be forced open to the economic dictates of the bloc to which it belongs and to a single world economy serving the interests of supranational concentrations of power. Those interests will more and more determine the policy of the separate nations, disturbing the balance governments are responsible for maintaining between the claims of economic productivity, public welfare, and social cohesion within the state. The probable outcome will be a great advance in technology and a greater imbalance in the distribution of its amazing benefits. There will be a three-tier society with sharp lines of demarcation. The very rich will climb into a strongly defended world of privilege, job security, and management power; a substantial middle group of technically well-qualified operatives, including the self-employed, will enjoy fairly secure work, more evenly dispersed than at present around a 'greener' countryside; and a superfluous population of unwanted people will be redundant in an absolute sense, an unavoidable burden on the state, unless it proves expedient to give them a more substantial minimum income to sustain a broader base of consumers. It seems merely utopian to hope that their frustration will be avoided by a resolute policy of job-sharing and an idyllic development of satisfying leisure.

The alternative must be escalating unrest, increasing repression, a heavier police presence, more racism aimed at poor blacks, tighter immigration controls, more retributive justice, more people in prison, more sophisticated surveillance, and a harsher hostility towards intellectual or activist sympathizers. Each step in this direction may be justified on grounds of necessity, and, in such an atmosphere of insecurity, an authoritarian regime will be surprisingly welcomed.

Fortunately this scenario is not inevitable in the 'developed' areas of the world. There is at least a chance that those who are ready to question the existing industrial-capitalist paradigm, which includes the traditional labour and trade union organizations, and to discern the direction in which it is moving, may combine to challenge and out-think its presuppositions so as to come forward with a convincing alternative. At present the various elements that might converge to achieve this are fragmentary and idealistic; but the slender success of the Green Party in West Germany points to the kind of catalyst round which an effective realignment could emerge.

But while the strong, developed nations can see positive glimmers of hope amid the forebodings of doom, in sub-Saharan Africa and in the nations now paralysed by debt the grim scenario seems all too accurate. The plight of the poorer nations is complex. Their rate of progress in average income, health, and education over the past fifty years has been much more rapid than was that of the industrial countries during their period of take-off. Their economic growth rate per capita between 1965 and 1982 was higher than that of the OECD's industrial market economy. In 1985 all the foreign aid, direct investment, and commercial loans received in the Third World amounted to less than 1 per cent of their combined national incomes. They are not rich compared to the USA, which accounts for a quarter of the world's annual consumption of resources. But they have the potential to raise themselves from poverty, as India and China are showing, if only the cards were not so ruthlessly stacked against them. The escalating wealth of the 'North' is not created solely by its advanced technology, but also by its tariff barriers and terms of trade, its use of cheap labour and control of commodity prices in the 'South', its exploitation of aid to enforce its exports and impose its ideology. The intolerable indebtedness of the Third World in the 1980s was largely created by the short-sighted self-interest of the reactions of the United States and the major European countries to the sharp increase in oil prices in 1973 and again in 1979. Popular awareness of the massive suffering that these things impose, adding its pressure to the reality of debt default and the need for healthy markets, will bring about some reluctant concessions and a temporary alleviation of one crisis after another. But it remains to be seen whether the basic paradigm of capitalism can be changed enough to allow a more equitable form of society to come into being in the developing countries, or whether it will actually create a harsher three-tier division there than the one taking shape in the North. In the absence of a keener moral imperative than appears to prevail at present no prediction can rule out the possibility of a future which one writer has depicted as 'an affluent lifeboat on a sea of poverty' from which the survivors beat back the multitudes of unwanted people who are desperately struggling to clamber aboard. If this hideous prospect is even remotely conceivable, its implications for the future of Christianity become starkly apparent when attention is given to the distribution of Christians among the different regions of the globe as the twenty-first century opens.

Impending Statistical Changes

Before concentrating on the prospects for Christianity it is important to see it in the wider perspective of the religious allegiance of humanity as a whole. It has been estimated that by the year 2000 32.3 per cent of the world's population will be nominally Christian, 19.2 per cent will be Muslims, 13.7 per cent Hindus, 5.7 per cent Buddhists, and 0.3 per cent Jews. Of

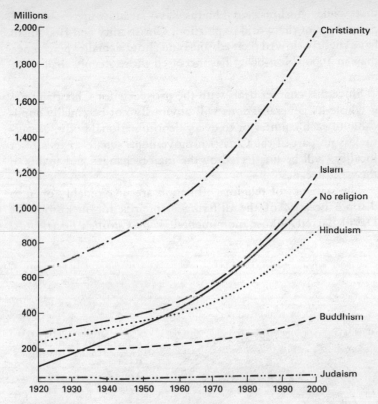

FIGURE I. Comparative growth of world religions, 1920–2000.

the remainder about 1 per cent will belong to one or other of the smaller religious groups, and 9 per cent will practise some form of tribal or animist religion. Figure 1 shows how the major world faiths have expanded since 1920. The steep rise in all but Judaism during the last thirty years reflects the population explosion as well as the gains in new adherents. It is significant that while Muslims and Hindus have steadily increased their percentage of the world population, Christianity and Buddhism have slightly slowed their advance and show a smaller percentage than in 1900. Non-belief has increased more steeply than all of them.

Since this chapter deals with the prospects for Christianity as a whole its generalizations will obviously not be equally applicable to each country or to every denominational body. Nevertheless no part of the Christian movement, whatever its size or locality, will be unaffected by the major changes and trends of the next decades.

The statistics of religious affiliation are unavoidably open to dispute because of the differing standards for inclusion. Dr David Barrett, whose monumental *World Christian Encyclopedia*

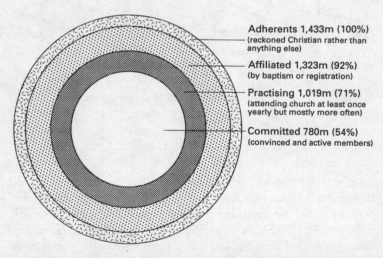

Adherents 1,433m (100%)
(reckoned Christian rather than anything else)

Affiliated 1,323m (92%)
(by baptism or registration)

Practising 1,019m (71%)
(attending church at least once yearly but mostly more often)

Committed 780m (54%)
(convinced and active members)

FIGURE 2. Levels of commitment of Christian adherents, 1980.

is often criticized for exaggerating the numbers, does actually apply a scale for measuring commitment by which his figures can be moderated for those preferring a more stringent criterion (Figure 2). This can be seen in his assessment of the number of Christians in the world in 1980. Because his is the most comprehensive and updated survey, Barrett's figures for adherents, unless otherwise stated, are used in this chapter. Those who prefer a more circumspect assessment of the totals will note that roughly 54 per cent of them can be regarded as committed and active Christians, 71 per cent as having some continuing contact with a worshipping congregation, and 92 per cent as having been at some time recognized members of a church. Such an adjustment of the figures will not affect the argument, since the point at issue is what *proportion* of all Christians is to be found in each of the several regions of the globe, and in which direction the change is tending.

Figure 3 shows the growth in the number of Christian adherents in each of the six major regions of the world during the present century. Because its numbers have been so much smaller, Oceania has been omitted, though its significance is considerable on other grounds. As a separate region it comprises Australia and New Zealand (where the Christian totals in millions are 4 in 1900, 14 in 1970, 16 in 1985, 20 projected for 2000), and the Pacific, where they have shown a more rapid growth (300,000 in 1900, $3\frac{1}{2}$ million in 1970, 5 million in 1985, 7 million projected for 2000).

The most striking fact to emerge from these figures is the speed with which the number of Christian adherents in Latin America, Africa, and Asia has overtaken that of Europe, North America, and the former USSR. For the first time since the seventh century, when there were large Nestorian and Syrian churches in parts of Asia, the majority of Christians in the world are not of European origin. This change can readily be appreciated from Figure 3. Moreover, this swing to the 'South' has, it would seem, only just got going, since the birth rate in those regions is at present so much higher than in the devel-

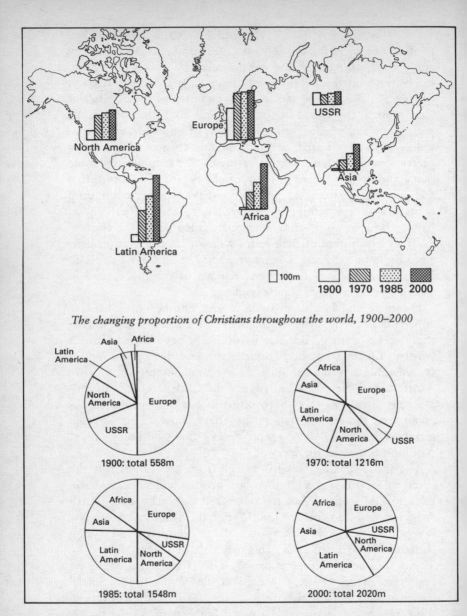

The changing proportion of Christians throughout the world, 1900–2000

1900: total 558m

1970: total 1216m

1985: total 1548m

2000: total 2020m

FIGURE 3. Growth in the number of Christians throughout the world, 1900–2000.

oped 'North', and lapses from religion are almost negligible compared with Europe. By the middle of the next century, therefore, Christianity as a world religion will patently have its centre of gravity in the Equatorial and Southern latitudes, and every major denomination, except possibly the Orthodox Church, will be bound to regard those areas as its heartlands, and embody the fact in its administration.

As has been said, the scale of the figures on the diagram is open to question, but the proportions are exactly the same when a more conservative estimate is followed. In fact the shift is even more startling according to the membership figures of the Roman Catholic Church. Walbert Bühlmann, in his book *The Coming of the Third Church*, quoted from the *Annual Statistics* for 1973 to show that there were 318 million Catholics in Europe and North America, and 367 million in Latin America, Africa, and Asia. He commented: 'It is by now an incontrovertible fact that the West has been dismissed from its post as *centre* of religious cultural unity for the whole of Christianity. . . . However, the West, as a field of religious cultural *influence within* the Church (no longer medieval), remains in existence.' (Italics mine.)

But while the pressure of these facts will grow more insistent in the next twenty-five years, there will be a prolonged comprehension gap, and the transition will be painful. Several factors will slow down the change. The first of these is language. In 1981 the language which was mother tongue to the greatest number of baptized or affiliated Christians throughout the world was Spanish (15.6 per cent) and the second most common mother tongue was English (14.8 per cent). The next in frequency were Portuguese, German, and French. So it is little wonder that all should continue to regard Europe as the homeland of their faith.

A second factor prolonging the status quo is the traditional method of representation on most conciliar bodies. This will impinge on the consciousness of Christians mainly on those occasions when they think in denominational categories, but all

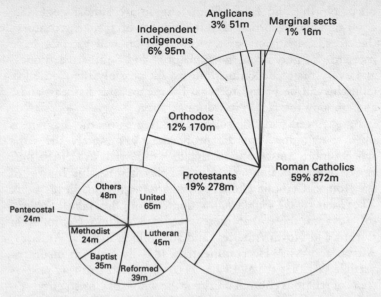

FIGURE 4. The relative size of the major Christian denominations in 1985.

the world confessional bodies will be affected in the same way. Any international meeting of bishops or clergy is bound to give a disproportionate presence to the metropolitan and older churches for the simple reason that the poorer churches have fewer clergy. Consequently the Lambeth Conference, for example, continues to look a great deal whiter than the Anglican Communion actually is. The various confessional bodies convene their occasional consultative synods and international assemblies as family gatherings, not as meetings of representative democracies; if, as the World Council of Churches does, they chose to represent the numerical strength of the various provinces or parts, they would present a truer image of their Communion, both visually and in the balance of their ideas. None the less, in spite of this factor, the African voice and presence exercised a powerful influence upon the Lambeth Conference of 1988, pre-saging an even greater ascendancy in the future.

The recognition of this change of balance is further inhibited by the fact that so few books and articles by the theologians of the southern continents are translated and published in the North. This perpetuates a serious underestimate of the intellectual weight that the South is able to bring to the counsels of the Christian world, and contrasts sadly with the openness of the world of science. Even the work of Kitamori, Takenaka, and Koyama of Japan, which economically and culturally belongs to the North, is generally ignored. The liberation theologians of Latin America suffer from the common label which prevents their individual voices from being heard with attention. But the theological schools of the West and the leaders of their churches are pursuing a blinkered scholarship while they remain ignorant of such writers as D. S. Analorpabadass, the liturgical scholar in South India; the Ghanaian, Kwami Bediako, with his application of patristic thought to modern Africa; Enrique Dussel of Chile, the historian; Jean Marc Ela of Cameroon, an important exponent of African theology; Edward Fasholé-Luke, a student of Cyprian and his relevance to the African church; the biblical scholar, M. P. John, in India; Kim Bockyong, the Korean theologian of society; Mulago Musharnene, who has written on traditional Catholicism, and Ngundu Mushete, student of French modernist theology, both in Zaïre; Samu Rayan, who has written on the Second Vatican Council in India, and Lamin Sannah of the Gambia, currently at Harvard, who expounds the uniqueness of Christ from an Islamic background.

Yet even when the contribution that the 'South' is making to the intellectual strength and the leadership of the world-wide Church can no longer be ignored, the assumption that the old Christendom is the sole guardian and arbiter of orthodoxy will tenaciously live on. What seems to be taking place is a transition from one cultural phase to another, and in the history of Christianity this has always been a slow process. Professor Andrew Walls of Aberdeen, in the Finlayson lecture for 1984, suggested that Christian history up to the present day and in the immediate future may be seen as a succession of phases, each representing Christianity's embodiment in a major cultural milieu. Each phase has entailed a transformation of Christianity as it penetrated another culture and received its impress. Each phase brought new themes to prominence, themes that would have been inconceivable to an earlier framework of thought.

Professor Walls identifies six of such phases. The first, very brief, was entirely Jewish. Just in time, before the destruction of the Jewish state, Christianity had entered the second, Hellenistic–Roman phase, otherwise it would have lingered only as a vanishing sect in the desert beyond the Jordan, whither the Jerusalem church fled before the advancing legions. The influence of Hellenism permeated all the regions into which Christianity now spread, including Egypt, Ethiopia, Armenia, and beyond, and what it gave to Christianity supremely was the idea of orthodoxy—of right belief formulated in propositions and a single desirable framework of civilized life. So Christianity took this into its system, and has never lost it. The time came when that culture eventually fell apart, and was overrun, first by northern barbarians and then by Arabs. But before that happened, Christianity had begun a new transposition into the tribal culture of the northern hordes. Among them the corporate identity of separate clans and peoples was the dominant reality, and, wherever Christianity was adopted, it became part of the custom that bound a tribal society together. In the new world of peasant cultivators and warriors Christianity evolved the concept of a Christian nation. The whole millennium of the Middle Ages can be perceived as the struggle between that pattern and the still surviving ideal of Hellenistic unity centred in Rome and Byzantium.

The sixteenth century saw the triumph of the less-than-Christian nation state, as much in Catholic Spain, Portugal, and France, as in England and Northern Europe, but not before the fourth cultural phase had already begun. This was not so much a geographical move as a psychological one. The great navigators enabled Western man to stand back in imagination from his small continent and see it differently. Copernicus invited him to take the same detached view of his planet. Descartes isolated the thinking individual as the first philosophical reality. The age was one of individualism and critical detachment and Christianity in its Western form adapted to it. So began a substantial recession from Christian faith and practice. All of this has continued up to the present, simultaneously with a quite different development which Walls identifies as a distinct, fifth phase, namely the extension of Europe's hegemony throughout the globe. In North America, Australia and New Zealand, and parts of Latin America, this became permanent settlement and even elsewhere the imperial presence and cultural penetration seemed set to last. So the Christianity of the West added to its long heritage a universal missionary vision of its task that no earlier generation had dreamt of.

That consciousness of mission, like each of the other insights that Christianity has acquired along its pilgrimage through one dominant culture after another, remains as a permanent possession, despite the passing of the empires, the continuing recession of Christianity in Western Europe, and the uglier face of neo-colonialism. If, at this moment before the dawn of a new century, the church in the industrial nations is confused, not knowing what to do with its inheritance, this is because it cannot yet see clearly the new cultural milieu into which it is already moving. If Andrew Walls is right, however, the church can take heart from the evidence that each time the cultural base of the Christian religion was about to crumble, Christianity has been saved by its diffusion into a new milieu. And if what Walls calls Christianity's 'infinite translatability' disturbs the guardians of orthodoxy, let them also find reassurance from this history. For it shows that, whatever undreamt-of forms the faith has evolved in each new phase, the dominant themes of former times have been added to rather than lost.

The Church of the Poor

The Christians of the next century, then, considered as a whole, will be young, since two-thirds of the populations of the 'South' are under 25; they will be dynamic, despite the apathy that accompanies malnutrition, because their hope is strong, as Bishop Newbigin pointed out in *The Other Side of 1984*; their organizations will be unstable and diverse; and they will be poor. All the churches in the industrial wealthy nations will be painfully adjusting their habit of thought to take in the fact that they are members of the church of the poor—no longer the church *for* the poor.

Hitherto the European and North American churches' comprehension of the poverty of fellow Christians in the southern continents has consisted mainly of news coverage, imagination, and generosity. It has perforce been a relationship of 'we' and 'they'. But as communication technology makes immediate personal contact across the world accessible to far more people, as business enterprises, even on the smaller scale, become transnational, as Christian leaders from the economically deprived countries play a frequent and prominent part in the international synods and assemblies of the churches, as the twinning of dioceses and congregations of the North with the South grows more personalized, and 'partnership' consultations become more mutually outspoken, and as the issue of poverty in the richer nations gets more perceptibly similar in structure if not in degree to that in the southern continents, sympathy will inevitably give place to solidarity, and it will be normal for Christian self-awareness to include all in a common 'us'.

Unhappily, it is too much to hope that this transition will be idealistically uniform. The mental habits of centuries are not surrendered without turmoil and the question of political activism for a church of the poor will be even more divisive than it is already. Yet it seems inescapable that this must be one of the 'themes' that will predominate in the Christian consciousness in its next phase, giving new shape and a different emphasis to the church's teaching and liturgy, her style of life, the preoccupations of her ministry, and her relation to the state. Intercession will tend to fade into petition: 'Have mercy on us all' rather than 'Help them'. Christians in the richer countries will probably be under strong moral pressure to pare down their own and their churches' extravagance, not as a means of directly sharing resources, but as a sign of identification with the vast majority of their fellow Christians and fellow humans. The change of emphasis from sympathy to solidarity will certainly be apparent in the agenda of whatever councils govern the life of the various churches. During the Second Vatican Council, Cardinal Lercato startled the assembly with his passionate complaint that not one of the conciliar texts spoke plainly of the church as the church of the poor. Their solidarity in poverty will be brought home with ever greater intensity to the churches in all parts of the world.

One thing is certain, however. Whatever the next act in the drama of history contains, neither the rich nor the poor will appear on the stage as ideological abstractions. In order to avoid the danger of such generalizations it is necessary to look separately at some of the main regions of the world and pick out indications of the way in which Christianity is likely to develop there. And, because of its significance for the theme that has emerged thus far, Latin America should come first.

Latin America

Four features dominate the broad view of the situation and seem likely to mould the immediate future of Christianity there.

1. Both numerically and culturally it is the most Catholic of the continental blocs, after 500 years of Roman missions, and with 91.8 per cent of its peoples nominally affiliated as late as 1973.

2. Though Protestant churches represent only a small minority, their rate of growth, especially that of the Pentecostal Churches, has been the highest in the world over the past twenty years. Today the charismatic movement, as distinct from denominations so named, has affected in part all the churches of Latin America.

3. The politico-economic situation of the area is arguably the most volatile of all, since it is the main 'sphere of interest' of the USA, its concentrations of urban poverty are the greatest (it is estimated that by the year 2000 the populations of Mexico City and São Paulo together will exceed that of the United Kingdom), and the burden of debt is the heaviest.

4. The spread of *comunidades eclesiales de base* (CEBs), as described in Chapter 12, has been on such an influential scale that they can now be justifiably regarded as a Latin American phenomenon. They are not evenly distributed throughout the area, being most numerous in Brazil, where over 100,000 communities were known in 1985, in Honduras, where lay community leaders, or 'delegates of the Word', number 10,000, and in Nicaragua and Peru.

This pattern of church life, however, did not originate in Latin America. If one recalls the *ecclesiolae in ecclesia* of the eighteenth-century Moravians and the camp meetings of American Negro slaves with their highly ambiguous spirituals, it is unwise to make too sharp a distinction between pietist and politically oriented groups. When oppressed, dispirited people gather for religious comfort and in other-worldly hope, the sharing of their troubles and the articulating of their prayers creates a space within their lives where the warrant of their helplessness does not run, and they find a personal freedom and a corporate identity. Their Bible reading, however heavenward looking, enriches their self-understanding with a new imagery of dignity, discipline, and responsibility. A selfhood is released that can fight back against apathy and alcoholism and, if those, then against other misfortunes as well. Since the groups depend mainly on lay leaders, both men and women participate in their meetings without inhibition. They are, as it were, already mobilized for change before any specifically political interpretation has been implanted.

It is impossible to generalize about the direction the CEBs are going to take in the future. Communities vary from country to country, and from region to region within countries. Protestant communities mostly fight shy of social activism, but even this is not uniformly true. In Central America theologically conservative Protestant groups of peasants and Indians have made common cause with Catholic communities in the struggle. In Guatemala alone there are 200 Protestant or ecumenical CEBs. The most striking model, which has caught the attention of Christians around the world, is that which combines celebration and scripture reflection with the cultivation of social and political consciousness. In their situation this naturally borrows insights from the Marxist critique of society, national and international, and also encourages CEB members to become active in the peoples' organizations contending for human rights. But it is a mistake to conclude that a preconceived ideology is therefore being insinuated into the *comunidades* by the priests or the group leaders. Liberation theology cannot be seen aright unless it is taken primarily as an attempt to give shape to an understanding of the faith that has genuinely sprung up from the experience of these simple Christians. The principal theologians of the movement—priests, like Gustavo Gutierrez, Leonardo Boff, Jose Marins, and Jon Sobrino, or the Protestant pastors Rubem Alves and Miguez Bonino—did their formative thinking and writing with their faces towards the people in the CEBs, and their ears open to their speech, as a part of their pastoral activity. It was when they turned to the world beyond and addressed their new insights to the wider church that their presentation became more doctrinaire. Then 'the poor' became idealized and, to that extent, less real. They were generalized to include under the one term 'marginalized races, exploited classes, despised cultures, and so on'. The modern concept of the class struggle was read back into the biblical affirmations of God's special love for the poor. And Christ, emptied of historicity, was presented as a symbol of triumph out of suffering, just as he had previously been a symbol of consolation under suffering. These weaknesses do not invalidate the witness of the CEBs to the world-wide church. They reflect the influence of Latin American Marxism upon this period of theological rethinking, but already there is evidence that Marxist ideology has run its course in Latin America. The struggle to break free from social and economic repression is too real to depend on a political theory, and will certainly continue into the next century.

The reactions of the different protagonists in the drama are predictable. Iberian Catholicism, still uniquely engrained in the history and culture of the whole continental bloc, will pay the price of having become a church of the poor by being divided even as society is divided. Its traditional parishes and institutions, with their confirmations, processions, and persevering priests, will survive as a matter of habit for a long time to come, massively crumbling, like an old cathedral in the sun. Though church attendance may in general decline, the participation of the poor will grow stronger still. Radicalized priests will grow more confident as they become aware that sections of the church elsewhere in the world are receiving the spiritual gift and challenge of the *comunidades*. They may draw new inspiration from indigenous Indian culture and values. Meanwhile right-wing governments will attempt to contain the popular movements with varying degrees of ruthlessness, sustained as 'democracies' by the USA and other industrial powers and by a diminishing conservative membership of the Catholic Church. The dichotomy will be felt most acutely by Rome, torn between her opposition to both insurrection and heterodoxy on the one hand, and, on the other, her fear of a breakaway by the CEBs if she is too intransigent. The Protestant churches, predominantly Pentecostal, will probably continue to grow, with a tendency to split into further divisions. The financial dependence of their considerable schools and hospitals will keep most of them closely attached to the USA and theologically and politically conservative, with notable exceptions. As such they will have an appeal to the élite and those in power, which some of their pastors will find problematic. As, in one way or another, the Latin American continent becomes financially viable, the church which has learnt to become a church of the poor, will have to think how it can remain that when circumstances have changed.

African Christianity

To turn to Africa is to find a continent intent on disengaging its history from a very recent colonial past. That preoccupation delays both the forging of new international relationships within the continent and the development of a sense of common identity. Already that past is an experience unknown to half the population of the new African nations, and they will move into the next century with quite different concerns. Yet, with the two exceptions of the Copts in Egypt and the ancient church of Ethiopia, the Christianity of Africa is sprung from that recent past. Among Christians in equatorial Africa and those with a concern for them one often meets with an exaggerated fear of the advance of Islam as an African religion of much longer standing. It is not justified by the facts. In the whole continent, including North Africa, the two faiths have been of roughly equal strength numerically throughout the century and by AD 2000 it is expected that 48 per cent of the population will be nominally Christian and 42.5 per cent nominally Muslim. Conversions from one to the other are infrequent, and both gain their new adherents mainly from among the traditional religions of Africa. Until recently there was a difference between the thoroughly rooted resistant Islam of West Africa and the Swahili Muslims on the east side of Africa who would more easily change their religion; but the new mood of fundamentalism has touched them also and given them a new firmness. Today they are making their presence felt as a confident minority in Zimbabwe. The frontier, if that is the right term, between

Islam and Christianity runs unevenly across the continent between latitudes 5 and 15 north of the equator. Christians outnumber all others in Ghana, Cameroon, and the Central African Republic; Muslims do so in Senegal, Mali, Niger, and the Sudan; and tribal religion still predominates in Sierra Leone. Chad surprisingly has 33 per cent Christians, Nigeria 49 per cent to 45 per cent Muslims. That kind of coexistence is natural in a loosely organized community, but nationhood invites conflict over who shall control the state. In the past there have been Islamic dreams of dominating the Nile to its source and these may be revived from time to time.

The amount of influence that African Christians exercise upon society and upon the state varies from one country to another, and does not coincide with their numerical strength. In Ghana the churches, when they present a common front, have proved to be the only element in society able to take on the government over an issue of justice or to mediate between two parties in a political conflict. In Nigeria also Christianity is a force to be reckoned with when it takes a united stand. Such courage and potential effectiveness in resistance attracts people, especially the young, to the church, irrespective of which government is being challenged. In Zimbabwe the Anglican Church has had difficulty in retaining its younger members since its ambivalent posture towards the independence movement, while the United Methodist Church, which was actively involved against the Smith regime, still holds its youth. Up in Malawi, too, what is felt to have been the failure of the churches to withstand Dr Banda is held against them. In this matter, however, as over so much else in Africa, pragmatism rules, and it is risky to draw conclusions that would be valid elsewhere. A very conservative pietism does not imply a detachment from social activism, and a readiness to be politically involved is not inconsistent with apparent passivity under tyranny.

The impulse to give Christianity a fully African expression has been inhibited by the fear of appearing to conform to the foreigner's image of a backward people; but now the movement is gaining impetus. An earlier generation of African theologians seemed anxious to demonstrate the Christian orthodoxy of their traditional ideas, but now they are asking what those ideas can contribute to a Christian's understanding and practice. Christianity in Africa in the next century will reflect its indigenous culture not only in worship and organization but in theology and discipline. It is unlikely that Rome can refuse for very much longer the demand of her African bishops for a married priesthood. Other churches may find that polygamy is on their agenda for reconsideration as an option under certain conditions. There will be changes in custom at funerals and memorial services that may be more Christian than those that have overtaken the churches in the West! Healing and exorcism will play a more prominent part in the ministry of the churches, and a doctrine of unbroken relationship with the departed will take its place more openly among Christian beliefs. And, during the final decades of the struggle in southern Africa, 'black theology' will become more interwoven with 'liberation theology', and, without either of these labels, permeate the thought of African Christianity. Throughout this development the rising generation will be ambivalent, welcoming the cultural autonomy, while resenting the autocratic role of 'chieftainly' bishops and elders, casting a sceptical scientific eye at the supernatural, while falling for the temptation to revert to magic and occultism to which the urbanized and alienated are peculiarly prone. In these ways the young will act as a spur, to impel the church to give cautious, responsible guidance.

The churches of the 'North' will find it hard to view with equanimity the emergence of such an African Christianity, and the old links of missionary contact and confessional solidarity and even economic support will be used as reins. But the era of conformity has passed, even for the Catholic Church. The deprivation of Archbishop Milingo of Lusaka in 1982 has to be one of the last examples of that kind of long-arm control. It led in the past to the formation of the African Independent Churches, which are now such a considerable element in African

Christianity. Many of them are ephemeral, inasmuch as they are a response to one charismatic healer or prophet. But others, like the $2\frac{1}{2}$ million Kimbanguists in Zaïre and Angola, are highly structured, disciplined churches. Such will continue, perhaps with the same phenomenal growth rate, as a reminder that the ties of a confessional family and the structures of a world-wide communion are no longer of supreme importance compared with responsible obedience to the gospel in the particularity of a given place and time.

Christianity in Asia

There have been Christians in parts of Asia for a very long time—from the beginning, in fact, in the Middle East. Yet it is still a small minority religion there. The contrast with Latin America and Africa is striking. Not that Asian Christians are few in numbers: they make up 10 per cent of the world total. Yet, apart from the Philippines, they average only 3.5 per cent of the vast populations and are submerged within the culture of other dominant religions. This is their burden and their peculiar strength. (The Philippines and their religious situation are in every respect like a Latin American state that has drifted across the Pacific, and, until they are absorbed into the political orbit of East Asia, their Christianity will share the same history as that of Guatemala or Ecuador.)

The immediate future for Christianity in the Middle East will turn on what is done by, and to, a reawakened Islam. The ancient churches may continue to rest secure in their status as *dhimmis*, religious minorities tolerated with a measure of cultural community, provided they concede—as the Maronites in Lebanon tragically ceased to do—the Islamic identity of the nation. The more recent small denominations of Western origin will be much more precarious if Muslim fundamentalism grows more militant. Membership of all the churches outside Iran is predominantly Arab, in sympathy as well as race, so whether 'Arabism' demands being Muslim will be increasingly under debate. All Christians will suffer a degree of psychic insecurity, inhibiting the influence they might have on the thought or the welfare of their society.

This minority-consciousness is acting as a drag upon the church in most other parts of Asia, hampering it from taking up the challenge of opportunities that are peculiarly its own. It is not their small numbers or lack of social standing that inhibits Asian Christians, as the boldness of Pakistani sweepers in forming themselves into a little church in Riyadh, whither they had been recruited by the Saudi government, demonstrates. It is the association of their faith with the bad history of Christian nations that makes them feel alienated from their own culture. There was a time when their links with all that was best in the West enabled Christians in Asia to give a lead in education, in the creation of a new legal tradition, and in service to the needy. Today it is often the adherents of the other religions who evince the spirit of justice and service. The foreign funds that maintain the Christian institutions serve to perpetuate not only administrative structures that are too top-heavy for today's church but also an estranged and inward-looking community life.

Most Asian churches can and will sever all their ties with the West except that of a common faith and mutual love. As they do so, confidence in their own identity will grow strong and change will come rapidly. There will be bolder inculturation as Western forms of worship, prayer, and custom are shed and a more Asian theology is preached and written. The organization of the church will begin to resemble the other Asian religions in being less uniformly structured, with many local variants. Base communities are likely to replace parochial units as, according to some sociologists, they are already starting to do in the churches in the West; and an openness between different traditions and their ministries will supersede the former laboriously negotiated schemes of church unity. There are signs also in many Asian churches that the younger generation will look for some more ideological approach to the structures of society instead of the old individual forms of social amelioration. And all of this, by making Christianity an unmistakably Asian religion, will improve its suppleness and confidence for the task of promoting continuous dialogue-in-life between faith and faith.

Religious pluralism will certainly be a significant fact of life in the next century and a new quality of relationship among the major religions is bound to develop. Instead of seeing one another as rivals, as Figure 1 might suggest, they are likely to become more aware of the rise of irreligion and spiritual indifference in the world, and may see themselves as fellow witnesses to the reality of God. At the moment this is commonly described as a Copernican revolution, but the metaphor is inadequate. It is better to think of entering a period of mutual testimony, in which the witnesses will not always agree. But each will contribute his conviction and try to grasp the inwardness of what the other is saying. And the Christian contribution is that God is Christlike. At present it is in Europe that interfaith dialogue seems to flourish. Is this because the church there is most conscious of the decline of faith, or emboldened by its knowledge that Christianity stands highest on the graph? It certainly should not desist. But ultimately a witness to the Christlike God may most effectively be given by a minority church in areas where the other faiths are strong.

Christianity in China

Potentially the most significant fact for the future of Christianity could be its phenomenal growth in China at the present time. The enforced severance of the churches from their foreign roots, and their suffering with everyone else under the Cultural Revolution, have for the first time established Christianity, in all its diversity, as a Chinese religion, part of the nation and its history. In 1992 it was responsibly estimated that Christians affiliated to the (Protestant) China Christian Council numbered between five and six million. In Zhejiang province alone there were a million communicants with nearly 2,000 churches and 3,500 other meeting points, mainly in people's homes. Catholics, though fewer in number, are spread more homogeneously throughout China owing to their more tightly structured organization, and they too have been overtaken by this unlooked-for expansion. In Shanghai city, with its thirteen million inhabitants, they account for over one per cent of the population. Church members, both Catholic and Protestant, are predominantly rural peasants who have found in the Christian groups an area of self-determination, a personal morality, and, often, a ministry of healing and exorcism through prayer. Many of the congregations are house churches, and the only effective authority is the local leader, who is as likely to be a woman as a man. This is the case even in the Catholic groups, in the absence of a priest.

Catholicism has the longer historical roots in China but it has preserved a rigid Tridentine ethos and a separatist, anti-Communist stance, though recently it has begun to adopt the insights of the Second Vatican Council. Being regarded as a fifth column, its members suffered most during the 1950s and 1960s. They were ordered to break their affiliation with Rome, to appoint bishops without papal approval, and to join the officially recognized Catholic Patriotic Association. Bishops who resisted were imprisoned and replaced. This does not mean, as is commonly believed in the West, that only the 'underground' Catholics remained faithful. Many priests and catechists were able to minister in the public church structures without belonging to the Patriotic Association. They continued to pray for the Holy Father and felt themselves to be in continuing communion with the universal Catholic Church. They hope for reconciliation with Rome, though without losing their newly won acceptance as one of China's indigenous religions. While Rome maintains the rhetoric of disowning the officially recognized bishops, a concordat was in fact firmly expected up to the moment of China's political reversion, signalled in Tiananmen Square in 1989.

The Protestants, in contrast, are much more loosely structured and include some distinctly heretical groups by any standard. In the past they were just as tied as the Catholics to their foreign bases, which were for the most part doctrinally conservative and congregational in structure. This had a natural appeal for the urban middle classes, among whom the missions worked, because of the Confucian tradition of rote learning and reverence for the precise written text. There were exceptions in the more liberal and socially aware ministry to students in the 1920s and the lively theology of the Anglican, T. C. Chao. Neither of these survived the trauma of the Cultural Revolution, but a firmer theological base had been built, politically radical and theologically fairly conservative, by such people as Y. T. Wu, the real author of the Three-Self Movement. That tradition of social awareness lives on in the Amity Foundation, a voluntary service organization initiated and administered by Chinese Christians within the Republic to promote health education and welfare among the neediest people in China. It represents a significant stirring of concern for the grinding poverty of those millions who are untouched by the present boom of prosperity.

Today all Christian bodies of non-Roman origin are federated through the China Christian Council at local, provincial, and national levels. Congregations adhere to their own church tradition and pay their pastors a small salary. The Christian Council structure provides voluntary workers' classes for the leaders of congregations, and organizes the ordination and placing of pastors. Bishop Ding expects to see a presbyterian style of pastoral eldership ministering to groups of congregations and exercising a corporate authority, while *guru* bishops give spiritual but not administrative leadership. There is little desire to re-establish denominational structures, since the Council itself has grown into an effective federation, joining the World Council of Churches as a member church in 1991.

There are few signs of dialogue between Catholics and Protestants, yet each group needs the strengths of the other, and both now face the same perils and the same opportunities.

Since 1989 official policy towards the churches has once more turned hostile and restrictive; there is a more rigid insistence on the registration of worship centres, and house meetings in many places have been closed down. But this has all the appearance of being the last throes of the ultra-conservatives, and reformers are biding their time. In 1986 Zhao Fusan, holding a significant post in the government of China, wrote a remarkable paper that argued for a new evaluation of religion on Marxist principles. He said: 'To omit the positive aspects of religion when exploring its role in history would hardly seem to be consistent with Marxist historical materialism.' This is typical of a rethinking which, notwithstanding reactionaries here and there, is taking place among the present generation of leaders. Bishop Ding said in the summer of 1992 that the intellectual, as distinct from the political, climate in China was more favourable than at any other time in forty years. Such reformers, like Gorbachev in Russia, look for a liberalizing of the economy and a humanizing of social control, but no shift of political ideology. For they recognize that, for a country of roughly the same size as the United States but with a population four times as large, *laissez-faire* economics would be a recipe for social chaos. Nor need their reformism fail as Gorbachev's was bound to do, since, apart from Tibet and, perhaps, Inner Mongolia, the Chinese, unlike the USSR, have enjoyed an immensely long history of centralized national unity. Without either the liberty or the licence of Western-style democracy they have accommodated themselves to a large measure of local entrepreneurship and foreign investment so that China's economy is currently growing at more than twice the rate of those of either Europe or the United States. Ironically the survival of the system is less endangered by the flaws of Marxism than by a possible overheating of the economy or the growing disparity between the rich and poor provinces, either of which could bring about a breakdown of social order on a vast scale.

It would seem, then, that three possible futures lie open to the church in China. If proselytizing sects, particularly those of

Chinese in other countries, try to exploit the greater openness of the Republic too aggressively they may provoke China's ancient xenophobia and condemn Christianity to a long-sustained rejection as an irredeemably foreign and subversive religion. There is a good chance that this may not happen. As a second possibility the predominant pietism of the Christians in China may so commend them in the eyes of officialdom for their good citizenship and freedom from corruption that their continuing expansion will be tolerated, if not welcomed. In the short term this is the most likely outcome, but it will mean that Christianity has little influence on the course of events. Or, in the longer term, if the Chinese Christians more generally were to take social concern on board as an element of the Gospel, they might become the representatives, not of a foreign but of an alternative ideology, challenging the swing towards unbridled capitalism and stimulating their statesmen to pioneer a truly 'third way' economy.

In the Former USSR and Eastern Europe

The sheer size of the Soviet empire, its natural resources, its military machine and nuclear arsenal, as well as the technical achievements of its scientists, blinded the rest of the world to its precarious infrastructures and moribund ideology. Many among the leaders in Russia were finding themselves compelled to rethink, the witness of Christian dissidents had made its mark, and dialogue between church people and Marxists was becoming fashionable at intellectual and street level. Patriotism was valued more highly than ideology, and the Orthodox Church has always been intensely patriotic. Religion as an influence was gaining ground, as was also the idea of liberalization. Gorbachev set out to reform Marxist–Leninism, but in Russia it was no longer capable of reform and he unleashed the breakdown of Soviet cohesion.

It is a sad fact of history that the victims of oppression have almost always reacted to their sudden release with a greedy scramble for privilege and a falling apart into rival factions, and

Christians in Russia, and outside Russia, have been no exception in their response to the collapse of Communism. The former hierarchies are still in place, singing the new tune, or even the old pre-1917 tunes. The Roman Catholic Church, though with notable dissenters within its ranks, seems to have adopted as its own the triumphalism of the West in establishing new missionary dioceses in what were purely Orthodox areas of Russia. Uniate and Orthodox bishops are bitterly at odds in the Ukraine. Orthodox exiles repatriated after two generations do not recognize the Moscow Patriarchate. Churches in Armenia, Georgia, and the Baltic states seem to have constituted themselves as the spiritual arm of the local nationalism. And there is no lack of fundamentalist or esoteric sects selling their wares along with the rest of the free world. In general the restoration of religious freedom is seen in backward-looking terms, with no recognition of the radical secularization of the present generation for whom the traditional Slavonic dream of Holy Russia is not gospel enough. There is a minority of young, mainly intellectual Christians, Orthodox and Baptist, who recall wistfully the years of a more heroic faith and grieve over the general reactionary trend. But, surprisingly, the Christian underground of former years has not thrown up the prophets and protesters who might address the chaos creatively. Perhaps they are at present too confused by their discovery of the spiritual bankruptcy of the only alternative to Communism so far on offer.

The same confusion besets the churches in all the recently liberated states of Eastern Europe, though they differ from each other by reason of their former histories. Romania was always a feudal fiefdom under autocratic rule, where religion was expected to endorse the actions of government. Under Ceauşescu's tyranny Orthodox bishops sat in a powerless parliament; after his murder, the Patriarch resigned only to re-emerge. There have been no confessions of complicity, no purging of collaborators, as in Bulgaria, Hungary, and East Germany.

In Hungary, where two-thirds of church members are

Catholic and one-third Protestant, the churches were accustomed to a system of state funding and surveillance, so Marxism brought no essential change of relationship. The tone of society continued to be secular rather than atheist, and generally more liberal than that of the churches. Christian base communities, critical of those churches, were lively during the Communist period; so it was no surprise that, when the regime was toppled, almost all the church leaders were removed. This spirit of independent judgement still persists among Hungarian Christians.

Czechoslovakia before the Communist take-over was the most secular country in Europe, and the churches actually gained more influence as a result of the popular reaction to state control. Today there is considerable indignation because Catholic priests who were active in the underground resistance cannot be recognized because they married during that time.

The East German Christians, mainly Lutheran, had been strongly affected by the 'Confessing Church' so they knew how to live in critical solidarity with Communism. Most of them had no wish to revert to capitalism; they were not a political opposition, but neither did they collude. They provided a habitat for those who had the will to oppose and, when the revolution broke out, they had much to do with it being bloodless. Many now feel that, though huge sums have been donated for the rebuilding of their churches, their positive witness under Marxism and their critique of capitalism count for nothing in a reunited Germany in such matters as the Church Tax, the maintenance of military chaplains, or the inclusion of denominational instruction in the schools curriculum.

The Pope's dream of a Christian Poland pointing the way for Europe seems, ironically, to have been shattered by the very liberation for which he longed. Under Marxist rule, popular devotion to Catholicism never waned. The Party needed that church's co-operation and the church used this advantage to maintain traditional values, leaving active resistance to other bodies such as the trade unions. But now Poland has opened its heart to secularization as well as to the market economy and has grown restless under the church's restraint on such issues as abortion. When Poland enters the European Community it will do so as a country very much like all the rest.

All the peoples, in fact, that have come out from under Marxist overrule now resemble Western Europe in turning back to the peculiarly European obsession with the independent nation-state, with its perilous underlying concomitant of ethnic identity. The haste with which Germany recognized the independence of Croatia in 1992, the swift but mercifully peaceful partition of Czechoslovakia, as well as Britain's horror of a federated Europe, are symptomatic of this passionate preference. Its bloodier aspect is being demonstrated in the Balkans and may all too easily appear in Azerbaijan, Armenia, and other republics of the former USSR. European Christianity, since the fall of the Roman empire, has had little in its history to equip it to withstand this atavistic nationalism or even to recognize that there are other forms of political organization beside the nation-state. So, in the present indeterminateness of Eastern Europe, Christians are divided between a majority who see their church indissolubly allied to their nation and a minority that is profoundly unhappy about this equation.

Western Europe and North America

There is no society more saturated with Christian influence than that of Western Europe. Yet the main thrust of that steep rise in the number of people in the world who are without religion, indicated in Figure 1, has occurred, not under anti-religious despotism, but in Western Europe. The dynamics of secularization have been analysed *ad nauseam*; what may have most significance for discerning its future is the fact that two distinct, though related, processes have been at work. Christianity as an intellectual framework was overtaken by the Enlightenment; Christianity as folk religion was broken up by industrialism. As the century draws to its close the assumptions of the Enlightenment are being modified radically, and a post-industrial era is making new changes in the structure of society. Will churches that were too slow to come to terms with both the previous changes, respond more effectively to the new ones?

Their reaction to the sudden change in the USSR and Eastern Europe does not hold out much hope of an affirmative answer to that question. The rapid advance of Catholicism into Russia, already mentioned, the influx of proselytizing sects, the unthinking acceptance of neo-nationalism, and the general conviction that Western Christianity has everything to give and nothing to learn—these seem little more than an echo of the triumph-song of the market economy. A spirit more open and critically independent than this will be required of Western Christianity if it is ever to undergird and shape a united democratic Europe, as some still dream it may. For, as T. S. Eliot constantly affirmed, and such pioneers of the European Community as Jean Monnet and Robert Schuman perceived, social and political cohesion grows only from cultural and spiritual roots. The roots of European identity, from the Urals to the Algarve, have already existed for a long time. They are Christian roots that run down into the soil of Israel, Greece, and Rome. The peoples who have recently broken free from absolutism and the churches that stood for decades in a dialectical relationship with a hostile ideology are more keenly aware of the regenerating power of those roots than are the ones that have faced only benign secularized indifference. East Europeans today have experienced the revolutionary character of Christian belief and, unless they have been subverted by the superficial success of the Western economies, their insights could contribute dynamically to the rediscovery of Europe's spiritual and cultural heritage and the search for a 'third way' economic system, resistant to the inhumanities of both East and West. Without that prophetic protest in its midst, a united Europe which imagined itself to be Christendom once again could do only harm to the world-wide Christian movement. For churches preoccupied with ecclesiastical conservation will be little aware of either the strengths or the needs of Christians elsewhere, and may all too easily identify themselves with the survivors in that 'affluent lifeboat on a sea of poverty'.

There is all the difference in the world between re-establishing a religion in society and re-establishing a society in religion. In the latter case religion is the root of the tree, in the former it is a mere rookery in its branches. For two centuries the churches in Western Europe have been struggling to rebuild the rookery, and the result has been a slow decline. The statistics of decline are familiar, yet there is hope. Falling church attendance, fewer marriages of any sort, chronic shortage of clergy, and religiously illiterate children are not the only evidence. The ratings of the best religious television are among the highest; church leaders are constantly in the news; more people visit the cathedrals and attend their worship than at any time in the past. Christian action and protest over the rights of immigrant labour, political refugees, penal reform, and so on is clearly influential; in Britain the social climate is far more affected by Christian impact than the strength of the churches would seem to warrant. And careful surveys reveal that nearly half the adult population recall some intensely private religious experience that remains significant for them, though only a minority see any connection between this and the institutional forms of Christianity. The most probable immediate future is one in which church membership is everywhere smaller and more committed, served by local, non-professional pastors, with a more theologically trained, mobile ministry to augment them. The network of parochial coverage may have broken down, in which case some other way will be found to co-ordinate the congregations in an area. House groups for prayer, study, and local action will play a more significant part in Christian spirituality and ecumenical experience, and the crucial issue will be whether such a church turns inward and becomes sectarian or sees itself as the base for critical and evangelistic participation in the life of society.

If Christianity has been *marginalized* in Western Europe, it has been *privatized* in the United States, and the one is just as inimical as the other in its spiritual effect. The outward appearances, however, are very different. North Americans are still emotionally the heirs of their founding fathers, men and women of various denominations and nationalities, who, at one moment or another in the past four centuries, turned their backs on Europe to escape from centralized uniformity. Many Roman Catholic priests, religious, and laity fear that Rome, by failing to appreciate this inheritance and insisting on the exercise of a rigid, remote control, may push their dioceses into schism before the twenty-first century has got under way. This pervasive tradition of individual liberty prompts, in all denominations, a strong attachment to a particular congregation as a mark of personal identity; so church-going remains a lively feature of the American way of life and, as David Edwards has sympathetically pointed out, Christianity is popularly valued as a major contributor to human fulfilment. The influence of the churches and synagogues on local and national policy is enormous. This has usually been effected, not by direct activism, but by the weight of the religious vote in the ballot box and the consideration that politicians have had to give it. The demonstrations and pronouncements of the churches over the last thirty years in regard to civil rights or foreign policy are still felt to be somewhat un-American, though they have become more necessary and inevitable since the USA achieved its unrivalled ascendancy in the world and in the United Nations Organization.

But now the Christian pressures are tending to cancel each other out. On the one hand Catholic bishops condemn the USA's nuclear strategy, economic injustices, and destabilization of left-wing governments in Latin America, while on the other hand fundamentalist churches commend an escalating defence budget, assume that poverty results from moral weakness, and find evidence of the left-wing conspiracy in all directions. The split between liberal and conservative seems bound to open more widely across all the denominations, except in the larger Black churches, where biblical conservatism and social radicalism walk hand-in-hand. The style of church organization is beginning more and more to embody this contrast. Hard-sell preachers of the huge auditorium or the 'electronic church' retain an authoritarian control over their followers through a high-powered central office or a network of supervisory 'house church' leaders, while at the same time an untidy profusion of base communities and other communal experiments, unworried over institutional structure or dogmatic exactitude, is becoming a significant influence within the mainstream churches.

The Coming Great Divide

That contrast seems to epitomize the issue which, above all others, will dominate the history of Christianity for the next half-century or more. This chapter's brief survey has revealed that, where Christianity is spreading most rapidly, it is distinguished by a multiplication of small, locally led congregations, as in Latin America, the Philippines, and China, a weakening of central control, as in many parts of Africa, and a preference for loose federations of churches, as in China and Zaïre, rather than interconfessional schemes of church union. The overall picture is one of vitality advancing hand-in-hand with diversity. At the same time there are political and psychological forces, allied to church traditions, working for clearer definition and firmer control in the spheres of organization, doctrine, morality, and relations between churches and between faiths.

Currently this polarization impinges most acutely for many Christians in the West through the theological and ecclesiological controversies between so-called radicals and conservatives. It seems to be sorting itself into three, rather than two, responses. There is a radicalism which appears to derive its arguments mainly from the reductionist science of the nineteenth century, but is actually moved by a much older proclivity of religious thought towards total introversion. This refinement, as its advocates perceive it, has in recent decades taken the form of an extreme scepticism as to the comprehensibility of the past, the content of religious language, or the actuality of any 'beyond-ness' in aesthetic or mystical experience. All is myth or symbol, which tell of nothing but our personal values and our self-realization. It has happened before in somewhat different terms at a certain level in the religions of South Asia, where events that conveyed revelatory significance in a distant past became first legendary, then mythical, and were finally interpreted as metaphors of the interior life. To some this process appears as a slow sinking of spiritual energies to an eventual state of entropy. Others believe that through it what seems to be lost will be given back in a more vital form. Whoever is right, it seems probable that in the next century the faith of the extreme radicals, mainly in Europe and North America, will come to look much more like a kind of Buddhism than traditional Christianity.

Apart from such thoroughgoing radicalism, the other two responses to which I have referred are the more familiar liberal and conservative schools of thought. This is currently demon-strated in the painfully divisive debate about the inclusion of women in the sacramental and episcopal ministries of the church. The differences between the two schools are a perennial feature of theology, as of politics, and have always been a matter of 'more or less' rather than 'either–or', since they derive from temperament rather than logic. It is Nature itself, as W. S. Gilbert observed, that 'does contrive That every boy and every gal, that's born into the world alive, Is either a little Liberal, or else a little Conservative!' The ability to see the conflict as comical may in the end be the salvation of the church, for comedy is inclusive, not dismissive. There are those who cannot abide an untidy home, while others prize above all a free and easy household. The temperamental difference is ultimately serious when it determines what the church thinks Christianity is, or what manner of society most truly reflects the Kingdom of God.

So the division that matters most for the church today and

tomorrow is not that between catholic and evangelical, or political right and left, but whether in any matter the form or the content is of prior importance. All must agree that the two are inseparable, yet in practice the question inevitably arises: which is paramount? It is care for the continuity of the Gospel committed to her that compels the church to pay scrupulous attention to the form in which it is transmitted. But custodial anxiety, especially in times of great and rapid change, can easily make the guardians mistake the form for the content. They then identify the meaning of God's self-revelation with the actual words of the Bible. The gift of ministry becomes dependent upon the manner in which it is conferred and the gender of the recipient. The structure of the church's government is confused with her catholicity; her uniformity becomes the measure of her faithfulness. Inevitably there comes a time when the Gospel itself, like the boy David, throws off the heavy armour so solicitously provided, and goes forward in its own vulnerable freedom. The contrast between these two attitudes was vividly presented to the bishops attending the Lambeth Conference of 1988 by Mrs Elizabeth Templeton when responding on behalf of the Reformed tradition to the Archbishop of Canterbury's paper on 'the Unity we seek'.

There are among us those who believe that the invincibility of God's love discloses itself in some kind of absolute, safeguarded articulation, whether of scripture, church, tradition, clerical line-management, agreed reason, charismatic gifts, orthopraxis, or any combination of such elements. And there are those among us who believe that the invincibility of God's love discloses itself in the relativity and risk of all doctrine, exegesis, ethics, piety and ecclesiastical structure, which are the church's serious exploratory play, and which exist at an unspecifiable distance from the face to face truth of God. What unity is possible in concrete existence between those on either side of the trans-denominational divide seems to me our toughest ecumenical question. If we can find a way through that one, I suspect that all our specific problems of doctrine, ministry and authority will come away as easily as afterbirth.

The question posed by this great divide will be the dominating issue for Christianity in the twenty-first century precisely because the shifting of its centre of gravity from north to south will entail a greater departure than has ever been made hitherto away from the Graeco-Roman concepts of orthodoxy and uniformity, and a greater level of confidence in provisionality and diversity. Father Vincent Donovan, the remarkable Catholic missionary who served among the Masai of Tanzania, saw this as the necessary outcome of the response to Christianity by non-European cultures on a global scale:

Historically a single form of this response to the Christian message has grown and thrived. . . . What we are coming to see now is that there must be many responses possible to the Christian message, which have hitherto been neither encouraged nor allowed. We have come to believe that any valid, positive response to the Christian message could and should be recognized and accepted as church. That is the church that might have been, and might yet be.

If within the coming century world-wide Christianity is compelled to embrace such a degree of diversity and provisionality and, indeed, to welcome this as intrinsic to its true nature, its pursuit of Christian unity will have to change direction. The preoccupations of this century's ecumenism, the painstaking search for verbal agreement, common ground, and mutual validation, will not have been in vain, and a future generation may look back and see it as a needful sacrifice, acceptable to God in its time. But as this century draws to its close the enthusiasm for that method of *rapprochement* is waning among most of the Christians in the world, nor is there any prospect of further schemes of union coming to fruition in the near future. Bilateral conversations have proved to be too blinkered to do justice to the pluralism of the Christian search for unity. The realities of global Christianity are such—and who is better placed to know them than the Vatican?—that all future talk of mutual 'recognition' must mean, not validation, as if by some body of examiners, but the glad realization that someone momentarily mistaken for a stranger is actually a member of the family. Recognition in that sense comes as a kind of revelation. Whether it comes soon or late, nothing less will carry much significance in the future.

Progress from a church meticulously defined to a church without boundaries will be rough going, and the divide may bring much painful misunderstanding and some grave schisms. A sombre view and a readiness for a long haul would seem to be the only realistic forecast of the next century in the history of Christianity. The flowering of the open, more loosely structured Christianity may have to take place in other soil than that of its former heartlands in Europe. It is too early to guess where that may be, but history suggests that, wherever it is, the seed will already have been sown. Moreover, the events of recent years have brought home one other truth of history that should not be ignored. A single member of the Soviet Politburo, scarcely known beyond the boundaries of Russia, set himself to bring about a better socialism and, in failing, ended an epoch. A decent, caring, but not very political Protestant pastor in Timişoara stood up to his supine bishop and unwittingly sparked off a revolution that brought down a tyrant in Romania. A devout electrician in the Polish shipyards, equipped with singular adroitness and tenacity, became the focus of the freedom movement. There is no inevitability in the process of history. Something close to free will in an individual person or a chosen few, even though they be the product of the social conditions in which they operate, can mean life or death for millions, life or death for the church. For this, if for no other reason, the shrewdest attitude towards both past and future is that taken by Chou En Lai who, when asked how he assessed the French Revolution, replied, 'It is a little too early to judge.'

Further Reading

General Reference

D. B. Barrett (ed.), *World Christian Encyclopedia* (Oxford, 1982).

H. Chadwick and G. Evans, *Atlas of the Christian Church* (London, 1988).

J. G. Davies (ed.), *A Dictionary of Liturgy and Worship* (London, 1972, 2nd rev. edn., 1986).

J. N. D. Kelly, *The Oxford Dictionary of Popes* (Oxford, 1986). By a distinguished scholar.

K. S. Latourette, *A History of the Expansion of Christianity*, 7 vols. (London, 1947). A vast and comprehensive survey.

E. A. Livingstone and F. L. Cross (eds.), *The Oxford Dictionary of the Christian Church* (2nd rev. edn., Oxford, 1983).

John Macquarrie, *Principles of Christian Theology* (rev. edn., London, 1979). A masterly summary of more recent thinking with a conservative inclination.

Christianity and History

What is the validity of the Christian story? How can historians examine spiritual things? How does God work in history? What is the goal or meaning of the process?

DISCUSSIONS BY HISTORIANS

H. Butterfield, *Christianity and History* (London, 1949).

—— *Writings on Christianity and History*, ed. C. T. McIntire (New York, 1979). See especially, 'The Christian and the Ecclesiastical Interpretation'.

H. C. Dawson, *The Historical Reality of Christian Culture* (London, 1960).

Boyd Hilton, *The Age of Atonement: The Influence of Evangelicalism on Social and Economic Thought, 1795–1865* (Oxford, 1988). A masterly study which also gives many clues for more general reflections.

C. T. McIntire (ed.), *God, History and Historians* (New York, 1977). Extracts from modern writers. The upshot for historians is, in C. S. Lewis's words, 'we must not say what it means, or what the total pattern is'.

Marjorie Reeves and Warwick Gould, *Joachim of Fiore and the Myth of the Eternal Evangel* (Oxford, 1987). The remarkable persistence of a medieval inspiration.

A. H. Toynbee, *An Historian's Approach to Religion* (Oxford, 1954).

—— *A Study of History*, 12 vols. (Oxford, 1934–61). The broad division into 'civilisations' is challenged, but the great work is full of insights and inspired with religious yearnings.

DISCUSSIONS BY THEOLOGIANS AND PHILOSOPHERS

J. Baillie, *What is Christian Civilisation?* (Oxford, 1945).

D. Bonhoeffer, *Letters and Papers from Prison*, ed. E. Bethge (London, 1971). Moving documentation of the role of suffering in Christian experience.

E. Brunner, *Christianity and Civilisation* (London, 1948). Parted company with Karl Barth on the question of creation as a source of our knowledge of God.

V. Langmead Casserley, *Towards a Theology of History* (London, 1965). Written in the shadow of the Bomb; our aim is 'to gain an understanding of what is at stake in history'.

R. Niebuhr, *Faith and History: A Comparison of Christian and Modern Views of History* (London, 1949). God works through human freedom. History shows 'the power of God to complete our fragmentary life'.

A. Richardson, *History Sacred and Profane* (London, 1964). Critics of the New Testament use sceptical techniques which the 'real' historians have outgrown.

Arend T. Van Leeuwen, *Christianity in World History: The Meeting of the Faiths of East and West* (London, 1964).

Christianity and Art

The multitude of monographs on individual artists cannot be mentioned here—there is room only for some general works.

INDISPENSABLE

Jane Dillenberger, *Style and Content in Christian Art* (London, 1986). Lucid and perceptive—shaped the views here presented.

Gertrud Schiller, *Iconography of Christian Art*, tr. Janet Seligman, 2 vols. (London, 1971). Classifies works of art by subject; much fuller is L. Réau, *Iconographie de l'art Chrétien*, 6 vols. (Paris, 1955–9).

PHILOSOPHIZING ON THE RELATIONSHIP

Jacques Maritain, *The Philosophy of Art*, tr. J. O. O'Connor (Ditchling, 1925). By the French Thomist philosopher.

Margaret R. Miles, *Image as Insight: Visual Understanding in Western Christian and Secular Culture* (Boston, 1985). Do images mean to us what they originally meant? Discussions concerning the fourth, fourteenth, and sixteenth centuries.

A. Nichols OP, *The Art of God Incarnate* (London, 1980). Art discloses new dimensions of life, and as such should be used as an analogy by theologians interpreting the incarnation.

Brooke Foss Westcott, 'The Relation of Art to Christianity', in *The Epistles of John* (London, 1883), pp. 319–60. Judicious defence of Christian art by a great biblical scholar.

ARTISTIC TREATMENT OF A PARTICULAR THEME

Collen McDonnel and B. Lang, *Heaven: A History* (Yale, 1988).

P. Thoby, *Le Crucifix des origines au Concile de Trente* (Nantes, 1959).

RELATIONSHIP OF CHRISTIANITY AND ART IN VARIOUS PERIODS

C. Christensen, *Art and the Reformation in Germany* (Athens, OH, 1979).

C. Garside, *Zwingli and the Arts* (New Haven, 1966).

A. Grabar, *Christian Iconography: A Study of its Origins* (London, 1969).

E. Panofsky, *Gothic Architecture and Scholasticism* (Latrobe, 1948). The 'visual logic' of the French Gothic cathedrals.

M. Wackernagel, *The World of the Florentine Renaissance Artist*, tr. A. Luchs (Princeton, 1981). Illustrates the pressures on artists and the complexity of their motivation.

TWENTIETH-CENTURY DEBATES

P. F. Anson, *Fashions in Church Furnishing, 1840–1940* (London, 1960).

F. W. Dillistone, *Traditional Symbols and the Contemporary World* (London, 1973). The problems posed by the ending of the world of symbols of the Middle Ages.

P. Hammond, *Liturgy and Architecture* (London, 1960).

W. S. Rubin, *Modern Sacred Art: The Church of Assy* (New York, 1961).

Basil Spence, *Phoenix at Coventry: The Building of a Cathedral* (London, 1962).

1. The Early Christian Community

GENERAL SURVEYS

H. von Campenhausen, *The Fathers of the Greek Church* (London, 1963), and *The Fathers of the Latin Church* (London, 1964). Gives brilliant portraits of the main figures.

H. Chadwick, *The Early Church* (Harmondsworth, 1967 and later edns.). Is a first introduction.

J. Daniélou and H. I. Marrou, *The Christian Centuries*, i (London, 1964).

L. Duchesne, *Early History of the Christian Church*, 3 vols. (London, 1909–24). Remains a classic.

W. H. C. Frend, *The Rise of Christianity* (London, 1984). Is less theological.

A. Grillmeier, *Christ in Christian Tradition*, 2 vols. (London, 1975–87).

A. Harnack, *The Mission and Expansion of Christianity* (London, 1908). Remains essential.

J. N. D. Kelly, *Early Christian Doctrines* (London, 1958 and later edns.) Surveys the history of theology.

H. Lietzmann, *The Beginnings of the Christian Church*.

—— *The Founding of the Church Universal*.

—— *From Constantine to Julian*.

—— *The Era of the Church Fathers* (London, 1937–51).

ETHICS

Peter Brown, *The Body and Society: Men, Women and Sexual Renunciation in Early Christianity* (New York, 1988).

C. J. Cadoux, *The Early Church and the World* (Edinburgh, 1925).
A. Harnack, *Militia Christi*, tr. D. M. Gracie (Philadelphia, 1981).

WORSHIP

G. Dix, *The Shape of the Liturgy* (Westminster, 1945 and later edns.).
J. A. Jungmann, *The Early Liturgy to the Time of Gregory the Great* (London, 1961).
—— *The Mass of the Roman Rite* (London, 1959).

BIBLE

H. von Campenhausen, *The Formation of the Christian Bible* (London, 1972).
A. Harnack, *Bible Reading in the Early Church* (London, 1912).

PERSECUTION

W. H. C. Frend, *Martyrdom and Persecution in the Early Church* (Oxford, 1965).

GNOSTICISM

There is a huge bibliography since the discovery of the Nag Hammadi library (all texts tr., ed. James Robinson, 1977).

F. C. Burkitt, *The Religion of the Manichees* (Cambridge, 1925).
—— *Church and Gnosis* (Cambridge, 1932). Both are short and masterly studies.
B. Layton, *The Gnostic Scriptures* (London, 1987).
S. Lieu, *Manicheism in the Later Roman Empire and Medieval China* (Manchester, 1985).
K. Rudolph, *Gnosis* (Edinburgh, 1983). An introduction.

THEOLOGICAL DEVELOPMENTS

H. Chadwick, *Early Christian Thought and the Classical Tradition* (Oxford, 1966 and later edns.).
G. W. Clarke's transl. and commentary on the letters is the best introduction to Cyprian, 3 vols. (New York, 1984–6).
R. M. Grant, *Greek Apologists of the Second Century* (London, 1988).
R. A. Norris, *God and World in Early Christian Theology* (London, 1966).
R. Williams, *Arius: Heresy and Tradition* (London, 1987).

CONSTANTINE

N. H. Baynes, *Constantine the Great and the Christian Church*, British Academy lecture, 2nd edn. (London, 1972).

A. H. M. Jones, *Constantine and the Conversion of Europe*, 2nd edn. (London, 1972).

ART

R. Krautheimer, *Early Christian and Byzantine Architecture* (Pelican, 1965).

F. van der Meer, *Early Christian Art* (London, 1967).

J. Stevenson, *The Catacombs* (London, 1978).

HAGIOGRAPHY

H. Delehaye, *The Legends of the Saints* (London, 1962).

2. From Rome to the Barbarian Kingdoms (330–700)

P. Brown, *Religion and Society in the Age of St Augustine* (London, 1972). A collection of important papers central to several themes of Late Antique Christianity.

—— *The Cult of the Saints* (London, 1981). A distinguished study of a major development in Late Antique religiosity.

H. Chadwick, *The Early Church* (Harmondsworth, 1967). Concise, readable, and authoritative.

C. N. Cochrane, *Christianity and Classical Culture* (Oxford, 1944). A pioneering work, still useful and readable.

H. Delehaye, *Les Origines du culte des martyres* (Paris, 1933).

J. Geffcken, *The Last Days of Greco-Roman Paganism*, rev. English transl. by S. G. MacCormack (Amsterdam, 1978). The fullest and most learned discussion.

R. MacMullen, *Christianizing the Roman Empire* (New Haven, Conn., 1984). Short, learned, and controversial.

R. A. Markus, *Christianity in the Roman World* (London, 1974). An idiosyncratic survey of the first 600 years.

H. I. Marrou, *A History of Education in Antiquity*, English transl. (London, 1956). A great work by one of the greatest of scholars in the cultural history of Late Antiquity.

H. Mayr-Harting, *The Coming of Christianity to Anglo-Saxon England* (London, 1972). Very readable.

A. Momigliano (ed.), *The Conflict between Paganism and Christianity in the Fourth Century* (Oxford, 1963). Collection of important studies.

P. Riché, *Education and Culture in the Barbarian West* (Columbia, SC, 1976). Now the best survey of its subject.

R. Van Dam, *Leadership and Community in Late Roman Gaul* (Berkeley, Calif., 1985). Stimulating.

J. M. Wallace-Hadrill, *The Frankish Church* (Oxford, 1983). An authoritative account and interpretation.

3. The West: The Age of Conversion (700–1050)

André de Fleury, *Vie de Gauzlin Abbé de Fleury*, ed. R. H. Bautier and G. Labory (Paris, 1969).

Geoffrey Barraclough, *The Medieval Papacy* (London, 1968). A contrast with the ideological approach of Walter Ullmann, see below.

John Beckwith, *Early Medieval Art* (London, 1964).

Donald Bullough, *The Age of Charlemagne* (Elek, 1965). As an introduction; a nice blend of critical scholarship and sympathetic understanding.

Carolingian Essays, ed. U.-R. Blumenthal (Catholic Univ., Washington, 1983). Containing Susan Keefe on baptismal treatises and also an excellent paper by Donald Bullough on Alcuin.

Roger Collins, *Early Medieval Spain: Unity in Diversity, 400–1000* (London, 1983). For Christian history in Spain.

K. J. Conant, *Carolingian and Romanesque Architecture 800–1200* (London, 1959).

Jean Dunbabin, *France in the Making 843–1180* (Oxford, 1985).

H. Fichtenau, *The Carolingian Empire* (Oxford, 1957). A brilliant but unsympathetic discussion.

E. H. Kantorowicz, *The King's Two Bodies* (Princeton, 1957). One of the most masterly books ever written on the Middle Ages.

T. Klauser, *A Short History of the Western Liturgy* (Oxford, 1969).

M. L. W. Laistner, *Thought and Letters in Western Europe 500–900* (Cornell, 1931).

W. Levison, *England and the Continent in the Eighth Century* (Oxford, 1946). For Willibrord, Boniface, and Alcuin.

K. J. Leyser, *Rule and Conflict in an Early Medieval Society: Ottonian Saxony* (London, 1979). Fundamental on the 10th century.

Rosamond McKitterick, *The Frankish Church and the Carolingian Reforms 789–895* (London, 1977). For episcopal handbooks and pastoral effort.

Janet Nelson, *Politics and Ritual in Early Medieval Europe* (London, 1986). An excellent set of papers particularly for ritual in the Carolingian age.

R. W. Southern, *Western Society and the Church in the Middle Ages* (London, 1970). An institutional and sociological study, written in limpid prose.

C. H. Talbot, *The Anglo-Saxon Missionaries in Germany* (London, 1954). With translations of material relating to St Boniface and his followers.

Walter Ullmann, *The Carolingian Renaissance and the Idea of Kingship* (London, 1969).

—— *A Short History of the Papacy in the Middle Ages* (London, 1972). Cf. Barraclough above.

J. M. Wallace-Hadrill, *The Frankish Church* (Oxford, 1983). Authoritative and goes up to 900.

4. Eastern Christendom

BYZANTINE CHRISTIANITY

W. H. C. Frend, *The Rise of the Monophysite Movement* (Cambridge, 1972). On the defence and criticism of Chalcedon during 451–681.

J. M. Hussey, *The Orthodox Church in the Byzantine Empire* (Oxford, 1986). The best general account; mainly historical.

B. Krivocheine, *The Light of Christ: St Symeon the New Theologian* (Crestwood, 1987). A detailed study, with many quotations.

V. Lossky, *The Mystical Theology of the Eastern Church* (London, 1957). A classic work; broader in scope than the title suggests.

C. Mango, *Byzantium: The Empire of New Rome* (London, 1980). On the religious outlook of the 'average' Byzantine rather than the scholar or theologian.

J. Meyendorff, *Byzantine Theology: Historical Trends and Doctrinal Themes* (New York, 1974). An excellent summary.

—— *St Gregory Palamas and Orthodox Spirituality* (Crestwood, 1974). Introductory, brief but illuminating.

—— *A Study of Gregory Palamas* (London, 1964). Still the basic work on the subject.

J. Pelikan, *The Christian Tradition: A History of the Development of*

Doctrine, ii. *The Spirit of Eastern Christendom (600–1700)* (Chicago, 1974). A useful supplement to Meyendorff's *Byzantine Theology*.

S. Runciman, *The Eastern Schism: A Study of the Papacy and the Eastern Churches during the XIth and XIIth Centuries* (Oxford, 1955). Better on history than on theology.

—— *The Byzantine Theocracy* (Cambridge, 1977). On church–state relations.

P. Sherrard, *Athos: The Holy Mountain* (London, 1982). Includes a section on the inner meaning of Orthodox monasticism.

K. (T.) Ware, *The Orthodox Church* (London, 1963). A general introduction; covers both history and doctrine.

RUSSIA AND THE SLAV CHURCHES

G. P. Fedotov, *The Russian Religious Mind*, 2 vols. (Cambridge, Mass., 1946, 1966). On Russian spirituality during the 10th–15th centuries; often misleading, but remains the fullest study in English.

—— *A Treasury of Russian Spirituality* (London, 1950). Well selected primary sources.

G. Florovsky, *Ways of Russian Theology*, i (Collected Works, 5; Belmont, 1979). Covers the 16th–19th centuries; a magisterial survey.

N. Gorodetzky, *Saint Tikhon Zadonsky: Inspirer of Dostoevsky* (London, 1951). A sympathetic portrait of an 18th-century Russian bishop.

P. Kovalevsky, *Saint Sergius and Russian Spirituality* (Crestwood, 1976). A helpful introduction to medieval Russian piety.

G. A. Maloney, *Russian Hesychasm: The Spirituality of Nil Sorskij* (The Hague, 1973). Careless on points of detail, but includes many quotations from the sources.

J. Meyendorff, *Byzantium and the Rise of Russia: A Study of Byzantino-Russian Relations in the Fourteenth Century* (Cambridge, 1981). Thorough and scholarly.

D. Obolensky, *The Byzantine Commonwealth: Eastern Europe, 500–1453* (London, 1971). On Byzantine–Slav relations; excellent.

N. Zernov, *The Russians and Their Church* (London, 1945). A lively introduction.

THE TURKISH PERIOD

The Philokalia: The Complete Text, compiled by St Nikodimos of the Holy Mountain and St Makarios of Corinth, tr. by G. E. H.

Palmer, P. Sherrard, and K. (T.) Ware, i–iii (London, 1979–84). The most important Orthodox book to appear in the Turkish period; transl. to be completed in 5 vols.

S. Runciman, *The Great Church in Captivity: A Study of the Patriarchate in Constantinople from the Eve of the Turkish Conquest to the Greek War of Independence* (Cambridge, 1968). The best general treatment, but relies more on Western than on Greek sources.

K. (T.) Ware, *Eustratios Argenti: A Study of the Greek Church under Turkish Rule* (Oxford, 1964). On Orthodox–Catholic relations.

THE ORIENTAL ORTHODOX CHURCHES

A. S. Atiya, *A History of Eastern Christianity* (London, 1968). A general survey, covering Copts, Ethiopians, Syrian Jacobites, 'Nestorians', Armenians, the St Thomas Christians of South India, Maronites.

R. Murray, *Symbols of Church and Kingdom: A Study in Early Syriac Tradition* (Cambridge, 1975). Goes up to the 5th century; richly illustrated by citations from the sources.

Paulos Gregorios, W. H. Lazareth, N. A. Nissiotis (eds.), *Does Chalcedon Divide or Unite? Towards Convergence in Orthodox Christology* (Geneva, 1981). On the recent *rapprochement* between 'non-Chalcedonian' and 'Chalcedonian' Orthodox.

LITURGY AND ART

P. Hammond, *The Waters of Marah: The Present State of the Greek Church* (London, 1956). Fine descriptions of Orthodox worship; applicable also to the Byzantine and Turkish periods.

C. Mango, *The Art of the Byzantine Empire 312–1453: Sources and Documents* (Englewood Cliffs, 1972). A good selection by an expert.

L. Ouspensky and V. Lossky, *The Meaning of Icons* (rev. edn., Crestwood, 1982). The best existing study on the theology and the liturgical use of icons.

D. J. Sahas, *Icon and Logos: Sources in Eighth-Century Iconoclasm* (Toronto, 1986). Includes the decisions of the 787 council in defence of icons.

5. Christianity and Islam

Norman Daniel, *Islam and the West: The Making of an Image* (Edinburgh, 1960). The first work in English to attempt an overall account of medieval Europe's attitudes to Islam, with useful bibliography.

Norman Daniel, *Islam, Europe and Empire* (Edinburgh, 1966). A study of 19th- and 20th-century European colonialism and Islam.

—— *The Arabs and Medieval Europe* (2nd edn., New York and London, 1979).

—— *Heroes and Saracens: An Interpretation of the Chansons de Geste* (Edinburgh, 1984). A stimulating investigation of popular literature as a source for medieval attitudes towards the Arabs.

Rana Kabbani, *Europe's Myths of Orient* (London, 1986). A powerful and often shocking exploration of the roots of European prejudice.

Benjamin Z. Kedar, *Crusade and Mission: European Approaches toward the Muslims* (Princeton, 1984). A perceptive study of the relationship between crusade and missionary activity in the reaction of medieval Europe to Islam.

Bernard Lewis, *The Muslim Discovery of Europe* (New York and London, 1982). A rare study of Muslim attitudes to Europe, largely post-medieval.

Hans Eberhard Mayer, *The Crusades*, tr. by J. Gillingham (2nd edn., Oxford, 1988). Far and away the best short account of the crusades.

James W. Powell (ed.), *Muslims under Latin Rule 1100–1300* (Princeton, 1990). A helpful and informative guide to the Muslim communities within Latin Christendom.

Edward W. Said, *Orientalism* (London, 1978). The fundamental critique of Europe's view of Islam.

Khalil Semaan (ed.), *Islam and the Medieval West: Aspects of Intercultural Relations* (Albany, NY, 1980). A collection of essays and round-table debate by an international group of scholars, including Muslims.

Irfan Shahid, *Byzantium and the Arabs in the Fourth Century* (Dumbarton Oaks, Washington, DC, 1984). The second of four works studying the relationship between Rome and Byzantium and the Arabs in the pre- and early Islamic periods; a challenging and provocative reinterpretation.

Emmanuel Sivan, *Radical Islam: Medieval Theology and Modern Politics* (New Haven, Conn., and London, 1985). The author of a perceptive and influential study of Islam and the crusades (Paris, 1968) here examines New Radical (Sunnī) Islam and traces its debt to medieval theology.

Richard W. Southern, *Western Views of Islam in the Middle Ages* (Cambridge, Mass., 1962). An elegant and civilized essay which, although slightly out of date, is still a joy to read.

John Spencer Trimingham, *Christianity among the Arabs in Pre-Islamic Times* (New York and London, 1979). The only general guide to this subject.

6. Christian Civilization (1050–1400)

G. Barraclough, *The Medieval Papacy* (London, 1968). An outline introduction.

R. Brentano, *Two Churches: England and Italy in the Thirteenth Century* (Princeton, 1968).

E. Christiansen, *The Northern Crusades* (London, 1980). Missionaries and militarism in the Baltic.

J. C. Dickinson, *An Ecclesiastical History of England: The Later Middle Ages* (London, 1979).

B. Hamilton, *Religion in the Medieval West* (London, 1986). A lively account of medieval attitudes.

N. Hunt, *Cluniac Monasticism in the Central Middle Ages* (London, 1971).

H. Jedin and J. Dolan (eds.), *History of the Church*, iii–iv (London, 1980). An excellent detailed survey.

D. Knowles, *The Monastic Order in England* (2nd edn., Cambridge, 1963). Of importance also for continental monasticism.

—— *Thomas Becket* (London, 1970). A good introductory book to a major figure.

M. D. Lambert, *Medieval Heresy: Popular Movements from Bogomil to Huss* (London, 1977).

C. H. Lawrence, *Medieval Monasticism* (London, 1984).

L. J. Lekai, *The Cistercians: Ideals and Reality* (Kent, OH, 1977).

Henrietta Leyser, *Hermits and the New Monasticism* (London, 1984).

R. I. Moore, *The Origins of European Dissent* (Harmondsworth, 1977). On growth of Western heresy.

J. R. H. Moorman, *A History of the Franciscan Order* (Oxford, 1968).

C. Morris, *The Papal Monarchy: The Western Church 1050–1250* (Oxford, 1989).

P. Partner, *The Lands of St Peter* (London, 1972). The history of the development of the papal state in Italy.

I. S. Robinson, *Authority and Resistance in the Investiture Contest* (Manchester, 1978). The best English account of the issues in dispute.

R. W. Southern, *Western Society and the Church in the Middle Ages* (Harmondsworth, 1970). A selective but brilliant discussion.

B. Tierney, *The Foundations of the Conciliar Theory* (Cambridge, 1955).

H. Tillmann, *Pope Innocent III* (Amsterdam, 1980).

W. Ullmann, *The Growth of Papal Government in the Middle Ages* (3rd edn., London, 1970). Learned and controversial.

7. The Late Medieval Church and its Reformation (1400–1600)

Roland H. Bainton, *Here I Stand: A Life of Martin Luther* (New York, 1955). Like all biographies of Luther, written by one person at one place at one time, but none the worse for that.

John Bossy, *Christianity in the West 1400–1700* (Oxford, 1985). A brilliant evocation which discusses the 'social miracle' and resolves to use the term 'Reformation' as sparingly as possible, since 'it sits awkwardly across the subject'.

C. M. D. Crowder, *Unity, Heresy and Reform 1378–1440: The Conciliar Response to the Great Schism* (London, 1977). An excellent selection of documents.

Jean Delumeau, *Catholicism between Luther and Voltaire* (London, 1977). Dates 'the rise of Christian Europe' from the 16th century rather than the 6th.

A. G. Dickens, *The Counter Reformation* (London, 1968, 2nd edn., 1989). The best general and factual introduction to the subject in English.

—— *The English Reformation* (London, 1964). Still holds its own as the standard history but more recent 'revisionism' may be compared in Christopher Haigh (ed.), *The English Reformation Revised* (Cambridge, 1987).

—— *The German Nation and Martin Luther* (London, 1974). A pioneering study of the sociotheological content of the Reformation.

—— and John Tonkin, *The Reformation in Historical Thought* (Oxford, 1985). An invaluable guide to four centuries of interpretation.

H. O. Evennett (ed.), with a postscript by John Bossy, *The Spirit of the Counter-Reformation* (Cambridge, 1968). Introduced a new and continental flavour to the theme.

Mark Greengrass, *The French Reformation* (London, 1987). An admirable short introduction.

Harro Höpfl, *The Christian Polity of John Calvin* (Cambridge, 1982). The most successful attempt to bring into line Calvin's political thought and action.

A. E. McGrath, *Reformation Thought: An Introduction* (Oxford, 1988).
—— *The Intellectual Origins of the European Reformation* (Oxford, 1987).
H. A. Oberman, *Luther: Man Between God and Devil* (London, 1985). The most theologically shrewd and informed of recent studies.
S. E. Ozment, *The Age of Reform 1250–1550* (New Haven, 1980). Authoritative and valuable for its generous scope but somewhat *devant garde* in its social assessments.
G. R. Potter, *Zwingli* (Cambridge, 1976). The definitive English study.
Menna Prestwich (ed.), *International Calvinism 1541–1715* (Oxford, 1985). Not quite what its title suggests but rather a composite history of Calvinism in many countries.
R. W. Scribner, *The German Reformation* (London, 1986). A brief introduction to modern approaches; see also his collected essays, *Popular Culture and Popular Movements in Reformation Germany* (London, 1987).
Ian Siggins, *Luther and his Mother* (Philadelphia, 1981). Strikingly original and illuminating; a most valuable by-product of Luther's fifth centenary.
Keith Thomas, *Religion and the Decline of Magic: Studies in Popular Belief in Sixteenth and Seventeenth Century England* (London, 1971). A vast extension to the hitherto conventional limits of what constitutes religious history.
John A. F. Thomson, *Popes and Princes 1417–1517: Politics and Polity in the Late Medieval Church* (London, 1980). A useful recent survey of what happened between the Great Schism and the Reformation.
G. H. Williams, *The Radical Reformation* (London, 1962). Encyclopaedic in its coverage of the Anabaptists and others.

8. Enlightenment: Secular and Christian (1600–1800)

GENERAL

John Bossy, *Christianity in the West 1400–1700* (Oxford, 1985).
Peter Burke, *Popular Culture in Early Modern Europe* (London, 1978).
G. R. Cragg, *The Church in the Age of Reason* (London, 1960). A brief summary.
S. C. Neill and H. Ruedi Weber, *The Layman in Christian History* (London, 1963). A slight sketch on a subject calling for fuller treatment.
R. Rouse and S. C. Neill, *A History of the Ecumenical Movement, 1517–1948* (London, 1954).

THE CHURCHES IN BRITAIN

John Bossy, *The English Catholic Community, 1570–1850* (London, 1975).

David Edwards, *Christian England*, 3 vols. (London, 1981–4). A biographical approach, very readable.

W. K. Jordan, *The Development of Religious Toleration in England*, 4 vols. (London, 1932–40).

Gordon E. Rupp, *Religion in England 1688–1791* (Oxford, 1988).

Michael R. Watts, *The Dissenters* (Oxford, 1978).

ROMAN CATHOLICS IN EUROPE

Owen Chadwick, *The Popes and European Revolution* (Oxford, 1981).

W. A. Christian, *Local Religion in Sixteenth-Century Spain* (New York, 1981).

J. Delumeau, *Catholicism Between Luther and Voltaire*, English transl. (London, 1977).

A. G. Dickens, *The Counter Reformation* (London, 1979).

H. O. Evennett, *The Spirit of the Counter Reformation* (Cambridge, 1968).

J. McManners, *The French Revolution and the Church* (London, 1960).

—— *French Ecclesiastical Society under the Ancien Régime* (Manchester, 1960). For religious life in a French town in the 18th century.

PROTESTANTS IN EUROPE

C. Bergendoff, *The Church of the Lutheran Reformation: A Historical Survey of Lutheranism* (St Louis, 1967).

A. L. Drummond, *German Protestantism since Luther* (London, 1951).

L. Kolakowski, *Chrétiens sans Eglise: La Conscience réligieuse et le lien confessionel au XVIIe siècle*, tr. from Polish by A. Posner (Paris, 1969).

E. G. Leonard, *A History of Protestantism*, 2 vols. (London, 1967).

J. T. McNeill, *The History and Character of Calvinism* (rev. edn., New York, 1967).

M. Prestwich (ed.), *International Calvinism, 1541–1715* (Oxford, 1985).

F. E. Stoeffler, *The Rise of Evangelical Pietism* (London, 1965).

J. Stroup, *The Struggle for Identity in the Clerical Estate: N. W. German Protestant Opposition to Absolutist Policy in the Eighteenth Century* (Leiden, 1980).

SPIRITUALITY

The great works of spirituality are generally available in modern edns.: J. Bunyan, *Pilgrim's Progress* (1678–84); W. Law, *A Serious Call to a Devout and Holy Life* (1728); R. Challoner, *The Garden of the Soul* (1740). There are translations of the French classics: St Francis de Sales, *Introduction to the Devout Life* (1609); J. P. de Caussade, *Abandonment to Divine Providence* (written before 1751, first published 1867).

H. Bremond, *A Literary History of Religious Thought in France*, tr. K. L. Montgomery, 4 vols. (London, 1928–36). A vast survey of astonishing insight by a believing Christian who admitted sadly that mystical experience had passed him by.

CHRISTIANITY AND THE MOVEMENT OF IDEAS

It is possible to offer only idiosyncratic choices out of a vast field.

R. Grimsley, *Rousseau and the Religious Quest* (Oxford, 1968).
Paul Hazard, *The European Mind, 1680–1715*, tr. J. L. May (London, 1953).
J. E. C. Hill, *The World Turned Upside Down: Radical Ideas in the English Revolution* (London, 1972).
J. McManners, *Death and the Enlightenment* (Oxford, 1981).
Keith Thomas, *Religion and the Decline of Magic: Studies in Popular Belief in Sixteenth and Seventeenth Century England* (London, 1971).

9. The Expansion of Christianity (1500–1800)

SURVEYS

K. S. Latourette, *A History of the Expansion of Christianity*, 7 vols. (London, 1947). III: comprehensive.
Stephen Neill, *A History of Christian Missions* (London, 1964). By a scholar who had been a missionary bishop.

BACKGROUND

D. Brion Davis, *The Problem of Slavery in Western Culture* (Ithaca, 1966).
J. H. Parry, *The Age of Reconnaissance* (London, 1963).
—— *Europe and a Wider World* (London, 1949).

Paul Tillich, *Christianity and the Encounter of the World's Religions* (New York, 1963). Convert or just co-operate?

ASIA

C. R. Boxer, *The Christian Century in Japan 1549–1650* (Berkeley, 1951).

R. Etiemble, *Les Jésuits en Chine, 1552–1733: La Querelle des rites* (Paris, 1966). The chapter roughly follows this view of the papal condemnation.

J. Gernet, *China and the Christian Impact: A Conflict of Cultures*, tr. Janet Lloyd (Cambridge, 1985). Shows from Chinese sources how cultural differences hindered communication between Jesuits and Chinese intellectuals.

K. S. Latourette, *A History of Christian Missions in China* (London, 1929).

A. Mathias and J. Thekkedath, *History of Christianity in India*, 2 vols. (New Delhi, 1982).

S. Neill, *A History of Christianity in India: The Beginning to 1707* (Oxford, 1984).

J. L. Phelan, *The Hispanization of the Philippines: Spanish Aims and Filipino Response, 1565–1700* (Madison, Wis., 1959).

NORTH AMERICA. See bibliography for Chapter 11.

SOUTH AMERICA

J. H. Parry, *The Seaborne Spanish Empire* (London, 1966). An excellent introduction.

The following books are meant to be evocative, rather than cover the theme.

P. Caraman, *The Lost Paradise: An Account of the Jesuits in Paraguay* (London, 1975).

C. Gibson (ed.), *The Black Legend: Anti-Spanish Attitudes in the Old World and the New* (New York, 1971). On the extent of the exaggerations of Las Casas and Protestant controversialists.

R. E. Greenleaf, *Zumárraga and the Mexican Inquisition, 1536–1543* (Washington, 1961). Christian attitudes to native religion.

L. Hanke, *Aristotle and the American Indians: A Study in Racial Prejudice in the Modern World* (London, 1959). See also his biography of Las Casas.

M. S. Klein, *African Slaves in Latin America and the Caribbean* (London, 1987).

G. Kubler and M. Sorce, *Art and Architecture in Spain and Portugal and their American Dominions, 1500–1800* (Pelican History of Art, London, 1959).

I. A. Leonard, *Books of the Brave: Being an Account of Books and of Men in the Spanish Conquest and Settlements of the 16th Century* (Cambridge, Mass., 1949). For the minds of the *conquistadores*.

M. Leon-Portilla (ed.), *The Broken Spears: The Aztec Account of the Conquest of Mexico* (Boston, 1962).

J. L. Phelan, *The Millennial Kingdom of the Franciscans in the New World* (Berkeley, 1970). For the minds of the missionaries.

R. Ricard, *The Spiritual Conquest of Mexico: An Essay on the Apostolate and Evangelizing Methods of the Mendicant Orders in New Spain*, tr. L. B. Simpson (Berkeley, 1966).

N. Wachtel, *La Vision des vaincus: Les Indiens du Pérou devant la conquête espagnole* (Paris, 1971). For the minds of the Indians.

ACCOUNTS OF MISSIONARY HEROISM

These are legion; e.g. for the Jesuits see:

F. Parkman, *The Jesuits in North America in the 17th Century* (Boston, 1878).

C. Wessels, *Early Jesuit Travellers in Central Asia* (The Hague, 1924).

PROTESTANT MISSIONS

C. R. Boxer, *The Dutch Seaborne Empire, 1600–1800* (London, 1965). Chapter on 'Gain and Godliness'.

J. E. Hutton, *A History of Moravian Missions* (London, 1922).

J. M. Parry, *Trade and Dominion: The European Overseas Empires in the 18th Century* (London, 1971). Background.

The great missionary societies all have their histories, e.g.:

W. O. B. Allen and E. McClure, *Two Hundred Years: The History of the Society for Promoting Christian Knowledge, 1698–1898* (London, 1898).

W. Canton, *A History of the British and Foreign Bible Society*, 5 vols. (London, 1904–10).

E. Stock, *The History of the Church Missionary Society*, 4 vols. (London, 1899–1916).

H. P. Thomson, *Into All Lands: A History of the Society for the Propagation of the Gospel in Foreign Parts, 1701–1950* (London, 1951).

MISSIONS OF THE RUSSIAN ORTHODOX CHURCH

S. Bolshakoff, *The Foreign Missions of the Russian Orthodox Church* (London, 1943).

AUSTRALIA

Ross Border, *Church and State in Australia, 1788–1872: A Constitutional Study of the Church of England* (1962).
T. L. Suttor, *Hierarchy and Democracy in Australia: The Formation of Australian Catholicism, 1788–1870* (1965).

10. Great Britain and Europe since 1800

GENERAL SURVEYS

H. Fey (ed.), *The Ecumenical Advance 1948–68* (London, 1970).
H. Jedin and John Dolan (eds.), *History of the Church*, tr. from the French (London, 1981). Is a judicious survey centred on Roman Catholicism:
  vii, by Roger Aubep *et al.*, *The Church Between Revolution and Restoration*;
  viii. *The Church in the Age of Liberalism*;
  ix. *The Church in the Industrial Age*;
  x. by Gabriel Adrianyi *et al.*, *The Church in the Modern Age*.
K. S. Latourette, *Christianity in a Revolutionary Age*, 5 vols. (London, 1959–63). I, II, and IV; the author is a Protestant.
R. Rouse and S. C. Neill (eds.), *A History of the Ecumenical Movement, 1517–1948* (London, 1954).

PARTICULAR COUNTRIES

D. A. Binchy, *Church and State in Fascist Italy* (Oxford, 1941).
Owen Chadwick, *The Victorian Church*, 2 vols. (London, 1966–70). A masterly and monumental study.
J. S. Conway, *The Nazi Persecution of the Churches 1933–45* (London, 1968).
A. Dansette, *Religious History of Modern France*, 2 vols. (Edinburgh, 1961), tr. J. Dingle from the French of 1948, with abridgements.

R. Davies and Gordon Rupp (eds.), *A History of the Methodist Church in Great Britain*, 4 vols. (1965–88).

A. L. Drummond, *German Protestantism since Luther* (London, 1951). A sound though dated sketch.

D. L. Edwards, *Christian England*, iii (London, 1984). Very readable.

J. R. Fleming, *A History of the Church in Scotland, 1843–1929*, 2 vols. (London, 1927–33).

Frances Lannon, *Privilege, Persecution and Prophecy: The Catholic Church in Spain, 1875–1975* (Oxford, 1987). A masterly study on a subject where there is so little available in English.

J. McManners, *Church and State in France 1870–1914* (London, 1972).

E. Molland, *Church Life in Norway 1800–1950* (Minneapolis, 1957).

E. R. Norman, *Church and Society in England 1770–1970* (Oxford, 1976). This and the following volume are indispensable.

—— *The English Catholic Church in the Nineteenth Century* (Oxford, 1984).

E. A. Payne, *The Free Church Tradition in the Life of England* (new edn., London, 1965).

C. S. Philips, *The Church in France 1789–1848* (London, 1929). A sparkling and readable account.

J. Wordsworth, *The National Church of Sweden* (London, 1911).

J. R. Wright, *Above Parties: The Political Attitudes of the German Protestant Church Leadership, 1918–33* (Oxford, 1974).

HISTORY OF THOUGHT

It is possible to do no more than indicate a few guides to an endless subject.

Owen Chadwick, *The Secularisation of the European Mind in the Nineteenth Century* (Cambridge, 1975).

B. M. G. Reardon, *Liberal Protestantism* (London, 1968). This author has also written books on Catholic thought in France (1975) and religious thought in Britain (1971) in the 19th century.

11. North America since 1800

Sydney E. Ahlstrom, *A Religious History of the American People* (New Haven, 1972). The comprehensive masterwork on the subject.

Henry Warner Bowden, *American Indians and Christian Missions: Studies in Cultural Contact* (Chicago, 1981). A fair minded treatment across cultural boundaries.

Jay P. Dolan, *The American Catholic Experience: A History from Colonial Times to the Present* (Garden City, NY, 1985). Stresses social history, the record of ordinary Catholics.

Edwin S. Gaustad, *A Documentary History of Religion in America*, 2 vols. (Grand Rapids, MI, 1982–3).

—— *The Historical Atlas of Religion in America* (New York, 1976).

Robert T. Handy, *Christianity in the United States and Canada* (New York, 1977). The only binational history.

James Hennessey, SJ, *American Catholics: A History of the Roman Catholic Community in the United States* (New York, 1981). Complements Dolan's work, with more accent on the official church.

Winthrop S. Hudson, *Religion in America* (New York, 1981).

William G. McLoughlin, *Revivals, Awakenings, and Reform* (Chicago, 1978). Offers a provocative thesis on 'revitalization'.

George M. Marsden, *Fundamentalism in American Culture: The Shaping of Twentieth-Century Evangelicalism: 1870–1925* (New York, 1980). The best informed, most judicious account.

Martin E. Marty, *Pilgrims in Their Own Land: 500 Years of Religion in America* (Boston, 1984). American restlessness, inventiveness; concerns itself with biographies of leaders.

Sidney E. Mead, *The Lively Experiment: The Shaping of Christianity in America* (New York, 1963). Classic essays on the 'religion of the republic'.

Albert Raboteau, *Slave Religion: The 'Invisible Institution' in the Antebellum South* (New York, 1978).

H. H. Walsh, *The Christian Church in Canada* (Toronto, 1956).

12. Latin America since 1800

R. Bastide, *The African Religions of Brazil: Toward a Sociology of the Interpenetration of Civilizations,* tr. H. Sebba (Baltimore, 1978). A landmark study of religious survivals and syncretism.

L. Cleary, *Crisis and Change: The Church in Latin America Today* (Maryknoll, NY, 1985). A brief, objective look at a field that has produced a plethora of partisan accounts.

R. Della Cava, 'Brazilian Messianism and National Institutions: A

Reappraisal of Canudos and Joaseiro', *Hispanic American Historical Review*, 48 (1968), pp. 402–20. A significant revisionist essay.

J. J. Kennedy, *Catholicism, Nationalism, and Democracy in Argentina* (Notre Dame, Ind., 1958).

J. L. Klaiber, *Religion and Revolution in Peru, 1824–1976* (Notre Dame, Ind., 1977).

J. Lafaye, *Quetzalcoatl and Guadalupe: The Formation of Mexican National Consciousness, 1531–1815*, tr. B. Keen (Chicago, 1976). A highly original treatment of certain facets of popular religion that found their way into 'high' religion and that still influence Mexican beliefs.

D. H. Levine, *Religion and Politics in Latin America: The Catholic Church in Venezuela and Colombia* (Princeton, 1981). A study in contrasts, focusing on the post-1945 era.

S. Mainwaring, *The Catholic Church and Politics in Brazil, 1916–1985* (Stanford, 1986). Utilizes the substantial body of published literature in the field as well as original research to produce fresh interpretations.

J. L. Mecham, *Church and State in Latin America* (2nd edn., rev., Chapel Hill, NC, 1966). Commencing with the colonial period, this book of magisterial sweep stands as the one true classic in the field.

R. E. Quirk, *The Mexican Revolution and the Catholic Church, 1910–1929* (Bloomington, Ind., 1973). Impeccable scholarship applied to a topic that often inspires emotional polemics.

K. M. Schmitt (ed.), *The Roman Catholic Church in Modern Latin America* (New York, 1972). A valuable selection of materials with an insightful introduction and a helpful bibliography.

J. H. Sinclair (ed.), *Protestantism in Latin America: A Bibliographical Guide* (South Pasadena, Calif., 1976). A comprehensive bibliography, with many of the entries annotated.

M. T. Taussig, *The Devil and Commodity Fetishism in South America* (Chapel Hill, NC, 1980). A strikingly original Marxist analysis of popular religion and mythology, focusing on Bolivia and Colombia.

F. C. Turner, *Catholicism and Political Development in Latin America* (Chapel Hill, NC, 1971). One of the best among a large number of books published during an era of excessive optimism about basic Latin American transformations to be spearheaded by the Catholic Church.

E. Willems, *Followers of the New Faith: Cultural Change and the Rise of Protestantism in Brazil and Chile* (Nashville, Tenn., 1967). A major study on a subject that lacks a comprehensive survey.

13. Africa since 1800

C. G. Baëta (ed.), *Christianity in Tropical Africa* (London, 1968). One of the earliest works to present an 'African' view of missionary history.

D. B. Barrett, *Schism and Renewal in Africa: An Analysis of Six Thousand Contemporary Religious Movements* (Nairobi, 1967). A sociological survey of independent African churches.

—— (ed.), *African Initiatives in Religion* (Nairobi, 1971).

T. A. Beetham, *Christianity and the New Africa* (London, 1967). A consideration of the future of Christianity in independent Africa.

D. Crummey, *Priests and Politicians: Protestant and Catholic Missions in Orthodox Ethiopia, 1830–1868* (Oxford, 1972).

B. Davidson, *Africa in History: Themes and Outlines* (London, 1968). A useful and succinct survey of African history from the very beginning, placing the colonial era in perspective.

J. W. de Gruchy, *The Church Struggle in South Africa* (Grand Rapids, 1979). A study of the opposition to apartheid.

G. S. P. Freeman-Grenville, *Chronology of African History* (Oxford, 1973).

L. H. Gann and P. Duignan (eds.), *Colonialism in Africa*, i (Cambridge, 1969). Specialist essays on the political implications of colonialism between 1870 and 1914.

C. P. Groves, *The Planting of Christianity in Africa*, 4 vols. (London, 1948). The last and most thorough of the older 'missionary' histories.

H. B. Hangen, *Mission, Church and State in a Colonial Setting: Uganda, 1890–1925* (London, 1984). A detailed study of one instance of the immensely complex relations between missions and colonialism.

A. Hastings, *African Christianity* (London, 1976). Description of the character of contemporary Christianity in Africa.

—— 'Emmanuel Milingo as Christian Healer', in C. Fyfe (ed.), *African Medicine in the Modern World* (Edinburgh, 1986).

P. Hinchliff, *John William Colenso, Bishop of Natal* (London, 1964).

K. S. Latourette, *A History of the Expansion of Christianity*, v (New York, 1943). Volume dealing with Africa from a monumental and exhaustive history of Christian missions.

J. McCracken, *Politics and Christianity in Malawi, 1875–1940* (Cambridge, 1977).

L. Nemer, *Anglican and Roman Catholic Attitudes on Mission* (St Augustin,

1981). Comparison of the organization of CMS and Mill Hill Fathers, providing useful background.

J. D. O'Donnell, *Lavigerie in Tunisia* (Athens, Ga., 1979).

R. Oliver, *The Missionary Factor in East Africa* (London, 1952). Pioneering modern work on missions in history.

G. Oosthuizen, *The Theology of a South African Messiah* (London, 1967). An examination of the beliefs of Shembe's Nazareth movement.

B. Pachai (ed.), *Livingstone, Man of Africa* (London, 1973). Essays marking the centenary of Livingstone's death, at once balanced and significant.

M. L. Pirouet, *Black Evangelists: The Spread of Christianity in Uganda, 1891–1914* (London, 1978).

T. O. Ranger and J. Weller (eds.), *Themes in the Christian History of Central Africa* (London, 1975).

B. Sundkler, *Bantu Prophets in South Africa* (London, 1948). Seminal study of independent churches.

—— *Zulu Zion and Some Swazi Zionists* (Oxford, 1976).

G. O. M. Tasie, *Christian Missionary Enterprise in the Niger Delta* (Leiden, 1978).

H. W. Turner, *African Independent Church*, 2 vols. (London, 1967). Detailed study of the history and beliefs of the Church of the Lord (Aladura).

J. B. Webster, *The African Churches among the Yoruba* (Oxford, 1976).

14. Asia since 1800

G. H. Anderson (ed.), *Studies in Philippine Church History* (Ithaca, 1969). Articles on Roman Catholicism and Protestantism in the Philippines.

Kaj Baago, *Pioneers of Indigenous Christianity* (Madras, 1969). A brief survey of prominent Indian Christians.

K. M. Banerjea, *The Arian Witness: Or Testimony of Arian Scripture in Corroboration of Biblical History and the Rudiments of Christian Doctrine* (Calcutta, 1875). An early version of the theory developed by Farquhar that Hinduism was fulfilled in Christianity.

R. H. S. Boyd, *An Introduction to Indian Christian Theology* (Madras, 1975). A broad survey of the subject.

G. T. Brown, *Christianity in the People's Republic of China* (Atlanta, 1983). A sympathetic account which ends on an optimistic note.

C. Caldarola, *Christianity: The Japanese Way* (Leiden, 1979). A socio-logical study of the Non-Church Movement, stressing the importance of such 'indigenized' forms of Christianity.

D. N. Clark, *Christianity in Modern Korea* (Lanham, 1986). A concise, balanced study of the period since the Second World War.

P. A. Cohen, *China and Christianity: the Missionary Movement and the Growth of Chinese Antiforeignism, 1860–1870* (Cambridge, Mass., 1963). The standard work on this theme.

Commission on the Theological Concerns of the Christian Conferences of Asia, *Minjung Theology: People as the Subjects of History* (rev. edn., London, 1983). A collection of articles by leading exponents of the Korean equivalent of liberation theology.

R. H. Drummond, *A History of Christianity in Japan* (Grand Rapids, 1971). A straightforward and reliable account which includes a section on the Russian Orthodox Mission to Japan.

D. J. Elwood (ed.), *Asian Christian Theology: Emerging Themes* (Philadelphia, 1980). A compilation of representative theological essays and church statements.

J. K. Fairbank (ed.), *The Missionary Enterprise in China and America* (Cambridge, Mass., 1974). Articles on various aspects of American missionary activity in China and the background to this activity in the United States.

J. N. Farquhar, *The Crown of Hinduism* (London, 1913). The standard exposition of the fulfilment theory.

C. F. Hallencreutz, *Kraemer towards Tambaram: a Study in Hendrik Kraemer's Missionary Approach* (Uppsala, 1966). An authoritative analysis of Kraemer in the context of changing Christian attitudes to other religions.

E. R. Hambye (ed.), *A Bibliography on Christianity in India* (Delhi, 1976). Fundamental.

H. Kraemer, *The Christian Message in a Non-Christian World* (London, 1938). An influential exposition of the Barthian view that Christianity is wholly different from other religions.

K. S. Latourette, *A History of the Expansion of Christianity*, v. *The Great Century in the Americas, Australasia and Africa*, A.D.1800–A.D.1914 (New York, 1943); vi. *The Great Century in Northern Africa and Asia*, A.D.1800–A.D.1914 (New York, 1944). A detailed and reliable narrative of events.

S. J. Palmer, *Korea and Christianity: The Problem of Identification with*

Tradition (Seoul, 1967). Explores the reasons behind the spread of Christianity in Korea.

Pro Mundi Vita: Dossiers (Asia–Australasia series), nos. 37–8 (Brussels, 1986). A balanced account of the role played by organized Christianity in the ending of the Marcos regime.

E. J. Sharpe, *Not to Destroy but to Fulfil: The Contribution of J. N. Farquhar to Protestant Missionary Thought in India before 1914* (Uppsala, 1965). A sympathetic analysis.

R. Streit and J. Dindiger (eds.), *Bibliotheca Missionum* (Münster, 1916–). An exhaustive bibliography of the history of missionary activities.

Kanzo Uchimura, *How I Became a Christian: Out of My Diary*, vol. i of *The Complete Works of Kanzo Uchimura* (Tokyo, 1971). A vivid autobiographical account, first published in 1895, of the formative experiences of the man who went on to found the Non-Church Movement in Japan.

15. The Orthodox Churches of Eastern Europe

T. Beeson, *Discretion and Valour: Religious Conditions in Russia and Eastern Europe* (London, 1982). A popular account based on the findings of a working party convened by the British Council of Churches.

S. Bolshakoff, *The Foreign Missions of the Russian Orthodox Church* (London, 1943). A useful, though brief, introduction.

J. S. Curtiss, *Church and State in Russia: The Last Years of the Empire 1900–1917* (New York, 1940). Well-documented analysis of the institutional and political aspects of church life; ignores spirituality, however.

J. Ellis, *The Russian Orthodox Church: A Contemporary History* (London, 1986). Wide-ranging, scrupulously researched, concerned yet dispassionate; a study of the years 1964–85.

C. Frazee, *The Orthodox Church and Independent Greece 1821–1852* (Cambridge, 1969). Deals with the unilateral decision of the Greek church to break with the patriarchate of Constantinople; closely based on primary sources.

Nikodimos of the Holy Mountain and Makarios of Corinth, *The Philokalia*. See Bibliography to Chapter 4.

D. Pospielovsky, *The Russian Church under the Soviet Regime 1917–1982*, 2 vols. (New York, 1984). A vigorously argued survey.

S. Runciman, *The Great Church in Captivity* (Cambridge, 1968). Masterly study of the patriarchate of Constantinople under Turkish rule.

P. Sherrard, *Athos: The Mountain of Silence* (London, 1988). An illustrated study, evocative and elegant.

K. (T.) Ware (ed.), *The Art of Prayer: An Orthodox Anthology*, compiled by Igumen Chariton of Valamo (London, 1966). An important source book for the hesychast tradition in its Russian form.

N. Zernov, *The Russian Religious Renaissance of the Twentieth Century* (London, 1963). Is concerned with the pre-revolutionary intelligentsia and its eventual role in communicating Orthodoxy to the Western world.

16. What Christians Believe

K. Barth, *Dogmatics in Outline* (SCM, 1966), (London, 1966). Lectures based on the Apostles' Creed by the outstanding 20th-century Protestant theologian.

J. Burnaby, *The Belief of Christendom* (London, 1959). A similar approach, but more directly in the form of a commentary on the Nicene creed.

H. Küng, *On Being a Christian* (London, 1977). An expansive commendation of Christian faith by the well-known radical Catholic scholar, which achieved remarkable sales in Germany on its first appearance.

J. Macquarrie, *The Humility of God* (London, 1978). Another small book by a leading British scholar with a strongly devotional emphasis.

A New Catechism, Catholic Faith for Adults (London, 1967). An outline of Christian faith from the Roman Catholic Church in Holland, written under the inspiration of the Second Vatican Council.

O. C. Quick, *Doctrines of the Creed* (London, 1938). An older, reflective account of Christian doctrine, loosely based on the structure of the creed.

K. Rahner, *Foundations of Christian Faith* (London, 1978). A less popular but more systematic account by another leading Catholic scholar of this century.

Ninian Smart, *The Phenomenon of Christianity* (London, 1979). A vivid descriptive account of the varied forms in which Christianity is to be found.

K. Ward, *The Living God* (London, 1984). A small popular presentation by a younger British scholar.

We Believe in God, A Report by the Doctrine Commission of the Church of England (London, 1987).

17. New Images of Christian Community

D. Barrett, *Schism and Renewal in Africa* (Oxford, 1968). A survey of the numerous independent and indigenous Christian movements that have arisen in recent years throughout Africa.

R. N. Bellah *et al.*, *The Habits of the Heart: Individualism and Commitment in American Life* (Berkeley and Los Angeles, 1985). An examination of the traditions and *mentalité* of contemporary American society, including religious attitudes and dispositions.

K. Dobbelaere, 'Secularization: A Multi-Dimensional Concept', *Current Sociology*, 29 (1981). This long essay occupies the entire issue of this journal and is the most comprehensive survey of the contemporary debate on the secularization thesis.

A. D. Gilbert, *The Making of Post-Christian Britain* (London, 1980). An analytical account that focuses specifically on religious and social change in 19th- and 20th-century Britain.

J. D. Hunter, *American Evangelicalism: Conservative Religion and the Quandary of Modernity* (New Brunswick, NJ, 1983). This work places the various manifestations of fundamentalism in America in the wider context of American social and religious change, and constitutes the best and most analytical study of the subject.

D. A. Martin, *A General Theory of Secularization* (Oxford, 1978). A profound and penetrating analysis of the circumstances in which secularization occurs or is impeded in various contemporary societies.

—— and P. Mullen (eds.), *Strange Gifts?* (Oxford, 1984). Collected essays on charismatic manifestations.

M. Marty, *The Modern Schism* (New York, 1969). A comparative analysis of processes of secularization.

H. Mol, *Religion in Australia* (Melbourne, 1971).

E. R. Norman, *Church and Society in England, 1770–1970* (Oxford, 1976). A useful work on the history of the Church of England over two centuries.

R. Quebedeaux, *The New Charismatics* (New York, 1976). A detailed account of the emergence and spread of the revitalization movement which, beginning in California in the late 1950s, has now come to influence many of the major Christian denominations.

B. R. Wilson, *Contemporary Transformations of Religion* (Oxford, 1976). A brief examination of the responses of religion to processes of social change.

—— *Religion in Sociological Perspective* (Oxford, 1982). Change in Christianity set in comparative perspective, with chapters on sects and secularization.

O. Wyon, *Living Springs: New Religious Movements in Western Europe* (Philadelphia, 1962). The 'new religious movements' of the title are new developments in monasticism and revitalization within the major churches which are briefly introduced and described.

18. The Christian Conscience

Robin Attfield, *The Ethics of Environmental Concern* (Oxford, 1983).

R. M. Hare, *Moral Thinking: Its Levels, Method and Point* (Oxford, 1981). A vigorous defence of the claim that a critical understanding of moral thinking can lead to the solution of moral problems.

Peter Hinchliff, *Holiness and Politics* (London, 1982).

John Mahoney, *The Making of Moral Theology: A Study of the Roman Catholic Tradition* (Oxford, 1987). A full and clear treatment of the subject.

—— *Bioethics and Belief* (London, 1984).

Alasdair Macintyre, *After Virtue: A Study in Moral Theory* (London, 1981). Argues that the modern world no longer has the capacity for rational discussion of moral issues.

J. L. Mackie, *Ethics: Inventing Right and Wrong* (London, 1977). A thorough and thoughtful presentation of the thesis that there are no objective moral values.

Basil Mitchell, *Morality: Religious and Secular* (Oxford, 1980). A study of the difference Christianity makes to ethics.

Oliver O'Donovan, *Resurrection and Moral Order: An Outline for Evangelical Ethics* (Leicester, 1986). Draws on the classical Christian tradition to illuminate contemporary moral problems.

Report of the Church of England Board for Social Responsibility, *The Church and the Bomb: Nuclear Weapons and Christian Conscience* (London, 1982).

Earl E. Shelp (ed.), *Theology and Bioethics: Exploring the Foundations and Frontiers* (Dordrecht, 1985).

19. The Future of Christianity

David B. Barrett, *The World Christian Encyclopedia* (Oxford, 1982). A massively comprehensive statistical survey, annually updated in the *International Bulletin of Missionary Research*; it suffers from a very inclusive standard of assessment and an idiosyncratic interpretation of 'evangelization', but as an indicator of the comparative proportions it accords with other, less comprehensive, surveys.

Walbert Bühlmann, *The Coming of the Third Church* (Slough, 1974). The one-time Secretary-General of the Capuchins made this early and bold attempt to alert the Catholic Church to the implications of the preponderance of the 'South' in the church of the future.

—— *The Church of the Future: A Model for the Year 2001* (Slough, 1986). An up-date of the above with a firmer outline of possible developments, and an epilogue by Karl Rahner.

David L. Edwards, *The Future of Christianity* (London, 1987). This is a magisterial treatment of its subject, written with brilliance and perception.

Christopher Freeman and Marie Jahoda (eds.), *World Futures: The Great Debate* (Oxford, 1978). Essays that make a more optimistic but still serious reappraisal of the ecological scare-mongering of the 1970s.

Keith Griffin, *World Hunger and the World Economy* (London, 1987). An expert, but readily comprehensible, examination of the economic realities.

Lesslie Newbigin, *The Other Side of 1984* (Geneva, 1983). An invitation to the church in the West to offer to our contemporary society a clear alternative to the Enlightenment culture which it has outgrown.

Karl Rahner, *The Shape of the Church to Come* (English edn., London, 1974). Arising from the synod of the Catholic Church in Germany in 1971, the book reveals the inadequacy of changeless presuppositions to provide a strategy for building up the church of the future, and outlines the hope of a more open church, oriented towards the world and the Kingdom of God.

Andrew F. Walls, 'Culture and Coherence in Christian History', article in *The Scottish Bulletin of Evangelical Theology*, 3/1 (1985). This is the Finlayson lecture for 1984 in which the Professor of Missions in the University of Aberdeen presents an interpretation of church history related to successive cultural phases.

Chronology

AD 29, 30, or 33   Crucifixion of Jesus: rallying of the disciples under Peter

*c.*44   Paul and Barnabas to Jerusalem on famine relief

*c.*49   Paul ends first missionary journey at Antioch

The first Christian Council in Jerusalem (Peter, Paul, and James ensure that the Jewish law will not be imposed on Gentile Christians)

*c.*50 (or 57–8?)   Paul's letter to the Galatian Christians

*c.*50   Paul establishes the Church in Corinth

51 or 52   Paul disputes with philosophers at Athens

*c.*58   Paul sends letter to the Romans from Corinth

60–100   The first three Gospels are written—Mark first

64   Great Fire of Rome; Nero persecutes the Christians— probable date of martyrdom of Peter

*c.*67   Paul executed in Rome

70   Fall and destruction of Jerusalem (the Jews had revolted against Rome in 66)

81–96   Domitian Emperor; renewed persecution at end of reign

84   Excommunication of Christians from Jewish synagogue

*c.*112   Letter of Pliny, governor of Bithynia, to the Emperor Trajan—the Christians are harmless

*c.*140–55   Hermas writes *The Shepherd* (visions and moral instructions)

144   Marcion excommunicated for the heresy of rejecting the Old Testament (he dies *c.*160)

*c.*155   The first *Apology* of Justin Martyr (the second *c.*161)

*c.*156–7 (or 172?)   Montanus begins to prophesy

*c.*178–200   Irenaeus bishop of Lyons

202   Origen escapes persecution in Alexandria (d. 254)

206   Tertullian (*c.*160–*c.*225) joins the Montanist sect

215   Death of Clement of Alexandria

250   Decius (emperor 249–51) persecutes the Christians Fabian, bishop of Rome executed

258	Martyrdom of Cyprian (bishop of Carthage since 248)
268	Paul of Samosata (bishop of Antioch from *c.*260) deposed for heresy
*c.*280	Gregory the Illuminator converts King Tiridates of Armenia
303	Diocletian (emperor 284–305) persecutes Christians
*c.*305	Antony of Egypt organizes colony of hermits
306	Constantine proclaimed emperor at York
311	Donatist schism begins in N. Africa
312	Constantine adopts a Christian symbol for his standards at the battle of Milvian Bridge
313	Emperors Constantine and Licinius meet at Milan and agree on a policy of toleration
*c.*315	Eusebius becomes bishop of Caesarea (d. *c.*340)
324	Constantine sole ruler
325	Council of Nicaea condemns theology of Arius and declares that Christ is 'one in essence with the Father'
330	Constantine inaugurates Constantinople (formerly Byzantium) as 'New Rome'—the ceremonies are Christian
*c.*330	Macarius of Egypt founds monastery in the desert at Wadi-el-Natrun
337	Constantine baptized on his death-bed
346	Death of the abbot Pachomius (Egypt), author of a famous monastic rule
361	Julian ('the Apostate') sole Roman emperor (killed in battle against the Persians 363)
364	Basil bishop of Caesarea
*c.*371	Fl. Gregory of Nazianzus (d. 389) and Gregory of Nyssa (d. 395)
374	Ambrose bishop of Milan (d. 397)
381	First Council of Constantinople: the see of Constantinople assigned 'seniority of honour' after Rome
382	Pope Damasus holds council and lists the canonical books of the Old and New Testaments
386	John Chrysostom preaching at Antioch
	Jerome (who translated most of the Bible into Latin) settles in monastery at Bethlehem (d. 420)
390	Bishop Ambrose excommunicates the Emperor Theodosius I for the massacre at Thessalonica
395	Augustine bishop of Hippo (d. 430): his theological writings against Donatists and Pelagians and his *City of God* dominate Western thought down to Aquinas
398	Chrysostom bishop of Constantinople
410	Sack of Rome by the Goths
416	Doctrine of Pelagius (a British monk) condemned in Council of Carthage

422–32	Pope Celestine I (is said to have sent Palladius to Ireland as its first bishop)
431	Council of Ephesus condemns Nestorius and reaffirms the faith of Nicaea: *Theotokos* ('Godbearer') is vindicated as the title of the Virgin Mary
451	Council of Chalcedon affirms Christ is one person 'in two natures': this is rejected by Christians in Egypt and Syria and elsewhere, who come to constitute 'Oriental' Orthodox Churches, separate from Constantinople.
455	The Vandals take Rome: Pope Leo the Great (pope 440–61) negotiates with them, as he had with the Huns
457	Barsumas, metropolitan of Nisibis (Persia), founds the Nestorian school there
c.460	Death of Patrick the 'Apostle of Ireland' (he was there from c.430)
469–c.480	Sidonius Apollinaris bishop of Clermont
496	Baptism of Clovis, king of the Franks
c.525	Execution of Boethius, author of the *Consolation of Philosophy*
527–65	Justinian emperor: reconquers N. Africa from the Vandals and Italy from the Goths
532	The Church of the Holy Wisdom (St Sophia) at Constantinople rebuilt by Justinian
c.540	Benedict of Nursia at Monte Cassino; here draws up his monastic rule
c.542–78	Jacob Baradaeus, disguised as a beggar, wanders east of Edessa founding Monophysite churches (Jacobite)
c.547	Cosmas Indicopleustes writes a topographical work which refers to Christians in India
553	The Second Council of Constantinople
c.563	Columba leaves Ireland with twelve disciples and makes Iona his centre (d. 597)
573–94	Gregory bishop of Tours (author of history of the Franks)
590–604	Gregory I pope
c.590	Columbanus leaves Ireland and introduces the usages of the Celtic Church in Gaul; later goes to Bobbio in Italy (d. 615)
597	Augustine, sent by Pope Gregory, arrives in Kent
c.600–36	Isidore bishop of Seville (his works a source of encyclopaedic knowledge for the Middle Ages)
622	The hegira, year 0 of the Muslim calendar
632	Death of Muhammad
635	Aidan bishop of Lindisfarne, having come from Iona (d. 651)

638	Arab conquest of Jerusalem
643–56	Final recension of the Koran; by now the Arabs have conquered Iraq, Syria, and Egypt
664	Synod of Whitby: Roman date for Easter prevails over that of the Celtic Church
681	Third Council of Constantinople re-emphasizes Chalcedonian Christology, saying Christ has 'two natural wills'
711–16	Arab conquest of Iberian peninsula
716	Boniface (Wynfrith) makes first missionary journey to Frisia
722	Boniface to Rome
726	Outbreak of the Iconoclast controversy
731	Bede completes his *Ecclesiastical History of the English People* (d. 735)
732	Charles Martel halts the Arab advance in battle near Poitiers
754	Martyrdom of Boniface in Frisia
768	Charles the Great and Carloman divide the Frankish kingdom between them (Charles sole ruler 771)
775	The see of the Nestorian Patriarch moved from Seleucia-Ctesiphon (on the Tigris) to Baghdad
781	Alcuin becomes adviser to Charlemagne—the 'Carolingian renaissance'
	The Sigan-Fu Tablet in China refers to a Nestorian missionary who was there 146 years earlier
787	Second Council of Nicaea upholds the veneration of icons
793	Northmen raid Lindisfarne (and Iona two years later)
800	Charlemagne crowned (Holy Roman emperor) by Pope Leo III
c.800	The Book of Kells (Ireland)
	Beginning of translations from Greek into Arabic at Baghdad—continue through the ninth and tenth centuries
815–42	Iconoclasm again
823	Arabs conquer Crete (begin conquest of Sicily 827)
c.840	*The Book of Governors* by the Nestorian historian Thomas, bishop of Marga
843	The 'Triumph of Orthodoxy'; the icons restored to the churches
848	Anskar archbishop of Bremen (evangelizes Denmark and Sweden c.830–65)
849	Synod under Archbishop Hincmar of Reims condemns the extreme predestinarian theology of Gottschalk (c.804–c.869), poet, grammarian, and critic
851–9	The martyrs of Cordoba

863–7	The 'Photian Schism': communion broken between Pope Nicolas I and Patriarch Photius of Constantinople
863	Cyril and Methodius, the 'Apostles of the Slavs', set out to Moravia: Bible and service books translated into Slavonic
871–99	Alfred the Great, king of Wessex, defeats the Danes and promotes Christian learning
877	Death of Scotus Erigena (Irish philosopher, head of the school at Laon)
909	Monastery of Cluny founded, becomes centre of reform
961	The great Lavra founded on Mount Athos by Athanasius the Athonite (d. 1003)
969–76	John Tzimisces's reconquest of some of the Asian provinces of Byzantium
988	Conversion of Russia: Vladimir, Prince of Kiev, is baptized by Byzantine missionaries
996–1021	Persecution of Coptic Church in Egypt under Caliph el-Hakim
1009	Destruction of the Church of the Holy Sepulchre, Jerusalem
1031	Fall of caliphate of Cordoba
1035	Creation of the kingdom of Aragon
1037	Unification of the kingdoms of Castille and Leon
1046	Synod of Sutri; Clement II pope
1049–54	Leo IX pope: beginning of effective papal reform
c.1051	The Monastery of the Caves is founded at Kiev
1054	Mutual anathemas are exchanged at Constantinople between Cardinal Humbert, representing the papacy, and Patriarch Michael Cerularius
1056	Death of Emperor Henry III; beginning of Patarini movement in Milan
1059	Decree places papal elections in hands of cardinal bishops
11th cent.–1492	Christian conquest of Iberian peninsula
1060–92	Norman conquest of Muslim Sicily
1071	Saljuk Turks defeat Byzantines at battle of Manzikert
1073	Gregory VII becomes pope
1076	Council of Worms deposes Gregory VII; Gregory deposes and excommunicates Henry IV
1077	Henry does penance at Canossa
1080	Second excommunication of Henry IV; election of imperialist Pope Clement III
1084	Bruno founds the Carthusian Order
1088	Building of great church at Cluny ('Cluny III') begun
1093	Anselm archbishop of Canterbury

1095	Urban II preaches First Crusade at Council of Clermont
1098	Anselm's *Cur Deus Homo* (theology of the atonement)
	Foundation of abbey of Cîteaux (the Cistercian Order spreads rapidly; over 600 houses by the end of the 13th century)
1099	Crusaders take Jerusalem
1101	Foundation of abbey of Fontevraud
1112	Bernard becomes monk at Cîteaux
*c.*1116	Peter Abelard teaching at Paris
1122	Concordat of Worms: Suger elected abbot of Saint-Denis
1123	First Lateran Council
1129	Templar Rule defined by Council of Troyes
1130	Disputed election at Rome of Popes Innocent II and Anacletus II
1139	Second Lateran Council
*c.*1140	Gratian, *Decretum* (*Concordance of Discordant Canons*)
1143	First clear evidence of Eastern influence upon Western heretics at Cologne
	Translation of Koran into Latin (Peter the Venerable, abbot of Cluny, organizing study of Islam)
1146	Preaching of Second Crusade by Bernard at Vézelay
*c.*1150	Bernard's treatise *De Consideratione* dedicated to Eugenius III
*c.*1157	Peter Lombard's theological treatise, *Sentences*, completed at Paris
1159	Schism at Rome between Alexander III and Victor IV, followed by dispute with Frederick Barbarossa
1170	Murder of Archbishop Thomas Becket of Canterbury
1174	Thomas Becket canonized
	Peter Valdes converted; forms 'the poor men of Lyons', beginning of the Waldensians
1177	Treaty of Venice settles schism between Alexander III and Barbarossa
	Third Lateran Council
1187	Capture of Jerusalem by Saladin
1189–92	Third Crusade
1189–1246	Muslim rebellions in Sicily
1198	Innocent III becomes pope
1202	Death of Joachim of Fiore
1204	The Fourth Crusade is diverted to Constantinople; Latin troops sack the city and a Latin empire is set up
1209	Francis of Assisi gives his friars their first rule
	Albigensian Crusade launched
1212	Children's Crusade
	Christian victory over Moors of Spain at Las Navas de Tolosa

1215	Fourth Lateran Council: annual confession ordered, doctrine of Eucharist defined, and the clergy forbidden to countenance ordeals
1216	Establishment of Dominican friars
1217–21	Fifth Crusade at Damietta
1220	General Chapter at Bologna: Dominic gives final form to his Order of Friars Preachers
1223	Franciscan rule approved by Honorius III
1226	Death of Francis of Assisi
1228–9	Jerusalem recovered by Frederick II (by negotiation)
1232	Papal inquisition established by Gregory IX
1237–40	Kievan Russia is over-run by Mongol Tatars
1239	Excommunication of Frederick II by Gregory IX
1244	Jerusalem finally lost to Muslims
1245	First Council of Lyon formally deposes Emperor Frederick II
1248–54	Louis IX on crusade in Egypt and Palestine
1250	Death of Emperor Frederick II
c.1255	Thomas Aquinas teaching at Paris (d. 1274)
1261	The Byzantine Emperor Michael VIII Palaeologus recovers Constantinople
1270	Death of Louis IX on crusade at Tunis
1274	The second Council of Lyon decrees union between Rome and the Orthodox, but its decisions are rejected in the Greek and Slav world
1281–1924	Ottoman state
1291	Fall of Acre (last crusader outpost and Frankish port in Syria)
1295	Conversion of the Mongol dynasty to Islam; destruction of the Nestorian Church (the 'Assyrian Christians' remain in mountains of Kurdistan)
1302	Boniface VIII, in *Unam Sanctam*, proclaims universal jurisdiction of the pope and the superiority of the spiritual power over the secular
1305	Election of Pope Clement V; beginning of the French exile of the papacy
1308	Death of Duns Scotus
1311–12	Council of Vienne rules in favour of the strict party in the dispute over Franciscan poverty
1312	Destruction of the Templars by pressure of Philip IV of France on Pope Clement V
1314	Latest date by which Dante's *Divine Comedy* is completed
1324	Marsilius of Padua, *Defensor pacis*: the church should be ruled by general councils, and its property depends on the state
1327–47	The Franciscan William of Ockham (born c.1285) criticizes the philosophy of realism and writes

	polemics against the papacy
1327	Death of 'Meister' Eckhart, the German Dominican mystic
1337	The hesychast controversy (the teaching of Gregory Palamas on the Divine Light is upheld by Councils at Constantinople, 1341, 1347, 1351)
c.1340	Sergii of Radonezh founds the monastery of the Holy Trinity near Moscow
1348–9	The Black Death
1361	Death of Johann Tauler, disciple of Meister Eckhart
1374	Conversion of Geert de Groote who founds the Brethren of the Common Life at Deventer (Holland)
1375–82	John Wyclif attacks clerical wealth, monasticism and authority of pope
1378	The Great Schism; two popes, Urban VI and Clement VII
1387	Monastery of Windesheim (Holland) founded by Florentius Radewyns, a disciple of de Groote
1413	Jan Huss writes the *De Ecclesia*: for reform of the church on Wyclif's lines
1414–18	Council of Constance affirms that general councils are superior to popes; Jan Huss burnt by the council, 1415; the election of Pope Martin V, leading to the end of the Great Schism in 1429
1418	First appearance of the *Imitatio Christi*, ascribed to Thomas à Kempis
1431–49	Council of Basle
1433	Nicholas of Cusa produces programme for reform of church and empire
1438–9	Council of Ferrara–Florence proclaims reunion of Rome and the Orthodox—rejected in the Orthodox world
c.1440	Reform of the Ethiopian Church by the Emperor Zara Jacob
1453	Constantinople falls to the Ottoman Turks
1478	Johan Geiler von Kaiserberg, 'the German Savonarola', begins to preach in Strasbourg
1479	Establishment of 'Spanish inquisition' with papal approval
1492	The Muslims expelled from Spain
1493–4	Pope Alexander VI partitions the new discoveries between Spain and Portugal
1498	Savonarola burned in Florence
1501	First bishopric in Hispaniola (Haiti)
1503	Conflict in Russia between two monastic parties, the 'Possessors' and the 'Non-Possessors'
1506	Pope Julius II lays foundation stone of St Peter's in

	Rome
1508	Michelangelo paints the ceiling of the Sistine Chapel in Rome
1509	Desiderius Erasmus attacks corruption in the church and criticizes monasticism
1510	Martin Luther visits Rome
1516	Concordat between Pope Leo X and Francis I of France Edition of the New Testament by Erasmus
1517	Luther posts the 95 theses at Wittenberg (31 October)
1519	Cortès strikes at the Aztec Empire of Mexico Luther disputes with Dr Eck at Leipzig and denies the primacy of the pope and the infallibility of general councils Huldrych Zwingli preaches in Zurich
1521	The papal bull *Decet Romanum Pontificem* excommunicates Luther (3 January); the Diet of Worms; Luther argues before Emperor Charles V
1522–3	Ignatius Loyola at work on the *Spiritual Exercises*
1524	The Franciscans arrive in Mexico The German Peasants' Revolt (to 1526)
1525	The Anabaptist Thomas Münzer executed after defeat of the peasants; William Tyndale's translation of the New Testament published at Cologne and Worms
1527–40	Vitoria (Dominican) lectures at Salamanca on the morality of the conquest of the Indies
1528	The Reformation adopted in Berne
1529	Diet of Speyer; reforming members (six princes and fourteen cities) make a formal *protestatio* against the Catholic majority (hence the term 'Protestant')
1530	Diet of Augsburg: the Lutherans present the Confession of Augsburg, drafted by Melanchthon Denmark adopts a Lutheran creed
1531	Zumárraga, first archbishop of Mexico, reports destruction of 500 heathen temples First bishop in Nicaragua appointed
1533–5	The Anabaptist Millenarian Commonwealth in Münster
1534	Act of Supremacy in England
1535	Execution of Thomas More
1536	John Calvin, *Institutes*; he arrives in Geneva
1537	Pope Paul III declares the American Indians are entitled to liberty and property
1539	Henry VIII's Great Bible printed
1540	Pope Paul III approves of Loyola's foundation of the Jesuits
1542	Francis Xavier arrives in India
1545	Council of Trent (suspended 1547, resumes 1551; suspended 1552; resumes 1562–4 December 1563)

1549	The First Book of Common Prayer in England
1551–94	Palestrina at Rome (from 1570 musical composer to the papal chapel)
1552	Las Casas publishes his account of the oppression of the South American Indians
	Second Book of Common Prayer in England
1553–8	Catholic reaction in England under Mary Tudor
1553	Michael Servetus burnt as a heretic in Geneva
1555	The Religious Peace of Augsburg: 'cuius regio eius religio'
	Bishops Latimer and Ridley burnt at Oxford
1556	Archbishop Cranmer burnt
1557	First *Index Librorum Prohibitorum*
1559	First National Synod of the French Reformed Church
	The Elizabethan religious settlement in England
1560	A reformed church established in Scotland (by John Knox)
1561	The Belgic Reformed Confession adopted in Antwerp
1562	The Heidelberg Catechism (for the Palatinate, Calvinist with Lutheran modifications)
	Spain seizes the Philippines
1562–1604	Faustus Socinus (Fausto Sozzini) spreads Unitarian doctrines
1564	Decrees of Council of Trent confirmed by Pope Pius IV (elected 1559: the first of the Counter-Reformation popes)
1566	Calvinist 'iconoclast' movement in the Netherlands; Philip II of Spain orders crushing of resistance
1570	Pope Pius V releases the subjects of Elizabeth of England from their allegiance to her
1572	Teresa of Avila reaches the mystical heights of 'spiritual marriage'
1573–81	Patriarch Jeremias II of Constantinople meets and corresponds with Lutheran theologians
1574	Calvinist university of Leyden established in Holland
	Torquato Tasso's epic poem, *Jerusalem Delivered*
1577	Formula of Concord: definitive statement of the Lutheran Confession
1579	The Jesuits at the Mogul court in India
	Union of Utrecht; the seven northern provinces defy Philip II of Spain, but the southern Low Countries make peace with him
1588	Defeat of Spanish Armada
	Molina (Spanish Jesuit) publishes a work defending free will against predestination
1589	Jeremias II visits Moscow; the Church of Russia becomes a patriarchate
1593	Henry IV becomes a Catholic, thus ending the wars of

	religion in France
1593	Sweden adopts the Lutheran Augsburg Confession
1594	Richard Hooker, *Treatise on the Laws of Ecclesiastical Polity*, Books 1–4 (Book 5, 1597)
1596	Council of Brest-Litovsk: majority of Orthodox in the Ukraine join Rome as 'Uniates'
1598	The Edict of Nantes gives guarantees to French Protestants
1599	Synod of Udayamperur: the Malabar Christians conform to Rome
1600	Giordano Bruno burnt in Rome
1601	Matteo Ricci, SJ, to Peking
1609	Francis de Sales, *Introduction à la vie dévote*
1611	Bérulle founds the French Oratory
	King James Bible (Authorized Version) published
1614	Prohibition of Christian worship in Japan
1618	Synod of Dort condemns Arminian doctrines
1620	The *Mayflower* sails from Holland and England to America
1622	Grotius, *De Veritate Religionis Christianae*
	Bull of Pope Gregory XV, *Inscrutabili*, creates the Congregation *de Propaganda Fide*
1624	Death of Jakob Boehme, mystic
1626	First Christian church in Tibet (Jesuit)
1629	Patriarch Cyril Loukaris issues a Protestantizing *Confession of Faith*
1633	The Sisters of Charity founded by Vincent de Paul and Louise de Marillac
1637	The Shimabara Rebellion in Japan (of persecuted Christians)
1640	Posthumous publication of the *Augustinus* of Cornelius Jansen (Jansenius), bishop of Ypres, confuting Molina on predestination
1642	Council of Iassy condemns the *Confession* of Loukaris and approves (with revisions) the Latinizing one of Peter of Moghila, metropolitan of Kiev
1643	Antoine Arnauld in France attacks the Jesuits and defends the memory of Jansenius
1647	George Fox begins to preach (organizes Quakers, later called Society of Friends)
1648	Peace of Westphalia ends Thirty Years' War
1649	The Iroquois destroy the Hurons and their Jesuit mission
1652–97	Antonio Vieira, SJ, works on behalf of the Indians of Brazil
1653	Bull *Cum Occasione* condemns five propositions; the Jansenists claim not to find them in Jansenius

1654	Pascal converted (23 November)—the night of 'fire' and 'the God of Abraham, of Isaac and of Jacob'
1655	The Duke of Savoy persecutes the Vaudois (Waldenses)
1656–7	Pascal's *Lettres provinciales* attack Jesuit ideas of grace and casuistry
1659	Laval-Montmorency vicar apostolic at Quebec (bishop 1674)
1660	Restoration of Charles II and of the Anglican Church in England
1662	The English Book of Common Prayer revised
	The 'half-way Covenant' in the churches of Massachusetts Bay
1666–7	Schism of the Old Believers in Russia
1667	Milton's *Paradise Lost*
1672	Council of Jerusalem endorses a Latinizing *Confession of Faith* by Patriarch Dositheus of Jerusalem
1673	English Parliament passes the Test Act; in force to 1829
1675	Philipp Jakob Spener, *Pia Desideria*, the origin of Pietism
1678	Richard Simon, *Histoire critique du Vieux Testament* (the beginning of Old Testament criticism)
	John Bunyan, *Pilgrim's Progress* (2nd part, 1684)
1682	The Gallican Articles in France (formally rejected by Pope Alexander VIII in 1690)
	William Penn founds Pennsylvania on the basis of religious toleration
1683	Second siege of Vienna; westernmost limit of Ottoman advance
1685	Louis XIV revokes the Edict of Nantes
1687	Lima earthquake—the Jesuits there institute the Three Hours Service of Good Friday
	Eusebio Kino, SJ, pushes into Arizona and California
	Pope Innocent XI condemns the Quietism of Miguel de Molinos
1688	James II (Roman Catholic) driven from the English throne
1689	English Parliament's Toleration Act (Catholics and Unitarians excluded)
	John Locke, *Letters Concerning Toleration* (others in 1690 and 1692)
1692	Imperial decree in China allows Christian worship
1698	Charter of East India Co. provides for chaplains to India
1699	Papal condemnation of Fénelon's quietism (after controversy with Bossuet)
1701	Society for the Propagation of the Gospel in Foreign Parts founded in London

1704	Papal legate arrives in the East to deal with Jesuit compromises with Chinese and Indian customs
1709–10	Louis XIV destroys the Jansenist centre of Port-Royal
1712	Christopher Codrington leaves Barbados property to the SPG
1713	The bull *Unigenitus*: Jansenists in France appeal to a general council
1716–25	The Eastern patriarchs correspond with Anglican Non-Jurors about reunion
1717	Bishop Hoadly's sermon begins the Bangorian Controversy
1719	Death of Ziegenbalg (Pietist) in India
1721	Peter the Great abolishes the Moscow patriarchate and puts church under the 'Holy Synod' (government-controlled)
1722	Count Zinzendorf founds the Pietist Herrnhut colony in Saxony
1723–6	Reign of Yung Chêng in China: Christians persecuted
1723–50	Johann Sebastian Bach at Leipzig where he composes the great religious works
1724	Church of Utrecht (Jansenist connections) separates from Rome
1726	Beginning of the 'Great Awakening' in N. America
1727	Conversion of Jonathan Edwards, the leading Calvinist theologian in N. America (d. 1758)
1728	William Law, *A Serious Call to a Devout and Holy Life*
1734	Voltaire, *Lettres philosophiques*
1736	Joseph Butler, *The Analogy of Religion*
1738	Conversion of John Wesley (24 May)
1740	Election of Benedict XIV, the great pope of the century (d. 1758)
	George Whitefield preaching in America (also 1754, 1764, 1770)
1742	First performance of Handel's *Messiah*
	Bull *Ex Quo Singulari* condemns the 'Chinese Rites'
1746	Christian Friedrich Schwartz to India
1749	Beginning of the 'Refusal of Sacraments' crisis in Paris; the Parlement supports the Jansenists
1756–72	The mystical writings of Emanuel Swedenborg
1759	British take Quebec; free exercise of religion guaranteed to Roman Catholics of Canada
	The Jesuits expelled from Portugal
1760	Kosmas the Aetolian sets out from Athos on first missionary journey (martyred by Turks, 1779)
1762	Rousseau's *Émile* (with the profession of the *Vicaire savoyard*, the supreme manifesto of sentimental Deism)

1807	First Protestant missionary arrives in China, although it is still illegal to propagate Christianity
1808	Vatican establishes Baltimore as first metropolitan see in United States
1810–24	The future republics of Spanish America struggle for independence (the Vatican takes the Spanish side)
1810	Formation of American Board of Commissioners for Foreign Missions
1813	Amendment to the Act renewing the East India Co.'s Charter facilitates the entry of missionaries into India
1814	Slave-trade made illegal in Holland
	Consecration of the Bishop of Calcutta, the first Anglican bishop in Asia
	Samuel Marsden's mission to the Maoris of New Zealand
1815	Unitarianism organized as split off US Congregationalism
1817	Union of Lutherans and Calvinists in Prussia and some other German states
	Robert Moffat, missionary, arrives in South Africa; works in Africa for over 50 years
1818–68	Theodore, emperor of Ethiopia
1819	First Provincial Council of US Catholic bishops at Baltimore
1820	Creation of Zulu kingdom
1820–51	Dr J. Philip LMS superintendent at Cape
1821	Greek revolt against Ottoman rule; execution of Gregory, patriarch of Constantinople
1822	Brazil obtains independence from Portugal
1826–30s	Widespread suppression of religious orders throughout Latin America
1826	Prohibition of widow-burning in British India
1829	Roman Catholic Emancipation in Britain
1830	*Protestant*, a magazine begun by US ministers, starts Nativist crusade against Catholics
	Death of the great Spanish American liberator Simón Bolívar, an anticlerical, who had finally been persuaded that the Catholic Church must play an influential role in the political order
1832	Autonomy of the Serbian Orthodox Church
1833	Start of the Oxford Movement in England
	Final disestablishment of a US church: Congregationalism in Massachusetts
	Slavery abolished in British territories
1834	Burning of Ursuline (Roman Catholic) convent in Massachusetts by Nativists

	of men, the Paulists
1858	Treaties of Tientsin imposed on China by Britain, France, Russia, and USA, resulting in the legalization of opium importation and the free entry of Christian missionaries into the interior
1859	Charles Darwin, *The Origin of Species*
1860–75	Ecuador's Gabriel García Moreno presides over one of the most staunchly Catholic administrations in Latin American history
1863	Bishop Colenso of Natal vainly deposed by the South African bishops
1864	Pope Pius IX's encyclical *Quanta Cura*, with the attached 'Syllabus of Errors'
1865	Samuel Crowther the first black Anglican bishop of Nigeria
	Foundation of the China Inland Mission
	Pius IX reiterates the ban on Catholic participation in Masonic associations: Brazil's Emperor Pedro II forbids promulgation of papal decree, precipitating a church–state clash (many of Latin America's nominal Catholics remain Freemasons)
1866	St Joseph's College founded at Mill Hill, London, by Herbert Vaughan (archbishop of Westminster, 1892–1903)
1867	Maximilian, briefly emperor of Mexico, is executed and the anticlerical laws of the 1850s are now implemented under Benito Juárez (d. 1872)
	The first Lambeth Conference of the Bishops of the Anglican Communion, 76 present
1868	White Fathers mission society founded by Lavigerie, archbishop of Algiers
1869–70	First Vatican Council: decree of papal infallibility, 18 July 1870
1870	Lobengula, Matabele ruler
	Establishment of an independent Bulgarian exarchate
1871	Formation of the Old Catholic Church
	Disestablishment of the Anglican Church in Ireland
1872	*Kulturkampf* begins in Prussia
	Condemnation of the Bulgarian exarchate by the patriarchate of Constantinople
1873	The end of open persecution of Christians in Japan, because of Western diplomatic pressure
1875	The World Alliance of Reformed and Presbyterian Churches formed at Geneva
1878–92	Missionary rivalry in Buganda
1879	Australian Methodist missions to the Solomon Islands begin

1879	Autocephaly of the Serbian Orthodox Church
1879–82	Jules Ferry promotes lay education as against the Catholic schools of France
1881	Westcott and Hort's Greek New Testament
1884	Tembu national Church founded
	Arrival of the first resident Protestant missionary in Korea
c.1885–1908	Congo Free State, personal possession of Leopold II of Belgium
c.1885	Simon Kimbangu, Congolese prophet
1885	Archbishop Benson of Canterbury establishes contacts with Assyrian Christians
	Foundation of the Indian National Congress, later known as the Congress Party
	Formation of the Romanian Orthodox Church out of the Wallachian, Moldavian, and Transylvanian dioceses of the Constantinople patriarchate
1886	Archbishop James Gibbons of Baltimore named cardinal; becomes most notable US Catholic leader
	Catholic and Anglican martyrdoms in Buganda
	Roman Catholic hierarchy established in India
1889	Brazilians, one year after abolishing slavery, oust Emperor Pedro II and establish a republic that proclaims separation of church and state
	Rhodesia founded
1890	Lavigerie, archbishop of Algiers, leads the 'Ralliement' to the French Republic on the orders of Leo XIII
	Anglicans, Methodists, and the LMS agree on spheres of missionary work in Australian New Guinea
c.1890	Garrick Braid, W. African prophet
	Prophet Harris, W. African revivalist
	Charles Helm, LMS missionary
	Bruce Knight, Anglican bishop in Rhodesia
	Fr. Prestage, Jesuit missionary in Rhodesia
1891	Pope Leo XIII's encyclical *Rerum Novarum* on the social problem
	Capt. Frederick Lugard occupies Buganda for British East Africa Co.
1892	Mangena Mokoni founds the 'Ethiopian Church' in South Africa; it later becomes the 'Order of Ethiopia' within the Anglican Church
1894	The Australian Labour Party draws strength from the Roman Catholic Church
	Dreyfus condemned by a French court-martial
1895	Beginnings of the World Student Christian Federation (or SCM)
1896	At Canudos (Brazil) millennialist movement headed by

a 'miracle-working' fanatic called the 'Counselor', ends in a blood-bath perpetrated by federal troops

Anglican Orders condemned as null and void by Rome

1898   In consequence of the Spanish–American War, Cuba, Puerto Rico, and the Philippines gain independence from Spain but fall under US hegemony

First Protestant missionaries enter the Philippines

1899   The first Bush Brotherhood in Australia

Pope Leo XIII in *Testem Benevolentiae* condemns 'Americanism'

1900   Uruguay's José Enrique Rodó publishes the influential book *Ariel*, urging Latin Americans to cling to the values of Hellenistic humanism while rejecting materialism

Boxer Uprising in China, during which many missionaries and Chinese Christians lose their lives

1902   Iglesia Filipina Independiente secedes from the Roman Catholic Church

1905   Nihon Kumiai Kirisuto Kyokai (Japan Congregational Church) becomes independent of Western missionary control (followed by other Japanese Protestant churches)

1906–7   Separation of church and state in France; the state takes church property

1907   Encyclical, *Pascendi*, condemns Modernism

Walter Rauschenbusch's *Christianity and the Social Crisis* proclaims the Social Gospel

1908   Catholicism in America (and Great Britain) removed from the Congregation *de Propaganda Fide*, as no longer a 'mission'

Federal Council of Churches founded for US Protestants

Union of Presbyterians, Congregationalists, and Dutch Reformed Churches in South India into 'the South India United Church'

Frank Weston bishop of Zanzibar

1910   Union of South Africa founded

World Conference of Protestant Missionaries in Edinburgh

1912   The Australian Inland Mission (and flying doctor organization)

1913   J. Chilembwe, nationalist prophet in Nyasaland

Albert Schweitzer, theologian, to Africa as a medical missionary

Kikuyu controversy; ecumenical proposal for E. Africa

Deportation of Russian monks from Athos on grounds of 'onomatolatry'

1914	The 'Assemblies of God', an affiliation of Pentecostal Churches in North America
	Act for Disestablishment of the Anglican Church in Wales (into effect 1920)
1914–18	First World War
1915	Birth of second Ku Klux Klan, anti-Catholic, anti-Jewish, anti-Black organization
1916	Charles de Foucauld, ex-soldier and hermit, murdered at the oasis of Tamanrasset: communities of 'The Little Brothers of Jesus' follow his teaching
1917	Re-establishment of the Georgian patriarchate
1917–18	Council of the Russian Orthodox Church; re-establishment of the Moscow patriarchate
1918	Decree on the separation of church and state in Russia issued by the new Soviet government
1919	World's Christian Fundamentals Association formed in the US
	Publication of US Catholic bishops' programme of social reconstruction
	Karl Barth's commentary on Romans
	Declaration of the patriarchate of Constantinople in favour of ecumenical collaboration between the churches
1920	Re-establishment of the Serbian patriarchate
	The Lambeth Conference of Anglican bishops issues appeal for Christian unity
1921	Church of Jesus Christ through the prophet Simon Kimbangu founded
1922–3	Spain's Cardinal Juan Benlloch y Vivó tours Latin America to promote *Hispanidad*, the idea that Latin American identity is rooted in Hispanic Catholicism
1924	Dissolution of Ottoman state and caliphate
	Autonomy of the Finnish Orthodox Church
	Autonomy of the Polish Orthodox Church
1925	J. O. Oshitelu, founder of the Church of the Lord (Aladura)
	Patriarchal status accorded to the Romanian Orthodox Church
1927	Faith and Order Movement founded at Lausanne
	A. Hinsley becomes first apostolic visitor to Catholic Missions in British Africa
	Declaration by Metropolitan Sergii Stragorodskii accepting recognition of the Russian Orthodox Church by the Soviet authorities
	Emil Brunner, *The Mediator* diverges from Karl Barth's theology
1928	Conference of the International Missionary Council at

	Tambaram, South India
1928	Alfred E. Smith defeated as first Catholic candidate for US presidency
1929	William Temple, archbishop of York; then of Canterbury, 1942–4
	Lateran Treaty, Rome
1932	Union of the United Methodist Church with the Wesleyan and Primitive Methodist Churches
	Reinhold Niebuhr's *Moral Man and Immoral Society* symbolizes arrival of a new critical realist Protestantism
1933	Paul Tillich, theologian, flees from Germany to the USA (d. 1965)
1934	Creation of Confessing Church in Nazi Germany (in defiance of the Nazi-sponsored church)
1936	Propaganda Fide accepts that Shinto rites are patriotic rather than religious
1937	Autocephaly of the Albanian Orthodox Church
1938	F. Buchman, founder of the Oxford Group, launches 'Moral Rearmament'
1939–45	Second World War
1940	Foundation of Taizé (ecumenical religious order) by Roger Schutz
1943	Concordat between the Russian Orthodox Church and Stalin
	George Bell, bishop of Chichester, condemns the bombing of German cities
1945	End of Japanese government attempts to control religion in Japan and elsewhere
	In the Communist-controlled north of Korea new restrictions imposed on religion
	The Evangelical Church in Germany: federation of the Protestant churches of East and West Germany (East German churches are forced to leave by state pressure in 1969)
1946	Abolition of the Eastern-rite (Uniate) Catholic Church in the USSR
1947	Independence of India and Pakistan
	Foundation of the Church of South India (union of Anglicans, Methodists, and the South India United Church)
1948	Foundation of the World Council of Churches, Amsterdam (patriarchate of Constantinople is a founder member)
1949	Billy Graham (Baptist) begins his evangelistic tours
	Communist triumph ends Christian proselytism in China

1950	Pope Pius XII proclaims the Virgin Mary's bodily assumption into heaven an article of Catholic faith
	National Council of Churches formed out of old Federal Council in the US; unites many Protestant and Orthodox churches for many causes
1951	Beginning of the Three-Self Patriotic Movement among Protestant Christians in China, accompanied by a similar movement among Roman Catholics, and the departure or imprisonment of most foreign missionaries
1953–63	Central African Federation
1953	Recognition of the Bulgarian Orthodox Church by the patriarchate of Constantinople
1957	The Democratic Labour Party breaking from the Australian Labour Party derives its strength from Roman Catholic dissidents
1958–64	Anti-religious campaign in the USSR under N. S. Khrushchev
1958	In China, election and consecration of the first Roman Catholic bishops by local priests, in spite of Vatican opposition
	Cardinal Roncalli becomes Pope John XXIII
1959–65	Fidel Castro comes to power in Cuba, establishes the first Communist dictatorship in Latin America, and seriously limits religious freedoms
c.1960	Death of Isaiah Shembe, founder of the Nazareth Movement in South Africa
1960	Election of John F. Kennedy, first Catholic president of the United States
1961	The Russian Orthodox Church joins the World Council of Churches, as do most Orthodox churches of Eastern Europe, but not the Roman Catholic Church
1962–5	Second Vatican Council: Catholicism's 'new opening' towards the modern world
1962	First performance of Benjamin Britten's *War Requiem* in Coventry cathedral (30 May)
c.1963	Alice Lenshina, Zambian prophetess. Had been evangelizing since the 1950s
1964–85	Military regimes in Brazil are criticized by the clergy for neglecting social justice and abusing human rights
1964–80s	Chile's Christian Democratic regime (1964–70) is replaced by the Communist-supported administration of Socialist Salvador Allende, who is ousted by a military coup in 1973; the civil rights abuses of the military dictatorship of Augusto

	Pinochet Ugarte elicit the clergy's condemnation in the 1980s
1966	Archbishop Ramsey of Canterbury visits Pope Paul VI in Rome
	Beginning of appearance of pentecostal and charismatic movements in mainline Protestant and Catholic Christianity
	Colombia's Camilo Torres, the most dramatic example of a priest who took up arms against the established order, is killed in a guerrilla skirmish
	Beginning of the Cultural Revolution in China; as part of a general campaign against religion the Red Guards close all Christian churches
1968	The papal encyclical *Humanae Vitae*, reiterating Church's ban on artificial methods of birth control, stirs dissent in Catholic circles
	Assassination of Martin Luther King, Baptist minister and civil rights campaigner
	Pope Paul VI becomes the first pope to set foot in Latin America when he inaugurates the Medellín bishops' conference in Colombia, with Protestant observers in attendance
1970	The World Alliance of Reformed Churches (i.e. the Congregational and Presbyterian Churches)
	Foundation of the Church of North India and of the Church of Pakistan
1972	The United Reformed Church in England formed from most of the Congregational Church and the Presbyterian Church of England
	Collapse of the proposals for Anglican–Methodist constitutional union
	Declaration of martial law in South Korea; the Christian churches and individual Christians are prominent in their opposition
1974–84	After death of Perón the Argentine military suppresses left-wing insurgency; after some delay the Catholic hierarchy condemns official terrorism; the bishops of Guatemala and Paraguay fail to denounce similar military excesses
1976	Election of 'Born Again' US President Jimmy Carter signals public importance of evangelical movements
1978	Election of Karol Wojtyta (Polish) as Pope John Paul II
1979	Churches in China reopened for public worship
	The Sandinistas come to power in Nicaragua, inaugurating a Marxist administration that soon encourages a 'Church of the People' largely removed from hierarchical control, but backed by many priests

Addressing the bishops' conference at Pueblo, Mexico, Pope John Paul II condemns excesses of liberation theology

Nobel Peace Prize to Mother Teresa for her work with the destitute in Calcutta since 1929

1980   El Salvador's Archbishop Oscar Romero, a zealous spokesman for social justice, is assassinated

1983   *The Challenge of Peace*, a pastoral letter of American Catholic bishops

1984   Visit of Pope John Paul II to Canada, one of three visits to N. America

The Vatican mediates a Chile–Argentina boundary dispute (one of a long line of similar papal mediations in Latin America)

1986   El Salvador's Christian Democratic administration is reluctant to accept earthquake relief from Catholic agencies owing to the clergy's alleged support of the 6-year-old leftist insurgency

In the Philippines, the Roman Catholic Church and other Christian bodies play a prominent role in the 'bloodless revolution' which brought an end to the Marcos regime

Desmond Tutu elected Anglican archbishop of Cape Town

1987–8   Scandals in television evangelism industry call attention to importance of this expression and to problems within it

1988   Election of a woman bishop in the Episcopal Church in the US

Millennium of Russian Christianity; prospects of increased toleration of religion by the Soviet state

Merger of three Lutheran bodies into an Evangelical Lutheran Church in America follows similar reunion of two bodies in the Presbyterian Church (USA) and continues trend of such mergers

1989   Catholic pressure for reform in Poland is a powerful element in the Solidarity movement

January. Security forces murder two Polish priests, and the murderer of Fr. Popietuszko (in 1984) is freed in April

11 January. Independent parties and organizations allowed in Hungary; Hungary demolishes border obstacles with Austria in May

April. Legalization of Solidarity in Poland

May. Student demonstrations in Tiananmen Square, Peking (brutally crushed in June)

30 June. Mgr Marcel Lefebvre, a traditionalist Catholic, excommunicated by the Vatican for consecrating four bishops

1989   *August*. East German exodus to West Germany;
        meetings in East German churches demanding
        freedom spill out into the streets

        Church leaders in Mozambique mediate between the
        rebel MNR and the government

        24 August. Tadevsz Mazowiecki of Solidarity becomes
        Prime Minister of Poland, after a sweeping election
        victory

        November. Collapse of the Communist regimes in
        Czechoslovakia and East Germany; hardliners ousted
        in Bulgaria

        1 December. Mikhail Gorbachev at the Vatican; the
        Ukrainian Eastern-rite (Uniate) Catholic Church
        (with three million adherents) is authorized in USSR

        15 December. Action of the Romanian dictatorship
        against pastor László Tokes, the defender of the
        rights of the Hungarian minority, sparks off the
        rising in Timisoara

        25 December. Execution of President Ceausescu of
        Romania

        Christian ceremonies for Christmas take place in all the
        Eastern bloc countries

1990   *January*. Anti-Armenian pogrom in Baku (Azerbaijan
        had blockaded the Christian people of Armenia since
        September)

        April. Lithuania (predominantly Catholic) insists on
        independence from the USSR; Russian economic
        blockade

        1 May. Christian elements in the demonstration against
        the Kremlin rulers in Red Square, Moscow; a priest
        with a life-size crucifix addresses Gorbachev, 'Christ
        is risen, Mikhail Sergeyevich'

1991   Relations between Rome and the Orthodox Churches
        begin to worsen progressively over alleged
        proselytism in Orthodox areas of Eastern Europe and
        property claims of the Uniate Church of the
        Ukraine.

        New ground broken in report of Roman Catholic/
        Methodist Joint Committee entitled *The Apostolic
        Tradition*.

1992   *March*. The assembly of the Council of Churches for
        Britain and Ireland, the new ecumenical body which
        includes the Catholics of Britain, meets for the first
        time.

        September. Catholic and Orthodox leaders in
        Yugoslavia appeal jointly for a cessation of war and

of 'ethnic cleansing'. The Bosnian president appeals
for aid from the Islamic nations.

November. Church of England decides to ordain
women to the priesthood. The possibility of
secession to Rome is explored by some of those
opposed to this, led by the former Bishop of
London.

Index

Index

OXFORD

MORE OXFORD PAPERBACKS

This book is just one of nearly 1000 Oxford Paperbacks currently in print. If you would like details of other Oxford Paperbacks, including titles in the World's Classics, Oxford Reference, Oxford Books, OPUS, Past Masters, Oxford Authors, and Oxford Shakespeare series, please write to:

UK and Europe: Oxford Paperbacks Publicity Manager, Arts and Reference Publicity Department, Oxford University Press, Walton Street, Oxford OX2 6DP.

Customers in UK and Europe will find Oxford Paperbacks available in all good bookshops. But in case of difficulty please send orders to the Cash-with-Order Department, Oxford University Press Distribution Services, Saxon Way West, Corby, Northants NN18 9ES. Tel: 0536 741519; Fax: 0536 746337. Please send a cheque for the total cost of the books, plus £1.75 postage and packing for orders under £20; £2.75 for orders over £20. Customers outside the UK should add 10% of the cost of the books for postage and packing.

USA: Oxford Paperbacks Marketing Manager, Oxford University Press, Inc., 200 Madison Avenue, New York, N.Y. 10016.

Canada: Trade Department, Oxford University Press, 70 Wynford Drive, Don Mills, Ontario M3C 1J9.

Australia: Trade Marketing Manager, Oxford University Press, G.P.O. Box 2784Y, Melbourne 3001, Victoria.

South Africa: Oxford University Press, P.O. Box 1141, Cape Town 8000.

RELIGION AND THEOLOGY FROM OXFORD PAPERBACKS

The Oxford Paperbacks's religion and theology list offers the most balanced and authoritative coverage of the history, institutions, and leading figures of the Christian churches, as well as providing in-depth studies of the world's most important religions.

MICHAEL RAMSEY
A Life

Owen Chadwick

Lord Ramsey of Canterbury, Archbishop of Canterbury from 1961 to 1974, and one of the best-loved and most influential churchmen of this century, died on 23 April 1988.

Drawing on Dr Ramsey's private papers and free access to the Lambeth Palace archive, Owen Chadwick's biography is a masterly account of Ramsey's life and works. He became Archbishop of Canterbury as Britain entered an unsettled age. At home he campaigned politically against racialism and determined to secure justice and equality for immigrants. In Parliament he helped to abolish capital punishment and to relax the laws relating to homosexuality. Abroad he was a stern opponent of apartheid, both in South Africa and Rhodesia. In Christendom at large he promoted a new spirit of brotherhood among the churches, and benefited from the ecumenism of Popes John XXIII and Paul VI, and the leaders of the Orthodox Churches of Eastern Europe.

Dr Ramsey emerges from this book as a person of much prayer and rock-like conviction, who in an age of shaken belief and pessimism was an anchor of faith and hope.

Other religion and theology titles:

John Henry Newman: A Biography   Ian Ker
John Calvin   William Bouwsma
A History of Heresy   David Christie-Murray
The Wisdom of the Saints   Jill Haak Adels

PAST MASTERS

General Editor: Keith Thomas

The people whose ideas have made history . . .

'One begins to wonder whether any intelligent person can afford not to possess the whole series.' *Expository Times*

JESUS

Humphrey Carpenter

Jesus wrote no books, but the influence of his life and teaching has been immeasurable. Humphrey Carpenter's account of Jesus is written from the standpoint of an historian coming fresh to the subject without religious preconceptions. And no previous knowledge of Jesus or the Bible on the reader's part is assumed.

How reliable are the Christian 'Gospels' as an account of what Jesus did or said? How different were his ideas from those of his contemporaries? What did Jesus think of himself? Humphrey Carpenter begins his answer to these questions with a survey and evaluation of the evidence on which our knowledge of Jesus is based. He then examines his teaching in some detail, and reveals the perhaps unexpected way in which his message can be said to be original. In conclusion he asks to what extent Jesus's teaching has been followed by the Christian Churches that have claimed to represent him since his death.

'Carpenter's *Jesus* is about as objective as possible, while giving every justifiable emphasis to the real and persistent forcefulness of the moral teaching of this charismatic personality.' Kathleen Nott, *The Times*

'an excellent, straightforward presentation of up-to-date scholarship' David L. Edwards, *Church Times*

Also available in Past Masters:

Muhammad   Michael Cook
Aquinas   Anthony Kenny
Cervantes   P. E. Russell
Clausewitz   Michael Howard

RELIGION AND THEOLOGY
IN OXFORD PAPERBACKS

...ord Paperbacks offers incisive studies of the philo-
...ophies and ceremonies of the world's major religions,
including Christianity, Judaism, Islam, Buddhism, and
Hinduism.

A HISTORY OF HERESY

David Christie-Murray

'Heresy, a cynic might say, is the opinion held by a minority of
men which the majority declares unacceptable and is strong
enough to punish.'

What is heresy? Who were the great heretics and what did they
believe? Why might those originally condemned as heretics
come to be regarded as martyrs and cherished as saints?

Heretics, those who dissent from orthodox Christian belief,
have existed at all times since the Christian Church was founded
and the first Christians became themselves heretics within
Judaism. From earliest times too, politics, orthodoxy, and
heresy have been inextricably entwined—to be a heretic was
often to be a traitor and punishable by death at the stake—and
heresy deserves to be placed against the background of political
and social developments which shaped it.

This book is a vivid combination of narrative and comment
which succeeds in both re-creating historical events and elu-
cidating the most important—and most disputed—doctrines
and philosophies.

Also in Oxford Paperbacks:

Christianity in the West 1400–1700   John Bossy
John Henry Newman: A Biography   Ian Ker
Islam: The Straight Path   John L. Esposito

POLITICS IN OXFORD PAPERBACKS

Oxford Paperbacks offers incisive and provocative studies of the political ideologies and institutions that have shaped the modern world since 1945.

GOD SAVE ULSTER!

The Religion and Politics of Paisleyism

Steve Bruce

Ian Paisley is the only modern Western leader to have founded his own Church and political party, and his enduring popularity and success mirror the complicated issues which continue to plague Northern Ireland. This book is the first serious analysis of his religious and political careers and a unique insight into Unionist politics and religion in Northern Ireland today.

Since it was founded in 1951, the Free Presbyterian Church of Ulster has grown steadily; it now comprises some 14,000 members in fifty congregations in Ulster and ten branches overseas. The Democratic Unionist Party, formed in 1971, now speaks for about half of the Unionist voters in Northern Ireland, and the personal standing of the man who leads both these movements was confirmed in 1979 when Ian R. K. Paisley received more votes than any other member of the European Parliament. While not neglecting Paisley's 'charismatic' qualities, Steve Bruce argues that the key to his success has been his ability to embody and represent traditional evangelical Protestantism and traditional Ulster Unionism.

'original and profound . . . I cannot praise this book too highly.'
Bernard Crick, *New Society*

Also in Oxford Paperbacks:

Freedom Under Thatcher   Keith Ewing and Conor Gearty
Strong Leadership   Graham Little
The Thatcher Effect   Dennis Kavanagh and Anthony Seldon